D1459802

DISEASES IN THE ANCIENT GREEK WORLD

Mirko D. Grmek

DISEASES IN THE ANCIENT GREEK WORLD

Translated by Mireille Muellner and Leonard Muellner

THE JOHNS HOPKINS UNIVERSITY PRESS
Baltimore and London

This book has been brought to publication with the generous assistance of the French Ministry of Culture and the David M. Robinson Publication Fund.

Printed in the United States of America

The Johns Hopkins University Press, 701 West 40th Street, Baltimore, Maryland 21211
The Johns Hopkins Press Ltd., London

The paper used in this publication meets the minimum requirements of American National Standard for Information Sciences—Permanence of Paper for Printed Library Materials, ANSI Z39.48-1984.

LIBRARY OF CONGRESS CATALOGING-IN-PUBLICATION DATA

Grmek, Mirko Drazen.
Diseases in the ancient Greek world.

Translation of: Les maladies à l'aube de la civilisation occidentale.
Includes bibliographies and index.
1. Diseases—Greece—History. 2. Diseases—Middle East—History. 3. Medicine, Ancient. I. Title. [DNLM: 1. Disease—history—Greece. 2. History of Medicine, Ancient. QZ 11 G86 G8m]
RA650.6.G8G7613 1989 616'.00938 88-45412
ISBN 0-8018-2798-1 (alk. paper)

Contents

Translators' Note

Our chief aim has been to produce a version of the original that is idiomatic and technically correct. The problems of translating a sophisticated interdisciplinary text from French into English are not slight, and we have sought—and received—assistance from many quarters. A secondary aim has been to make this book accessible to an audience beyond physicians and historians of science, who perhaps constitute its primary readership, and we hope that nonspecialists equipped with a standard medical dictionary can read the English-language edition without difficulty.

We are truly grateful to those who have helped us in this effort—first of all, to the author, who took great pains to fix and chasten our version as well as to revise and correct his original. Two expert readers, Caroline Hannaway and Dr. Gert Brieger, were chosen by the Press to review the manuscript, and they, too, have saved us from error. The manuscript has benefitted much in addition from the attentiveness and skill of its copy editor, Mary Yates, as well as from the care of Eric Halpern and Barbara Lamb. We thank the following persons for their technical advice: Dr. Christian Baecker, Pierre-Yves Jacopin, John Kirsch, Dr. Anne-Marie Moulin, and Dr. Robert Torchin.

—M. M. and L. M.

Author's Preface

How much uncertainty and obscurity does the passage of time cast over history, if false displaces true even for recent events, which took place right before our eyes?

—Plutarch, *The Banquet of the Seven Sages*

This book is a history of diseases, not a history of medicine. It is not, nor does it try to be, a history of professional and popular knowledge about nosological entities, nor is it even a history of the means of combating diseases. Its purpose is to discover the pathological reality hidden behind ancient medical and paramedical texts. The ideas people have held in the past about diseases and ancient efforts to effect cures for them will detain us only insofar as we can gain enlightenment about the existence of pathogenic agents and their consequences on the individual or social level. In fact, I will devote the greatest possible attention to certain ancient conceptualizations of disease precisely because they can shed light on pathological realities. And yet I will dispense with the details of medical treatment in antiquity because until the beginning of the nineteenth century, therapeutics and prophylaxis had practically no effect whatever on the nature and frequency of the diseases present in any society.

My initial aim was to encompass the whole of the ancient world, but the complexity of the problems presented by such a global approach forced me to modify my ambitions and to limit my investigations in this first phase to the eastern Mediterranean, the so-called Greek world. I hew to this convenient term knowing full well that, in probing prehistoric civilizations for evidence or by including places such as Macedonia and the territories of Magna Graecia, the purview of my research is not, strictly speaking, limited to the Greek populations. My choice of the Aegean as a bridgehead for exploring the diseases of the European past is in no way arbitrary. At least two powerful reasons dictate it: first, the antiquity and relative abundance of its written sources and archaeological sites, and, second, its unique geographical position, at the crossroads of three continents, which resulted in the region's playing a decisive historical role.

Texts in ancient Greek are in fact our oldest testimony from physicians on diseases of the West. But deciphering them is not always as easy as is often believed. Translation into a modern language, while it may be adequate when it comes to an ancient author's theoretical teaching, is less so for the concrete experience on which the theory is based. In this respect, the medical texts are even notably obscure. For instance, understanding technical terms, particularly the names of diseases themselves, presents grave difficulties even if we are content to accept an approximation of their sense, that is, their translation into popular medical language as against the terminology of modern medicine. The problem stems from the abstract nature of the concept of disease and the partly conventional character of medical discourse.

In this work, the mode of presentation, the investigative method, and even the degree of historical analysis vary from one chapter to the next. The heterogeneity is intended. It results from my wish to open new horizons by using different approaches and to place in the service of history certain recent developments in the biological and medical sciences. Despite the diversity of its methodologies and an ampleness that surpasses my expectations and intentions, this book cannot pretend to exhaust its subject, even within the geographical and chronological confines imposed upon it. Not all the diseases of the past have been studied; for instance, mental illnesses have been left to one side. It is my intention to devote another book to plagues in antiquity and to write a series of articles on the descriptions of pathological states in Greek tragedy and on the relationship between myths and diseases.

Several chapters of this book have already been presented at colloquia or published, in whole or in part, as articles. All such texts have been reviewed, revised, elaborated, and updated. I thank the editors and directors of the journals in question; their kind permission has made possible this reprinting and recasting.

This book would never have seen the light of day without the initiative of Fernand Braudel at a time now distant, or without the encouragement which that famous historian of Mediterranean civilization was willing to lavish upon me. The lengthy gestation of this work was linked to my teaching in the Fourth Section of the Ecole Pratique des Hautes Etudes, and its final form is shaped by the original rules of an institution that ties research to teaching and prefers knowledge in the making to the ready-made kind. I am indebted to my colleagues, especially Pierre Huard, Guy Beaujouan, and Marc Ferro, as well as to the audience of the seminar on the history of medicine and the biological sciences. I could hardly overestimate the stimulus from exchanging ideas with such interlocutors, nor that of discussions with my philologist friends, Fernand Robert, Jacques Jouanna, Jackie Pigeaud, and Danielle Gourevich, all so willing to share with me their critical observations. I express to them my deepest gratitude.

For the American edition of this work, I have corrected some errors that crept into the French version, filled out the bibliographical references with special attention to English-language publications, and added some new thoughts and information. These contributions are strictly limited to materials published before the appearance of the original version (1983).

DISEASES IN THE ANCIENT GREEK WORLD

Introduction

THE CONCEPTUALIZATION OF PATHOLOGICAL EVENTS

It is impossible to apprehend correctly the significance of an ancient text concerning a pathological event unless we rid ourselves as completely as possible of the ontological notion of disease embedded in our everyday language. Notions of disease and even of particular diseases do not flow directly from our experience. They are explanatory models of reality, not its constitutive elements. To put it simply, diseases exist only in the realm of ideas. They interpret a complex empirical reality and presuppose a certain medical philosophy or pathological system of reference. So, for example, one can say that there exists a person who is sickly, coughs, spits blood, and grows thin, and one can say that the bacillus that pervades his organism and produces characteristic lesions on his lungs and other organs also exists in the strict sense of the word, but one cannot say the same for tuberculosis. Its existence is bound up with a well-articulated conceptual structure and a particular medical ideology.[1]

The history of Western medicine, as well as the comparative study of medicine in diverse societies, shows clearly that diseases are not inevitably conceptualized as they are nowadays.[2] How they are conceptualized depends as much on the scientific sophistication of a society as on the pathological realities of a given historical moment in a specific geographical area. The Hippocratic medical teachings are rich in instances of this. The theory of humors is at once the logical consequence of Ionian philosophy and a faithful reflection of the pathological and clinical features of the ills actually suffered by Mediterranean populations. If the Hippocratic doctrine of critical days can reasonably be interpreted as the result of a desire to introduce number into the explanation of nature, it is no less true that such a notion was well supported in a region where the majority of patients suffer from malaria or pneumonia. Bouts of tertian or quartan fever succeed each other with perfect regularity due to the biological cycle of the parasite in question; similarly, patients with simple pneumonia undergo a crisis right at the end of a week of fever. A medical practitioner in Scandinavia would never have devised a theory of acute fevers comparable to the Hippocratic one.

Establishing a link in specific cases between observed reality and nosology is the essence of medical diagnosis. It used to be a relatively simple activity that never really went beyond the difficulties any process of classification gives rise to. But all that changed when the definition of disease was transformed from a clinical to an anatomical notion. Instead of describing and classifying a disease according to its symptoms, its apparent characteristics, one must now discover the fundamental lesion, the hidden injury. As a result, the historian of diseases is continually troubled by the inevitable uncertainties that arise when passing from a diagnostic system of the first kind to a more modern one.

We have no choice but to express ourselves in the medical idiom—using the terms and, more significantly, the concepts—of our own time. Yet between us and Hippocrates the pathological systems of reference have changed, not just the names of the diseases (actually, the names themselves are remarkably static, even at the expense of a continual change in their meaning). To put it simply, a delimitation of pathological reality based on clinical symptoms and on a theory of disease that attributed a preponderant role to the fluid parts of the organism has now been replaced by anatomical and etiological diagnosis that sometimes even includes a molecular definition of lesion—which is to say, by a set of criteria that, except for certain surgical syndromes, was completely unavailable to ancient practitioners. In order to make ancient medical texts understandable to modern readers, then, we have to resort to interpretations that take us beyond a purely philological approach. Understanding the real pathology underlying a Hippocratic text can significantly elucidate its content; hence the interest in completing our understanding of that reality by access to nonliterary sources. Unavoidably, much space in what follows will be given to the results of anthropological and medical examination of ancient human remains. Useful information on the diseases of the past can also be gleaned from the study of bas-reliefs, paintings, statuettes, and votive offerings in the shape of bodily organs.[3] Such sources offer the advantage of being nonlinguistic and thus skirting certain interpretative pitfalls.

The Concept of Pathocoenosis

Until very recently, the history of diseases has almost always been undertaken analytically, examining separately the history of each disease or of groups of related diseases in isolation from one another.[4] At least in the first phase of historical exploration such a simplification is necessary and justifiable in terms of its results. Nevertheless, it obscures numerous facts of capital significance regarding the interconnections among diseases. To facilitate a more synthetic approach I introduce the concept of *pathocoenosis*.[5]

Three propositions can serve to define this neologism: (1) Pathocoenosis is the ensemble of pathological states present in a specific population at a given moment in time. It consists of a system with precise structural properties that should be studied so as to determine its nosological parameters in qualitative and quantitative terms. (2) The frequency and overall distribution of each disease depends on the frequency and distribution of all the other diseases within a given population (in addition to various endogenous and ecological factors). (3) A pathocoenosis tends toward a state of equilibrium expressible in relatively simple mathematical expressions; that state is especially perceptible under stable ecological conditions.

Two diseases belonging to a single pathocoenosis can be in a state of symbiosis, antagonism, or indifference to each other. Cases of symbiosis are numerous. They arise either from the fact that the same environmental conditions favor two or more diseases (for instance, the diseases resulting from stress in a technologically advanced society), or from an etiological link at the level of the individual (for instance, the link between angina, rheumatic fever, and endocarditis), or to genetic synergy, or to a complex interplay of factors operating at the level of the society and the individual (for instance, avitaminosis, anemia of various types, typhus, or in general the coexistence of malnutrition with certain serious infectious diseases).

In investigating pathocoenoses of the past, the results are more illuminating when the pathological states in question are antagonistic. Antagonism between two diseases can stem from a conflict between man's genetic state and the germ causing a specific disease (as in the relationship between malaria and thalassemia discussed later in this book), or—this is more often the case—conflict can appear as the last consequence of a complex chain of heterogeneous causes. Infectious diseases due to poor hygiene and bad water (typhoid fever, dysentery, etc.) are antagonists of so-called degenerative diseases (arteriosclerosis, cancer, etc.) for the simple reason that people die of the former before they can run the risk of growing old and contracting the latter.

In reality there is no such thing as a synergistic or antagonistic relationship between two isolated diseases, only a complex interdependence of all the diseases present in a given population. The mass of reciprocal dependencies can be studied globally by looking at the distribution of diseases by frequency in a given population during a relatively short time-frame. The problem closely resembles that of determining the distribution of animal and vegetable species as a function of the number of individuals living in a biotope. Modern investigations show that the distribution of living species due to their quantitative importance corresponds to the log normal series, that is, the series x, $x^2/2$, $x^3/3$ . . . , which expresses the probability of the distribution of variations whose classes are expressed by a geometric progression (as the Gaussian curve expresses the probability of an arithmetic progression). Indeed, it seems that a pathocoenosis, when it is in the state of equilibrium that is only really noticeable in a relatively closed, ecologically stable population, presents a mathematically regular structure. That structure corresponds to the conjunction of several kinds of distribution but with a preponderance of the log normal type, which therefore gives its character to the whole.[6]

How can the mathematical regularity in the distribution of diseases be accounted for if they are actually only a logical construct? In my opinion, the regularity remains even if it is admitted that the conceptualization of diseases is not entirely determined by direct experience, by objects in the strictest sense of the word. However, the nosological categorization process must be logically consistent and conform to pathological reality. The changeover to a different, and, in its own way, consistent, conceptualization will change the numerical data and to a certain extent the general shape of the curve of frequencies, but the structured character of the pathocoenosis will not disappear.

To be sure, it is impossible to apply true mathematical analysis to the diseases of peoples as ancient as those that are the subject of this book. The data on such distant pathological events are quantifiable only in a uselessly hypothetical and approximate way. Nevertheless, our research can be and should be inspired by one consequence in particular of such analysis. It is clear, from logarithmic and log normal distributions, that each pathocoenosis must have a small number of common diseases and a great number of rare ones. This corollary permits—or, rather, forces—us to discover and explore the dominant diseases in a given historical setting.

The study of a pathocoenosis consists primarily in establishing the synchronic relationship among diseases during a given historical period. Yet a static description is not enough: it is also necessary to observe the way diseases evolve over time. Accordingly, I have introduced the notion of pathocoenotic dynamism. Future historians will surely scrutinize the two most distinct phases of these diachronic processes, the times when a pathocoenosis is in equilibrium and the times when it is in disarray, for example, the Neolithic agricultural revolution, the beginnings of urbanism, the times of the great migrations, colonial expansion, the industrial revolution, and so on. But the concept of pathocoenosis is still in its infancy, and no one can yet predict its practical value or its limitations.

Pandora's Jar

A sense of justice prevented men of old from believing that diseases had afflicted mankind from the start. Such a terrible perquisite of the human condition could only be due to a moral error committed by man himself. Myths of the Golden Age or of paradise evoke a primordial time without blame or disease. As Hesiod puts it, "First of all the deathless gods who dwell on Olympus made a golden race of mortal men . . . they lived like gods without sorrow of heart, remote and free from toil and grief: miserable age rested not on them; but with legs and arms never failing they made merry with feasting beyond the reach of all evils (*kakôn*)."[7] The silver race, of inferior biological quality, replaced the golden race, only to be replaced in turn by the race of iron. Men of the iron race, the Boeotian poet's contemporaries, "never rest from labor and sorrow" but still "have some good mingled with their evils." In the end they, too, will be supplanted, by men who "have grey hair on their temples at their birth."[8] For the mythographer, all humanity is like a man climbing a staircase, his fading vigor marked from one landing to the next.

Although the myths may suppose diseases were absent at the moment of creation, no time is wasted introducing them into the world, often as the result of an original sin: without disease the true human adventure is unimaginable. In Greek mythology the artificial woman Pandora is presented by all the Olympian gods as a gift to Epimetheus. Actually she is a gift to the whole human race, and she brings as her deadly dowry diseases shut up in a jar.[9] As Hesiod says,

> For ere this the tribes of men lived on earth remote and free from ills and hard toil and heavy sicknesses (*noûsoi*) which bring the Fates upon men; for in misery men grow old quickly. But the woman took off the great lid of the jar with her hands and scattered all these and her thought caused sorrow and mischief to men. Only Hope remained there in an unbreakable home within under the rim of the great jar and did not fly out at the door; for ere that, the lid of the jar stopped her, by the will of Aegis-holding Zeus.[10]

As I shall show in the first chapter of this book, Pandora's diseases have the peculiar quality of affecting men without being brought on by personal error or direct divine intervention.[11] So the myth sanctions a general feeling that, more often than not, disease has no apparent ethical justification at the level of the individual. Plato later rationalized the myth of the Golden Age, asserting that in a natural state man has no need of doctors and that most of the diseases in his day were due to luxury, by which he meant laziness and too much fancy food.[12] Plutarch and a host of later moralists repeat Plato's argument that diseases are the result of the blandishments of civilization. Even the medical treatises echo it. In the famous preface to *De medicina,* Celsus voices an opinion that must have been widely held in his time:

> It is probable that with no aids against bad health, none the less health was generally good because of good habits, which neither indolence (*desidia*) nor luxury (*luxuria*) had vitiated: since it is these two which have afflicted the bodies of men, first in Greece, and later amongst us; and hence this complex Art of Medicine, not

needed in former times, nor among other nations even now, scarcely protracts the lives of a few of us to the verge of old age.[13]

The myth of the Golden Age was founded on no true historical inquiry, nor does it reflect any real memory of an era of well-being. It is just a faulty notion with a psychological origin: the myth externalizes and unduly generalizes individual recollections of a strong and happy youth. But nowadays this mythical notion of historical degradation has given way to an idea of progress that, in its absolute form, is no less deluded.

Greek and Roman attempts to shed light on the origin of diseases in their world never went beyond legendary tales or moralizing. Being as far as we are from the events under study, can we moderns really do better? The answer to this rhetorical question should be affirmative, and the present book intends to provide some proof that it is. Despite the scarcity of sources, the occasional opacity of written testimony, and the hypothetical nature of most retrospective diagnoses, I believe in the possibility of reconstructing the nosological reality of the ancient societies of the eastern Mediterranean. What encourages me is the certainty that, despite the historical vicissitudes of both things and words, there must be verifiable constants in language and ideas as well as in external reality.

Semantic Constants and the Difficulties of Retrospective Diagnosis

I begin with what seem to be the most straightforward of constants, those in the meaning of words. It is not risky to assert that the term *peripneumonía* always designated a respiratory ailment. Moreover, it is almost certainly a disease of the lungs—I say "almost" because the persistence of meaning in the names of diseases derived from organs is not absolute. Hippocratic *peripneumonía* may well be a disease of the same localization as modern pneumonia, but inferences of this kind are not always true. For instance, the Hippocatic terms *nephrîtis* and *splēnîtis* refer to various pathological states some of which, as we now know, are not localized in the kidneys or spleen. Roughly speaking, *karkínos* or *karkínōma* designate what we call "cancer," and etymological considerations are adequate clues to the generic sense of terms like *arthrîtis, ophthalmía, húdrōps, apepsía,* and so on. The meaning of terms tends to persist particularly for symptoms or simple syndromes, like jaundice, hemorrhage, diarrhea, urinary or anal incontinence, loss of hair, blindness, toothache, and so on.

Unhappily, there are also several traps. Most dangerous are the shifts in meaning—the word remains, the concept changes. Sciatica (*iskhiás*) is indeed the same disease now as in the time of Hippocrates, but the term refers to two entirely different concepts: for them, hip pain, for us, neuralgia of the sciatic nerve. Frequently such shifts in meaning are so subtle that only the most nuanced exegesis reveals their extent. For instance, terms like *phthísis, pleurîtis, apoplexía, erusípelas,* or *eileós* are used by the ancient Greek physicians in senses that in some ways correspond to their modern meaning but in others differ profoundly from it. The ancient Greek word *kholéra* designates, as it does in English, a disease marked by vomiting, severe but blood-free diarrhea, and colics. But for the physicians of antiquity cholera was an acute, nonspecific, gastrointestinal syndrome, while for us it is an infection caused by *Vibrio cholerae,* a distinct and particularly dangerous disease. The word has existed at least since Hippocrates, yet the ailment it now designates is an endemo-epidemic disease from India unknown in Europe until the nineteenth century. So the medical historian could almost be more at ease with terms whose meaning has changed completely (e.g., *lépra* and *kardialgía*) or those whose usage and significance are now completely lost (e.g., *kaûsos, phrenîtis,* and *kardiogmós*).

The manuscript tradition of the classical medical texts and its critical restoration by the painstaking, tireless effort of philologists have made it possible for modern doctors to make a retrospective diagnosis of some diseases from symptoms described by ancient clinicians. Such a procedure assumes that the semantic context and the biological processes in question are unchanged, but it also assumes a certain constancy in Western medical thinking.[14] At times we can arrive at solid results without much difficulty. There are some diseases whose retrospective diagnosis, based on the clinical descriptions of the classical era, can be considered certain: epilepsy, mumps (with associated inflammation of the testicles), lobar pneumonia, pulmonary tuberculosis, pleural empyema, peritonitis, tetanus, dysentery, hemorrhoids, cancer of the breast and of the uterus, gout, acute intestinal obstruction, ordinary fractures and dislocations, and so on. Even so, we cannot stress too much the difficulty and frailty of retrospective diagnosis. Always hypothetical, it is often dubious and rarely exclusive of other diseases.[15] Where we wish to recognize in Hippocratic accounts rabies, meningitis, rheumatic heart disease, anthrax, gas gangrene, adrenocortical virilization, Behçet's disease, gastric carcinoma, or peptic ulcers, the identification is in fact only plausible and uncertain.

The paradox is that the progress of medicine in the past few decades has made our picture of the past even more questionable than before. Our knowledge of the great diversity of rare pathologies makes us suspicious of any diagnosis based on a few clinical symptoms. Such diagnostic excogitations are usually dependent on an evaluation of statistical probabilities. But for historical periods and societies whose pathocoenosis is poorly understood, we run the risk of being circular: our diagnoses only prove what we have previously supposed was true. A patient, for instance, is said to cough up red blood. Without hesitating we would pronounce the person tuberculous, since the last few centuries' clinical experience has taught us that pulmonary tuberculosis is the main cause of this symptom. Yet it is not the only imaginable pathogenic reality. It is not impossible that in certain pathocoenoses of the past, the rupture of varicose veins in the esophagus (e.g., as a function of a high incidence of cirrhosis of the liver) was a more common pathological complication than tuberculous blood-spitting. In the future, computers will be capable of producing almost exhaustive lists of the diagnoses possible for a goodly number of ancient clinical accounts, but they will not be able to match each possibility with a statistical probability.

The Constants of Human Geography

The pathocoenosis of a given population is determined by its geographical setting, by the presence in it of pathogenic parasites and their hosts, by its gene pool, and by its social life. Moreover, the state of affairs in a pathocoenosis at a given historical moment depends on the previous distribution of diseases in its population. All of these factors are interconnected in an extremely complex, even inextricable way.

These remarks about pathocoenosis in general can and must apply to the study of diseases among the ancient populations of the Greek world. Such a study presupposes that for the past few millennia biological laws, especially those that govern pathological events, have undergone no changes and that the properties of the human body have changed but little. To us it seems entirely reasonable to assert the immutability of natural laws as an epistemological postulate, at least on the scale of human time and human space. As for the biological evolution of man, the scientific evidence currently available points strongly to its slowness. Accordingly, we infer that the regulatory mechanisms and pathological reactions of the human body on all the levels of its organization are the same now as in the past, particularly from the Neolithic period to the end of the classical age. So an epileptic fit, an attack of apoplexy with its aphasic and paralytic aftereffects, the spread and ulceration of a cancer, functional disorders as a result of physical trauma, and even allergic reactions of the skin must have taken place in the human of the past as they do in the human of the present. The Hippocratic texts confirm this biological constancy. Where differences exist between the diseases of ancient Greece and those of today, they must stem from changes in external factors (such as food, habitat, work and leisure, therapeutic procedures, and so on) or in the relations between man, pathogenic germs, and their hosts. With regard to the latter, there have been considerable changes, but it is worth noting that they obey certain rules. Recent discoveries in immunology and epidemiology allow us to make some fairly plausible hypotheses about the historical evolution of infectious diseases and to use the results in various parts of the present book.

Certain diseases are surpassingly ubiquitous. They are so linked to essential vital processes that they seem "programmed" ahead of time. Either they derive from inevitable flaws owing to the constraints of the phylogenetic past,[16] or their manifestations, so harmful to the individual, provide biological advantages to a population or even the species as a whole. In particular I have in mind the so-called degenerative diseases, most of which are unavoidable consequences of the aging of the human body. Plainly, the inhabitants of Greece, just as those of the rest of the world, suffered since time immemorial from senility and arteriosclerosis and the host of local complications they bring.

Other, relatively less frequent diseases also look programmed, since they affect man because of inherent flaws in the functioning of his genetic equipment. The root of several complex clinical pictures can actually be traced to relatively simple abnormalities in the karyotype, in either the structure or the distribution of chromosomes. Structural anomalies are transmitted as hereditary diseases in the strict sense. They can be localized to the synthesis of a particular molecule necessary for the proper functioning of the organism ("inborn errors of metabolism"), and their frequency is determined by a kind of equilibrium between the mutation rate and the selection pressure of the environment. In studying hereditary anemias in Greece, especially thalassemia, we shall see that selection can have a positive as well as a negative effect on the genetic trait. The history of favism will serve to illustrate the persistence of such traits. When the abnormality lies in the number of chromosomes, the resultant disease is innate but not necessarily hereditary. The standard example is Down's syndrome (mongolism), a deformity accompanied by mental retardation that is due to one supernumerary autosomal chromosome in the fertilized ovum (trisomy 21).

Biological considerations lead us to believe that the risk of an abnormality due to the absence of disjunction of a chromosomic pair during meiosis did not change between antiquity and the beginning of the modern demographic explosion. In other words, the frequency of Down's syndrome and sex chromosome abnormalities was about the same in the classical age and the eighteenth century. The only factor known to change the frequency of Down's syndrome is the age of the mother at conception. This consequence of maternal aging was uncovered in statistical analyses by L. S. Penrose in 1934, and subsequent research has indeed confirmed his finding. Among the present populations of Europe, the overall frequency of Down's syndrome is 1 in about 600 live births. If the mother is younger than 30 years old, the rate drops to 1 in 2,500. Accordingly, one can suppose that in archaic and classical Greece at least 1 newborn in 2,000–2,500 had trisomy 21. As for trisomies affecting the sex chromosomes, the frequency of Klinefelter's syndrome in boys could not have been far from 1 in 500–1,000 male births; likewise, the frequency of Turner's syndrome in girls should have been 1 case in about 2,000–3,000 female births.

I hesitate to supply figures for diseases caused by an inborn error of metabolism. Their frequency is determined by the genetic load, something that varies from population to population, and the mutation rate, which depends, in turn, on environmental factors like radiation and chemical pollution. However, certain of these molecular diseases now occur with a distinctly different frequency than the mutation rate, a fact that forces us to assume their existence in the remote past of the human race. Phenylketonuria is a good example of this. It is an autosomal, recessive disease clinically manifested as serious mental disorders sometimes accompanied by epileptic fits. First described by I. A. Folling in 1934, this hereditary disease strikes approximately 1 newborn in 10,000. Its mutation rate has been calculated at 25 per million loci. It must be a very old inheritance, since its frequency is at once too high and too consistent among all current Caucasion populations to be explained as the result of recent mutations. The same inference can be made about mucoviscidosis or cystic fibrosis of the pancreas, a disease now occurring in Europe at the rate of 1 newborn per 2,000–2,500 or about hereditary deaf-mutism and albinism, even though the frequencies of the latter vary considerably among different populations.

In a paper presented in 1980 to the Paleopathology Congress at Caen, Valfredo Capecchi maintained that congenital clubfoot is due to "a genetic mutation at least 100,000 years old, that is, pre-existing the glaciation of Würm." He reached this conclusion from two premises, namely, that (1) "this deformity occurs throughout humanity, irrespective of race, at a rate of approximately 0.12 percent," and (2) "its recessive hereditary transmission is considered proven." Its selective disadvantage, especially for a primordial society of hunters, would have been offset by the attribution of magical powers to its carriers. In this regard one can cite the mythological deformity of Hephaestus.[17]

Regrettably, Capecchi's argument is not probative. If we leave aside his incomplete and too approximate statistical data on the worldwide distribution of clubfoot, his inferences concerning its past are very weak since its etiology is not simple and unique. Long ago, Hippocratic physicians saw that congenital clubfoot could derive from a lesion developed during intrauterine life.[18] Not all occurring cases are of chromosomic origin, and even when they are, the defect is polygenic and can be attributed not to the antiquity of the genes responsible but to some relatively recent mutations. So the trait's advantage would not consist in some link between its external, phenotypic expression and the environment, such as social protection justified by magical beliefs, but in some particular, internal feature of the human genome itself, whose structural stability might demand weakness in specific genetic loci.

It seems to me that a similar argument could be made about some hereditary forms of diabetes and other endocrine disorders. Such a hypothesis would not allow us to judge the real impact of these diseases within the pathocoenoses of the past, nor could we assert that their frequency is unchanged, but it would suffice to establish their existence at the dawn of human history. Although the Hippocratic writings make mention of clubfoot and know certain diseases are hereditary (generalized epilepsy, pulmonary consumption, strabismus, among others),[19] the truth is that most congenital diseases were unknown to ancient physicians. The causes of this were, above all, the faint interest in medical treatment of very young children and the extremely high childbirth and infant mortality rate; together, they simply prevented doctors from seeing such diseases.[20]

Nevertheless, certain of them have such typical symptoms lasting on into adulthood that the silence accorded them by the physicians of antiquity can be considered meaningful. Hemophilia is a good example. It is a hereditary enzyme disorder transmitted recessively and linked to gender. Disorders in the blood coagulation system inevitably result in serious hemorrhages. The two classic forms of this disease appear only in males, not necessarily from birth but generally soon after, for instance, when the child learns to walk. In the past, hemophilic boys usually died of accidents before reaching puberty. But the transmission of the disease was maintained by females as heterozygous carriers of the gene that their own bodies did not express.

The literature of the Greco-Roman world seems to contain no mention of the kind of hemorrhagic episode that suggests hemophilia, and the silence persists in medieval writings from Byzantium and western Europe. By contrast, Jewish and Arabic writers of this period offer several unimpeachable descriptions of the disease. The Talmud notes not only that it was hereditary but also that it was transmitted in the female line. Furthermore, nineteenth-century doctors remark on the absence, or at least the extreme rarity, of family-linked hemophilic syndrome among native inhabitants of Greece, Italy, and Turkey, and at the same time they note its frequency among Jews and descendants of the northern barbarians. The inescapable conclusion seems to be that hemophilia did not exist in ancient Greece and Rome.[21]

But things are not so simple. Current research suggests that hemophilia has a particularly high mutation rate. The trait must have appeared relatively often without familial antecedents, and in ancient populations it could only have produced short-lived hereditary lines. Among Jews and Islamic peoples the practice of circumcision facilitated its early discovery. However, none of these considerations explain the important distinctions that exist in the geographic distribution of hemophilia.

In fact there is no way to understand actual pathological events until we thoroughly grasp the idea that most diseases result from the conjunction of an innate weakness with a wide variety of environmental factors. In the great majority of cases, diseases occur at the intersection of two causal chains, one genetic and the other external. Consider hypertension as an example: the frequency of this disease—an important one in a pathocoenosis because of its multiple complications—increases with the quantity of salt in food and with stress, but it is also genetically determined by a particular permeability of the cellular membranes to sodium and potassium. The disease is an organism's response to attack, so its occurrence depends as much on the force of the attackers as on the vulnerability of the attacked. This kind of twofold causality is apparent as well in certain forms of cancer. In this regard Jacques Ruffié has stressed the difference in the frequency of carcinoma of the nasopharynx in Asia where it is common, and in Europe, where it is rare. In Macao it occurs among the Chinese but never the Portuguese. It is thought that the difference is due to racial differences, particularly as concerns tissular antigens, but even so environment is not blameless in the etiology of this disease (distinctive diet, viral infections, and so forth).

The factor of race is sometimes adduced for diseases whose causes are still unclear. It has been said, for instance, that hemorrhoids are especially common among inhabitants of the Mediterranean basin, but no serious study has been able to prove it. Certain societal habits, such as sitting for long periods of time on high, hard chairs, favor this disease in Europe nowadays. But that did not prevent the inhabitants of classical and probably also archaic Greece from having it too although they did not lead the sedentary life of a modern civil servant. We recall that a whole treatise of the Hippocratic corpus is devoted to hemorrhoids, and the disease is often mentioned in other classical texts.[22]

Diabetes, a disease whose early history needs further study, offers a fine example of double causality. As an inherited trait, diabetes is indeed ancient, doubtless as old as the human race. Yet it is possible that for a long time this inborn error of metabolism was advantageous or at least had no practical consequences in most cases because there was no excess of sugar. Beekeeping had to be invented for diabetes to become a true disease. Once there was regular honey production, man had the possibility of putting the functional capacity of his pancreas to the test. But changes of a social nature had to take place, along with modifications in the eating habits of several levels of society, before diabetes could appear to be a common disease. Unknown in the time of Hippocrates, probably because of its rarity, diabetes mellitus becomes an important disease for medical writers of the Imperial period (Aretaeus, Celsus, Galen).[23]

I note in passing that, according to modern knowledge of its pathogeny, another disease of the endocrine glands, exophthalmic goiter (Graves or Basedow's disease), must have occurred sporadically. The silence of ancient Greek writings in regard to it is surprising to us. As for endemic (hypothyroid) goiter, today we know it is linked with iodine deficiency and probably associated with nutritional and genetic factors. According to V. M.

Goldschmidt, the decline in iodine was due to the expansion of the glaciers. In fact, F. Merke has shown that the confines of the worldwide distribution of endemic goiter and of its derivative, cretinism, correspond to the furthest extension of the glaciers during the most recent stage of glaciation.[24] So it must have always been rare in Greece. And indeed, this kind of goiter was described in antiquity only by Latin authors well informed on the Alpine regions.

Despite the constancies we have just instanced, diseases do change not only in their frequency but also in their clinical aspect and in certain epidemiological peculiarities. It is worth stressing that these changes are especially common for two groups of diseases: those caused by germs (viruses, bacteria, protozoa) and those stemming from environmental changes introduced by man. To be sure, the first of these groups is far more important than all other diseases combined. In the past, infectious diseases completely dominated the pathocoenosis. In today's world, the second group has had an unequaled impact on human health.[25]

The history of infectious diseases could be told in epic style.[26] One could speak of legions of corpses and ineffable suffering, of an incredible variety of microbes and their biological plasticity, of population density and the progressive acquisition of genetic resistance to common germs, of violent responses to relatively new or rare germs, of struggles between diseases, of the presence of animal carriers and germ reservoirs, and so on. As for killer diseases, theirs is a terrifying drama with a varied cast: humanity, the parasite, the parasite's enemies, the carriers. After the initial invasion, there is a long period of mutual adaptation between host and germ. Bubonic plague, for instance, is only secondarily a human disease, and that only for short periods of time, since it destroys its own biological props too radically. A human can only be a subsidiary host of Yersin's bacillus. Actually, plague is a disease of rodents, among which it has achieved biological equilibrium between parasite and host.

Syphilis today is not what it was in the recent past, but still less is it like sixteenth-century syphilis, a disease whose violent clinical manifestations resemble smallpox. In this book we will study the immunological phenomena that typify humanity's adaptation to germs as well as some of the germs' strategies against biological defenses. Sometimes such study yields results about past epidemiological states. For instance, yellow fever is a relatively benign disease for Africans. When introduced in modern times in Greece, it took a terrible toll on the inhabitants. One can only conclude that their ancestors had no opportunity to build a biological defense.

I insist on the fact that changes have taken place for just two particular groups of diseases in order to make it clear that the spectacular aspect of those changes is only very recent. Until the nineteenth century, humanity did not know how to combat infectious agents directly. As for the way Greek peasants live, that has changed more in the past fifty years than it did in the previous three millennia.[27] A modern medical inquiry, such as the one recorded by Richard and Eva Blum during their fieldwork in Greece from 1957 to 1962, can produce useful information and unexpected insights even for a specialist in classical medicine. The inhabitants of three Greek villages were interviewed and examined by this American medical team and were found to be suffering from the following important ailments: malaria, typhoid fever, amebic dysentery, pulmonary tuberculosis, scrofula, diabetes, jaundice and hepatitis, pneumonia, meningitis, diphtheria, undulant fever, scarlet fever, cataracts, and eye diseases. Acute respiratory diseases, gastrointestinal disorders, and rheumatic pains constituted the overwhelming majority of ills seen by the team in this population of peasants and shepherds. If we include the relatively frequent diagnosis of nutritional dystrophy, high blood pressure, tonsillitis, peptic ulcers, hernia, gout, and sciatica, it is striking how closely this pathocoenosis resembles the one suggested to us by reading the Hippocratic texts. Aside from a decline in malaria, the villages of Dhadhi, Panorio, and Saratzani confronted these American researchers with a nosological reality essentially the same as the one confronting an itinerant physician in the fifth century B.C.[28]

The Greek Pathocoenosis in the Classical Period

Texts offering direct evidence of the relative frequency of diseases in antiquity are very rare. I cite three of them here in order to give the reader a general orientation, since the unavoidably analytic discussions in most of the subsequent chapters of this book can obscure a wider perspective.

According to the *Regimen of Acute Diseases,* a Hippocratic treatise from the last third of the fifth century B.C., acute diseases "kill the greatest number of people."[29] The rest of the passage makes clear what diseases it concerns: "Acute diseases are those which men of old have called *pleurîtis, peripneumonía, léthargos,*[30] *kaûsos,* and all others dependent on them whose fevers are generally unremittent. In the absence of an epidemic of some kind of pestilence (*loimṓdēs noûsos*), when diseases are sporadic, as many or more people die of acute diseases as of the rest."[31]

As for the frequency of nonfatal diseases, a valuable piece of evidence is provided by Plato, who puts the following words in Socrates' mouth when he wishes to show that the whole of a concept must not be confused with its most common elements: "Does it seem to you necessary that every sick person be gouty or feverish or afflicted with ophthalmia? Can't one be sick without having one of these diseases, since there are many others and they are not the only ones?"[32]

The Hippocratic writings offer profuse details, notably in the description of the seasonal morbidity on the island of Thasos[33] and in the following, more general medical-geographic evaluation:

A city that lies exposed to the hot winds . . . The heads of the inhabitants are moist and full of phlegm that runs down into them from the head . . . The endemic diseases are these. In the first place, the women are unhealthy and subject to excessive fluxes. Then many are barren through disease and not by nature, while abortions are frequent. Children are liable to convulsions and asthma, and to what they think causes the disease of childhood, and to be a sacred disease. Men suffer from dysentery, diarrhoea, ague, chronic fevers in winter, many attacks of eczema [*epinuctís,* a particular kind of dark pustule], and from hemorrhoids. Cases of pleurisy, pneumonia, ardent fever [*kaûsos*], and of diseases considered acute, rarely occur. These diseases cannot prevail where the bowels are loose. Inflammations of the eyes occur with running, but are not serious; they are of short duration, unless a general epidemic takes place after a violent change. When they are more than fifty years old, they are paralyzed by catarrhs supervening from the brain, when the sun suddenly strikes their head or they are chilled. These are their endemic diseases, but besides, they are liable to any epidemic disease that prevails through the change of seasons.

But the following is the condition of cities with the opposite situation, facing the cold winds that blow from between the summer setting and the summer rising of the sun, being habitually exposed to these winds, but sheltered from the hot winds and from the south . . . The natives must be sinewy and spare . . . Their endemic diseases are as follow. Pleurisies are common, likewise those diseases which are accounted acute. It must be so, since their digestive organs are hard, and the slightest cause inevitably produces in many patients abscesses, the result of the stiff body and hard digestive organs. For their dryness, combined with the coldness of the water, makes them liable to internal lacerations. Inflammations of the eyes occur at last; they are hard and violent, and rapidly cause rupture of the eyes . . . Instances of the diseases called "sacred" are rare but violent . . . As to the women, . . . their menstrual discharges are not healthy, but scanty and bad. Then childbirth is difficult, though abortion is rare. After bearing children they cannot rear them, for their milk is dried up . . . cases of phthisis are frequent after parturition, for the violence of it causes ruptures and tears. Children suffer from dropsies in the testicles while they are little, which disappear as they grow older.[34]

If we are not distracted by the essentially false etiological discussions of the Hippocratic writer, we can look at his text as a deposition of exceptional value on the nosological reality of long ago. It is a faithful account of what itinerant Greek physicians of the fifth century B.C. really came across in the regular practice of their profession. This is not to say it is a faithful account of what actually took place in the bodies of their patients. At least two factors come into play to deform this testimony. The first is dogmatic prejudice, and the second is what one might call the invisibility of the familiar. An anecdote can illustrate what we mean here. In an ancient anthology of funny stories, we find the following joke: "We were talking about indigestion (*apepsía*), and the backslapper said he never got it. But when we asked him if he'd ever a sour or nasty-tasting burp, he said, 'That I get every day.' "[35] As for the doctrinal obstacles, it is enough to note, as an example, that their medical theories prevented Greek and Roman practitioners from perceiving the true frequency of heart disease.

As we do, Greek doctors distinguished endemic, epidemic, and sporadic diseases. The most awful endemic diseases were, in modern terminology, malaria, tuberculosis, acute forms of gastroenteritis (particularly typhoid fever and other diseases caused by salmonellae and enteroviruses, bacillary dysentery, and amebiasis), ophthalmias, and skin diseases, especially purulent ones. These diseases were so frequent that the ancient doctors divided them into a great number of distinct nosological entities, some epidemic, others sporadic. Diseases from contaminated water must have been the principal cause of the elevated infant mortality rate.

The Historical Impact of Disease

Disease is one of the factors forging human destiny. Its importance in the footnotes of history, in the private life of everyone, is a truism, yet biographers inhibited by exaggerated modesty have not always been equal to its scope. By studying the effects of disease on the public activity of some famous persons, an attempt has also been made to introduce pathology into history proper.[36] Couldn't the diseases of leaders determine the lot of their peoples? Greek historians, from Herodotus to Plutarch, were convinced of it, and the idea is not inappropriate to an era when the personal genius of a few great men was granted a preponderant role on the stage of history. What would the destiny of the ancient world have been if Nikias had not been sick during the Athenian expedition to Sicily, or if Alexander had not abused alcohol and gone to an early grave from malaria? These are truly naive questions, on the order of Pascal's famous joke about Cleopatra's nose and Cromwell's kidney stone.[37]

Traditional history aims to describe the most extraordinary political, military, and cultural events and to give homage to "great men," but its proper opposite is a more complete vision of the past of humanity, a history of daily life, a sociological approach especially interested in the fate of the "common man." In this global historical vision, diseases take on prime significance as mass phenomena affecting economics, demography, and social behavior.[38] There are epidemic diseases, plagues whose terrible consequences are so stunning and vast that their role in history escapes no one. I note that the best accounts of exceptionally serious epidemics in antiquity are not provided by professional physicians but by historians or other men of letters. It is enough to mention Thucydides' account of the "Great Plague," which was an event of decisive importance for the outcome of the Peloponnesian War and the future of Athenian imperialism.[39] The significance of such disasters needs no proving, but the same is not true of endemic diseases, with their slow evolution. Yet they affect the biological potential of a society much more profoundly and in more enduring ways.

Chapter One

LITERARY REFLECTIONS OF PATHOLOGICAL REALITY

The Hippocratic corpus is a collection of about sixty fairly heterogeneous medical treatises traditionally attributed to Hippocrates (ca. 460–377 B.C.), the most prestigious member of the guild of Asclepiadae on the island of Cos. Together they make up the oldest professional account of diseases in the Greek world. The dates of composition vary from one treatise to the next, but no one of them is older than the fifth century B.C. Since my purpose is to go as far back in time as possible, I am obliged to appeal to other written sources that are more venerable but much less relevant to my actual subject. This means scouring archaic inscriptions and, above all, what survives in Greek from the oldest poetic, historical, religious, philosophical, and legal works.

In the Introduction I stressed that the modern reader must confront a special obstacle to understanding ancient names of various diseases, the fact that they conceptualize morbid states in a way that is not our own. This change in the system of reference for the terminology of disease is a hindrance even in the highly technical texts from antiquity in which it is possible to glimpse a link between concept and clinical reality. In other chapters of this book there are several concrete instances of the difficulties to be faced in the modern interpretation of diseases described by Greek medical treatises. Clearly, the task of the historian of disease is that much more arduous when he must track down the pathological states of the past with nothing more to guide him than literary passages that refer to them incidentally, as subjects of casual concern, and usually without mention of symptoms. The project that awaits is a kind of "linguistic archaeology," with all that such a locution implies with respect to both significance and frailty. It would be hard to overstate the pitfalls in this field of study.

Language as Historical Evidence and the Linear B Tablets

In itself language is a source of information about realities that can be much older than the moment when certain words are attested for the first time in surviving documents. The Greek language as we know it through inscriptions and the oldest literary works appears and develops in the Mediterranean world after invasions of the Balkan peninsula by people speaking an Indo-European language. The arrival of the tribes who made the decisive contribution to the birth of the "Greeks" took place in the Bronze Age, more precisely toward the end of Old Helladic II, in the last centuries of the third millennium B.C. The Greek language developed from the idiom of the newcomers and of the indigenous peoples. The Linear B inscriptions prove that this language was dominant no later than the time of the expansion of Mycenaean civilization, that is, by the middle of the second millennium B.C. It is interesting to note that, according to specialists, the majority of Greek medical terms are of Indo-European origin.[1] This is especially the case for the ancient vocabulary of pathology.[2] In fact there is no Greek word for a disease, disability, or symptom that is securely identified as of proto-Balkan, Semitic, or Egyptian origin.[3] The richness of Greek terms inherited from Indo-European is particularly striking for visible disabilities and ailments on the surface of the human body: deformities, paralyses, injuries, tumors, hernias, a very wide variety of skin and eye afflictions. The same is true of the main intestinal and cutaneous parasites. The number of words referring to hunchback and other chronic trunk and limb deformities goes way beyond the normal need for synonyms. There was a refined differentiation among such states that reflects their social significance.[4]

Since it contains no identifiable proto-Balkan medical terms, the Greek language offers no information on the diseases found by the Indo-European tribes on arriving in their new homeland. Instead, it preserves the memory of those that the invaders brought with them. Even so, care is necessary in applying this sort of reasoning to concrete philological analysis: we must remember that the Greek language is hospitable to the creation of neologisms formed from a stock of old lexemes whose meanings modulate with changed circumstances. The fact that a Greek word has an Indo-European root does not always guarantee its antiquity or, *a fortiori,* that of the concept it is thought to signify.

The decipherment of Linear B by M. Ventris and J. Chadwick in 1952 has made available Mycenaean epigraphy, a treasure-house of Greek words from the Late Bronze Age, in particular the period from the fifteenth to the twelfth century B.C. It is now possible to read the inscriptions found in great numbers at Mycenae, Knossos, Pylos, and, more recently, Thebes. Most of the texts deciphered are inventories that relate almost exclusively to the administration of the palaces; unfortunately, none concerns medicine directly.[5] From reading these documents the medical historian can recover a few simple terms of external anatomy and glean some information concerning diet and various medicinal plants.[6] Among the occupations mentioned, he will find an unguent-boiler, a female bath-keeper, and, to be sure, a doctor.[7] But he will search in vain for the names of diseases or disabilities. Nevertheless, it may well be that a terminology of pathology is hidden in the onomastic evidence. In most languages, there are hypocoristic personal names with a negative tinge that allude to an individual's (or his ancestor's) physical idiosyncrasy. According to Oscar Landau, author of a meticulous study of Mycenaean personal names, the proper name *Ku-ra-no* is derived from the same root as *kullós* 'crippled, deformed,' while *Ku-jo* and *Ku-ja-ro* mean 'lame,' *A-ra-i-jo* 'thin,' *A-pa-u-ro* 'weak,' *Pa-ra-ro* 'bald,' *No-da-ro* 'toothless,' and *Nu-o* 'dumb.'[8] The name *No-sa-ro* attested on a tablet from Knossos is etymologically related to *nósos* and would have once designated a sickly person; it also constitutes a proof of the great antiquity of the generic term in Greek for disease.[9]

Life and Death in the Homeric World

In the second half of the eighth century B.C. the oldest work of Greek literature, the *Iliad,* assumed the form it has today, with the exception of a few interpolations. The *Odyssey,* probably but not necessarily composed by the same poet, appeared a little later. The events related in the two epics[10] are for the most part imaginary, but it is generally accepted, especially since Schliemann's excavations, that the historical background is not wholly fictitious. Achaean warrior kings did rule over peasant populations in the geographic sites mentioned by the poetic narrative. They did indeed wage a war against Troy, and they destroyed that city toward the last third of the twelfth century B.C. Using a general framework transmitted orally from generation to generation, a genius poet was able to create a dazzling world in which gods, heroes, and plain mortals undertake the most varied activities and in which the ordinary and the marvelous, the mundane and the sublime, seamlessly commingle.[11]

In this epic world, medicine has a privileged place, but only one of its aspects will preoccupy me here: the way pathological states are conceptualized and the historical reality that underlies them. I pass over in silence the Homeric understanding of biological phenomena in general as well as pharmacology, the treatment of wounds, hygiene, the identity and social status of doctors and healers, and so on.[12] Thorny questions about the real existence of Homer as well as the genesis and unitary or composite character of the poems ascribed to him are not my concern. Nevertheless, insofar as I accept the *Iliad* and the *Odyssey* as sources of information on some aspects of daily life in Greece, it is incumbent on me to make plain my opinion regarding the historical era pertinent to the Homeric evidence that does interest me.

The Homeric world is formidably ambiguous from a chronological point of view. Properly speaking, the story takes place in the grand days of the Mycenaean kingdom. But what is actually the case? To be sure, the representation of material and social conditions, of customs and beliefs, is deliberately archaizing. The bard wished to convey to his hearers a vision of an old-fashioned civilization, of a lost heroic age. But after four dark centuries in which even the memory of Mycenaean writing was lost, what was still known about the actual way of life of Achaean society before the Dorian invasion? Aside from a few broad strokes of history, the poet evoking this glorious past was free to invent what he wished. And he could not do otherwise, since the object of his enterprise was essentially aesthetic and pedagogical. Even so, as far as daily life is concerned, for the material details of existence he was dependent on the state of knowledge of his own time. The believability of his narrative was based on its everyday realism. The poet could introduce the extraordinary and revel in fantastic events, but only if he carefully respected part of the daily experience of his public. Such veracity was particularly important with regard to my object of study, namely, the sufferings of the human body, diseases, and medical practices. When touching upon such subjects, which are frankly secondary in the epic purview, the Ionian bard could not deviate perceptibly from his own historical and geographic milieu.[13]

The *Iliad* begins by invoking the funeral pyres on which the corpses of countless warriors slain by the arrows of Apollo are burning, and it concludes with a description of the funeral of Hector. Death is present in it at every moment.[14] Nor does its author tire of relating, in detail and without fear of repeating the most significant expressions, how a sort of vital principle *(thumós)* and the soul *(psukhḗ)*[15] quit the bodies of those who succumb to their wounds: a dark cloud covers the dying man, his nostrils cease to inhale air, his vision swirls and black night veils his eyes, his knees bend and give way, he sleeps a sleep of bronze and breathes out life through his mouth or a wound.[16] Sarpedon, wounded by Patroclus "where the *phrénes* encircle the stout heart," falls "like an oak," calls out to his companion, Glaucus, and "the end of death *(thánatos)* covers his eyes and nostrils." Then Patroclus places his foot on his victim's chest, pulls on the bronze spear, and "draws out at once Sarpedon's soul and the point of his spear."[17]

On the physical side, Homer is aware not only of simple facts like the fatal results of a massive hemorrhage but also of the rare and striking phenomenon called cataleptic rigidity: Mydon, the squire and charioteer of a Paphlagonian chieftain, dies almost instantly after a sword blow to the temple. His body falls head first from the chariot, sticks well into the sand, and "stays upright for some time" until his horses knock it down on the ground.[18] As for psychological phenomena, Homer describes men's paralyzing terror in the face of imminent death and stresses the fading sense perceptions and progressive loss of consciousness in the dying.

When Hector is killed by a bronze lance through his neck, "his soul leaves his limbs and goes off, flitting to Hades', bemoaning its fate, abandoning its strength and youth."[19] The *psukhḗ* that escapes from the body persists after death and leads a pitiful existence in the underworld, like a shadow or faded image of the living person. That is where Odysseus learns from the shade of his mother, Anticleia, what the profound reality of death is in the Homeric scheme of things:

> That is the law of mortal men, when they die:
> the tendons *(ínes)* no longer hold together the bones and the flesh;
> the mighty fury of fire destroys all, once life *(thumós)* has left the calcined bones
> and the soul *(psukhḗ)* has flown away like a dream.[20]

The *psukhḗ* of a man, declares Achilles in his passionate speech to Odysseus, can neither return nor be seized or captured "once it has crossed the barrier of one's teeth."[21] Once breathed out, life can never be regained. But despite death's definitiveness, there are states comparable to it that are entirely reversible: Homer describes several cases of syncope.[22] The poet conceives of it as a provisional loss of breath, in other words, a temporary departure of the vital principle manifested by a sudden dimming of consciousness and an overall weakness in the limbs—serious symptoms, but brief ones. Such syncopes result either from a physical injury, for example, the spear-shot that wounds Sarpedon in the thigh or the boulder-throw that crushes Aeneas's hip or smites Hector's breastbone,[23] or a psychological shock, as in Andromache's emotional response to Hector's corpse or Laertes recognizing Odysseus.[24]

To return to the subject of death: the Homeric world clearly distinguishes four types—namely, death by overt violence (combat, accident, sacrifice), death as the result of debilitating disease, sudden death without apparent external cause, and death from grief. The first type, violent death, predominates throughout ancient poetic and historical texts. It fascinates by virtue of its tragic dimension. Its frequency is extremely high in war narratives (as in the *Iliad*), but that does not mean it is considered the most common way to die in peacetime conditions. Accidents while hunting or working, drownings, and fatal falls could not have been rare. They are only rarely spoken of because they are humdrum. I recall the story of Elpenor, one of Odysseus's companions, who drank too much and went out on the roof to get some air: falling head first, he broke his cervical vertebrae and died immediately.[25]

Whom the gods love dies young: such is the sentiment of a poet who abhors death caused by chronic disease. But the third type, sudden death, stands between violent death and natural death from disease. Sudden death without visible external cause (i.e., from the modern point of view, natural death from acute internal disease) is, for Homer, simply violent death by divine intervention. When Menelaus returns home, at the moment his ship touches Sunium, the sacred promontory off Athens, the pilot Phrontis dies holding in his hands the steering oar of the running ship. Though modern medicine is hesitant in the face of such an event and can only cautiously suggest the possibility of a vascular mishap affecting heart or brain, Homer is sure of the facts and expresses his etiological diagnosis clearly through the mouth of Nestor: the valiant pilot of Menelaus's ship succumbed to the gentle arrows of Apollo.[26] In wishing death on someone, the convention was to cry out, "May Apollo strike him today!"[27] But not wanting to make the heavenly bowman a murderer of women, the Greeks attributed to Artemis the power, not to call it the job, of destroying with her arrows persons of her own sex. In the myth of Niobe as Homer tells it, that proud mother lost her twelve children in one day, Apollo killing the boys and Artemis the girls.[28] If pestilence *(loimós)* rages in the Achaean army before Troy, the reason is, according to Homer, the wrath of Apollo who fires his arrows at their mules, their dogs, and finally at the men.[29] So sudden death is a sign of divine anger. Yet the epic tradition is not unequivocal on this point. The usual, accepted epithet of these murderous arrows is "gentle." The fact is that in this archaic world, long suffering is more to be feared than sudden death.

For simple mortals, the interventions of Apollo and Artemis were of the order of the invisible, but they also knew of a kind of divine punishment that put before their very eyes the reality of such phenomena, namely, thunderbolts. Zeus, master of lightning, so slew Asclepius and, above all, Capaneus, one of the seven Argive chieftains to attack Thebes. Such tales are known only from relatively late texts, but they assuredly belong to the distant past of the Greeks.

As for the fourth type, death provoked by grief, it is enough to cite the answer that Anticleia's shade provides to her son's question about the reason for her demise:

> It was not the unerring archer, Artemis, who slew me at home with
> her gentle arrows; neither was it a disease that drives out the
> *thumós* by the hideous consumption of flesh. It was my
> regret, my worries, noble Odysseus, my longing for you that stole
> the honey-sweet *thumós* from me.[30]

I have not dared translate the term *thumós* in this passage, since its polysemy is deployed advisedly by the poet. Suffice it to say that besides its more abstract sense, it connotes the spark of life.

Health and Sickness in Heroic Times

Each individual human being is the result of inborn and acquired factors, the product of both heredity and environment. A human is like any living organism, carrying within itself the combined history of its ancestry and of its own formation. The human organism's biological quality and state of health depend on them. Early on, the Greeks understood fully these two aspects of man's rootedness. According to the oldest epic and dramatic poets, a person's health and predisposition to disease and death are determined not only by the unforeseeable will of the gods but also by blood and by the climate of the place where he or she is born and lives. Blood must be understood to mean the stock or biological link between the members of a family conceived as a succession of generations. When Glaucus, the son of Hippolochus, presents himself to Diomedes, he lists his ancestors and proudly declares, "That is the stock, the blood from which I claim to be descended."[31] And Menelaus says of Telemachus, the son of Odysseus, that his blood is noble.[32] The Homeric epics describe an aristocratic world in which gallantry, passion, and strength properly belong to the members of the dominant class. So it is socially obligatory to believe that the warrior virtues as well as physical force and good health are hereditary. That is why genealogical considerations are customarily used to account for and rank the physical traits of the various heroes. In the *Iliad*, only one man of low birth dares to speak during an assembly, and it is no accident that this representative of the lower classes, Thersites (of whom more later), is described by the poet as an inferior being, ugly and deformed, disabled from birth. Homer refrains from giving eugenic advice,[33] but an echo of such precautions is audible in Hesiod:

> Bring home a wife to your house when you are of the right age,
> while you are not far short of thirty years but not much above;
> this is the right age for marriage. Let your wife have been grown
> up four years, and marry her in the fifth. Marry a maiden, so that
> you can teach her careful ways, and especially marry one who lives
> near you, but look well about you and see that your marriage will
> not be a joke to your neighbors. For a man wins nothing better than a
> good wife, and, again, nothing worse than a bad one, a greedy soul
> who roasts her man without fire, strong though he may be, and
> brings him to a raw old age.[34]

The overt purpose of most of these recommendations is the happiness, health, and longevity of the patriarch, not the qualitative and quantitative preservation of his race. But closer observation reveals that, for Hesiod and moralists of his stripe, the welfare of the progeny is basically at stake. Taken as a whole, this advice seeks to bring about a state of affairs held to be especially favorable for biological reproduction and the preservation of the patrimony.

The farmer's experience teaches that the use of first-rate seed is a favorable but not sufficient condition for the production of a good harvest. The crop's worth also depends on the soil and the weather. Should it not be the same for human beings? In the land of the Phaeacians, for instance, the climate is very mild: the crops never fail there, since the west wind's blowing fosters the sprouts and ripens the full-grown fruit. The poet of the *Odyssey* remarks that the character of the Phaeacians reflects their land's: not remarkable as boxers or wrestlers, they are fast on their feet and excellent sailors, with a love for feasting, the lyre, singing, changing clothes, warm baths, and bed.[35] Still more important for my purposes is the neatherd Eumaeus's description of his homeland, the island Syria:

> Not so much a populous island, but a good one, good for
> cattle and good for sheep, full of vineyards, and wheat raising.
> No hunger ever comes on these people, nor any other
> hateful sickness, of such as befall wretched humanity;
> but when the generations of men grow old in the city,
> Apollo of the silver bow, and Artemis with him,
> comes with a visitation of painless arrows, and kills them.[36]

Even if Syria truly exists and the soil of this little island of the Cyclades has simply been depleted over the centuries, this passage is still nothing other than an evocation of a fatherland forever lost, an imaginary paradise. But that is not the issue. What interests me is the implicit correlation of climate and substance with long life and the absence of chronic disease. It is not said that the land where life is especially pleasant is the cradle of the best men. The fantastic tale of the Phaeacians expresses the same thought as the proverb Herodotus puts in the mouth of Cyrus:

> "Soft countries," he said, "breed soft men. It is not the property of any one soil to produce fine fruits and good soldiers, too."[37]

Ideas like these, already outlined in archaic times, reach their acme in the great treatises of the Hippocratic corpus.[38]

As a rule, the Homeric heroes are well-built, of unfailing health, and, at least in the *Iliad,* durable to an extent that defies experience. Even old age does not stop these stout-hearts: Nestor, wise king of Pylos and eloquent orator, accomplishes deeds of valor even though "he had already seen two generations of mortal men pass."[39] Binges of slaughter leave them unharmed: the *Iliad* knows nothing of disabled veterans, despite its horrendous battles. But there is nothing surprising in that: the epic disdains the other side of the coin.

Yet there is an exception, an anti-hero *par excellence* named Thersites. This is how he is caricatured:

> This was the ugliest man of those who came beneath Ilion.
> He was bandy-legged and went lame of one foot,

with shoulders stooped and drawn together over his chest,
and above this his skull went up to a point with the wool grown sparsely
upon it.
Beyond all others Achilles hated him, and Odysseus.[40]

Thersites the Insolent is turricephalous, almost bald, stooped, bow-legged, and lame. According to Christos Bartsocas, this Homeric passage and the iconography it gave rise to are evidence for ancient knowledge of a congenital dysplasia called dysostosis cleidocranialis by modern medicine.[41] That is possible but unproven. Whatever the case may be, Thersites' deformity is above all a dramatic *tópos:* this personage is the court buffoon, the show-off, and the whipping-boy of Odysseus, who does not flinch from smiting him with the scepter and raising, as though it were needed, a "bloody welt."[42]

Skipping over the hump of Eurybates, the senile kyphosis of Aegyptius, the ugliness of Dolon (whose appearance is disturbing but whose feet are swift), and the twisted foot of the god Hephaestus,[43] I focus my attention instead on the most frequently mentioned infirmity in epic and in classical tragedy: blindness. Enraged by his boasts, the Muses punished the Thracian bard, Thamyris, with it,[44] and the gods themselves saw fit to blind the Theban seer Tiresias.[45] In ancient belief, loss of sight was linked by a kind of compensation magic to clairvoyance and the gift of poetic creation, song, and enchantment. Thus the bard Demodocus, who sang so well the events of the Trojan War, was blind as a result of the Muse's special affection: the Muse "gave him both good and evil. / She reft him of his eyes, but she gave him the sweet singing / art."[46] Some have seen in this bard the poet's self-portrait.[47] Was Homer blind? If we accept the attribution to him by Thucydides and Aristophanes of the majestic *Hymn to Apollo,* he must have been blind, since the author of that poem describes himself as "a blind man *(tuphlòs anḗr)* living in harsh Chius."[48] But modern criticism is not inclined to date the composition of this hymn earlier than the beginning of the seventh century B.C. or to consider it a work by the author of the Trojan epic.

Several of the *Lives of Homer* mention the great poet's blindness, but all of them are late. According to the biography of Homer transmitted in the chrestomathy of Proclus, "Some claim that he received his name as a result of his blindness; according to them, the Aeolic peoples call blind men *homḗroi.*"[49] That is an old opinion. There is a trace of it in Ephorus, the fourth-century Greek historian. According to him, the poet's original name was Melesigenes. He changed it to Homer because of his blindness, since that was what blind people were called as a result of their using guides *(tȏn homēreuóntōn).*[50] The etymology is patently false, but the need for such a philological digression in Ephorus proves that learned men of his time thought of the father of epic poetry as a sage and venerable personage who had lost the use of his eyes. In Plato there is a strange parallel between Homer and the great lyric poet Stesichorus, who had been "deprived of his eyesight for having cursed Helen."[51] The iconographic tradition, which goes back at least to the classical period, provides us with a few magnificent busts of Homer as a blind old man. At times they can barely be distinguished from busts of Stesichorus.[52] But it is important to note that in some ancient representations, for example, a fourth-century B.C. coin from Ios, Homer is a sighted figure with a piercing gaze.

Ancient writers were not unaware of the contradiction between a tradition that wished the bard to be blind and the fact that visual experience of the world is necessary to describe it well in poetry. On the one hand, says Cicero, the tradition portrays Homer as blind; on the other, the text he left is so rich in descriptions of places and events that it more nearly resembles painting than poetry.[53] In short, to cite the Homeric biography handed on by Proclus, "Those who have called him blind are themselves poor observers, since no man has seen as much."[54] Lucian is similarly ironic about Homer's supposed blindness and pokes fun at everything thought known about the poet's life.[55] But such critiques could not gain headway against a notion so deeply rooted in psychological, as against historical, compulsions. According to Dio Chrysostom, poets catch blindness from Homer as though it were an infectious ophthalmia.[56] To be sure there were a hardy few who claimed, out of a taste for paradox or to underline the marvelous nature of divine inspiration, that Homer was blind from birth or youth.[57] But generally the perfection of Homeric descriptions was a major reason for asserting a relatively late date in the poet's life for the onset of his blindness.

Pausanias says explicitly that Homer lost his eyesight exactly like Thamyris before him. Although in both cases the ultimate cause of the blindness was on the divine level, for Pausanias it is still true that it was actually produced through the agency of an eye disease.[58] According to Heraclides Ponticus, "There is evidence that Homer traveled from the Tyrrhenian Sea to Cephalonia and Ithaca, where it is said that he lost his sight as the result of an eye ailment."[59] According to a biography falsely attributed to Herodotus, Homer contracted ophthalmia in Ithaca and went blind in Colophon.[60] Such accounts are of some interest as historical evidence concerning eye ailments current at the time of their invention, but they have no value for the diagnosis of the disease of the historical Homer or for the nosological realities of the archaic period.[61]

A variety of causes can be invoked to account for the cases of acquired blindness that are spoken of in the epic, including the possible but unproven case of Homer himself. Infectious ophthalmias were most likely the cause of bilateral blindness in those days. Despite the absence of direct proof, for paleo-epidemiological reasons it must be admitted that trachoma, a disease present in Egypt since Pharaonic times, occurs around the eighth century B.C. along all the other shores of the eastern Mediterranean.[62] The multiplicity and richness of Homeric expressions for the functions of the eye and for visual perception are remarkable[63] and make it difficult to imagine that their author hadn't the benefit of personal experience. So saying, we rejoin the argument in Proclus. It does not exclude the possibility of acquired blindness. On the contrary, the point can be turned around and used as a proof of the poet's sensitization to visual phenomena after sight loss. In my opinion, this kind of reasoning is too weak to be taken seriously. I cannot consider it a scientifically sound idea that the special structure of Homeric dreams is a proof of their author's blindness,[64] or that the imprecise color terms in Greek epic diction prove that the Hellenes were color-blind or "immature" in their sense perception.[65]

Trojan War Wounds

The *Iliad* and the *Odyssey* present us with the circumstances surrounding the death of about 200 named individuals. In the majority of cases death results from combat wounds. In accord with the differences in their subject matter, martial violence has a greater role in the *Iliad* than the *Odyssey.* The tale of Odysseus's wanderings contains a score of woundings, most of which occur in book 22 and are part of the massacre of the suitors. From a medical point of view the descriptions are relatively summary and stereotyped. By contrast, the author of the *Iliad* describes with remarkable anatomical precision, and not without some delight, a great number of highly varied wounds visited upon the warriors fighting before the walls of Troy. In some ways these descriptions constitute the oldest surgical report of losses in a military campaign.

What could be more tempting for a modern physician than to take the epic literally and consider these descriptions surgical evidence from which to compile statistics? In 1865 Charles Daremberg was the first to scour the text of the *Iliad* to establish, with prudent restraint, just the numeric distribution of wounds over various regions of the human body.[66] A German army doctor, Hermann Frölich, revised Daremberg's statistics to complete them[67] and to include both the result of each wound and the weapon used.[68] Frölich's table is reproduced in Table 1.

Other, more recent writers have contributed to Homeric wound statistics by comparing them with modern evidence and by remarks on some questions of detail, but they have not succeeded in changing in any essential aspect the opinions formulated long ago by Daremberg and Frölich.[69] The statistical method brings out correlations hidden in the Homeric narrative, but it is important not to get carried away by numbers and lose sight of the fact that the *Iliad* is not an exhaustive or even a representative report on the surgical state of affairs during a specific war. Statistical analysis

TABLE I. *Statistical Table of Wounds in the* Iliad

Body part	Result	Weapon				Total
		Stone	Sword	Spear	Arrow	
Head	Fatal	4	8	17	2	31
	Not fatal	0	0	0	0	0
	Unclear	0	0	0	0	0
Neck	Fatal	1	4	8	0	13
	Not fatal	0	0	1	0	1
	Unclear	1	0	0	1	2
Trunk	Fatal	1	4	59	3	67
	Not fatal	1	0	5	3	9
	Unclear	0	0	3	0	3
Upper Limbs	Fatal	1	1	0	0	2
	Not fatal	0	0	6	1	7
	Unclear	0	0	1	0	1
Lower Limbs	Fatal	1	0	0	0	1
	Not fatal	2	0	3	2	7
	Unclear	0	0	3	0	3
TOTAL		12	17	106	12	147

SOURCE: H. Frölich, *Die Militärmedizin Homer's* (Stuttgart, 1879).

is only applicable to the poetic discourse by analogy; consequently, I refuse to use percentages or other statistical parameters arrived at by computation. They are based on false assumptions, and the refinement of the mathematical operations in such figures endows them with only deceptive legitimacy. To put it briefly, the conclusions to be drawn from statistical analysis of Homeric wounds must be limited to the detection of tendencies in the poet's thinking, which then allow us to make guesses about his familiarity with military medicine in his own time and to discern some specific aspects of it.

In terms of the number of victims, the most formidable weapon is the spear (by "spear" I mean all casting weapons with a haft: spear, pike, and javelin). However, in terms of lethal wounds, the sword is the most dangerous of archaic weapons. In the *Iliad,* no one wounded by a sword survives. The deadliness of the result is less certain when the wound is from a spear or a stone. Finally, the bow leaves one with a fair chance of surviving: roughly one hero of every two hit by an arrow does not succumb to his wound. In general, the greater the distance between adversaries when a given weapon is used, the less effective that weapon becomes.

Homeric warriors know where to strike to finish off their enemies quickly. In the *Iliad,* the result of a wound depends more on the region and the organs hit than the weapon used. The Homeric descriptions of woundings attest to an excellent knowledge of vulnerable points in the human body, of the anatomical disposition of the principal organs, and of the most likely consequences of lesions to each. Aeneas, Aphrodite's mortal son, is struck by a huge rock on the hip, at the place called the "cup-socket," where the thigh turns into the hip-bone. The blow tears the skin, "breaks the two tendons" (these could be the ilio-femoral and the pubo-femoral ligaments, or the tops of the crural and vastus externus muscles), and crushes the cotyloid socket. Although the rock was thrown with superhuman force (its weight was such that "no two men could carry / such as men are now"), Aeneas does not die from this wound—he doesn't even lie down on the ground immediately. He falls to his knees and faints from the pain: "The fighter / dropping to one knee stayed leaning on the ground with his heavy / hand, and a covering of black night came over both eyes." In this state of shock, he would have been an easy mark for enemies wanting to slay him and plunder his weapons, but his mother, Apollo, and Artemis protect him. Transported miraculously to a distant sanctuary, Aeneas is cured so quickly and completely that he returns to combat the same day, full of vim and vigor.[70] This narrative is a skillful interweaving of realities experienced in daily life with the marvels of an imagined world. While the presentation of the wound and its consequences is realistic, the rapid cure and above all the integral restoration of the damaged body are contrary to observed experience in similar cases—but those events are expressly attributed to divine intervention.

With all his might, Patroclus hurls a jagged rock at Hector's charioteer, Cebriones, and it hits him right on the forehead: the rock crushes both brows and, unhindered by the bones, dislodges his eyeballs from their sockets. Wounded mortally, the Trojan warrior "vaulted to earth like a diver."[71] His fall resembles the fall of the Paphlagonian charioteer mentioned above: struck on the temple by the sword of Antilochus, he falls "gasping . . . from the carefully wrought chariot / headlong, driven deep in the dust."[72] There are thirteen other instances when mortally wounded warriors fall forward, and fourteen when they fall backward. Each time there is a good reason, either physiological or physical, to justify what the poet says. Men die in the *Iliad* falling backward or forward, stiff or sagging, gasping or crying out, but always in a way compatible with what a modern physician would predict given the localization of the wound in question.[73]

Head wounds are rightly considered especially dangerous. Once a lesion on that part of the body is sufficiently important, death is inevitable. Wounds to the face from a spear or sword are particularly shocking. An example will reveal the atrocity and the realism of their description:

> Idomeneus stabbed Erymas in the mouth with the pitiless
> bronze, so that the brazen spearhead smashed its way clean through
> below the brain in an upward stroke, and the white bones splintered,

and the teeth were shaken out with the stroke and both eyes filled up
with blood, and gaping he blew a spray of blood through the nostrils
and through his mouth, and death in a dark mist closed about him.[74]

Actually, a warrior's face was only partially covered by his helmet, which served to protect him fairly well from cutting and thrusting weapons. To be sure, the helmet was vulnerable to an especially violent spearcast, as in the sad case of Hippothoos, the Pelasgian chieftain. The Telamonian Ajax leaped at him and

struck him at close quarters through the brazen cheeks of his helmet
and the helm crested with horse-hair was riven about the spearhead
to the impact of the huge spear and the weight of the hand behind it
and the brain ran from the wound along the spear by the eye-hole,
bleeding. There his strength was washed away.[75]

Nor was it enough to be helmeted to be safe from the dread consequences of a blow to the head from a hard and heavy object like a club or a rock. Here, for instance, the Trojan warrior, Erylas, is struck by a rock on the dome of his skull: "All the head broke into two pieces / inside the heavy helmet, and he in the dust face downward / dropped." On the Achaean side, Epeigeus died in exactly the same way.[76] But during his battle with Diomedes, Hector's helmet saved his life. Diomedes' javelin struck the top of it, but bronze repelled bronze. Shaken up, Hector withdrew at a run, then fell to his knees in a faint. Finally, he "got his wind again," stood up, and remounted his chariot.[77] The epic repeats here verbatim the lines used to describe Aeneas's loss of consciousness when wounded on the hip.[78] From a medical point of view, however, the situation is a little different: Hector has no visible wound.[79] He has suffered a concussion, a disturbance of the brain that causes a transient loss of consciousness.[80]

Nowadays, concussions are almost inevitable for boxers. In view of the boxing rules in antiquity, it was even worse then than now. Here is the Homeric account of a sporting event during the funeral games of Patroclus, which pitted the Argive leader, Euryalos, against the warrior Epeios, skilled in boxing:

Their heavy arms were crossing each other,
and there was a fierce grinding of teeth, the sweat began to run
everywhere from their bodies. Great Epeios came in, and hit him
as he peered out from his guard, on the cheek, and he could no longer
keep his feet, but where he stood the glorious limbs gave.
As in the water roughened by the north wind a fish jumps
in the weeds of the beach-break, then the dark water closes above him,
so Euryalos left the ground from the blow, but great-hearted Epeios
took him in his arms and set him upright, and his true companions
stood about him, and led him out of the circle, feet dragging
as he spat up the thick blood and rolled his head over on one side.
He was dizzy when they brought him back and set him among them.[81]

Wounds to the neck are relatively frequent, considering the small size of this region of the body. This is because it is at once very delicate and poorly protected by the warrior's armor.[82] Plotting Hector's removal, Achilles was eyeing his "splendid body, to see where it might best / give way." All the rest of his body was covered with armor,

> yet showed where the collar-bones hold the neck from the shoulders,
> the throat, where death of the soul comes most swiftly; in this place
> brilliant Achilles drove the spear as he came on in fury,
> and clean through the soft part of the neck the spearpoint was driven.
> Yet the ash spear heavy with bronze did not sever the windpipe,
> so that Hector could still make exchange of words spoken.[83]

In several other instances, a warrior plunges his spear into his enemy's throat, cutting the carotid arteries[84] or the whole neck from one side to the other. Sometimes decapitation is the *coup de grâce* administered to a powerless, fallen enemy. Deucalion, his arm already transfixed by Achilles' spear, awaits death resignedly: "Achilles struck with the sword's edge / at his neck, and swept the helmed head far away, and the marrow / gushed from the neckbone."[85]

The number of wounds to the trunk or abdomen is particularly high in the epic. They account for more than half of all wounds whose localization is specified. Doubtless this high frequency is consistent with what actually happened in the Bronze and Iron Ages, when the decisive role in battle was played by soldiers in heavy armor. It is explicable in view of the central position and relative size of the trunk as a target for casting weapons and arrows. The chest itself was heavily protected, as much by body armor as by the shield, which was carried in the left hand and covered the cardiac region.[86] As a result, Homeric champions sought to hit their enemies at waist level and on the right-hand side, "under the *phrénes,* in the liver."[87] According to Homer, a wound to this organ inevitably resulted in death. In fact, given the prevalent conditions, there could only have been very rare exceptions to this rule. The experience of modern army surgeons attests to the extreme seriousness of sword wounds that cut across the diaphragm and thus open both the thoracic and abdominal cavities.[88]

The belly was also a region where wounds were unforgiving.[89] Having wounded Diomedes in the foot with an arrow, Paris shouts in delight that he did not miss his enemy but is unhappy that he failed to hit a fatal spot: "You are hit, and my arrow flew not in vain. How I wish / I had struck you in the depth of the belly and torn the life from you."[90] For instance, Agamemnon kills Deïkoön by driving his spear through the man's shield and belt into his belly.[91] Or Meriones took Adamas's life by a similar wound:

> Meriones dogging him threw with the spear
> and struck between navel and genitals where beyond all places
> death in battle comes painfully to pitiful mortals.
> There the spear stuck fast driven and he, writhing about it,

gasped as an ox does when among the mountains the herdsmen
have bound him strongly in twisted ropes and drag him unwilling.
So he, stricken, gasped for a little while, but not long,
until fighting Meriones came close and wrenched the spear out
from his body, and a mist of darkness closed over both eyes.[92]

Like decapitation, the death-blow to the belly was a *coup de grâce* dealt to a defeated but not yet dead enemy. The account of the battle between Thoas and Peiros shows that the epic poet knew that abdominal wounds were more serious than wounds to the lungs:

Thoas the Aitolian hit Peiros as he ran backward
with the spear in the chest above the nipple, and the bronze point fixed
in the lung, and Thoas standing close dragged out the heavy
spear from his chest, and drawing his sharp sword struck him
in the middle of belly, and so took the life from him . . . [93]

After Patroclus, a victim of divine terror, had already been struck by surprise in the back between the shoulder blades, Hector finished him off with a blow to the same region.[94] Wounds to the lower belly at once produce a state of shock. They are not always immediately fatal, but it was not known how to combat internal hemorrhaging or peritoneal infection caused by the spilling of intestinal contents or the consequences of the intra-abdominal effusion of urine. Lesions of the bladder were doubtless frequent and deadly. The case of Pherekles serves as an illustration of a lethal wound to that organ by a strange but anatomically possible route:

This man Meriones pursued and overtaking him
struck in the right buttock, and the spearhead drove straight
on and passing under the bone went into the bladder.
he dropped, screaming, to his knees, and death was a mist about him.[95]

Going from back to front and from below to above, the spear traversed the gluteus maximus, the ischio-pubic foramen, the bladder, and the pubic arch.[96]

I now come to wounds of limbs.[97] There are relatively few of them, and, as should be the case, most often they are not mortal. Their relative infrequency in the epic is certainly not in conformity to reality, to the abundance of banal wounds to arms and legs. The poet prefers to relate serious and spectacular events. One case merits attention. When Teucer is drawing the string of his bow, a sharp rock thrown by Hector hits him "at the side of the shoulder, where the collar-bone separates the chest from the neck, at the decisive spot." The shock broke the string and "his arm went dead at the wrist."[98] The scene suggests a basis in observed reality (lesion of the brachial plexus?), since details like these do not arise from imagination alone. The same is true for remarks about the convulsive movement of the jaws caused by a fatal wound to the nape of the neck,[99] or the "shooting pains" from a relatively light leg wound that arise only after "the sore place was dry, and the flow of blood stopped,"[100] or, again, the attack of "hard pain [coming] over his flesh" not at the moment of an arrow wound to the foot but when the arrow is extracted.[101]

A few overly enthusiastic medical historians could not keep themselves from calling Homer the oldest Greek doctor known. Before becoming a poet, he was an army surgeon, or at least a kind of priest with access to medical lore accumulated over centuries.[102] According to Otto Körner, the Diomedeia (*Iliad* 5) is different from the rest of the poem in its surprising knowledge of "anatomical topography."[103] It is tempting to conclude that its author had medical training, that he was a real precursor of Hippocrates! Sadly, such hypotheses, however attractive they may be to a medical audience, are unprovable.[104] The Homeric epics contain no more medical knowledge than a "gentleman" of the eighth century B.C. with some experience of warfare can be expected to have had.

Homer has brief but undeniably realistic descriptions of cuts or surface wounds.[105] Their treatment is fairly crude (rational in the *Iliad* and magical in the *Odyssey*), and the poet only speaks of it for fresh wounds.[106] The *Iliad* calls the loss of tegumentary continuity *hélkos,*[107] a term taken up by the Hippocratic physicians in a technical sense that for a long time comprises both cuts and ulcers.[108] The word *traûma* never occurs in Homer, despite numerous occasions in which it could have been used.[109]

It is a surprising and completely abnormal thing that the Homeric heroes are never sick as a result of their wounds. They either die of them or return very quickly to normal activity. Hector fights like a lion after suffering a concussion and a thoracic contusion that makes him spit blood. Teucer, whose shoulder injury and arm paralysis were discussed above, is in such a state after it that he sobs and has to be carried back to the ships by his companions. One day later, he is already fighting bravely against several adversaries. Agamemnon, Odysseus, and Diomedes all participate successfully in the funeral games for Patroclus, but they were all wounded in battle the day before. The rule in Homer is that the heroes either die or reemerge in good health; that wounded persons can be in a state of traumatic shock, but never have any fever; that cuts bleed but are never inflamed; that tissues can be torn and smashed but never suppurate. To be sure, these distortions of reality reinforce the poetic design and flow from the very nature of epic narrative, which will not stand for inactive personages on the scene. The heroic life is inconceivable in the absence of physiological completeness. Death on the field of battle in the prime of life is glorious; slow decay is its shameful opposite. Even in the background, chronic diseases would be incongruous in this imagined world.

True Diseases in Homer

Other than the pathological states discussed above, which are disabilities,[110] and the sudden deaths attributed to the invisible arrows of Apollo and Artemis or the thunder of Zeus, and aside from wounds whose etiology is obvious, the Homeric epics do speak of mental aberrations and cases of intoxication, they mention a few banal pathogenic factors, and last, in an unfortunately off-hand way, they talk about internal diseases.

Several verses of the Homeric poems tell us that the gods can disturb a man's spirit, cloud his reason, and strike him with madness. Nevertheless, having decided not to include mental illnesses in my inquiry, I pass over the depressiveness of Bellerophon and the manic behavior of a few others. In any case the Homeric texts add little to the medico-historical knowledge of psychic health. Not until Greek tragedy do the poets provide us with masterful, almost clinical descriptions of neuroses and psychoses.[111]

Rage *(lússa)* poses a separate problem. Although in Homer this term denotes a kind of fury and not the disease (rabies) that will later bear the same name, it is likely that there are very old links between the fury of fighting men and rabid dogs.[112] Two other words that are part of modern medical terminology are already attested in the *Iliad:* aphasia *(amphasíē* or *aphasía)* and asthma *(ásthma)*. For a physician nowadays these names are attached to specific diseases. Such is not their meaning in archaic literary texts or even in the classical and Hellenistic Greek medical writers. Aphasia in the ancient sense of the word is nothing more than difficulty in speaking when one is the victim of violent emotion. Antilochus has just learned from Menelaus of the death of Patroclus and is stupefied by the news. Stricken with horror, for a long time he is seized with "aphasia," that is, he can't say a word.[113] The modern nosological sense of the word "aphasia" (speech disability caused by lesions in a specific region of the brain) dates only from 1864. Likewise, if Hector is struck by a rock and suffers from asthma and perspiration, this simply means that he has trouble breathing and is sweating.[114] His complaint is dyspnea as the result of a contusion of the chest and not an attack of suffocation strictly speaking. The word *asthmázō* is used now and then in ancient literary texts to indicate that a person is panting, either after running or some other form of exertion or during death-agony. In the Hippocratic corpus asthma denotes accelerated and difficult breathing, or shortness of breath. Despite technical usage in nosological contexts, it remains a term for a clinical symptom. In specific cases it can be used for patients with bronchial or cardiac asthma, but that is by no means the rule.[115]

Homer knows of the poisonous effect of snakebite, the use of poisoned arrows, and the existence of venomous plants. The Homeric word *phármakon* is a middle term between our concepts of poison and of medicine. As for banal pathogenic factors, I recall that Hector recommends disorienting the Achaeans with smoke[116] and that Odysseus speaks of the deleterious effects of cold, specifically of morning frost, on persons who are scantily clad.[117] People have always known that great exertions can break a man. This is how the poet describes Odysseus's state when he lands on the Phaeacians' island, after days on a raft at sea and an exhausting swim to reach dry land:

Now he let limp both knees
and his ponderous hands; his very heart was sick with salt water,
and all his flesh was swollen, and the sea water crusted stiffly
in his mouth and nostrils, and with a terrible weariness fallen
upon him he lay unable to breathe or speak in his weakness.[118]

Was such prostration, brought on by plainly natural factors and easily relieved by rest alone, really considered a *noûsos,* a disease strictly speaking, by the Greeks of the archaic period? It is doubtful that it was. In the Homeric world, true disease has a divine etiology. The Cyclopes, for instance, who are Odysseus's dupes, so answer Polyphemus's call for help: "If alone as you are none uses violence on you / why, there is no avoiding the sickness sent by great / Zeus."[119] Long ago, Celsus drew attention to the fact that during the Trojan War the doctors, "in the Homeric account, were of no help against pestilence *(pestilentia)* or against various diseases *(in variis generibus morborum)* since they are only presented as treating wounds with remedies and by the knife."[120] And the poet does call the destructive plague that is started by the arrows of Apollo an "evil disease."[121] Along with a notion that sudden death and chronic disease are of divine origin, since earliest antiquity and especially in regard to pestilence there was also a specific belief that invoked impurity or the violation of tabu as a causal explanation.[122]

Returning to the exhaustion of the shipwrecked Odysseus on the shore of Scheria, some modern medical historians have wished to consider that passage the oldest description of seasickness.[123] I do not find such an interpretation satisfactory. Instead another passage in the *Odyssey* reminds me of that syndrome, the one in which Odysseus tells how he and his men sailed off the coast of Crete, slipping along smoothly "like sailing downstream" and "without sickness" *(ánousoi).*[124] Greek sailors must have known seasickness, since it is practically certain that during at least the last few ten thousand years there have been no essential changes in the anatomical structures and functions of the inner ear that are responsible for this sickness provoked by the movements of a ship in water. Nevertheless, other, more serious diseases must have haunted the sailors of old, and the poet could well have mentioned them and not just a minor, transitory, and, frankly, somewhat silly ailment. Indeed, the word for seasickness is attested in Aristophanes.[125] Although it does not occur in Homer, the nosological term *nautía* (or, in Ionic dialect, *nausíē*) is assuredly very old. Its primary meaning, seasickness, or more precisely ship-sickness, allows for no doubt despite the fact that in its oldest occurrence, in some satirical lines of the lyric poet Semonides (late seventh century B.C.), it denotes nausea in general.[126]

Since ship-travel in Homeric times was only coastal, the sailors had no fear of scurvy, but the frequency and proximity of ports-of-call did not protect them from infectious diseases, and in fact they must have been especially exposed to diseases endemic to coastal zones, principally infestation by pathogenic protozoa. Water and insects, both germ carriers, must have been the chief factors in archaic naval pathology. Although the important role they played was unknown, their consequences could not be ignored. It is not hard to understand why Odysseus considers it remarkable that at one stage of his voyage no one on board was sick. There is every reason to believe that sailors in those times suffered often from typhoid, malaria, and dysentery. Those who reached Africa must have had schistosomiasis. Unfortunately, our literary sources are silent on the subject.

Likewise, in a military camp, and especially during a prolonged siege, infectious diseases and those caused by various deficiencies could not have been absent. And yet the Homeric heroes never have intestinal or renal colic—they don't even catch cold. The historian of diseases can only regret that moral and aesthetic considerations heeded by the epic deprive him of information about the one category of pathology that is fundamental to his investigation.

The scene of a sick man in bed, according to Daremberg, is completely alien to the epic; no hero takes time out for a bout of pneumonia or a case of diarrhea.[127] As far as I know, only one passage in archaic Greek literature speaks of a sick man in bed. Homer uses the metaphor of the curing of sickness to express the joy Odysseus feels once he senses the shore after thrashing about in heavy swells:

> And as welcome as the show of life again in a father
> is to his children, when he has lain sick, suffering strong pains,
> and wasting long away, and the hateful death spirit has brushed him,
> but then, and it is welcome, the gods set him free of his sickness.[128]

The poet gives the epithet *stugerós* 'hateful, abominable, odious' to the malevolent spirit who causes suffering *(álgea)* and who slowly dissolves *(tēkómenos)* one's flesh. In other Homeric texts, this epithet applies to disease itself, as in

> many times the good old man Polyidos had told him
> that he must die in his own house of a painful sickness *(noúsōi hup' argaléēi)*
> or go with the ships of the Achaians and be killed by the Trojans.
> He therefore chose to avoid the troublesome price the Achaians
> would ask, and the hateful sickness *(noûsón te stugerḗn)*
> so his *thumós* might not be afflicted.[129]

Homer never speaks of diseases but only of one disease, or rather, the disease. This disease *par excellence* is a kind of chronic wasting away or consumption. The historian of diseases would like to be able to say it is phthisis (pulmonary tuberculosis) or malarial cachexia, but the poet's language is too imprecise. Without any doubt, these two diseases were the major components of the nosological reality behind the Homeric texts. I can be positive in this regard thanks to cross-checking from nonliterary sources, since the testimony in Greek texts prior to the Hippocratic corpus is too generic and ambiguous to support, by itself, the diagnosis of tuberculosis and malaria. In a lovely passage cited above, Odysseus's mother draws the distinction between gentle death from divine arrows or grief and death from the disease "that drives out the *thumós* by the hideous consumption of flesh."[130] To begin with, it is worth noticing that the epithet *(stugerós)* given elsewhere to the malevolent spirit and the disease itself is here applied to consumption. The word I translate "consumption" is *tēkedṓn* and not *phthísis,* a term that does not appear in Greek literature before Herodotus. But there is no doubt about the meaning of this substantive, which is a derivative of the verb *tḗkō* 'melt, dissolve' (applied, for example, to melting snow). The authors in the Hippocratic corpus use this verb often in connection with pulmonary consumption.[131]

Some historians believe that the latter disease is mentioned by two tragic poets of the classical period, but the texts in question are very vague. In the play of Sophocles that bears her name, Antigone is told by the chorus that she "departs toward the hiding place of the dead without being wasted by consuming diseases."[132] And in Euripides' play about Alcestis, the heroine is dying to save the life of her husband and the servant woman says that "the disease consumes her."[133] From a strictly medical viewpoint, these passages do not support any specific diagnosis.

The situation is no better for the attestation of malaria in literary texts. Speaking of the star called Orion's Dog, Priam says that "it is a sign of evil / and brings on the great fever for unfortunate mortals."[134] By 1700 Adam Brendel was interpreting this passage as an allusion to the upsurge in malarial fevers during summer and fall. For the Greeks the rising of Sirius with the sun heralded hot weather, the dog days. This was the time that malaria raged.[135] But Charles Daremberg opposed Brendel's hypothesis and refused to accept that *puretós* in this passage means fever in a medical sense. According to him, it is "quite simply a period of intense heat that just exhausts poor mortals."[136] This may seem a surprising idea, but it only takes up where an ancient quarrel leaves off. A scholium teaches us that the learned men of antiquity were unsure of the meaning of this Homeric line: "Note that the word *puretós* occurs only here and that it is used in its ordinary sense and not, as some assert, to denote hot weather."[137] To me it seems that Daremberg's interpretation renders the Homeric text banal and pointless. I prefer to leave *puretós* in its medical sense, which is well-attested all through Greek literature. However, Brendel and in his train Körner and a good number of other historians seem to me to have gone too far in reducing at all cost these Homeric fevers to the intermittent and pseudo-continuous fevers of modern pathology. The epidemiology of infections due to salmonellae is cautionary in this regard: the fact that acute endemic fevers rise in summer and autumn does not prove they are malarial. When all is said and done, the real interest of the remark in Homer is not that it proves the existence of malaria in Homeric times, but as Fernand Robert did well to emphasize, that the relation between seasons and epidemic diseases had been observed, prefiguring, albeit from afar, Hippocratic medicine.[138]

From Hesiod to the Presocratics

After reading and rereading Homer, I pass on to Hesiod, the shepherd from Boeotia. According to Herodotus, these two poets gave the Greeks the genealogies of the gods and their names and functions. Hesiod's *Theogony* retells the birth of the world, the cosmogonic struggle of the new forces, and the origin of civilization. It is a mythological account transposing reality into symbolic tales. Such an approach is hardly conducive to the recording and transmission of concrete pathological information. Even when such information is in the myth, we cannot be sure of decoding correctly the language and images in which it is embedded.

Mythology likewise predominates in the second of the two principal poems of Hesiod, although, as its title suggests, *Works and Days* is a didactic poem closer to earth than sky, closer to men than gods. Conspicuous in it are the myth of the successive generations of men and the myth of Pandora. I have already spoken of them in the Introduction, since these two related myths provide a solution, a still prerational solution, to the problem of the origin of diseases. Since ancient times and still today, there have always been learned men who think that these tales of Hesiod relate, in their own way, a historical truth, namely the progressive decline in health during protohistorical times that resulted in the sudden appearance of new diseases. Even if this is true, the myth is no proof. Doubtless Hesiod did not invent the notion of a Golden Age, a legendary time when the gods spared men the misery of disease. He adopted it from a very old popular tradition. But it makes little difference, since the theme of paradise lost did not have its origin in a confused collective memory of medically idyllic times. It is a fantasy whose creation and projection onto the distant past of humanity have to do with depth psychology and not historical recall. The myth of a Golden Age has various functions, among them the satisfaction of a psychological need stemming from the irretrievable loss of childhood and the desire to justify certain social changes. A historian might conclude that, in reviving this old theme and elaborating it by making himself the prophet of the Iron Age that will take over from the Age of Heroes, Hesiod bears witness to a social crisis in his time and to the necessity that peasants like him leave behind the aristocratic ideology of

Homer. All this is surely true, but it does not advance the study of disease in ancient Greece.

Even so, once he has transferred his attention from the lofty deeds of war to the rigors of daily labor, Hesiod teaches us a few details about the demands and the risks of rural life that are determinants of health. For instance, he exhorts the Boeotian farmer to prepare himself a shelter and to provide himself with nourishment for the cold season,

> lest bitter winter catch you helpless and poor and you chafe a swollen foot with a shrunk hand. The idle man who waits on empty hope, lacking a livelihood, lays to heart mischief-making.[139]

This is the first mention in history of starvation edema.[140] Today we know that lack of protein provokes diffuse, cold edemas localized in the lower body parts (as a result of gravity). Hesiod provides the perfect clinical picture of this deficiency as he describes the characteristic attempt of the sufferer to reduce the swelling by applying pressure around the ankles and as he emphasizes in the fewest words the contrast between swollen foot and withered hand. Crises of subsistence are also responsible for a famous line of his in which famine *(limós)* and pestilence *(loimós)* sit side by side. Hesiod also knows that winter's cold aggravates rheumatism ("breaks the back").[141] But despite Plutarch's view that "it appears that Hesiod was a physician,"[142] research on his vocabulary is disappointing: he hasn't a single term of pathology that is not already known from the Homeric texts.[143]

Nevertheless, two points are peculiar and worthy of comment. First, there is the fact that a work devoted to country life makes no mention whatever of fever. Jones finds the silence especially deafening since Boeotia was marshy country with a climate favorable to mosquitoes.[144] It is known that later on malaria was rampant there. Was it not yet endemic around the end of the seventh century B.C.? The absence of evidence is only a weak indicator, but it could become significant in the presence of other arguments.

Second, Hesiod speaks of *diseases,* that is, he uses the word *noûsos* in the singular and the plural, unlike Homer, who uses it only in the singular: "Countless plagues wander among men; for earth is full of evils and the sea is full. Of themselves diseases come upon men continually by day and by night, bringing mischief to mortals silently; for wise Zeus took away speech from them."[145] So for this author diseases are numerous and can attack men of themselves, as they please *(autómatoi)*—by a kind of intrinsic causality and not by an individual divine decision in each case. For Homer, disease is outside nature: altogether alien to man and dependent on divine whim, it escapes the order of nature. By contrast, Hippocratic doctors consider diseases disturbances in man's natural equilibrium. Though unharmonious, they are still part of nature and consequently obey certain rules. Hesiod is a witness to the reclaiming of disease by nature, of nosology by physiology.[146] Although he stopped halfway, the philosophers of the sixth century B.C. did resume the destruction of the metaphysical and ontological concept of disease and its replacement by a natural and functional concept.

Around 500 B.C. Alcmaeon of Croton stated clearly what a natural disease is. His formulation borrows a political metaphor. It is important not only as an expression of Pythagorean ideas about evil as a loss of equilibrium, but also, especially as regards my subject, because it reflects the concrete experience of contemporary physicians concerning the main centers of pathological disturbance and their apparent causes:

> Health is maintained by the equal rights *(isonomía)* of the qualities of the wet, the dry, the cold, the hot, the bitter, the sweet, etc., but exclusive power *(monarkhía)* among them produces disease. Exclusive power of one [of the opposites] corrupts. Cases of disease can be explained as to their causes by an excess of heat or cold and as to their occasion by an excess or deficiency of nourishment; as to their locale, blood, marrow, and brain are affected. However, diseases also arise from external occasions, such as certain waters, a place, expense of effort, torture, or the like. Health is the mixture of the qualities in proper proportion.[147]

According to this statement, diseases are not the result of direct actions by the gods, nor are they whimsical demons whose behavior cannot be foreseen. Even so, one disease in particular kept the epithet *hierós* 'holy' long after Alcmaeon.[148] An epileptic fit strikes the whole of one's being suddenly, without warning, and in spectacular fashion it twists and shakes the body and deranges the mind, to such an extent that it suggested an extrahuman presence and could not at all be thought of as comparable to other diseases. Thus epilepsy was considered a sacred disease, or rather, the sacred disease: *hē hierḕ noûsos.*[149] It is so designated from the first line of a famous treatise in the Hippocratic corpus, which, despite its traditional title, the *Sacred Disease,* is actually concerned to rebut the reason for this name and thus to storm the last citadel of the magico-religious concept of disease:

> As for the so-called sacred disease, this is the way it is: I hold it to be no more divine or sacred than the other diseases; it has a natural origin from which it derives just like other diseases. Men have regarded it as divine because of their confusion and their wonder at its resemblance to no other disease . . . Those who first attributed a sacred character to this disease were men whose kind one can still find today: magicians, exorcists, charlatans, quacks.[150]

The clinical descriptions found in this treatise and in other Hippocratic texts fully justify the usual retrospective diagnosis of the sacred disease: generalized epilepsy, more precisely grand mal epilepsy, is its central element. Still, the features in the clinical picture are vague enough to permit the inclusion of several other pathological states, for instance, certain other forms of epilepsy, convulsions caused by encephalitis, severe spasmophilia, eclampsia, and, to be sure, hysteria. Despite this possibility of a contamination by other clinical entities, the conceptualization of the sacred disease would not have occurred had there not been, as its basis, a profound, long-term, and direct acquaintance with grand mal epilepsy.

So there is not a shadow of a doubt concerning the antiquity of epilepsy.[151] The Hippocratic physician's observation of the role of heredity in its genesis[152] shows that the disease in question must mainly be what is today called "essential" epilepsy, not just its symptomatic forms. It is true that the treatise cited above, which gives the first secure description of epilepsy, only dates from the end of the fifth century B.C., but the polemic it opens sets back the origin of the disease's name to such a distant past that the identity of its inventors was unknown. The true origin of the name "sacred disease" was already long forgotten.[153]

Cambyses II, king of Persia from 530 to 522 B.C., was regarded as an epileptic. In a fit of anger, he kicked his pregnant wife until she miscarried and died as a result. To explain this misdeed and a host of other abnormal actions of Cambyses, Herodotus says that "there is, in fact, a story that he had suffered from birth from a serious complaint which some call 'the sacred sickness.' There would then be nothing strange in the fact that serious physical malady should have affected his brain."[154] Greek mythology accuses Heracles of an attack of madness during which he killed his sons. And one of the ancient names for epilepsy was "Heracles' disease." It is not uninteresting that modern medicine fully confirms the occurrence of episodes of homicidal delirium in some epileptics. Diogenes Laertius ascribes to Heraclitus of Ephesus the opinion that falsely imagining something is the same as suffering from the sacred disease.[155] The authenticity of the passage is not assured.[156]

On the other hand, tradition links to the life of Heraclitus, in a reliable way despite considerable disagreement about the details, the mention of another disease, dropsy, of which he himself was a victim. Here is the principal variant on the philosopher's death:

> He became so misanthropic that he withdrew and went off to live on herbs and plants in the mountains. But when this diet made him dropsical, he returned to the city and consulted the doctors, asking them about his condition in the form of a riddle: could they change wet weather into a drought? Since they did not understand, he shut himself up in a stable, hoping to cure himself and dry up the water by the heat of manure, with which he covered himself. To no avail—he ended up dead of it at age sixty.[157]

It would be pointless to hold forth on the possible causes of Heraclitus's death. In terms of modern medicine, dropsy is not a disease but a syndrome. A strict vegetarian diet can result in hypoproteinemic edema, but the term *húdōr* (or *húdrōps*) most likely indicates significant effusions in the body cavities and swelling of the abdomen. One should consider, in the case of a 60-year-old leading the life of an anchorite, a very serious ailment such as peritoneal tuberculosis, heart failure, or cirrhosis of the liver. Whatever the correct diagnosis, the medical historian will lend his credence to the above account rather than that of a certain Ariston, according to whom Heraclitus "was cured of dropsy and died of another disease."[158]

Lyric Poets of the Seventh and Sixth Centuries

From the standpoint of chronology, it is now incumbent on me to scrutinize the works of the first Greek lyric poets. Sadly, they have survived only in bits and pieces whose existence we owe to citations in later authors and to papyri from Hellenistic Egypt. Despite the fragmentary and disjointed nature of this historical documentation, we owe it great respect since the message it transmits is true-to-life. Unlike Homer and Hesiod, the lyric poets of the archaic period are not fond of telling tales of far-off gods and heroes, nor of teaching proper social behavior; what they want and what they do is to sing, to purge themselves of their own miseries, their most intimate problems. In this genre of poetry, the main theme is immediate, personal experience of the world, so it would be surprising not to find in it reference to disease and death.

The oldest lyric poet whose work is at least partially accessible to us is Archilochus of Paros (first half of the seventh century B.C.). He is a strong personality, an anti-hero.[159] Enamored of life and passionately attached to the sensual exaltation it can offer, he is a soldier who demythologizes heroic death. Dead bodies, he says, serve only as fertilizer. He confesses, without pretending to be ashamed of it, that he once left behind his shield on the field of battle. And he waves off the moral significance of the act by exclaiming: I saved my life! He admits it freely, just as he declares publicly through his poetry that he is a bastard, born of an aristocratic father and a slave mother.[160] A realist, Archilochus bursts the seamless unity of virtue and physical beauty that was the rule in Greek poetry until his arrival. According to him, it's better to have as your officer "a squat fellow with knock knees" and a good heart than a slender dandy infatuated with his own curls. But the poet much esteems his mistresses' beauty, and, the ultimate inconsistency, gets himself killed on duty.

A line of Archilochus contains the following expression: "tumor between the thighs."[161] The word used is *phûma* 'tumor, swelling, abscess.' Daremberg noted that the only interest of this passage lies in its use of a word from the vocabulary of pathology.[162] But more can be said if we accept the reconstruction of Archilochus's *Epodes* proposed by François Lasserre, who joins several fragments by analogy with Horace's *Epodes*.[163] The verse that mentions the tumor between the thighs was probably part of a satirical description by the poet of his former fiancée, featuring ridicule, not to say caricature, of an aging woman who still thought herself beautiful. This verse seems to follow a fragment that evokes her withering skin and other ravages of old age. In this context, the *phûma* in question could be a prolapsed uterus or vaginal wall, if not a hernia or a vulva edema.

A scholiast in Theocritus noted that Archilochus also used the word *phutón* in the sense of *phûma.*[164] By chance the line was found on a papyrus from Oxyrynchus.[165] The context is mutilated, but something like the following is still readable: " . . . physician . . . cutting . . . since I know an excellent remedy, a very different one, for this kind of tumor . . . I propose . . . evils . . . be very careful . . . of linen . . . "[166] It is impossible to be sure of the meaning of this fragment. Bonnard thinks that "the mention of a physician, the words for swelling and cure could mean that poverty had cost the poet his health." In other words, the poet is describing starvation edema. His poem would then have inspired an epode in the *Catalepton Vergilianum* that speaks of a person whose feet are swollen from hunger.[167] Even though Archilochus complains impressively in other poems of the paucity of food on Paros,[168] I doubt that Bonnard's explanation is the right one. The term *phutón* has botanical connotations and suggests an excrescence rather than a diffuse edema. It would seem to indicate a newly formed tumor, unless it is being used simply in an erotic sense without any medical connotation.

According to Daremberg, Archilochus spoke of "ablation of the genitals" and "perhaps knew of pediculosis."[169] That is unprovable, since the texts in question are short fragments without context. In the first case, the phrase "he cut the tendons of his limb / member"[170] could refer not to castration but, as Lasserre suggests, to a fable in which a lion eats a conceited deer. In the second, there is nothing to indicate that the expression "devoured by vermin"[171] is an allusion to a disease. Nor is it likely that the curse invoking Sirius and the heat of the dog days has any relation whatever to malaria.[172]

Finally, and not surprisingly, Archilochus sings of love, its passion as well as its physical aspect. To describe the passion of love, he uses language that recalls the clinical description of a disease: love's desire excites the heart, sheds a dense mist over the eyes, and robs one of hearing; it "breaks the limbs," takes one's breath away, and causes terrible pains that pierce the bones.[173] Alcaeus also sings of the disease of love, and Sappho does so superbly: the heart melts in one's breast, one cannot speak a word, the tongue breaks, a subtle fire runs under one's skin, a mist comes over one's eyes, the ears buzz, sweat streams down one's body, a shudder seizes the man seated across from the loved one, one gets greener than grass and feels like dying.[174] To be sure, this is a poet speaking, at least in part, through metaphors. But that does not alter the fact that Archilochus, Sappho, and Alcaeus proceeded to examine almost clinically the "madness of love," and that their poems are the oldest detailed descriptions of a psychosomatic state perceived to be abnormal. Medical literature and countless anecdotes from antiquity show that the passion of love was in fact lived, diagnosed, and treated like a disease.[175]

The Greek lyric poets appreciated almost as much another thing that beautifies life and can also threaten health: wine. In the Homeric epics, the heroes never miss a chance to mix bowls of wine "as sweet as honey." A line in the *Iliad* declares that it greatly swells the might of a tired warrior. The lyric poets go further in the same line, praising drunkenness as an ecstatic experience. The success of Anacreon's drinking songs illustrates the role of alcoholism in Greek society. Poets and doctors described, each from their own viewpoint, alcoholic intoxication.[176] However, chronic alcoholism as a pathogenic factor completely escaped medical interest.

Is wine really more dangerous than water? The answer cannot be given outside a specified historical framework. It depends on the supervision of water quality, mean longevity, social activities, and so on. Wasn't it preferable for an ancient Greek to risk cirrhosis of the liver at an age beyond average life expectancy than dysentery from water in the flower of one's youth? Anacreon, a great drinker, "exceeded the limits of human life" according to Valerius Maximus; he died after the age of 85. An example like him did not inspire abstinence. Still, the Greeks preached temperance early on. Theognis of Megara insists in one of his elegies that "it is bad to abuse wine; used in moderation, wine helps, not hurts."[177]

As a rule, wine was mixed with water and not drunk straight, in contrast to the customs Greeks attributed to Scythians and Thracians, who were considered nations of drunkards. According to Herodotus (VI, 84), the Spartans ascribed the madness (perhaps a case of delirium tremens) that destroyed their king, Cleomenes, to the fact that he had learned from the Scythians to get drunk often and on unmixed wine. In this connection I cannot resist the temptation to cite a funerary inscription that is, to be sure, late, but whose topicality is not restricted to a single moment in Greek history: "Asclepiades, son of Anaxippos, an Ephesian. Twenty-two years of age, I drank in one gulp a large amount of unmixed wine and died, spitting blood."[178] If this victim had not been so young, the most tempting diagnosis would be rupture of esophageal varices caused by cirrhosis of the liver. Actually, the fatal hemorrhage could easily have been pulmonary or gastric as well.

The poet Alcaeus draws a strange picture of Pittacus (ca. 650–570 B.C.), the tyrant of Mytilene who was canonized as one of the Seven Sages. If we believe this account, Pittacus was less appealing to look at than to hear:

> Alcaeus calls him *sarápous* or *sárapos* ('splay-footed'), because he had flat feet and shuffled; *kheiropódēs* ('chapped-footed') because he had cracks and chapped skin on his feet; *gaúrēx* ('braggart') because he was arrogant; *phúskōn* and *gástrōn* ('potbellied') because he was obese, and again *zophodorpídas* ('dining in the dark') because he was stingy with lamp oil, and *agásurtos* ('slob') because he was slovenly and dirty.[179]

The ancient world has left us other portraits of this kind in which, taking off from the real or imaginary appearance of an Aesop or a Socrates, their aesthetic defects border on the pathological.

Hipponax of Ephesus, a great lyric poet of the mid-sixth century B.C., was so ugly as to be the butt of jokes in his home town. In exile at Clazomenae, his life was miserable. His poetry calls up the life of the pauper: Hipponax knows what it is to be hungry and to shiver with cold.[180] He complains that the god Plutus must be blind, since he gives him nothing.[181] In Hipponax's surviving fragments, there is mention of famine, chilblains *(khimétla),* blisters *(phōídes),* incest, and castration.[182] The poet says of a rival that he is ill from gluttony. In this highly mutilated text, the word *gastríē* meaning "abdominal cramp, colic" appears. At least that is the explanation given by a scholiast commenting on the passage in a second-century A.D. papyrus.[183]

It is a shame that only a few scraps survive of a poem by Hipponax on a subject that may have medical implications. Long ago Daremberg remarked that in the fragments of this poet is to be found a passage depicting "an unknown man who passed blood in his urine and bile from his anus."[184] He even proposed as his diagnosis a vesico-rectal fistula. But Daremberg only knew a single verse of the poem that is cited as an example in a work of the Alexandrian grammarian Herodian. The discovery at Oxyrynchus of a papyrus that contains the beginning of the verse allows for an improved understanding of its context.[185] Here is the verse Herodian cites to illustrate the usage of the verb *omikheîn* 'make water, urinate': ". . . he urinated some blood and discharged some bile." On the papyrus the passage continues as follows: "but as for me . . . and my teeth are all chattering in my mouth . . . I run crazed . . . fearing . . . this person . . ."[186] Little is clear, and unfortunately the larger whole suggests less medical significance than the single verse had led one to hope for. According to Olivier Masson, the subject is two victims of a great fright: first, the narrator, whose fear makes his teeth chatter, then the other person, "on whom the fear has a violent effect."[187] If this interpretation is correct, the expressions that seem to designate hematuria and bilious stools must be considered metaphorical. Fright, no matter how terrible, cannot cause blood to appear in the urine of a healthy person. The most common cause of this symptom in classical and Hellenistic antiquity was stones in the urinary tract. So the line from Hipponax does retain some interest for the history of diseases in Greece.

In the second half of the sixth century B.C. Theognis, an aristocrat from Megara, stresses in his elegiac poems the hereditary aspect of physical virtues and defects[188] and maintains that poverty is worse than fever *(ēpíalos).*[189] "Let's nip in the bud," he exclaims, "the ills of those near and dear; let's try to find a salve for the ulcer as soon as it forms."[190]

I conclude this chapter by citing a few verses from an ode of the lyric poet Pindar in which he speaks of the primordial diversity of diseases. True, this text belongs to the fifth century B.C. (it was composed probably ca. 473), but it clearly preserves a reflection of the tripartite division of diseases and their treatments that, as Benveniste and others think, was an archaic characteristic of Indo-European thought.[191] While telling the tale of Asclepius and his apprenticeship to the centaur Chiron, the poet describes as follows the latter's medical technique:

> They came to him with ulcers the flesh had grown,
> or their limbs mangled with the gray bronze, or bruised with the stone flung from afar,
> or the body stormed with summer fever, or chill; and he released each man and led him
> from his individual grief. Some he treated with guile of incantations,
> some with healing potions to drink; or he tended the limbs with salves
> from near and far; and some by the knife he set on their feet again.[192]

According to this text, there are three sorts of diseases: those born in the body without visible cause, those due to wounds, and those caused by climate. Likewise, their treatment is of three kinds: charms, medicines, and surgical interventions. For the history of diseases, I take note of the importance given to "spontaneous ulcers," that is, skin diseases.

With the cultural flowering that takes place in the fifth century B.C., the literary documentation in Greek texts becomes extremely rich and varied. Historians like Herodotus and Xenophon provide priceless information about diseases and about medicine.[193] The same is true for the poets and philosophers of the Age of Pericles. The theater becomes a more and more valuable source of evidence for understanding all aspects of daily life. However, for my subject all this documentation can take on only secondary significance, since it is displaced by the appearance of technical writings by physicians. Therefore I will only use these historical, philosophical, and poetic texts insofar as they complement or illuminate what we learn from the Hippocratic corpus. But before taking up that subject, a different perspective based on unwritten sources demands attention. Until now their contribution to the study of pathology in ancient Greece has been neglected, at least in works of historical synthesis.

Chapter Two

PALEOPATHOLOGY
Evidence from Ancient Bones on Diseases in Greece

The anthropological and medical examination of ancient human remains is all the more valuable as a source of evidence for its being "objective" and so dispensing with both the benefits and the drawbacks of language. Nevertheless, the exploitation of this nonverbal source material has only recently been embarked upon. Before that could happen, archaeologists had to bring to light a sufficient quantity of ancient human remains and date them correctly. Another necessary precondition was that the rapidly expanding field of pathological anatomy forge the conceptual tools to proceed from the identification of structural changes to their clinical and epidemiological significance. Finally, the two disciplines, archaeology and pathology, had to meet and adjust to their respective requirements and techniques.

The Historical Development of Paleopathology

Paleopathology, defined in 1913 by Sir Marc Armand Ruffer as "the science of diseases whose existence can be demonstrated on the basis of human and animal remains from ancient times,"[1] made its discreet and timid debut toward the end of the eighteenth century, that is, after the founding of organic anatomopathology by Morgagni. In 1774, J. F. Esper recognized a fracture of the pelvis in a Pleistocene mammal and described a bone tumor on the femur of a prehistoric cave bear. Modern examination of this femur supports the diagnosis of a fracture with excessive callus formation; but it is important, historically speaking, that Esper thought he had found a primitive malignant tumor, an osteosarcoma.[2]

The first investigators in this field, such as Cuvier and Walther, limited their interest to gross traumatic pathology and to so-called rheumatic lesions in animal fossils. Not until the second half of the nineteenth century did anthropologists and doctors attempt human paleopathology. Indeed, it would have been fruitless to do so before the complete revision, undertaken by Rokitansky and by Virchow, of the doctrine and methods of pathological anatomy. Rudolf Virchow (1821–1902), the founder of cellular pathology, himself made several major contributions to paleopathology. However, as is often the case with great pioneers, at the same time as he opened new horizons, he also engaged in misguided research. In order to explain the frequency and special characteristics of osteoplastic lesions on the vertebrae of prehistoric men and bears, Virchow created the nosological concept of *Höhlengicht* (cave gout), an unfortunate term because of the incorrect etiological and pathogenetic explanations that its etymology suggested. Worse still, Virchow interpreted as signs of rickets features that were actually an anthropologic peculiarity of Neanderthal man. But these blunders of an illustrious pathologist should not blind us to the value of his other work for the constitution of a new branch of medical history.

Thanks especially to Rudolf Virchow and to the anthropologist and surgeon Paul Broca (1824–80), the existence of pathological vestiges on prehistoric human remains was accepted, and the interest of their systematic study was recognized. Parrot, Le Baron, Bartels, and others followed in their footsteps, examining prehistoric and Gallo-Roman remains in western and central Europe. Despite the incorrect interpretation of certain lesions as rachitic or syphilitic, the work of these scientists produced new and incontestable medico-historical knowledge. By the end of the nineteenth century, the presence of various ailments in ancient bones from Europe had been proven: traumas, purulent and tuberculous inflammatory processes, neoplasms, rheumatic ailments, tooth decay, rickets, and so on.

The first three decades of the twentieth century amount to a kind of Golden Age of paleopathology. Profiting from the overall progress of knowledge in bone pathology and bacteriology, and with effective use of the technique of histological sections and radiography, anthropologist-doctors of this period identified a relatively high number of diseases that left their traces in the remains of human and animal bodies. For reasons having as much to do with methodological principles as with convenience, the objects of choice were mummies and bones found in Egypt and on the American continent (pre-Columbian civilizations) as well as prehistoric bones exhumed in western Europe. The scientific achievements of this period are recorded in the monographs of Marc Armand Ruffer, Roy L. Moodie, and Léon Pales.[3]

Paleopathology has been said to have made such progress that it should no longer be satisfied with a simple medical examination of ancient lesions, but that "in contributing to the study of the evolution of pathological processes and pathogeneses, it belongs to general pathology."[4] In short, pathology should serve history at the same time as history serves pathology. But despite such a noble goal, paleopathological research seems to have lost its inspiration. From the 1930s to the middle of this century, it confined itself to confirming diagnoses made before or to multiplying them. Pharaonic Egypt, pre-Columbian America, and prehistoric Europe continued to fascinate some paleopathologists. Here and there one can find a few cases cited for Roman Gaul or the European Middle Ages. Aside from the first studies of John Lawrence Angel, which are still totally unknown to historians of medicine, absolutely nothing is known about the paleopathology of Greece and Italy in the classical era.[5] This explains why E. H. Ackerknecht, when taking stock of modern paleopathological research, even in 1953 defined as its domain "the pathology of prehistoric animals and man in prehistoric and unlettered societies."[6] The restriction proposed in this definition was soon shown to be inappropriate by subsequent developments in paleopathology. Even when written documentation of pathological events is at hand, paleopathological investigation is not superfluous. Standing at the crossroads of medicine, anthropology, and history, paleopathology is currently undergoing extraordinary growth in the quantity and quality of specialized publications, in the scope of its field of interest, in new modes of analysis, and in the organization of special institutions.[7] In my view, three tendencies characterize recent progress in paleopathology: the use of new scientific methods; the movement from the study of isolated cases to the paleopathological investigation of whole populations; and the widening of the research area to include classical antiquity, the Middle Ages, and even modern societies.

Today, microradiography is a useful complement to paleopathological research. Calvin Wells has shown the importance of certain calcification lines whose X-ray study makes it possible to evaluate the exposure of children in an ancient population to famine or disease. It is known that the long bones grow along the epiphyseal line and that the process can be interrupted by undernourishment or by certain infectious or parasitic ailments. When growth begins again, a transverse line of dense calcification, called "Harris' line," forms between the diaphysis and the epiphyses of the two sides. Harris' lines mark the bones permanently, and their number indicates the frequency of distress during an individual's childhood. So by examining all the tibias or femurs in a necropolis for such lines, we can obtain valuable information on morbidity and subsistence crises.[8] By similar observations of healing lines on the female pubic symphysis, it is possible to guess the number of times a woman has given birth, and, by multiplying such results, to estimate the fertility of an ancient population. Likewise, analysis of the microscopic structure of teeth provides information about eating habits and nutritional deficiencies.

Among the new techniques, the most promising and extraordinary are those of paleo-immunology. This branch of paleopathology is still in its early stages. Thanks to sophisticated microserological processes, it may become possible to determine the blood type (ABO system) of persons long since deceased even if only a small quantity of dessicated bone remains. The results obtained so far are encouraging, though it cannot be ruled out that post-mortem impregnation of bone tissue by bacteria or molds can falsify this type of serological reaction. Without much concern about this as a possible source of errors, systematic research has been done on the frequency of ABO groups among the ancient Etruscans, the prehistoric inhabitants of southern Italy, Egyptians of the Pharaonic period, the ancient Khmers, and pre-Columbian American Indians. Given the genetic stability and the relatively simple mode of transmission of these blood traits, knowledge of their distribution in the past and today allows the historian to reach significant conclusions about the origin and migration of peoples. However, in the present state of our knowledge, this study sheds no light on the history of diseases, since there is not a significant enough correlation between blood groups and pathological phenomena.

From the viewpoint of paleopathology, it would be much more important to be able to determine, from an examination of bone remains or at least of mummified tissues, histocompatibility types of the HLA (human leukocyte antigen) system. Jean Dausset, who proposed this system in 1958, and his collaborators and followers have shown in their recent studies, first, that the genetic traits of the HLA complex are true "biological markers" that allow one to follow human migrations, and, second, that there are associations between HLA antigens and certain diseases. For instance, a carrier of tissue group HLA-B27 is 120 times more likely to contract ankylosing spondylitis than an average person; the risk is increased 500-fold if the carrier of the tissue group is male. These medical discoveries could open new horizons in paleopathology if a way is found to perform antigenic HLA typing on ancient biological materials. Some as yet uncertain results have been obtained on the tissues of pre-Columbian mummies.[9]

All hope is not lost that specific immunological tests for various infectious diseases can be applied in paleopathological research. There is nothing surprising about the failure of numerous attempts at specific immunological diagnosis from ancient bone or tissue: if the molecules of antibodies are still present in them, it could only be in infinitesimal quantities. To succeed, perfection or wholesale revision of traditional serological methods will be necessary. In the near future, scanner electron microscopy will perhaps make it possible to localize blood corpuscles, large organic molecules, and pieces of nuclear chromosomal matter. Once identified in this way, such highly specific organic structures as these can probably be subjected to chromatographic and serological analysis.

Sometimes the ancient remains of human corpses contain the eggs of fossilized parasites and traces of bacteria, the true nature of which can be difficult to determine. However, as against the consistent frustration of current paleo-immunological research on the antibodies that pathogenic agents give rise to in a host organism, it has been possible to prove, by a standard immunological technique, that pathogenic bacterial antigens are present in ancient organic materials: in 1976, a team of American researchers was able to demonstrate the existence of salmonella antigens (most likely type D, i.e., *Salmonella typhi,* the agent of typhoid fever) in the intestinal contents of a Peruvian mummy.[10] Microscopic examination of coproliths and deposits found during archaeological excavations in latrines or similar places makes possible the discovery of eggs and cysts of various intestinal parasites, as has been shown in several cases going back to the Middle Ages or the Roman Empire.[11] In addition, we have at our disposal today methods of chemical microanalysis that can serve to determine the concentration of normal elementary components of bone tissue—the calcium, strontium, and phosphorus values are especially useful indicators of health—or to detect the presence of inorganic toxic substances, for instance, lead in the bones of ancient potters.[12] None of these new techniques has yet been exploited in paleopathological studies of materials from Greece. The reason I have stressed the possibilities that they offer the historian in search of original approaches is to sketch a program and open perspectives, not to criticize better, in the rest of this chapter, the results already obtained. My purpose is to call attention to a lacuna in historical research on archaic and classical antiquity.

Careful examination of human remains can provide information not only on serious diseases and grave lesions but also on small, almost normal factors, such as wear and tear from age or work, longevity, the state of bodily development, or undernourishment. Just as in political or economic history, the interest of contemporary researchers is moving away from exceptional events and closer to common facts, to quantifiable evidence about daily life. At first, the curiosity of paleopathologists was piqued by the somewhat baroque aspect of certain "cases" and by the antiquity of the specimens. Nowadays the preference is for a necropolis instead of an unusual skull, interest is not limited to singular "discoveries," and there is great willingness to emerge from the domain of prehistory. Indeed, it is not important to have paleopathological proof of the existence of a disease within a historical population for which written documentation of that fact is to hand. What matters—and this in itself transforms paleopathological investigation—is evidence of the anatomopathological peculiarities, the diachronic and geographic prevalence and distribution of the disease in question. By offering information on gender, lifespan, height, body build, and even fertility, the systematic examination of bones and mummies enriches historical demography and makes possible the creation of a new branch of it, called "paleodemography." The American anthropologist John Lawrence Angel has spelled out in brilliant fashion the ideological and methodological bases of this new approach, and he has demonstrated concretely its practical applications. Nor is it without interest for our subject that Angel had done most of his work on Greek necropolises.[13]

All ancient populations have several characteristics in common: reduced longevity, frequency of inflammatory processes and of trauma, rarity of tooth decay, and presence of tuberculosis, among others, but in numerical variations that can be significant. We emphasize the crucial importance of the statistical analysis of paleopathological evidence. The main advantage of paleopathology is to by-pass the mediation of language and consequently to become the complement or even the replacement of written sources. However, the nature of the material remains, chiefly the hard portions of the human body, poses severe limits on the number of diseases and the biological facts that can be arrived at in this way. Considering that each ancient human bone is a historical witness and that in its examination the borders between normal and pathological fade, Vilhelm Møller-Christensen has proposed that the branch of science that concerns itself with them be called "osteoarchaeology."[14] Its area of study is in one sense broader than that of paleopathology, since it also studies the nonpathological aspects of bones. In another sense, osteoarchaeology is narrower, since its purview includes no direct evidence of disease other than bones and teeth of human or animal origin. In any case, the definition of osteoarchaeology is well-suited to the conditions of research in Greece, given the absence of mummified tissue and the significance of demographic data. Moreover, the term appropriately brings to mind the links of this discipline with archaeology.

Earliest Osteoarchaeological Research in Greece

Paleopathology has taught us more about the character and frequency of diseases in Egypt in the time of the Pharaohs, and even during the Hellenistic and Roman periods, than the most determined and ingenious analysis of the literary tradition. But the situation in Greece is altogether different. The results obtained up to now are very incomplete, especially for the classical period. We will not waste time blaming the archaeologists who, while excavating archaic and classical sites, too often treated human remains in a way that has made it difficult if not impossible to undertake paleopathological examination of the unwritten medical documentation. The famous Heinrich Schliemann (1822–90) tells how, during his first excavations at Hissarlik, Mycenae, and Tiryns, he would come across skeletons that he could neither examine with the necessary care nor preserve for subsequent study. Here is an excerpt from his account of the excavations of 1876:

One of the most interesting objects I found at Tiryns is the skeleton of a man, at a depth of five meters. The bones are petrified, but I attribute this phenomenon to the nature of the soil in which the skeleton happened to be encrusted. Some of the bones are considerably swollen because of the humidity; this is probably why the lower jawbone is of such enormous thickness. Unfortunately, I could only preserve a portion of the skull.[15]

It is really a shame that this specimen was lost, since we doubt that Schliemann's opinion on the pseudo-pathological, post-mortem nature of the mandibular swelling is well-founded.

In the midst of his archaeological discoveries, Schliemann made the acquaintance of Rudolf Virchow, at the time not only the greatest authority on pathology but renowned as well for his competence in archaeology, anthropology, and ethnography. A friendship grew up between the two.[16] The Berlin professor's backing was a great help to Schliemann who, as a dilettante, was having difficulty gaining an audience in certain official scientific circles. In 1879, Virchow traveled to Greece and Turkey, examined skulls found in ancient tombs and kept at Athens, participated in the excavations at Hissarlik by Schliemann's side, and made a series of medical observations in the region.[17] Schliemann entrusted him with the bulk of his osteological finds and deposited his collections at the Museum of Ethnology in Berlin.

The formidable challenge of making the first detailed analyses of the bones exhumed at Troy thus fell to Rudolf Virchow. He met it with the publication, in 1882, of a monograph on the Trojan skulls, in which he described the bone finds from Hissarlik as well as several skeletons discovered by F. Calvert at Ren Köi and Hanai Tepe.[18] At the outset, Virchow expresses his regrets concerning the small number of specimens analyzed and their poor state of preservation. The archaeologists, he says, often damaged, simply destroyed, or just buried bone finds, especially bones other than the skull. At the time it was thought that only the skull was relevant to anthropological research, the main goal of which was the determination of racial types. Although he was theoretically critical of this attitude, Virchow generally adopted it himself in the practical portions of his study. To be sure, he observed some anomalies of no consequence for pathology (metopic suture, platycnemia, and the like), and he described some pathological lesions as well, such as fusion of the cervical vertebrae and the fracture of long bones. He determined skeletal sex and age group and observed the way teeth were worn. He stressed the existence of sturdy trochanters and hypertrophied bumps at points of muscular insertion, signs that some males were exceptionally strong. But these are marginal comments. In truth, the great pathologist neglected paleopathology. In reality he was only interested in measuring skulls for supposed racial attributes. So, for example, he explicitly excludes the examination of two skulls from Ren Köi because they were obviously pathological and therefore might invalidate the racial significance of his measurements. Nothing can be said against such a procedure, but it is astonishing that Virchow does not offer a word on the nature of the pathological distortions in question, and that he completely excludes the two skulls from his investigation. When bones from the ancient world were before him, this expert in modern pathology became engrossed in purely anthropological problems.

In 1884, Virchow published a second study of Greek skulls.[19] In it he analyzed bones from Behram Köi (ancient Assos in the Troad) and from Cyprus. This publication includes an excellent presentation of two cases of skull trauma. In 1890, another trip to Greece provided Virchow with the opportunity to examine skulls dug up at new excavations in Athens. Finally, the discovery of a skeleton thought to be the mortal remains of Sophocles resulted in the description of a very strange case of asymmetry in the brainpan.[20] Several aspects of this work are admirable: the analyses it contains are very precise, and its conclusions are original, perceptive, and well thought out. I shall speak of it again in the systematic portion of this chapter.

Clon Stephanos (1854–1914), a Greek doctor who had assisted Virchow during the latter's trip to Athens, published an article in 1884 on Greece in Dechambre's medical dictionary.[21] In point of fact, it is the best overview of Greek medical geography in the nineteenth century. A paragraph in it on anthropology informs us that at that time there was knowledge of only about 90 ancient skulls exhumed in Greece and the lands it colonized (29 from Attica, 22 from Troy, 16 from Ionia, 4 from the islands, and 19 from southern Italy and Sicily). They had been measured and studied by Virchow, Nicolucci, Quatrefages, Broesike, and Zaborowsky, whose overall conclusions were that the so-called "Pelasgians" were brachycephalic while the "Hellenes" were dolichocephalic. Stephanos expresses himself circumspectly on this subject, stating that the ancient Greeks were, as distinct from the Pelasgians, "in great part dolichocephalic, though it isn't possible to state absolutely that the early Greeks were dolichocephalic." He stresses that the number of skulls examined was relatively small and that for most areas in Greece not one ancient skeleton was known. Furthermore, Stephanos draws attention to the fact that most Greek statues of nonmythical persons are brachycephalic.[22]

According to the measurements of Virchow and Nicolucci, the average cranial capacity of Greek skulls was "one of the lowest known to anthropology" (1388.7 cc. was the average for 18 skulls; more exactly, 1418 for males and 1276 for females). The only explanation for this surprising and embarrassing statistic was to judge it provisional and insignificant because of the small number of specimens under examination.[23]

The anthropologists discussed up to this point took no notice of bones other than the skull, and as for pathology, their interest went only as far as the mention of a few healed fractures. In sum, Greek osteoarchaeology began promisingly, but after the initial bursts of enthusiasm, scientific curiosity in the subject seemed spent. Virchow's work had no immediate successors. Even though continuing archaeological investigators brought new bone material to light, its study was neglected. We do note the work of the anthropologist Ionnis G. Koumaris, who published, in the beginning of the twentieth century, several sets of skull measurements and an article on nonpathological variations in Greek skull bones (especially metopic sutures).[24] As a whole, paleopathological research in Greece was stagnant just when it was achieving its greatest successes in Egypt, America, and France. In the basic works on paleopathology, that is, the monographs of Ruffer (1921), Moodie (1923), and Pales (1930), there is no information whatever about Greece. That fact corresponds to the complete lack of osteoarchaeology in Greece during the first three decades of the twentieth century.

In 1951, Sigerist summarized the progress that had been made in paleopathology around the world during the first quarter of the twentieth century and compiled a fine bibliography on the subject.[25] He also was completely silent on the subject of Greece. But the silence was no longer justified, since in the meantime C. M. Fürst had published studies on skeletons from the Argolid and Cyprus,[26] E. Breitinger had analyzed bone finds from the German excavations of the Kerameikos in Athens,[27] and, most important, J. L. Angel had begun the anthropological and paleopathological investigation of the new American excavations and had already undertaken a complete review of all ancient Greek bones.[28] While Fürst and Breitinger perfected the purely anthropological approach and still limited themselves to gross pathology (fractures, bony growths, etc.), Angel gave Greek osteoarchaeology a new direction.

John Lawrence Angel, a British (born London, 1915) anthropologist working in American scientific institutions—he was curator of the Division of Physical Anthropology at the Smithsonian Institution in Washington—is at the moment the almost unique representative (one might almost call him the personification) of the osteological paleopathology of prehistoric, archaic, and classical Greece. Angel's first trip to Greece goes back to the fall of 1937 when, as a young graduate student, he joined the team excavating the Athenian Agora. From the start he wished to unravel the social biology of this area, or, more precisely, to find, at the very place where Western civilization had been born, anthropological responses to the racialist ideas of Nazism.[29] His ambition was to make a systematic study of the changes in the biological substratum of the populations that had succeeded one another in Greece and the neighboring regions since prehistoric times. Accordingly, he tried to localize and examine all the ancient skeletal remains from Greek lands, whether they were in private or public collections. At the time of this, his first review of osteoarchaeology in 1937–38, Angel was able to analyze 455 skulls and 132 skeletons dating from Neolithic times up until the Byzantine period. In his publication of the results of this inquiry, he remarks on the poor state of preservation of the bones due to marked seasonal fluctuations in Greek soil conditions, specific burial customs during some periods of Greek history, and the carelessness of archaeologists with human remains.[30]

As for the attitude of the archaeologists, the situation has changed since the 1930s and especially since World War II. So Angel was able to profit from the rich harvest of human bones excavated by D. M. Robinson at Olynthus, H. A. Thompson in the Athenian Agora, J. L. Caskey at Lerna, G. Daux and P. Courbin at Argos, C. W. Blegen at ancient Pylos and in the Troad, P. Dikaios at Khirokitia (Cyprus), J. L. Benson at Bamboula (also Cyprus), R. J. Rodden at Nea Nikomedia, M. J. Mellink at Karataş, T. W. Jacobsen in the Franchthi Cave, J. Mellaart at Çatal Hüyük, S. Dietz at Asine, and others. By 1973, Angel had examined the mortal remains of approximately 2,200 persons from the Paleolithic up until the modern era. For the first time, it was possible to study systematically the sum-total of bones found in the relatively important necropolises, and to draw sure conclusions about the biological traits of populations, not just individuals. From this point of view, Angel's monograph *The People of Lerna* is a model of the genre.[31]

Besides this American research, one should cite the studies by Robert P. Charles on the skeletons discovered during the French excavations in Argos and on those of the ancient inhabitants of Crete, the examination of bones from the Kitsos Cave in Attica done by J. Dastugue and H. Duday, the articles by N. G. Gejvall and F. Henschen, C. S. Barsocas, A. D. Tsouros, H. G. Carr, and D. M. Hadjimarkos on specific paleopathological and paleodental questions, and the work of V. G. Vallaoras and M. S. Senyürek on paleodemography.[32] Even so, Greek osteoarchaeology is a branch of scholarly research in which much remains to be done. Though the current total of skeletons examined surpasses 2,000, oftentimes the specimens are incomplete and fragmentary. They are also scattered in time and space. The contents of prehistoric burials are now better known than those of the classical period, for which the number of skeletons examined is well below 200. For most archaeological sites, the local sample is very small. There is a relative abundance of bones from peripheral areas, such as Anatolia, Macedonia, and Cyprus, and although some places of major significance are well-represented (Athens, Mycenae, Lerna, Argos, etc.), regrettably, the most interesting places for historians of medicine are totally lacking in osteoarchaeological finds. We know nothing of the paleopathology of Cos, Cnidus, Thasos, or Epidauros, to mention a few sites.

Traumas

Wounds to the skin, muscles, and internal organs are only by exception amenable to paleopathological investigation. The opposite is true for fractures, which affect the solid and long-lasting parts of the body and also leave recognizable traces even when they heal perfectly. The percentage of Aegean bones that were fractured during life is not excessive. It is on the order of 10 percent (of the number of individuals, not the number of bone specimens). The real frequency of fractures must have been greater, since a negative diagnosis cannot be confirmed in the case of incomplete skeletons, which are, unfortunately, especially numerous. Despite the need for this correction, the frequency of fractures in ancient populations does not seem close to that of current societies with developed technologies. The difference is explicable partly in terms of increased longevity, partly in terms of new activities, such as transportation by powerful and relatively dangerous vehicles, sports, and so on.

As far as the prehistory and ancient history of Europe (including Greece) are concerned, it appears that the risk of fracture is inversely related to the progress of civilization.[33] The oldest completely preserved skeleton found in Greece dates from the Mesolithic era (ca. 7000 B.C.). It was discovered by Thomas W. Jacobsen in the Franchthi Cave, a prehistoric site along the Gulf of Nauplia. It is not a coincidence that this skeleton is that of a man who perished at around age 25 from a series of blows to the front of his skull. So the most remarkable bone evidence from prehistoric Greece makes its entrance in a context of violence, of struggle between men.[34] In most osteoarchaeological cases of skull trauma, the locale and nature of the lesions make it clear that they result from conflict, from intended acts and not from accident. The Franchthi man was bashed on the head by a rock or a club, and the scars and oblong dents on certain skulls of the Bronze and Iron Ages lead one to suspect the use of blades. Of two individuals with head wounds at Karataş (the only two cranial traumas in 560 skeletons from the Early Bronze Age), one succumbed to a fracture of the temporal bone (skull *522 Ka.*), while the other survived a wound to the top of the skull that reached a depth of 5 millimeters (*165 Ka.*).[35] Among the princes or aristocratic warriors buried in Grave Circle B at Mycenae (Middle Bronze Age, 1650–1450 B.C.), two were wounded in the head. One skeleton (*59 Myc.*) is that of a sturdy man, very tall and well-built, with noticeable depressions in the skull vault above the left eye and behind the left parietal boss. These are apparently the results of rugged combat, yet they did not cause this chieftain's death, which overtook him at the age of 50 years or more. The other skeleton (*51 Myc.*) is that of a 30-year-old man of exceptional strength. On the right of his frontal bone he has an oblong, shallow depression (23 mm. long) that is the mark of a healed wound, and higher to the left the traces of a fatal fracture, unsuccessfully treated by a surgical intervention.[36] Such details are indeed reminiscent of the exploits and destinies of the Homeric heroes.

Among the skeletons from Lerna, most of which date from the Middle Bronze Age, Angel has counted 10 cases of cranial trauma. Of the 10, 8 are relatively mild or, at least, completely healed. Among those with well-healed unions, 4 are on male skeletons (*18, 23, 66,* and *132 Ler.*) and 4 on females (*38, 59, 178,* and *182 Ler.*). To take a closer look at one example, consider the skeleton *59 Ler.:* it's a young woman, about 25 years of age, short and slight; on her skull, just to the right of the vertex, there is a sharp, traumatic depression without loss of substance.[37] In 2 of the 10 cases from Lerna the wounds probably resulted in death (*181* and *189 Ler.*), as the skull splits and the state of the fractured edges indicate. The skeleton *181 Ler.* is the mortal remains of a man about 45 years old, short but with an athletic body, who suffered from deformations of the vertebrae. His skull presents an irregular fracture with loose bone fragments; the inner table is split off and curled as if by an imploding force.[38] He might have been hit by a stone or club, or taken an especially bad fall. Wounds similar to this one are described in the Hippocratic corpus.[39]

On a skull from the main necropolis of Argos (*168 Arg.*; protogeometric tomb, tenth century B.C.), probably of a female in her middle twenties, R. P. Charles noticed that the bone wall over the left frontal eminence was crushed as the result of a violent trauma. It is interesting to note that despite the seriousness of the lesion, which certainly did significant damage to the central nervous system, the victim survived the accident: the inside of the bone shows breaks that were completely healed.[40]

In the Kerameikos cemetery in Athens, Breitinger found an old man's skull with a scar of traumatic origin in the form of a crater on the left side of the frontal bone (*100 C Keram.*). The cervical vertebra of an adolescent whose head was buried in the protogeometric era near the Hephaisteion in the Athenian Agora has the marks of decapitation.[41] During the older excavations at Assos in the Troad (now the Turkish village Behram Köi), a male skeleton was discovered (*1 Ass.*) dating from the time of the Lydian conquest or the first Persian occupation (sixth century B.C.). The skull shows signs of two wounds that were made by a sharp weapon. On the frontal bone, there is a fracture line 30 millimeters long, well healed, which stretches diagonally from the middle of the forehead to the middle of the top edge of the left eye socket. An additional scar, parallel to the first but very short, cuts across the lower edge of the same socket. Also in this spot, the blade of the weapon detached and lifted a small splinter of bone that managed to heal in an abnormal position. This man, probably a warrior, certainly lost an eye and probably suffered brain damage from the shock, but he did not succumb to the blows whose traces we have just described.

He died at an advanced age, as his heavily worn teeth, among other things, attest. On another male skull (*2 Ass.*) uncovered in the same place as the previous one but dating from the third century B.C., Virchow recognized the signs of a broken nose.[42] Three persons of the protohistoric era in the Argolid, two men at Lerna (*18* and *50 Ler.*) and one woman at Asine (*18 FA.*), have broken noses, probably the result of accidents or combat. One the same occasion the woman from Asine also lost several of her front teeth. There are exostoses above her right wrist, interlocking radius and ulna; they suggest a defensive response to violence. Two women from Çatal Hüyük (*86* and *108 CH.*) and a man from Karataş (*189 Ka.*) had their lower jaws broken near the chin. All three healed solidly.[43]

As might be expected, skull injuries, especially the more serious ones, occur more often in men than women and statistically tend to be situated on the left- rather than the right-hand side. Discussing such wounds in the people of Lerna, I mentioned the skeleton *59 Ler.*, that of a slight woman hurt on the right side, purposely to stress the existence of atypical cases. The localization on the left side is more frequent because, then as now, usually the right hand wielded the weapons. The greater number of wounds in males is easily understood if we assume that skull traumas are mainly caused by violence between people. The same preponderance of the male also occurs, though to a lesser degree, in the statistical distribution of certain long-bone fractures that are usually the result of accidents. Taking all fractures together, the relation between female frequency and male frequency is on the order of 1:4. Males were more exposed to the danger of fractures not only as warriors and fighters but also by the nature of their activities outside the home.

Angel drew attention to the fact that fractures in children are rare. Of 100 children's skeletons in Lerna and Argos, he noticed only 1 with a damaged bone, and that was probably caused by a difficult birth, not an accident thereafter.[44] Does this mean that the children of certain Greek populations were especially well protected and watched and that they led a relatively uneventful life? The exceptional specimen just mentioned is an infant, dead after scarcely a month of life, whose right collarbone shows a swelling, probably a callus, at the junction of its middle and outer thirds (*162 Ler.*).

Generally, fractures of the collarbone (for instance, an adult case in Çatal Hüyük and also one in Karataş) and of the humerus are accidental. Three instances deserve mention here. On a Neolithic humerus from Çatal Hüyük (*101 CH.*) belonging to a 40-year-old woman, the shaft, which had broken midway, at deltoid insertion, has knitted solidly and with slight medial angulation, but the upper piece is rotated. The rotation must have resulted in functional difficulties. A male skeleton from Asine (*110 As.*) has a right humerus fracture below midshaft with about 15° angulation, shortening, and thickening, along with arthritic lipping at the elbow and erosion of the capitulum.[45] On the other hand, a comparable midshaft fracture in a woman from Mycenae (*58 Myc.*) healed remarkably well.[46]

If a much larger number of specimens were at our disposal, it would be possible to use the way upper and lower arm fractures heal to date the introduction and spread of the therapeutic practices codified in the Hippocratic corpus. According to the author of the treatise *Fractures,* "The treatment of a fractured arm is not difficult, and is almost any practitioner's job."[47] After this peremptory statement, the Hippocratic author goes on to describe in minute detail how carefully to proceed in fitting together the fragments, how to put a limb in traction in some cases, and in every case how to keep the broken bone in place with bandages and devices.[48] The case *58 Myc.* of a perfectly healed arm fracture belongs to the Middle Bronze Age. This woman, who was buried in a royal tomb, was an aristocrat. As a consequence of her social position, she could call upon highly qualified physicians. When the skeletons of persons of the same era but of lower social standing can be examined, as with the inhabitants of Asine and Lerna, more often than not fractures of the arm have faulty unions, healed in abnormal positions. However, in the case of Lerna it should be noted that we find fractures of the forearm and not of the humerus.

Two types of fracture of the forearm dominate the Greek osteoarchaeological record: (1) breaks of continuity in the middle of the ulna resulting from a defensive movement (holding up the arm to parry blows aimed at the head or the trunk) and (2) lesions of the lower portions of the radius and the ulna caused by falls (from breaking a fall with one's arm). In prehistoric times most fractures like these healed poorly and resulted in persistent dysfunctions. Forearm bone trauma disabled its victims and was a nagging, unsolved problem for the bonesetters of the day.

To exemplify the first type of fracture, we cite a Neolithic case from Çatal Hüyük: in a 30-year old male, the left ulna had been broken in the middle of the shaft. The fragments are joined together by a kind of fibrous pseudo-arthrosis with a cauliflower formation from the bridging callus (*184 CH.*),[49] Such overdeveloped pseudo-arthroses form when the broken bone is insufficiently immobilized during the repair process. The same type of fracture of the ulna as the result of a defensive movement has been remarked on two other skeletons from Çatal Hüyük as well as on bones from the Kitsos Cave (also Neolithic) and the necropolises of Karataş (Early Bronze Age), Asine, and Lerna (Middle Bronze Age). Often the union is imperfect and shows signs of periostitis. Again, a man from Lerna, aged about 50, has both bones of his right forearm broken, radius and ulna, at the junction of the lower quarter (*73 Ler.*). A blood clot filled the space between the two bones, which became fibrous and mineralized, and a bony bridge formed, fusing the radius and the ulna in a slightly pronated position.[50] In Athens, in the Kerameikos, a skeleton was exhumed from tomb 93 (Iron Age, twelfth–tenth century B.C.) of a man about 50 years old. His right ulna has the marks of a well-healed fracture.[51] This probably means that by his time effective methods for the extension and immobilization of fractures were becoming known in Greece.

All the fractures of the ulna just mentioned are of the first type, the result of a blow to the forearm raised in a parrying movement. The other common type of forearm fracture occurs when a person falls forward onto an outstretched hand, a reflex gesture that is intended to break the fall (the so-called Pouteau-Colles fracture). It particularly affects the lower end of the radius, with or without involvement of the ulna. As examples, I can cite two cases, one from Çatal Hüyük (*51 CH.*, Neolithic) and the other from Lerna (*207 Ler.*, Middle Bronze Age). The first is an isolated fracture of the radius of classic form in a young male. The second is more informative: a woman, who gave birth more than once and died at about age 30, had undergone, probably during adolescence, a fracture of the right radius in the typical place. Along with it was a spiral fracture of the right ulna. The bones healed solidly, but a dorsal deviation at the wrist and a slight shortening of the forearm resulted.[52]

Fractures of the metacarpal bones in the hand are attested in two individuals from Lerna, a man (*89 Ler.*) and a woman (*7 Ler.*). Usually such lesions are the result of a direct, violent action, such as blows to the hand with a blunt object. In the great majority of cases, fractures of the leg are caused by accidents, usually falls. Angel catalogues four fractures of the femur on Neolithic skeletons from Çatal Hüyük. The case of *165 CH.* is typical: the left femur of a woman who perished at around age 25. On the upper third of the shaft there are traces of an old so-called greenstick fracture, an incomplete break in which the outer layer of the bone is not ruptured through its whole circumference. The bone healed well, without being shortened or developing a large callus, but with slight medial angulation and rotation of the upper fragment.[53] Two healed cases of greenstick fracture of the femur were found at Karataş (*117* and *122 Ka.*). Lesions of this kind are characteristic of children or adolescents—they are the result of falling from a certain height, as from a ladder or when scaling a wall. Proper fusion of such fractures is more the work of nature than of the physician's art. The left femur of a female (*137 CH.*) provides another example of a greenstick fracture in which the young bone's elasticity saved it from a complete break. In a protohistoric inhabitant of Asine in the Argolid, the shaft of the femur was broken clear through, and the pieces were thrown out of place, with the upper jammed askew into the lower. The result was a spontaneous fibrous union, with a tough callus in very poor position, shortening the leg and twisting it.[54]

An accident may well be the cause of the deformation of a man's foot in the Middle Bronze Age (*127 Ler.*). And I mention in passing a fractured seventh rib in a man from Lerna (*88 Ler.*), an ordinary mishap that needs no special attention for a good repair. Fractures of the spinal column are much more important, for they often give rise to troublesome complications on the part of the nervous system. If the spinal column of a woman from Nea Nikomedia (Neolithic, ca. 6000 B.C.) was really broken clear through before death, as Emily Vermeule suggests, then death surely followed. The Macedonian tomb in which she was found provides a moving glimpse of a family tragedy: the miraculously well-preserved skeleton of an adult female, tall, sturdy, with excellent teeth, is curled up in a fetal position and holding in her arms the skeletons of two children. Plainly, they perished along with her.[55] Fractures of the vertebral bodies have been described in another woman of the Neolithic era found at Çatal Hüyük (*52 CH.*), in a Middle Bronze Age denizen of the Argolid (*76 Ler.*), and in a Mycenaean prince from the Late Bronze Age (*25 Myc.*). In all three cases, the fractures are relatively benign and seem not to have brought on paralysis.

The skeleton *25 Myc.*, exhumed long ago by Schliemann from Grave 5 of Circle A of the royal burials at Mycenae, appears, like the others, to be a robust and muscular man who died at about the age of 40. Aside from a few signs of spondylitis on the thoracic and lumbar vertebrae, there is a definite wedging of the third lumbar vertebral body that is strongly reminiscent of a well-healed youthful fracture.[56] A similar case has been noticed among the skeletons from Lerna (*76 Ler.*). It is a man who died at about age 40, but unlike the Mycenaean prince, he was on the slender side. His skeleton shows a disk injury between the ninth and tenth thoracic vertebrae as well as a fusion (with a possible old fracture) between the eleventh and twelfth thoracic vertebrae.[57]

The process of repairing a fracture is often complicated by inflammatory reactions due to infection. In about one-third of the prehistoric and protohistoric skeletons, the callus that results from the union of the fracture shows traces of periostitis. There are also bone lesions in the absence of fractures that attest to the existence of wounds in soft tissue that, as a consequence of inflammation, have affected the adjacent bone tissue. Thus a serious inflammation of the left ischium has been remarked in a 40-year-old male from Çatal Hüyük (*97 CH.*), probably caused by an infected wound of the buttocks. According to Angel, it might be the result of being gored by a bull.[58] Comparable wounds sometimes occur in contemporary bullfights. Even so, there is no reason to exclude the possibility that a weapon did the damage. It was indeed a weapon, either a javelin or a sword or the like, that pierced the back and made an elliptical hole in the right shoulder blade of a stout warrior from the Middle Bronze Age (*91 Ler.*).[59] The inflammation around the perforation proves that the wounded man, a 40-year-old, did not immediately succumb. In another man of the same era and vicinity (*175 Ler.*), periostitis in the lower part of the left fibula is the tell-tale sign of an infected leg wound.[60]

Cranial Trepanning

By means of archaeological dating of trepanned skulls exhumed in various regions, it has been determined that the surgical procedure of trepanation goes back to Neolithic times.[61] In Greece, we now know of at least five sure instances of it, all dating from the Bronze Age or the archaic period. On the skull of a young girl from the Neolithic era found at Çatal Hüyük (*256 CH.*), the diagnosis of trepanation before death is possible but doubtful. The skull has two small round holes 6 millimeters in diameter, penetrating the right parietal bone near bregma and separated by only 15 millimeters, which does not suggest a surgical procedure with therapeutic objectives. According to Angel,[62] the holes were made after death. If the procedure was performed on a living subject, it had a magical-religious purpose, namely, ritual murder. In this connection, we should mention the strange marks on the skull of a Bronze Age man found at Arkhanes (Crete). The skull in question (*65 Ar.*) features two arc-shaped bony growths situated symmetrically on the right and left parietal bones. A. Tsouros suggests that they are lesions from "initiatory surgery," in other words, a violent ritual operation on the scalp which irritated the bone beneath.[63] Indeed, the nature and regular placement of these bony growths on the skull cannot be explained by any disease. They must be a kind of scar consequent upon an inflammation brought on by some form of torture. For example, the application of a burning metal crown to the victim's head would have left such marks as these.

In 1979, not far from Arkhanes, at Anemospilia, the Greek archaeologists Efi and Yannis Sakellarakis brought to light a small temple from the Minoan era (ca. 1700 B.C.). Destroyed by an earthquake and the fire that resulted from it, the temple has remained in the state in which the catastrophe left it. Three persons were inside at the fatal moment. The state of their skeletons shows that two were crushed to death by the falling walls—the defensive position of their arms in front of their faces and a recent fracture of the thigh are notable signs of this—while the third, a strapping 18-year-old, has had his throat cut at an altar! The earthquake had interrupted the performance of a human sacrifice.[64] Robert P. Charles has found on five Argive skulls (two from the Mycenaean necropolis of Deiras and three from geometric tombs in Argos) multiple circular holes of modest size drilled into the bone wall. The holes are not unlike those in the Neolithic skull 256 from Çatal Hüyük. They were made with a bit-brace on perfectly healthy bones. There is no trace of scarring or infection. So they must be the results of post-mortem interventions that, in the absence of medical purposes, point to the survival of a very old mortuary cult.[65]

We return to trepanation on living subjects. In the classical period, the goal of this procedure was exclusively medical and rationally conceived. From the time of the oldest Greek surgical texts, it is a well-codified operation, described with great precision and thorough knowledge of its indications and complications. The Hippocratic treatise *Wounds in the Head* advocates trepanation for the treatment of skull trauma. The indications are concise: bruising and above all fracture of the skull. Cuts or depressions in the skull do not call for it. Chapters 30 and 31 of the treatise describe how to clean and scrape the wound, the technique for perforating the bone, whether with a cylindrical saw or a boring trepan, and bandaging after the operation to prevent purulent inflammation of the bone and decay of the brain membranes.[66]

Osteoarchaeological finds in the ancient Greek world support the hypothesis according to which the origin of trepanation is not to be found in rational medical practice. It makes its initial appearance as a ritual act first performed upon corpses, then on the heads of living persons. Experience taught that humans could survive the opening up of their brainpan, and a crude technique for doing so was learned, which eventually made possible the medical use of trepanation. In the presence of magical indications—as among certain primitive peoples of the nineteenth century who trepanned those suffering from convulsions or headaches in order to provide a way out for evil spirits—or rational ones, such as fractures of the skull vault, they began to operate on the afflicted. In the Mycenaean age, professional surgeons had already mastered the technical side of this operation and formulated its indications: they were on the path that led ultimately to the Hippocratic codification.

A female skull found in Karataş and dating from the Early Bronze Age (*81 Ka.*) has a relatively small (10 mm.) round opening on it and no trace of any preexisting wound. Is it a magical trepanation? Another skull from the same necropolis (*522 Ka.*) shows the failure of an attempt to trepan a terrible traumatic rupture in the temporal region.[67] The skull *33 Ler.* found by J. L. Caskey at Lerna in a Middle Bronze Age tomb is still more informative. It belongs to a young man about 22 years old who died from a cranial trepanation, the indications for which cannot be discovered. On his forehead there is a large (40 mm. by 60 mm.) opening of irregular outline with a beveled edge (at least, the outer diameter is greater than the inner one). The part of the bone that was cut out is broken into two pieces that remain in place. They must have stayed there after the operation, adhering to the skin. In the case from Lerna, the operating technique seems very crude.[68]

By contrast, an examination of the skull *51 Myc.* evokes admiration for the surgeon's skill. True, this time the patient was an aristocrat, perhaps a prince, who could afford to have a good practitioner. The skeleton in question was exhumed by G. Mylonas from Grave Circle B at Mycenae and is the mortal remains of a man of exceptional strength who was killed at about age 30, probably in battle; the two wounds on his frontal bone were discussed above. In addition, on the upper left of his frontal bone, at a distance of less than 1 centimeter from the coronal suture, is an oval hole (measuring 27 mm. by 30 mm.), with a clean-cut, slightly conical edge to it (the inner diameter is greater than the outer one). Two laminae of the outer table of the vault, which fit the opening exactly, are preserved in place, as though they had remained attached to the scalp. The corresponding laminae of the inner table and the diploë have disappeared. Two vertical fracture lines start from the hole down to the lower part of the frontal bone: probably they represent the initial lesion that, along with complications inside the skull, motivated the surgery. The bone is cut surprisingly cleanly, as though by a machine, and the edges of the opening are perfectly smooth. From this we can draw two conclusions. First, the surgeon must have had considerable experience performing this kind of operation as well as hard, well-sharpened instruments. And second, the patient did not long survive the wound, since otherwise the reaction of the bone tissue would have rounded off the edges.[69]

Like the two just mentioned, the fourth case also comes from the Argolid during the Middle Bronze Age. The Scandinavian excavations at Asine recently brought to light the well-preserved skeleton of a man who died around age 35, some time after a surgical operation on his head (*107 As.*). On the left mid-parietal, about 30 millimeters from the sagittal suture, there is an elliptical trepanation hole (17 mm. by 20 mm.) with a healed bevel around it. This may represent, says Angel, the surgical removal of fragments after a battle-axe wound, as in *51 Myc.*, but with survival of the patient.[70]

The last of the five cases is a young man in his early thirties whose skeleton was removed from a burial in Argos. Judging from its archaeological characteristics, the burial belongs to the early geometric period (900–850 B.C.). According to the description by R. P. Charles, a cup-shaped indentation caused by a deep-seated focus of infection is visible over the left eye socket. A very distinct semicircular groove runs to the left of the indentation. There was an attempt to treat the infection by surgical intervention. Plainly, the intervention was unsuccessful, since the trepanation was never completed. Probably the cutting of the skull was abandoned owing to the patient's demise.[71]

The "Skull of Sophocles" and the Portrait of Menander

Schliemann's dazzling archaeological discoveries were made on the basis of an attentive and naive reading of classical texts. Inspired by the success of this method, a Danish civil servant by the name of Münter decided, in 1893, to look for the tomb of Sophocles, using as a guide his own interpretation of the written traditions about the great poet's last resting place. According to the biographical account preserved in the *Vita,* Sophocles was buried in a family tomb situated along the road to Dekeleia, exactly 11 stades from the walls of the city. Traditionally, this was understood to be the walls of Athens, since the tomb would then be in the deme of Colonus, his birthplace. When excavations at Colonus brought forth nothing that could be construed as the poet's burial place, Münter thought that the walls in question might well be the walls of Deceleia, whose site had just been identified as the mound now called Palaiokastro. Using his compass on the military map of this region, he fixed the point 11 stades distant from Palaiokastro along the old road from Deceleia to Acharnae (modern Menidi). On that spot Münter dug up three sarcophagi, one of which, made of marble, contained the skeleton of a male whom the joyous discoverer immediately proclaimed to be Sophocles. Beside the skeleton, there was an iron strigil, a wooden stick, and some alabaster and clay pots datable to the fifth century B.C.[72]

It turned out that the three sarcophagi at Menidi had been broken into at a relatively early date, so that the inscriptions normally found on them were gone. As a result, identification of the skeleton by archaeological means was impossible. Münter's hypothesis was violently attacked by German philologists with strong and fairly convincing arguments, but they do not constitute an absolute refutation.[73] The skull thought to be Sophocles' was sent to Berlin, then to the Universal Exposition in Chicago; it was finally deposited in a Copenhagen museum. In May 1893, Rudolf Virchow made a detailed report on this anthropological specimen to the Prussian Academy of Science.[74] According to Virchow's analysis, none of the various characteristics of the skull from Menidi went against the identification Münter had proposed. Sophocles died about 406–405 B.C., a very old man, probably in his nineties, and according to a consensus of historical witnesses, he was hale and strikingly handsome. Despite the length of his life, the *Vita* has him dying by accident, choking on a grape.[75] According to Virchow, the skull Münter found is that of a tall, vigorous old man. However, the state of preservation of its teeth, the abrasions on them, and the overall degree of osteoporosis do not correspond to what one usually sees in people over the age of 90. Unfortunately, Virchow says nothing about the rest of the skeleton. Probably it had been destroyed.

Anthropological examination of the skull could have disproved the identification of the Menidi bones with the last remains of the tragic poet, but it is not sufficient to confirm it. What interests us here is not so much the historical identity of the skull as the report of certain anomalies on a specimen that is securely dated to the fifth century B.C. This particular skull is markedly asymmetrical because the left rear section of it has been flattened (technical term: plagiocephaly). The deformation is due not to the skull's senile involution but instead to a pathological process in childhood that began with the complete union of the suture that joins the left parietal bone to the temporal bone. According to Virchow, the union must have been caused by an accidental trauma, such as a blow to the head or a fall, and not by an artificial deformation of the skull. Since the synostosis hindered growth in one direction, the skull developed, compensatorily, in other directions. The asymmetry of the bone structures brought about the displacement of the brain and an asymmetry in its hemispheres: the right half must have been relatively larger than the left.

"According to current conceptions," wrote Virchow in his 1893 report (p. 694), "one can deduce from it a predisposition to criminal activity, though older pathologists would instead have associated it with the eccentricities of a poet or a utopian." Neither opinion is acceptable to modern anthropology. There is renewed interest in such questions from the perspective of neurophysiological experimentation with bisected brains. The experiments of Sperry and Bogen show that the left hemisphere predominates in verbal activities, arithmetic operations, and literary expression, while the right is better at realizing nonverbal thought and the perception of shapes.[76] But the effect of pronounced cerebral asymmetry on intellectual and psychosocial aptitudes is still unclear. The results of Sperry's experiments cannot serve to identify the man whose skull was found at Menidi. If it could, the predominance of the right hemisphere would suggest a Phidias rather than a Sophocles.

No literary source speaks of Sophocles' plagiocephaly. The comparison of the Menidi skull with ancient busts of the poet is not at all favorable to the identification, but the argument is not decisive, since hair can mask asymmetry of the skull vault. Only copies of the idealized portrait of Sophocles have come down to us. I mention in passing what Plutarch tells us about the head of Pericles (ca. 495–429 B.C.):

> Agariste once had a dream that she had given birth to a lion, and a few days later she was delivered of Pericles. His physical features were almost perfect, the only exception being his head, which was rather long and out of proportion. For this reason almost all his portraits show him wearing a helmet, since the artists apparently did not wish to taunt him with this deformity. However, the comic poets of Athens nicknamed him "schinocephalus" or "squill-head."[77]

Ancient sculptures can be informative about some pathological characteristics of historical personages. It is also true that the blindness of Homer, the snub nose of Socrates, and the hunchback of Aesop are clichés whose sculptural or pictorial expression stems from legend, not clinical reality.

Perhaps that is not the case for the facial asymmetry that can be seen on a very lovely Hellenistic head in marble, now in the University Museum in Philadelphia. After a careful morphological examination of this sculpture, the American neurosurgeon Temple Fay asserts that it faithfully represents a kind of facial asymmetry whose pathological character is beyond doubt and whose subtlest details correspond to a precise nosological category. According to this doctor, the late-thirties man represented in the Philadelphia sculpture suffered, sometime before the tenth year of his life, a lesion to the fronto-parietal region of the left hemisphere of the brain that resulted first in spastic hemiplegia ("cerebral palsy") and in underdevelopment of the right side of the face and neck.[78] Although this childhood accident may have had no negative effect on his intellectual gifts, its consequences were not confined to an asymmetry in the physical development of the body. If Fay's diagnosis is correct, this handsome man with a melancholy look suffered from disturbance of his motor functions and was even, perhaps, epileptic.

One must be very cautious in proposing a clinical interpretation in such cases. From a recent study that reviewed substantial archaeological material and made rigorous use of the quantification of morphological parameters, we learn that asymmetry of the face and the brainpan in Greek statues and bas-reliefs from the fifth to the third centuries B.C. occurs with a regularity that clearly surpasses normal anatomical variation.[79] These are representations of gods, anonymous warriors, idealized and unidentifiable individuals. According to L. A. Schneider, there is a correspondence between facial asymmetry and the position of the head, either in relation to the activity being expressed by the body as a whole, or in relation to the position of the neck. This scholar has not extended the research to portraits of historical persons, but from now on one should take account of the fact that, from the fifth century B.C. on, exaggerated asymmetry of the face is a technical tool, a craftsman's trick intended to enhance the aesthetic effect of a work of art.

The Philadelphia head is not the bust of a man standing still in a conventional attitude, looking straight ahead. It is a fragment of a statue. The head is bent on the neck and turned toward the right. So a certain asymmetry in the face would be completely within the rules of art. The Philadelphia statue is the copy of a lost Greek prototype. Several other ancient copies of the same original have survived (in Boston, Dumbarton Oaks, Venice, Copenhagen, and elsewhere). All have clear facial asymmetry. According to a consensus of art historians, the statue is the realistic portrait of a historical personage. The prevailing view is that it represents the Athenian poet Menander (about 342–291 B.C.), the leading figure in Greek New Comedy. The identification is very probable but not absolutely certain.[80] It was recently corroborated by the discovery of some third-century A.D. mosaics found in the Khorapha quarter of Mytilene: they contain ten scenes relating to the plays of Menander and a portrait of the poet labeled with his name. The technique of this portrait is a little crude, almost like a caricature, but even so one can see that the figure has crossed eyes and a facial asymmetry that are not the result of an artist's botch. Here, then, is an argument in favor of the "verism" of the Philadelphia head's asymmetry, that it is the reflection of a real pathological phenomenon and not a clever sculptor's trick. Still, one cannot help mentioning that the underdeveloped part of the face is on the right in the sculptures but on the left in the mosaic. Perhaps that is a consequence of the way paintings and mosaics were copied.

Written sources are very chary of details on the private life and bodily characteristics of Menander. According to the *Suda,* he was cross-eyed, but his spirit had piercing vision. If Alciphron can be believed in one of his letters, Menander complains of poor health. According to an ambiguous discussion in Phaedrus, he had an effete and langorous gait. He died at the age of 52, probably trying to swim the harbor of the Piraeus. These few biographical details are favorable to a diagnosis of infantile spastic paralysis, but they are not a straightforward confirmation of it. Other events in Menander's life, particularly his service as an ephebe and his success as a lover, do not easily accord with the medical label of a handicapped person and certainly exclude any serious or even moderate form of chronic motor disability.[81]

According to Jean Dastugue (1974), an adult atlas (first cervical vertebra) found in a Neolithic cave near Laurion (*2/337 Kitsos*) has an asymmetrical posterior arch probably due to a difference in the diameter of the vertebral arteries. If this etiology for the bone malformation in question is correct, it is reasonable to suppose that the person in question suffered from cerebral hemiatrophy.

Congenital Malformations, Tumors, and Metabolic Disorders

Anomalies of the spinal column, especially with regard to the number of vertebrae and their fusion, are frequent among contemporary inhabitants of Europe and Asia. The lumbosacral region is the part of the spine most subject to variations. This same genetic instability is very pronounced in the ancient skeletons thus far exhumed in Greece. Of particularly high frequency is the six-segment sacrum, which is chiefly due to the sacral incorporation of the fifth lumbar vertebra.[82] There is a genetic tendency for the pelvis to ascend and the lumbar curvature to lessen. Actually, these phonomena are not properly a part of my inquiry, since they lack direct pathological significance. However, certain vertebral fusions, especially in the neck area, can give rise to neurological problems, and anomalies at the lumbosacral joint can be a predisposition to lumbago and arthritic breakdown. As an example, I can cite the case of a Mycenaean aristocrat (*58 Myc.*) whose fifth lumbar vertebra, by a congenital anomaly, was incorporated into the sacrum and who had, at age 35, traces of degenerative arthritis on the other lumbar vertebrae.[83]

Another example deserves mention here even though it belongs to a relatively late period. While excavating a Roman camp at Corinth in 1960, H. S. Robinson discovered a tomb containing the well-preserved skeletons of two persons buried at the same time, one next to the other. The

Swedish experts N. G. Gejvall and F. Henschen state that they are the remains of an adult female and an adult male, both tall (181 and 158.5 cm.) and both afflicted with congenital spinal malformations. In the man, the first cervical vertebra is fused with the base of the skull, and the second is squat and has a very short denticulate apophysis. In the woman, the first cervical vertebra is not completely formed (it consists of the two lateral halves kept together by a pseudo-arthrosis), and the second is misshapen, shortened, and fused in a block with the following two cervical vertebrae; there is also a block fusion of the fifth and sixth cervical vertebrae and the first, second, and third thoracic as well as a partial fusion on just one side of the fifth lumbar vertebra with the sacrum.[84] Occipitalization of the first cervical vertebra is a rare anomaly. In the male skeleton from Corinth it surely is of genetic origin, as is the whole series of spinal malformations on the female skeleton from the same tomb. Very likely the two were linked by blood, not marriage. In both, the bone anomalies are so serious that they must have been accompanied by significant neurological problems. To be sure, parallelism in suffering does not explain their simultaneous demise, unless we suppose it was a double suicide. For the record, a case of spina bifida has recently been discovered on the skeleton of a young woman from Tiryns (geometric period, ca. 900–700 B.C.).[85]

In 1912, the French physicians Maurice Klippel and André Feil described for the first time in a precise and detailed way a case of congenital absence of the cervical vertebrae resulting in the ascent of the thoracic cage to the base of the skull. This same anomaly, the Klippel-Feil syndrome, is represented with stark realism in a Hellenistic figurine from Smyrna. A coroplastic artist gave the clay the shape of a little fellow without a neck (aplasia and fusion of the cervical vertebrae) whose face expresses suffering. The diagnosis is secured by the symmetrical position of the head (which excludes a stiff neck), atrophy of the mastoid region, and the presence of a pterygium colli. Often deafness and mental retardation are associated with the Klippel-Feil syndrome. The cervical malformations compress the spinal nerves and cause painful disorders.[86]

On a terra cotta head from Corinth that dates from the middle of the fourth century B.C., a Greek artisan has rendered with the precision of a scientific observer all the morphological characteristics of a unilateral cleft lip (cheiloschisis) as well as the secondary consequences of this congenital malformation for the overall structure of the face.[87]

On two female skeletons from the Late Bronze Age excavated in the Pylos region, Christos C. Bartsocas has good but not definitely convincing reasons to recognize two specific bone ailments, Paget's disease on one and cleidocranial dysplasia on the other. The first (osteitis deformans, identified by Paget in 1877) causes remodeling of bones and deformities in old people; it attacks several bones and progresses slowly. Heredity seems to play a significant role, but the etiology of the disease is unknown. The second disease is a congenital disorder in skeletal development causing defective formation of the skull, the collarbones, and the vertebral arches. The same scholar has diagnosed this disease in an ancient iconographic representation of Thersites, the deformed anti-hero of the Homeric epic.[88]

A 35-year-old male whose skeleton was found at Argos in an old geometric tomb (*16 Arg.;* ca. 900–850 B.C.) suffered from congenital dislocation of the hip due to a malformation of the left hip socket, which is open too wide. With the head of the femur out of place, excessive pulling on the ligaments of the joint resulted, which then caused the production of osteophytes on the vertebrae, the trochanter, and the hipbone. According to the osteoarchaeological description of Robert P. Charles, the location and quantity of these bony proliferations suggests an ankylosis of the left hip as the final complication of an apparently minor congenital malformation.[89] Another case of congenital hip dislocation with less serious consequences has been reported by John Lawrence Angel on a Greek skeleton of the Mycenaean age.[90]

Angel has also described cases of clubfoot on two skeletons from the necropolis of Lerna. The first is an unusual calcaneo-navicular joint, probably a talipes valgus, in the left foot of a boy about 15 years old (*122 Ler.*). The femur on that side is thinner than its mate on the other side. Is it a congenital clubfoot or one caused by an acquired pathological state? The paleopathologist cannot decide one way or the other for this case or a second one: the disability in the right foot of a 45-year-old man (*127 Ler.*) is associated with a noticeable shortening of the right lower limb. The talus is rotated laterally and downward, which completely unbalances the ankle joint. The navicular, the cuneiforms, and the metatarsals are underdeveloped, while the calcaneus seems to have been fractured. It is possible that this abnormal state results from a traumatic dislocation with fracture during adolescence, but it could just as well originate in a congenital malformation.[91]

The Hippocratic physicians were perfectly well acquainted with congenital hip dislocation as well as the principal forms of clubfoot. According to them, congenital dislocation of the hip is not inherited but is rather the result of a lesion arising during embryonic development. They accounted for permanent deformities of the foot and ankle in the same way, evoking mechanical factors like intrauterine compression or infantile trauma, not knowing of their genetic determination and paralytic etiology.[92]

It is practically certain that since his origin man has been subject to disturbances in the biological controls on cell growth that are manifested clinically as malignant tumors, leukemias, and the like. However, the frequency of these ailments has not necessarily been the same in different eras and throughout the range of geographic and sociocultural environments. Cancer, in the widest sense of the term, is a common disease for modern man: in developed countries it is now the cause of death for two out of ten persons. The growth of such neoplasms often leaves traces on skeletons, either when a tumor arises from the bony tissue itself (e.g. an osteosarcoma), or when bones are attacked by the expansion and spread of a malignant soft tissue proliferation. In modern man there are metastases into bone in at least one-quarter of all cancer victims. It would suffice to examine fewer than 100 skeletons from a twentieth-century cemetery to be almost sure of finding a case of cancerous disease, but the results of osteoarchaeological investigations in no way match these statistics. Though it is true that the mark of cancer can be observed on human bones from any and every age, the fact remains that its presence is exceptional in specimens before the Renaissance. For the epochs stretching from prehistoric times up to the sixteenth century, its frequency is difficult to quantify but certainly is a lot less than 1 case for every 1,000.[93]

To our knowledge, no certain case of a malignant tumor has yet been identified on ancient Greek bones. Angel mentions a probable case of cancer metastases in one Late Bronze Age skeleton (unpublished). As for neighboring areas, an Etruscan example of malignant cranial metastasis has been reported.[94] Aside from a few instances of benign tumors, notably two osteomas of the femur in Karataş, the osteoarchaeological evidence for neoplastic diseases in Greek prehistory and history is extremely poor. One should not draw hasty conclusions from this situation. Some works of art appear to show that the Greeks knew of and portrayed both breast cancer and sarcoma of the eye-socket, but such diagnoses from medical archaeology are not unimpeachable.[95] On the other hand, literary sources offer abundant, reliable information on the existence of various malignant tumors in the classical period. However, their frequency was so low that the absence of traces of them in the osteoarchaeological record is not surprising. Considering the total number of skeletons that have been examined, the current negative result does not allow us to state positively, for example, that cancer was rarer in Greece than in certain geographic and cultural regions for which there are positive paleopathological finds (prehistoric Iran and northern Europe, Pharaonic Egypt, and pre-Columbian America). The infrequency of cancerous disease in ancient populations as compared with our contemporary societies is partly explicable in terms of differences in average life expectancy, chemical pollution, and the quantity and nature of some particular radiations. All these circumstances are undeniably significant, but it does not appear that they adequately account for the magnitude of the change in frequency from then to now. Whatever the solution, genetic factors seem less to blame than environmental ones.

Among the "inborn errors of metabolism" (A. Garrod, 1909) that leave their marks on bones, the most important in the eastern Mediterranean are hereditary anemias and gout. The former raise such complex problems that I must devote a separate chapter to them. As for gout, osteoarchaeological reports and literary texts both attest to its antiquity in the Greek world. A 35-year-old man whose skeleton was found at Lerna in a Middle Bronze Age tomb (*70 Ler.*) must have suffered from it in his big toe, the classic locus of urate deposits. The surfaces at that joint of his right foot are markedly arthritic, and an interphalangeal enlargement of the space between it and the next toe corresponds to the place taken, during the man's lifetime, by a tophus, an accumulation of urate crystals. Although the presence of arthritic exostoses on the rear part of this foot might raise doubts about the diagnosis of gout, it is confirmed by the presence of a yellow-purple deposit on the same man's left elbow.[96] An affliction common in the experience of the Hippocratic writers,[97] gout is cited by Plato along with fever and ophthalmia as a typical disease.[98] Yet it seems to have been unknown to the physicians of Pharaonic Egypt. No mention is made of it on papyri, and physical signs of it have not been detected on mummies of the high period. As long ago as 1910, Elliot Smith and Wood Jones described a spectacular case of primary generalized gout with subcutaneous tophi and incrustations within the joints on a mummy found near the temple at Philae (one urate deposit measures 5 by 10 by 23 mm.), but the case is of relatively recent date: the gouty old man in question was a Christian living under the Roman occupation.[99]

Another case of gout from Roman times (second century A.D.) was diagnosed by Calvin Wells on a skeleton from the necropolis of Cirencester in Gloucestershire. As is to be expected, it is also a man—gout is much more common in men than in women—of mature age with gout in several joints and, interestingly enough, a relatively high social status: of the 268 people in this Roman British cemetery, he and another individual are the only ones to be buried in sarcophagi.[100] Without wanting to take up at this point the difficult question of the reasons for the spread of gout in the Roman Empire and for its outbreaks during certain historical periods, I note that there is paleopathological confirmation of the antiquity of the gene in just those regions in which this disease will plague the ruling classes (Byzantium, Christian communities in Africa, and Britain).[101]

According to modern medical research, the metabolic processes leading to an excess of uric acid and its deposit in tissue are basically dependent on genetic factors. By contrast, environmental factors are responsible for various concretions that are deposited in the urinary tract. The climate of coastal Greece and certain dietary habits make probable on a priori grounds a high incidence of urinary stones. In fact the exceptionally rich historical documentation of bladder stones in Greece, in the classical age as well as the Byzantine period and on into the nineteenth century, confirms their commonness and especially their frequency in children. Paleopathological methods allow the identification of urinary calculi among the prehistoric human remains of Egypt and western Europe.[102] A kidney stone from the

Bronze Age was found in Hungary, at the limit of the Greek world, but no paleopathological example from Greece itself has yet come to light.[103] No doubt the cause of this lack of evidence is the difficulty of finding such small stones after bodily decomposition.

Specialists in the prehistory of disease in Greece have been more fortunate with gallstones. In 1954 J. L. Angel found several in one of the tombs of Grave Circle B in Mycenae (Middle Bronze Age). These reddish brown aggregates, with green patches, several facets, and rounded edges, were found between the lowest right ribs and the pelvic brim of the skeleton of a massive man around 55 years old (*131 Myc.*).[104]

In a man of the classical period (skeleton *65 AK.*, found in the Kerameikos in Athens and dated around 450 B.C.) about 40 years of age, osteoarchaeological examination has revealed a strange condition of the larynx. It had become rigid, almost ossified, as the result of calcification of the thyroid and arytenoid cartilage.[105] The same skeleton shows spinal hyperostosis (with ankylosis of several thoracic vertebrae even to the point of their fusion with certain ribs) and scattered osteophytosis, which suggest generalized metabolic disease. This individual also suffered from a large tooth socket abscess and gum disease. Without X-rays and histological examination, the diagnosis of systemic disease in this citizen of Periclean Athens cannot be specified. Nor can the medical historian add anything to the laconic report in Herodotus concerning the bone anomalies observed during the creation of an ossuary for the victims of the battle of Plataea in Boeotia (victory of the Greeks over the Persians in 479 B.C.): "When the corpses were fleshless, they discovered—this was after the Plataeans put all the bones in one place—a skull without any sutures, a single, continuous bone; also a jawbone, the upper jaw, with all the teeth attached to one another, both the front teeth and the molars all made of one bone; and also the bones of a man five cubits tall."[106] What were the shape and dimensions of this skull "without any sutures"? Since it belonged to a warrior, who must have been an adult male without handicap, the skull could not have been fused into a single bone since birth. Herodotus's summary description, however, is insufficient for a retrospective diagnosis. As for the strange "dental ankylosis," we can mention two famous historical parallels: it is said that Pyrrhus, king of Epirus (ca. 319–272 B.C.), and Prusias Monodus, son of King Prusias of Bythinia (second century B.C.), had single, continuous bones by way of teeth for their upper jaws. These are probably extremely rare forms of dental agenesia, a specific recessive genetic disorder. The pathological state has only recently been recognized.[107]

As for the giant, his size is given in round numbers. Five cubits corresponds roughly to 7.5 feet (2.3 meters). For a learned man in ancient times it was not easy to determine the exact height of a man using bones as the only clue. When discussing another giant from Persia, a military engineer named Artakhaies who "fell ill and died," Herodotus is more precise: he "measured six royal cubits less four fingers," that is, about 8 feet 2 inches (2.55 meters).[108] Relatively proportional gigantism can be a matter of constitution with no accompanying metabolic anomalies. Often, especially in extreme cases like those mentioned by Herodotus, it is due to endocrine disorders, in particular to a hyperactive adenohypophysis before the physiological end of growth. An excess of growth hormone after puberty results in acromegaly. The tokens of this disease (namely, excessive growth of extremities, facial peculiarities like a projecting jaw and an oversized nose, lateral and convex spinal curvature, etc.) are visible in several Hellenistic statuettes.[109] Finally, I mention only in passing the iconographic representation in antiquity of several other syndromes due to chromosomal anomalies or endocrine disorders: achondroplastic dwarfism, Down's syndrome, hermaphroditism, hydrocephalus, and Cushing's syndrome.[110]

Vitamin Deficiencies

From what is known of the diet and climatic conditions in ancient Greece, it is fair to posit the existence of vitamin A deficiency (which causes night blindness and xerophthalmia), the rare and sporadic appearance of vitamin B_2 deficiency, osteomalacia, rickets, and scurvy, and, finally, the absence or extreme rarity of beriberi and pellagra. Only rickets, osteomalacia, and scurvy (two forms of vitamin D and vitamin C deficiency) affect the bone system. No other vitamin deficiency can be identified by osteoarchaeological methods.

Rickets is a systemic disease of bones and cartilage in infants and children. By far the most common clinical form of the disease is associated with a lack of vitamin D_2 (ergocalciferol) and insufficient exposure to sunlight, for solar radiation is indispensable to the synthesis in the skin of vitamin D_2 from previtamins that are not often lacking in the food chain. It is easy to understand why fog, heavy clothing, and staying indoors continually are, along with a restricted diet, factors associated with the development of rickets. The disease's main characteristics are nonmineralized growth and bone deformities. Its diagnosis can be made as easily on the skeletons of children as on those of adults, thanks to its permanent consequences. If the vitamin D_2 deficiency arises after growth ceases, that is, in adulthood, the result is a bone disease called osteomalacia. Unlike rickets, it only occurs under conditions of extreme deprivation of vitamin sources, general malnutrition, and heavy drain on the body's calcium resources (particularly in pregnant women). That is why, as a rule, osteomalacia is much less common than the childhood form of vitamin D deficiency.

In view of what has just been said about the etiology of rickets, it is not surprising to learn that almost all cases of the disease observed up to now on prehistoric, protohistoric, or medieval bones come from the misty regions of northern Europe and from Siberia. A few fairly dubious identifications have been put forth for pre-Columbian peoples in the Americas, but all the osteoarchaeological documentation now extant proves that rickets only became a relatively common ailment along with the urbanization of Europe after the Middle Ages.[111] There is no rickets on early Greek and Egyptian bones. Harris' lines and striations on dental enamel are insufficient to sustain a diagnosis of this disease. Nor is the existence of hunchbacks, which has been confirmed by osteoarchaeology, iconography, and literary texts, proof of the antiquity of the disease.

A possible but highly problematic instance of rickets is the case of a young girl from Centuripe in Sicily (first century B.C.).[112] A thickened frontal bone and a curved tibia are indeed suggestive of the disease, but the skeleton in question, which is now housed at the Archaeological Museum in Syracuse, should be reexamined by a pathologist well versed in modern paleopathological technique. Two cases have been identified by Guyla Regöly-Mérei on skeletons from the Roman era found at Fazekasboda near Pécs (in ancient times Sopianae, capital of Lower Pannonia). The poor wretches were undoubtedly natives of the region, not Roman soldiers or colonists.[113] Aside from instances of hunchback, whose connection with vitamin D deficiency is far from unequivocal, the marks of rickets are missing from archaic and classical iconography. But some have thought they recognized the disease on certain Hellenistic terra cottas found in Asia Minor and Italy.[114]

The Hippocratic writings contain no allusion whatever to pathological phenomena that could be interpreted as rickets. And a decisive argument for the rarity of vitamin D deficiency in classical Greece consists of the complete absence in gynecological treatises of reflections on pelvic deformations and their obstetrical significance. The flat pelvis was unknown to Hippocratic physicians, nor is it mentioned in the medical texts before Soranus. Osteoarchaeology confirms the rarity of pelvic anomalies and the relative broadness of the pelvis in Greek females. Not until Roman times did urban density, changes of diet, and the impoverishment of one part of the population unite to bring about conditions favorable to rickets and to making its ravages apparent to medical practitioners.[115]

Did endemic bone dystrophy exist in the classical period among certain neighbors of the Greeks, chiefly the Persians, as Herodotus seems to suggest? On a visit to Pelusium, a harbor on the eastern branch of the Nile and the site of Cambyses' great victory over the Egyptian army in 525 B.C., Herodotus tells us he found the following:

> At the place where the battle was fought I saw a very odd thing, which the natives had told me about. The bones still lay there, those of the Persian dead separate from those of the Egyptian, just as they were originally divided, and I noticed that the skulls of the Persians are so thin that the merest touch with a pebble will pierce

them, but those of the Egyptians, on the other hand, are so tough that it is hardly possible to break them with a blow from a stone. I was told, very credibly, that the reason was that the Egyptians shave their heads from childhood, so that the bone of the skull is indurated by the action of the sun—this is also why they hardly ever go bald, baldness being rarer in Egypt than anywhere else. This, then, explains the thickness of their skulls; and the thinness of the Persians' skulls rests upon a similar principle: namely that they have always worn felt skull-caps to guard their heads from the sun. I also observed the same thing at Papremis, where the Persians serving under Achaemenes, the son of Darius, were destroyed by Inarus the Libyan.[116]

Travelers reaching Mesopotamia would have encountered cases of scurvy, a deficiency disease marked by serious hemorrhaging and disorders of the bones and joints. But Greek physicians did not know of it.[117] Even during famines, it was never vegetable products containing ascorbic acid (vitamin C) that were lacking to the inhabitants of Greece and Italy, and sea travel was still just coastal navigation. The only occasion on which scurvy could have had a significant impact was the prolonged siege of a city, but historical accounts of the subject are lacking.[118] It may well be that scurvy appeared sporadically, for instance, among people who were bedridden or in prison, even in a society in which the necessary supply of vitamins was abundant. We cannot exclude some incidence of infantile scurvy or Barlow's disease, which seriously interferes with bone growth. Unfortunately, diseases of the newborn were not well observed or differentiated by ancient physicians. Their pathology is historically invisible. In any case, no osteoarchaeological case of scurvy is known until the Middle Ages.[119]

Rheumatic Ailments

Traces of "rheumatism" are very common on prehistoric and protohistoric human bones, and their diagnosis is the most common in osteoarchaeology.[120] Nevertheless, I take the precaution of putting the name of this disease in quotes, since the ancient concept of rheumatism has survived in modern medicine only at the cost of its pathological coherence. It broke up to form a host of various osteoarthropathies. On a dry bone, the morphology of rheumatic lesions is relatively uniform—rough joint surfaces with local compressions and erosions, bony excrescences on the edge of these surfaces—but that does not mean that their etiology is not complex, very diverse (wear and tear, traumas, infections, metabolic disorders, autoimmune reactions, genetic defects with delayed aftereffects, etc.), and, in general, still inadequately understood.[121] So it was to be expected that such lesions would occur on bones from Greece and that we would have to confront the difficult problems of differential diagnosis that they present.

Degenerative joint disease (degenerative arthritis or, better, osteoarthritis)[122] is the most common of all the rheumatic ailments that lend themselves to osteoarchaeological diagnosis. It manifests itself in living subjects as a progressive deterioration of articular cartilage that is, on the one hand, either a secondary phenomenon resulting from a malformation, a trauma, an intra-articular deposit, or an attack of fever, or, on the other, a primary one, without some other pathological state being its "cause." Bony lesions are associated with the erosion and ulceration of the cartilage: underlying bone tissue thickens in certain places (zones of osteosclerosis) and makes fissures in others; at the edge of the transformed joint, bony protuberances called osteophytes begin to grow. The synovial membrane is either normal or slightly inflamed. In modern man, primary degenerative joint disease is seen chiefly after age 50, and its frequency increases with age. Its basic pathogenetic process is wear and tear on joints linked with mechanical stress and changes due to aging.[123] The disease is often confined to a single joint or acts in bilateral symmetry. It attacks the hip, the knee, the shoulder, the wrist, the fingers, the joint of the jaw, and frequently the spine. Its localization on the spine can be either anterior or posterior. Degenerative joint disease of the limbs is often disabling, while in the spine it is usually well tolerated.

Osteophytes grow as the result of ossification under the periosteum or within the bone. Their presence at the margin of the articular cartilage together with marginal lipping reinforces a diagnosis of degenerative joint disease. However, their number or size is not an indicator of the seriousness of the degenerative process. The etiology of osteophytes is multiple, so that it is not easy to detect, especially on a dry bone that is not well preserved, the pathological event that is at the origin of an isolated growth of them around a joint without accompanying joint lesions. Divergences in the statistical data of different paleopathologists could be due to differences in their diagnostic evaluation of isolated osteophytes.

There are good reasons to think that at the dawn of mankind the food consumed called for considerable feats of chewing. Two consequences of such a functional strain are especially common on ancient human remains: dental abrasion and wear on the joint that is involved in chewing. The presence of degenerative osteoarthritis in the temporo-mandibular joint has been reported on several Neanderthals (Krapina, La Chapelle-aux-Saints, La Ferrassie, etc.), on some specimens from Taforalt, an epi-Paleolithic necropolis in western Morocco, and in numerous Neolithic specimens from central and western Europe. According to W. M. Krogman, 9 of 110 mandibles from Tepe Hissar, an Iranian necropolis dated 4000–2000 B.C., have sure signs of degenerative joint disease on their condyles.[124] That amounts to a little more than 8 percent; the real percentage should be higher, since dubious or mild cases were not taken into account.

There should be no shortage of similar signs on prehistoric jawbones in the eastern Mediterranean. Unfortunately, currently available information provides only a sketchy picture of the frequency of this disorder. These modifications of maxillary condyles and their sockets in the mandible are relatively slight and easily go unnoticed. Angel has reported osteoarthritis of the temporo-mandibular joint in 11 of 43 individuals at Çatal Hüyük (Neolithic), which is 25.5 percent of those examined (31.5 percent among men and 21 percent among women).[125] A systematic study of prehistoric jaws in Anatolia has been undertaken by B. Alpagut, a Turkish researcher, who, in a preliminary survey, was able to diagnose one serious case of bilateral temporo-mandibular degenerative joint disease (adult male of the Early Bronze Age) and three cases in which the condyle is affected unilaterally (adults, Neolithic and Chalcolithic).[126] For the Peloponnesus, I can cite, as an example, a very pronounced case in a prehistoric inhabitant of Lerna (*125 Ler.*), who also suffered from periodontal disease on the same side.[127] For Attica, I can report an adult lower jaw from the Kitsos Cave (*2/518 Ki.*) that has signs of degeneration of the joint on the left condyle, probably associated with bite disorders resulting from a major loss of molars.[128]

Degenerative joint disease in the limbs is not unusual in ancient bones from Europe. Its role in Greek osteoarchaeology has been stressed by C. M. Fürst (with special reference to specimens from the Middle Bronze Age found at Asine)[129] and studied in detail by J. L. Angel. The latter found that on noninfantile bones from the Helladic necropolis at Lerna, osteoarthritis of the limb joints affected 41 percent of the men and 18 percent of the women.[130] During the classical, Hellenistic, and Roman periods these frequencies diminish by about half. When degenerative joint disease affects the joint of a limb, it is often associated with a malformation or a fracture that has healed in an abnormal position. Their association on ancient skeletons makes it possible to establish, in some cases, the causal links that result in a joint's degeneration. Degeneration can also result from especially harsh and repetitive physical labor. The osteoarchaeological proof of such labor is sometimes provided by the increase in bone ridges to which muscles are attached. As an example, there is the female skeleton *137 Ler.*, which shows, on the one hand, scars in the form of an enlargement of the scalene muscle insertions on the first right rib, and, on the other, traces of degenerative joint disease on the surfaces of the right scapulo-humerus joint and along the biceps groove of the right humerus. It is probably a case of occupational shoulder osteoarthritis in a weaver.[131]

As against the observations of J. L. Angel, Robert P. Charles has only rarely been able to report the presence of degenerative joint disease on ancient skeletons from the Argolid. According to him, although signs of rheumatism are usually very common on the prehistoric bones of western Europe, he has seen only three cases of it in Argos: some "rheumatic exostoses" (that is, osteophytosis) on the clavicle of *93 Arg.* (from a protogeometric tomb), on the humerus of one of the specimens from tomb *15 Arg.*, and on the vertebrae as well as at the level of the left hip joint on skeleton *16 Arg.* (a man with congenital hip dislocation; see above, p. 71). A new investigation was able to add only one more case: *XXXVI-1 Deiras,* the remains of a woman from the Mycenaean era, aged about 35, with mild spinal osteophytosis.[132]

Without doubt, the most common disease diagnosed by paleopathologists is degenerative osteoarthritis of the spine.[133] In the great majority of cases, one should not even call it a disease in the usual sense of the word, since the bone changes in question, although they are morphologically impressive and plainly pathological, do not result in serious functional disorders and are generally not experienced by the person affected as a sickness. In some cases, vertebral osteophytes can become so important that they form massive bony bridges across intervertebral discs and make some portions of the spine rigid. Ankylosing vertebral hyperostosis, whose anatomical and clinical profile has been clarified by Jacques Forestier, is a severe form of osteophytosis. It is marked by vertical ossifications between the thoracic and lumbar vertebrae that have the appearance of dripping wax. Despite its impressive anatomical modifications, this disease is usually without major clinical symptoms.[134]

Paleopathological "rheumatic bone growths" were first discovered in the prehistoric bear (F.J.K. Mayer, 1854). At first their etiology was thought to be the cold and dampness of caves, whence the name "cave gout" coined by Virchow (1895). The hypothesis seemed confirmed by the description of similar lesions on the vertebrae of Neanderthal men, specifically Krapina man (D. Gorjanovic-Kramberger, 1906) and the man from Chapelle-aux-Saints (M. Boule, 1911). But evidence began accumulating that this disease had also been common among the Neolithic populations of Europe, who were relatively well protected from the elements, and in particular among the inhabitants of Pharaonic, Hellenistic, and Roman Egypt. To the pioneers of paleopathology, nothing could be more astonishing than widespread endemic rheumatism in a dry, hot climate. To save the prevailing hypothesis, Wood Jones did not scruple to invoke, as an etiological factor, "dabbling in the water of the Nile." Then, for a while, the trend was to explain vertebral osteophytosis as a reaction to a primary infectious focus. A causal link was suggested between tonsillitis or periodontitis, everyday diseases in all epochs, and proliferating rheumatism of the spine. In the middle of this century, osteoarchaeology finally drew its lesson from the fundamental distinction between acute articular rheumatism and degenerative joint disease, and it realized that the common form of spondylitis was basically independent of climate and of microbes.

In a study of the biological history of the spinal column,[135] I insisted on the fact that, in man, it has obvious weaknesses. I attempted to account for them as a result of its partially contradictory functions and of the adaptation, perforce inadequate, of a structure initially designed for another role. The present form of the spine is the result of a compromise among several functions that it has to fill, each of which has a shaping influence that either complements or competes with the others. On the one hand, the spine must be both an endoskeleton that serves as a mechanical support for the body's system of locomotion and also an exoskeleton that must shelter and guard the central nervous system. On the other hand, the spine is shaped from the beginning like a mechanical support for a marine animal of soft consistency; stretching out into a horizontal position, it developed like the hydrodynamic axis of animals that swim, only to adapt itself thereafter to locomotion on dry land (first crawling, then walking on all fours, then walking erect). This series of readaptations is the source of certain spinal ailments, notably degenerative spondylitis. Unknown among most animals, this disease appears among the larger saurians of the Cretaceous and among the crocodilians, then in the cave bear and prehistoric man. In the former, it is the price of their size and their passage from water to earth. In the latter, it is the price paid for the vertical orientation of a relatively heavy trunk. Just as that orientation creates lowered resistance in the lumbosacral region, the development of the hand, cephalic flexure, and cephalization define another in the cervical region. Moreover, degenerative diseases of this kind are promoted by the fact that the mechanism of natural selection does not work after the conclusion of the sexual cycle. The spine must function appropriately only until the end of the reproductive phase. Selection cannot correct genetic errors that become apparent only during senescence.

The Greek osteoarchaeological record offers a few spectacular examples of degenerative osteoarthritis of the spine. The most famous is that of a Middle Bronze Age man from Asine (*3 FA.*) described by Carl M. Fürst in 1930. In this stalwart individual between 40 and 50 years of age, numerous vertebrae have osteophytes, and six vertebral bodies of the lower thoracic region are fused into a single block. According to Fürst, "This man suffered from a very serious case of *arthritis deformans chronica anchylopoetica.*"[136] The diagnosis of the Swedish anthropologist seems correct; it only has to be translated into current medical parlance. The man from Asine had degenerative ankylosis of the lower spine, most likely Forestier's ankylosing vertebral hyperostosis. The same diagnosis (Forestier's syndrome or even Resnick's DISH [diffuse idiopathic skeletal hyperostosis]) can be considered in the case, mentioned above in a discussion of calcification of the larynx, of the skeleton *65 AK.* exhumed in the Kerameikos in Athens.[137] On a skeleton from Grave Circle B at Mycenae (*59 Myc.*), one can see three thoracic vertebrae (T 9–11) fused together through ossification of the disk portions of the anterior longitudinal ligament and numerous osteophytes on the cervical, lower thoracic, and lumbar vertebrae. These are the remains of a warrior prince who died at about age 50, a particularly fit and sturdy fellow.[138] Surely some extraordinary stress on the spine (athletic training and wrestling?) contributed to the development of this ailment. The man has exostoses at almost every tendon attachment, so that other etiological factors were certainly involved. Again, the spinal column of the specimen *181 Ler.,* a fairly muscular 40-year-old male, shows pronounced exostoses of the vertebral bodies. There are also some indications of spondylolisthesis (forward slippage of one vertebra over the one beneath it). All of which suggests that heavy work and trauma were at the origins of this case of spinal joint disease.[139]

Among the many vertebral osteophytes found in Greece, some are due to cases of herniated disk, an exclusively human disease that sometimes takes the form of severe sciatica. The syndrome in question is described in the Hippocratic corpus.[140] On prehistoric and protohistoric bones, degenerative spondylitis usually occurs in the thoracolumbar region; its second choice is the cervicothoracic. Fürst reported an instructive instance from Asine (*4 FA.*),[141] while Angel has stressed the relative frequency of cervical spondylitis among the ancient inhabitants of Lerna.[142] As for the statistical frequency of degenerative osteoarthritis of the spine in the eastern Mediterranean, J. L. Angel has estimated that this ailment (including all forms of spinal osteophytosis) occurs in approximately 70 percent of prehistoric specimens and that the percentage drops to about 40 percent for the historical periods of antiquity.[143] In subsequent publications, Angel provided the following figures: 74 percent at Nea Nikomedia in Macedonia (Neolithic), 61 percent at Çatal Hüyük in Anatolia (Neolithic), and 62 percent at Karataş in Lycia (Early Bronze Age).[144] The same order of magnitude is in force at Lerna, but there is a significant split between the men and the women. With the former, spinal osteophytosis reaches 75 percent, while among the latter it is only at 50 percent.[145] To be sure, the majority of the cases counted are mild and of no import clinically. But the statistic remains very interesting to the historian because of the role played by stress, especially physical labor, in the etiology of degenerative osteoarthritis: the numbers given show that a clear improvement in conditions of life, above all in working conditions, took place during the archaic period and at the beginning of the classical period. The statistical effect of this change of conditions in the social environment is all the more significant since a concurrent increase in the average life expectancy should have influenced the numbers in the opposite direction from the one they take.

Nevertheless, it would be incorrect to conclude that reduction in the frequency of this ailment is a continuous and regular historical phenomenon. For example, spinal osteophytosis was rare among the Hittites of central Anatolia prior to the time it was common in Greece; it was much more widespread in medieval Byzantium than in Greece during the classical period. The difference between masculine and feminine morbidity is essentially due to social factors, such as sexual discrimination in occupation, not to biological differentiation. On bones from Kalinkaya, a proto-Hittite necropolis in central Anatolia dated 4000–3000 B.C., spinal osteophytosis occurs in 50 percent of the women and 33 percent of the men.[146]

Wedge-shaped deformation of certain vertebral bodies and the existence of Schmorl's nodules (hernias of the pulpy nucleus in the spongy matter of the vertebral body) make likely (e.g., in *69 Ler., 182 Ler., 196 Ler.,* and *62 Myc.*[147]) the diagnosis of Scheuermann's disease, an affection of both bone and cartilage during growth. Its etiology is unknown, and it occurs as kyphosis in adolescents, often evolving into degenerative joint disease of the spine. According to G. Bergmark, this disease is represented on an ancient statue of Antinoos of Bithynia, Hadrian's lover.[148]

Differential osteoarchaeological diagnosis is especially difficult in the case of arthritis.[149] A joint's inflammatory reaction can be septic, that is, due to a direct microbial influence, or rheumatic, that is, not linked to the local presence of microbes. Septic arthritis in the strict sense of the term, particularly suppurating joints brought on by nonspecific pyogenic bacteria and tuberculosis of the bones and joints, will be touched upon elsewhere. The limited resources of osteoarchaeology do not allow for the diagnosis of oculo-urethro-synovial syndrome (RS or Reiter's syndrome or, more correctly, the Fiessinger-Leroy-Reiter syndrome), whose infectious origins have recently been proven, nor for certain kinds of multiple joint arthritis whose etiology is still unknown (Felty's syndrome, lupus polyarthritis, psoriatic rheumatism).

Unfortunately, the same is true of the most important of all the rheumatic diseases, rheumatic fever or Bouillaud's disease. This form of multiple joint arthritis appears after a streptococcal sore throat or an outburst of festering infection in some other focus—the bacteria act at a distance, without local infection of the joints affected. The disease especially strikes children and young adults, and it often brings with it serious cardiac complications. A very common disease in Europe and America before the antibiotic era, it was surely present in the Greek world from prehistoric times. According to the oldest Greek medical texts, red sore throat with pus (streptococcal tonsillitis) was commonplace. The Hippocratic corpus contains a concise yet readily identifiable description of Bouillaud's disease.[150]

So rheumatic fever existed in ancient times, but since it produces no bone changes we can provide no osteoarchaeological proof of its presence. By contrast, rheumatoid arthritis, which is now the most common form of chronic inflammatory arthritis, does leave enduring marks on bones but perhaps did not yet exist in antiquity. This disease develops in irregular stages, affecting the limb joints, especially the wrist and the fingers, and is frequently symmetrical. It generally prefers women to men, and although it can arrive at any age, it usually begins after age 40.[151] First defined as a clinical entity in 1800 by A. J. Landré-Beauvais (under the name "goutte asthénique primitive" [gout that begins with weakness]), rheumatoid arthritis seems to have been an unusual disease before that date. Its clinical aspect is very striking—the effect on hands can be disabling—and, as was said above, among present populations it is common. So it is all the more surprising that clinical descriptions, pictorial representations, and osteoarchaeological evidence prior to the nineteenth century that might relate to this disease are so rare. It is possible to prove its existence in the seventeenth century—from a description by Thomas Sydenham and paintings by P. P. Rubens—and to suspect its existence in the Middle Ages—the case of the Byzantine emperor Constantine IX, a passage in the eighth book of the encyclopedic treatise *De proprietatibus rerum* by Bartholomew Anglicus, some Flemish paintings going back to about 1400, and some dubious osteoarchaeological cases—but nothing enables us to follow its history further back in time.[152] A diagnosis of the disease was posited by E. G. Smith for an Egyptian mummy of the Fifth Dynasty, but specialists who have looked into the case since consider it only an unconvincing possibility. To explain the paucity of historical information about the existence of rheumatoid arthritis, C. L. Short offered the hypothesis that it is a relatively recent disease that appeared as the result of a genetic transformation of the factors responsible for ankylosing spondylitis.[153] The cause of rheumatoid arthritis is still unknown, but certain immunological phenomena that go with it suggest the intervention of an autosensitization process with an immunological attack of the organism on its own tissues. The appearance of the disease at a certain moment in human history and its spread can be explained as immunogenetic events. In support of the etiological role of genetic factors, we can adduce the familial grouping of victims and the very high frequency among such groups of the histocompatibility antigen HLA-Dw4.[154] Nevertheless, the possibility cannot be excluded that rheumatoid arthritis is an infectious disease caused by a slow virus. In that case, the diachronic fluctuations in its prevalence could be still more easily accounted for.[155]

A discovery on Greek bones has just come up in the debate on the origin of rheumatoid arthritis. According to Linda Klepinger, a skeleton from the Hellenistic era (ca. 300 B.C.) found at Morgantina in Sicily has joint lesions and osteophytes that resemble no currently known rheumatic disease. According to Klepinger, it could be an intermediate stage between ankylosing spondylitis and rheumatoid arthritis, that is, a kind of archaic rheumatoid arthritis. In that case the skeleton would be a paleopathological proof of the hypothesis Short made as the result of medico-historical research and epidemiological considerations.[156] Eminent rheumatologists reject any idea of a historical kinship between the two diseases in question. The paleopathological diagnosis of Linda Klepinger has been strongly criticized, and the debate is still unresolved.[157]

As for ankylosing spondylitis itself (pelvispondylitis ossificans, Strümpell-

Marie's disease, or Bechterew's disease), the supposed or disputed ancestor of rheumatoid arthritis, all specialists agree that it goes back to the dawn of mankind. A disease that is from every point of view comparable to ankylosing spondylitis has been observed in monkeys.[158] Its prehominid origin seems likely. It is a chronic disease of unknown etiology that by preference strikes young adult males. Beginning insidiously with a painful, ankylosing inflammation of the sacroiliac joints, it then attacks one vertebra after another, going from lower to higher. The involvement of peripheral joints is morphologically indistinguishable from rheumatoid arthritis. Genetic predisposition plays an incontestable role. Hereditary transmission of the disease takes place by an autosomal dominant factor. In more than 9 of 10 victims the histocompatibility antigen HLA-B27 is found, while its frequency in the general population is on the order of 4 percent. A viral infection may trigger the disease. For instance, this form of spondylitis may follow Reiter's syndrome, whose infectious origin is a certainty.[159]

The oldest osteoarchaeological case of ankylosing spondylitis was reported in France on a Neolithic skeleton.[160] According to E. G. Smith, Wood Jones, M. A. Ruffer, and A. Rietti, this disease was very common in Pharaonic Egypt. But there is a basic error in the statistical estimates of these paleopathologists: they thought they saw ankylosing spondylitis where there was only ankylosing vertebral hyperostosis.[161] It remains true that in certain cases from Egypt the old diagnosis seems utterly justifiable. My conclusion is that ankylosing spondylitis existed in Egypt at least since the Third Dynasty (ankylosed spine of a man named Nefermant), but it was relatively rare.[162] Among the Macedonian soldiers of Alexander the Great whose tombs are at Chatby near Alexandria, two doubtful cases of the disease have been found, though a firmer diagnosis can be made for a female mummy of the Ptolemaic era.[163] Ankylosing spondylitis has not been reported, as far as I know, on ancient vertebrae from Greece or Italy. Hippocrates probably observed it, since he mentions rigid curvature of the spine as a consequence of old age or "from giving in to pains."[164]

Notes on Infectious Diseases

Pathogenic germs have often framed the destiny of individuals and societies. If humanity succeeded fairly quickly in gaining mastery over the animals, until the last 100 years it was defenseless against countless living creatures who were so tiny that they escaped notice and so powerful that for millennia they were by far the most significant cause of disease and death. Bony lesions of microbial origin are only a minor component of the pathology of infectious disease. Even so, they offer direct proof of the antiquity of pathogenic parasitism, and, for the historian of diseases, they constitute the only visible portion of a huge iceberg whose submerged portions are lost in the past.

I have devoted a whole chapter to the commonplace germs that cause nonspecific festering inflammations in affected tissue, bony or otherwise. Other chapters of this book are concerned with treponematoses, leprosy, and tuberculosis, which are the main specific inflammatory diseases. I found it necessary to include the osteoarchaeology of these diseases in a medico-historical inquiry of wider scope, one that takes special notice of the most recent microbiological, epidemiological, and immunological research. A single endemo-epidemic disease caused by Protozoa, malaria, affected the course of Greek history more than any other pathological factor. Though it has no direct effect on bones, malaria does leave traces on them since it promotes certain hereditary defects that affect bone marrow. A separate chapter is also devoted to this subject.

What malaria was to Greece in decisive moments of its history, schistosomiasis (bilharziasis) was to Egypt. It is a debilitating disease caused by the parasitic worm *Schistosoma haematobium*, a species of fluke whose calcified eggs have been found in the kidneys of Egyptian mummies from the Twentieth Dynasty.[165] No such discovery can be made in Greece, since Greeks did not mummify corpses. Schistosomiasis seems to have been known to the physicians of the classical era, although it was not seen in Greece itself. Actually, climatic conditions and the aquatic fauna of the country have not been hospitable to the life cycle of this parasite, in particular with regard to its intermediary infestation of aquatic gastropods.

Acute viral diseases spare bone tissue. However, it is possible for the paleopathologist to discover traces of their consequences. Thus one can imagine that the extremely slender left femur shaft of a 40-year-old male from Lerna (*95 Ler.*) is the result of a partial paralysis that suggests, in turn, infection by the poliomyelitis virus.[166] In such cases, the diagnosis is very hypothetical. If we use it to prove the existence in antiquity of this viral disease, there is a strong possibility that the argument is circular. Some scholars think they recognize traces of smallpox on Egyptian mummies.[167] Considering the contagiousness of that virus and the existence of commercial links between all lands bordering the Mediterranean, such traces would be indirect proof of at least an episodic presence of the scourge of smallpox in ancient Greece.

The spinal deformation in an Iron Age woman exhumed in Greece may have been brought on by blastomycosis,[168] a fungal infection of the skin and internal organs, but a diagnosis of tuberculosis seems more likely. According to Jean Dastugue, Paleolithic man in Cro-Magnon times was already the victim of another fungal disease, actinomycosis or lumpy jaw.[169] A new examination of this specimen suggests that its lesion had a noninfectious origin. It seems that *1 Cro-Magnon* died a victim of malignant eosinophilic granuloma (a disease now called histiocytosis X).[170]

Chapter Three

PALEODEMOGRAPHY

Evidence from Ancient Bones on the Conditions of Daily Life in Greece

To obtain even a vague idea about the health of the ancient inhabitants of the Greek world, it is useful, if not indispensable, to know beforehand something of their demographic traits. The pathocoenosis of these peoples would be completely obscure were it not possible for us to ascertain at least the order of magnitude for such parameters as the total number of inhabitants, their demographic density, their degree of urbanization, their distribution by gender and age cohort, their fertility, average lifespan, and average height, and the frequency among them of certain bodily defects. The absolute values of such parameters at a single time and place concern us less, however, than their geographic and chronological fluctuations.

This list of demographic traits that can serve to profile a pathocoenosis leaves out birth and death rates, for the simple reason that in our present state of knowledge about ancient Greece there is no way to make adequately secure inferences concerning them. As for the parameters I have listed, osteoarchaeological examination provides information precise enough to justify, as was said in the previous chapter, the recent flowering of a specific discipline called paleodemography.[1] Insofar as paleodemography is based on the osteological and archaeological record, it is not limited strictly to historical periods. But when it does concern itself with history, availing ourselves of written sources can usefully enhance osteoarchaeological methods.

Estimates of the number of inhabitants, their demographic density, and their degree of urbanization are a crucial ingredient in our understanding of the epidemiology of the past, given that certain infectious diseases take different forms depending on the size and structure of the populations they attack, and given also that they invariably pass over populations whose size and density fall short of a certain threshold. Average height as well as tooth and bone characteristics yield general information about diet. In chapter 2 we saw how the percentage of rheumatic lesions allows inferences about stress from physical labor. All these data, along with estimates of average lifespan and the proportion of infant to adult skeletons, make possible a synchronic overview of the health of a population at a given moment in its history. For diachronic study, such data enable us to take a global look at the variations in health and bring to light periods in which the equilibrium of a pathocoenosis is broken.

The Dynamics of the Ancient Greek Pathocoenosis

For the sake of clarity, I interrupt for a moment the logical thread of my exposition to offer a perspective on the dynamics of the Greek pathocoenosis. Fuller argumentation will follow.[2]

The transition in the Neolithic period from hunting and gathering to agriculture and cattle-rearing must have had a profound effect on the state of health in human groups.[3] Earlier than most, the Balkan peninsula and the islands of the eastern Mediterranean were the domain of this changeover from a predatory to a producing economy. The Neolithic revolution began on several fronts at once. One of the most ancient of these, perhaps the most ancient in the world, was western Asia. From there the new civilization spread slowly into Europe, where its first manifestations are visible in what would later become the Greek world. Humans become sedentary and settle in villages. They work the land and domesticate animals without giving up hunting or fishing. Judging by carbon 14 dating of a sample from Nea Nikomedia, the oldest villages in this region date from 6200 to 4500 B.C.

Each Paleolithic human required approximately 5 to 10 square kilometers of land to sustain himself. In the Neolithic period, a smaller lot sufficed to ensure a more varied and abundant diet, and the resultant increase in resources facilitated an extraordinary demographic expansion that had complex repercussions for general health. Relative overpopulation tends to slow improvements in the food supply, or even to reverse here and there an initial trend toward abundance. Loss of mobility and concentration in villages inevitably brings outbreaks of new infectious diseases as well as the revival of certain old ones. With humans and domesticated animals living under the same roof, certain infectious diseases developed that were common to both, and a particular group of viral diseases arose. Moreover, communal life in a fixed locale caused serious problems with the supply of drinking water and the disposal of waste and excrement. Cycles of reinfection began establishing themselves, allowing several parasitic diseases caused by bacteria, protozoa, and intestinal worms to become endemic. The settling of villages in fertile areas near bodies of water and the irrigation of fields fertilized by manure favored the spread of several especially noxious diseases. In addition to these pathogenic factors, there were changes in climate as well as the beginnings of the division of labor and social stratification. As a result, silicosis appeared among stonecutters, lead poisoning among potters, mercury poisoning among the producers of cinnabar (notably at Vinča), higher mortality among women than men owing to their servitude at hard labor, and, generally speaking, the first differentiations of pathology in relation to social class. The first irreversible transformations of the environment, like deforestation and pasturing, were to have long-term public health consequences. Most Neolithic sites were small, comprising scarcely more than a few hundred souls, but recent archaeological excavations have brought to light the existence of important communities that have almost the same proportions as true cities.

The ease and speed of sea travel has played as significant a role in the history of diseases as demographic expansion. Just as stone tools were transported throughout Greece (the inhabitants of the Franchthi Cave were already using obsidian from Melos in the Mesolithic period), so were disease germs carried quickly and easily from one place to another throughout the region. As a result, most places in the eastern Mediterranean during the Neolithic period came to share a pool of infectious diseases. Time would only reinforce their unity in this regard.

The conditions of daily life during Neolithic times were perhaps not as bleak as the exclusive consideration of new pathogenic factors makes them out to be. The biological advantages of a sedentary life in a protected habitat, with essential needs for survival more or less assured, probably won out over the health problems, or at least compensated for them. That seems especially true for Greece—more so than for Asia—where the sun, the climate, the fauna, and other special features of the ecology were not favorable to the great killers from Africa and Asia, except for tuberculosis, malaria, and typhoid. Although the evidence leads us to believe that certain viral diseases arose in Mediterranean lands after the domestication of animals and once the population had surpassed a certain critical density, it does not seem that their origins can be located in the Mediterranean. Even in Hippocrates' time, Greeks still did not know of smallpox, measles, or plague, nor did they ever face scourges like bilharziasis or yellow fever.

And yet average age and various other characteristics of Neolithic bone remains point to a generally poor biological state. These indicators do not change significantly during the whole prehistoric period, except in relation to the salubriousness of particular sites. Even in the Early Bronze Age they remain about the same, which amounts to saying that the conditions of life neither improved nor worsened during the long series of centuries stretching from the seventh to the third millennium B.C. The apogee of Minoan civilization and the beginning of Mycenaean civilization in the

Middle Bronze Age (ca. 1900–1600 B.C.) and the flourishing of the Mycenaean sea empire in the Late Bronze Age (ca. 1600–1200 B.C.) go hand in hand with a clear improvement on the paleodemographic plane in physical well-being.[4] For instance, lifespans lengthen perceptibly, and the frequency of porotic hyperostosis decreases to a spectacular degree. Though the latter phenomenon (the sign of a drop in endemic malignant malaria, or perhaps of improvement in the nutrition of children) begins in the Neolithic period, the jump in longevity takes place all of a sudden. It is probably as much a result of changes in physical surroundings and social structures as of the arrival of a mass of new genes. There is no way for us to discern with certainty the role ascribable to each of these factors.

It is certain, however, that the inhabitants of Greece in the Bronze Age are no longer pure biological descendants of the tribes whose skeletons fill the Neolithic cemeteries. From the end of the third millennium B.C., several waves of Indo-Europeans invaded the Aegean area, first destroying the old economic centers, especially in the Argolid, and then building Mycenaean palaces, fortifications, and villages. Only after the "arrival of the Greeks" is a true physical improvement noticeable. I wish to stress particularly the biological importance of the extraordinary genetic variety of the mixture that is at the origins of the Greek people. This "racial impurity," this heterogeneity, gave the Greeks their vigor, adaptability, and resistance to the often noxious forces in their environment. So on the one hand, chance encounters and the need to survive at any price made the *phúsis* (nature) of the Greeks a rich and versatile one, especially adept at surviving all kinds of biological and social adversities. On the other hand, this physical well-being could never have been realized without the rapid development of a "civilized" society that knew how to control a number of pathogenic factors. For instance, the bookkeeping that went on in the Mycenaean palaces reflects a fussy organization of the production and distribution of victuals. There is archaeological evidence to suggest a concern for cleanliness and, at least among certain classes, an interest in personal hygiene and fashion in clothing. And there is striking proof of technical progress in supplying water and constructing sewers. In any case the growth of the population and the crowding of people into palaces and feudalistic settlements bespeaks the need for sanitary arrangements.[5]

Opulent, fortified centers had one great enemy: overpopulation. Available resources dictated the size of the towns that utilized them. Emigration and colonization were insufficient to overcome such constraints. From time to time people must have suffered subsistence crises, and by the Late Bronze Age the Aegean population had attained the density necessary for the outbreak of catastrophic epidemics. Paleodemography reveals to us a clear worsening in the condition of women, and the higher mortality rate for them than for men does not cease climbing until the Golden Age of the classical period.

The archaeological record signals the material decline and collapse of the bureaucratic states organized around the palaces during the period from 1200 to 1100 B.C. Then the Dark Ages of Greek history began, marked by the Dorian invasion and the arrival of a civilization based on iron.[6] By the ninth century, the demographic shock seems to have been absorbed. A new type of society emerged with even more anthropologically variegated populations that suffered from infighting. There was still a tendency toward unity of culture and biological homogeneity. The general improvement in health that began in the Bronze Age halted or even reversed itself during the Iron Age, only to take off again with renewed and surprising vigor beginning around 800 B.C.[7]

Several generations before the classical period (strictly speaking) begins, the height of the inhabitants of Greece increases, and their physical aspect changes (e.g., the relative length of long bones and the roundness of their shafts, or the depth of the pelvic inlet). The frequency of lesions from chronic wear and tear as well as infantile mortality both diminish, while the average lifespan reaches limits that it will not attain again until the twentieth century. In fact, the supply of food, the fit between human and habitat, the physical condition of people, and general well-being were never better in the West during antiquity.[8] To be sure, there were a number of shadows across the landscape. Warfare was unceasing, work was often harsh and exhausting, and the variety of diseases was greater than ever. The heaviest threat was still overpopulation. Well-being generates a strong demographic surge, and that, in turn, forces colonial expansion, the export of human beings, which was particularly intensive from the eighth to the sixth century B.C.

Beginning in the sixth century a profound transformation seems to have taken place in Greece. From an essentially agricultural land, it became, at least in some regions, an important industrial power with outside trade substantial enough to permit population growth without an increase in agricultural productivity. The import of grain and other foods made colonization less pressing. The age when communities begin to live not just from agriculture but also from the products of their artisans and from trade marks the real debut of urbanization in Greece—one can cite, for example, the concentration of people and wealth in Athens and Corinth—even though the *pólis* is of modest proportions compared with certain urban centers in Asia and with what the city of Rome would become.[9]

By 600–500 B.C. the pathocoenosis of Greece was in a rarely attained state of equilibrium. Humanity seems to have adapted well enough to the forms of parasitism native to Mediterranean agriculture, and endemic malaria seems to have abated. Thus, at the dawn of the classical period, the inhabitants of the Aegean region enjoyed exceptional health, but that situation would not last for long. The change took place over the fifth century B.C., not abruptly, but still profoundly and inexorably. The flourishing of "scientific" medicine under the name of Hippocrates could not halt the decline; from the perspective of public health, its contribution was merely psychological. In fact scientific Greek medicine arose at the time when the pathocoenotic equilibrium was crumbling; as it developed, the health of the Greeks was deteriorating. Some might consider that a kind of paradox.

The success of the Greeks in adapting themselves to their environment and in mastering pathogenic factors in it was in great part due to their cultural development. Good health fed upon the Greek miracle and added to its ampleness. However, the new forms of civilized life carried within themselves the seeds of misfortune. Without knowing of the paleodemographic arguments at our disposal nowadays, the great historian Jacob Burckhardt (1818–97) once remarked that the fifth-century Greeks had a heightened need to consult their doctors. They were more sickly, said Burckhardt, not because of an easier life but from their unbridled passions, "from an unhealthy activity throughout the city."[10] While Burckhardt and several other historians of the nineteenth century saw only moral causes, current medical concepts force us to seek out material ones. The decline in public health was still understated during the Peloponnesian War, apart from the "plague of Athens" and its aftereffects, but it became obvious during the fourth century B.C. According to Angel, "It was a response to social conditions before it was a response to disease organisms. The direct causes of the increase in such diseases as malaria, typhoid, and tuberculosis must have been: (1) rural dislocation through constant petty warfare, with inevitable breakdown of proper swamp drainage and irrigation; (2) urban overcrowding and inadequate expenditure on sewers or sanitary inspectors; (3) wandering of war refugees."[11] Just at this time the shores of the Mediterranean were forming, as was said above, a shared pool of infectious diseases. Near the end of the Hellenistic era and in Roman times, this pathocoenosis would again be seriously disturbed by exchanges of microbes with pools originating in the Far East and Africa.[12]

Geographic Unity and Genetic Variety among the Inhabitants of Greece

Historically, Greece consists of the promontory of the Balkan peninsula (mainland Greece), some islands of the eastern Mediterranean, and the west coast of Asia Minor. Outside this Aegean region, the Greeks colonized some adjacent lands, for instance, southern Italy, Sicily, Syria, and the coast of Egypt. But their colonial expansion never went beyond the banks of the Mediterranean. At no point does the Greek world leave the temperate zone behind. Wherever Greeks settled on a long-term basis, they were able to introduce a way of life that they had devised in perfect accord with the geographical conditions of their civilization's birthplace.[13]

In Greece, climate varies perceptibly from one region to the next, although some traits ascribable to the preponderant influence of the sea persist everywhere. "Nothing to excess"—this maxim of the Greek wise men mirrors the profile of their natural environment. Situated between the cold of northern Europe and the warmth of the African continent, maritime Greece revels in its temperate heat, etesian winds, the regularity of its seasons, its dry summers and wet winters. As a whole, the climate is remarkably healthy, hospitable to a free-spirited life favoring productive labor, sports, and intellectual activity.[14]

By virtue of its position at the crossroads of the continents, the Greek world forms a bridge between Asia, the northern coast of Africa, and western Europe.[15] It served as a link between the Mediterranean basin and central Europe, and the great routes of infectious disease went straight through it.[16] Not only did the first great historical pestilences pass through Greece on their way north and west, but it also saw the slow, insidious penetration of endemic disease (like tuberculosis and malaria in the distant past and, more recently, leprosy). On the other hand, its temperate climate acted as a barrier against the diffusion into Europe of the so-called tropical diseases whose vectors or germs could survive only under specific physical or biological conditions. Sheltered from yellow fever, schistosomiasis, sleeping sickness, filariasis, and perhaps acute cutaneous treponema infection as well, to cite only a few of the large number of diseases that ravaged lands with less merciful climates, the Greek world nonetheless suffered terribly from one African pestilential disease: malaria. I will discuss it in detail elsewhere, but it deserves mention here since, as its name suggests, it represents a disease closely tied to ecological factors. The "malarial complex," as defined by Max Sorre, existed in Greece from prehistoric times in its most typical form. A significant portion of Greece is marshland (I recall in this regard Aristotle's statements that the swamps were a cause of the depopulation of certain parts of the Argolid).[17]

Greek soil is on the poor side. Even in our time less than a fifth of it is fertile, and since the Greeks practiced biennial crop rotation, at most only a tenth of the land was harvested in any given year. Deforestation from protohistoric times and especially in the Hellenistic era increased the amount of ploughland but brought with it changes in microclimate that were unhealthy for both air and water. To the modern observer, Greece proper is a small country. Its total surface area is approximately 132,000 square kilometers, while Attica has only about 2,800 (more like 2,600 in the classical period) and the Peloponnesus about 21,500. These relatively modest dimensions are surprising, considering the role that this land and its inhabitants have played in the political and cultural history of mankind. Greece lacks great plains, which tend to favor huge concentrations of humanity. So to a certain extent its political partitioning in the archaic and classical periods reflects its topographic compartmentalization. Plato tells us that citizens actually left Crete and the Peloponnesus because in the cities the population had "surpassed the number that the land can feed."[18]

The links between physical surroundings and the constitution of those who inhabit them, not to speak of their political institutions, did not escape Greek intellectuals. In fact, it is the central topic of the treatise *Airs, Waters, and Places,* one of the most charming texts in the Hippocratic collection. For many historians of medicine, it is the most authentic work of the great master from Cos. Whatever the case may be, its dating to the fifth century B.C. and its Coan origin can hardly be doubted. The first section of the treatise lays down the foundations of medical geography: it tries to ascertain the effects of winds, waters, and the placement of cities on the health of their inhabitants. In the second part, there is an explanation in ecological terms of the differences between Greeks, Scythians, and Asiatics with respect to certain physical and psychological traits and their political consequences.[19] This treatise "places mankind under a strict determinism" that is, as R. Joly judiciously remarks, "very exaggerated and too often incorrect."[20] But all the reservations one can have about the correctness of the etiological positions taken by the author of this treatise do not detract from its value as a descriptive witness to the salient nosological elements of the pathocoenosis of the Greek city-states near the end of the fifth century B.C.

I have spoken elsewhere of the work's epidemiological content.[21] Here I will cite a few passages from its second part that have to do with climatic changes and their effect on the general constitution of Hippocrates' contemporaries. After speaking of the Scythians, the author portrays the rest of the Europeans (meaning, as far as he is concerned, the Greeks) as follows:

> The other people of Europe differ from one another both in stature and in shape, because of the changes of the seasons, which are violent and frequent, while there are severe heat waves, severe winters, copious rains and then long droughts, and winds, causing many changes of various kinds . . . It is for this reason, I think, that the physique of Europeans varies more than that of Asiatics, and that their stature differs very widely in each city . . . For the frequent shocks to the mind impart wildness, destroying tameness and gentleness. For this reason, I think, Europeans are more courageous than Asiatics.[22]

The extraordinary variety in the inhabitants of archaic and classical Greece is fully confirmed by the anthropological study of their skeletons. The variety is due above all to their genetic polymorphism, to the wealth of their gene pool. The climate has something to do with this state of affairs, but in ways not foreseen by the Hippocratic writer.

Demographic Density

The study of the demographic history of the ancient eastern Mediterranean seems relatively secure as regards the determination of general trends in the evolution of populations, but we encounter insurmountable obstacles when we come to the degree of precision in the actual numbers it supplies. For prehistoric periods, we can make hypotheses that stand up to criticism only if they are limited to a relatively imprecise order of magnitude. For the classical period, we have to be content with the vague information given by ancient historians and topographers. Manipulation of this information does not provide incontestable results.

The total number of hunters scattered over the European biotope during the Paleolithic period was probably, at any single moment in their history, fewer than 100,000. In the Mesolithic period, after the last Ice Age, the number increased perceptibly, but it was not until the beginning of the Neolithic that, by virtue of a sedentary way of life and a broader variety of means of subsistence, the overall population of Europe reached or even surpassed 1 million. For centuries, these primordial farmers lived in a natural environment so empty that the average density was equal to or less than 1 inhabitant for each square kilometer. Over the long term, this figure increased slowly but steadily. At the beginning of the Bronze Age, the population of Europe rose to a few million, and by 1000 B.C. it had reached about 10 million. Speculation on the actual density is useless, since the distribution of people was extremely uneven. Most Europeans kept to the south, where the climate was more forgiving. According to Colin McEvedy and Richard Jones, "By the end of the Bronze Age in 1000 B.C., the density of population was higher than the European average by a factor of three in Greece and more than two in Italy. This is the demographic background to the emergence of classical society. Greece set the pace. Between 1000 and 400 B.C., the population of Europe doubled, increasing from 10 to 20 million; in the same period the population of Greece tripled, reaching a final total of three million, an amazing figure for the era."[23]

Neolithic civilization entered Europe by way of the Balkans. That is where it bore first fruit on the continent, and where it initiated the European demographic upheaval. In 5000 B.C. about a quarter of a million farmers were already living on the Balkan peninsula. At the apogee of Mycenaean civilization, their number reached about 2 million, with almost half of them living in continental and insular Greece.

Of all the guesses that have been made about the number of inhabitants in prehistoric Greece, the one most worthy of respect at the moment is by Colin Renfrew. It is based on a scrupulous analysis of the number and importance of the archaeological sites, especially necropolises, in the Aegean region.[24] The first villages in this geographic area were small. Nea

Nikomedia or Çatal Hüyük counted several hundred inhabitants, but most other villages had scarcely a hundred. Houses were scattered here and there without concern for common, fortified protection. The concentration of persons was very low, about 200 per hectare of village land. The demographic density was approximately 1 inhabitant per square kilometer. By Renfrew's calculations, it ranged from 0.85/km.^{2} in Laconia and central Macedonia to 1.77/km.^{2} for Messenia, with the Cyclades at 1.20/km.^{2} and Crete at 1.53/km.^{2}

The history of the Aegean population from the beginning of the Neolithic to the end of the Bronze Age is typified by almost exponential growth (that is, it was constantly accelerating) in some regions, notably Crete and Messenia, and by growth of the same general intensity but with a marked decline during the Early Bronze Age in other regions, for instance, in Laconia or the Cyclades. The first type of growth can be considered "natural" or in conformity with a relatively favorable biological state of affairs and free from dire external disturbances. The second type of growth shows that a catastrophe, or rather a series of them, intervened and struck the population of certain parts of Greece between 2500 and 1900 B.C. In this case the catastrophe was certainly the invasions by Indo-European peoples and the disturbances resulting from them, but the information available does not allow us to say to what extent this prolonged disaster was caused by political events and to what extent biological factors, including pathology, contributed to the situation. In any case we can rule out pestilential diseases, since they would not have spared the most populous areas.

Here are Renfrew's estimates, in round numbers, for the demographic density of several regions during the Bronze Age—the three numbers indicating, successively, the situation during the Early, Middle, and Late Bronze Ages—Crete: 9, 26, and 31 per square kilometer; Messenia: 8, 46, and 63; Cyclades: 14, 8, and 12; Laconia: 7.5, 8, and 14; and central Macedonia: 2.5, 2.5, and 4.5. The population of Crete increased from 75,000 in the Early Bronze Age to 250,000 in the Late; Messenia jumped from 23,000 to 178,000, while Laconia went from 26,000 to 50,000 and the Cyclades decreased from 34,000 to 29,000.[25] For the eastern Mediterranean in general, J. L. Angel maintains that the demographic densities for all three Bronze Ages were, respectively, 10, 18, and 30 inhabitants per square kilometer.[26] To be sure, all these statistics are conjectures that can only serve as general indicators.

During the Middle Bronze Age, fortified towns proliferated and villages grew. On average, they had a total of 500 inhabitants. So, for instance, Lerna in the Argolid was at that time a town of about 120 dwellings, each occupied by a relatively small family (5–7 members). At the height of Mycenaean civilization its total population approached 800, according to Angel. The state of public symphyses among its female inhabitants shows an average of 5 childbirths per adult (equivalent to 5.5 per fertile woman, assuming a sterility rate of 10 percent). With a birthrate of about 44–45 and a death rate slightly higher than 40 per 1,000 inhabitants, there was an annual growth of 0.4 percent, which is high for a preindustrial society.[27] All these figures were arrived at from the results of osteoarchaeological analysis, and despite the exiguousness of the sample studied and uncertainty about some basic values, they seem to us relatively secure, at least in their order of magnitude.

Examination of the female pelvis, including the state of pubic symphyses, makes it possible to estimate fecundity, here defined as the number of childbirths per woman beyond the age of sexual maturity. Over the land of Greece, fecundity varies between 4 and 5, with a rise during the Neolithic and the Middle Bronze Age and a fairly clear drop during the Early Bronze and the Iron Age. The number of children per adult woman may seem small, given the likely absence of contraception, but it is explicable in terms of the shortness of life and thus of female genital availability: on average, a woman's period of fecundity did not exceed a dozen years.[28] When the classical period opens, the Greeks are in the midst of demographic expansion. The population of the eastern Mediterranean grows without respite from the ninth to the fifth century B.C., despite emigrations and a slowing birthrate: pubic scars on female adult skeletons of the archaic and classical periods suggest an average of 4.3 childbirths. In the fifth century B.C., in the time of Pericles and Hippocrates, the total number of inhabitants of Greece was not much more than 3 million, 2 million of whom lived on continental Greece (surface area 56,000 km.^{2}), with another 800,000 on the Peloponnesus (surface area 21,500 km.^{2}) and some 400,000 on the islands. So the demographic density, excluding the islands, amounts to 36 inhabitants per square kilometer.[29]

In fact, as Pierre Salmon has shown, we should distinguish between different regions: those of low demographic density, from 10 to 30, like Aetolia, Achaea, and Thessaly; those of average density, from 30 to 100, like Laconia (33), the Argolid (36), and Boeotia (60); and those of high density, like Corinth with 110 and Attica with 160 inhabitants per square kilometer. The enormous density of people in the isthmus and in Attica is ascribable to urbanization, itself a consequence of the development of an artisan class, of sea traffic, and of the slave trade.[30]

Without any doubt, the figures supplied are conjectures, since no real census of the Greek population exists from before the modern era.[31] To arrive at the values cited above, it was necessary to use evidence from historians on the number of citizens in assemblies and on the number of persons a city could put in the field in case of general mobilization, the lists of ephebes, information on wheat consumption, what the archaeological record reveals about the surface area of towns, and so on. Thucydides' testimony on the military force of Athens around 431 B.C.[32] has inspired very close analysis and informative debate about the population of Attica.[33] The upshot is that there were plainly more than 300,000 inhabitants in Attica at that time, probably as many as 420,000. The uncertainty stems from the difficulty in knowing the quantitative relationship between citizens, resident aliens, and slaves. These last seem to have been more than half of the total population. So the community consisting of Athens and the Peiraeus had, at the time Thucydides considers the high-water mark of Athenian imperialism, a population surpassing 200,000 souls. For the conditions of life in Greece, this concentration of human beings was an extraordinary break with centuries of custom and habit. In the classical period, Greeks lived in the countryside. Thucydides tells us that the majority of Athenians themselves "had only known life in the countryside" and that being cooped up within the city's walls in wartime for protection was to them a painful ordeal.[34]

During the fourth and part of the fifth century B.C., the population of Greece remained almost unchanged overall, though the social and geographic distribution of persons did not. On the one hand, the population of slaves increased perceptibly compared with that of free persons; on the other, urban centers became more populous at the expense of the countryside.[35] By the middle of the second century B.C., the demographic decline is striking.[36] Inscriptions confirm the accuracy of this withering glance by the historian Polybius: "All of Greece suffers from a halt in reproduction and a dearth of persons; the cities are being depopulated. The problem is that men nowadays, in their love of splendor, money, and idleness, too, no longer want to get married, or if they do, to raise a family. It's all they can do to let one or two children enjoy their wealth and grow up in luxury."[37]

Knowledge of demographic realities is useful, even indispensable, for any epidemiological investigation. It is certainly no coincidence that the "plague of Athens," the first catastrophic epidemic in the West whose symptoms and progress are really known, broke out just at the time and place of the greatest human concentration in Greece. At the beginning of this chapter, I said that certain infectious diseases cannot subsist in populations that fall short of a certain threshold in size and density. That is especially true for certain viral diseases that either destroy their host or confer lasting immunity, are transmitted from one person to the next without any animal reservoir, and have a relatively brief acute phase; the most important of these are measles, smallpox, and mumps. Because of their epidemiological traits, specifically their extreme contagiousness, their viral aggressiveness, and their capacity to immunize, they manifest themselves most often as acute fevers in children. Unfortunately, we do not know the exact values of the demographic thresholds each of these viral diseases requires.[38] According to studies recently made among the Amazonian Indians, and according to epidemiological observations of peoples on certain isolated islands, demographic densities comparable to those in Neolithic Greece are inadequate to support measles.[39] It therefore seems that that disease had no chance of sustaining itself in Greece until the Middle Bronze Age. Its premature introduction from a more densely populated region outside Europe could have caused a deadly, but short-lived, epidemic tide. It is perhaps worth noting that Neolithic bones from Çatal Hüyük suggest a relatively low infant mortality rate. It may well be that the situation changed with the arrival of Mycenaean civilization. It surely did so at the beginning of historical times, growing worse and worse all through the classical and Hellenistic periods.

Osteoarchaeological Data on Lifespan

Longevity is an essential feature of a pathocoenosis. We now have at our disposal sufficiently sophisticated ways of recognizing the approximate age of an individual from skeletal remains and, as a consequence, a way of calculating the average age of persons buried in a necropolis.[40] From such osteoarchaeological data, we can draw some conclusions as to the average lifespan in a larger prehistoric or historic population. The value of those conclusions depends, on the one hand, on the size and representativeness of the sample, and, on the other, on the validity of some demographic hypotheses. The numerical estimates reached in this way are valid only until the next research effort modifies them.

In 1947, John L. Angel attempted an osteoarchaeological demographic study for ancient Greece.[41] Here are the main results of his investigation: over the whole period in question, the mean age at death was 35.4 years (men, 39.8; women, 31); for the Neolithic and the Early Bronze Age, 32.1 (men, 34.7; women 29.6); for the Middle Bronze Age, 34.7 (men, 39.3; women, 30.1); for the classical period, 38.1 (men, 42.6; women, 33.7); for the Roman era, 36.8 (men, 42.1; women 31.6); and for the Byzantine period, 33.7 (men, 36.5; women, 31). On about fifty adult male skulls from the classical period (that is, in Angel's study, from 650 to 150 B.C.), signs of senility occurred on about 10 percent, while on a group of about thirty adult female skulls of the same era, they were apparent on only 3.7 percent.

Angel was fully aware of the provisional character of this pioneering study and of problems in the numbers he produced. His sample consisted of only 384 adult skulls spread out over the period from 3500 B.C. to A.D. 1300. Using just the state of cranial sutures as a criterion of aging, the average age of this same sample was appreciably lower: 27.4 years overall, and 29.1 for the classical period, including both sexes. Intermediary figures were obtained if age was determined for a few dozen skeletons as a function of the ossification of the pubic symphysis: 31.9 years (men, 35.5; women, 27) for all the periods of antiquity together.[42] In the osteological material examined at the time by Angel, there was a shortage of skulls of children and old people, a fact attributable at least in part to the selective destruction of their bones. It was out of the question to establish average longevity, that is, the life expectancy of an individual at birth.

Even so, three demographic peculiarities arise clearly from these data: (1) the shorter lifespan of women than of men; (2) the rarity of the tokens of senility; and (3) the increase in average lifespan until the classical period and its progressive diminution after it (at least for persons who reached puberty). Between the Neolithic and the classical period the gain in longevity was, according to Angel's statistics, 6 years, or 8 years for men and only 4 for women.

Infant mortality was assuredly very high, but it is difficult to arrive at figures for it. Pertinent information can be obtained from the numerical relationship between children's and adult's tombs as provided in excavation reports. For instance, in the classical necropolis of Olynthus, the proportion is 290:294, which means that death overtook 49.7 percent of this particular population before it reached adulthood (infants, 28.3 percent; children, 21.4 percent).[43] In six cemeteries of the Mycenaean age the percentage of nonadults increases to at least 55 percent. Furthermore, an examination of 30 prepubescent skeletons of various dates allowed Angel to state that more than half of these young persons did not live beyond the age of 5.[44]

For the last thirty years, research on this subject has been continuous. Angel has revised his figures on the basis of an ever-larger number of bone specimens.[45] Progress has been made by restricting statistical analysis to samples that are better defined in time and space. The order of magnitude of Angel's initial results has not been changed, but relatively subtle modifications have been made, lowering the figures slightly for very ancient times and raising them a little for historical times. The result is an even clearer rise in longevity at the time that Hellenic civilization came into flower. Also, estimates of infant mortality are slowly becoming more exact.

Since the work of Henri-Victor Vallois,[46] we know that inhabitants of the European continent during the Paleolithic and Mesolithic died most frequently during childhood and between the ages of 21 and 40. Infant mortality was tremendous. There was a drop between the ages of 11 and 20, then a strong rise into the forties, beyond which most people did not live. This overall picture conforms with the one given by Jean Noël Biraben after minute study of skulls from the epi-paleolithic necropolis of Columnata in western Algeria (ca. 6000 B.C.). According to his reconstruction of the table of survival, the average lifespan was only around 21 to 22 years, which presupposes, for a stationary population, a raw death rate of 46 to 47 per thousand. However, it is important to state that Biraben used a method, classification by age groups according to the state of cranial sutures, that produces lower results than the reality it targets. Moreover, Biraben himself thinks that, all things considered, his osteoarchaeological data suggest not a stationary population with a very short lifespan, but a different demographic model: an average lifespan of 25, an annual growth rate of 0.5 percent, and the periodic occurrence of catastrophes.[47]

In demographic studies based on the state of fossilized bones from the Greek world, there has been general reluctance to calculate average lifespan in the strict sense because of lack of confidence in the data on prepubescent mortality. All of Angel's numbers on this provide only the average age at the moment of death of persons who have reached adulthood. He tries to determine the length of adult life, not what modern demographic statistics call the average lifespan or life expectancy at birth (e_0). In modern life tables, his numbers correspond approximately to life expectancy at age 15 (e_{15}).

According to Angel's revised (1972) paleodemographic picture, the average length of adult life reached 32 for men and 24.9 for women in the Mesolithic period (based on 71 specimens), 33.6 for men and 29.8 for women in the Early Neolithic period (259 specimens), and 35.7 for men as against 28.2 for women in the Late Neolithic period (40 specimens). The Mesolithic bones come from various parts of Europe, the Early Neolithic ones from Çatal Hüyük and Nea Nikomedia, and the Late Neolithic ones from Kephala (the island of Kea).[48] The most representative and homogeneous sample of bones, relatively speaking, for these very early periods is the series of almost 300 skeletons unearthed by James Mellaart at Çatal Hüyük in Anatolia.[49] The adults whose bones were found in this Neolithic necropolis (ca. 6500–5700 B.C.) died on the average at age 31.5 (men, 34.3; women, 29.8). The numerical proportion of infants' (ages 0–4) to children's (ages 5–14) to adults' (15 years or more) tombs is 7:4:10, which bespeaks considerable infant mortality. Angel stresses the demographic improvement since the Mesolithic period. The increase in the average duration of life is not very large, but even so it reveals a change in the conditions of life, especially since women benefit more than men. It seems reasonable to attribute this enhancement of survival to the greater security offered by sedentary village life.[50]

From the classification into age groups established by Angel,[51] I have constructed a table of survival and calculated that, assuming a demographic situation fairly close to a stationary state, the average lifespan (e_0) for the Neolithic population of Çatal Hüyük might have been around 23 or 24 years (both sexes). By this hypothesis, the raw death rate exceeds 40 per thousand. If we return to Angel's table, the average age of deceased adults in the Early Bronze Age was 33.5 for men and 29.6 for women (estimated on the basis of 400 specimens); in the Middle Bronze Age it reached 36.7 for men and 31 for women (183 specimens); in the Late Bronze Age, 39.3 for men and 32 for women (286 specimens); and in the Iron Age, or more exactly near the end of the twelfth century B.C., 38.8 for men and 30.4 for women (164 specimens).[52]

The best osteoarchaeological series for these periods is one of about 500 skeletons from the necropolis of Karataş in Lycia, the burial ground of the inhabitants of a fairly typical village of the Early Bronze Age (ca. 3000–2000 B.C.). The adults in this sample died on average at age 31.7 (men, 34; women, 30). The proportion of infants' to children's to adults' tombs seems to be 6:5:10. Actually, skeletons of small children are rare and the proportion given is an extrapolation on the basis of finds in a well-preserved portion of the necropolis.[53] According to more recent excavations, the proportion of infantile (ages 2–14) to adult deaths is 4:10, which is the same as at Çatal Hüyük and better than in the Mycenaean tombs at Lerna.[54] Relatively speaking, the situation elsewhere was by no means as good. So, for instance, the length of life was appreciably shorter among the inhabitants of Aghios Cosmas (Attica) at the same period.[55]

Excavations in the Mycenaean parts of Lerna in the Argolid uncovered 234 skeletons, of which 35 percent are less than 5 years old, 21 percent are children from 5 to 15 years old, and 44 percent are adults (proportionately, 8:5:10). By comparison with the populations of Neolithic hunters and villagers, this proportion suggests an increase in the mortality of little children and at the same time a decrease in the mortality of bigger ones. As for the adult inhabitants of Lerna in the Middle Bronze Age (ca. 2000–1600 B.C.), death overtook them on the average at age 34 (men, 37; women, 31). As was said above in a discussion of the number and density of this population, each adult woman had an average of 5 childbirths. According to the demographic model suggested by Angel on the basis of these data, the average period of fertility for a woman lasted 12 years, and the birthrate seems to have been a little less than 45 per 1,000, while the death rate was slightly higher than 40 per 1,000. Despite significant infant mortality (of 1,000 births, more than 300 died before the age of 5), this Helladic population sustained noteworthy growth.[56]

If we insist on figuring the average lifespan according to principles that are in force for populations whose essential parameters are precisely known, for the ancient inhabitants of Lerna we would obtain an extremely low figure for e_0 because the very high death rate for children has a powerful effect on the average. It would create an essentially false impression of an overall decline in longevity between the Neolithic period and the Middle Bronze Age. Even though, strictly speaking, life expectancy at birth probably did decline because of the accumulated risks of the early years (risks that were probably due to infectious diseases), life expectancy is on the upswing once the age of 5 is attained.

The royal graves in the two circles of tombs at Mycenae (ca. 1650–1450 B.C.) offer an especially welcome opportunity to compare the length of life for common people who lived in the Mycenaean Argolid, the people of Lerna, with analogous data for aristocrats of the same region toward the end of the same era. Judging from the bones of the princely families that are in the Archaeological Museum at Nauplia, the average age at time of death was not more than 35.9 for the men of this ruling class, while women treated to the same funeral honors reached age 36.1. Deeds of warfare exposed these chieftains to mortal danger so often and so early that their average lifespan was equal to that of their subjects, if not shorter. As for the ladies of the Mycenaean aristocracy, they profited from their material well-being to the extent of living longer than both their lower-class counterparts and the men whose social preeminence they shared. Nevertheless, it is important to realize that to the 22 male skeletons of this princely sample, there correspond only 5 female skeletons, which is far from a representative number.[57]

Robert P. Charles, combining his own conclusions about the age of Helladic skulls in Argos with the older observations of Fürst, arrived at results that favor a much rosier picture for the Middle Bronze Age than Angel's for the analogous osteoarchaeological series at Lerna. Of 44 specimens examined, a little more than a quarter died before puberty. The death rate slows considerably between 15 and 30 years of age, only to accelerate vigorously thereafter, leaving few the chance to live beyond their forties. Longevity is greater, Charles writes, in the men than in the women: the maximum death rate is about 40 years of age for the former and about 35 for the latter.[58]

According to Charles's osteoarchaeological investigations in Crete, the average lifespan there was markedly higher than in continental Greece, at least in Minoan times. Among the Cretans of the Middle Bronze Age, the highest mortality among adults is at age 50 or thereabouts (between 50 and 59 in men, and between 40 and 49 in women). That tends to associate, Charles asserts, "the state of health of the island's populations with those of the Middle East and to distance it even more than Greece from the deplorable conditions in western Europe."[59] Although it is altogether likely that life was not only more pleasant but also, on average, longer in Crete than on the Peloponnesus or in Attica, the figures proposed by Charles seem to me too optimistic. Study of a Bronze Age population in Rumania yields an average lifespan of 25, with 30 percent dead before adulthood and only 1 percent surviving to age 60.[60] In Anatolia, research by M. S. Senyürek fixes the average age of deceased adults in the Bronze Age at 35 for men and 28 for women.[61]

For Greece in classical times, Angel's work (1973) gives 41.7 years as the average age of adults at the moment of death, specifically, 45 years for men and 36.2 for women (based on 146 specimens), or in a recent report (1983), 44.1 years for men and 36.8 for women (with the number of specimens increased to 230). The proportion of infants' to children's to adults' tombs is 5:3:10. Most of the adult bone specimens come from Athens and Corinth, while the calculation of the proportion between children's deaths and adults' is based mainly on results of excavations at Olynthus.[62] These figures show a general improvement of health conditions in continental Greece around the seventh century B.C. The average lifespan has lengthened, but impressively so only for men. From the Neolithic period to the Middle Bronze Age, males reaching adulthood died about 4–6 years later than females. By the end of the Bronze Age and in archaic times, the difference became even greater, around 7–8 years, and it did not diminish in the classical period. This higher mortality of women between the ages of 15 and 40 was essentially due to the harmful results of pregnancy, childbirth, and breastfeeding. Variations in it attest to the influence of social factors on the biological risks inherent in female reproductive functions.[63]

In our present state of knowledge, available osteoarchaeological materials provide only an approximate overall estimate of life expectancy at birth in the classical Greek world. In my opinion, the results cited above support a hypothesis that the Greek populations living in these times should be placed between level 15 and level 20 on the typical life tables established by the United Nations.[64] Accordingly, the life expectancy varied between 27 and 30 years. It is very likely that the latter figure was reached and surpassed around 600–500 B.C., the time when general health was at its best in the history of ancient Greek society. At that time the death rate probably went down to 30–33 per 1,000. But in "natural" biological conditions, when there is no possibility of a truly effective struggle against the most deadly diseases, a demographic situation of this sort could occur only at intervals and for relatively short stretches of time.

The decline in average lifespan probably began in the fifth century B.C. and became apparent in the fourth century. For comparison's sake, I can cite data for Hellenistic and Roman times that were gathered from Greek bones by the same techniques as were used for more ancient periods. Around the fourth and third centuries B.C., the average age at death for adults is only 42.4 in men and 36.5 in women; by the second century A.D., it is about 38 years of age (men, 40.2; women, 34.6). It is worth noting that the decline, especially in its early stages, affects female longevity much less than male. This demographic drop is a lasting one. Not until the second half of the nineteenth century do demographic indices reach the levels of the classical age.

The osteoarchaeological methods used to arrive at average lifespans of the past are open to criticism. In the first place, the number of specimens examined is still relatively small. They are scattered in time and space, and by looking at individuals born over a relatively long time-span as though they were a single generation, we open ourselves to error. Furthermore, statistical calculations presuppose a fairly stable and closed population, which was certainly not always the case. Determination of age by the state of cranial sutures and wear and tear on teeth has risks, especially toward underestimation. Finally, there is no guarantee that the population of corpses in a cemetery is always an accurate statistical reflection of the living population that uses it.

All these criticisms, and many more as well, have a good deal of weight to them. To counter them and for reassurance, I can point to the convergence of results and insist on the reality of the trends rather than on the values themselves. And for historical times, it becomes very interesting to compare data obtained in this way with data available from written documentation.

Determination of Average Lifespan from Inscriptional Evidence

From the writings of historians, lexicographers, and biographers, information can be culled about the longevity of numerous Greek personages from the classical, Hellenistic, and Roman eras. Although this information constitutes an impressive mass of pertinent data, it is of no value whatever for determining average longevity. The process of selection operating in the writing down and transmission of the data renders the resultant statistical sample unrepresentative of the population as a whole. At most, we could try to use it to get a notion of the death rate among the oldest members of the most privileged classes.

By consulting biographical documents, we remain prisoners of the anecdotal approach and are deprived of a demographic perspective. So historians of the ancient world have tried another approach that is at first sight more promising: statistical analysis of epitaphs. Very elaborate demographic studies have been made of Latin funerary inscriptions, but relatively little has been done with this aspect of Greek epigraphy. The reason is that Latin epitaphs generally include the age of the deceased, while Greek ones do so only randomly. Age specification became customary only under Roman influence. For the Greek material, the monograph of Bessie Ellen Richardson published in 1933 is still the main reference work.[65] She collected the data on 2,022 Greek tombstones that specify the age of the deceased. The series of epitaphs stretches from the classical period to the beginning of the Middle Ages, with a clear majority from Hellenistic and Roman times. B. E. Richardson distributed the cases into five-year age brackets and calculated first the percentage belonging to each bracket, then what she calls "average expectancy of life." According to her, this expectancy is as high as 29.4 years in her sample.[66] This figure was arrived at by dividing the sum total of ages by the number of individuals. So it is the arithmetic average of the ages at death and should approximately correspond to life expectancy at birth. Richardson did not provide separate statistics for the two sexes, perhaps because that would have made still more plain the strange distribution of frequencies in her sample. Her book also has an appendix containing a catalogue of all the inscriptions used, which enables us to complement the transverse study she made with an attempt at a longitudinal one. In order to be able to compare this sample with the results of osteoarchaeological research, I first submitted it to the method by which Angel calculated his averages. In Richardson's sample, the average age of adults at the moment of their death is only 36.5. This is a lower number than the one obtained from the osteoarchaeological record. I have tried to concoct life tables; the estimate of average life expectancy at birth (e_0) by this method is 27.4 years.

With this e_0 value, the tables of male and female mortality fall into level 15 of the United Nations typical life tables. However, comparison of the mortality quotients of the epigraphic series and of the typical tables brings to light various serious anomalies—in fact, they are demographic impossibilities. In Richardson's sample, the death rate is extraordinarily high between 10 and 20 years of age, too high between 20 and 35, and much too low before 5 years of age and after 55. No real population can provide a curve like this one, especially if it is supposed to represent death rate as a function of age over a period of time long enough to temper the effects of catastrophic events.

Our calculations presuppose that all the individuals in this series belong to the same generation of a relatively closed and stable population. Even though it is a false assumption, the results of the calculation of death rate quotients could not be so patently atypical unless the sample itself were utterly unrepresentative of the real populations from which it was selected. Numerous factors could be the cause of such deviation: the inadequate number of available inscriptions; their excessive scatter over time and space, which in turn mixes data about populations with differing demographic characteristics (several epitaphs in Richardson's catalogue are in Greek but contain the names of barbarians or persons from non-Greek lands, especially Italy and Egypt); funerary beliefs and customs (such as relative indifference at the death of infants, or the need to erect a status symbol at the death of a young wife); the social selectivity of the sample; and so on. Since Richardson's monograph appeared, there has been an effort under way to mitigate the heterogeneity of her sample by grouping epigraphic data and analyzing them according to better-defined geographical categories and shorter historical periods. For example, funerary inscriptions of the fifth and fourth centuries B.C. put the average age at death between 29 and 30 years of age,[67] while those of Greece under Roman occupation put it at about 29 years[68] and those of Greco-Roman Egypt at about 24 or, if analyzed by locale, between 22 and 40.[69] For the Roman Empire, age at death varies from province to province between 21 and 47 years, with the lowest figure in Rome itself and the highest ones in the African colonies.[70]

Seasoned demographers have recently denied that these results are representative of ancient demographic realities, and they characterize any attempt to determine the death rate from funerary inscriptions as illusory. Experience has shown that even under conditions much more favorable than those prevailing in Greek and Roman epigraphy—for instance, when a relatively high number of inscriptions from a single cemetery is to hand—the results arrived at are generally absurd. The distribution of ages inscribed on tombstones, according to Louis Henry, teaches us more about how funerary honors vary with the age of the deceased than about the prevailing death rate in a given era.[71]

With this methodological obstacle in mind, let us return to the classical Greek world and two literary documents. The first is Aristotle's advice that the ideal age for marriage is 37 for a husband and 18 for a wife, a difference of 19 years that is desirable "in order to synchronize the cessation of sexual activity."[72] The second is Thucydides' assertion about the age structure of the Athenian populace on the eve of the Peloponnesian War: "The Athenian youth was more numerous than at any other time in history."[73] These young people were then decimated by the war with Sparta, the plague, and the Sicilian expedition. Was the situation much different a century later? The question is all the more interesting since for the last quarter of the fourth century B.C. lists of adolescents *(éphēboi)* and arbitrators *(diaitētoí)*, that is, of hoplites at the first and last phases of their service, at ages 18 and 60 respectively, have come down to us. Around 330–325 B.C., there were approximately 500 adolescents and 100 arbitrators.[74] According to the typical life tables, in a population where for every five men between the ages of 18 and 19, only 1 survives to age 60, the life expectancy at birth is extremely low, around 22 or 23 years. Admittedly, one should hesitate to generalize from such a picture, since the sample in question is a portion of the inhabitants of Athens who were subject to high risk in the prime of their lives.

Old People and Maximum Longevity

Average longevity, otherwise known as life expectancy at birth, is the average age reached by a group of persons born in a given period and living in a given environment. I have noted the way it varies over the history of the Greek world, interpreting its fluctuations as an important indicator of changes in health conditions. As such it is an *ecological longevity* (Bodenheimer, 1938) that does not coincide with *physiological longevity* or *maximum longevity.*[75] Ecological longevity is determined above all by the death rate prior to the beginning of aging. In ancient populations it is almost unaffected by death rate quotients in age brackets above the fifties.

Although old people were relatively rare in the past, they were often remarkably active. In our present state of knowledge, their scarcity forbids any study of the biological and social impact of old age in prehistoric societies. In the classical and archaic periods, great respect was shown to men in their sixties. According to the *Iliad,* in Nestor's time "two generations of mortal men had perished, / those who had grown up with him and they who had been born to / these in sacred Pylos, and he was king in the third age."[76] This septuagenarian king fights alongside young warriors beneath the walls of Troy, and although he no longer takes part in athletic contests ("my limbs," Homer has him say, "are no longer steady . . . nor my feet, neither / do my arms, as once they did, swing light from my shoulders"),[77] he excels in counsel and in moderating impetuous behavior. He has the role of a symbol in the epic. In the political system of Greek city-states, true gerontocracies are not uncommon. It is enough simply to recall Solon at Sparta and the institution of the *gerousía* (the senate, literally the council of elders) as well as the role played by the *diaitētoí* in the public life of Athens. In a famous speech that Thucydides puts in his mouth, Pericles at age 60 makes the peremptory assertion that he is "still in the prime of life."[78] Nicias, a sage in his sixties, declares before the Athenian Assembly that Alcibiades at 36 or 37 is too young to command the expedition to Sicily[79]—this at a time when, by Thucydides' own account, the population of young people at Athens was larger than ever.[80] The existence of flourishing old people is also well-attested in the theater and in classical iconography.

I define physiological longevity as the length of life usually attained when the principal causes of death other than aging are ruled out. Its limit is reached when death from old age wins out over premature or accidental death. Modern statistical and physiopathological observations place physiological longevity at around age 80.[81] It is a more biological than social parameter that does not seem to have changed since protohistorical times. The Bible considers 70–80 years as the normal span of human life.[82] According to Herodotus, for the Persians in the time of Cambyses II, "The longest life a man can hope for does not exceed 80 years," and although the Ethiopians, as Cambyses' spies explained, live to age 120, that is only due to the miraculous effects of a fountain of youth that existed in their part of eastern Africa.[83] Finally, the assertion that the human lifespan is an ideal number, nine squared, is attributed to Plato.[84] To be sure, experience taught that under exceptional circumstances one could live beyond one's eightieth or even ninetieth birthday. Prodigious ages were attributed to Thales, Pythagoras, Democritus, Xenophanes, Hippocrates, and, perhaps, advisedly so, to Gorgias.[85] Does a truly insuperable limit exist, and if so, what is it? According to modern demographic statistics, maximum longevity, which is the highest age actually attained, does not exceed 112 years. It is highly likely that man never has and, except by techniques as yet unknown, never will surpass a limit that demographic calculations put at age 115.[86]

Some authors of the Empire, such as Pliny and Censorinus on the Roman side or Phlegon Trallianus and Pseudo-Lucian on the Greek, inquired into the maximum longevity of men in their own time and in the past of their civilizations. By our lights they are all very credulous, especially Pliny, although, strange to say, not more so than some of their modern successors. In any case, these ancient authors deserve our esteem for having collected interesting gerontological documents, especially in the treatise *Vitarum auctio* that passes for the work of Lucian of Samosata (second century A.D.). To demonstrate the existence of famous nonagenarians in classical Greece, it is enough to mention the rhetorician Isocrates (98 years of age), the poet Philemon, the philosopher Cleanthes, and, not least, the tragedian Sophocles. There were famous centenarians as well: the musician Xenophilos, perhaps the historian Hieronymus of Cardia, the writer Alexis of Thurioi, and most likely the sophist Gorgias of Leontini (who lived 105 or perhaps even 109 years). On Greek funerary inscriptions the oldest age attested is 110.[87] Egyptian storytellers in Pharaonic times were in the habit of saying that human life could not be prolonged beyond 110 years except by means of magic, and even then for only a single additional year.[88] The astrologer Epigenes placed the limit of human life at 112 years.[89]

Variations in Height and Some Consequences of Malnutrition

In prehistoric times prior to the introduction of agriculture, the average height of inhabitants of the eastern Mediterranean was relatively great, exceeding 170 cm. in men and 158 cm. in women. It begins dropping in the first villages of the early Neolithic period: the men at Çatal Hüyük were about 169 cm. tall and those at Nea Nikomedia about 168 cm. In the Late Neolithic period, average height stabilizes between 166 and 167 cm. in men and between 153 and 156 cm. in women. These figures, arrived at from the dimensions of long bones, do not change again until the classical period. By the seventh century B.C. a discernible increase has begun (men, 170 cm.; women, 156.3 cm.) that continues into the Hellenistic age (men, 171.8 cm.; women, 156.6 cm.).[90]

Height is a phenotypic expression of the genetic program. As a result, average height is conditioned as much by hereditary racial traits as by the influence of environment during an individual's growth. Among external factors the most important is nutrition—the quality, quantity, and regularity of food—especially in early childhood. The height of the inhabitants of the Greek world seems to have been determined above all by external factors. It should be stressed, for instance, that the Indo-European invasions had no noteworthy effect on the average height of the populations derived from the mix of newcomers and autochthons. However, it did modulate negatively at the time of the changeover from hunting and gathering to agriculture, and positively when the quality of life improved as a result of the development of industry and trade.

The stability of average height should not blind us to the importance of individual variations. The gap between shortest and tallest was remarkably large, especially from the Bronze Age on. It reflects both the genetic polymorphism of Greek populations as well as strong social differentiations. As an example, we can look at the situation in the Middle Bronze Age. The inhabitants of Lerna at the time averaged 166.3 cm. (men) and 154.2 cm. (women) in height, those of Pylos 167 cm. (men) and 152 cm. (women), and those of Kato Zakro (Crete) 167 cm. (men) and 157.5 cm. (women).[91] Although these figures correspond in order of magnitude to the body size of the people of Mycenae, the same is not true for the size of the aristocrats of that citadel. The 14 persons of male gender buried in the royal tombs at Mycenae had an average height of 171.5 cm., and their 3 female companions exceeded 160 cm. Despite the small size of the sample, the difference of 5 cm. in the height of the princes as against the common people appears to be significant.[92]

The inhabitants of Greece in the Mycenaean, archaic, and classical periods were thickset and sturdy, with relatively short lower limbs. The image of their general appearance that one obtains from osteoarchaeological evidence does not coincide with the idealized representation of the human body in Greek sculpture.[93] Although the average man had neither the slender grace of a statue of Apollo nor the force concentrated in one of Heracles, he did have a supple, vigorous body attuned to the grind of daily life.

In Greece as elsewhere, the historical variations in average height were largely dependent on nutritional customs and possibilities. I limit myself to a few remarks on this theme, since nutrition and its social and medical implications are such a huge, complex subject that they merit a monograph in themselves of no mean proportions.[94] A radical change in nutritional customs took place during the agricultural revolution of the Neolithic period. The new system in itself does not seem to have been superior to the one it displaced. A decline in average height suggests that there was even a deterioration in the physical conditions linked to nutrition. Actually, hunting and gathering is a very successful way of life for relatively small human groups,[95] though it cannot adequately maintain populations that exceed a certain density. The changeover to agriculture took place under the pressures of a serious nutritional crisis caused by demographic expansion.[96]

On the other hand, a sedentary life reduces the variety of nutrients, and that in itself can give rise to deficiency diseases, particularly those caused by lack of a regular supply of proteins, vitamins, and certain minerals.[97] Moreover, dependence on agricultural products allows for the periodic appearance of famine. Both the climate and the flora of Greece seem to have protected its inhabitants from serious vitamin deficiencies like rickets, osteomalacia, scurvy and beriberi, or the harsher forms of proteino-caloric malnutrition like kwashiorkor. But that does not mean they did not suffer often from lesser vitamin deficiencies and lack of essential amino acids, conditions that markedly reduce resistance to infectious disease.

From Neolithic times, people grew wheat, barley, lentils, and peas in Greece and raised goats, sheep, pigs, and cattle there. As early as the Bronze Age they were cultivating olive trees, figs, and the grape, as well as raising farmyard animals, which eventually included bees. Meat was becoming an ever more precious foodstuff, and most mortals did not partake of it daily. Although game was becoming scarce, technological improvements in fishing fostered growing exploitation of the wealth of the sea. So the necessary nutritional supply of proteins came from milk, cheese, eggs, and fish; that of carbohydrates from bread, honey, and dried figs; and that of fats from olive oil and, less dependably, pork products.

A person's basic caloric intake consisted of bread and wine. Homer and Plato knew what they were talking about when they praised them. The wily chieftain Odysseus so addresses hotheaded Achilles:

> Rather tell the men of Achaia here by their swift ships, to
> take bread and wine, since these make fighting fury and war-craft.
> For a man will not have strength to fight his way forward all day
> long until the sun goes down if he is starved for food. Even
> though in his heart he be very passionate for the battle,
> yet without his knowing it his limbs will go heavy, and hunger
> and thirst will catch up with him and cumber his knees as he moves on.[98]

And here is how Plato imagines the life of the inhabitants of "the first city":

> First of all, then, let us consider what will be the manner of life of men thus provided. Will they not make bread and wine and garments and shoes? And they will build themselves houses and carry on their work in summer for the most part unclad and unshod and in winter clothed and shod sufficiently. And for their nourishment they will provide meal from their barley and flour from their wheat, and kneading and cooking these they will serve noble cakes and loaves on some arrangement of reeds or clean leaves. And, reclined on rustic beds strewed with bryony and myrtle, they will feast with their children, drinking of their wine thereto, garlanded and singing hymns to the gods in pleasant fellowship, not begetting offspring beyond their means lest they fall into poverty or war.[99]

After this speech from the mouth of Socrates, Glaucon undertakes to praise the refinements of civilization; he proffers a less harsh diet as the requisite of perfect health:

> True, I forgot that they will also have relishes—salt, of course, and olives and cheese, and onions and greens, the sort of things they boil in the country, they will boil up together. But for dessert we will serve them figs and chick-peas and

beans, and they will toast myrtle berries and acorns before the fire, washing them down with moderate potations. And so, living in peace and health, they will probably die in old age and hand on a like life to their offspring.[100]

In this system of reference, Plato faults the luxury of his contemporaries, a luxury that promotes idleness and too rich a diet, as the main cause of the city's diseases "to which the clever sons of Asclepius have attached names like flatulence and flux."[101]

The history of medicine can accept this line of argument only with reservations that deprive it of all its vitality: though it is true that sybaritic luxury and culinary novelties can be blamed for an increase in some diseases, especially gout and vascular failures caused by obesity and arteriosclerosis, the dominant pathology is one of deficiency even at the height of the economic boom of the Greek city-states. The frequency of bladder stones in Greek children of the fourth and fifth centuries B.C. is relevant to this assertion.[102] Idiopathic bladder stone disease in children is a different disease from urolithiasis in adults. It is rare in modern societies, except those rife with poverty and nutritional deficiencies. Reports presented to the symposium on idiopathic bladder stone disease organized by the World Health Organization in Bangkok in 1972 stress that the incidence of the disease in children is a direct reflection of a country's socioeconomic state and a close correlate of malnutrition.[103]

Though it has almost disappeared in western Europe and North America, idiopathic bladder stone disease is endemic in Turkey, Egypt, Iran, India, and several Southeast Asian countries. Its etiology remains obscure. It is known, however, that its cause must lie in a person's nutrition during the first three years of life and in factors determining water metabolism. Possibly vitamin A deficiency favors the formation of bladder stones as well as a hot climate, but the decisive etiological factor is precocious weaning coupled with a relatively dry and protein-poor diet. This usually occurs when breastfeeding is disturbed because of protein deficiencies in the mother or wet-nurse.[104]

It emerges from several Hippocratic texts that idiopathic bladder stone disease was a common ailment affecting children, especially boys, in ancient Greece.[105] Its symptoms are well described, and its surgical treatment is known and forbidden in the famous Hippocratic oath. The author of the fourth book of the treatise *Diseases* even says that "the principle of this disease is milk, when a child suckles impure milk. And the milk of a mother or wet-nurse is impure when her diet consists of mucous food, impure food and drink."[106] Hippocratic physicians explained the formation of bladder stones as a process of sedimentation of impurities contained in milk or water. Though false in their detail, such explanations do point to a fundamental truth, namely, the pathological results of faulty breastfeeding and of the improper nutrition of the wet-nurse.

The natural resources of Greek soil were mediocre at best. Aridity placed limits on the cultivation of grains. According to the calculations of A. Jardé, annual consumption of wheat was about 3 hectoliters per person, while the average output of the soil was about 10 hectoliters per hectare. From this Jardé deduces that "the food supply became inadequate as soon as the population density surpassed 36 inhabitants per square kilometer."[107]

In the classical age, most of the continental portions of Greece maintained an equilibrium between the production and the consumption of wheat. Only Thessaly had a surplus, since it was a relatively sparsely populated (about 30 inhabitants per square kilometer) breadbasket. The inadequately supplied areas were chiefly Corinth, the Megarid, Attica, and the island of Aegina. Their inhabitants survived thanks only to the industry and commerce that made possible the importation of sustenance. Along with imported grain, a new disease reached Greece from time to time and in waves, namely, ergotism, a kind of food poisoning caused by a parasite in rye. Rye was not cultivated in Greece itself.

Traces of malnutrition on Greek bones have not been studied sufficiently. A first desideratum is the radiological determination of Harris' lines on the long bones from a Greek necropolis. Microanalytic determination of the minute variations in the elementary composition of bones, specifically the relation between the amounts of strontium and calcium, is beginning to give us clues about the level of meat consumption among ancient Mediterranean populations (S. C. Bisel, 1980; G. Fornaciari et al., 1982).

Paleo-odontology

Abrasion of the hard tissues is a very common special feature on the anatomical crown of teeth. It is seen among adults of every human population, though there are important statistical variations with respect to the earliness of its first appearance, the swiftness of its progress, and the seriousness of the final lesions. It can range from mild wear and tear on the enamel, hardly more than a physiological phenomenon, to the total abrasion of tooth enamel on the occlusive surface with partial destruction of the dentine and, in the most serious cases, disclosure and secondary infection of tooth pulp. Its etiology is essentially mechanical, a function of the hardness of the substances that the teeth grind up. So the degree and the frequency of dental abrasion can offer clues about the kind of foods that a given population eats.

According to several authorities, dental abrasion is chiefly attributable to the presence of particles of sand in food, especially in flour milled by stone and foods ground up in stone mortars. However, nowadays it seems more likely that this factor, although assuredly not negligible, is less important than just the slow, steady way people chew food of a certain firm or rubbery consistency. In this kind of chewing, the teeth themselves wear each other away.

Dental abrasion, which is very pronounced in Paleolithic teeth, does not appear to decrease in the Mesolithic period or at the beginning of the Neolithic period.[108] For these remote times, a true statistical analysis of the frequency of this lesion is not possible, at least at present, since our knowledge is based on such small samples. As for more recent periods, the number of specimens examined is becoming significant, although a difficulty remains. How can the figures given by different authorities be compared when we do not yet really know how to measure the parameter in question, with the result that we are basically dependent on subjective estimates?

Dental abrasion is very marked on Neolithic human teeth from Iran and in Europe, among the Sumerians, and among the inhabitants of predynastic and Pharaonic Egypt. In the latter, considerable abrasion occurs throughout the social ladder. M. J. Becker has reported very marked abrasion on anatomical crowns in 74 persons exhumed in 1973 at Kato Zakro (a necropolis dating from Middle Minoan times). According to him, such extensive wear and tear is due to the use of stone mills and the consumption of coarse grains. Furthermore, this Cretan populace, whose cultural development was relatively high, suffered from tooth decay—in fact, almost everyone over the age of 40 was toothless.[109] Robert P. Charles has described a male skeleton aged 30–35 found in a protogeometric tomb (ca. 900–850 B.C.) from the Argive necropolis *(16 Arg.)*. This person had a complete and perfectly preserved set of teeth, free from decay, but all of them, both uppers and lowers, were "very worn."[110] I cite these two reports as examples. They are instructive, but, statistically speaking, in themselves they are not significant. The authors who tell us that dental abrasion was "very marked" in Minoan and archaic peoples rarely produce figures and fail to specify whether the level of abrasion they speak of is in comparison with Neolithic teeth, those of classical antiquity, or those of modern times. They are probably right if their frame of reference is the dentition of the current inhabitants of western Europe. But if we keep the phenomenon in its own historical context, our judgment will be more cautious: dental abrasion in the inhabitants of Bronze Age Greece is plainly less than that of the first farmers of the Neolithic period, and it is probably still less than that of Greeks in the classical period. At least, that is the upshot of John Lawrence Angel's studies, and his statistics have the advantage of being based on the judgment of one and the same researcher, a factor that eliminates differences in classification criteria and neutralizes subjectivity in their use.

Angel distinguishes between five stages of dental abrasion: absent, slight, medium, pronounced, and very pronounced. According to him, 50 percent of adult skeletons at Nea Nikomedia (Early Neolithic period) fall into the latter two categories, while the proportion is 30.8 percent at Karataş (Early Bronze Age), 28 percent at Lerna (Middle Bronze Age), and 40 percent overall for the sum-total of archaeological sites in classical Greece.[111] However, this picture is complicated to some extent by the fact that study of the skeletal remains at Çatal Hüyük (Early Neolithic period) finds only 30.8 percent of the skulls with pronounced or very pronounced dental abrasion.[112] As for the figures on classical Greece, they derive from the examination of the remains of 87 individuals without common origins. Given the interest we have in any token of the evolution of living conditions from the seventh to the fourth century B.C., at some future time it would be useful to undertake a detailed analysis of the classical evidence that would take account of differences in the age and provenience of each specimen. It is hard to accept the notion that the sophisticated citizenry of Athens, Corinth, or Sybaris at their height suffered from dental abrasion. In the Middle Bronze Age, the aristocrats at Mycenae were much less prone to it than the common people. Scarcely 15 percent of the skeletons from the royal tombs evince pronounced or very pronounced abrasion, while the number rises to 28 percent among the rural population of the Argolid.[113] Did a similar difference exist between the Athenians' teeth and those of the Spartans?

Whatever the case may be, the jump from 28 percent among the Mycenaean inhabitants of Lerna to 40 percent in the Greeks of the classical period does not actually signify what it seems. Across the sample from Lerna, strong dental abrasion is much more common in men (38 percent) than in women (15 percent). This is partly due to the greater force of the chewing muscles in men and partly to the fact that the average age of the women in the sample is 6 years less than that of the men.[114] Probably the classical sample favors its masculine component over the feminine one. Dental abrasion increases with age, and the only valid comparison is between equivalent age groups. However, the average age in the Mycenaean sample (35 years) is 6 years younger than that of the classical one (41).[115]

The bread eaten in the Bronze Age and in classical times must have been much less hard on dental enamel than the grain eaten in the Neolithic period. Around the sixteenth century a new change in diet in Europe affected the way people chew: from then on, dental abrasion subsides, but dental caries increases. The rural population of Greece has lagged behind in this overall change. Angel states that about a third of modern adult Greek males (average age, 38 years) have markedly worn down the grinding surfaces of their teeth.

It is often—but falsely—said that dental caries is a "disease of civilization." The presence of its typical lesions can be confirmed on the teeth of Australopithecine man.[116] There is no human population that has completely escaped it. Nonetheless, it must be admitted that dental caries is much more frequent nowadays than it was in the past. In Europe, its frequency begins mounting in medieval times and markedly accelerates in the modern period.[117] There is no doubt that the fundamental cause for this increase is progressive change in eating habits. Probably sugar and white bread are the single most important factors in the current high rates of caries, since they actually stimulate the action of the microbes in dental plaque. But so simple an explanation cannot possibly suffice. The etiology of tooth decay is very complex and for the most part still unexplained. The foods eaten are significant at various levels, since they supply the proteins, vitamins, and minerals necessary for the proper formation of dental tissues, maintain metabolic equilibrium, determine the mouth's acidity and the creation of dental plaque, elicit local mechanical activity, and so forth. It is clear that poor people's food and rich people's food both have their advantages and disadvantages. In any case, given a minimum supply, an excess of food seems to have more damaging consequences for dental tissue than a lack of it. As a rule, the well-to-do have more decayed teeth than the poor.

Factors other than diet are implicated in the pathogenesis of dental caries, such as the genetic determination of dental microstructure, the physiopathology of salivation, climatic factors, the mineral content of drinking water, the evolution of microbial flora, social and individual habits regarding dental hygiene, and so forth. This plurality of factors favoring or curtailing dental caries means that variations in its frequency from one population to the next are difficult, if not impossible, to reduce to a common model.

Among the inhabitants of ancient Greece, the incidence of caries is distinctly greater than in analogous populations of western Europe and in Egypt. For the totality of European and North African populations in the Mesolithic period, its frequency nears 7 percent of the teeth examined. For the necropolis of Taforalt, the figure is around 6 percent. Later on, the incidence of this disease falls considerably in the European, North African, and Asiatic populations studied, but not in Greece, where it appears to increase in the Early Neolithic period, only to subside and then remain steady until the classical period at about 6 decayed teeth for every 100 examined.[118]

In comparing published results, it is essential to take into account differences in reference systems. Some rates refer to the number of teeth actually examined, others to the number of teeth likely to have existed on extant jawbones and individuals. The rate based on teeth actually examined underestimates the real frequency of the disease, since it neglects lost and destroyed teeth. Accordingly, the analysis of teeth must be complemented by an analysis of jawbones. The sum-total of decayed and missing teeth, expressed either as a percentage of "possible" teeth or as the average number of dental lesions per mouth, overestimates the frequency of dental caries.

For ancient Greece, in round numbers, the rate of decayed teeth as against teeth actually examined is a little more than 6 percent; the rate of decayed and lost teeth as against "possible" teeth from extant tooth sockets is as high as 20 percent. This latter number corresponds to a figure of 6.5 lesions per mouth. But there were significant local variations. The aristocrats at Mycenae had only 1.3 lesions per mouth, of which 0.8 were actually instances of caries, while their contemporaries at Lerna had close to 7 lesions per mouth, more than 2 of which were actually caries.[119] According to C. M. Fürst, dental caries was common in skulls from Argos, but R. P. Charles reports its rarity at the same site.[120] The disease was unequivocally common among the Cretans of the Minoan era, especially at Knossos (9 percent caries in a survey of 1,500 teeth actually examined) and at Kato Zakro.[121]

These local variations are upsetting insofar as an undeniable improvement in the conditions of life and especially in diet increased the incidence of dental caries in the palaces of Crete but drove it down in spectacular fashion among the warrior princes of Mycenae. In their case it is tempting to postulate the existence of hereditary factors. Contrary to what one might expect, the urban way of life of the classical period brought on no deterioration in Greek teeth. In fact the frequency of dental caries was less than before, though it remained relatively high compared with the situation elsewhere in Europe as a whole. Angel's initial research on Greek teeth in this era resulted in the following statistics: 5 percent of the teeth were actually decayed or lost, which corresponds to 4.5 lesions per mouth. New paleo-odontological specimens have brought down this latter figure to 4 lesions per mouth, with just 0.8 of the teeth in it actually decayed.[122] In Bronze Age Cypriot tombs typical cases of dental caries have been found (at times resulting in osteitis of the jawbone, as in *9A Kition*) as well as very marked dental abrasion, to the extent of laying bare tooth pulp.[123]

It is hardly likely that the relatively high frequency of caries among the Greeks is attributable to racial traits. For instance, there is no caries on any of the numerous human teeth from the Greek-Etruscan necropolis of Spina (fifth to third centuries B.C.) in northern Italy, nor on those of the Greek colonists at Pithekussai (eighth to seventh centuries B.C.) in southern Italy.[124] Among the external factors that could favor dental caries among the inhabitants of protohistoric and classical Greece, I should mention the relative abundance of sugar in their diet. To be sure, we are not referring to refined sucrose, which was still unknown, but to honey and fruits high in sugar content, chiefly fresh or dried figs. In asking himself, "Why do figs that are ripe and sweet impair the teeth?" the author of an Aristotelian *Problem* was handing on an old empirical observation.[125]

In modern times, it seems that the population of Athens enjoys some resistance to dental caries. According to recent research, this is due to a high concentration of fluoride and still more to a weak concentration of selenium in the teeth. Chemical analyses of several undecayed teeth from Athenian tombs of the eighth and eleventh centuries B.C. reveal that even in remote times fluoride was abundant and selenium did not surpass a critical threshold. Although drinking waters in Athens are not and doubtless never were rich in fluoride, a supply of it is guaranteed from sea salt and the consumption of fish.[126] There is the report of a modern endemic of fluorosis at Laurium in Attica caused by an excess of fluoride in the drinking supply. When Henri Duday found a predominance of mottled enamel (enamel hypoplasia) in the dental pathology at the Kitsos Cave, he speculated on such a phenomenon as its etiology, given the fact that the cave itself was situated precisely in the mining district of ancient Laurium. So a hypoplastic tooth was analyzed by X-ray diffraction, with the result that the possibility of fluorosis was excluded.

Such linear hypoplasias of tooth crowns are especially interesting for the paleopathologist. Actually, their significance is analogous to that of Harris' lines. Appearing as horizontal furrows parallel to the free edge of the tooth, they represent defects in the generation of enamel, arrested growth processes. They testify to attacks on the organism in early childhood: acute infectious diseases or chronic ones with acute crises, such as childhood fevers, gastrointestinal troubles, and famine. Although it is not possible to distinguish among their possible causes, these hypoplasias are valuable indicators of the overall state of health of a given population. So in the case of the Neolithic inhabitants of the Kitsos Cave, Duday came to the conclusion that they must have "paid heavily for the illnesses of early childhood, inasmuch as the skeletons of young people are relatively numerous (10 children of the 18 individuals enumerated) and inasmuch as the teeth of older persons bear the marks of severe, repeated childhood afflictions."[127] Arrested enamel growth is relatively rare among the Neolithic inhabitants of Çatal Hüyük, but abundant in the most recent population of Lerna. Comparative study of these phenomena is hampered by the lack of an objective, accepted method for quantifying them.

Chapter Four

COMMON PURULENT INFLAMMATIONS

Any wound that breaks the continuity of the skin tends to produce pus and to be complicated by pathological manifestations in originally unharmed body parts or even the whole organism. Such events are caused by infection, that is, by the penetration of microbes into the body, by their particular biological activity, and by the reactions of the organism under attack. Penetration of pathogenic microbes into the human body can also come about by natural, as opposed to traumatic, pathways: through the respiratory tract, the digestive tract, and so forth.

Infection is an invisible event in the strict sense of the word, since it takes place on a microscopic level. For a very long time it was invisible to the eyes of the intellect as well, because the almost ubiquitous presence of pyogenic bacteria in the human environment obscured their necessary role in purulent inflammation. The very banality of infection in its best-known form was the reason for its elusiveness to medical science. The production of pus appeared as a "normal" phase in the healing of wounds.[1]

The Paleopathology of Nonspecific Purulent Infections

Gram-positive[2] cocci classified in the Micrococcaceae family (in particular, *Streptococcus, Staphylococcus, Enterococcus, Pneumococcus,* and *Micrococcus*), when found on wounded human body parts or on those with lowered local resistance, provoke acute inflammatory reactions and the production of pus. Upon the body's return to clinical health, these microbes continue living peacefully as saprophytes on the skin or in the mouth, the throat, or the intestines. The same events can take place with gram-negative bacilli belonging to the Enterobacteriaceae family *(Escherichia coli, Proteus, Kleb-*

siella), which are optionally pyogenic bacteria that remain in the human organism and harm it only in exceptional cases. These bacteria are perfectly adapted to man, who for his part has at his disposal powerful immunological mechanisms to defend himself against their attack. In fact, the formation of pus is the expression of the mobilization of this defense system. The mutual adaptation established between the majority of pyogenic germs and man proves that their coexistence is indeed old.

During the last two decades, paleontologists have proved the existence of microbial life in the Precambrian era. J. W. Schopf, E. S. Barghoorn, and several other specialists in the microanalysis of rock have discovered petrified remains of the cells of various kinds of microbes from more than 2 billion years ago.[3] R. Cameron and F. Morelli even believe that they have found, deep in the soil of the dry valleys of Antarctica, frozen bacteria capable of reproducing themselves after living in suspended animation for several hundred thousand years. It is somewhat surprising to a historian of biology that the current state of scientific knowledge makes it plausible to credit such extraordinary contentions. Only a few decades ago experts would have had difficulty accepting them. I should stress that even if subsequent research disproves the Precambrian origin of true procaryotes or the ability of prehistoric bacteria to revive, there can be no doubt about the presence of many different kinds of bacteria in the biosphere during geological periods prior to the appearance of the higher animals.

We know neither when nor how certain groups of heterotrophic microbes were specialized into parasites that disturbed the biological equilibrium of Metazoa. Though there are fossil microbes that present the typical structure of *Eubacteria* and even correspond in their general aspect to the Micrococcaceae, the fact that they are found at large in rocks and not contained in organic tissue prevents us from witnessing their pathogenic role. In any case, it is absolutely certain that the ancestors of numerous pyogenic bacteria adapted themselves to parasitic life on higher organisms before the appearance of mammals and therefore well before the appearance of man on the planet. Man inherited pyogenic germs by vertical transmission from his ancestors.

Roy L. Moodie described fossil bacteria in the bones of prehistoric animals afflicted with osteomyelitis, but doubts have been expressed about his interpretation of the slides.[4] Even if we cannot accept the existence of bacteria in Moodie's bone sections, there is no denying his diagnosis of osteomyelitis, which in and of itself suffices to establish the existence of pyogenic bacteria—though they cannot be identified with known free-living fossil bacteria. Among the cases Moodie describes, the oldest is that of a saurian of the Permian period in which a spine fracture is complicated by a purulent bone infection. Traces of osteomyelitis have been reported on a Cretaceous dinosaur, a Pleistocene lion, and so forth.

Among the hominids, an osteoarchaeological proof of the antiquity of pyogenic germs is provided by the traces of alveolar pyorrhea on the lower jaw of *Sinanthropus lantianiensis* (about 450,000 B.C.).[5] Periodontal abscesses are also present in Neanderthal man and in fact occur in practically every prehistoric population of *Homo sapiens*. Such infections arise from saprophytic microbes in the mouth. Among the Neanderthals of La Ferrassie, an abscessed osteitis of the tibia and fibula has been conjectured; in Chapelle-aux-Saints man, some have recognized the secondary infection of a crushed phalanx; in Rhodesian man, there is a convincing paleopathological diagnosis of mastoiditis.[6] From the Neolithic period on, there are definite traces of osteomyelitis and osteoperiostitis on various European and African bones. Most often they are localized on the tibia and the temporal bone.[7] But the present rarity of very old and well-preserved bone specimens makes unwise any statistical study of the possible variations in frequency and virulence of pyogenic infections during the Stone Age.

Pyogenic germs are transmitted from one human to another directly or by way of infected objects. They do not require an animal to serve as their reservoir. Unlike certain viral diseases that are directly transmitted between humans, purulent inflammations do not demand a minimal population density for epidemiological continuity. To repeat, this perfect mutual adaptation, which makes the pyogenic microbe a saprophytic companion of mankind, is the best proof of the antiquity of the common suppurative diseases.[8]

Mastoiditis, a purulent inflammation that usually results from the extension of an inflammation of the middle ear, was relatively common in Pharaonic Egypt. Its occurrence on American pre-Columbian skulls, as reported by E. A. Hooton and H. U. Williams, suggests that the germs responsible for it, especially the streptococcus and pneumococcus, had adapted themselves to man before the first colonization of the American continent. The results of Egyptian paleopathology are not irrelevant to a study of ancient diseases in the Greek world, for it is plain that a germ capable of living in equilibrium with man and not requiring special climatic conditions or vectors or social customs to ensure its survival would of necessity be present (or, for that matter, lacking) throughout the eastern Mediterranean. Sir Marc Armand Ruffer proved the existence of gram-positive cocci in the lung tissue of a twelfth-century B.C. Egyptian mummy.[9] Since the individual died of pneumonia—his pulmonary tissue was in the stage of hepatization—it is very likely that the cocci in question belong to the genus *Diplococcus,* or at least to the family Micrococcaceae. This is grounds for suspecting that the inhabitants of archaic Greece were exposed to lobar pneumonia and therefore to heightened mortality during cold and wet seasons.

Let us pass on to a survey of actual cases of common pyogenic infections on ancient bones from the Greek world. In a man from Lerna *(88 Ler.)* living in the Middle Bronze Age, traces of periostitis and of ankylosis of the last joint on the thumb and on the little finger of the right hand are the result of a typical V-shaped phlegmon: after a wound to the wrist or palm, infection by pyogenic germ propagated along the synovial bursae and the flexor tendon sheaths of the hand. Although cured of the acute purulent inflammation—and also, by the way, of a fracture of his right seventh rib—the subject was left with a slight handicap until the end of his life (at about age 35).[10] Another man of the same era, whose skeleton was found at Argos *(123 Arg.)*, suffered from cranial osteomyelitis: on the occipital bone, to the left of the inion, the external surface is deeply corroded, and the wall has become very thin (actually, it is perforated, but as the result of a post-mortem accident). Such damage to this bone can be a complication from a carbuncle on the nape of the neck, which is generally caused by a staphylococcus infection.[11] Osteomyelitis was also reported by V. V. Bobin in 1964 on bones from Neapolis in the Crimea (Greco-Scythian necropolis, third–first centuries B.C.).[12]

In the relatively complex case of a male child from Lerna *(130 Ler.)*, dead at age 3, it may well be, as Angel supposes, that a mastoid infection brought on a thrombosis of the meningeal sinus on the left side, which caused, in turn, the development of collateral venous channels.[13] If this is actually what took place, meningitis and intracranial hypertension were certainly part of the clinical picture. However, other explanations (for example, the existence of a congenital malformation) might account for the state of this child's skull.

Traces of a purulent infection on the upper jawbone can be detected on the skeleton of an athletic, 50-year-old chieftain exhumed from a royal grave at Mycenae *(59 Myc.)*. A cystic formation in the area of the upper second molar testifies to the existence of an old abscess. His gum infection propagated in the maxillary sinus, whose thickened bony walls bear the marks of an inflammation of the mucoperiosteum—in other words, a sinusitis.[14]

From osteoarchaeological research it is clear that alveolar pyorrhea is a disease whose commonness among the ancient inhabitants of Greece and the lands adjacent to it should not be underestimated. The bones of Aghios Kosmas, Lerna, the Kitsos Cave, and Argos offer a whole series of instructive examples of it.[15] H. Graham Carr states that up to 80 percent of the ancient jawbones from Knossos bear signs, however slight, of periodontal disease.[16] To conclude the discussion of this aspect of bone pathology, it is enough to recall one more case whose special feature is that it belongs to the classical age: some traces of alveolar pyorrhea and a large abscess of the jawbone are to be found on the skeleton of an Athenian citizen *(65 AK.)* who died around 450 B.C. and who was buried in the Kerameikos.[17]

A separate problem is posed by the pyogenic germs of the Neisseriaceae family, in particular the gonococcus and the meningococcus. These gram-negative cocci lack the ability to coexist as peacefully with the human organism as other pyogenic germs. Unlike the Micrococcaceae and the Enterococcaceae, the Neisseriaceae do not appear to be parasites that must have accompanied man since the dawn of humanity and in all societies. Did gonorrhea and epidemic meningitis flourish in Greece in early antiquity?[18] Osteoarchaeology cannot answer this question. Even though the gonococcus and the meningococcus can leave traces of their pathogenic activity on bones, such lesions are not specific to them and are indistinguishable from those of pyogenic microbes in general.

Ancient Explanations of the Formation of Pus

Pus is a thick whitish or yellowish liquid that results from the infection of the tissues in higher animals by various kinds of bacteria. At the points at which these bacteria enter into contact with the host organism, a local inflammatory reaction can be observed, which ancient physicians described very precisely in terms of its four cardinal symptoms: heat, redness, swelling, and pain. These, in turn, are soon associated with the production of pus. Microscopically, the pus consists of an exudate swimming with live and dead bacteria, tissue waste products, and above all numerous degenerated polynuclear white blood cells (pyocytes or "pus globules"). Actually, the production of pus is an immunological defense, and pus is nothing more than an accumulation of bacteria and cellular "corpses."

I have offered the preceding brief summary of the views of modern medicine on the nature of pus in order to make it clear why in the evolution of medical ideas, the correct interpretation of the pathological mechanism of suppuration and an understanding of its proper biological role are unimaginable before the advent of cellular pathology, microbiology, and immunology in the nineteenth century. Although this phenomenon was inaccessible at the microscopic level, wherein lay the key to its nature, it was perfectly accessible on the macroscopic level and must have fascinated healers at all times and places. The etymology of the words for pus in the Indo-European languages confirms the earliness of its existence as a concept. The Greek word *púon* or *púos,* like the Latin word *pus* and its homographic descendant in French and English, derives from the same root as the verbs *púthomai* in Greek and *pūyati* in Sanskrit (meaning "rot, putrefy, decompose"). According to Chantraine, this whole family of words stems from a protestation of disgust, *pu* or *pū.*[19]

In Homer, the verb *púthō* is used on several occasions to designate the decomposition of corpses, especially their bones, under the earth. Although descriptions of wounds abound in the Homeric epics, pus is never mentioned. The silence is probably one imposed by the heroic perspective and high style of the poetic narrative, which deliberately ignores life's little woes in favor of great exploits on the field of honor. The term *púon* is attested in Empedocles, who claimed that the milk of a pregnant woman "on the tenth day of the eight month is in the state of whitish *púon.*"[20] This Presocratic philosopher and physician seems to have taught that all transformations within an organism, including physiological digestion, the formation of milk and tears, and the pathological modifications of the humors, derive from a ripening process that he called *sêpsis.*[21] This explains his comparison of foremilk to pus. Some have translated *tò púon* in this passage as "colostrum," which is usually designated by the Greek term *ho pūós* with long *u,* but that cannot be justified in view of Aristotle's testimony on the matter.[22] Here are his remarks: "Milk is blood that has been cooked to perfection, not putrefied. Empedocles erred or used an inappropriate metaphor . . . , for rotting *(saprótēs)* is the opposite of cooking *(pépsis),* and pus *(púon)* is rotten, while milk is a substance that has been perfectly cooked."[23] Aristotle, along with the peripatetic philosophers and most later medical authors of the fourth century B.C., was indeed careful to distinguish cooking *(pépsis)* from rotting *(sêpsis, sēpedṓn, saprótē).* One term designates ascent to a higher state, the other a process of degradation.

Hippocratic terminology in this regard was not so well defined. To be sure, one can detect a general tendency toward the use of the *pep-* family in a more positive sense than *sēp-* /*sap-* , but semantic indecisiveness and inconsistent usages from one treatise to the next affirm that the basic theories of Greek medicine concerning digestion, assimilation, the formation of pus, and the elimination of harmful substances were still in flux. In the Hippocratic corpus, the verb *sḗpō,* the noun *sêpsis,* and their derivatives designated decomposition through putrefaction, the deterioration of the humors, the formation of pus, and at the same time the digestion of foodstuffs, especially its final stage.[24] The verb *pepaínō,* the noun *pépsis,* and their derivatives are used by the Hippocratic writers above all to designate the "maturation" that corrects disturbances in the humors, a kind of cooking that allows an organism to overcome and eliminate harmful substances.[25] This process can also produce pus. In a medical observation collected on the island of Thasos, there is talk of patients "in whom the disease resulted in suppuration *(empúēma)* or some similar coction *(pepasmós).*"[26] This *pepasmós,* or cooking of the body humors that are in an abnormal state, appears as well in other medical texts, always in connection with the formation of pus. There is no need to see a paradox in this: for the Hippocratic physicians, suppuration was not necessarily an evil process implying degradation. It could also be a transformation of raw and very dangerous pathogenic substances into a liquid that was separate from the rest of the body and ready to be expelled.

The treatise *Nutriment* teaches that "pus comes from flesh" and that "the purulent humor comes from blood and liquid."[27] In short, the opinions in the Hippocratic corpus are that pus is formed either from decaying battered flesh or extravasted blood or, more rarely, from the aqueous humor, or even from phlegm.[28] After having remarked on the abundant suppuration of head wounds caused by blunt, hard, heavy objects, the author of a surgical treatise explains that "the crushed, wounded flesh in such cases is inevitably transformed into pus and dissolves."[29] Modern medicine confirms the clinical side of this statement: it is really true that contusion favors the suppuration of a wound.[30] According to the Hippocratic writers, wounding implies significant movement of blood, not just the hemorrhage, but also and even especially an inflammatory afflux.[31] This engorging of the wound with blood causes suppuration: the wounds "suppurate once the blood is modified or warmed until it is putrefied and passes into the state of pus."[32] A passage in the fourth book of *Diseases* is the key to understanding how the surgical experience of the suppuration of wounds served as a model for the Hippocratic explanation of the formation of pus inside the body in the absence of a violent external lesion:

> If an injury *(traûma)* occurs, the flesh is harmed and a wound *(hélkos)* ensues; I call that a disease *(nósēma)*. If a contusion occurs as the result of a blow, a fall, or another injury of that kind, and if there is swelling *(oídēma)*, the blood, which has been forthwith warmed by the violent act, flows back towards the open vessels and, since it has no means of escape, for all its abundance, it hardens: that is the origin of the swelling which lasts until evacuation either through the pathways mentioned or when, at the same place where the swelling occurs, by surgical intervention or otherwise, the blood finds an exit, whether or not it has changed into pus with the passage of time.[33]

The use of the term *nósēma* 'disease' for a traumatic lesion may surprise the modern reader. It seems to me very significant for understanding the ancient Greek physicians' logic. The author of the treatise *Fractures* even goes so far as to ask "if one can say that other diseases (that is, nontraumatic diseases) are not themselves wounds."[34] The double meaning of the word *hélkos,* at once "wound" and "ulcer," is troubling. Probably the word originally meant traumatic lesion,[35] though it is important to be properly cautious in saying so in order not to falsify the archaic way of thought by introducing later conceptual distinctions. On the level of the external lesion, the confusion between wound and ulcer must have been total: in the protohistoric and classical Mediterranean world, every open wound was infected, so there could have been no distinction between healing by primary scar formation and the results of secondary infection.[36] This initial confusion is precisely what permitted the extension of the notion "wound/ulcer" from an external traumatic event to a spontaneous external or internal lesion, that is, one that appeared in the absence of an external act of violence.

Extravasated blood discharged in a part of the body that is foreign to it, for instance, in a cavity in which it is not normally found, changes into pus. If that is not an absolute truth for the modern physician who knows well the indispensable role of infection, at least it is an opinion that was firmly upheld by certain Hippocratic treatises,[37] which could thereby account for various clinical observations. According to the Hippocratic writers, there were at least three process by which blood could change into pus without there being an external lesion on the body: plethora and stagnation of blood; "spasms"[38] of the flesh with secondary rupture of small blood vessels; and "spasms" of the blood vessels. The pathological mechanism is described in several passages of the first book of the treatise *Diseases,* for instance, in chapter 14 on abscesses in the thoracic cavity and in chapter 17 on abscesses in the abdominal cavity.[39] According to this same treatise, pus can also come from phlegm: the empyema arises from the rotting of phlegm that comes from the head and empties into the pleural cavity.[40]

The distinction that was made in prognosis between "good" and "bad" pus had dramatic significance. A suppuration that was white, homogeneous, not bloody, and not malodorous was valued as a good omen, while a purulent discharge with the opposite qualities was considered the reverse.[41] There is some truth, to be sure, in this rule of prognosis, since the quality of the pus depends on the germ that induces its production, and yellow, cloudy, fetid pus is generally caused by very harmful bacteria. However, if one believes that the suppuration of wounds is inevitable, the difference between "good" and "bad" pus is made in a misleading context. The "good" kind of purulent inflammation seemed desirable, and instead of combating it, various means were used to stimulate it. This tragic mistake was reinforced, in daily practice, by the observation of cases in which the abscence of a pyogenic response actually was a bad sign due to failure in the immune system, or again by cases in which suppuration visibly helped the healing process by the destruction of necrotic tissues in open wounds before the practice of preventive debridement. From a theoretical point of view, this false conclusion was facilitated by its elegantly simple integration into the Hippocratic teachings about the pathology of humors. For these teachings, suppuration and the subsequent evacuation of pus were means by which an organism's *phúsis* eliminated harmful substances and prevented relapse: "All suppuration toward the exterior runs counter to a relapse, since therein lies a coction that is both crisis and abscession."[42]

The First Descriptions of Traumatic Purulent Inflammations

The historian Herodotus tells how an accident slew the Persian king Cambyses II at the very moment when he wished to rush out and defeat a usurping Magus:

It was clear to him now that the murder of his brother had been all to no purpose; he lamented his loss, and at last, in bitterness and anger at the whole miserable set of circumstances, he leapt upon his horse, meaning to march with all speed to Susa and attack the Magus. But as he was springing into the saddle, the cap fell off the sheath of his sword, exposing the blade, which pierced his thigh—just in the spot where he had previously struck Apis the sacred Egyptian bull. Believing the wound to be mortal, Cambyses asked what the name of the town was, and was told it was Ecbatana. There had been a prophecy from the oracle at Buto that he would die at Ecbatana; and he had supposed that to mean the Median Ecbatana, his capital city, where he would die in old age. But, as it turned out, the oracle meant Ecbatana in Syria . . . some twenty days later he sent for the leading Persians who were present . . . and when the Persians saw the king in tears, they tore their clothes, and showed their sympathy by a great deal of crying and groaning. Shortly afterwards, the bone decayed and the putrefaction spread quickly over his thigh, and the sickness took away Cambyses son of Cyrus.[43]

This took place near the end of the summer in 522 B.C. I pass over the various magical and religious aspects of Herodotus's narrative (such as the divine etiology of the wound superimposed on the physical one; the oracle; the prophetic dreams; the king's mental illness; and so forth) to focus on its medical content. The diagnosis is straightforward: Cambyses died a victim of traumatic osteomyelitis with septic complications.

A similar misadventure overtook Miltiades. This famous Athenian general, the victor at Marathon, had an accident during the siege of Paros in 489 B.C. When he returned to Athens in a sorry state and without having conquered the town he had besieged for twenty-six days, he was accused of having deceived the Athenians: "Miltiades, though present in court, was unable to speak in his own defense because his leg was putrid; he lay on a couch and his friends spoke for him . . . The popular verdict was to spare his life, but to fine him fifty talents for his offense. Shortly afterwards the rot in his thigh grew worse and he died."[44] Herodotus, who reports this event as an undeniable historical fact, informs us as well concerning the origin of Miltiades' ailment, but not without some reserve. According to the Parians, who were the only ones to say so, Miltiades entered the holy precinct sacred to Demeter that was situated on a hill before the town of Paros. There, on the very threshold of the sanctuary, he was overcome by fright and would have returned, except that "in jumping back over the stone wall he broke his thigh, or, as others say, he smashed his knee."[45] The infection's point of entry was therefore a compound fracture of the thigh or perhaps a skinned knee. It could not be just a hip dislocation, as certain commentators have allowed. Herodotus does not cast doubt on the reality of the initial wound, and if he speaks of it with rhetorical circumspection that is only because of the Parians' insistence on Miltiades' sacrilegious behavior. In this case and that of Cambyses, the serious consequences of an apparently harmless wound inevitably suggest divine intervention.

That interpretation was no longer acceptable to the physicians of the classical era. The Hippocratic writers knew perfectly well the dangers inherent in any break in the continuity of the integument. Even without any conceptual knowledge of infection and the lymphatic system, they had carefully observed the pathological changes now called nonspecific lymphangitis and lymphadenitis. They knew that when a cut is inflamed, the flesh in the immediate vicinity swells up, and swelling and heat spread from there along the blood vessels. If a wound is in the leg, tumors form in the groin; if it is in the arm, their preferred site is the armpit. A local injury, warmed by the afflux of humor, makes the whole body febrile. One can die of it, especially on odd-numbered days.[46]

These Hippocratic physicians say that if a wound is deep enough, suppuration affects bones as well as flesh. In that case local necrosis can be observed (*sphákelos* or *gángraina*) along with the generalization of symptoms. This happens especially in the case of compound fractures. If a leg bone protrudes through the skin, reduction must not be attempted, says Hippocrates, since

> the patient who undergoes such a reduction successfully will surely succumb within a few days; only a few last more than seven; the spasm[47] kills them; it can also happen that both leg and foot are attacked by gangrene *(gangrainoûsthai)*.[48] Should there be a fracture or a wound, for example of the leg or the thigh, and should the ligaments or the tendons communicating with these body parts lose their spring, or should the heel become gangrenous due to an uncorrected bed position, serious complications will follow. Other than local necrosis, very high and quickly fatal fevers can occur, along with weeping, trembling, and mental disorders, and also lividity of large blood vessels which then extravasate blood, and finally gangrene.[49]

Among the patients whose histories are recorded in the seven books of the *Epidemics,* there are numerous cases of traumatic infection with suppuration of flesh and bone and typical sepsis whose likeliest cause is the ancestor of the *Staphylococcus aureus*.[50] We know today that bony tissue can also be infected in the absence of any wound by the hematogenous route, with microbes spreading from a focus inside the organism. These "spontaneous" bone suppurations did not escape the attention of the Hippocratic physicians. The treatise *Joints* contains this remarkable passage: "When the joint is dislocated and started from its socket by disease—such things often happen—if necrosis of the thigh-bone occurs in some of these cases, chronic abscesses are formed . . . and there is some denudation of bone. Likewise, both where there is and where there is not necrosis of the bone, it becomes much shorter, and will not grow correspondingly with the sound one."[51]

This is without doubt a description of hematogenous staphylococcic osteomyelitis, a disease well known in modern times and one that was much feared before antibiotics.[52] It is a juvenile form of osteomyelitis related to the rate and time of osseous growth. It has a marked predilection for the long bones of the lower limbs. The importance that the Hippocratic corpus accords to head caries leads me to believe that in Greeks of the classical period another preferred site of osteomyelitis was the skull.[53]

Probably the reason for this was the very high frequency of infections in the area of the mouth, nose, and ears, especially in children.

In ancient times as well as in the not so distant past, tiny skin wounds or subcutaneous injuries were often followed by purulent reactions that were generally benign but sometimes were serious or even deadly: furuncles, whitlow, phlegmon of the foot, erysipelas, and so forth. The Hippocratic treatises describe cases in which the progress of the infection was stunning. For instance, an inhabitant of Thasos died the second day after a phlegmon began forming on his big toe;[54] or a shoemaker succumbed in three days to a swelling of his thigh caused by an accidental puncture with one of his tools.[55] In both these cases the infection of an apparently insignificant cut is followed by violent inflammation and fatal sepsis. The likeliest agent is an especially virulent streptococcus, probably a betahemolytic *Streptococcus pyogenes*.

The Hippocratic description of erysipelas is the best proof of the existence of harmful stocks of this bacterium in classical Greece. To be sure, the term *erusípelas* in ancient Greek medical parlance designates various diseases that "redden the skin" and also diffuse, purulent inflammations of internal organs, but in its commonest sense it designates a group of skin diseases with hot, painful, reddish swelling, now thought to be streptococcic dermatitis.[56] The Hippocratic term *erusípelas* may also cover another disease, erysipeloid, the human form of a disease affecting pigs, but that is only a guess. By contrast, it is well established that it did cover gas gangrene, a particularly serious disease caused by the infection of wounds with certain species of *Clostridium, Aerogenes,* and *Bacteroides*.[57] These anaerobic bacteria are found in soil the world over. (Among other possibilities for the infection of wounds, I should mention in passing tetanus[58] and anthrax.[59])

Wounds to the abdomen regularly resulted in peritonitis, a disease caused by various microbes introduced from without or from the intestinal content. Here is a case observed at the battle of Delos, which took place around 357 B.C.:

> A man from Ainos wounded at Delos by a javelin on the left side in the back suffered little from the wound itself, but on the third day, he had sharp abdominal pain. No stools. An enema brought some excrements at night. The pain did not subside, but became localized in the testicles. On the fourth day, waves of pain in the pubis and over the whole abdomen. He could not stay still; he vomited dark bilious matter; eyes like those of people fainting. He died after the fifth day. There was a slight fever.[60]

The Oldest Medical Evidence on Purulent Inflammation of Internal Organs

There is hardly an organ that cannot be the site of a staphylococcal, streptococcal, or pneumococcal suppuration. In the Greek medical writings of the classical period, there are clinical accounts of purulent inflammation in numerous internal organs. In interpreting these descriptions, a modern physician can say that the following sites were either the commonest among the sick of those days, or, to give a better account of historical reality, the most striking to ancient healers: tonsils, the ear and the cranial sinuses, the meninges, the lungs and pleura, joints, the kidneys and the perirenal region, the biliary organs, the peritoneum, the rectum, and the uterus and its annexes. Of all this abundant and varied pathology I can cite only a few instances, which will offer at least a glimpse of the necessarily great number of diseases with this bacterial etiology.

Membranous pharyngitis, peritonsillar abscess (Duguet's angina), and Ludwig's angina were soon isolated as specific clinical entities.[61] Inflammation of the tonsils was thought to promote submaxillary adenitis, to spread to the lungs, and even to destroy its victim with the typical symptoms of sepsis. There is no doubt for a modern physician that sore throats like these must have often resulted in rheumatic fever with cardiac and renal manifestations.

Suppurative otitis media was also a well-known disease, and the Hippocratic physicians knew its usual symptoms (flow of pus from the external auditory meatus, severe pain, hearing loss) as well as those of its most spectacular complications, like mastoiditis, phlebitis of the lateral sinus, or meningitis.[62] Here is a clinical history of it told in exemplary fashion:

In Kydis's son, near the time of the winter solstice, shivering and sweating, headache and earache in the right ear. This kind of misery had begun when the boy was still a baby, and it continued, with fluxions and fistulas and horrible smells. When he was in this state, it was usually painless, but on this occasion the pain was terrible, especially in the head. On the second or third day of it, when moving his bowels, he began vomiting bile that was as viscous as an egg, slightly bilious, slightly ochre in color. On the night of the fourth day and during the fifth, a little delirious; the pain in his head and ear were terrible, as was the fever. On the sixth, his stomach was emptied by the administration of Mercurialis annua; the heat seemed to have subsided and the pain along with it. On the seventh day, it was as if he was cured, but the beating in his temple persisted; he did not sweat at all. On the eight, he kept down some boiled barley, and in the evening some beets, then during the night, the pain stopped completely. On the ninth day, too, he remained himself until sunset, but during the night the pain in his head and ear were terrible; and there was also this, that the ear was purulent precisely when the pain was at its height, just after it started. During the whole night of the ninth day, as well as during the next day and most of the next night he recognized no one but did not stop groaning. At daybreak, he was himself again, the pains subsided, he was less hot. On the eleventh day, he took some mercurial, and his excrement consisted of foul-smelling phlegm and mucus. Twelfth and thirteenth days: in a moderate state. On the fourteenth, he began sweating from tip to toe, from morning till evening, with much sleep or sleepiness: waking him was a task. Toward the evening, he awoke, and his body cooled off satisfactorily, but the beating in his temples persisted. On the fifteenth and sixteenth days, he ate some boiled food. On the seventeenth, pain returned to the same places, there was some delirium, and there was a flow of pus. On the eighteenth, nineteenth, and twentieth days, the pain was unleashed: he shrieked and tried to stand up, but could no longer control the movement of his head; he stretched out his hands, and kept on chasing something in the void. On the twenty-first day, a little sweat on the right side, the chest, and the head. On the twenty-second, his face sweated profusely; as for his voice, by this time, if he tried very hard, he could succeed in saying everything he wanted to, but if he let himself go, he only half succeeded; besides, his mouth was limp and his lips and jaws were always moving, as if he wanted to say something; his eyes were often moving and glancing, and there was a tinge to his right eye, like one we call "bleeding" eye; the upper lid was swollen, and the end of his jaw was reddish; and all the blood vessels in his face stood out; and as for his eyes, he never closed them and had a fixed stare, and he opened the lids upward, as when something gets stuck in your eye. When he was drinking, as it went down through his chest to his stomach, a noise like that observed in the case of Chartades. Breathing always satisfactory and moderate; tongue, like patients' with peripneumonia, light yellow. From the beginning and without a letup, pain in the head; neck always fixed, so that he had to turn his whole body along with his head; the spine from the neck down was rigid and impossible to bend. Bed positions as described, and not always on the back. Pus from that time on was milky white and abundant, a trial to clean up, with an excessive smell. At the end, completely insensitive to being touched on the feet.[63]

Cases of meningitis and meningoencephalitis are brought up in the Hippocratic writings, but the nosological accounts confuse these diseases with tetanus, cerebral abscess, and even intracranial hemorrhage.[64] As for unspecific inflammations of the thoracic organs, Greek physicians of the classical era often came across lobar pneumonia, bronchopneumonia, and serofibrinous pleurisy, as well as empyema and abscess of the lung.[65] The Hippocratic disease called *peripleumoníē* is in most cases what we call lobar pneumonia. Besides a form of it that is assuredly caused by a pneumococcal infection, the author of *Diseases,* III, described one clinical variant that corresponds exactly to streptococcal or staphylococcal pneumonia.[66] Similarly, Hippocratic *pleurîtis* is actually most often either bacterial or viral pneumonia.[67] Pleuritis in the modern sense of the word had no name as yet. The author of *Diseases,* II, mentions typical serofibrinous pleurisy as an ailment that occurs "if the lung collapses against the side."[68] These diseases, *peripleumoníē* and *pleurîtis,* are often said to change into *empúos,* a term that includes pulmonary abscess and empyema in the modern sense of the word (purulent pleurisy).[69] The Hippocratic practitioners had remarkable familiarity with purulent lung diseases. For instance, they knew the diagnostic value of clubbing or the use of wet clay to determine the exact spot with the largest accumulation of pus, and so forth. They practiced the drainage of empyemas by thoracic paracentesis, and they also operated on perinephric abscesses, which are common complications of renal lithiasis and were probably caused by staphylococci.[70]

Nontraumatic purulent inflammations of the main abdominal organs were poorly known. Only with the greatest reservations can one propose a retrospective diagnosis of cholecystitis (inflammation of the gall bladder) or appendicitis on the basis of vague and confused descriptions. By contrast, the Hippocratic writers were not ignorant of metritis, still less of puerperal fever.[71] In the two oldest books of the *Epidemics,* there are no fewer than five clinical histories with fatal consequences in which a diagnosis of puerperal sepsis can be made without the least hesitation.[72]

Chapter Five

THE ORIGIN AND SPREAD OF SYPHILIS

Syphilis, leprosy, and tuberculosis are infectious diseases whose impact on the life and destiny of human societies cannot be overestimated. Unlike "plagues," acute epidemic fevers that fire the imagination of chroniclers with their brutality and their ephemeral or exceptional aspects, these three chronic diseases keep a low profile and, insofar as they are long-term phenomena, tend to be passed over in silence by contemporary accounts. Yet they are the great hidden killers.

All three of these diseases share a common property that is especially important for the historian: they produce lesions on bone tissue that are specific from the anatomopathological point of view, unlike those produced by inflammations due to common germs. In other words, in cases of syphilis, leprosy, and tuberculosis, the morphological analysis of bone lesions often supports an etiological diagnosis, that is, the identification of a causal agent. Until now, no trace of syphilis has been found on the ancient bones exhumed in Greece and its vicinity. As for leprosy and tuberculosis, no truly certain osteoarchaeological case is yet known. But caution is necessary in the face of such negative results. They have value only as indicators, and they must be evaluated in the light of biological as well as historical considerations. In my opinion, syphilis did not exist in the ancient Greek world; leprosy may well have been present but only sporadically, not becoming endemic until the end of antiquity; and tuberculosis had flourished there since mankind's arrival, or at least since the Neolithic Age.

The Problem of the Unity of the Treponematoses

The question of the origin of European syphilis continues to interest and divide medical historians.[1] In earlier days, scholarship seemed to vindicate those who held that syphilis was imported into Europe by Columbus's sailors as late as the last decade of the fifteenth century. But now eminent specialists are adducing biological arguments in favor of historical speculations that the disease was distributed throughout the world at a very early date. At least the microbe that is its cause was so distributed, though the pathological consequences varied depending on its geographical and social context.

For those who value opinions founded uniquely on literary sources, the "American" theory is beguiling. Modern medical-historical investigation has dismantled little by little the dossier assembled by scholars of the nineteenth century[2] to support the antiquity of venereal syphilis.[3] Actually there is no information from written documents or the oral or iconographic traditions that justifies the hypothesis of the existence of this disease in ancient populations of the Mediterranean. If the question is asked about venereal syphilis in western and southern Europe during the Middle Ages, although a negative answer is less certain, there, too, no serious literary proof has been found for a positive one.

In discussing the existence of syphilis in ancient Europe, I have taken care not to omit the epithet "venereal," since it is necessary to distinguish between at least four forms or types of syphilitic infection. First, there is syphilis in the strict sense of the term, a sporadic disease of urban populations that is chiefly transmitted by genital contact. Its etiological agent is the pale spirochete, *Spirochaeta pallida,* discovered in 1905 by F. Schaudinn and today called *Treponema pallidum*. The second form is endemic syphilis (otherwise known as treponarid), which is nonvenereally transmitted, localized in hot, dry climatic zones, known by various regional names (for example, bejel in Syria and North Africa, dichuchwa among the Bochimans of Botswana, and scherlievo on the Adriatic coast in the nineteenth century), and occurring among nomads or poor rural populations. Caused by what appears to be the same germ as venereal syphilis, the endemic form of the disease presents clinical features that distinguish it from the sporadic one. The third disease of this group is yaws (other names: frambesia, pian, and bouba), a serious skin and bone ailment that is transmitted directly, and usually not venereally, among humans. Yaws flourishes in warm, wet, forested regions, especially in central Africa. Its etiological agent, *Tr. pertenue,* was described by its discoverer, A. Castellani, as a slightly different germ from Schaudinn's treponeme. The fourth and last form is pinta (other names: caraté, mal de pinto), a relatively benign skin disease limited to the tropical zone of Latin America. Pinta bears little resemblance to ordinary syphilis, despite the fact that the latter is a multiform disease *par excellence*. I speak of it here only because its etiological agent, *Tr. carateum*, is indistinguishable from *Tr. pallidum*.

The three forms of *Treponema* just mentioned appeared morphologically close to one another at the time they were discovered. Bacteriologists took them for cousins, descendants of one particular branch in the evolution of microbes. But to our surprise, it has emerged in the present state of knowledge that these pathogenic treponemes do not just resemble each other, they are absolutely identical, both as to their appearance (even under the electron microscope) and in their responses to staining and in their antigenic structure as well. No serological test can distinguish among them, and immunity given by one has crossover value for secondary infection by the others.[4] Are we then faced with a single microbial species, or with several different species or varieties whose distinctiveness resides only in their pathological effects? Can the yaws treponeme produce ordinary syphilis in the right conditions? And can that of venereal syphilis be transformed into the germ of bejel and vice versa? In a word, are there several treponematoses or is there just one treponematosis whose clinical manifestations vary according to environmental conditions?

This taxonomic problem is not devoid of interest for a reconstruction of the historical past of syphilis. Unfortunately, we do not yet know which of the two answers to this question is the right one. No definite conclusion can be drawn from experiments on the specificity of treponemes isolated from patients with known diseases that were then inoculated into animals. I have no choice but to flesh out, one after the other, the two contradictory hypotheses.

Hudson's Hypothesis: A Sociocultural Explanation

The identity of the germ and the unicity of treponematosis were hypothesized, and the hypothesis along with its medical-historical consequences were carefully elaborated, by the American hygienist Ellis Herndon Hudson.[5] According to him venereal syphilis, bejel, yaws, and pinta are four syndromes of a single disease, treponematosis, which is produced by a single germ, *Tr. pallidum*. The diversification of these syndromes occurred as a biological response to the challenge of abrupt changes in climatic and sociocultural conditions. The four syphilitic syndromes are therefore, according to Hudson, epidemiological phases of a single nosological entity, and they can be converted according to a biological gradient in which endemic syphilis resides between yaws and venereal syphilis.

Pursuing this idea, Hudson arrives at a series of speculative conclusions: that the cradle of treponematosis was equatorial Africa, where the disease may have started in Paleolithic times with clinical manifestations almost identical to those of yaws. The germ *Tr. pallidum* was derived from a saprophytic treponeme. This disease then accompanied primitive hunter-gatherers as they migrated over the African continent. With them, it crossed the Mediterranean and arrived in Europe, and it also crossed Arabia to reach as far as Indonesia. Outside hot, wet, forested zones, treponematosis changed its aspect. Skin eruptions gave way to mucous lesions, and yaws changed into bejel. The principal cause of this change, according to Hudson, was the change to an arid climate. Among the inhabitants of the desert regions that border the tropical rain-forests, the skin is not moist enough for treponemes, which retreat to the mouth, axilla, and groin. A sociocultural factor reinforced the effect of climate, namely, the appearance of villages. In the Mesolithic and Neolithic periods, endemic syphilis found an especially favorable environment for itself in the Fertile Crescent. So treponematosis was established in this part of the world as an endemic childhood disease not linked to sexual activity. In comparison with other dangers to life and limb in the past, it was relatively benign and socially obscure. Once it arrived in Ceylon, the endemic form of the disease could revert to yaws. Leaving India and Indonesia, it spread over the islands of the Pacific to New Guinea and Australia. In the Neolithic period, again in its endemic form, it crossed Siberia, Alaska, and North America, ultimately reverting to the tropical climate of its African birthplace in Central America, which allowed it to transform itself into pinta and yaws.

The final phase of this speculative history, again according to Hudson, was the appearance of venereal syphilis. He attributes its rise to the urban way of life. Treponematosis became a sporadic disease affecting adults, attacking parenchymal internal organs and the central nervous system and transmitted genitally. Its expansion no longer depended on climate. The transition from endemic to venereal syphilis took place in many places at various times wherever rural life changed into urban life. Endemic and venereal forms must have coexisted in Mesopotamia and Egypt starting between 6000 and 4000 B.C., and in Greece at about 900 or 800 B.C. Beginning in the classical period, says Hudson, syphilis was confused with leprosy, a similar, chronic disease of the skin and bones, which "probably came out of Africa during the prehistoric migrations." At the latest, endemic syphilis spread into Europe during the Roman period and was present there, especially in rural areas, throughout the Middle Ages. So the poor sailors of Columbus are not to be blamed for having introduced venereal disease into Europe after all, even if we admit that they brought with them a few more treponemes. Environmental factors, chiefly climate and social habits, were paramount in determining the character of treponematosis in each epoch and country. It is worth noting, in conclusion, that Hudson's putative history is evolutionist, but it insists on the sociocultural evolution of the host (man) rather than the biological evolution of the parasite.

Hackett's Hypothesis: A Microbiological Explanation

The opposite point of view has been maintained by the British anatomopathologist Cecil John Hackett.[6] According to him, mankind suffers from four treponematoses. Venereal syphilis, bejel, yaws, and pinta are not four forms of one disease but truly four different nosological categories. Their etiological agents differ among themselves by their pathogenic properties and cannot be transformed into each other simply as the result of environmental changes. Though it is true the four microbes resemble one another to a great degree, that is because they are very closely related, all being derived from a common ancestor from which they differ only in a few details of fine biochemical structure.

According to Hackett, the existing microbe that is the closest to the primitive stock is *Tr. carateum,* the etiological agent of pinta. Either it is the ancestor of the group or a precocious offshoot of it, the derivative of a treponeme that lives parasitically in animals. To justify his opinion on the relative antiquity of pinta, Hackett points both to the length of time it is contagious, a characteristic that permits the disease to maintain itself over time even in small populations, and, more important, to its geographic limits—at present it is isolated among Indians living in humid areas of America. According to Hackett, the first human treponematosis appeared somewhere in the Old World, at the borders of the three continents, "perhaps before about 20,000 B.C.," through the mutation of a germ causing treponematosis in simians. Migrations of primitive hunter-gatherers spread it throughout the inhabited parts of the earth, except for Europe and northwestern Asia. The date 20,000 B.C. seems to have been chosen by Hackett to make the origin of pinta older than the land-bridge across the Bering Strait (around 15,000–10,000 B.C., according to the geophysical theory accepted by him), the likeliest point of its passage into America. But in Hackett's hypothesis it is not clear what determines the *terminus post quem* of the initial mutation.

The wet and hot climate of "Afro-Asia" (*sic*) favored the most invasive and destructive stock of *Tr. carateum* and fostered its mutation into *Tr. pertenue* around 10,000 B.C. As a result, yaws invaded all of Africa, the Middle East, and the Far East, the islands of the Pacific, and Australia, but without reaching Europe or the Americas before the Bering Strait was flooded. Wherever it established itself, yaws eliminated pinta. The arid climate that ruled certain parts of the earth after the Ice Age was responsible for a new birth, by natural selection of mutants of *Tr. pertenue:* the appearance of *Tr. pallidum* around 7000 B.C. From this time on, yaws remained the only treponematosis within the tropics, but endemic syphilis took its place in the northern and southern zones, invading the eastern Mediterranean and central Asia.

Finally, the change of a nonvenereal treponematosis in rural children into venereal syphilis in urban adults took place, in Hackett's view, during the postglacial climatic optimum around 3000 B.C., in the now arid lands of the eastern Mediterranean and southwestern Asia. Venereal syphilis, says Hackett, was probably carried by ship along the Mediterranean coasts, and later on, especially after the Roman conquests in the first century B.C., throughout Europe, "which was a treponemally uncommitted area." The map accompanying Hackett's study shows clearly that for him, venereal syphilis must have been present between 3000 and 100 B.C. in the Balkan peninsula, North Africa, Asia Minor, Italy, and on the French and Spanish coasts.[7]

The anthropologist Don Reginald Brothwell basically accepts Hackett's view of the general history of treponematoses, but he proposes a different date and locale for the mutation that created *Tr. pallidum*. By his lights, syphilis appeared in the Far East "*at least* two thousand years ago." This cautious assertion suggests an appreciably later date than the one proposed by Hackett. If it is correct, the spread of venereal syphilis from Asia into the Americas via the Pacific islands and into Europe via the expanding Arab world could not have taken place until the end of the Hellenistic period.[8]

Cockburn's Views

Aidan Cockburn, a well-known epidemiologist who is both bold and concerned with scientific precision, takes Hudson's side. He believes that the treponematoses "are in fact merely forms or variants of one basic infection, the differences being due chiefly to modes of transmission, climate, geography, humidity, etc."[9] At the very beginning of the pathogenic treponemes, says Cockburn, there was a free-living form whose descendants include certain current nonpathogenic protozoa living in the soil *(Tr. zuelzerae)*. At some very distant moment in the past, well before the origin of man, free spirochetes began attaching themselves to the higher animals to live symbiotically in their skin and the orifices of their bodies. Did man inherit the treponemes from his ancestors, or was he infected horizontally by an animal species in his ecosystem? Cockburn first hesitated on this issue, since the distribution of treponemes in the animal kingdom is poorly understood (mainly because it is necessary to take into account the symbiotic treponemes that are not pathogenic to their hosts). His most recent opinion is that the original infection was produced several million years ago in a common ancestor of man and the higher apes.[10] There are some signs pointing to the existence of a clinically hidden autochthonous treponematosis not unlike yaws in African gorillas and baboons.[11] However, the only form of syphilis known to exist in animals whose microbial agent has been definitely isolated is one that affects not apes but rabbits. That microbe, *Tr. cuniculi,* differs only slightly from *Tr. pallidum.* Even their serological reactions are identical. Did man catch the germ from rabbits, or did they catch it from him, or did both catch it from another reservoir of treponemes? The domestication of the rabbit was relatively late and the disease does not seem to affect other Leporidae, so that the transfer from man to rabbit seems much more likely than the other way around.

According to Cockburn, *Homo sapiens,* whether he first appeared in Africa or Asia, brought with him, when he crossed the Bering Strait, the germ of a primitive form of treponematosis, a disease older than mankind. The different modern forms of that disease resulted from geographic segregation and from environmental differences. Thus the peculiar features of pinta were due in part to the modification of the microbe (*Tr. carateum* is the only one that resists all forms of inoculation into animals), and in part to certain genetic traits of a group of American Indians. This is why the disease remained restricted despite the possibility of its expansion in modern times. Yaws, in Cockburn's opinion the form of the disease closest to the original treponematosis, flourished in climatic zones hospitable to it in which sociocultural conditions facilitated direct, skin-to-skin contact between men. In Europe, treponematosis took the form of endemic syphilis. Until about A.D. 1000, says Cockburn, treponemes cohabited with all of the world's human populations, either as commensals or as parasites, but they produced only mild, chronic disturbances since population density was low. The wearing of clothes hampered treponematosis in temperate regions, where the improvement of hygienic conditions and increased prudery brought about the disappearance of endemic syphilis and, through the survival of strains with a predilection for the genitals, the appearance of venereal syphilis. The discovery of America and the pandemic of venereal syphilis are not causally related but are parallel results of one common sociocultural factor, namely, the transformation of society due to the Renaissance and the Reformation.

The Osteoarchaeology of the Treponematoses

The historical and epidemiological reconstructions of Hudson, Hackett, and Cockburn are based on general biological considerations and the current distribution of four syphilitic diseases. They neglect specific historical information, and all of them face a major difficulty: the osteoarchaeology of the eastern Mediterranean. They do not take account of the fact that no trace of syphilis has been discovered on more than 25,000 skeletons and mummies from ancient Egypt and the Sudan or on several tens of thousands of prehistoric, ancient, and medieval skeletons exhumed in Europe and Asia Minor.[12] In particular, it has not been possible to detect this disease on any ancient bone from the Mediterranean. To be sure, that part of the globe is not the central preoccupation of the scholars cited, but it is still an indispensable part of their demonstrations.

Venereal syphilis, endemic syphilis, and pinta produce bone lesions that can often support a positive diagnosis of treponematosis.[13] Still, it is not possible to distinguish among them just by anatomopathological examination. This failing of paleopathology led Hudson to the conclusion that "the use of such bones to prove, or to disprove, theories about the place of origin of syphilis is not justified,"[14] which is a strange remark. In the present state of knowledge, not being able to distinguish between the treponematoses on bones seems to me secondary when what confronts us is the complete absence of the diseases in question.

Let us recall briefly the present state of osteoarchaeological research on syphilis. This disease, or another caused by treponemes, has been reported on several pre-Columbian bone specimens from different regions of the Americas: Argentina, Peru, Guatemala, Mexico, the mouth of the Ohio River, Arizona, New Mexico, Florida, and even the Antilles.[15] On the Mariannas in Oceania the skull and long bones of a 13-year-old child have been found to bear syphilitic lesions. According to carbon 14 dating, these particular bones are from the Middle Ages, probably the ninth century. Stewart and Spoehr offer a diagnosis of yaws,[16] a likely hypothesis, but it is well to be less precise and say that it is a case of treponematosis. The disease has also been reported on the remains of Australian aborigines.[17] On the other hand, no human remains older than 1500 and bearing sure signs of a treponematosis have been found in Europe, Africa, or Asia.[18]

To explain the absence of paleopathological proofs of the pre-Columbian existence of treponematoses in the Old World, the "anti-Americanists" stress the relative rarity of the remains that have been examined. Such an argument was perfectly valid when it was still believed that syphilis was present in the European populations of the protohistoric period and of antiquity in the form of sporadic cases and small epidemics. Yet the hypotheses of both Hudson and Hackett are obliged to assert the presence of endemic syphilis in the eastern Mediterranean, either alone or in concert with venereal syphilis. However, the conservation of endemic syphilis demands very high morbidity, so high that it makes no sense for the disease to have escaped osteoarchaeological detection. Moreover, it seems unbelievable that an endemic disease of such scope could have escaped the notice of Greek physicians. Another argument of the "anti-Americanists" does not withstand criticism either. It is said that Old World treponematoses were confused with leprosy. The famous medical historian Karl Sudhoff said the same for the Middle Ages, not without justice, but this argument has no value if we also apply it, as Hudson does, to classical antiquity. The osteoarchaeological proofs of the existence of leprosy in Europe are very late. Physicians of the classical period could not confuse the endemic presence of syphilis with leprosy for the simple reason that they did not know of either one.

Tr. Pallidum: *An American Mutant*

The biological hypotheses on the origin of syphilis certainly deepen knowledge and exercise ingenuity, but they must be modified in order to harmonize with the osteoarchaeological and historical evidence. I think that the four human treponematoses are caused by three kinds of microbes that, although they are morphologically alike, are distinguished by biological properties and do not transform themselves into each other under the influence of environment. They are the result of an evolutionary process that cannot really be reversed. I speak of three and not four kinds because it seems to me very likely that *Tr. pallidum* is responsible for endemic as well as venereal syphilis. Historical studies demonstrate the reality of the change from one to the other according to sociocultural circumstances. But history contains no known instance of a parallel conversion for yaws and pinta. It may well be that an as yet undiscovered technique of biostructural analysis will determine the degree of relationship between the three pathogenic treponemes and make it possible to decide which of them is the closest to their ancestor.

For the moment a decision on that matter cannot be made on a purely biological basis. The chief considerations must still be historical and geographic. Hackett's hypothesis, which gives the right of primogeniture to *Tr. carateum,* seems to me incompatible with his guess on the Afro-Asian origin of that disease. According to modern taxonomic principles, particularly according to the cladistic rules of Hennig and Brundin, a species that is isolated in a territory at the edge of the geographical area in which its group has expanded should not be considered plesiomorphous or primitive. That is precisely the case with *Tr. carateum,* if its origin is to be situated in the center of the Old World. If we admit that it is the conservative branch of pathogenic treponemes, its provenance must be the tropical zones of the New World. We can suppose that, in the Americas, natural selection among mutants produced *Tr. pallidum,* which can flourish in temperate regions. Once it had spread over the world, from the fifteenth century onward, this germ caused endemic syphilis and venereal syphilis. Only in relatively recent times, when it was restored to a hot, moist climate in equatorial Africa, did it sire the microbe *Tr. pertenue,* the specific agent of yaws. Although this hypothesis runs counter to common notions, no fact now known really contradicts it.

But I favor a different historical explanation. The original treponematosis was, in my opinion, indeed a disease that mankind inherited from the ancestors of his species. For the initial phase, I accept Cockburn's hypothesis. But, believing as I do in the specificity of the three extant pathogenic treponemes, I suggest that the original one produced, in the Old World, a plesiomorphous branch, *Tr. pertenue*. Yaws, not pinta, is the ancient clinical manifestation of this microbial group. From remote times, yaws flourished in hot, moist, forested regions, but it was never able to reach the territory of the great Mediterranean civilizations in significant proportions. In America, which it reached via the Bering land-bridge, the original germ had a different biological evolution. It bifurcated into *Tr. carateum* and *Tr. pallidum*, with the first, more conservative branch confined to tropical zones, and the second, an apomorphous one, fit to conquer the world. Introduced from Haiti into Europe by sailors in the fifteenth century, *Tr. pallidum* spread rapidly over the three continents of the Old World, producing either venereal or endemic syphilis, depending on sociocultural circumstances. Pockets of endemic syphilis existed in the nineteenth and twentieth centuries on the Balkan peninsula, notably in Bosnia. Historical research shows that these pockets are relatively recent, not earlier than the seventeenth century, and that endemic syphilis was preceded there by sporadic cases of venereal syphilis.[19] In any case, the Greek world knew of no syphilitic disease, no treponematosis. There might have been scattered cases brought in by way of contacts with black Africa, specifically cases of yaws, but that disease could not propagate in an environment so hostile to the survival of its specific germ.

The Mythology of Venereal Plague

Trustworthy historians like Ackerknecht and Henschen inform us that both the experience and the concept of the venereal transmission of pathological states were acquired at the dawn of human history and incorporated into archaic myths: the Assyrian poem that tells of the trials of Gilgamesh, the legend of Dionysus, and, above all, the story in the Bible (Numbers 25) of the disease that afflicted several thousand Israelites after their debauchery with the daughters of the Moabites.[20] Yet it is surprising, if this is truly the rational kernel of certain myths, that philosophers and physicians of the classical age did not know enough to distinguish it and lay it bare. The fact is that no author from antiquity expresses clearly and directly the notion of infection by sexual contact. Were they blinded by the appeal of theories that left no place for magical defilements of this kind? Or were they really lacking in actual experience of venereal disease? And if so, isn't the blindness then ours, when we project an empirical content onto myths that is based on our own knowledge where once there was only a notion of punishment for breaking a tabu?

The notion of punishment is not just antiquity's prerogative. Medical and historical writings of the eighteenth and the first half of the nineteenth century are still imbued with it. For a goodly number of historians of medicine prior to Pasteur, Koch, Neisser, and Schaudinn, that is, before the discovery of the real nature of contagion and when the etiology of venereal diseases was not yet securely established, the hoary antiquity of syphilis and other venereal diseases was "proven" indirectly by means that a modern reader would consider not only unsatisfactory but also inadequate, inept, and even stupefying. For example, Julius Rosenbaum (1807–74), a physician at Halle and a broadly educated humanist, was convinced he had proved the existence of syphilis in Greco-Roman times by laying out irrefutable documentation of certain erotic practices and morals that he considered to be corrupt. I cannot resist the temptation to quote his methodological justification (I could not summarize it without distorting its content and losing the flavor):

> The reproduction or preservation of a species being a law imposed on the genital organs, it is not likely that this function, when exercised in conformity with its purpose, would produce disease in these parts. Indeed, experience shows that, in a rational marriage whose natural goal is the procreation of children, diseases of the genital organs are rare or do not exist at all. Therefore we are obliged to admit that there still exist other kinds of sexual functions beyond the natural goal, or at least in which that goal becomes secondary; these other types of function have sensual pleasure as their only purpose, and the use of the genital organs to achieve this purpose is lust. However, just as all abuse redounds not only to the detriment of the organ but of the organism as a whole, the same must be true for the sexual organs. In lust, in the abuse of the pleasures of love—that is wherein we must seek the principal cause of genital diseases. An exact knowledge of the history of lust becomes indispensable in order to arrive at the history of diseases of the reproductive organs.[21]

According to Rosenbaum, syphilis derives from the abuse of the genital organs, which were devised for procreation and not enjoyment. In that nineteenth-century universe, he is not by any means the only one to imagine venereal disease as the price humanity must pay for its quest for sexual pleasure, for the "excitation of debilitating titillation." In this view, the etiology of syphilis is more moral than medical. Since every venereal disease was essentially just a form of divine punishment, the historian of syphilis and all other diseases involving the genitals was obliged to study in detail the sins of all peoples and all historical periods. This is why, after a hypocritical sigh ("what a sad task it is for the historian to pursue the degradation of humanity down to its most hideous details"), Rosenbaum exposes with courage (his term) and not without a certain delight (evident but not confessed) all the "lubricious" sexual practices that for him are the cause of syphilis and so represent arguments in favor of the early occurrence of the disease. He goes so far as to assert the syphilitic nature of certain "Syrian ulcers," particularly in connection with the masterly description of diphtheria by Aretaeus of Cappadocia, since for him they are the fatal consequence of fellatio, just as *leukê* and aphthae are "just retribution" for cunnilingus.[22]

For the modern historian, debauchery, supposing that this moral term can be part of a discourse about social behavior, can only be one factor among many in the propagation of venereal diseases. Their appearance must be based on the presence of certain microorganisms. The existence of venereal diseases should be proved either by paleopathological examinations or medical exegesis of the clinical descriptions of the past. Did diseases transmitted by sexual intercourse really exist in ancient Greece? To answer this question, I will review the literary evidence on diseases of the external genitals, and so that nothing significant will be overlooked, I will not limit my survey to venereal disease in the strict sense.

Gonorrhea, Spermatorrhea, and Leukorrhea

In modern times, surely no venereal disease has been better known and, at least before antibiotics, more common than gonorrhea. It is a contagious disease caused by a pyogenic bacterium, the gonococcus *(Neisseria gonorrhoeae)*. As a rule it is transmitted by coitus, and in its acute phase it causes urethritis in men or vulvovaginitis in women. Frequently the infection propagates in the genito-urinary tract, extends into adjacent organs, and becomes chronic. It can produce pathological symptoms in joints, skin, and eyes.

The inflammatory reaction of tissues in the presence of the gonococcus is not specific. As a result, diagnosis of gonorrhea is not possible through osteoarchaeological investigation. The etiological interpretation of ancient clinical descriptions that may relate to this disease is very uncertain, since instances of urethritis and vulvovaginitis comparable to those produced by the gonococcus can also be produced by other germs (staphylococci, intestinal bacteria, and so forth). So it is not surprising that historians do not agree whether gonorrhea existed in the Greco-Roman world. According to E. H. Ackerknecht and M. L. Brodny, it was mentioned in the Bible and described by Hippocrates, Celsus, and Galen.[23] Folke Henschen thinks he recognizes it in certain passages of the *Papyrus Ebers,* the Hippocratic corpus, and the work of Aretaeus of Cappadocia.[24] Adalberto Pazzini rejects this retrospective diagnosis and asserts that gonorrhea was unknown in antiquity.[25] The same negative view is expressed vigorously by several British doctors who have recently researched the whole issue.[26] The critical examination of literary evidence does not make it possible to resolve the debate.[27] On the one hand, the diagnosis of gonorrhea is compatible with certain ancient descriptions, and on the other, for none of those descriptions is it the sole interpretation possible.

The origin of the germ causing gonorrhea is unknown. It probably came into being as a result of the mutation of a Neisseriaceae saprophyte, but in our present state of knowledge that is an undatable event. For Oriel, it took place after the end of the Old World.[28] I prefer to push back the birth of the gonococcus to a date prior to the classical era of Mediterranean civilization, since it seems to me that such a hypothesis takes better account of the myths of venereal plague, the relatively common references to urethritis, semen discharge, and vulvovaginitis in the ancient medical treatises, and, last, the biological properties of the germ itself.

The name of this disease, gonorrhea, in Neo-Latin scientific terminology and several modern languages is a term that goes back to Greco-Roman antiquity and that originally meant "semen discharge." Although the Greek substantive *gonórrhoia* occurs only in relatively late authors (Aretaeus, Galen, Soranus, Oribasius), a verbal formula occurs as early as Hippocrates. For modern physicians, this term has nothing to do with its original sense, since it applies to the discharge of pus by the urethra or the vagina and not to the discharge of sperm. Greek physicians used it to designate what they saw as a real loss of the masculine or feminine seminal substances, that is, as spermatorrhea in men and some forms of leukorrhea in women. When the Hippocratic writers speak of semen discharge in men, that is actually what they intend: they are referring to pollutions, frequent acts of intercourse, and pathological spermatorrhea, not the "gonorrhea" of modern medicine.[29]

The Hippocratic description of "dorsal phthisis" *(nōtiàs phthísis),* a disease that "especially affects newlyweds and men who have surrendered themselves to sexual pleasure" and whose chief symptom is abundant spermatorrhea following urination or defecation, is evidence of an inflammation of the seminal vesicles in the context of a complex nosological entity.[30] This type of vesiculitis may well be due to the gonococcus, but that is only one among many possibilities. Several ancient cases of spermatorrhea are doubtless functional, nervous disorders. It remains no less certain that other such cases were caused by nonspecific pyogenic bacteria or the tubercle bacillus. The predilection of such germs for the genito-urinary tract is obvious from the importance given in Hippocratic texts to clinical pictures that correspond in modern pathological terminology to pyelonephritis and cystitis. Both are often due to secondary infection of a primary urinary lithiasis.[31] Thus a Hippocratic text mentions as a common event the formation of "abscesses in the urethra" that "suppurate and burst."[32]

The third book of the *Epidemics* contains a description of the principal diseases observed on the island of Thasos by a Hippocratic physician, probably Hippocrates himself, during an especially rainy year in the last decade of the fifth century B.C.[33] In the spring of that year "erysipelas" began, abscesses in the throat and on the gums, *kaûsoi* ("ardent fevers") and "phrenitis"; there were also other affections:

> Many had aphthae *(aphthṓdea)* and sores *(helkṓdea)* in the mouth. Fluxes *(rheúmata)* about the genitals were copious;[34] sores *(helkṓmata),* tumors *(phúmata)* external and

internal; the swellings which appear in the groin *(boubônas)*. Watery inflammations of the eyes *(ophthalmíai)*, chronic and painful; growths on the eyelids, external and internal, in many cases destroying the sight, and which are called "figs" *(sûka)*. There were also often growths on other sores, particularly in the genitals.[35]

When interpreting this Hippocratic text in the light of modern pathological knowledge, nineteenth-century physicians separated the eye symptoms from those of the mouth and genitals. The first, they said, were due to trachoma.[36] Though it is as vague as can be, the description of genital symptoms here was considered the best direct proof of the existence of a venereal disease, either syphilis or gonorrhea, in classical antiquity.[37] However, in 1937 a Turkish dermatologist, Hulúsi Behçet, identified a particular syndrome that combines uveitis and hypopyon in the eye with the formation of aphthae in the mouth and ulceration of the genitals.[38] Behçet's disease (or Adamantiades-Behçet syndrome) also brings with it, aside from the basic clinical triad, attacks of fever, skin eruptions, neurologic lesions, and retinal complications that can lead to blindness. The agreement between Hippocrates' clinical sketch and modern descriptions of this disease is perfect but for one detail, an outward excrescence of the eyelids.[39] Nowadays this is a sporadic disease linked to certain geographic areas, with a clear predilection for the Mediterranean basin, especially the lands that once constituted the ancient Greek world, and Japan. Men contract it much more often and suffer from it more grievously than women. A genetic predisposition to it is confirmed by the high frequency of the tissue histocompatibility antigen HLA-B5 in people with the disease. Behçet's disease results from the action of an exogenous factor on an organism with a specific immunological predisposition. That the exogenous factor is viral seems very likely, although this has yet to be really proven.

In the Hippocratic text cited above, there is mention of *boubônas* 'buboes, swellings in the groin.' To be sure, Greek physicians did not know about lymph nodes and their physiological and pathological role, but that did not prevent them from noticing causal relationships between suppurating wounds, transient fevers, and swelling in the joints of the arms and legs.[40] Aside from this text, the medical writers of the classical period noticed no link between genital ulcerations and buboes. It is true that in Aristophanes' *Lysistrata* the herald, who has an erection for all to see, is asked the question, "Do you have a bubo from all your traveling?"[41] This is a joke meant to draw attention to the physiological state of the character who has just come on stage, but a bit of medical-historical information can be drawn from it: Aristophanes' public knew that travel, with the risk it at that time entailed of infection to the lower limbs, could produce swollen glands in the groin. But I have not found the least allusion anywhere in the literature of the classical era—in comedy, erotic texts, or elsewhere—to swelling in the groin in conjunction with ulceration of the penis or urethritis. Galen, a Greco-Roman physician of the second century A.D., knew of the link; he explicitly says that swelling in the groin is at times a consequence of genital ulcers. He is amazed that the ancient practitioners speak of this so rarely, and he tries to explain their silence by stating that "those with fever caused by swelling in the groin do not summon a physician but prefer to take care of themselves."[42]

In the gynecological discussions of the Hippocratic corpus, a distinction is drawn between the discharge of female semen and other common forms of white or yellowish spotting, but it is difficult, if not impossible, to grasp the pathological reality on which the distinction is based: "If the semen flows *(ḕn dè ho gónos aporrhêē̃)* pure and uninterrupted, the woman does not like to have sex with her husband; she does not become pregnant; her loins hurt; there is a stubborn fever, weakness, and fainting; sometimes the uterus is out of position."[43] This description of "gonorrhea" in the etymological sense of the term is at once true-to-life and also lacking in differentiating information. It relates a syndrome that has been observed with admirable precision but that has no specific significance for modern pathology. It would be useless to wish to provide it with a modern diagnosis, since a substantial number of different diseases have these same symptoms. Chronic, continuous, and nonfetid leukorrhea, dyspareunia, sterility, lower back pain, fever, adynamia—all this can be found in chronic gonorrhea or, even more readily, in a patient with tuberculosis, nonspecific salpingo-oophoritis, hormonal disturbances, and many other diseases.

Writers of the Imperial period, and Galen in particular, will tell us that female "gonorrhea" is not a disease of the lower genital tract through which the semen flows but a functional disorder of the vessels that constitute and concentrate it in the abdomen.[44] The treatise *Diseases of Women,* II, subdivides leukorrhea into five types, but this multiplying of the symptomatic categories is done in such a way as to confuse the modern clinician instead of helping him define the pathological processes behind the ancient nosological categories.[45] Here is the first of the five:

> The discharge is white like a donkey's urine; the face swells, especially below the eyes; they are watery and look poor; their shine is gone; they are bleary and eyesight is cloudy. The complexion is sallow, and the skin is covered with vesicles. The lower abdomen swells. A reddish, small, watery, malignant eruption gradually spreads over the jaws. The legs get swollen; if you press them with a finger, an imprint forms as in dough. The mouth fills with saliva. The woman has pain in her *kardía* on an empty stomach, and she vomits some kind of sour water. If she goes up an incline, she is soon out of breath. She suffocates; her legs get cold; her knees are wobbly. Aphthae form in her mouth. The uterus is unnaturally dilated and weighs like lead on its orifice. There are shooting pains in the thighs. All the lower limbs grow cold, from the lower abdomen to the feet; the soles of the feet are numb, and she cannot walk. In these cases a cure is difficult, since the patient

is no longer youthful, and the symptoms go from bad to worse, unless by a stroke of luck the disease spontaneously disappears.[46]

According to Paul Diepgen, who was an experienced gynecologist and medical historian, the description of this first type of leukorrhea "recalls the clinical picture of chlorosis or pernicious anemia."[47] M.-T. Fontanille sees here "the description of pelvic peritonitis with a generalization of the infection and serious anemia."[48] I would add that a diagnosis of myxedema is also possible, nor can one exclude the diagnosis of several other systemic diseases that disturb the metabolism as well as both cardiac and renal function. Whatever the case may be, it is only indirectly a disease of the external genital organs. Contrary to opinions expressed in the nineteenth century by some medical historians and repeated since then only by inertia, it is hard to admit that this disease has venereal origins.

Generally speaking, the cases of white, yellow, and brown spotting described in the Hippocratic treatises correspond to common types of parasitic, mycotic, or bacterial leukorrhea and minor metrorrhagia. Biological arguments make it very likely that such infestations of the genital organs with protozoa and fungi are both ancient and ubiquitous. Greek women in the time of Hippocrates are likely to have suffered from vaginitis caused by *Trichomonas vaginalis* and *Candida albicans* or by ancestors of this parasitic species. *T. vaginalis,* a flagellate discovered in 1836 by A. Donné "in purulent substances and the products of secretions from male and female genitals," causes foaming, yellowish or greenish, fetid leukorrhea that irritates the vulval region. Trichomoniasis is often but not necessarily transmitted by sexual contact. No classical text describes this disease as a separate entity, but it is probably included in nosological descriptions that speak of yellowish, fetid discharges. The microscopic fungus *C. albicans* is to blame for several pathological states: a vulvovaginitis marked by leukorrhea; a mycosis localized in the large folds of skin and the nails; rarely, septicemic complications; and, last, some common diseases of the mouth, tongue, and bronchi. The most typical of the latter is thrush, a candidiasis of the mucous membranes of the mouth. Its appearance is characteristic: erythematous patches with a creamy white membrane in the middle that are scattered throughout the mouth in small children and malnourished adults. The white membranes of thrush were the points of departure for the studies in 1841 by F. D. Berg in Sweden and, independently of him, by D. Gruby and C. Robin in France, that succeeded in isolating the mycotic agent and demonstrating its pathogenic role. Ancient accounts of leukorrhea do not permit a differential diagnosis of vaginal candidiasis, but the existence of its germ is confirmed by the mention of aphthous eruptions in children and pregnant women. Probably the aphthae in newborns discussed in the Hippocratic *Aphorisms* are related to thrush.[49] According to Galen's commentary to the *Aphorisms,* aphthae in the mouths of breast-feeding babies are superficial, inflamed ulcerations of the soft tissue that come from bad milk or the inability to digest milk properly.[50]

Other Diseases of the External Genitals

Hippocratic aphthae are not localized in the mouth alone. These discrete, whitish, superficial ulcerations can also be found on a woman's genitals[51] and even in the trachea.[52] According to Jacques Jouanna, the change in meaning from a mouth ulcer to one on the orifice of the uterus was facilitated by the fact that both openings are called *stóma* in Greek.[53] The "aphthous fluxions" in pregnant women[54] are especially reminiscent of candidiasis, a disease that occurs during pregnancy, especially in the last trimester, and is marked by copious discharges and whitish ulcerations on the vaginal walls. The trachea becomes aphthous from tuberculosis.[55] The genital aphthae in Hippocratic texts probably include candidiasis, aphthosis in the modern sense (especially Behçet's disease), lymphogranuloma venereum (LGV or Nicolas-Favre disease), tuberculous lesions, and vulvovaginal diphtheria, as well as ulcerations due to nonspecific pyogenic bacteria and several other dermatological diseases.

Herpes eruptions can also appear as aphthae. The presence of genital herpes simplex (in the modern sense of the term)[56] in patients of the Hippocratic doctors seems to me to be strongly suggested by a clinical observation that in cases of the formation of *phlúktainai* 'blisters' associated with menstrual flow, it happens that "the edges of the [genital] labia are ulcerated *(helkō̃thē)*."[57] Though these vesicular or blistery eruptions, when they are situated on the orifice of the uterus,[58] could be nabothian follicles, that they are herpetic is practically assured by the statement that they appear during menstruation and cause erosion on the edges of the labia. I note that a passage in the sixth book of the *Epidemics* probably alludes to herpes labialis (cold sores), which coincide with accesses of fever.[59] This disease, in its genital and labial forms as well as when it produces aphthae in the mouth, is assuredly relatively benign, more of a nuisance than a danger. But that does not diminish the significance of its mention in the Hippocratic corpus for the medical historian: it constitutes proof of an ancient pedigree for at least one kind of herpesvirus, a viral agent that is perfectly adapted to the human being with which it lives, in most cases, as an almost totally unnoticed parasite. It has recently become known that it can also produce serious complications, that infection with genital herpes in the mother can actually be fatal to the newborn child.

As for lymphogranuloma venereum (a sexually transmitted disease typified by a small, pseudo-herpetic, genital or anal chancre and severe adenopathy in the groin) and nonspecific reappearing urethritis, their existence in the ancient Greco-Roman world seems to me very likely, given the recent discovery that they are actually caused by the same microbe, *Chla-*

mydia trachomatis, as endemic trachoma. Trachoma was the bane of ancient Egypt, and there is every reason to believe that it did not spare other coasts of the Mediterranean.

Often in the past, but rarely nowadays, women developed ulcers on their external genitals after giving birth. Such puerperal ulcers are caused by the maceration and superinfection of obstetric tears and scratches. Here is a description of one from the Hippocratic corpus: it begins by a local inflammation "resembling an aphtha" and ends with the formation of a "mushroom," an excessive scar that closes the two lips.[60] Ancient Greek doctors also knew of condylomas, which are soft, wartlike growths of viral origin that can be encumbering. In men, they occur on the glans penis and the prepuce and are relatively small. In women, they are localized on the vulva and the external part of the vagina. In both sexes, they can develop around the anus. The author of the Hippocratic treatis *Wounds* says that a plant called parthenion microphyllon removes the *thúmia* from the prepuce.[61] Celsus explains that for the Greek physicians tumors resembling warts have special names depending on their shape. Thus "that which is named thumion projects above the surface like a little wart, narrow near the skin, wider above, hardish and at the top very rough. . . . The worst, however, are situated on the genitals, and there they bleed the most."[62] For the Latin medical writers, condylomas resemble figs rather than thyme flowers, whence their Latin names *ficus* (especially in its adjectival form, *ficosus*) and *marisca*. An assumption that this disease is transmitted by sexual congress, especially pederastic, underlies some satiric lines in Juvenal and Martial. It is possible that the assumption is correct. In the classical period, condylomas were successfully removed by surgery.[63]

One Hippocratic author speaks of ulcers *(hélkea)* that seem particularly dangerous.[64] According to Paul Diepgen, they sound like cancer.[65] Unfortunately, the Greek text contains no details that would make it possible to support such a diagnosis. Serious ulcerations of the genital organs are produced by tuberculosis, chancroid, neoplastic diseases, and some others already mentioned in this chapter. Nowadays we know that tuberculosis can be directly transmitted genitally. A man with renal or epididymo-orchitic tuberculosis can give his female sexual partner a vulval or cervical tuberculous chancre. A diagnosis of urogenital tuberculosis is very likely in the suicide of a Roman couple. The husband suffered from a chronic, ulcerous disease of the private parts.[66] Chancroid or soft chancre, that is, the venereal disease caused by *Haemophilus ducreyi,* is not described in the classical and Hellenistic Greek texts, but its existence has been recognized by some in the medical encyclopedia of Celsus.[67] There is also a historical example that is doubly dubious, in that it is both late and embedded in a moralizing narrative: in Alexandria, in the fourth century A.D., a fallen eremite is said to be afflicted with a corrosive ulcer on his penis.[68] This is the moment to recall as well the unfortunate fate of the Alexandrian rhetorician Apion (beginning of the first century A.D.): "He was circumcised of necessity, to treat an ulcer on his genitals; moreover, the circumcision did him no good, as his flesh became gangrenous and he died in excruciating pain."[69] Josephus tells this story with the explicit goal of showing how a traitor to the ancestral laws suffered by divine will a symbolic punishment befitting his impiety. Even if it were historically reliable, it would be hard to pin down the diagnosis: phagedenic ulcer? Kaposi's sarcoma? or cancer of the penis? Cancers of the penis or the vulva are not clearly described until the Imperial period (Celsus, Galen, etc.), but it is hard to believe that they have not existed since the remotest times in human history. When the Hippocratic writers speak of discharges resembling beef glaze that are so corrosive that they produce skin ulcerations, the modern physician immediately thinks of cancer of the uterus.[70] The diagnosis is very likely, if not certain. Finally, it is difficult to know what to make of the "disease of the genital organs" contracted by Otanes, a Persian general of the fifth century B.C. Herodotus's narrative tells us only that his sickness, in conjunction with a dream, induced him to repopulate the island of Samos.[71]

Chapter Six

LEPROSY
The Gradual Spread of an Endemic Disease

Most scholars who have taken up the history of leprosy or of tuberculosis have made the mistake of treating their subject in isolation, without concern for the historical and epidemiological consequences of the kinship between the microbes of the two diseases. This strong kinship—it consists of a close genealogical relationship between the bacilli that cause the diseases—demands an approach not unlike that of the paired lives of Plutarch: a parallel presentation of both diseases, concluding with a confrontation between them.

Leprosy is a chronic, infectious disease that mainly affects the skin, the peripheral nervous system, and bones. It is caused by a specific germ, *Mycobacterium leprae,* that was discovered by A. Hansen in 1871. Human beings are the only source of contagion; its manner of transmission, which can take place through direct contact as well as by the intermediary of common objects or animal vectors, is still poorly understood. As a general rule, it seems that a single infection by the microbe is not sufficient: contamination takes place as the result of repeated and prolonged contact. The clinical evolution of leprosy is very slow, but in the absence of modern chemotherapy the progress of the disease is inexorable. It results in deformities and mutilations that provoke communal disgust. Although in the short run it is less dangerous than an acute fever or a cancer, leprosy produces such horrifying external effects that it was considered, especially in the Middle Ages, no less a curse than the plague.

Four clinical forms of the disease have been distinguished, two of which are fundamental: lepromatous leprosy and tuberculoid leprosy. The third form is the initial stage of the disease, indeterminate leprosy, which then evolves into one of the two main types or the fourth, intermediary form. The basic lesion, which enables early diagnosis and which ancient physicians found especially striking, is a hypochromic macule, a nonelevated spot whose degree of discoloration varies from a slight decrease in pigment to an ashen color. The initial spots are isolated and not numerous; their preferred locale is the face, but they can also occur on the buttocks, the legs, the arms, or the trunk. Contour and size vary greatly. Lepromatous leprosy is the most serious clinical form of the disease. It is characterized by (1) papules and nodules (lepromas) that are distributed fairly symmetrically over the face, on the inner surfaces of the limbs, and over the rest of the body, (2) diffuse mucocutaneous infiltrations, and (3) erythematous or coppery, polymorphous macules that may contain anesthetized zones. The skin infiltrations and nodules can give the face an appearance that evokes the head of a lion (leontiasis or facies leontina): general swelling, erythema, pronounced wrinkles, ears becoming full of nodules and detaching, hypertrophied lips and nose, loss of beard and eyebrows. Tuberculoid leprosy is a relatively benign form whose chief skin manifestations are pale spots that are clearly demarcated and numb. A bilateral attack on the peripheral nerves causes pain, loss of feeling, muscle weakness, and trophic disorders (ulcerations, resorption of bones). Intermediary or borderline leprosy has clinical features that lie between these two polar forms of the disease.

In order to arrive at a satisfactory explanation of the origin and initial dissemination of leprosy and, more especially, to formulate a valid hypothesis on the time of its arrival and on its prevalence in the eastern Meditteranean, it is necessary to survey and reconcile evidence deriving from five distinct domains: osteoarchaeology, iconographic representations, the oldest literary sources, the geographical distribution of the disease in modern times, and biological considerations about the properties of the germ and its relationship to the tubercle bacillus.

Leprosy leaves an enduring imprint on bones. The exact morphology of these lesions was practically unknown until the osteoarchaeological investigations of Vilhelm Møller-Christensen. Since 1948 this paleopathologist has studied skeletons from a lepers' cemetery in Naestved, Denmark, and he has described bone stigmata whose specific character has been confirmed clinically and radiologically on living victims of the disease.[1] Beginning with the initial phase of leprous infection, there are observable, pathognomonic lesions on the bones of the face. Leopold Glück, a dermatologist from Sarajevo in Bosnia, identified these lesions as early as 1897 in an anatomopathological and clinical study, but the significance of his observations was not grasped, probably because of the lack of radiological evidence (X-rays had just been discovered at the time).[2] So the definition of a syndrome that is very useful for early diagnosis of leprosy had to await the work of a specialist in osteoarchaeology. It was not until 1952 that Møller-Christensen and his co-workers described the facies leprosa, an osteoarchaeological entity whose medical equivalent was dubbed Bergen's syndrome in 1953. This entity is characterized by the following pathological conditions: atrophy of the anterior nasal spine; erosion of the lateral margins of the nose; atrophy of the alveolar processes of the maxilla, often accompanied by loss of the incisors; inflammatory modifications of the hard palate. The surface of the atrophied parts resembles pumice stone. Leprosy also leaves characteristic traces on the tibia and the fibula (periostitis and striation) and on the small bones of the hand and foot (atrophy beginning in the distal phalanges and progressing proximally to the metatarsals or metacarpals).[3]

After an examination of approximately 20,000 specimens, Møller-Christensen was able to confirm the presence of leprous lesions on eight individuals who lived prior to A.D. 1000. Although they come from three different regions, all eight cases date from the same, surprisingly late era: the sixth century A.D.[4] The specimens from Egypt were the first described, in 1910. They consist of two Coptic mummies found in the same spot (El-Bigha near Aswan) and dating from the same era (about A.D. 500). One of these mummies, a male, presents typical bone destruction on his hands and feet. Its case was recognized as leprosy at the first osteoarchaeological examination. The second mummy, a female, has the characteristic marks of facies leprosa. At the time of its first examination, the existence of a chronic rhinitis was affirmed, but its true nature could not be specified. During a visit to Cambridge, Møller-Christensen made a diagnosis of leprosy from the skull and the small bones of this Coptic specimen.[5]

I stress the absence of any trace of leprosy on the human remains from Pharaonic Egypt. However, in a recent publication, the Polish researcher T. Dzierzykray-Rogalski brings to light a find of truly exceptional significance: of 31 skulls found in a necropolis of the second century B.C. in the Daklah Oasis, 4 had typical leprous stigmata. Although the great majority of the inhabitants of this oasis were Negroid during the Ptolemaic era, the skulls in question are not. Situated in the Libyan desert, the Daklah Oasis is not only the largest but also the most isolated of the seven major oases of ancient Egypt. Accordingly, the Polish paleopathologist suggests that it may have served as a deportation zone for lepers of the Egyptian elite during the reign of the Lagides.[6]

For France, about 1,000 skeletons dating from the Neolithic era to A.D. 1000 have been examined; a single skull from the Merovingian era (sixth century) has leprous stigmata. Five cases of leprosy have been described in bones from Great Britain dating from the period A.D. 550–650, to which two doubtful cases from the fourth and fifth centuries must be added.[7] No leper has been found among several hundred ancient inhabitants of the Jordan Valley (cemetery of Lachish, near Jericho); the bones were very closely scrutinized in the expectation of a diagnosis of the disease.[8] Moreover, all paleopathological research in the New World has failed to produce evidence for the pre-Columbian existence of leprosy.

In 1970, John L. Angel identified a possible case of leprosy that is of extraordinary importance, if his diagnosis is accepted.[9] The skeleton in question is that of a man from the Early Bronze Age found at Karataş in Lycia *(416 Ka.)*. The metatarsal bones of this subject, who died at age 40, are atrophic and pitted on their anterior extremity, in a way that is characteristic but not truly pathognomonic of leprosy. There is a kind of symmetry in the lesions affecting metatarsals 1, 2, and 3 on the left side and metatarsals 1, 2, 3, and 4 on the right, a feature that favors a diagnosis of leprosy. Unfortunately, it cannot be confirmed by typical stigmata on the facial bones. A nonleprous etiology for this atrophy of the lower extremities can be devised, such as a serious metabolic, toxic, infectious polyneuropathy, or gangrene following a crushing wound. If this man from Karataş is leprous, his case is doubly interesting, first, since it is the oldest concrete evidence for the disease, and second, as proof of the early presence of Hansen's bacillus in Greece. It is a shame that the ambiguity of the lesions makes it necessary to consider the case a possible indicator rather than a sure argument.

At the risk of appearing repetitious, I underline the following cautions: the absence of traces of a disease on the bones of a region and a period does not constitute proof of the actual absence of it in the region and during the period in question. It is only a potent argument against the endemic presence of the disease in question. The results of osteoarchaeological investigation do not, therefore, exclude the sporadic existence of leprosy in the ancient Greek world, even if we refrain from a sure interpretation of specimen *416 Ka.*

Artistic Representations of Leprosy

Leprosy is a disfiguring, mutilating disease. Its appearance is unforgettable. Might not an artist's eye, like the photographer's lens, have fixed upon the image of such a horrible disease (in horror there is always an element of the sacred and bewitching) and might not his hand have reproduced it in an iconographic message that modern medicine can decipher? Historians of disease have pored over ancient artistic representations of the human body in the hope of discovering in them the deformities that would justify a retrospective diagnosis of leprosy.

Such a medico-historical process is full of pitfalls. Here is an example: since the discovery of the golden masks of Mycenae, scholars have tried to detect the imprint of leprosy on their hieratic faces. The idea elicited passionate debate at the end of the nineteenth century among certain German historians.[10] Yet an unprejudiced glance at these splendid products of the Mycenaean goldsmiths' craft is enough to show that the so-called pathological signs (loss of eyebrows, subsidence of the nose) are nothing more than the consequences of stylization.

The medical and art historians who believe they have found the ravages of leprosy on the faces of a series of Hellenistic figurines use more serious criteria. Thus a small terra cotta statue that probably dates from the third century B.C. has been described as the representation of an individual whose facial marks, dress, and overall bearing show that he suffered from leprosy.[11] This object, once kept in the Polytechnic Institute of Athens, is now in the National Archaeological Museum there (inv. no. 5871). The retrospective diagnosis of leprosy seems plausible, but not convincing enough to make it certain that the figurine's creator actually saw someone with the disease.

Leprosy has been mentioned in the description of several Hellenistic clay heads belonging to the collections of the Louvre. One of these statuettes was found at Troy, all the others at Smyrna. After examining them personally, I disagree with Félix Regnault's appraisal of the Trojan head. The deformities it presents have nothing to do with the usual stigmata of leprosy.[12] The terra cotta figurines originating in Smyrna are of two sorts. In the first, the facial expression is horrifying; according to Simon Besques, it is "a death's head, or a leper at the last stage of the disease, with teeth exposed, a nose without flesh, a hole in the forehead that may be a wound."[13] In the second, the subject's nose is crushed, its lips thickened, its eye sockets gnarled, and its face furrowed.[14] In molding the first kind of head, with a face deprived of flesh and without the infiltrations that suggest lepromas, the Smyrnan coroplast wanted to create an image of death. He produced it without being inspired by any special disease and without necessarily having seen a leper. As for the second type, the diagnosis of leprosy is plausible but not at all obligatory. On these heads, most of which express horrible suffering, there is nothing pathognomonic of leprosy. That is only one nosological explanation among many others that are no less likely.

Similar caution is appropriate regarding two Hellenistic figurines in limestone found at Alexandria. Angélique Panayotatou presents them as an artistic image "of the terrible disease that so ravaged Egypt."[15] As evidence for her diagnosis of leprosy, Panayotatou notes "the absence of eyelashes and eyebrows, the thickening of the skin, the nose partly destroyed, the nostrils shut by the thickened skin, the thickening of the lips, the projecting upper jaw."[16] All this appears convincing indeed, but unfortunately the description is based on the presumed diagnosis: it evokes the disease with much greater force than the photographs of the objects themselves. The rounded eyes, the absence of eyebrows, the nose more swollen than eaten away, the thick lips, and the mouth wide open actually give the impression of a mask, of an actor in the theater, not a sick person. This impression is strengthened once comparison is made with some Alexandrian clay figures at the Benaki Museum, where the grotesque, caricatural nature of the subjects is obvious.[17] I also recall here the possible diagnosis of leprosy in the case of a Gallic limestone bust found at the source of the Seine (early Christian era).[18]

Rudolf Virchow and Ivan Bloch believed that they recognized leprosy on some pre-Columbian anthropomorphic vases from Peru and Bolivia that depict facial mutilations and tumors. But the identification has not carried conviction among specialists, who prefer to see in them uta (New World leishmaniasis), if not bartonellosis, blastomycosis, or even syphilitic gummas. However, a Canaanite clay anthropomorphic jar found during excavations of the Late Bronze Age settlement of Bet She'an in Israel and dated to about 1300 B.C.—that is, before the Hebrews' conquest of the Promised Land—shows features resembling facies leontina and strongly suggests a diagnosis of lepromatous leprosy.[19]

The Oldest Literary Evidence of Leprosy

Leprosy has long been known in the literature of ancient India.[20] It may well be that it is alluded to in a text as venerable as the hymns of the *Atharvaveda,* but there is some uncertainty. The Vedic term *kilāsa,* which is used in the archaic sacred texts and is customarily translated "leprosy" in modern Western editions and commentaries, etymologically denotes an "ashen" disease. According to its usage in classical medical works, it denotes a disease of the skin (exclusively) that presents discolorations, desquamations, and localized inflammations.[21] From the vantage point of modern pathology, that is a vague notion covering a host of skin ailments. In Vedic times, *kilāsa* may have included, in addition to other diseases of the body surface, true leprosy. However, the semantic evolution of this term in Indic medical literature suggests that leprosy was not its principal reference. A "white" disease, leukodermic and psoriatic, that corresponds to the meaning of the term *lépra* in the Hippocratic texts (discussed below), instead of its modern sense, was the dominant element in the epidemiology of dermatoses in early India.

With the great Sanskrit medical treatises, namely the collections of the Susruta and Charaka, doubt disappears: Hansen's disease is unimpeachably described in them under the name *kustha.* This term of classical Hindu nosography has two senses: a broad one, in which it designates all kinds of cutaneous diseases (the Susruta distinguishes nineteen of them), of which leprosy is just a subset; and a narrower sense, especially when prefixed by the word *maha* 'great,' in which it applies to leprosy proper in its various clinical forms.[22] According to the Susruta, *kustha* is a contagious disease transmitted either by sexual activity or by touch and respiration or by the use of objects previously handled by a diseased person.[23] This astonishingly precise knowledge of leprosy among the classical Hindu physicians—sophisticated early diagnosis, correct description of various symptoms in their proper order of appearance, precise prognosis, and awareness of the danger due to contagiousness—and the existence of legal measures concerning lepers that go back to the fourth century B.C. show that Hansen's bacillus must have been rampant in India during the first millennium B.C. and was particularly severe during the last centuries of that era.[24]

In China, leprosy is mentioned in the oldest medical treatises that have come down to us. The famous *Nei-ching,* a compendium of classical medicine, describes a disease that "swells and ulcerates the flesh . . . produces paresthesias . . ., spoils the blood, which becomes cloudy, and results in a collapse of the nasal structure, an altered skin color, and skin ulcerations."[25] The consensus of the historians of Chinese medicine is that this passage refers to true leprosy (other identifications would not be impossible, especially given the chapter in which the passage occurs). These specialists do not, unfortunately, agree on the date of this text. The edition we know comes from the eight century A.D., but the essential parts of the *Nei-ching* certainly go back much further. The question is, How much? For traditionalists, the text is a faithful record of the conversation of the legendary emperor Huang-ti in the third millennium B.C. To modern, critical historians, its origins cannot precede the fourth century B.C., and J. Needham does not hesitate to date it only to the second century B.C. Other Chinese medical texts that speak of leprosy (for instance, the *Prescriptions for Emergency* of Ko Hung, a Taoist physician of the fourth century A.D.) are all clearly later than the beginning of the Christian era.[26]

In almost all the handbooks and encyclopedic reference books that treat of the history of leprosy, it is confidently assumed that this disease raged in China from the earliest historical periods. This conviction, which has become general by virtue of its being repeated, actually rests on documentation that is both thin and weak. Its only basis is, first, the orthodox dating of the *Nei-ching* (which can no longer be upheld) and, second, the traditional interpretation of a Confucian anecdote. In the celebrated *Lun Yü* (Conversations) that were gathered by Confucius's followers, one of the disciples, Po-niu, contracted leprosy. The master, visiting him, did not wish to see him but restricted himself to touching the sick man's hand through a window; Confucius then exclaimed, "Fate kills him. For such a man to have such a disease!"[27] The event took place in the sixth century B.C. There is no doubt of the authenticity and antiquity of this story. Its source is respectable, but its purpose is moral, and the information it contains is hardly satisfactory from a medical point of view. The disease of Po-niu is not described or even specifically named: the hero suffers from *chi* 'disease (in general).' The notion of leprosy was introduced by later commentators like Pao Hsien in the first century, who accounted for Confucius's behavior on the basis of the unpleasant appearance of his disciple ("the disease," says the commentator, "was a disfiguring one").[28] It is possible that leprosy was spread throughout China during the first millennium B.C., but the silence of the documents forces us to count on its presence in that part of the Far East only in the very last centuries of the period.

Since 1937, as the result of an ingenious and bold conjecture by the Danish missionary physician and renowned Egyptologist Bendix Ebbell, a passage concluding an Egyptian medical treatise of the sixteenth century B.C. (the *Papyrus Ebers*) has been considered the oldest literary description of leprosy. However, that conjecture has been strongly criticized, and the latest edition of the text implicitly rejects any possibility of such an interpretation.[29] Without this evidence, there is no substantial sign of leprosy in Pharaonic Egypt. Paleopathological research makes its endemic presence most unlikely.

By contrast, one can reasonably share the opinion that this disease was known in Mesopotamia as early as the second millennium B.C. Since J. Oppert and C. W. Belser, pioneers in the decipherment of cuneiform inscriptions, first proposed translating the Akkadian terms *saharšubbŭ, išrubŭ,* and *garābu* as "leprosy" or at least a disease like leprosy, Assyriologists have consistently done so. The disease in question is mentioned in imprecations inscribed on milestones from the Kassite period. It "covers the whole body," and those whom it disfigures are excommunicated, chased outside the walls to live "like wild-asses." The only additional information given by Babylonian texts is not so reassuring about the traditional diagnosis: *saharšubbŭ* seems to be associated with dropsy. A disease called *sibtu* that is cited in the Code of Hammurabi as a sufficient reason to cancel a contract for the sale of a slave has been identified, uncertainly at best, with leprosy. The main argument in its favor is its parallelism with expressions used in similar Greco-Egyptian contracts.[30] The ancient Babylonians suffered from a chronic, incurable disease with symptoms on the body surface. They considered it a contagious disease, like a tabu, and their means of combating it was to isolate the victims of it. The disease is not necessarily leprosy in the modern sense; the evidence that exists is inadequate for that diagnosis. But there is more: the key to Mesopotamian leprology is a Babylonian omen text that was published only in 1957. Here is a translation of the decisive passage, as interpreted by J. V. Kinnier Wilson: "If the skin of a man exhibits white patches *(pūsu)* or is dotted with nodules *(nuqdu)*, such a man has been rejected by his god and is to be rejected by mankind."[31] Kinnier Wilson sees this text as solid proof of the existence of leprosy in ancient Mesopotamia and also, even at that time, of a clinical distinction between the two chief forms of the disease, the depigmented macular (that is, tuberculoid) type and the nodular (that is, lepromatous) one. This specialist in the history of Babylonian medicine realizes that the nosology of this civilization lacks the precision required by modern medicine and that, as a result, other diseases could be included in the "leprosy" of the past, notably pellagra. This does not negate the fact that, in his view, Hansen's disease is the major constituent of Mesopotamian leprosy. Wilson's opinion has been criticized by Stanley G. Browne, a competent leprologist whose judgment in this case seems conditioned by his previous, strongly held position against the leprous nature of the Biblical dermatosis.[32] In my opinion, the medical exegesis of the omen text VAT 7525 must be undertaken by way of a careful review of the information about leprosy among the Hebrews. The Babylonian evidence and the Biblical prescriptions have a common origin and elucidate each other.

Leprosy in Palestine and Persia

The exact meaning of the Hebrew word *Ẓarāʿat* has been much debated. It is common knowledge that the Bible declares "lepers" impure and demands their isolation, or rather, their expulsion from society. According to Leviticus, any person with a swelling, scab, or shiny spot on the skin is under suspicion of being afflicted with a lesion of *Ẓarāʿat* and must be brought before the priest *(kohen)*, who will decide if certain signs are present or not. The presence of these signs, which are carefully described in the Biblical text, requires that the person in question be declared impure. If the first examination reveals questionable signs on the skin, the priest has the person isolated for seven days. Then a second examination takes place. If the signs on the skin are unchanged, a second period of isolation—again, for seven days—is necessary before a definitive declaration of purity or impurity can be made. If declared impure, the affected person must withdraw from the community, wear torn garments, and live alone, far from the camp.[33]

To a mind not biased in favor of a purely medical interpretation for any ancient account of a pathological state, one thing is clear: *Ẓarāʿat,* the mark of divine wrath, is not a medical notion but a ritual one. It can be and is applied in the Bible not only to a person but also to clothing or a house. Clearly a house can be "leprous" only by metaphorical extension of a medical notion, while a house can be afflicted with *Ẓarāʿat* in the strict, nonmetaphorical sense of the word. The diagnosis of *Ẓarāʿat* is a matter for the priest, not the doctor, and the length of the period of isolation is determined by the ritual significance of the number seven.

Still, the description of the signs of *Ẓarāʿat* should reflect a medical reality and refer to a concrete pathology that the historian of medicine can try to outline as closely as possible.[34] To be sure, several details of the clinical picture provided in Leviticus do not correspond to true leprosy. Taken as a whole, the signs of *Ẓarāʿat* correspond to no disease known to modern dermatology. The only reasonable conclusion is that the Biblical text refers to a set of skin diseases. Some of these are relatively benign (psoriasis, vitiligo, steatoid pityriasis, perhaps favus and some forms of eczema), but they have been confused with one or even a few diseases that have serious consequences for the affected person and those around him. In short, I am in agreement with E. Jeanselme, R. G. Cochrane, J. G. Andersen, S. G. Browne, E. V. Hulse, and other recent authorities who reject a pure and simple identification of *Ẓarāʿat* with leprosy. But if the two terms and the notions they refer to actually belong to two different semantic fields, and if the pathological substratum of the first cannot simply be equated with that of the second, it does not therefore follow that the Biblical prescripts are altogether foreign to leprosy. Leprosy could well be an essential element of *Ẓarāʿat* without being its sole constituent.

A short time ago, E. V. Hulse drew attention to an error in the usual translation of the Biblical passages that describe the skin of persons suffering from *Ẓarāʿat*. The passages usually rendered "white as snow" actually say "like snow," and according to Hulse the simile suits scales that detach themselves from the skin like snowflakes, not the white color of diseased skin.[35] On this interpretation *Ẓarāʿat* is essentially a scaling disease whose ritual impurity stems precisely from such "waste" or loss of integument.[36] Whatever the case may be, Leviticus speaks explicitly of patches on the skin whose hair turns white and of lumps or nodules that recall Babylonian divinational terms as well as the early signs of leprosy. To be sure, Leviticus is not a medical handbook; the expulsion of "impure" persons is a matter of tabus, not infections in the medical sense. Still, medicine itself existed only in the shadow of ritual and without distinction from it. It is hard to believe that such a radical social rejection of persons infected with a certain disease is simply the result of mistaken religious ideas about completely benign symptoms. So I vigorously support the opinion of Julius Preuss in his masterly summation of several centuries of historical exegesis: leprosy is the only chronic skin disease whose seriousness justifies the social remedies of the Biblical legislation.[37]

The difficulties of a medical analysis of Leviticus stem from the fact that the purpose of this text is not the complete description of one or more skin diseases but the schematic specification of rules for an early, differential diagnosis of a physical state of impurity. Insofar as they are actually interested in leprosy, the authors of Leviticus are concerned only with its initial, indeterminate phase. So it is understandable that certain important signs of leprosy have escaped their attention. If such a practical definition of *Ẓarāʿat* also includes some harmless skin diseases, isn't this because it seemed preferable to err in overestimating its severity rather than risk the consequences of dangerous diseases? I add here that at least the Talmudic commentators know that spots of *Ẓarāʿat* are numb, so there is no doubt that for them the disease includes true leprosy.

Some recent writers have raised doubts about Biblical knowledge of leprosy on the basis of the negative results of osteoarchaeological research in Palestine.[38] It is a weak argument, at least given the current state of knowledge. The absence of leprous remains in a great necropolis like that of Lachish in the Jordan Valley (600 skeletons examined by V. Møller-Christensen) could be due to segregation of the diseased. And the sum-total of pre-Hebraic and Hebraic remains found throughout the Near East in scattered cites and then subjected to paleopathological tests is still too small to validate conclusions about the incidence of leprosy.

The priestly code that contains the prescripts against *Ẓarāʿat* is the most recent section of the Pentateuch. Modern Biblical scholarship dates its definitive form to the fifth or fourth century B.C., contemporary with the Hippocratic corpus. However, its content is much older. The Biblical text only codified laws that the tradition attributes to Moses and dates to the time of the Exodus from Egypt (thirteenth century B.C.). Is there any evidence that leprosy was known to the Jews at the time of their enslavement in Egypt, or did it begin to spread only after their arrival in Canaan? In fact, the anthropomorphic vase of Bet She'an (about 1300 B.C.) and some Babylonian cuneiform texts make it probable that leprosy existed in the Promised Land before the arrival of the Hebrews. It was not, then, the Jewish people who brought it with them, but even so they may have suffered from it before the thirteenth century. It is plain that the Biblical remedies for *Ẓarāʿat* are inspired by ancient Babylonian beliefs and practices, and this influence could as easily precede as follow the Egyptian period in Jewish history. If the latter, then the Jews first came into contact with leprosy in Phoenicia/Palestine, where they adopted into their religion magico-hygienic prescripts against it that the native Canaanite populations had learned from Babylonian sources. Otherwise, the Jews would have known of leprosy before the Exodus and probably even before their departure from Chaldea.

Historical sources favor the second hypothesis and actually affirm it, but they are late and must be used with great caution. The information in them may be distorted by indirect transmission, and in any case they are often contradictory and obscure. The oldest is Manetho, a Heliopolitan priest of the third century B.C. who wrote, in Greek, a history of Egypt "according to the sacred books of his land." The work itself is lost, but the Jewish historian Flavius Josephus cites extracts from it. Just like the fragments of the Alexandrian writers Chairemon and Lysimachus, who wrote after Manetho, Josephus's extracts concern "lepers" at the time of the Exodus.

Manetho tells how a Pharaoh had all the "lepers" and "other impure persons" of Egypt rounded up—80,000 of them in a single day—to put them to work in quarries far from the rest of the Egyptians. Among them were several learned priests, also victims of this horrible disease. With the priests as their guides, especially one who changed his name to Moses, the impure left Egypt, joined the shepherd-kings of Jerusalem, and made war against the Pharaoh. Chairemon tells of 250,000 "polluted" men who were exiled from Egypt as the result of a prophetic dream that came to Amenophis. And according to Lysimachus, "the Jewish people, afflicted with leprosy, scabies, and other diseases" were eliminated from Egypt in the time of King Bocchoris: the "leprous" and "itchy" were drowned and the rest were chased into the desert. The accounts of Manetho, Chairemon, and Lysimachus, which I have given in bare resumé, are full of unlikely events and deliberate slander of the Jews, especially in the case of Lysimachus. Josephus (first century A.D.) has no difficulty pointing out their contradictions and inconsistencies. However, he casts no doubt whatever on the presence of leprosy in Egypt at such an early period. It is not the presence of the disease among the Jews that offends him but the statements that Moses was afflicted with it and that only Jews contracted it.[39] Josephus is aroused because Manetho deliberately "confuses the Jewish people with a collection of leprous or otherwise diseased Egyptians."[40] Several other ancient authors echo the accounts Josephus cites, especially Tacitus, who repeats the slanders of Lysimachus, Justinus, who does the same, and Diodorus Siculus, who explains the Exodus as the result of a plague that broke out of old in Egypt. The Egyptians blamed it on the Jews, who were chosen as scapegoats because of their strange customs and ceremonies.[41]

In presenting opinions from ancient sources on the causes of the Exodus, I have taken care to put the words "leprous" and "leprosy" in quotation marks. In the extracts of his work in Josephus, Manetho designates the disease in question by the Greek word *lépra* and calls those afflicted with it *hoi leproí*. Lysimachus uses the terms *lépra* and *psṓra*. Justinus translates them into Latin as *vitiligo* and *scabies,* while Tacitus, more descriptively, calls the disease *tabes quae corpora foedaret* (a corruption that befouls bodies). Josephus himself translates the Biblical *Ẓarāʿat* by the term *lépra,*[42] as does the first translation of the Pentateuch, the Septuagint, which was produced in Alexandria during the third and second centuries B.C. This is how the word "leprosy" came into the Vulgate and acquired its medieval and modern meaning. But the problem for the historian of diseases lies in the surprising revelation that in strictly medical treatises from antiquity the term *lépra* has nothing whatever to do with the disease we now call leprosy. Was it the wish of these Jewish and Egyptian authors writing in Greek during the Hellenistic and Roman era—Manetho, Lysimachus, Josephus, and the authors of the Septuagint—to identify the Biblical term *Ẓarāʿat* with the relatively benign skin disease called *lépra* in the Hippocratic writings? Or did they use this word for lack of a better one to designate a disease still without its own name in the current medical terminology?

A passage in Herodotus, the fifth-century B.C. Greek historian, is enlightening in this regard. Of the Persians, he says that "if one of their fellow-citizens has the scaly-disease *(lépra)* or the white disease *(leúkē),* he does not go in town or trade with the other Persians; they explain that he suffers these ills for having sinned against the Sun; any foreigner with these diseases they expel from their land."[43] These Persian customs recall the Babylonian and Biblical prescripts. The comparison of three families of historical sources suggests the identity of the ailments Herodotus speaks of with the *nuqdu* and the *pūsu* of Babylonian divinational formulas as well as the *Ẓarāʿat* of Mosaic law. But why, then, does Herodotus use the word *lépra* in this context, a word used by Greek physicians of his time for a benign disease that is much too banal to justify legal repression? I believe that an explanation lies in the absence of precise technical terms for Hansen's disease in the medical vocabulary of the fifth-century Greek. When forced to inform his audience of pathological states still unknown in his own land, Herodotus, like all good ethnographers, uses approximations, words from his own language that express the essential sense of foreign terms. It is revealing that words like *leúkē* and *lépra* correspond in their etymological senses to the Babylonian terms *pūsu* and *nuqdu,* with the former referring to white spots and the latter to roughness of the skin. From Herodotus's choice of words to render the sense of the Persian nosological terms, one can conjecture that the learned caste of Persia knew of the two chief forms of leprosy (in the modern sense), a knowledge surely drawn from the sacred traditions of ancient Babylonia. One of these two forms, called *leúkē,* is characterized by pale spots, while the other, *lépra,* features swollen lumps or nodules. Herodotus's *lépra,* then, is a rough, scabrous disease rather than the scaly one modern commentators have in mind. Later on, in the second century A.D., the historian Justinus applied exactly the same mental process to the translation of Greek terms as Herodotus applied to the Persian ones. As mentioned above, he translates the twofold terminology of leprosy into the Latin words *vitiligo* and *scabies,* with due respect for their original meaning, not for their current, strictly medical usage.

Aeschylus mentions a disease comparable to leprosy called *leikhḗn.* Orestes is in danger of being afflicted with it for neglecting to avenge his father. The disease attacks flesh and devours the body, covering it with white splotches. Coming from Apollo, it marks the man afflicted with it as proscribed by divine law.[44] But it is a mythic disease with a deliberately vague and emotive profile. In classical Greek medical literature, the word *leikhḗn* designates various benign rashes and has absolutely none of the seriousness ascribed to it by Aeschylus. Isn't it likely that the tragic poet had access to the same information as Herodotus on the ancient customs of the Persians and likewise found himself without a proper medical term? To my mind, his verses confirm my intuition that true leprosy was only rarely observed by practicing physicians in the Greek world.

Lépra, Leúke, Alphós, *and the Phoenician Disease in the Hippocratic Corpus*

The etymology of the Greek noun *lépra* poses no problems. It is derived from an adjective *leprós* (rough, scabrous) whose root is a verb meaning "peel, strip off bark or skin."[45] The oldest attestation of this adjective in the sixth-century poet Hipponax has nothing to do with medicine, but in the Hippocratic corpus *leprós* occurs with its derivatives in a precise technical sense. It refers to a particular pathology of the integument and not the scaly aspect of surfaces in general. The original sense has been displaced without being altogether lost, as is clear from Nicander's use of the word *leprúnomai* in a medical poem to describe the normal state of the skin of certain snakes.[46]

In the Hippocratic texts the disease called *lépra* comes up often, but unfortunately it is never the subject of a description precise enough to ensure its identification with a clinical entity of modern medicine. What can be gleaned from the medical treatises runs counter to its being a mutilating disease like the one caused by Hansen's bacillus and even suggests relatively benign skin ailments. If we take account of the word's etymology as well, the first possibilities that come to mind are psoriasis and eczema. In classifying the main diseases by their prognosis, the treatise *Diseases,* I, places "leprosy" next to "arthritis" and "lichen" among changes in health without serious consequences, that is, not entailing death.[47] *Aphorisms* teaches us that "the diseases of spring are maniacal, melancholic, and epileptic disorders, bloody flux, quinsy, catarrh, hoarseness, cough, leprosies, lichens, loss of skin pigmentation *(alphós)*, exanthemata mostly ending in ulcerations, boils, and arthritic affections."[48] Hippocratic "leprosy" first presents itself as a kind of eruption on the skin's surface, an abscession *(apóstasis)* on the skin that results from the expulsion of humors in disequilibrium. For this reason, Hippocratic physiopathology considers hemorrhoids a guarantee against "leprosy."[49] But when the abscession of corrupt humors is not expelled downward, there is the danger of various pathological phenomena such as "suppurations, ulcers, exanthemata, peeling of the skin *(lópoi),* loss of hair, loss of skin pigmentation *(alphós),* leprosies, or their like–ills that will settle by way of considerable movement."[50] As abscessions, some skin diseases such as ulcers, suppurations, "leprosies," are at times useful for the health of the whole organism, at times harmful, and at other times without consequence.[51] When all is said and done, the Hippocratic physicians fear the suppression of a "leprous" eruption more than they fear its initial appearance. Treatment is contemplated only in exceptional cases, and even then only the mildest remedies are used: no caustics, no revulsive agents, only the topical application of salt dissolved in vinegar[52] or "quicklime in water, so as not to produce ulceration."[53]

The Hippocratic writers already had a sense of the difference between simple surface reactions on the skin and true dermatoses. Their "leprosy" can be one or the other, depending on the circumstances.[54] If it appears suddenly in the adult, it is only a passing purificatory eruption. But in its chronic, evolving form, "leprosy" is considered a disease in the fullest sense. According to the *Prorrheticon, leikhḗnes, léprai,* and *leúkai* are all pathological phenomena of the same type, "and if one of these appears in youth or childhood, or it grows little by little over a long period of time, the eruption must be considered not an abscession but a disease (*nósēma*); on the contrary, it is an abscession when the eruption makes a sudden, massive appearance." The same paragraph goes on to say that "leprosies and lichens are atrabilious diseases" and that "the younger the patient and the tenderer or plumper the affected body part, the easier the cure."[55] Another Hippocratic text asserts that "certain leprosies and articular ailments provoke itching before a rainfall."[56] The regular use of the plural form *léprai* highlights the absence of the real nosological unity of this concept within the framework of Hippocratic medicine. Instead, the term refers to skin and mucous membranes of a particular appearance that may well correspond to a variety of pathologies. That is why Greek physicians can speak of a "leprous" disease of the bladder in the case of an inflammation (cystitis) with exfoliation; or of an appearance "comparable to that of leprosy" in the case of an Athenian suffering from thickening skin and general itching.[57] In fact the Hippocratic term is so polysemous that it even includes phenomena outside the proper domain of pathology. In a stationary–that is, chronic and not evolving–state, the skin's "leprous" appearance betokens neither abscession (*apóstasis*) nor disease (*nósēma*) but merely represents an aesthetic blemish (*aîskhos*). This explains the passage in the treatise *Affections* according to which "leprosy is a deformity rather than a disease."[58]

For Theophrastus, *lépra* is a skin manifestation without consequence for the overall health of the body. He mentions it along with "scabies" *(psṓra)* and "lichen" *(leikhḗn)*. And in the *Characters* he describes the "disgusting" individual who neglects to care for his body as repulsive in appearance because of his rashes and pimples, his black fingernails, his *lépra,* and so forth.[59] Clearly, this "leprosy" is no great disease. In another work that belongs to the Aristotelian tradition, the *Problemata,* it is stated that *lépra* can pass from a sick person to a healthy one just like scabies because they are both diseases of the surface.[60] The concern here about the contagiousness of "leprosy" is absolutely foreign to the Hippocratic writings, but even in this new context the word *lépra* does not seem to refer to a serious, mutilating, incurable disease.

In the Greek medical writers of the classical period, *lépra* is often associated with two other skin ailments, *leúkē* and *alphós*. Judging from their etymologies, these diseases were characterized by local loss of pigmentation. The Hippocratic texts do not justify the conclusion that *leúkē* and *lépra* are affections that often occur together in individual patients but only that the association of their names is due to a similarity in their nature. Pausanias tells us that the name of the town Lepreon in the Peloponnesus implies that its founders suffered from "leprosy." In the town's vicinity, he writes, was a "grotto of the Anigrides Nymphs. Anyone afflicted with *alphós* or *leúkē* who entered it was first obliged to pray to the Nymphs and promise them a sacrifice, then to wash his body; then, by crossing a stream, the worshipper left behind his sickness and emerged completely cured, his skin healed." In fact archaeological investigation has shown that a spring existed there and that its water was sulfurous: therapeutic baths in sulfurous water are actually effective in treating some relatively benign skin diseases.[61]

The Hippocratic usage of *lépra* and *leúkē* cannot be taken the same way as the Herodotean, since the two terms do not designate two complementary forms of a single disease. Hippocrates includes in the same class with them "lichens," scabies, exfoliations, ulcerations and so forth. If "leprosy" and "lichens" arise from perturbation of the black bile, as the classical theory of humors avers, *leúkē*, by contrast, is caused by phlegm.[62] Acquired *leúkē* does not develop before puberty, and it must be distinguished from congenital *leúkē*.[63] Aristotelian texts and the case of Atossa show that the terms *leúkē* and *alphós* apply to diseases that are not especially serious.[64] However, Aristotle's *leúkē*, a skin disease that whitens all body hair, does not entirely match the nosological domain of the Hippocratic term. For the author of *Prorrheticon*, II, considers "the *leúkai* among the fatal diseases, like the so-called Phoenician disease."[65]

We are now in a different arena: after benign ailments of the skin that have more to do with cosmetics than medicine, dread and deadly diseases confront us. What in the world is this so-called Phoenician disease that is mentioned in passing and not without some horror in the chapter on skin disease of a Hippocratic treatise? It is a serious disease, in some way belonging to the same clinical category as *leúkē* and *lépra*, scarcely known in Greece but apparently thought common among the Phoenicians. That is all we know with certainty, since the expression *noûsos phoenikíē* occurs only here in the *Corpus Hippocraticum*.

Galen comments on this passage, "Phoenician disease: common in Phoenicia, and in other Oriental regions; the disease in question seems to be elephantiasis."[66] What Galen means by elephantiasis is without any doubt what medieval authors call leprosy, that is, Hansen's disease. The wording of the gloss betrays Galen's embarrassment: his first statement is banal, his second a guess projecting on the past the epidemiological reality of Imperial Rome. Though it cannot be proven, Galen's hypothesis still remains the most plausible explanation of the true nature of this mysterious disease.

For Greek physicians of the fifth and fourth centuries B.C., true leprosy seems not to have been a disease they encountered in the normal practice of their profession. It was only an exotic disease limited to eastern lands or sporadically arriving in Greece from them. A "pestilential" *(loimṓdēs),* that is, contagious, form of *leúkē* is said to have afflicted the Delians. "Their faces were covered by a *leúkē,* their hair grew white, their necks and chests swelled, but they felt no fever or great pain, and their lower limbs remained utterly unharmed." It was thought to be a punishment by Apollo for their having buried a man on the island, a violation of sacred law. Perhaps this story reflects true leprosy, but what date can we ascribe to it? It is found in a letter addressed to Philocrates by Aeschines, the famous orator of the fourth century B.C. Nowadays the letter, which is said to relate the latter's travails on a journey, is considered a forgery not older than the second century A.D..[67]

Elephantiasis: The Outbreak of True Leprosy in Europe

In the works that have come down to us, the terms *eléphas* and *elephantíasis* do not occur in a nosological sense until the first century B.C. (Lucretius has a Latin translation of them). They then become current in the first century A.D. (Dioscorides, Celsus, Aretaeus, Scribonius Largus, and Pliny). However, the fragment of a treatise of Rufus of Ephesus transmitted to us in the great medical encyclopedia of Oribasius (fourth century) makes it possible to go back, for the history of this disease, as far as Straton, the pupil and secretary of the physician Erasistratus, who lived in Alexandria during the third century B.C.[68] Here is the text in question:

> The ancients have taught us nothing about elephantiasis; there is reason to wonder how such a serious and common disease escaped the notice of men capable of pondering everything in the tiniest detail; only Straton, the disciple of Erasistratus, has provided us with some notion of this disease, which he calls cacochymia; for the book concerned with this disease, which is attributed to Democritus, is plainly apocryphal. The physicians who lived shortly before us established the types of this disease: they called it, in its early stage, leontiasis, because those affected with it take on a bad odor, and their cheeks collapse, and their lips thicken; but when their eyebrows swell and their cheeks are flushed and they are seized with a desire for sexual gratification, these physicians call it satyriasis, which, however, is different from the disease of the genitals called by the same name; for the latter has gotten its name from a continual erection of the genitals, while the former has it also from its character; when the symptoms invade the whole body, the physicians in question call it elephantiasis. Now its symptoms are not hidden: they consist in livid and black embossments that resemble ecchymoses; some on the face, others on the arms, still others on the legs; many also develop on the back, the chest, and the stomach; at first, the embossments are not ulcerous; later, they ulcerate in the most hideous way, since their ulceration is accompanied by a swelling of the lips and so deep a decay that in some cases the tips of the fingers fall off and the ulcers never succeed in scarring. So it appears to be a superficial disease, since it

makes its appearance on the skin; but the difficulty of curing it, a difficulty that comes close to impossibility, suggests to us that it has a deeper origin, an origin not easy to penetrate; it is even as deep as that of carcinoma, by common opinion; in truth, Praxagoras accepts a deep origin above all for carcinoma.[69]

This enumeration of the symptoms of elephantiasis by Rufus of Ephesus (early second century A.D.) corresponds perfectly with the clinical profile of low immune resistance leprosy.[70] Straton is said to have provided the first information on this disease in Alexandria, but only the Greek physicians who lived shortly before Rufus—that is, not until Roman times—get credit for describing it well, distinguishing among its phases, and naming them. With a single exception,[71] elephantiasis was not related to or identified with the Hippocratic *lépra* or *leúkē,* even though these names continue to be used in Greek medical literature of the Hellenistic and Roman periods to denote dermatoses such as eczema, psoriasis, and vitiligo.

The Seventy were victims of a regrettable confusion, unless those erudite rabbis actually thought that Biblical *Ẓarā'at* corresponded more closely to ancient Hippocratic *lépra* than to the serious ailment that was gaining the attention of physicians at that very time and in the very city in which they were laboring. Whatever the case may be, it is unlikely that these translators had at their disposal a generally accepted Greek medical term that signified leprosy. Straton's cacochymia is more a pathogenetic explanation than a specific name for a disease. And the satyriasis of which Aristotle speaks in the *Generation of Animals* is not necessarily leprosy, even though the diagnosis cannot be excluded with certainty.[72] The novelty, variety, and vagueness in the terminology prove that the Greek physicians were grappling with a disease that they perceived as a new arrival and concerning which they found no adequate information in the great masters of the past.

To Lucretius, the Roman poet and natural philosopher who died in 55 B.C., *elephas morbus* was still a strange and foreign disease confined to the banks of the Nile.[73] About two generations after him, Celsus can still affirm that "*elephantia,* which the Greeks call *elephantiasis,* is a chronic disease hardly known in Italy and very common in certain lands."[74] Pliny the Elder expressly states that it is a "new disease," one of those that, like *lichen* or *mentagra, carbunculum* and *colum,* "were unknown in past years not only to Italy but also to almost the whole of Europe."[75] He continues:

Elephantiasis did not occur in Italy before the time of Pompeius Magnus, and . . . though the plague usually begins on the face, a kind of freckle on the tip of the nose, yet presently the skin dries up over all the body, covered with spots of various colours, and uneven, in places thick, in others thin, in others hard as with rough itch-scab, finally however going black, and pressing the flesh on to the bones, while the toes and fingers swell up. The plague is native to Egypt. When the kings were afflicted, it was a deadly thing for the inhabitants, because the tubs in the baths used to be prepared with warm human blood for its treatment. This disease quickly died out in Italy.[76]

The evidence I have been citing in fact only concerns the presence of leprosy in Egypt and Italy. As for Greece proper, the information is somewhat later and less explicit. Aretaeus of Cappadocia, Galen, and Plutarch, who all speak often of elephantiasis, would certainly have stressed its absence from the Greek world if such had been the case in the first and in the beginning of the second century A.D. Plutarch takes up the subject in a chapter of *Quaestiones conviviales* in which he undertakes to consider "if it is possible that new and unknown diseases can arise."[77] The question is debated at a symposium in which the physician Philo, the philosopher Diogenianus, and Plutarch himself speak one after the other. Philo maintains that "elephantiasis has only been known for a short time, since no ancient physicians speak of it." Plutarch takes an opposing position, proffering the evidence of Athenodorus, the author of a treatise on epidemic diseases according to whom "not only elephantiasis but also hydrophobia were first observed in the time of Asclepiades." For the modern reader, Plutarch's remark runs counter to its stated intention: it confirms the newness of leprosy for physicians in Greece instead of debunking it, since Asclepiades of Bithynia lived around the year 100 B.C. and, moreover, his writings basically reflect the state of affairs in Rome. Plutarch's dinner guests were divided between two opinions that they found equally surprising: either such diseases really appeared for the first time and there are, therefore, changes in nature itself, or all diseases have always existed but they have not always been noticed by physicians. Although such a blind spot is astonishing for a disease as great and serious as elephantiasis, most of the participants in the symposium plump for the second opinion, "not being able to believe that nature, in the human body as in the city, can enjoy inventing novelties." Diogenianus makes a peroration to this effect, emphasizing that psychic phenomena and, *a fortiori,* somatic ones do not change as a whole but simply vary within certain limits. The constancy of causes and the conservative character of the very nature of the living organism are opposed to fundamental innovation in the domain of nosology. To explain the arrival of apparently new diseases, one has only to consider the pathological variations brought on by changes in diet and in bathing habits. Plutarch cites, only to reject it, the hypothesis of Democritus according to which the spillage of extraterrestrial atoms could be the cause of epidemics and unusual diseases.[78] The rest of the discussion only secondarily concerns the history of leprosy.

Though the descriptions of elephantiasis by Celsus, Pliny, Rufus of Ephesus, and Galen validate the retrospective diagnosis of lepromatous leprosy, they leave much to be desired with regard to precise knowledge of the clinical unfolding of the disease and the possibility of confusing it with other disorders of lesser proportions. Still, by the first century A.D., Aretaeus of Cappadocia, a physician thought to have studied at Alexandria and to have lived at Rome, had given a thorough description of the clinical characteristics of elephantiasis, a disease that he thinks is as great, frightening, and enduring among diseases as the elephant is among animals.[79]

True, Aretaeus has some wrong ideas about the etiology and pathogenesis of leprosy, but he know perfectly well its main symptoms, their clinical course, and their hopeless prognosis. His description of the insidious start of the disease, the lepromas, the facies leontina, and the final mutilations is masterful. He still confuses true leprosy with some manifestations of less serious dermatoses (whence, for instance, his mention of alopecia or localized lichenoid eruptions on the fingers and joints), but these are trifling objections: the clinical picture he paints has great rigor and is on the whole very distinct. It guarantees an unequivocal diagnosis. The reason Aretaeus is ignorant of the anesthetic patches in tuberculoid leprosy must be that his description is based on direct experience with the low immune resistance form of the disease. Even so, one can detect in his account a certain knowledge, albeit vague and shadowy, of dimorphic leprosy.

Pliny's conclusion about the rapid extinction of leprosy in Italy was overly optimistic. Far from being extinguished, henceforth this disease ceaselessly and surreptitiously spreads throughout the Roman Empire. But it was to become an important endemic pestilence in Europe only after the collapse of ancient civilization and the abrupt change in the conditions of life that marks the beginning of the High Middle Ages.

More and more, leprosy evokes a holy terror that is fostered by the actual propagation of the disease as well as by the spread of Judeo-Christian religion. Aretaeus of Cappadocia gives eloquent voice to the fear that leprosy inspired in common people:

> Who would not wish to escape these diseased people, and who does not turn away from them in horror, even if one's own son, father, or brother is among them? We fear the transmission of the disease *(metádosis toû kakoû)*. For this reason, there are those who abandon their most cherished relatives in the desert and the mountains, from time to time bringing them provisions, or they leave off doing even that and let them perish.[80]

Though modern medicine justifies this common fear that ancient physicians were at pains to accept, there is a strange paradox in the situation: the contagiousness of leprosy was recognized, though it is a disease with a relatively low risk of infection, while the contagiousness of most acute fevers was denied.[81] The underlying motivations for flight from lepers and their forced isolation were at first basically magico-religious in nature.

The first leprosaria in Europe date from the sixth century A.D., if not the fifth. Gregory of Tours (about 538–594) speaks of "ladreries," leper houses, in France. The edict of the Lombard king Rothari (643) imposes social death on lepers and regulates their settlement on the margins of the community. From the sixth century on, the lepers of Rome were crammed into a hospice called Saint-Lazarus.[82] Walafrid Strabo (808–849) attributes to Saint Othmar, abbot of the Benedictine community of Saint Gall, the founding of "a small hospice, situated not far from the monastery but removed from the homes of the rest of the poor, and devoted to the housing of lepers who customarily live apart from other people." That took place around 736. During the same century, Pippin the Short (in 751) and Charlemagne (in 786) intervened to strengthen the social repression of leprosy. But none of the measures they took succeeded in stemming the progress of the disease.[83] There is no agreement among modern historians as to the effect of the Crusades on the spread of leprosy. It is certain that the disease was present in the West before they took place, and yet endemic leprosy reached its apogee between the eleventh and fourteenth centuries.

Medieval leper houses were for rounding up the sick and localizing the social canker they represented, not for providing care. Lepers were thought to be incurables. Actually, people did not even suppose that complete isolation of lepers was possible. In the available evidence, there is nothing to show that lepers were shut in or kept by force in certain places. They were able to circulate in the region but had to avoid urban areas, to refrain from entering homes or churches, and to give notice of their presence from afar. So, for example, in the Republic of Dubrovnik, they had to wear white. From time to time, in fact very often, the measures taken against them were relaxed. Then lepers invaded towns and took up their places in the midst of street crowds, where begging was profitable. The people of medieval times believed that leprosy was contagious, but that belief was tempered by a specific restriction: the transmission of the disease should obey causes of a moral order. To a medieval person, leprosy was above all a form of divine punishment, more an affliction of the soul than a disease of the body.[84] Byzantine physicians (first among them, Paul of Aegina in the seventh century) and Arabic-speaking physicians (notably, Abul-Qasim, who lived in Andalusia in the tenth century) realized the importance of the neurological symptoms of leprosy. Was this due to a greater exactness in their clinical observations, or a real change in the disease itself? I opt for the latter hypothesis: the disease was really changing its appearance, since the high immune resistance forms, that is, tuberculoid leprosy, were becoming more and more frequent.

Nosological terminology itself also changed in the course of the Middle Ages. *Elephantiasis quam vulgus lepram vocat,* says a passage in the *Collectio Salernitana.*[85] The homilies of Gregory of Nazianzus show that in the fourth century the words *elephantiasis* and *lepra* were synonyms, at least for those not initiated in the medical art. The Second Synod of Orleans (549) consecrated the legal use of the terms *lepra* and *leprosus*. The physicians bowed to the *vox populi,* or rather, the *vox ecclesiae,* and agreed to the nosological term *lepra* in a sense closer to that of Greek and Latin translations of the Bible than the Hippocratic tradition. The term *elephantiasis* was not abandoned, but instead, and still worse, it was reused to denote a totally different disease, namely a lymphatic ailment accompanied by swelling of the limb affected and roughening of its integument; the main cause of this disease was infestation by filaria, nematode worms of the warmer regions.

Origin and Worldwide Distribution of Leprosy

Although leprosy as an endemic disease was extinct in Europe long before the effective use of chemotherapy against it, it is still rampant on a global scale. The number of lepers in 1982, according to the World Health Organization, is surprising: 15 million. The disease has four main epidemic foci: India and Southeast Asia, China, black Africa and Madagascar, and Latin America. For the record, one should add the remnants of its medieval endemic in Europe, especially in Greece, southern Italy, Portugal, and, until recently, Scandinavia. Current estimates are that there are approximately 1,000 lepers in London and at least as many in France, though they are imported cases. Little is said of them in public, and people have no direct experiences of these victims, but that is a conspiracy of silence. The seal of infamy still rests heavily on this disease.[86]

According to some authorities, for instance, D. Zambaco Pacha and G. Barbézieux, leprosy is a universally distributed disease as old as humanity itself. Its geographic limits and historical outbreaks are simply due to ups and downs in social conditions.[87] This view is no longer shared by specialists in the historical pathology of leprosy. Though it is true that the geographic distribution of leprosy is for the most part coterminous with the third world, this need not mean that in the past social conditions were not only necessary, as they are today, but sufficient causes for an outbreak of endemic leprosy in a region. The distribution of leprosy in ancient times depended not only on appropriate social environments but also on the special history of Hansen's bacillus and its migrations.

Some foci of leprosy are obviously older than others. The disease was probably born after the global dispersion of *Homo sapiens*. However, even though it is possible to reach general agreement that the introduction of leprosy on the American continent and in Oceania is relatively recent, the question of the disease's original focus remains open. It was first brought to America by Spanish and Portuguese sailors, then by the black slave traders, and last by Norwegian immigrants. Though it has been invading the New World since the sixteenth century, it never took root in the northern continent, which was predominantly populated by Anglo-Saxons. Eskimos and certain other isolated Amerindian peoples have never known leprosy. In Oceania, it dates only from the nineteenth century. The current situation in western Europe and North America, in which continuous immigration of lepers and the absence of special measures for the protection of society against the disease have had no serious epidemiological consequences, can serve as a model and helps to explain why, or at least makes it plausible that, leprosy did not exist in an endemic state in the Greek and Roman world during the archaic and classical periods despite the introduction from that time on of sporadic cases.

As for the place where leprosy first appeared, it may be black Africa, or the Far East, or the Middle East. In asking himself whether leprosy originated in Africa or Asia, R. Chaussinand states that "this problem is part of a larger problem concerning the origin of the human species."[88] From this point of view, the most seductive hypothesis is surely the African one. According to T. A. Cockburn, leprosy is an infection with a mycobacterium inherited directly from the ancestors of man.[89] The place of origin of the human race, which recent anthropological research situates in East Africa, would thus coincide with that of the origin of leprosy. But this argument does not seem to me convincing. The hypothesis of the vertical transmission of leprosy from hominids to humans, taking place during the Pleistocene era along with the evolution of *Homo sapiens,* is far from proven and even seems unlikely. It comes up against two difficulties: the absence of a common leproid affection in existing primates (or at least our ignorance of any such) and the nonubiquity of leprosy, a fact that suggests a hypothesis of the appearance of Hansen's bacillus after the first colonization of the New World.

Another argument in favor of African origins is provided by immunology. The high frequency of high immune resistance leprosy among the autochthonous inhabitants of black Africa suggests that this geographical area is an ancient endemic focus of the disease. For instance, in Senegal, there are ten times as many lepers as in Mexico (calculating, to be sure, by thousands of inhabitants), and yet the number of lepromatous cases is about the same in both countries. Approximately 10 percent of the lepers in Senegal have lepromatous leprosy, while in Mexico 80 percent are evolving toward the more serious form.[90] It is tempting to interpret these data as a sign of the greater antiquity of African leprosy in comparison with American leprosy. However, that is not the only possible explanation, and in any case the situation is more complex if we compare African morbidity with that of Asia (and not that of the New World). I doubt that this argument can be valid when extrapolated into a time as remote as that of the formation of the germ of leprosy. In the current state of knowledge, immunology cannot decide the case between Africa and Asia.

Those who suppose that leprosy originated in Asia base their belief on the antiquity of the literary evidence for the existence of the disease in the Far East and Mesopotamia. The Indian focus is probably older than the Chinese one, but there is still no way of deciding whether India, Mesopotamia, Persia, or East Africa should be considered the cradle of the disease. These contiguous lands form a vast domain all of which was invaded by leprosy in the beginning of the second millennium B.C. at the latest, but it remains impossible to say where inside it the disease was born and how it was first spread.

From the critical examination of historical sources undertaken above, it emerges that endemic leprosy spread from Mesopotamia toward the west up to the Asian shores of the Mediterranean, that is, up to Phoenicia. Around the fourteenth century B.C., it was present in Canaan (Phoenicia-Palestine), brought there either by Babylonians who came from Chaldea in the eighteenth century B.C., or by Hebrews who also came from there and mingled with the Canaanite populations (seventeenth to sixteenth centuries). One Hebraic tribe descended into Egypt, returning from it later on to take over the Promised Land around the twelfth century B.C. The Biblical prescripts about *Ẓarā'at* date from this period. Egypt, Greece, and Italy—actually, the whole Mediterranean except the Phoenician coast—were still free from leprosy around the fifth and the first part of the fourth century B.C. A certain tradition of much later date than the events of which it speaks held that the Hebrews, during their sojourn in Egypt, were infected with leprosy and brought back the disease to their new homeland. That is possible, but it is more likely that they found it in Canaan, where they also may have left it in the first place. It remains true that leprosy did not take root in Egypt at such an early date.

Leprosy respects a certain form of civilized life and does not take up residence in all societies, even if it is introduced into them sporadically. Certain sociocultural conditions whose essential parameters are still unknown, though they are plainly correlate with misery, close quarters, and a low level of hygiene, are needed for the transformation of sporadic into endemic leprosy. It is indeed instructive that the disease spared Greece and Italy for a long time despite the significant contacts these countries had with Phoenician sailors and Persian soldiers and merchants.

Leprosy did not acquire visibility to Greek medical eyes until around 300 B.C. At that time, the endemic of leprosy in Egypt had already taken on considerable amplitude. It was especially rife in Alexandria, the new city. For all that it was the most brilliant instance of ancient urban life and the center of Hellenistic civilization, Alexandria, like Rome after it, sheltered its share of hovels in the shadow of grandiose monuments. As a result of the concentration in this city of the poor and the sick as well as the learned, the inevitable finally took place: leprosy was seen and taken for the special calamity it was.

Modern leprosy specialists maintain that the disease was brought to Egypt from India by the armies of Alexander the Great on his return from the great eastern expedition of 327–326 B.C.[91] Indeed, there is nothing to prevent us from thinking that the wars of Alexander, like the campaigns of Darius and Artaxerxes before him, contributed to the spread of leprosy into the West. However, there is no proof at all that it was the first introduction of leprosy into Northeast Africa, nor that Alexander's soldiers caught the disease in India. It is very likely that leprosy had long since existed in Persia and at Babylon, where Alexander succumbed to an attack of fever in 323 that was almost certainly malarial.

At the beginning of the Christian era, Roman legions brought leprosy to the heart of the Occident. If Pliny is to be believed, it began expanding into Europe at the time of Pompey, who, once he had conquered Mithridates of Pontus, put down Armenia, and crossed the cities of Greece in triumph, then disembarked on the coast of Italy at the head of an army laden with microbes from the East (61 B.C.). There, for the moment at least, my inquiry into leprosy will end. I will return to it after a glance at the other panel of this medico-historical diptych: the history of tuberculosis.

Chapter Seven

TUBERCULOSIS
A Great Killer

The length of this chapter is not in proportion to the importance of tuberculosis in the history of humanity in general and the history of Greek and Roman antiquity in particular. If the exposition is slightly shorter than that in the previous chapter, which is devoted to leprosy, the reason lies in the less complex and less ambiguous nature of the sources and, above all, in the quantity and quality of the monographs on the history of tuberculosis.[1]

The Clinical Forms and Paleopathology of Tuberculosis

Currently, tuberculosis is defined as a disease that results from the inflammatory reaction of organic tissue to infection with a specific microbe discovered in 1882 by Robert Koch (*Mycobacterium tuberculosis*), or by certain microbial species very close to it. For clinical nosology, tuberculosis is not, strictly speaking, a disease, since it has no symptomatic homogeneity. Because it is defined exclusively by its etiology, tuberculosis includes a quantity of diseases that differ among themselves in the place affected, the symptoms, and the seriousness of the prognosis. Aside from a specific microbe, the tuberculous diseases also have in common the histological appearance of the fundamental lesion, namely the tubercle and the caseous destruction of cellular structures.

The favored locale for these lesions is, at least in modern times and developed countries, pulmonary tissue. Pneumonic infiltration, granulomatous reaction, and the caseous degeneration that often ends up as significant local destruction (cavities), as well as the general poisoning of the organism by the microbe's metabolic products, all result in the classic profile of consumption: wasting away of the whole body, continuous fever, fatigue, cough, and blood-spitting. The evolution of the lesions varies depending on the immune resistance of the patient. Not unlike leprous infection, tuberculosis can develop in two ways: one is characterized by excessive exudation along with ulceration and rapid dissemination, the other by fibrosis and calcifications that isolate the tuberculous foci. In inhabitants of industrialized nations, the infection usually evolves in both ways at once (fibrocaseous tuberculosis), as though there were a sort of compromise taking place between the two basic forms.

The localization of tuberculosis in the lungs is favored by the abundant oxygen in that organ and, at least in modern man, by the fact that Koch's bacilli are usually transmitted in the air we breathe. Among their localizations, which are numerous and varied, I mention the intestines and mesenteric lymph nodes (typical when the bacilli are ingested orally in massive quantity, as with infected milk), the lymph nodes of the neck (scrofula), the genito-urinary organs, the meninges, and, last but not least, the bones and joints. On the skeleton, Koch's bacillus prefers to attack the diarthroses (tuberculous osteoarthritis of the knee, hip, wrist, ankle, elbow, and so forth), the spine, and the areas of hemopoetic marrow in long bones. The tuberculous affection can attack the cranial vault. Its most common skeletal form is Pott's disease, which is a tuberculous spondylodiscitis that destroys adjacent vertebral bodies. The caseous destruction can lead to a paravertebral abscess that extends downward and burrows under the sheath of the psoas major muscle. The collapse of one or several vertebral bodies produces a sharp hump (angular kyphosis) with a distinctly different appearance from the round one due to rickets and most other factors that deform the spinal column.

Though anatomopathological observation of osseous tuberculosis is relatively simple and secure when one can proceed to a microscopic examination of fresh tissue, the diagnosis of this disease is much less simple when only dry, even petrified, bones are available. Though pathognomonic in principle, the tuberculous lesion equivocates within the material constraints imposed by osteoarchaeological study.[2] In cases in which the diagnosis of tuberculosis can be based only on iconographic documentation, the chief indicator, at least for prehistoric and ancient art, is provided by the presence of an angular hump. However, it must be admitted that several pathological processes that are not tuberculous (for instance, traumas, congenital malformations, and pyogenic osteomyelitis) sometimes produce kyphoses that at least externally mimic exactly the consequences of Pott's disease. From modern clinical experience, vertebral tuberculosis is the most common cause of angular hump, but it would be circular to project the frequency of such an etiology on a distant past whose epidemiological conditions are scarcely known. So Pott's disease is only one possibility among others that must be invoked with respect to hunchbacks in ancient art.[3] As for the iconographic representation of emaciated individuals, the usual diagnosis of "consumption" must be taken loosely. Overall decline is not necessarily tuberculous in origin. Pictorial information alone cannot justify a diagnosis of pulmonary tuberculosis. There is no question of invoking certain prehistoric rock paintings, Hindu sculptures, Greek statuettes, or Roman mosaics that represent extremely thin, relatively young persons as evidence of the antiquity of tuberculosis.

Tuberculosis is not exclusively a human disease. However, in the publications that I have had occasion to consult, no mention is made of this disease on the bones of prehistoric animals. Likewise, no lesion suspected of being tuberculous has been reported on human bones of the Paleolithic period. There is no need to draw hasty conclusions: the former lack may be explained by the insufficiencies of paleopathological research into animals, and the latter by the very small number of bones in question.

An osteoarchaeological diagnosis of tuberculosis has been proposed for several cases from the Neolithic period and the Bronze Age in western Europe (France, Belgium, Germany, Denmark).[4] The best-known example is a Neolithic spine (about 5000 B.C.) excavated at the beginning of the century from a cemetery near Heidelberg and described by Paul Bartels; at the time of its publication, the find seemed to prove irrefutably the prehistoric existence of osseous tuberculosis in western Europe.[5] The case presented partial destruction of the bodies of the fourth and fifth thoracic vertebrae with complete fusion and an angular kyphotic deformity, which is indeed an anatomopathological feature of Pott's disease. Some doubts were expressed as to the solidity of the diagnosis, since, as H. U. Williams remarked, a healed fracture of the spine might well have produced the same paleopathological condition. Since the apophyses of the Heidelberg thoracic vertebrae are intact, the likelihood that the deformation of the vertebral bodies was due to an act of violence or an accident instead of tuberculous infection seems to me slight, although it cannot be entirely ruled out.

It is not absolutely impossible that all the European prehistoric cases diagnosed as Pott's disease are actually traumatic destructions or nonspecific purulent inflammations, and also that all the presumed cases of tuberculous osteoarthritis from the Neolithic period (such as the ankle from Aumède in Lozère or the hip from Grenelle in Paris) actually result from the action of staphylococci, not Koch's bacilli. Still, such an interpretation of the osteoarchaeological discoveries accumulated up to now seems to me untenable. Even if a critique can be made of each case, the sum-total of prehistoric lesions described as tuberculous justifies a strong presumption in favor of the diagnosis.[6]

An unshakable case of osseous tuberculosis was recognized by G. Elliot Smith and Sir Armand Ruffer on an Egyptian mummy of the Twenty-first

Dynasty (about 1000 B.C.). The mummified corpse of this young man, a priest of Ammon, presents both an angular kyphosis brought on by the destruction of the lower thoracic and upper lumbar vertebrae and a huge abscess in the area of the right psoas muscle.[7] More than 30 other osteoarchaeological specimens from Egypt and Nubia have lesions that perfectly resemble those of vertebral tuberculosis. Even if some of the cases are debatable, that does not detract from the worth of those that resist criticism and whose evidence is, as a whole, undeniable.[8] The oldest tuberculous specimens go back to 3000 B.C., the time of the First Dynasty. So it is very likely that in that part of the Mediterranean, osseous tuberculosis was already established in the Neolithic period, at least in its latest stage.

Several Egyptian figurines represent hunchbacks, and some of them have the hump at right angles. So they could be referred to Pott's disease. One of the statuettes is probably predynastic (about 4000 B.C.) and therefore constitutes an indication in favor of the antiquity of tuberculosis.[9] The presence of osseous tuberculosis in ancient Egypt allows us to credit the existence of pulmonary, intestinal, and glandular tuberculosis. However, the statistical correlation between these various forms cannot be extrapolated for such a distant past. In other words, knowledge of the frequency of one of these forms does not support specific conclusions as to the frequency of the others. Certain pleural adherences that might derive from a tuberculous attack have been noticed on mummies, but it has never been possible to find tuberculous lesions on the mummified pulmonary tissue.[10] Such examinations are very difficult, since the embalmers removed the viscera from the cadavers and deposited them in Canopic vases in which the tissues of parenchymal organs quickly underwent important changes.

The Oldest Literary Evidence of Tuberculosis

According to Charles Coury, pulmonary tuberculosis was once a rarity in Egypt, "a hot, dry land whose climate was even in ancient times considered healthy for consumptives."[11] The fact is, Egyptian medical texts of the high period nowhere mention consumption. Was it present in Mesopotamia at the dawn of the historical period? Yes, probably, but the affirmation rests more on biological considerations that on concrete evidence. Literary sources, notably the tablets of Assurbanipal, contain incantatory formulas against coughs and against a disease that for philological reasons seems to be consumption. In some Assyrian texts, we can recognize the description of pneumonia and bronchitis, but even so their tuberculous character cannot be established. A medical historian can find proof of the frequency of respiratory diseases in this part of the Old World, but he cannot specify their etiology.[12]

In the Far East, pulmonary tuberculosis is a disease that was known very early on. In the laws of Manu (ca. 1200 B.C.) consumption is a defect or impurity that can be transmitted to one's descendants. Ayurvedic medicine dubs it "the royal disease" *(rājayakṣma)*. The *Susrutasaṃhitā* contains an excellent description of its symptoms and stresses its sociodemographic importance as well as its resistance to medical treatment.[13]

The *Nei-ching,* the basic treatise of Chinese medicine, contains some allusions to pulmonary disorders whose tuberculous nature is highly likely. According to the annalists, the prime minister of Emperor Kao-tsung (ca. 1300 B.C.) was afflicted with a hunchback "as angular as a fish fin." Descriptions of chronic coughing, blood-spitting, cervical adenopathy, "infantile consumption," "osseous fever," and deformities of the spine abound in the classical medical literature of the Celestial Empire. In the seventh century A.D., Tswei Che-ti assembled the various forms of tuberculosis into a masterful clinical tableau; apparently the disease was becoming more and more devastating.[14]

Protohistory of Tuberculosis in America and Greece

The existence of this disease among the peoples of pre-Columbian America has been cast into doubt by specialists as competent as R. Moodie, A. Hrdlička, and, more recently, Dan Morse. The numerous representations of hunchbacks in American Indian art, especially in pottery, do not of themselves constitute incontestable proof of the presence of Pott's disease. As was said earlier, other ailments can mimic the tuberculous hump. To back up the diagnosis, tuberculous stigmata should be identifiable on pre-Columbian bones. By 1960, 15 osteoarchaeological cases suggesting tuberculous disease on the spines of American Indians had been published. Morse reviewed them all and came to the conclusion that only 4 of them (a Peruvian mummy, a child's skeleton from Pueblo Bonito, and 2 spines of adult males from Hopewell Mound and Chucalissa, Memphis) are typical enough to justify a strong presumption of spinal tuberculosis. In 1 of these cases, a pre-Columbian date is not certain, and in all 4, according to Morse, other diseases could have caused the same paleopathological picture.[15]

Morse's hypercritical approach and his rejection of prehistoric tuberculosis in American Indians has been contradicted by osteoarchaeological research carried out in a systematic and sophisticated fashion on human remains discovered during the last two decades in sites as diverse as Sonoma (California), Pueblo Bonito (New Mexico), Nazca (Peru), and Chavez Pass near Tempe, Arizona. Of the 44 skeletons from Sonoma, dating from the sixth to the third century B.C., 1 case of osseous tuberculosis has been recorded. On the more recent American Indian bones from Chavez Pass, which date only from the twelfth to the fourteenth century A.D., Marc

Kelley has been able to identify 3, if not 4, very probable cases of tuberculous infection.[16] The diagnosis of pre-Columbian osseous tuberculosis is supported by the philological interpretation of an oral tradition according to which the Maya and the Inca of the historical period prior to the conquistadors used special terms to designate pulmonary consumption.[17]

According to Charles Coury, "Tuberculous affections were decidedly more rare among the red men and the other autochthonous Indian tribes before the massive contamination of the American continent by Europeans that began in the seventeenth century."[18] However, this same authority cautiously notes that in order to ascertain the morbidity and mortality due to tuberculosis in general and to its more serious internal forms in particular, one cannot proceed by extrapolating from the frequency of osseous tuberculosis. The sample of human remains thus far subjected to study is too small and statistically insignificant, and, also, the correlation index between Pott's disease and pulmonary tuberculosis is too uncertain. "The fact that in a set of skeletons the percentage of those with traces of tuberculosis is 3.5 percent for Neolithic France, .22 percent for ancient Egypt between 6,000 B.C. and A.D. 600 (Møller-Christensen), or 4.5 percent in California from the sixth to the second century B.C. (Roney), does nothing to inform us on the frequency of tuberculosis in general."[19] The notion that tuberculosis was relatively rare among native Americans before the conquest is based on observations suggesting a high mortality and special virulence in the tuberculous conditions among them from the time of their contact with whites. Was it Europeans who brought into the New World special strains of the human tuberculous bacillus, fiercer than those already there, or did they introduce the very first strain of the bacillus, assuming that the Indians had known only bovine tuberculosis before the whites' arrival?

Being unable to answer this question, I return to my main subject and the shores of the eastern Mediterranean. Though the introduction of tuberculosis into Greece certainly goes back to prehistoric times, sure osteoarchaeological examples of it are still lacking. J. L. Angel has reported a single, doubtful case, in which the collapse of the vertebral bodies and their kyphotic fusion in a young girl of the Early Iron Age (Argos, ca. 900 B.C.) might be explained as tuberculosis.[20] The representation of hunchbacks is fairly common in Greek art, but the works in question are relatively late. Literary sources confirm the presence of pulmonary, osseous, and glandular tuberculosis in the Greek city-states during the classical age and support the hypothesis of an endemic worsening during the Hellenistic and Roman periods. According to Krause, the demographic disturbances that followed the great invasions from the fifth to the sixth century A.D. produced a regression of tuberculosis; then there was a strong resurgence of it in cities that were overpopulated and at a generally low level of hygiene.[21]

The Ravages of Consumption in the Classical Age

Received opinion nowadays sides with the bold medical historians who have detected pulmonary tuberculosis in a few vague references in Homer and the tragic poets to a sluggish, devastating disease without a single other specific trait.[22] In this matter, I prefer a more reserved judgment. It remains true that tuberculosis sufferers were an important segment of the clientele of the Hippocratic physicians, who had found out the essential traits of the clinical picture of pulmonary consumption.[23] I haven't the slightest doubt about the presence of tuberculosis in archaic Greece, but in all candor it must be admitted that the myths and ancient poetic works say nothing substantive about it. The omission is made good from the earliest medical literature on. The concept of pulmonary consumption appears in the oldest parts of the Hippocratic corpus, in the most authentic epidemiological texts of the Coan physicians as well as in passages that go back to the *Cnidian Sentences*.

In ancient Greek the word *phthísis* 'consumption, phthisis' has a more general sense than the purely medical meaning of its calques in modern languages. When Aristotle speaks of the *phthísis* of the moon, he simply means that it is waning. The same word can be applied to the setting sun, to any kind of extinction, and to any diminution of an object that will conclude with its disappearance. *Phthísis* in its original sense is nothing more than a state of diminution or withering. The noun is derived from the verb *phthínō* 'wither, diminish, be consumed,' whose root is Indo-European.[24] Once part of the technical vocabulary of Greek physicians, this family of words kept its original meaning: the expressions dorsal phthisis, nephritic phthisis, phthisis of an eye or a limb, are used to designate not tuberculosis but atrophy of those organs. Galen and Aretaeus use a similar expression for the shrinking of the pupil of the eye. But that does not prevent the word *phthísis* and its derivatives from appearing in the classical medical literature without qualification and in a narrower sense, that is, as the name of a specific nosological entity.

The first attestation of the word *phthísis* is in Herodotus. The historian is telling how, at the time when Xerxes' army was preparing to conquer Greece, one of the three generals of the Median cavalry, Pharnuches, had to be "left behind, sick, at Sardis." This took place in or about the year 481 B.C.: "When the army was leaving Sardis, he met with an unhappy accident: a dog ran under his horse's feet, and the horse, taken by surprise, reared and threw its rider. As a result of the fall Pharnuches began to spit blood; and his sickness finally turned into consumption *kaì es phthísin periē̂lthe hē noûsos)*.[25] According to Bruno Meinecke, *phthísis* is here "clearly mentioned" in the modern sense of pulmonary consumption.[26] That is not the opinion of Fridolf Kudlien: the last phrase of the passage cited seems to him so vague that he proposes to translate it simply by the words "the disease became chronic." Pharnuches was left at Sardis in the same way as Philoctetes was abandoned at Lemnos in the Trojan cycle. In both cases, the long-term consequences of an accident made the military leader incapable of exercising his functions. In Herodotus, says Kudlien, the substantive *phthísis* does not yet have the more restricted meaning "pulmonary consumption." It only denotes a general decline, which is the primary characteristic of every serious chronic disease.[27] I tend toward a more finely shaded interpretation, one that lies between those of Meinecke and Kudlien. The former is incorrect in identifying Herodotus's *phthísis* with pulmonary tuberculosis; and the later exaggerates, to my mind, by denying any nosological specificity to this *phthísis*. Pharnuches' hemorrhage[28] was brought on by a trauma, so it seems unlikely that the disease that followed it was tuberculous. Unlikely—but not excluded, since the accident could have activated a latent specific bronchopulmonary process. In any case our retrospective judgment on the pathological reality of this posttraumatic illness is of only secondary importance for an appreciation of Herodotus's medical terminology. Pulmonary hemorrhage with complications, hemopneumothorax, abscess, bronchiectasis or caseation—the Greek historian, or the physician who served the Persian army and whose diagnosis he relates, did not err in calling it *phthísis:* though it did exist as a clinical entity and not just as a vague idea of decline, as yet it only partly comprised tuberculous consumption.

In the Hippocratic texts, the concept of *phthísis* becomes more limited and more precise, and it takes on an anatomoclinical meaning at once richer in details and narrower in its definition of a nosological field. *Diseases*, I, a normative Hippocratic treatise of exceptional value as a repository of extensive medical experience, enumerates the diseases that, once they have declared themselves, inevitably lead to death: at the head of the list stands *phthísis*. In the same treatise, mention is also made of *phthóē,* which takes first place in a list of diseases that are necessarily of long duration.[29] According to K. Deichgräber, *phthóē* is nothing more than the "Cnidian term that replaces *phthísis*."[30] But both words occur in the same chapter of a single work (*Morb.*, I, 3) whose Cnidian affiliations are doubtful; and moreover, the treatises that are generally considered Cnidian commonly use the term *phthísis*. The split Deichgräber proposes seems to me difficult to accept. It remains true that there are philological arguments in favor of the synonymy of the two words, for they are just two grades of the same root.

In the *Definitiones medicae* attributed to Galen but perhaps compiled a little before him, the following explanations occur: "*Phthísis:* ulceration *(hélkōsis)* of the lung or the chest or the throat; it brings on coughing and light fevers, along with wasting of the body. *Phthísis* differs from *phthóē* in that *phthísis* generally is used to designate any thinning down or consumption of the body, while *phthóē* is used especially for the consumption and thinning down that are the result of an ulcer *(eph' hélkei)*."[31] It is not easy to grasp the clinical significance of this distinction. Attested as it is in a late text, it is not necessarily valid for the classical period. The term *phthóē* is used only twice in the Hippocratic corpus, as against 42 usages of the noun *phthísis* and 30 of the adjective *phthinṓdēs* (which applies to persons as well as diseased organs). I will return later to the second mention of *phthóē*, noting for the moment that it relates to the clinical description of a pulmonary disease with pyogenic internal ulcers.[32] A glance at the passages in which *phthísis* and *phthinṓdēs* occur without qualification is enough to reveal the duality in their use: in some instances, the original and broad sense of a consumptive disease is at the forefront, and in others, which are more numerous, the narrower and more precise one must be understood. As a whole, the latter corresponds to the Pseudo-Galenic definition that speaks of a clinical triad (cough, fever, consumption) and derives it from pulmonary or at least intrathoracic ulceration. The nosological vocabulary of the Hippocratic corpus is fluid, and the word *phthóē* appears as a kind of abortive attempt to eliminate the technical annoyance of the double meaning of *phthísis*. The attempt failed at least in part because some masters of the Greek medical thought on principle refused subdivision and rigidity in the nomenclature of diseases, doubtless out of fear that it would cause a loss of perspective on the individuality of concrete cases.

By the end of the fifth century B.C., the nosological conceptualization of pulmonary consumption took the form of clinical profiles that fixed the symptoms of tuberculosis sufferers for centuries to come. Its most striking example is the three consumptions of the treatise *Internal Affections:*

> The first consumption . . . begins with a dull fever and chills; there is pain in the chest and back; from time to time, an overpowering coughing fit; lots of aqueous, salty spittle. Those are the signs of the beginning of the disease, but as it progresses, the body grows thin, all but the lower limbs, which swell up. Finger- and toenails become curved; the shoulders become thin and weak; the throat is full of a kind of down and produces whistling sounds, as from a reed flute. For the duration of the disease, a terrible thirst, and total body weakness. After a year, the patient succumbs wretchedly to the devastation.[33]

> The second consumption: it comes from exhaustion. The manifestations are about the same as in the previous case, but the sickness has more remissions and it slackens in the summer. The spittle is thicker; the cough is overpowering especially in the mornings; there is more pain in the chest—it feels like a stone; the back, too, is painful, the skin sweaty, and with the least exertion the patient pants and breathes heavily. In this disease, death overtakes the victim usually after three years.[34]

> The third consumption . . . First, the person becomes black and somewhat swollen, with yellowish skin below the eyes; the body's vessels are distended and yellow, but some take on a bright red color; the most visible are those under the armpits. The spittle is yellow when there is any, the patient chokes and at times cannot cough even if he wants to; sometimes, too, the choking and the need to cough bring on abundant vomiting either of bile or phlegm or often also of food,

when the patient has eaten; immediately afterward, the patient feels lightened, but the improvement does not last long, and the same suffering begins again. The voice is more shrill than when well. From time to time, there are chills and fevers accompanied by sweating . . . Usually the disease lasts for nine years; after that time, though in a wasted state, one can last; but few escape, it is so severe.[35]

The first type of consumption is described still more vividly in *Diseases,* II:

When there is lung ailment, the patient spits up slimy substances that are thick, greenish, and sweet; there is grinding of teeth, pain takes over the chest and back, a slight whistling can be heard in the throat; the throat is dry, the hollows beneath the eyes are red, the voice lowers, the feet swell and the nails bend; the upper body wastes away and the patient grows thin. The slimy spittle is disgusting to the patient when it is brought up and is in the mouth. He coughs especially in the morning and the middle of the night, but also at other times. The disease tends to attack younger women rather than older ones. Then, if hair falls out and the head is bald as after a sickness, and, when the patient spits on charcoal, if the slimy substance gives off a strong smell, the end is near and the cause of death will be diarrhea.[36]

The chapter that follows immediately upon this description is entitled "another *phthóē.*" One can therefore conclude that the preceding pulmonary ailment was indeed, for the author of this treatise or for one of its ancient editors, a kind of consumption. Despite some differences of detail, the clinical identity of the pathological states described in *Internal Affections,* 10 ("the first consumption"), and *Diseases,* II, 48, is not in doubt. As for the second *phthóē,* essentially it corresponds to the third consumption of *Internal Affections,* but with a fairly important difference in the presentation of the symptoms. Here is the semiological part of *Diseases,* II, 49: "The patient coughs; his spittle is abundant and moist; at times, without effort, he spits up pus like a hailstone; crushed between the fingers, this pus is hard and malodorous. The voice is clear, and the patient feels no pain. He is not attacked by fever, but sometimes by heat; above all, he is weak . . . The disease lasts seven or nine years. In this case, if the patient is treated from the start, he is cured."[37] Another clinical portrait of the same pathological category is drawn in chapter 50 of this treatise. It speaks of the "aphthous pulmonary flute," "the raucous voice," slimy spittle that sometimes contains "hard pieces that resemble a fungous growth from an ulcer," "growing thin," "reddening cheeks," "curving nails," as well as rapid death "amidst the spitting of blood and pus."[38]

To be sure, in the descriptions I have just been citing, the nosological distinctions are not those of modern medicine. All the various kinds of consumption have symptoms that may signify pulmonary tuberculosis in the current sense of the term, but at the same time, each of them goes beyond the framework of the modern disease. In all the examples, the symptomatology is based on concrete observation of pulmonary tuberculosis, but it also includes clinical experience with cavities and suppurating ailments that are not tuberculous: abscesses, fistulated empyemas, excavating cancers, bronchiectases, and so forth. The "first" consumption corresponds perfectly to the serious forms of ulcero-caseous tuberculosis in the adult, but at the same time it also corresponds to the clinical appearances of a pulmonary abscess or a bronchopulmonary cancer. The picture in *Diseases,* II, 50, is of the typical tuberculosis sufferer as we know it, especially from descriptions of the first half of the nineteenth century. Tuberculosis is no doubt its major component, but some symptoms, especially the seriousness of the morning cough and the qualities of the sputum, also recall bronchial dilatation.[39] Black skin coloration and extreme debility could also have been seen in cases of tuberculous affection of the adrenal glands (Addison's disease). Strident respiration is a sign of the stenosic form of tracheobronchial tuberculosis. In the description given by *Diseases,* II, 50, it is also easy to recognize tuberculous pharyngitis, a common complication of pulmonary tuberculosis. But just as Hippocratic consumption extends beyond pulmonary tuberculosis in the modern sense of the word, it is also true that some other classical nosological entities, for instance, empyema and pleurisy, comprise clinical forms due to infection of the lungs and pleura by Koch's bacillus. It seems to me that the importance of pleurisies in the writings of the ancient Greek physicians[40] can only be explained by the predominance of tuberculosis in their etiology.

The modern physician can admire the subtlety of the Hippocratic symptomatology and appreciate the judiciousness of its prognostic. In the descriptions given above, the high points are the observations of secondary signs in addition to wasting away, hemoptysis, purulent sputum, and mitigated fever: the curved nails, which are part of the phenomenon now known as clubbing;[41] the quality of the sputum and the nature of the cough; the examination of sputum over hot coals; the smell of the patient's breath; the hair loss and the diarrhea in the terminal phase of consumption. The existence of passages parallel to these in the form of aphorisms elsewhere in the Hippocratic corpus shows how much value was attached to such signs: "In persons affected with consumption, if the sputa that they cough up have a fetid smell when poured on burning coals, and if their hair falls out, then it is fatal."[42] In a similar text, there is the added detail that "there is a strong smell of burnt meat."[43] In fact, this method makes it possible to detect the presence of pulmonary tissue debris in the sputum.

When consumptives spit in sea water and the pus falls to the bottom, danger is imminent. The water should be in a copper vase.[44]

Consumptives whose hair falls out die from diarrhea; and all consumptives with diarrhea die.[45]

Those who cough up foaming blood without feeling pain beneath the diaphragm are getting it from their lungs.[46]

Foaming blood in the absence of abdominal pain is precisely the difference between hemoptysis and hematemesis. This particular aphorism suggests that the Hippocratic physicians saw both tuberculosis of the respiratory tract and gastric ulcer in daily practice.

According to the medical texts of the classical era, the basic form of consumption is marked by pathological events whose origins lie in the lungs. The disease arises from the fluxion of phlegm that descends from the head to the lungs and brings on suppuration[47] or, rather, from an accumulation of phlegm and bile. These humors, existing to excess, stay in the lungs, gather there, and, becoming tainted, form "tumors" or masses of pus; the evacuation of this pus by expectoration transforms the masses into cavities, which either can become totally dessicated (after the patient is cured) or can continue to suppurate (with a fatal result marked by the dessication of the body and by diarrhea).[48] The pathological mass in the lungs, which today we call the tubercle, is called *phûma* in the Hippocratic texts. It is a technical term with a very broad sense, encompassing "any unnatural tumor that arrives spontaneously";[49] it is especially appropriate for suppurating tumors. So the word *phûma* corresponds primarily to our terms "abscess" and "tubercle," but it also functions as the name for certain forms of cancer and hydatid cyst. In a context that assuredly refers to tuberculosis, the author of the treatise *Joints* mentions intrapulmonary *phûmata* that are "hard and raw." Impressed by this medical knowledge, Charles Daremberg exclaimed that "the ancients assimilated lung tubercles to true abscesses, with periods of being unconcocted and of coction, perceiving the overall progress of the disease and the nature of the expectorate that accompanies the suppurated tubercles, while our word tubercle refers instead to the origin, form, and first stage of an accidental pathological process."[50]

I will not go into detail on the pathogenetic explanation of consumption, since my task is to make out the reality of diseases and not to follow the tortuous byways of medical theorizing. Still, I cannot suppress my amazement at the anatomopathological realism of the nineteenth chapter of *Diseases,* I, whose subject is the formation of tubercles and their cavitation. Doesn't such knowledge of facts that are invisible from the outside of the body imply recourse to autopsy?[51] An alternative, historical explanation seems superior: recourse to analogy with animals from butchers or sacrifices. In *Youth and Old Age* Aristotle said of the death of animals in general, "Animals die without violent pain, and the deliverance of their souls is utterly insensate. All the diseases that harden the lung, whether by tubercles *(tòn pneúmona sklēròn ḕ phúmasin)* or secretions or an excess of unhealthy heat, as in accesses of fever, make breathing frequent."[52]

An Epidemiological Observation and Two Clinical Cases

Book 2 of *Diseases* and the treatise *Internal Affections* are traditionally associated with the medical community of Cnidus and are said to have found inspiration in the nosological descriptions recorded in the *Cnidian Sentences,* a work with major contributions from Euryphon, Hippocrates' senior colleague. However, it is worth noting that the same clinical notion of consumption occurs in works thought to be the most authentic, that is, those attributed to Hippocrates himself or at least to the physicians of Cos during the last quarter of the fifth century B.C. Here is an itinerant Coan physician's account of diseases seen over the course of a year on Thasos:

> Beginning early in the summer, throughout the summer and in winter many of those who had been ailing for a long time took to their beds in a state of consumption, while many also who had hitherto been doubtful sufferers at this time showed undoubted symptoms. Some showed the symptoms now for the first time; these were the ones whose constitution inclined to be consumptive. Many, in fact most of them, died; of those who took to their beds I do not know one who survived even for a short time. Death came more promptly than is usual in consumption, and yet the other complaints, which will be described presently, though longer and attended with fever, were easily supported and did not prove fatal. For consumption was the worst of the diseases that occurred, and alone was responsible for the great mortality. In the majority of cases the symptoms were these. Fevers with shivering, continuous, acute, not completely intermitting, but of the semiterian type; remitting during one day they were exacerbated on the next, becoming on the whole more acute. Sweats were continual, but not all over the body. Severe chills in the extremities, which with difficulty recovered their warmth. Bowels disordered, with bilious, scanty, unmixed, thin, smarting stools, causing the patient to get up often. Urine either thin, colourless, unconcocted and scanty, or thick and with a slight deposit, not settling favourably, but with a crude and unfavourable deposit. The patients frequently coughed up small, concocted sputa, brought up little by little with difficulty. Those exhibiting the symptoms in their most violent form showed no concoction at all, but continued spitting crude sputa. In the majority of these cases the throat was throughout painful from the beginning, being red and inflamed. Fluxes slight, thin, pungent. Patients quickly wasted away and grew worse, being throughout averse to all food and experiencing no thirst. Delirium in many cases as death approached. Such were the symptoms of the consumption.[53]

This account is the nosological core of the first *katástasis* of Thasos.[54] The observations in question date from around 410 B.C. Their author is not conveying bookish knowledge but reporting what he actually saw. To be sure, he saw the clinical events by way of a medical theory. Charles Daremberg provides an especially insightful commentary on this passage: "This picture of consumption is strikingly realistic. Even so, it is useful to note that the disease is here described more as a general ailment than a chest disorder, and that the description of general symptoms exceeds that of local ones in terms of the space and significance accorded them by Hippocrates."[55] For the historian of diseases, the interest of this first *katástasis* lies primarily in the fact that it studies consumption as a collective phenomenon. There is no doubt that it attests to the seasonal exacerbation of a tuberculous endemic on the island. The limitation of such an endemic to a single island seems unlikely, and this Hippocratic testimony should be thought of as a valuable reminder of the prevalence of tuberculous diseases at the time of the Peloponnesian War.[56]

The Hippocratic physicians knew that consumption could be a social phenomenon, a disease affecting several people at once, but they still did not believe in infection.[57] To account for the epidemic outbreak of consumption, Hippocrates appealed to the noxious effects of certain ecological factors and especially to the determining role of climate. However, since all persons inhabiting the same places were subject to the same climatic conditions, it was necessary to explain in theoretical terms the empirical fact that only a portion of those individuals exposed to the unhealthy factors actually fell ill. Hippocrates' explanation is simple, skillful, and based on precise clinical observation: the disease results from the coincidence of external factors (meteorological as well as earth-bound conditions—diet, exercise, and so forth) with individual predispositions, with a personal "constitution" that reacts pathologically to changing local conditions.

For most Greek physicians of the classical period, the constitution of an organism was nothing more than a global expression of its individual mixture of bodily humors. Since they could not acquire direct experience of this humoral mixture, Hippocrates and his disciples studied the relations between the habitus of patients and their diseases in order to deduce the features of temperament and, in the last analysis, the constitutional weaknesses of each person. They knew that predisposition to tuberculosis depended on age, sex, mental state, heredity, and prior way of life. According to the Hippocratic texts, "Consumption commonly occurs between age eighteen and thirty-five."[58] Women in particular are threatened by it, especially during pregnancy.[59] The prognosis is very poor when it breaks out after amenorrhea.[60] Phthisis frequently supervenes after childbirth.[61] The author of the treatise the *Sacred Disease* asserts in explicit terms the decisive role of heredity not just in the case of epilepsy but also in our disease: "One consumptive is born from another"![62] In *Prorrheticon,* II, consumption is mentioned, along with dropsy, gout, and epilepsy, as a disease whose cure is difficult when there is a genetic predisposition.[63] The predisposition itself can be recognized from the overall appearance of the body—at least that was the teaching of the Coan physicians. In an account of his yearlong observations of the diseases prevailing in Thasos at some point in the last quarter of the fourth century B.C., Hippocrates or a physician close to him noted that "consumption afflicted men with smooth skin, whitish, with freckles, ruddy, blue-eyed, with soft, puffy flesh and shoulder blades shaped like wings."[64] A late Hippocratic text adds to this profile a flattened thoracic cage.[65] The notion of habitus phthisicus caught on, and Hippocrates' description, especially his mention of the winged shoulder blade, was repeated by Celsus and Aretaeus of Cappadocia. It continued to influence the diagnosis and prognosis of pulmonary tuberculosis up to our time. The modern physician can confirm, with admiration, the acuity of the ancient Greek practitioners' clinical eye, though he repudiates their theoretical conclusions, which go beyond observed correlations.

For physicians at the end of the nineteenth century, at the apogee of medical bacteriology, "this habitus is not the cause, it is the sign of the disease."[66] Around the middle of the twentieth century, some famous experts returned to the classical opinion that the habitus was, if not completely, at least in some of its essential components, the hereditary constitutional condition of pulmonary consumption. The modern notion of "germ" does not supplant the ancient concept of "terrain"; it only opens a new dialogue between the acquired and the inborn.

I leave aside these problems in medical theory in order to look more closely at the concrete nosographic experience of the Greek practitioners, at the bedside reality of consumption. Here is a typical description that gives, in condensed form, information about a sequence of morbid events whose dramatic aspects do not accord with the cold style of the narrative:[67] "The wife of Simos, shaken during childbirth, had a pain in the chest and the side; coughing, bouts of fever, slightly purulent expectorates;[68] consumption, then things returned to normal;[69] then, for six months, bouts of fever and constant diarrhea; at the end, the fever stopped; then the bowels tightened up; seven days later she died." In this case, consumption is enunciated as a symptom among others and not as a generic term for the whole clinical picture. The initial stages are sketched rapidly. The author wishes to make plain the pathogenic role of childbirth or, to state his opinion more precisely, that of succussion during it. The reference is to a therapeutic procedure whose use is actually recommended in some gynecological treatises in the same collection.[70] Although this procedure, which is undisguisedly condemned in the text cited above, can have no justification in the eyes of a modern physician, it still cannot be accused of having caused the consumption that ended the life of the wife of Simos. On the other hand, pregnancy and the stress of childbirth surely aggravated a heretofore latent tuberculous condition in her.

I now cite another case history that is reported in greater detail by the same Hippocratic writer from the fourth century B.C.:[71]

In the wife of Polycrates, around the dog days of summer, fever; difficulty breathing, less so in the morning, worse from midday on, when it became a little more rapid; coughing and immediately sputum that was purulent from the start; within, along the throat and windpipe, husky wheezing; good coloring on the face; red cheeks, not dark red but, on the contrary, fairly bright. As time went on, voice becoming hoarse and body wasted, scabs on the loins, and bowel movement on the watery side. The seventieth day: the fever grows very cold externally; on the temples, no throbbing;[72] but the breathing becomes more and more rapid. After this respite, the breathlessness is so heightened that the patient remains seated until the moment of death. In the windpipe, there was a lot of noise; also, terrible sweats; looks full of understanding up to the final moment. Once, her fever lightened for more than five days. After the first few days the patient did not cease spitting up purulent substances.

This clinical picture is grippingly real, and except for its silence about blood in the sputum, corresponds completely to the unfolding of pulmonary consumption with a specifically concomitant laryngitis. Nevertheless, one should realize that this retrospective diagnosis is not altogether certain: though the sequence of symptoms corresponds exactly to that which laryngeal and pulmonary tuberculosis can provide, it is also compatible with several other serious diseases of the respiratory organs. One can imagine a diagnosis of cancer of the larynx, trachea, or bronchi, which would produce respiratory wheezing as well as dyspnea turning into orthopnea along with cancerous cachexia. Still, the striking redness of the cheeks tells against malignant consumption and in favor of tuberculous infection.

Notes on Consumption in the Hellenistic and Roman Eras

The Roman encyclopedist Celsus (first century A.D.) tells us that the Greek physicians distinguish three kinds of consumption (*tabes*), the first two of which, *atrophia* and *kachexia,* were thought to be the result of nutritional insufficiencies or of the body's inability to profit from nutrients even when abundant. "The third and most dangerous kind is the one the Greeks call *phthísis;* it usually begins by attacking the head, then it attacks the lung, where it produces an ulcer that is accompanied by a small, dull fever that comes and goes. The patient coughs a lot, spits up pus and sometimes blood."[73] It would be hard to find a more succinct definition of pulmonary tuberculosis. But what Celsus describes simply and compendiously, an Alexandrian physician of the same era, Aretaeus of Cappadocia, can relate in minute and judicious detail: his chapter on consumption is the high point of medical symptomatology in antiquity.[74] Even a physician of today could learn by reflecting upon his text. Yet I cannot stop to analyze it, since the chronological framework of my study forces me just to mention it along with the passages on consumption scattered in the wordy *oeuvre* of Galen as well as the finicky account in Caelius Aurelianus.[75]

Knowledge of consumption advanced substantially from Hippocrates to the beginning of the Christian era. Is this due to an increase in the number of consumptives during the Alexandrian period? We do not know, nor is such an inference inevitable. On the other hand, it is certain that at no time during the classical, Hellenistic, and Roman periods was consumption a rare disease. All post-Hippocratic medical writers consider it at once a serious but not necessarily mortal disease that is banal, ubiquitous, and well known. Aretaeus says that even an *idiṓtēs,* an average person without professional medical knowledge, can recognize the disease effectively when he sees a pale and worn-out invalid who coughs.[76] This statement unintentionally suggests the commonness of a disease that can supposedly be diagnosed by everyone and anyone one may come across in daily life. But relatively few famous persons of antiquity are said to die of consumption. That is not a proof of the rarity of the disease, since it tends to favor the young, who have not lived long enough to acquire notoriety. Actually, pulmonary tuberculosis appeared rarer among the old than it really was. Though easy to recognize in young people, it was mistaken for senile cachexia or *peripneumonía* in the old. Perhaps one can understand the relative rarity of consumption in the pathological histories of the famous as a sign of the disease's social selectivity, since it attacked primarily the poor. Still, it had its victims: the Greek general Aratus of Sicyon (ca. 271–213 B.C.) and the Macedonian king Antigonos II Doson (ca. 263–220 B.C.). The former died as the result of hemoptysis and a wasting away that he himself thought were signs of poisoning;[77] the latter likewise expired after spitting blood.[78] The dietitian Herodicus of Selymbria and the comic author Theopompus of Athens (fifth century B.C.) were consumptives—the second claiming that he was cured by the divine intervention of Asclepius.[79] In the Athenian sanctuary of the god of medicine there was an *ex voto* statue of Parian marble of a severely emaciated Theopompus reclining on his bed.[80] Votive stelae at Epidaurus relate the miraculous story of Thersandrus of Halieis, who, down with consumption, was healed by the sacred snake of Asclepius (second half of the fourth century B.C.).[81]

In such sanctuaries, the cure for consumption was a matter at once of diet, climate, and divine intervention. For this particular disease, such an approach was certainly superior to strictly medical treatment. Celsus only repeats an old adage when he advises consumptives to "take long cruises, change your climate, and move to a thicker air than the one you leave behind." The dry climate of Egypt was especially prized: consumptives get better, says Celsus, "passing from Italy to Alexandria."[82] Following this recommendation, Pliny the Younger sent his freedman Zosimus to Egypt to treat his consumption. When he returned from Africa to Rome, Zosimus had a relapse and Pliny dispatched him for a stay in subalpine Forum Iulii (Cividale).[83] No doubt, climatic therapy along with rest and good food was the most effective means at the time in the struggle against tuberculosis on an individual level. From a public health standpoint, such trips for consumptives had the disadvantage of spreading the contagion outside of Rome, a city that had become one of its havens since the Hellenistic period or earlier.

It is worth noticing that Pliny the Younger and his circle at Rome believed in the contagiousness of the disease. The fact emerges clearly from the moving eulogy of Fannia, a young, dedicated noblewoman who was caring for the Vestal Virgin Junia and caught a disease with the typical symptoms of pulmonary tuberculosis: "continuous bouts of fever, worsening cough, emaciation, great weakness."[84] For Fannia's fellow citizens, the diagnosis was beyond doubt; for a modern physician reading Pliny's epistles, it is very likely.

Extrapulmonary Tuberculoses

Medical texts confirm the presence in the classical Greek world of certain extrapulmonary forms of tuberculosis. They confirm rather than disclose it, since the documentation of pulmonary consumption suffices in itself to postulate the existence of other localizations for tuberculous infection. Although the documents in question are explicit enough to leave no doubt about the retrospective diagnosis, they unfortunately provide no information on the relative frequency of tuberculous attack on various organs. That frequency may well have undergone historical fluctuations. Even though we can extrapolate from the current situation about the physiopathological progress of tuberculous inflammation and the clinical aspects of its chief localizations, it is not possible to do the same with regard to their statistical distribution.

The unity of tuberculosis was not hinted at until the eighteenth century, nor was it demonstrated until the full flowering of the new medicine of the nineteenth century.[85] The physicians of antiquity could not conceive of this unity, since it is based on the anatomopathological traits of the specific microbial lesion. In ancient times, tuberculosis was only known as a host of subdivided, autonomous ailments. In any case, that was a legitimate analysis of the nosological reality as long as a disease was defined by its symptoms. For the physicians of yore there was in principle no reason, apart from their possible coexistence, to associate pulmonary consumption, scrofula, white swelling (of the joints), lupus, and certain inflammations of the genito-urinary organs.

It is therefore all the more remarkable that the Hippocratic physicians noted the coincidence and even established a causal link between the pulmonary form of the disease and acquired angular gibbosity. According to a Hippocratic aphorism, "Those who become hunchbacks before puberty as a result of dyspnea *(ásthma)*—are lost."[86] A chapter in the treatise *Joints* devoted to the curvature of the spine from internal causes provides more detail:

When the spinal vertebrae are drawn into a hump by diseases, most cases are incurable, especially when the hump is formed above the attachment of the diaphragm . . . When humpback occurs in children before the body has completed its growth, the legs and arms attain full size, but the body will not grow correspondingly at the spine; and those limbs are spindly. And where the hump is above the diaphragm, the ribs do not enlarge in breadth, but forwards, and the chest becomes pointed instead of broad; the patients also get short of breath and hoarse, for the cavities which receive and send out the breath have smaller capacity . . . They have also, as a rule, hard and unripened tubercles *(phúmata)* in the lungs; for the first appearance *(próphasis)* of the curvature and contraction is in most cases due to such gatherings, in which the neighboring ligaments *(tónoi)* take part. Cases where the curvature is below the diaphragm are sometimes complicated with affections of the kidneys and parts about the bladder, and besides there are purulent abscessions in the lumbar region and about the groin, chronic and hard to cure; and neither of these causes resolution of the curvatures.[87]

There can be no doubt about this author's familiarity with Pott's disease.[88] His text was to be retained and paraphrased by Celsus and Galen; the disease in question seems to have been a common one. This allows us to consider reasonable the diagnosis of tuberculosis of the spine in a certain number of cases that make up the rich iconography of hunchbacks in the Hellenistic and Roman eras.[89]

Osteoarticular tuberculosis can attack all bones and joints. In modern times it has a clear predilection for the spine, but tuberculous caries also can reside relatively often in the articular regions of the lower limbs. In ancient descriptions of coxalgia and knee arthritis, tuberculosis must surely play a part, but it is hardly possible to make a differential diagnosis. Visceral forms of tuberculosis readily accompany skeletal affections. Tuberculous peritonitis certainly existed in ancient Greece, but we are once more faced with the impossibility of distinguishing, just on the basis of a clinical description, tuberculosis from other inflammatory diseases of the gut or even diseases of an altogether different type.

The dropsy of antiquity, particularly ascites (effusion of liquids into the peritoneal cavity), can originate in tuberculosis of the serous membranes, but that is only one among many pathogenetic possibilities. As for the "eloquently laconic" Hippocratic aphorism to the effect that "the cough supervening in dropsy is bad," Charles Coury thought it sensible in the context of a tuberculous pathology.[90] But in its clinical context, this cough may well be the symptom of pulmonary edema arising from a cardiac disorder, which can also produce ascites as a result of circulatory insufficiency.

I can cite a concrete instance in which the diagnosis of visceral and osteoarticular tuberculosis is perfectly suitable but still not obligatory: "Bion, after a prolonged dropsical state, had no appetite for several days and suffered from strangury; a deposit formed on his left knee; suppuration; death."[91] Was this patient a victim of tuberculosis? Or did he succumb to the complications of a gonococcal infection? Or, again, did he have Bright's disease and, independently of it, acute arthritis of the left knee? We do not know Bion's age. Another example: osteoarticular tuberculosis often strikes children and kills them by miliary spread. There is a strange funerary inscription in Greek that deserves mention in this context, even though it belongs to a relatively late period (third century A.D.). The medical-historical interest of this epitaph is considerable, since it relates a true clinical history, namely, the sufferings of one Lucius Minicius Anthimianus, who died at age 4½ after a painful disease of the testicles, the decay of his metatarsal bones, and a swelling of his viscera that was accompanied by a wasting of his body. The retrospective diagnosis is uncertain, since it cannot be ruled out that the three diseases (orchitis, osseous caries, and an abdominal disorder) were autonomous. But if we interpret all the pathological manifestations of this brief life as phases of a single disease, by far the most likely diagnosis is tuberculosis. Other possibilities are leukemia and lymphosarcoma.[92]

The Hippocratic corpus contains a description of scrofula *(khoirádes)* that, though somewhat confused, agrees with the modern profile of tuberculous cervical adenitis.[93] The kinship between scrofula and pulmonary tuberculosis was not even suspected, despite the fact that the Hippocratic writers insisted on explaining the two diseases by the same pathogenetic process, namely, local corruption of the plhegm flowing from the head. In the case of consumption, the fluxion was by way of the lungs, and in scrofula, it passed to the tonsils, where it brought on an inflammation of the throat and of one or both ears and, finally swelling of the glands in the neck, the armpits, or the groin.[94] The Greek physicians of the classical period knew of the painless but insidious nature of scrofula, its sluggish progress, and the difficulties of treating it. From the evidence in a Hippocratic text of the fourth century B.C., it was very common in children.[95] Though it was rare from age 42 to age 63,[96] it became a common disease once again among the old.[97]

It is perfectly reasonable to suggest the tuberculous nature of certain nephrites, cystites, endometrioses, meningites, otites, kerato-conjunctivites, iridocyclites, and serious dermatoses that are mentioned here and there in the Hippocratic corpus and the works of Aretaeus, Celsus, Rufus, Galen, and other physicians. However, the diagnosis in these cases cannot with certainty pass the anatomoclinical level to reach that of a specific etiology. In the genito-urinary region, the ravages of tuberculosis were important, but they evade historical analysis: the symptoms of genito-urinary tuberculosis are confused with those of nonspecific inflammations of those organs.

The texts we have been examining prove that from the first medico-historical documentation, there existed in the Mediterranean, alongside the pulmonary form of tuberculosis, osteoarticular, visceral, and glandular diseases that can be ascribed to Koch's bacillus or its ancestor. But what was the frequency of these diseases? Was there a preponderance of extrapulmonary as against pulmonary forms of tuberculosis? Was the pulmonary form more often serious or fibrinous? All questions of this type must unfortunately remain unanswered. Our sources are silent about the kind of quantitative information that is so important for the reconstruction of the natural history of mycobacterioses.

Chapter Eight

LEPROSY AND TUBERCULOSIS

Their Biological Relationship

A study of the protohistory of leprosy and tuberculosis would be incomplete without a comparative examination of their pathogenic microbes, of the biological relationship between them and their hosts, and of the immunological phenomena that arise when their infections cross.[1]

The germs of leprosy and of human and bovine tuberculosis are so closely related to each other that there can be no doubt as to their derivation from a common bacillus. They are all mycobacteria, species belonging to the genus *Mycobacterium,* which was defined in 1896 by K. B. Lehmann and R. O. Neumann. Mycobacteria are clearly distinguishable from other microbes by their slender, sticklike form and their immobility, as well as by a lipoid envelope that is dyed red by the Ziehl-Neelsen reagent and cannot be discolored by nitric acid: they are acid-fast bacilli. Though it is relatively simple to recognize this genus, determining the differences among the species that compose it can be difficult. Aside from the three "classic" pathogenic species, namely *Mycobacterium leprae, M. tuberculosis,* and *M. bovis,* we know today of a large number of so-called "atypical" species. To confirm a specific diagnosis, certain bacteriological culture characteristics must be taken into account (such as optimal growth temperature, growth speed, pigmentation), as well as biochemical and enzymatic tests, immune properties, pathogenic capability in various animals, and sensitivity to certain antibacillary substances.

Mycobacteria are spread throughout nature, either as free-living organisms (for instance, *M. terrae* and *M. aquae*), or as commensals on various animals and man without the least pathological consequence (for instance, *M. phlei* and *M. smegmatis*), or as parasites producing diseases whose seriousness varies from slight ulcerations to the fatal destruction of tissue and organs. Some species produce diseases in animals whose local lesions resemble human tuberculosis histologically: *M. marinum* (pathogenic agent in saltwater fish), *M. piscium* (agent in freshwater fish), *M. ranae* (agent of amphibian tuberculosis, to which reptiles are also susceptible), *M. thamnopoecilus* (agent of reptilian tuberculosis), *M. chelonei* (agent of pulmonary tuberculosis in turtles), *M. microti* (agent of glandular tuberculosis in certain rodents), *M. avium* (agent of aviary tuberculosis, especially affecting chickens but also pigs and humans), and so on. For cattle, in addition to *M. bovis,* I should mention two pathogenic species: *M. fortuitum,* which produces purulent adenitis, and *M. paratuberculosis,* which is the agent of diarrheic hypertrophying enteritis. In contrast to this broad spectrum of animal tuberculoses, there is only one known species of *Mycobacterium* that specifically produces leprosy in animals: *M. lepraemurium,* agent of murine leprosy. It is a parasite chiefly in rats, though it can occur in mice and hamsters.

Aside from the three species that are strongly pathogenic in humans, several "atypical" mycobacteria (especially *M. kansasii, M. avium, M. intracellulare, M. gordonae, M. scrofulaceum, M. balnei, M. ulcerans*) can produce pulmonary, glandular, cutaneous, and more rarely osseous, genito-urinary, and septicemic diseases in humans. These "paratuberculous" affections have been attracting increasing interest among physicians since the middle of the century. Their frequency—at least in the pulmonary form—seems to be mounting to a disquieting degree in countries with highly developed health care systems. The rise in "atypical" mycobacterioses (in some areas of the United States they account for up to 30 percent of the clinical cases of pulmonary tuberculosis) may be linked to a disequilibrium in the pathocoenosis of industrial societies that is caused by recent successes in the chemotherapy of "classic" tuberculosis and of other diseases with very virulent microbes.[2]

The worldwide distribution of mycobacteria and the variety in their habitats, ranging from free aquatic and terrestrial species to commensals and parasites of all classes of vertebrates, support Aidan Cockburn's opinion that the appearance of the first representatives of the *Mycobacterium* genus must go back several hundred million years. He explains the evolutionary birth of most mycobacterial species as a radiation parallel to the phylogenesis of their hosts. There was a "vertical" transmission of parasitic species, starting from a common ancestral form that infected salt- and freshwater fish on one side and reptiles, birds, and mammals on the other. This diachronic infection sequence produced the specialization or rather the ramifying specification of pathogenic mycobacteria that in some ways parallels the appearance of certain great animal phyla. That would account for the appearance of, among others, *Mycobacterium marinum,* a pathogenic bacterium for fish; *M. avium,* which infects birds; and the mycobacterium responsible for Johne's disease in cattle. The parasitism of most mycobacteria is not strictly elective: for example, *M. marinum* does not seem different from *M. balnei,* which produces cutaneous lesions in humans; *M. avium* plays a certain role in the etiology of tuberculous ailments in pigs as well as humans; and so forth. However, the human species has the privilege of harboring a highly specialized mycobacterium, *M. leprae.* According to Cockburn, leprosy is vertically derived from our ancestors and is therefore a very old disease in terms of human history, as old as humanity itself.[3]

But where does *M. tuberculosis* come from? Cockburn devised a fine hypothesis in this regard: that human tuberculosis was acquired from bovine tuberculosis by interspecific, "horizontal" transmission of the germ during a relatively recent era, the Early Neolithic Age (about 7000 B.C.). The appearance and spread of Koch's bacillus resulted from the domestication of cattle—apparently they did not suffer harm from it in the wild—and from the development of agriculture, a sedentary lifestyle, and the beginnings of urbanization. A mycobacterium weakly pathogenic to mammals was the ancestor of *M. tuberculosis.* It profited from changes in the ecological conditions of its hosts to increase its virulence and adapt itself via a bovine form to human populations living in more and more crowded towns.[4] According to Ronald Hare, "It would seem probable that pulmonary tuberculosis, caused by the human strains of *M. tuberculosis,* did not make its appearance anywhere until about the second millennium B.C. If this be so, it is possible that the human strain is a mutant of the bovine which had previously become established in the dairy cattle that were domesticated during the Neolithic period."[5] He also stresses that the germ of bovine tuberculosis has never been isolated from wild animals that were not in contact with their domesticated counterparts.[6] The bovine strain is infectious for humans, in whom it is transmitted mainly by way of milk and tends to produce abdominal, glandular, and osseous tuberculosis. For the Mediterranean societies, historical proofs of the existence of tuberculosis in domesticated cattle go back to classical antiquity.[7]

These hypotheses of Cockburn and Hare open new vistas on the study of the "natural history" of mycobacteria. I hope to contribute to it by modifying and complementing their ideas, especially as regards the genetic relationship between *M. leprae* and *M. tuberculosis.* But before formulating my own opinion on this subject, I should mention, however briefly, some immunological and epidemiological facts.

The Epidemiology of Leprosy

From an epidemiological standpoint, there is continuity between human tuberculosis and animal tuberculoses, but there is almost none between leprosy and animal mycobacterioses. Mammals living in proximity to men, particularly certain domestic animals and captive apes, easily fall victim to human strains of Koch's bacillus. The tuberculous diseases they suffer from hardly differ from those attacking humans. The situation is different in the case of the leprosy bacillus. Handbooks tell us that *M. leprae* is not pathogenic for any animal species, that it cannot be cultured, and that it cannot survive normally in an environment other than the human body. Research done in the last few years has shown that such categorical statements are not totally justified. For one thing, it has been discovered that Hansen's bacillus can be cultured on the footpads of mice, a finding that can have great practical value but sheds no new light on our theoretical problem, since the disease does not become generalized in an animal infected in this way. I mentioned a specific form of murine leprosy. More interestingly, recent observations suggest that some other animals may become leprous. Even though descriptions of leprosy in cats or frogs are unconvincing—like the strange observation of a "leprous" buffalo published in 1936, and unheard of since—apparently the existence of a leprous disease in armadillos is to be taken seriously. Research on the subject is ongoing, and it is not easy to get a clear picture at the moment. I merely point out a recently published finding that is adequately documented and upsets several accepted notions: two American researchers observed in 1977 that one of their laboratory animals, a chimpanzee, was suffering from a cutaneous disease similar to leprosy. They isolated a bacillus in the creature that possessed all the traits of *M. leprae* apart from some minimal enzymatic differences.[8] This chimpanzee had been captured in Africa, in Sierra Leone, which is a region with endemic leprosy. Probably the infection is transspecific, having spread from human to ape, and not an independent, simian type of leprosy.

None of this alters the fact that leprosy is above all a human disease, our prerogative, and that it is, moreover, strictly limited to human populations with a certain sociocultural profile. Its current geographic distribution testifies loud and clear to the role of poverty in the maintenance of its endemic zones. Leprosy, like tuberculosis, is a by-product of indigence. However, there is a great difference that is both evident and unexplained in the way poverty operates in regard to each disease. The causal chain in the case of tuberculosis is fairly clear—easier contamination in close quarters without aeration and sunlight, diminished resistance to infection as a result of malnutrition and exhausting work—but in the case of leprosy, the way poverty fosters the disease is largely a mystery to epidemiology. To be sure, population density, migrations, and the absence of personal hygiene all favor endemic leprosy, but these factors are insufficient to explain completely the vagaries of its geographic and sociocultural distribution. As for climatic conditions, they seem to play a secondary role, in contrast to what happens with treponematoses, malaria, and some tropical parasitic diseases. Leprosy as well as tuberculosis has been rampant in all climates, from the Far East and black Africa to Scandinavia. Moreover, sociocultural and geographic factors cannot account for historical fluctuations in the contagiousness of leprosy. They are probably linked to changes in the bacillus itself and perhaps even more to complex immunological phenomena, such as a biological balancing process between the populations of this parasitic microbe and those of its sole host.

Nowadays leprosy is, relatively speaking, just slightly contagious. Only a small number of individuals exposed to it become leprous, and the majority of persons who contract the disease undergo no malignant clinical evolution. That is true even in the absence of any protection or treatment (we do have at our disposal fairly effective chemotherapy for leprosy). A single figure is enough to convince us of the current low contagiousness of the disease, even though its chronic nature should favor, as in the epidemiology of tuberculosis, the wide dissemination of its bacilli: cases of conjugal leprosy are less than 3 percent of the total. The difference, then, between leprosy and tuberculosis is striking, for tuberculosis is clearly a familial ailment that is often transmitted by cohabitation.

The situation of lepers in Greece in the nineteenth century is a good illustration of how socially innocuous this disease can be, unless certain and, to repeat, still unknown conditions are met that facilitate its spread.[9] During the whole century, the number of lepers in Greece remained more or less constant—a few hundred cases, about 150 according to official statistics.[10] They were grouped into small colonies that were not strictly isolated from the rest of the population. Moreover, numerous lepers were married to healthy persons who themselves did not suffer from the disease. Clon Stéphanos relates that in the village of Keneri, where 150 families lived in great poverty beside an open leper house, not a single healthy villager was known to become infected with the disease.[11] It is almost certain that the clinical form leprosy takes depends on the "terrain," that is, the host's resistance, not the intrinsic properties of the germ that is responsible for infection in a given case. Tuberculoid leprosy is the high resistance form of reaction to Hansen's bacillus, while lepromatous leprosy is the low resistance form. Resistance itself is partly the result of hereditary, hormonal, nutritional, and other factors whose nature and mechanism are still mostly obscure,[12] and partly the result of previous contacts with Hansen's bacillus or other mycobacteria that set in motion immunological defense processes.

The presence in an individual of specific antibodies can be detected by Mitsuda reaction (a reaction to the intradermic injection of lepromin, a sterile extract from tissue rich in Hansen's bacillus). This reaction is negative in young children, the majority of adults not exposed to leprous infection, and persons who have contracted lepromatous leprosy. Mitsuda reaction is positive (that is, it proves the presence of a specific defense against bacillary antigen) in persons with tuberculoid leprosy, healthy persons who live around lepers, and a certain number of adults who have never had contact with lepers. The positive result of this test in the last group, at first very surprising, can be explained as a consequence of immunological affinities between various species of mycobacteria: it has been shown that the first stages of infection with tuberculosis as well as BCG (bacille Calmette-Guérin) vaccination can produce a positive Mitsuda reaction.[13] This makes plausible the hypothesis that infection by tuberculous mycobacteria provides relative immunity against leprosy.[14]

Clearly, such a hypothesis has important consequences both for public health professionals and for historians of diseases. For the latter, the hypothesis provides an elegant and unforeseen solution to the problem of the disappearance of the medieval leprosy endemic in western Europe.[15] From the standpoint of an antagonism between leprosy and tuberculosis based on immunological competition, it seems possible or even probable that the retreat of leprosy in the West was linked to a rise in tuberculosis, which for its part coincided with the social, economic, and demographic changes of the fourteenth century.[16] In the domain of public health, BCG vaccination has been undertaken in leprous endemic zones to determine whether it provides increased resistance to Hansen's bacillus, either by inciting the production of paraspecific antibodies or by arousing some nonspecific protective factor. The results now available are not statistically significant. Though they do not confirm the initial hypothesis, they do not refute it either.[17]

Whatever the case may be, the relations between leprosy and tuberculosis are very complex and cannot be reduced to a simple case of antagonism. To begin with, there is no real cross-allergy. Koch's bacillus can make Mitsuda reaction positive, but not always, and, more importantly, the inverse is not true: infection with Hansen's bacillus does not produce a positive Mantoux reaction (intradermic tuberculin test). So if, theoretically, tuberculosis may compete with leprosy, leprosy can have no effect on tuberculosis. In criticizing Chaussinand's ideas about the antagonism of leprosy and tuberculosis, several recent authorities have noted that (1) the number of observed cases of tuberculosis-sufferers with secondary leprosy is fairly high, (2) systematic radiological examinations have uncovered the presence of tuberculosis in Africa hard by havens of leprosy, and (3) the disappearance of tuberculosis in Scandinavia has not resulted in the recrudescence of leprosy.[18] These arguments effectively destroy the notion of a simple antagonism between the two diseases. But they do not, in my opinion, destroy the historical explanation for the disappearance of leprosy in medieval Europe, according to which it was the result of competition between two related mycobacteria, with the issue depending on numerous ecological factors and the dynamics of the European pathocoenosis as a whole.

In any case, the third argument of the three given above is of no weight at all, since the recrudescence of leprosy in Scandinavia is impossible because of a total change in sanitary conditions. The suppression of tuberculosis is only one component of the complex struggle against infectious disease in general. The second argument is banal and irrelevant to our problem. The coexistence of leprosy and tuberculosis in a given region is an undeniable fact that historical studies repeatedly confirm. But such coexistence does not exclude the possibility of a balanced relationship between the two diseases, of a subtle competition that in certain circumstances could swerve sharply in favor of one and make the other almost disappear. At the moment when leprosy invaded Europe, tuberculosis was well established, but we do not know its frequency or its preferences among social and age classes. If tuberculosis really did become an effective antagonist of leprosy across the population of Europe at a moment in history near the end of the Middle Ages, it may have been the result of specific epidemiological conditions, of a sociobiological disturbance in the pathocoenosis whose underlying causes we do not yet understand.

Finally, the first argument calls for the kinds of experimental investigation and meticulous observation that perhaps will provide the basis for an answer to my remarks above on the riddle of pathocoenotic equilibrium among the mycobacteria. It is undeniable that tuberculosis and leprosy, especially lepromatous leprosy, can be associated in the same patient. There is even an osteoarchaeological instance of it.[19] However, this only proves that the relation between Koch's and Hansen's bacillus is not a simple antibiosis—no one said that it was—and that in some individuals resistance to both germs can be lacking at one and the same time. It is enough that a tuberculous infection can protect even a relatively limited number of individuals against leprosy; that could produce, on the level of populations, a complex antagonism between the two diseases. An essential and often neglected factor in this is the age of the patient at the time of infection. We know the receptivity of children to leprosy. Does age at the moment of first infection with tuberculosis play a role in the ultimate reinforcement of an individual's resistance to the germ of leprosy? The question is interesting because the average age of first contact with the tubercle bacillus is closely dependent on sociocultural factors. In long-term processes, a slight shift can ultimately reverse tendencies and make one disease dominate or even almost eliminate another.

The Epidemiology of Tuberculosis

In today's world, tuberculosis is a ubiquitous disease with an incalculable number of victims. According to cautious estimates published by the World Health Organization, there are now on this earth more than 15 million cases of flourishing, infectious tuberculosis. At least 1 million to 2 million tuberculosis-sufferers die each year. New medicines have strongly reduced tuberculous mortality. However, it seems that current reductions in the frequency of this disease are less the result of specific chemotherapy than of BCG vaccination, genetic increases in resistance, and, above all, the improvement of hygiene. In developing countries, especially in Africa, it is still one of the major causes of disease and death. In some underdeveloped countries, more than 70 percent of the children 14 years of age are infected with it, as against 2 percent in countries with more favorable socioeconomic conditions. Tuberculosis beds well with debilitating parasitoses like malaria and schistosomiasis and especially well with malnutrition. One can speak of a true pathocoenotic symbiosis of these diseases. In Greece, that symbiosis has been plain to see since the Turkish occupation. In some rural regions, it lasted into recent times.[20] We should not forget that even in the 1930s respiratory tuberculosis still held a place in official Greek statistics as one of the chief causes of death.[21]

In the history of modern Europe, the spectacular rise in pulmonary tuberculosis, which reached its climax between the latter half of the eighteenth and the first half of the nineteenth century, has often been ascribed to large-scale urbanization. That can only be partially true. The medical historian must take account of the fact that tuberculosis also raged in rural environments, which were certainly its original haven. In ancient societies, an important factor in its spread was horizontal, transspecific transmission made possible from close contact with domestic animals, as when farmer and cattle live in a single dwelling. In modern times the transmission of tubercle bacilli is mainly from human to human, and in this regard no one could deny the importance of demographic density and crowded living spaces. But in themselves they cannot explain the historical vagaries in the distribution of malignant forms of tuberculosis. R. and J. Dubos devised a felicitous expression for the set of conditions mentioned above that are capable of igniting a tuberculosis endemic: physiological misery.[22]

Unlike leprosy, tuberculosis is an extremely contagious disease. Its bacilli enter the human body chiefly by inhalation and ingestion, but infection can also take place via the skin or placenta. The clinical form that the disease assumes depends largely on the resistance of the individual infected. The immediate result of infection is often subclinical or even completely lacking. From my point of view here, it is not insignificant that resistance to tuberculosis is genetically based. The immunity acquired after contact with Koch's bacillus is a particular form of "infection immunity" called premunition; its persistence is determined by the continuous presence in the human body of the infecting agent. It follows that in the epidemiology of this disease, the notion of "virgin ground" that is helpful, say, in the study of some viral diseases must be used with extreme caution. In the case of tuberculosis, acquired immunity is not preserved after the destruction of the germ in the host organism. The eventual growth of resistance in healthy individuals cannot result from acquired immunity but is the expression of genetic increases in natural resistance by the process of selection. This is a historical process that, if it takes place at all, must be very slow.

Different ethnic groups do not all offer the same natural resistance to tuberculosis. For instance, blacks and American Indians are less resistant than whites. Family differences can also be very pronounced. K. Pearson has shown that, in the incidence of overt forms of pulmonary tuberculosis, statistical correlations are much greater between parents and children than between spouses. Experimental research by Lewis and Lurie on laboratory animals has shown that any acquired resistance to tuberculosis is just a specific increase from the mechanisms of natural resistance. The physiological misery mentioned above gets in the way of these natural immunological mechanisms and so becomes a dominant factor.[23] Finally, I point out a recent discovery by French researchers, the isolation of *Mycobacterium africanum,* an agent of human, bovine, and perhaps simian tuberculosis with traits intermediate between those of *M. bovis* and *M. tuberculosis.*[24]

Diagram of the Evolution of Mycobacteria

Does Koch's bacillus derive from Hansen's, or vice versa? The question is a poor one, and it is not surprising that all those who have sought to answer it, however learned, have gone astray. No living species can derive from another existing species. These bacilli can only have a common ancestor whose form and other properties can and even should be closer to one of the two species (conservative or plesiomorphic branch) than the other (anagenetic or apomorphic branch). That is why the genetic relations within a monophyletic group must be represented not by a genealogical tree but by a cladogram.[25]

The genus *Mycobacterium* derives from a common ancestor (I have called it *M. archaicum*) whose descendants diversified and specialized themselves for subsistence in very different environments. The degree of specialization in the way of life of a given species is a valuable indicator of its apomorphy. The founding species lived in a free state. From it derive, on the conservative line, current free-living species and probably some saprophytic ones. The anagenetic branch includes species that live in association with multicellular organisms as pathogenic parasites. At the origin of this branch were species that became associated with sea animals (probably placoderms) in the very distant past. On the conservative line, their descendants are the current parasites of fish, and on the anagenetic side, the parasites of all other vertebrates. The initial association of mycobacteria with animals must have taken place before the passage of vertebrates from aquatic to terrestrial life. I would date it around the Upper Devonian period, a geological era that goes back more than 300 million years. As for the rest of the evolution of parasitic mycobacteria, until humans appeared it was parallel to the evolution of the host organisms. Basically it seems to be the result of the evolution of the vertebrates and the vertical transmission of their parasites. To be sure, that is only a hypothesis offered up for criticism and skepticism.

In an article that is relatively recent yet largely outdated in its microbiological and phylogenetic documentation, J. Grober asserts that the hypothesis of a parallelism between the evolution of mycobacteria and their hosts is not more likely than an alternative explanation, that of "furtive multiple introduction" by repeated mutation of free saprophytes into a variety of host species.[26] In my opinion, he is wrong. His alternative hypothesis would perhaps be defensible if the number of mycobacterial parasitic species and that of their host species were as small as he seems to believe. It is a theory that demands too many coincidences. Moreover, the microbes living as saprophytes on Metazoa (for instance, *M. smegmatis*) are more likely to be descendants of an originally pathogenic germ than the ancestor of such an agent.

The cladogram I have established (Figure 1) on the assumption of evolutionary parallelism corresponds to the real morphological and biochemical "distances," insofar as they are known to current research, between the various mycobacteria. As for the genetic relation between Koch's bacillus and Hansen's, it is my opinion that (1) a direct mutation of the ancestor of the tuberculous branch into an ancestor of the leprous branch or vice versa is ruled out, and (2) the separation of the tuberculous branch is prior to that of the leprous branch. Against Cockburn, I think it is not likely that leprosy is a mycobacterial disease transmitted vertically from one generation to the next, from the fossil hominids to *Homo sapiens*. One can suppose that *M. leprae* results from a horizontal infection not older than the Neolithic Age that resulted in the mutation of a parasite of rodents, either *M. lepraemurium* or a species that has disappeared or is as yet unknown. If humans have mycobacteria that are proper to them as the result of a parallel evolution, they must be found among the microbes that now inhabit their bodies in silence or are responsible for minor complaints, not among the germs of leprosy and tuberculosis. Tuberculosis was transmitted as far as cattle, either vertically or by a horizontal infection originating in birds. From there it passed into humans as an unfortunate consequence of the domestication of animals and a settled way of life.

The biological "distance," that is, the difference in specific properties, between *M. leprae* and most of the other mycobacteria (except for the tuberculous group) is greater than that separating the tuberculous branch from the rest. I have already listed the traits of *M. leprae* that attest to its maximal specialization, its perfect and almost exclusive adaptation to humans. That adaptation in itself suggests that leprosy is an "ancient" disease in terms of human history (the realization of an immunological equilibrium between the germ and its host means that leprosy is older than plague, for example), but on another level, that of the history of mycobacteria, extreme specialization is a sign that a species is "young" in relation

Figure 1. Cladogram of the Genus *Mycobacterium*

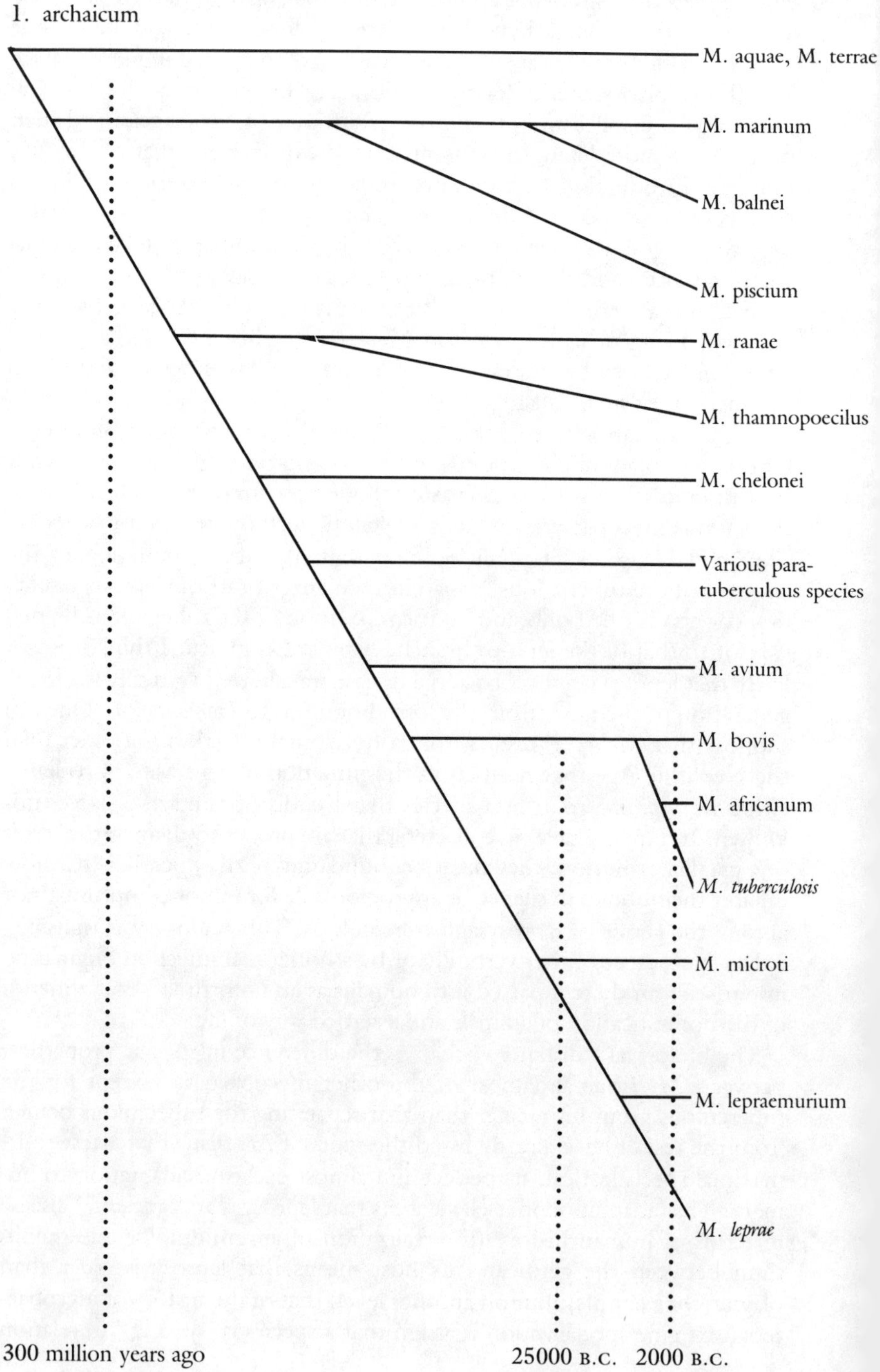

to other species of the same genus. The absence of leprosy from the pre-Columbian New World is no mean argument in favor of its "youthfulness." It suggests a *terminus post quem:* the appearance of leprosy should have happened after the interruption of prehistoric human migrations between Asia and America, that is, after the disappearance of the land-bridge across the Bering Strait.[27] The date of this interruption is not precisely known: more timid hypotheses place it around 10,000 B.C., and the most rash at around 25,000 B.C. What seems to me most reasonable is to place the date of the origin of leprosy, of the birth of *M. leprae,* between this date and, as I showed above in the analysis of historical documentation, the beginning of the second millennium B.C.

Some historical and biological considerations lead one to believe that the origin of *M. tuberculosis* does not go further back than the Neolithic Age. At first tuberculosis spread from cattle to humans. With the development of herding in sedentary populations,[28] this infectious disease became more common, and a strain of ancient tuberculous microbe adapted itself for survival in richly oxygenated human pulmonary tissue. It seems likely that *M. tuberculosis* appeared even later than *M. leprae.* That would contradict neither my cladogram nor what I was just saying about the differentiation of mycobacteria. To be sure, in that case it must be asserted that the pre-Columbian osteoarchaeological cases in the New World are all due to humans being infected with *M. bovis,* or more precisely to a mycobacterium of which *M. bovis* is the plesiomorphic descendant. There is no need to confuse the origin of *M. tuberculosis* with the older origins of the tuberculous branch, that is, of the common ancestor of the existing species *M. bovis, M. africanum,* and *M. tuberculosis.* The birth of *M. tuberculosis* probably took place in Africa from a "bovine" form (that is, by horizontal transmission) and through the intermediary of the "African" form. In classical Greece, *M. tuberculosis* was already present alongside *M. bovis.*

Chapter Nine

THE HARM IN BROAD BEANS
Legend and Reality

The physicians of classical Greece understood clearly how important environment can be for keeping the components of an organism in equilibrium.[1] They were aware, that is, of the ecology of health. Treatises attributed to Hippocrates—actually, the very ones it has become customary to praise to the skies—have a valid appreciation of the role that air, soil, and water play in the etiology of disease. Other texts in the Hippocratic corpus treat with remarkable philosophical insight and impressive technical mastery the medical issues of diet and exercise. These writers had observed the hereditary nature of epilepsy, strabismus, and certain deformities. In special cases, such as gout, a disease that corresponds better than any other to the explanatory principles of the pathology of humors, or pulmonary consumption, ancient practitioners began to understand some rules of the complex interaction between the innate and the acquired. They caught glimpses of the necessary nexus of internal and external factors, of disposition and triggering cause. But there are pathological states in which this two-sided causality is so complex that reason is no longer able to track down all the interconnections. In such cases, physicians can just refuse to see parts of reality in order not to compromise the rationality of the overall system. It is possible that in order to satisfy such needs for coherence certain intuitions from the archaic period had to be suppressed. A good example is the notion of infection, which, since it was cloaked in the magico-religious concept of pollution, found no quarter among the champions of rational medicine. Out it went, and as a result certain events in the day-to-day practice of medicine became literally invisible. A core of truth too well hidden in mystical trappings ended up on the trash heap of superstition. The event ultimately hindered subsequent attempts at a theory of infection that better answered to the demands of scientific rigor. It is my purpose now to examine closely the history of a certain medical theme in which, at one point, magical thought was probably nearer reality than strict reason.

A Pythagorean Prohibition and Its Justifications in Antiquity

A surprising rule of conduct, *kuámōn apékhesthai* 'abstain from broad beans,' is included among the Pythagorean *súmbola,* or pithy teachings, whose esoteric meaning escaped the common run of mortal men.[2] Since classical antiquity philosophers and historians have been fascinated by this prohibition. It was attributed to Pythagoras himself, the famed sage of the sixth century B.C., but Aristotle was aware that by his time the personal lucubrations of the master could not be clearly distinguished from the mass of material from his school. The person and teachings of Pythagoras are veiled in legend, transformed in the image of late accounts that divinize a charismatic leader and drown his original thought by systematizing it into a Platonizing doctrine that is more Hellenistic than archaic.[3]

At the outset I wish to stress two special aspects of the historical documentation on which our knowledge of the Pythagorean teaching about broad beans rests. First, the existing texts that attest to it directly are not earlier than the first century B.C. (they are Latin authors, like Cicero and, in a fairly obscure allusion, Horace), or if we consider only Greek sources, not earlier than the second century A.D. (Plutarch, Lucian of Samosata, Artemidorus, Clement of Alexandria). No information has come down to us on the exact words that Pythagoras used to formulate the tabu. The only way we happen to know of Empedocles' and Callimachus's verses about broad beans as well as the opinions of some fourth-century B.C. authors is through readers' citations.[4] On the other hand, the multiplicity of Greek and Roman witnesses on this subject, their recourse to earlier authors, and the already incomprehensible (to their eyes) nature of the prohibition lead me to believe that it is indeed older than the classical period in Greece. In a word, it seems to me that one can reasonably attribute to Pythagoras or the Pythagorean community at Croton a particular attitude toward broad beans; but one cannot determine that it originated there or what exactly its original form was. The Samian master's words, the famous *ipse dixit,* have not fled the barrier of time. Scarcely a few generations after the death of Pythagoras, the express motivation and original justification for the tabu were totally lost.

What, precisely, does the Pythagorean prohibition consist of? To begin with, it concerns a legume called *kúamos* in Greek and securely identified with the broad bean, *Vicia faba* L. (*Faba vulgaris* Mönch; also called horse bean or fava bean). The broad bean comes either from the region south of the Caspian Sea or from North Africa. It flourished in the wild in Persia and on the northwest coast of Africa. Its use as food, its cultivation, and its spread around the Mediterranean go back to prehistoric times.[5] Its seeds have been found in very ancient archaeological sites in Italy, in Swiss lake-dwellings, and in Egyptian tombs from the Pharaonic period. They have also been reported in Mycenaean tombs and in the ruins of Troy, beginning with the layers that date from the Early Bronze Age. Homer compares an arrow glancing off Menelaus's breastplate to the way "blackskinned broad beans" fly at winnowing time, which presupposes that his audience was familiar with this peasant activity.[6]

Ancient broad beans were smaller than modern ones, but they were doubtless ancestral varieties of *Vicia faba,* not a similar species that has by now disappeared or is not appreciated by modern farmers. From the botanical description in Theophrastus, it is certain that the Greek term *kúamos* (consistently translated by the Latin *faba*) denotes in the first place the broad bean, the whole plant as well as the seeds meant for eating.[7] However, a distinction should be drawn between the substantive *kúamos* by itself or the expression *kúamos Hellēnikós* 'Greek broad bean' and the expression *kúamos Aigúptios* 'Egyptian broad bean'; they are set apart implicitly in the Hippocratic corpus[8] and explicitly by Dioscorides.[9] The former designates the broad bean as such, while the latter is the pink lotus, an exotic plant known in Greece for its medicinal uses, not as a food.

The existence of this *kúamos Aigúptios* and of the chapter Dioscorides devotes to it has led some historians and botanists since the sixteenth century to consider the Pythagorean *kúamos* to be the edible seeds of the nelumbo (*Nelumbium speciosum* Willd. [*Nelumbo nucifera* Goert. and *Nymphaea nelumbo* L.]).[10] No author from antiquity suffers from such a confusion. Herodotus and Theophrastus discuss the two separately. It was known in antiquity that the latter, a kind of lotus, was considered sacred by certain Oriental peoples, though they did not forbid their priests to partake of it. In the modern literature on this subject some incorrect statements are to be found that result from a vicious circle: the identification of *kúamos* in Herodotus and Pythagoras with the nelumbo is made and then used to prove that it is correct. Pliny, who speaks of both "broad beans" (he call the first *faba* and the second *faba Aegyptia* or *colocasia*), mentions the Pythagorean prohibition only apropos of the common broad bean.[11] Plainly, his opinion in that regard was shared by other ancient authors, since it is hard to see why they would have discussed the subject at such length if in their opinion the Pythagorean rule concerned only a plant that was not usually eaten, was little known in Europe, and was considered sacred by foreigners to boot. What fascinated these thinkers was precisely the fact that the Pythagoreans forbade the consumption of a very popular food.

Several other botanical identifications have been proposed by modern scholars. I think they are to be rejected. Out of sheer ignorance some physicians translate *kúamos* as "haricot bean" (*Phaseolus* sp.), a plant not introduced into the Old World until the discovery of America.[12] Still more anachronistic is the desire to identify Pythagoras's bean with a toxic species similar to the Calabar bean. L. Livet believes that "the bean of which Pythagoras speaks is none other than henbane."[13] He stresses that the word *huoskúamos* (which designates henbane, *Hyoscyamus niger* L.) is composed of *hús* and *kúamos* and means "wild boar bean." Consequently, Pythagoras and his pupils could have meant this plant and used only the generic portion of its usual name. Actually, henbane, which is a poisonous plant inspiring holy terror, was well known to ancient Greek and Latin authors, who were careful not to confuse it with a harmless legume.[14] Livet's hypothesis, which is all conjecture, tries to explain the Pythagorean prohibition by reducing it to something so obvious that the interest it generated among ancient philosophers becomes incomprehensible: with or without a tabu, no one would be tempted to think of a notoriously toxic plant as food.

But it is worth considering whether or not the Pythagorean rule originally envisaged the use of broad beans as food. The wording most likely to be closest to the original formulation occurs in two citations that besides being early are also in verse. As a result, they were less exposed to corruption in the process of being transmitted, whether orally or in writing. Empedocles of Agrigentum, a philosopher and physician of the fifth century B.C. who in some ways was a perpetuator of Pythagorean teachings in Magna Graecia, says, "Unhappy, very unhappy one, do not touch broad beans."[15] Callimachus, a poet of the third century B.C., authored this couplet: "Do not touch broad beans, a food some devour, I tell you this just as Pythagoras did."[16] It is striking that both these writers use the same warning formula: *kúamōn apò cheîras ékhesthai* (or *ékhein*), which literally means to keep broad beans far from one's hands. Certainly the significance of this recommendation is far from clear. Its ambiguity has allowed divergent interpretations, as I will illustrate in the course of this historical analysis. However, the appositive "a food some devour" in the citation from Callimachus suggests strongly that the context is nutritional. Other testimonia, numerous but late, are more explicit in the same direction. So Cicero brings up "the Pythagorean prohibition against eating broad beans";[17] Iamblichus speaks of it in his chapter on the food of the Pythagoreans, in which he places it alongside the prohibition against eating an animal's heart or its brain, two types of saltwater fish, and mallow.[18] Diogenes Laertius insists that Pythagoras "above all forbade the eating of mullet and sea perch as well as animal hearts or broad beans."[19]

So the broad bean was not the only food that Pythagoreans were forbidden to eat. But it is readily apparent that the context of the prohibition, though it is, broadly speaking, nutritional, is not really concerned with health in the medical sense. It is a section of the sacred diet, not a chapter on profane nutritional hygiene. The prescriptions cited above derive from the principle of ritual purity, not health. The distinction emerges clearly in a text that Alexander Polyhistor, a writer of the first century B.C., says he found in the *Memories of Pythagoras:* "Purity is obtained by purifications, ablutions, sprinklings, from not having had contact with a corpse, a woman, or any other defilement, and by abstaining from the meat of dead animals, mullets, blacktails, eggs, birds born from eggs, broad beans, and all the things forbidden by those who are in charge of celebrating the rites in sacred ceremonies."[20] According to Artemidorus, the broad bean is forbidden in all religious ceremonies.[21] Porphyry says that "initiates into the Eleusinian mysteries must abstain from domestic birds, fish, broad beans, peaches, and apples."[22] Pausanias must be alluding to the same custom in the following passage from his description of the Sacred Way at Eleusis: "On the road a small construction of Cyamites has been built; I cannot say whether this hero was the first to have cultivated broad beans or if he has his name from the fact that it was impossible to attribute the creation of broad beans to Demeter; those who have witnessed the celebration of the mysteries at Eleusis or who have read the Orphic poems know what I am referring to."[23] The Orphics' horror of broad beans is likewise attested in several other Greek texts.[24] The abstinence from broad beans in the myth of Amphiaraus, the divine dream-interpreter, belongs to the same current of mysticism.[25]

This particular attitude toward broad beans is not the only link connecting Orphic teachings, Pythagoras, and Empedocles. In all three there is a philosophical and religious system with cosmological elements and ethical or ascetic consequences whose common roots are undeniable and at whose core are the magical, pantheistic concept of nature and the notion of the immortality and transmigration of the soul.[26] Analogous concepts and practices mark ancient Hindu philosophy. It has even been said that the tradition of the Ayurveda imposes abstinence from broad beans on the sacrificer and that the superstition is therefore an Indo-European one that the Achaeans brought with them when they migrated into the Mediterranean basin.[27] That is highly uncertain. Greeks could have received philosophical ideas from India in the archaic period once they were well settled along the perimeter of the Mediterranean basin. It is generally admitted that by the time of Pythagoras Hindu philosophical thought had already reached Persia. In recognizing this cultural link, one should not overlook the possibility of intellectual exchange in both directions. If the prohibition against eating broad beans actually occurs in the religious or medical practice of India, I see in that a borrowing from the West instead of the other way around. Natural historians maintain that the broad bean was not cultivated in prehistoric India or the Chinese world: The plant itself has no native name in Sanskrit or in any modern Indian language. Those who assert the contrary are mistaken in the botanic identification of the ancient terms.[28]

If abstention from broad beans is not a practice invented by the Greeks themselves, it could only have come to them from western Asia or North Africa. That is the inescapable conclusion from geographic data concerning the spread of the bean's culture. The same conclusion also rests on historical documentation. To quote Herodotus, "as for [broad] beans, [the Egyptian priests] cannot even bear to look at them, because they imagine they are unclean (in point of fact the Egyptians never sow broad beans, and even if any happen to grow wild, they will not eat them, either raw or boiled)."[29] That was surely the situation around the middle of the fifth century B.C., when Herodotus was writing, and perhaps also during a more or less lengthy period before then, but it does not seem to have been the case in Pharaonic times. Broad beans have been found among the mortuary offerings in ancient burials, and Egyptian documents nowhere condemn the cultivation or use of the plant.[30] In any case, what Herodotus says proves that the Egyptians of his day knew of broad beans. The plant grew there, either wild or cultivated by persons whose hunger got the better of their religious scruples—and as de Candolle remarks, it was probably grown on farmland, since the soil suited to it was generally farmed. In the Egyptian scheme of things, the prohibition against the broad bean was relatively recent, but it still can be older in Egypt than in Greece.

Pythagoras is said by all three *Vitae* to have been a disciple of the Egyptian priests. Modern opinion is reluctant to credit the late stories about Pythagoras's visit to the temples of Memphis and his knowledge of Egyptian language, but even so one cannot reject as nonsensical the opinion of Isocrates about the Egyptian background of Pythagorean philosophy or of Herodotus on the theory of metempsychosis.[31] Essentially, Herodotus says that the Egyptians were the first to formulate the idea that the human soul is immortal and that it migrates from a dying body to another, living one. The chapter on this subject concludes with a transparent allusion: "This theory has been adopted by certain Greek writers, some earlier, some later, who have put it forward as their own. Their names are known to me, but I refrain from mentioning them."[32] Most likely Herodotus had his contemporary Empedocles in mind, along with the ancient Orphic poets and, to be sure, Pythagoras.

Is it a matter of chance that all those who espoused the transmigration of souls forbade the eating of broad beans? Is it possible to understand the prohibition as a practical consequence of the general idea of metempsychosis? From antiquity to the present, there have been those who thought so. Celsus—not the medical writer but the anti-Christian polemicist of the second century—was clearly trying to be systematic when he said that

"Pythagoras and his disciples ate no broad beans or anything else that had life."[33] But matters are not that simple. Although it is relatively easy to deduce the prohibition against killing animals and eating their flesh from the overall doctrine, it is hard to see why the same should be true for a plant. And exactly why should it be the broad bean? Besides, it is not even certain that the Pythagoreans advocated strict vegetarianism. Aristotle maintained that they "abstained from the womb and the heart of animals, from the sea-anemone and other animals like it, but used everything else."[34]

But before examining the various attempts to get at the underlying sense of Pythagoras's rule, it is crucial to highlight one aspect of it that is often neglected. The Pythagorean dread of broad beans did not stop at the prospect of simply eating them; it implied that one should not even set foot in a field of them. It was forbidden to trample them.[35] It is not known whether this prohibition is a corollary of the original one or a secondary extension of it. Whatever the case, legend ascribes it to the master himself and makes his obedience to it in exemplary fashion part of the story of his death. It relates how Pythagoras at a venerable age surrendered himself to death out of weariness with life, or, alternatively, was killed after an attempted flight was cut off by a field of broad beans that he chose not to cross. Diogenes Laertius was inspired by the latter account to compose the following verses:

> Alas! Why did Pythagoras so dread the broad bean?
> Behold him dead with his disciples.
> There lay a field of broad beans, and so as not to trample them,
> He died at the fork, slain by the Agrigentans.[36]

Diogenes also tells us how Pythagoras and his followers were attacked by the Agrigentans. The house where they were lodging was set on fire by a man who was disappointed at not having been chosen as one of the philosopher's disciples. Pythagoras fled: "He was met near a field of broad beans; he refused to cross it, saying that he preferred to be killed than to trample the beans with his feet, and adding that he preferred to die rather than to speak. His attackers put him to death and most of his followers along with him—there were about forty."[37]

This story does not hold together and is totally fabricated, but it contains a moral that proves the importance and the extent of the tabu about the broad bean in the Pythagorean tradition. The statement by Pythagoras that it is better to die than speak does not follow from what precedes it. Armand Delatte was right to see it as a sign of the contamination of the story of the master's death with another legend from the hagiographic cycle of the Pythagoreans. Here is that other story as told by Iamblichus, in a version he says he had from Hippobotus and Neanthes, philosophers and historians of the end of the third and the beginning of the second century B.C.: Dionysus, the tyrant of Syracuse, wanted to learn the secrets of the Pythagoreans. So he ordered his henchmen to bring him, even against their will, some members of the sect. An ambush was staged near Tarentum and a group of ten Pythagoreans was taken by surprise. They disengaged themselves and began to flee; making headway on their attackers, who were heavily armed, they had the misfortune to arrive at the edge of a broad bean field in full flower. Stopping there and "not wanting to violate the prohibition against touching broad beans," Pythagoras's disciples were massacred in obedience to the teaching that it is better to die than be captured. On their way home, Dionysus's men met Myllias of Croton and his wife Timycha of Sparta, Pythagoreans who were lagging behind their group because the woman, who was pregnant, had a hard time walking. Her state also permitted Dionysus's men to capture the couple and bring them before him. The tyrant then demanded that they reveal the mysteries of their sect. Despite his threats and enticements, Myllias and Timycha refused to betray their secrets. Dionysus insisted and ordered them on pain of death at least to explain to him the reason why their fellows had been unwilling to walk on the broad beans. Myllias answered, "They chose death so as not to trample on beans, and I myself would rather trample on beans than reveal the reason for the prohibition." His wife, a Spartan, proved the extreme loyalty of her character by biting off her tongue and spitting it out in front of the stupefied tyrant.[38]

Voltaire said that martyrs make converts. It matters little that the story of Myllias and Timycha is a tissue of improbabilities. At the time its main purpose was moral edification and propaganda for a sect. For us, it endorses a broad interpretation of the bean tabu in the Pythagorean communities and confirms the fact that the official justification of it was utterly esoteric. Chances are that, being reserved for a closed circle of initiates, said justification was mythical rather than physiological, mystical rather than rational. But nothing in all this is certain. At least the Pythagorean role of silence explains why the persons in antiquity who dared write on this subject were already in the dark. Aristotle—the "master of those who know," according to Dante—says that Pythagoras "proscribed broad beans either because they have the shape of testicles; or because they resemble the gates of hell, for they alone have no hinges; or again because they spoil, or because they resemble the nature of the universe, or because of oligarchy, for they are used for drawing lots."[39] The multiplicity of reasons advanced proves that the justification Pythagoras and his immediate disciples gave was unknown. And the wealth of explanations is no embarrassment to the eclectic Iamblichus, who states that "one should abstain from broad beans for several reasons, some religious and natural and some having to do with the soul."[40]

Did people really believe that broad beans could be the home of souls in the process of transmigrating? It is tempting to understand an obscure

Orphic line in those terms: "Eating broad beans and gnawing on the head of one's parents are one and the same."[41] According to Pliny, some writers were convinced that Pythagoras condemned the use of this plant "because the souls of the dead are in the bean." And he adds that "in any case, that is why they are used in offerings for the dead" and that "according to Varro, that is why the *flamines* do not eat them."[42] In the *Dream,* a comic play by Lucian, a rooster with the gift of speech comes on stage and introduces himself to a shoemaker as the reincarnation of Pythagoras. The shoemaker is confused and says the rooster must be lying—he is too talkative, and he ate some broad beans. Here is a portion of the argument that the shoemaker addresses to the rooster: "If you are really Pythagoras, you have broken your own laws, and when you swallowed the beans you committed a sacrilege as great as eating the head of your own parents." The rooster, more of a sophist than a Pythagorean, answers that different rules of behavior are appropriate for each form of life, and that he abstained from broad beans when he was Pythagoras but as a rooster he is no longer obliged to heed the tabu.[43]

In another work by Lucian, *Sects for Sale,* there are several philosophers auctioning off their ideas and praising their own moral and dietetic prescriptions. This is the way Pythagoras presents his way of life: "I feed myself nothing that has been alive; I eat everything else except broad beans." When a buyer is surprised by this exception, Pythagoras explains: "I consider broad beans sacred. Their nature is in some ways to be admired, for they encompass in themselves all kinds of procreation: if you shell them when green, you will see that they closely resemble a man's testicles; and if, after cooking them, you expose them for several nights to the moonlight, they bleed."[44] So it seems that in Pythagorean thought, the broad bean is actually related to humanity not so much by way of metempsychosis but in terms of mystical analogies and cosmic speculation. Aristotle adduced the resemblance of the seeds to testicles. The flower also has its symbolic aspect: "Pythagoras says that one should not eat broad beans, because there are letters of mourning in their flowers."[45] The Orphic line that likens broad beans to the head of one's parents is cited by Plutarch during a discussion of the egg, its cosmological significance, and the prohibitions concerning it. According to Porphyry, the Pythagoreans taught that humans and beans sprang from the same original matter. Broad beans in flower, he declares, if they are closed up for some time in a terra cotta vase and kept moist, can be transformed into the head of a child or female genitals.[46]

Critical observers of nature must have found such tales amusing. It is not surprising if some found the sacred dread and magical mystique of beans just so much superstition. For a rationalist, there were two ways to preserve Pythagoras's prestige: to deny the tabu of broad beans (that is, to give it a sense different from the accepted one), or to provide it with a "physiological" justification. Both ways of keeping up appearances were tried, and not infrequently. The oldest testimonia on the tabu itself are not free from the rehabilitation of magic through reason. At the end of Aristotle's list of widely divergent explanations, he mentions the use of beans for drawing lots in political life. Here is an interpretation that negates the nutritional one: actually, Pythagoras was prohibiting his disciples from touching broad beans not as food but so that they would not take part in the public responsibilities of a democratic city-state. Plutarch takes up and develops this idea, considering the Pythagorean adage a rule for social order.[47] But Iamblichus denounces this explanation, saying that it comes from a political pamphlet by Ninon whose purpose was to pervert the ideas of Pythagoras in order to stir up the people of Croton in opposition to the teachings of his immediate successors.[48]

Aristoxenus of Tarentum, a disciple of Aristotle and the Pythagorean Xenophilos of Chalcis, took another tack. As a musical theoretician, he appreciated the work of Pythagoras, but in his loyalty to peripatetic rationality, he had no love for the mystic side of Pythagoreanism. If we are to believe Gellius, Aristoxenus said in a book on Pythagoras that Pythagoras "never enjoyed a single vegetable more often than broad beans, since it was food that gently calmed and soothed the stomach." This is the opposite of what is known from other sources. Aristoxenus's words were, "Broad beans were the vegetable Pythagoras preferred, calling them soothing and laxative; he enjoyed them often."[49] Gellius, who reports and appropriates this correction "of an old error that has carried away many," also sets about ridding the famous verse of Empedocles of any dietary content:

> People thought that *kuámōn* 'broad beans' designates the vegetable, as in ordinary usage. But those who have interpreted the poems of Empedocles with greater care and sophistication say that *kuámōn* refers here to testicles, and that he called them beans in a secret, symbolic way, after the fashion of Pythagoras, because they are *aítioi toû kúein* 'to blame for pregnancy,' and because human procreation gets its impetus from them; so Empedocles in this verse was not trying to keep men from eating broad beans but to abstain from sexual pleasure.[50]

Another way to rehabilitate the Pythagorean precept was, as I said above, to find natural, "physiological" justifications for abstinence from broad beans. It is a vegetable that provokes flatulence, a bloated abdomen, and rumbling in the stomach, which are improper during sacred rites or in a sanctuary, as Artemidorus tells us.[51] But the release of flatulence was less fearful in antiquity than its retention within the organism. Otherwise it rose to the head, disturbing the reason of those awake and giving false dreams to those asleep. That is Cicero's opinion: "Plato prescribes caring for one's body on going to bed in such a way that nothing leads the soul into error or disturbance. It is thought that the Pythagorean prohibition against broad beans derives from that, since they cause substantial flatulence, which is against the search for the tranquillity of the soul."[52] Here are some other passages in the same vein:

> The broad bean is said to blunt the senses and stimulate dreams; that is why the teaching of Pythagoras condemns it [Pliny the Elder].[53]

> One should abstain from broad beans, since they are full of wind and take part in the soul, and if one abstains from them one's stomach will be less noisy and one's dreams will be less oppressive and calmer [Diogenes Laertius communicates this version of Pythagoras's teaching; he thinks it superior to others].[54]

> The naturalists say that broad beans dull the stomach of those who eat them. That is why they prevent a person from having true dreams, since they cause flatulence [an anonymous Byzantine author who was probably dipping into Didymus of Alexandria][55]

A rationalizing explanation that is peculiar and unknown to others occurs in Clement of Alexandria (second century A.D.): the lawgivers, he tells us, forbade the eating of the broad bean because it made women sterile.[56]

Before concluding this review of the ancient evidence, we should consider the enigmatic expression that bedecks a Horation verse: *faba Pythagorae cognata.*[57] What does "broad bean, sister of Pythagoras" mean? At first sight, the poet seems to want to establish a close kinship between the bean and the human race. The expression belongs in the mystical tradition on the common origin of the two species and the transmigration of souls. But that is not the only interpretation: it is possible that the broad bean is called Pythagoras's sister because they are both equally untouchable for him. So a relationship is established not so much between humans and beans as between the incest tabu and eating broad beans.

Blinkered Physicians and the Discovery of Lathyrism

Tradition says that Empedocles was a physician, and Pythagoras himself is considered an expert in the healing art. But in the eyes of posterity, both are personages endowed with charisma and exceptional power; they are sages, thaumaturges, or educators rather than scholars, clinicians, and writers on technical subjects. Their magical and religious attitudes toward nature and the healthy or sick person found no favor among the technician-physicians of the fifth and fourth centuries B.C. whose works have come down to us under the name of Hippocrates. Greek medicine in the classical period was an art (*tékhne*), and as such it purged itself of all notions of the sacred and the supernatural, of transcendance of the determinism in the existence of living beings and their relations with the environment. So, interestingly enough, subsequent to the two putative fathers of the prohibition against broad beans, not a single other physician in antiquity wished to take the trouble to speak of it. All the evidence cited above derives from writers whose occupation was not medicine.

The Hippocratic writers could not have been ignorant of the Pythagorean diet. They knew the writings of Empedocles.[58] But the tabu against broad beans is never mentioned in their treatises. Plainly, they considered it outside the competence of medical art. The texts do confirm that the *kúamos* was a common food in classical Greece. As for its dietetic properties, the treatise *Regimen of Acute Diseases* limits itself to the following: "Beans afford an astringent and flatulent nourishment; flatulent because the passages do not admit the abundant nourishment which is brought, astringent because it has only a small residue from its nourishment."[59]

Elsewhere, information of this kind is still more meager. Cooked broad beans are prescribed as treatment for the dysenteric syndrome *(dusentería)* or, more generally, for upset stomach *(tarakhḕ gastrós)*.[60] Dioscorides (first century A.D.) provides a good overview of the place held by broad beans in the Greek *materia medica*. The chapter he devotes to this plant begins with a summary of the common view that we have already seen in several nonmedical writers: "The broad bean swells the stomach and makes one break wind; it is hard to digest and produces bad dreams." According to the sequel, these beans are nourishing and put flesh on one's bones. It is suggested that they be eaten as treatment for coughing and vomiting. Once cooked, seasoned with vinegar, and swallowed pods and all, broad beans are said to put a stop to diarrhea, especially dysentery. The preferred way to eat them is boiled in two waters, of which the first is to be thrown out, since "green broad beans discomfit the stomach and cause more flatulence." External application of broad bean flour (in the form of a powder, or a plaster, or an ingredient in salves) and even of fresh seeds cut in two is suggested as treatment for various diseases and wounds.[61]

Modern medicine essentially confirms these dietetic observations and therapeutic indications. Broad beans contain some indigestible oligosaccharides that cause flatulence, but they can also be beneficial in the treatment of some forms of diarrhea of infectious origin. However, though the beans do tighten up the stomach when the digestive tract is in certain states, that is not due to the slightness of their residue, as the author of the *Regimen* believes, but, to the contrary, the large amount of it. It is doubtful that the undeniable influence that the ingestion of broad beans has on psychic activity, specifically on dreams, is solely due to the flatulence they produce. Broad beans contain a fairly high concentration of levodopa (L-dopa), a substance used nowadays in the treatment of Parkinson's disease. The administration of this substance increases the quantity of dopamine, a precursor of norepinephrine, in the central nervous system, which can produce insomnia, nightmares, or even hallucinations, as well as increase nervous tension and stimulate sexual activity.

I have surveyed the use of words in the Hippocratic corpus that are close in meaning to *kúamos*, that is, those denoting various leguminous plants and their edible products. In book 7 of the Hippocratic *Epidemics*, there is a very long list of foods that are supposed to be possible causes of "bilious incidents" *(kholeriká)*. The items are so varied—overcooked pork, crabs, leeks, onions, lettuces, pastry with honey, fruit, milk, wine, and so forth—that from the standpoint of modern medicine their only common pathogenic feature is that they are capable of feeding infection. So the "incidents" in question are acute kinds of gastroenteritis caused by infected food. However, the list also includes the chickpea *(erébinthos)* and the bitter vetch *(órobos)*; for them, their own toxic effects cannot be ruled out.[62] In general, the Hippocratic writers thought that "all leguminous plants are flatulent" and that "one should not partake of them without bread," since "each has its own disadvantages." Thus the chickpea "causes some pain" and the lentil is "astringent and causes distress if eaten with its pod."[63] A passage in the *Epidemics* that is included in book 2 and repeated as such in book 6 is especially instructive in this regard: "At Ainos, in the course of a famine, those who ate pulse continually became powerless in their lower limbs; the condition lasted; and moreover, those who ate bitter vetch had pain in their knees."[64] Since it belongs to the second group of books of the *Epidemics* (2–4–6), this account goes back either to the last decade of the fifth century or the first half of the fourth century B.C. It refers to Ainos, a town in Thrace that was suffering from war and severe economic collapse.[65]

Two key terms arouse attention: *ospriophagéontes* and *orobophagéontes*. Although these words only occur here in Greek, their meaning is transparent. The first denotes those who eat *óspria* 'pulse.' It does not specify the nature of the plants eaten, for how long they were eaten, or even whether or not other foods were eaten along with them. However, in context the term conveys the impression that the people of Ainos fed themselves almost exclusively for a certain period of time on vegetables with low nutritional value. In his commentary on this Hippocratic text, Galen says that *óspria* are the seeds of leguminous plants not usually used for making bread. The inhabitants of Ainos ate them for a long while, without eating bread made from wheat flour even occasionally.[66] Littré says nothing of the famine. Indeed, the V manuscript and most of the *recentiores* derived from M (which has a lacuna here) contain, in the first phrase of the passage at *Epid.*, II, 4, 3, the incomprehensible words *en aimō* or *enaíō*. Littré suppressed these words, considering them a faulty repetition of *en aínōi* 'in Ainos.' There is indeed a transcriptional error, and a very old one, but of another kind: the correct reading is *en limôi* ('during a famine,' which is preserved twice in Galen's commentary, once in his note on *Aph.*, III, 16, and again in his note, known only in the Arabic version, on *Epid.*, VI, 4, 11.

As for the *orobophagéontes,* they are eaters of bitter vetch, since *órobos* in classical texts is indeed *Vicia ervilia* Willd. (*Ervum ervilia* L.), a plant used for forage and known in Greece since prehistoric times.[67] Bitter vetch was a substandard human food with medicinal uses. The Greeks knew that if eaten in certain proportions it could have toxic effects. According to Dioscorides, bitter vetch causes headache, disturbance of the bowels, and lower cavity hemorrhages.[68] Pliny considers it harmful to humans, since ingesting it is followed by headache, vomiting, and diarrhea.[69] According to Galen, it is eaten only when food is scarce.[70] The Hippocratic writer attributes pains in the knee to the consumption of this leguminous plant by the inhabitants of Ainos, but he does not elaborate on the clinical features. The observation was made amid nutritional difficulties of such a kind that the modern physician must suspend judgment. I suspect that the pathogenic factor responsible for the joint disease described was deficiency rather than poisoning.

But though pain in the knee is too vague a symptom to allow valid inferences about its etiology, the same is not true of permanent paraplegia, the major symptom mentioned in the first part of the Hippocratic account. A loss of mobility in both legs after prolonged ingestion of pulse on an epidemic scale among the inhabitants of a Thracian town—that suffices for a retrospective diagnosis: lathyrism. Such is the name that the Neapolitan physician Arnoldo Cantani gave to poisoning by certain species of pea or vetch.[71] It is by far the likeliest diagnosis of the chronic disease afflicting the poor "ospriophagic" inhabitants of Ainos. Their paralyses would then have been caused by excessive consumption of a bread prepared with flour made from a species of *Lathyrus,* either *L. sativus* (chickling pea) or *L. cicera* L. (chickling vetch).[72]

The first modern information in the West regarding this neurotoxic syndrome dates from the middle of the seventeenth century. During the Thirty Years' War, terrible famines forced people to find a substitute for bread. In the Duchy of Wurtemberg, the population fed itself on such legumes, not without major mishaps. In 1691, Bernardino Ramazzini, the founder of occupational medicine, described pea intoxication in subjects living in the Duchy of Modena. All during the eighteenth and nineteenth centuries, isolated cases or small epidemics of the affliction were noticed in Europe.[73] The cultivation of chickling was particularly common in India, Syria, North Africa, and Greece. Most of the neurotoxic accidents due to the ingestion of seeds or flour from this plant are situated in these geographical areas. In India, lathyrism has long been known.[74] There were often very serious poisonings from it, and at times they took on the proportions of epidemics. In the Greco-Roman world, chickling pea was cultivated not just as fodder but also for human consumption.[75] People made barley bread and added vetch or chickling pea flour to it.[76] Use of the latter as food is attested in the comic poets.[77] Such uses are explicable since only excessive or exclusive consumption of the plant produces the neurotoxic syndrome. Lathyrism became a medical problem only when food was scarce, when a type of pea meant to feed the livestock became the main ingredient in everyday bread, and when its consumption was associated with important quantitative and qualitative deficiencies.

The pathogenic factor resides only in the seeds, but its nature is not yet wholly clear. The pure chemical substances that produce lathyrogenic effects in experiments on animals have been isolated and even synthesized. They are chiefly derivatives of aminopropionitril.[78] The absorption of the seeds in considerable quantities leads to selective attack (degenerating lesions) on nerve cells in the lumbosacral marrow. The clinical picture is dominated by muscular asthenia in the legs and vasomotor disturbances. It evolves into spasmodic paraplegia.[79] This irreversible paralysis of the lower limbs is the symptom that the Hippocratic writer describes with typical, inimitable concision.

So Greek physicians of the classical age saw lathyrism. But they noticed no accidents following the ingestion of broad beans. Couldn't we interpret this silence as an indication of the absence of favic idiosyncrasy in Greece? That is a hasty conclusion to come to. Favism certainly existed in Greece in the eighteenth century, and yet no physician saw, wished to see, or rather was able to see attacks caused by broad beans. To be sure, physicians noticed serious malaise and abruptly appearing jaundice, but they set aside any causal link with broad beans. Lathyrism is a kind of poisoning. That is why it poses no conceptual problems. But the situation with broad beans is altogether different, since in the everyday experience of most people they are a totally harmless food.

The Reality of Favism

Since the end of the last century, Western medicine has officially taken cognizance of certain individuals whose habitus and way of life seem entirely normal but who suffer from a strange idiosyncrasy: give them a few broad beans to eat, or let them just cross a field of these papilionaceous plants in flower, and they fall into a hemolytic crisis. The first modern mention of this intolerance is in the letters-to-the-editor section of a Lisbon magazine. In a letter dated May 3, 1843, one Manuel Pereira de Mira Franco reported, "as a curiosity," the case of an inhabitant of the town of Cuba (Portugal) who reacted to each ingestion of green broad beans with an attack of jaundice.[80] Though validated today by the historian's backward glance, this observation by a Portuguese practitioner escaped the attention of the learned men of the day and had no influence on the development of medical knowledge. Under the prevailing mentality of physicians in the middle of the nineteenth century, at the moment of the full flowering of their new rationality, it was just a tale. The publication of the letter itself in a periodical of general interest rather than a specialists' journal seems to me to suggest that for official medical circles of the day an idiosyncrasy of this kind was still something marginal, inexplicable, even inadmissible. It defied the postulate of the interchangeable biological nature of individuals of the same species and, still worse, appeared to threaten the postulate of strict determinism in physiological reactions.

Sicilian physicians of the second half of the nineteenth century were the first to admit the reality of such a personalized hypersensitivity. First in 1856, Antonio Minà La Grua drew attention to the peculiar "endemic jaundice" of peasants in Castelbuono (a village in the hinterland of Cefalù) "caused by the fragrance of the flowers of broad beans."[81] Other practitioners, particularly Di Pietra-Leone from Piazza Armerina, Mulè Bertolo from Villalba, and Rizzo-Matera from Syracuse, confirmed La Grua's observations, noted the presence of this ailment in several Sicilian communes and in Calabria, discovered its hereditary nature, and, in polemics with colleagues who thought that the jaundice was ascribable to malaria, insisted on the etiological role of the broad bean in triggering it. Mulè Bertolo reported that the clinical picture regularly includes hematuria.[82] Taking the region of the Nebrodi Hills to be the cradle of this disease, La Grua called it *malattia vegetale nebrodese.* In 1894, at the Eleventh Congress of International Medicine in Rome, Dr. Montano proposed the name *favismo* to designate the set of troubles brought on in subjects who were particularly sensitive to the ingestion of broad beans or to the inhalation of the pollen of *Vicia faba.*[83] Short, expressive, and easily convertible into other tongues, this term quickly entered the nosological vocabulary of all lands.

Apparently, among the people of Sicily, there was a dialectal word, *zàfara,* that denoted malarial jaundice and also, particularly, the jaundice that resulted from crises of favism—this was long before the latter was recognized by physicians.[84] Doubtless the first impetus for the scientific study of favism is to be found in Sicilian folklore. Pietro Messina alludes to popular belief, in his *Mediche osservazioni sopra non ovvie rilevanti infermità* (published in Catania in 1851, and so prior to the monograph of La Grua), when he says, "Not unknown to us is the miraculous influence on the formation of bile in some subjects brought about by the fragrance of the flowers of the broad bean." The story of Salvatore Greco, a young peasant from the province of Syracuse who suffered, like his maternal grandfather, from favism, attests to the endurance or at least the prescientific revival of ancient tradition. Without any medical intervention and solely on the basis of his own experience and that of his grandfather, Greco "long since and scrupulously abided by the Pythagorean teaching that forbids the consumption of broad beans" (Rizzo-Matera, 1878).[85] This Syracusan peasant's name is probably a reminder of the Greek origin of his family.

On the threshold of the twentieth century, physicians understood that the central physiopathological event in favism is hemolysis, the decomposition of the red cells in blood. In his communication to the Congress at

Rome in 1894, Montano states that the hematuria of favism is actually hemoglobinuria. The miscroscopic and chemical examination of peripheral blood during an acute reaction to the ingestion of raw broad beans enabled him to report diminution in the number of red blood cells, discrete leukopenia, and the presence of hemoglobin in solution in the serum. Thereafter, all the other symptomatology of favism could be explained as a secondary consequence or complication of hemolytic crises. Montano also expresses very clearly the distinction between "the determining cause (broad bean) and the predisposing cause (particular individual idiosyncrasy)," a distinction that saves biological determinism. He stresses the important role of "determining cause" played by a chemical factor that is essentially toxic, that is, not microbial; as for the "predisposing cause," he stresses the familial factor. In this conceptual context, Montano denies the influence of climate on the appearance and geographical distribution of favism.[86] His clinical experience rested on the meticulous examination of several dozen patients observed in Lavello in the province of Potenza (Basilicata). Other typical cases of favism were discovered in central Italy (Girotti, 1899; De Camillis, 1901; and so forth), in Sardinia (Piga, 1899; Stevani, 1904), and in Greece (Ducas in Lamia, 1895; Skavenzos on the island of Skopelos, 1895; Cawadias in Leukas, 1897; Vellopoulos in Atalante, 1898; Kontogouris in Leukas, 1900; Tselios in Thebes, 1904; and so forth). Despite this extension of the cases diagnosed outside the area (Sicily, Calabria) in which the disease was first recognized, it still seemed that favism was limited to the inhabitants of a relatively narrow zone of the Mediterranean basin.

Thanks to careful epidemiological studies undertaken before World War I,[87] the clinical picture of favism has been refined, the patients have been classified according to their specific degree of sensitivity, the familial nature of their predisposition has been confirmed, and a tendency for the disease to appear in young persons and preponderantly in males has been reported. These studies have revealed the seriousness of the defect in question: according to Fermi's statistical survey, for 72 Sardinian communes, the morbidity, amazingly, was greater than 5 per 1,000 in 1905, with a lethality at 8 percent (that is, the number of deaths as against the number of sick persons). From then on, favism stopped being a rarity of interest only to collectors of medical oddities. It has its due as one of those endemic diseases that have real consequences for the public health of certain regions.

Although they defined favism impeccably as a clinical entity, the physicians of the first half of the twentieth century still did not know the true nature of its underlying pathogenic processes. Montano, Fermi, and other pioneers in the clinical and epidemiological exploration of the disease thought of it as poisoning by a chemical substance with a molecular structure and a kind of action that were as yet unknown. However, among the various proteinic and glucosidic substances isolated from the seed of the broad bean and tested in appropriate dosages on laboratory animals, none seemed to present toxic properties. In particular, none displayed hemolytic powers great enough to account for the crises of favism in terms of direct action on red cells. And between the second and fourth decades of this century, several researchers uselessly persisted in wanting to reduce favism to ordinary poisoning by cyanhydric acid.[88] But the concentration of this poison in the beans does not reach the critical threshold, its action mechanism (enzymatic blocking of tissue respiration) suits poorly the symptoms of favism, and, last but not least, the "toxicological" hypothesis is of no help in accounting for the enormous differences in individual sensitivity.

In the description of favism, the triggering cause was well accounted for, but the intrinsic cause remained totally obscure. By what biochemical mechanism does the hemolysis start, given that the substances in the beans themselves are not toxic in the usual sense of the word? What is the actual role of heredity? How can one explain the possibility that an individual who is "predisposed" genetically can eat the fatal bean with impunity, after having reacted violently to a previous ingestion of it? So many questions, long without answers.

From the time of the definition of the concept of allergy by Clemens von Pirquet (1904), the existence of a pathological reactivity as individual and specific as that of favism recalled the mechanism of allergic sensitization. In most medical handbooks of the 1930s and 1940s there is a vague suggestion of the "allergic" nature of the clinical manifestations brought on by broad beans. However, this analogy met an impasse: instead of immunity sensitization by previous contact with the substance responsible for favism, one was faced with an innate idiosyncrasy that was largely independent of prior chemical conditioning.

The actual point of departure for the discovery of the complex etiology of favism was the observation by American physicians that absorption of synthetic antimalarials can produce a hemolytic anemia in some individuals that can be very serious. Actually, in 1896 Pucci had already noted at Catanzaro in Calabria (a place not far from the ancient location of the Pythagorean community at Croton) that certain persons who could not tolerate broad beans had a similar intolerance for quinine. Once pamaquine (plasmoquin) was introduced in 1926, disturbances like those of favism were noticed as side effects of the medication. To be sure, these were just occasional observations whose pathogenic mechanism no one knew how to explain. Finally, during World War II, the struggle against malaria in the American army, in particular the preventive oral administration of primaquine (like pamaquine, a derivative of 8-aminoquinoline), brought to light significant individual intolerances in many blacks and in some whites with family origins in southern Italy and Greece. In 1948, A. Turchetti made the connection between drug-induced anemia in American blacks and Mediterranean favism.[89] Subsequent research showed that in both cases there was an innate enzymatic deficiency, a lack in the activity of glucose-6-phosphate dehydrogenase (G6PD). This is a red blood cell enzyme that intervenes in the breakdown of glucose, permits the maintenance of reduced glutathione, and fights against the tendency toward oxidation in red blood cells, thus protecting the hemoglobin in its function as a gas carrier. A true epidemic of intolerance to primaquine was observed during the Korean War among blacks in the American expeditionary force; this facilitated systematic research. Decisive hematological and biochemical research was performed in a prison laboratory in Joliet, Illinois, with selected volunteers from among the prison's inmates. In 1956, Paul E. Carson and an excellent multidisciplinary team at the prison succeeded in proving that deficiency in G6PD was actually responsible for the hemolytic distress occurring in individuals sensitive to the absorption of primaquine.[90] It quickly became clear that the same deficiency was at the origin of other drug-induced, bacteriotoxic, and nutritional idiosyncrasies. Among the latter, the place of honor belongs to favism, as William A. Crosby remarked during a trip to Sardinia in 1956, shortly after Carson's ground-breaking publication.[91]

Nevertheless, there must be some difference between primaquine intolerance and favism, since individuals who are sensitive to antimalarials or other artificially synthesized drugs do not necessarily have a hemolytic reaction to the ingestion of broad beans. The two diseases are not to be confused and are not necessarily associated. It seems that the molecular lesion is not identical in both cases, and in addition, favism demands a specific seric disorder besides the exogenous cause and the enzymatic deficiency. K. L. Roth and A. M. Frumin have reported that the serum of persons vulnerable to the crises of favism lacks a protective factor that is present both in normal individuals and in most carriers of the G6PD genetic defect.[92] So favism is the result of the intersection of three factors: (1) introduction in the organism of one or of several specific substances of vegetal origin; (2) biochemical fragility of erythrocytes due to a hereditary deficiency of G6PD; and (3) seric deficiency (lack of a protective substance?).

The noxious vegetal principle in favism is still poorly understood. It is probably a whole family of chemical substances whose basic representative is vicine, a substance isolated in 1962 by J. Y. Lin and K. M. Ling.[93] This agent is present in the broad bean, of which there are two main varieties, *Vicia faba major* and *Vicia faba minor*. The two varieties are equally harmful. Beans (*Phaseolus* sp.), although they belong to the same family as broad beans, are not dangerous for favic individuals. Hemolytic anemias occurring in persons with favism have been described upon ingestion of peas *(Pisum sativum)* or stinking bean-trefoil *(Anagyris foetida)*. Do these plants contain the same noxious molecules as the broad bean but in smaller quantities, or do they act through the presence of a similar chemical substance? It is possible, even likely, that such an agent occurs in several plants that do not serve as food. For instance, it is likely that the pollen of verbena *(Verbena hybrida)* when inhaled is the cause of a hemolytic anemia like that of favism. Called Baghdad Spring anemia, this ailment is known chiefly from the observations of R. Lederer among Iraqi Jews.[94]

The most spectacular incidents of jaundice and hematuria are provoked by the ingestion of raw fresh broad beans. Dried broad beans or flour made from them can also bring on hemolytic crises, but boiled beans are not at all dangerous. The harmful substance is destroyed by heat. However, it is transmitted in the milk of nursing women or goats, which explains the frequency of hemolytic anemias among newborns in regions like Greece, where, from antiquity up to the present, a high degree of hereditary enzyme deficiency has coexisted with extensive cultivation of broad beans. The pods, leaves, and pollen of the beans also contain the harmful agent, but in lesser quantities than the seeds. Simple contact with the pods or the inhalation of particles emitted by the broad bean's flowers can provoke relatively mild hemolytic episodes or, more often, migraine headaches. Sometimes minute quantities are enough to trigger a pathological reaction. Serious distress has been reported in persons who simply lingered at a distance of several hundred feet from a field of broad beans in flower.[95]

As was said above, since the work of Carson and his collaborators, we have known that the biochemical basis for individual hypersensitivity is a deficiency of glucose-6-phosphate dehydrogenase (G6PD). But research performed in the past twenty years in the domain of molecular pathology has shown that behind the phenomenon thought of as a simple deficiency of G6PD, that is, as a purely quantitative lack of a single molecule, there lies hidden a complex and diverse reality consisting in qualititative anomalies of the enzyme in question. Instead of being an enzymopeny in the strict sense of the word, the G6PD deficiency actually constitutes a family of erythrocytic enzymopathies. The first step toward the discovery of this pathogenic heterogeneity was the observation in 1962 of a normal electrophoretic polymorphism in G6PD. In a healthy population there exist two fully functional variants of this enzyme (types A+ and B+).[96] The second and decisive step was bringing to light abnormal enzymatic molecules.[97] It became necessary to admit the biochemical and genetic diversity in the G6PD deficiency. So this "inborn error of metabolism" consists in different mutations at the level of the gene that specifies G6PD. The abnormal variants that result are probably to be distinguished by different substitutions located on one amino acid. Their phenotypic expression consists in qualitative and quantitative modifications of the enzyme that vary according to the nature of the particular mutation. The intolerance in blacks for primaquine is very likely due to a mutation that hits the allele of type A+. Accordingly this variant is designated by the symbol A−. In whites with favism, especially in Italy and Greece, the common normal allele of type

B+ is replaced by the so-called Mediterranean variant (B−). These two abnormal variants are frequent, as is a third that was discovered in some Chinese suffering from drug-induced hemolysis and sometimes also favism (the so-called Canton variant).[98] However, these three main pathological forms of the G6PD deficiency hardly exhaust the polymorphism of the disease. Worldwide, about 100 abnormal forms of G6PD have been identified, but it appears that only the 3 main variants have a major statistical incidence of morbidity.[99]

The study of the hereditary transmission of favism entered a new phase when consideration of its biochemical basis (latent favism recognizable through tests of enzymatic deficiency) replaced that of its clinical phenotype (overt favism). Research carried out mainly in Sardinia by U. E. Carcassi, P. Larizza, and other Mediterranean experts confirmed for favism what B. Childs and his associates had already found for intolerance to primaquine: the locus determining the synthesis of G6PD is part of the X chromosome (called the Gd locus). It is situated near the loci responsible for hemophilia and color blindness. Favism is a defect whose heredity is sex-linked. It can be fully expressed in males and is partially expressed in females with the defect, who play the role of carriers in its genetic transmission.[100]

G6PD deficiency is a very widespread genetic trait that most often remains latent in clinical terms. At the moment there are more than 100 million individuals with this defect, and yet true cases of favism are relatively rare. The enzymatic anomaly, especially the B− variant, is an indispensable but not a sufficient condition to make a person hypersensitive to broad beans. As was said above, a second anomaly must intersect with the first. It is probably expressed in the serum, but its true nature remains unclear. In any case, we must assume that it, too, is determined by a specific, probably autosomal genetic mechanism. From this standpoint, favism is still an enigmatic idiosyncrasy.[101]

The typical clinical profile of favism is acute hemoglobinuric jaundice. In the hours following alimentary contact with raw broad beans, gastroenteritis with acute abdominal pains is followed immediately by hemoglobinuria—the urine can become black—severe anemia, bouts of fever, and moderate jaundice. These symptoms disappear after a week, but the crisis leaves behind an anemia that can last for several months. The milder reaction is expressed as general discomfort, with headache and nausea. In about one case in twelve, the hemoglobinuria can be so violent that it results in death from anoxemia or acute renal failure.[102] Modern Greek pediatricians have reported that G6PD deficiency is an important cause of severe forms of neonatal jaundice, which is relatively frequent in Athens and various regions in Greece. At times the children can be saved only by exchange transfusion.[103] To be sure, this jaundice is not triggered by broad beans. In children the anemia that follows the crises of favism can produce cranial lesions that resemble porous hyperostosis from thalassemia.[104]

Historically, the main haven of favism is the territory of Magna Graecia (southern Italy, including Sicily), Sardinia, certain parts of what is now Greece, especially several islands, Anatolia, Corsica, and the Mediterranean coast of Africa (Egypt, Algeria, etc.).[105] If we consider only the B− variant of the G6PD deficiency, the genetic defect is practically restricted to the Mediterranean basin. For my purposes, it is not important to note the geographical distribution of the A− variant (widespread in Africa), the Canton variant (Far East), or the countless other mutations of G6PD scattered throughout the world. There is no longer any doubt that their origin is polyphyletic, without links to the birth and spread of Mediterranean favism.

Before the modern mixing of populations and the massive migrations of southern Europeans, the frequency of favism in northern Italy was minimal, as it was in other countries of northern Europe. The ancient homelands of the Etruscans and Latins have only very recently been tainted by the disease. By contrast, the B− variant of G6PD deficiency is extremely common in Sicily, the fatherland of Empedocles, in Sardinia, and in the parts of Calabria where the Greek colonies once stood and Pythagoras held forth. There, up to one-third of the autochthonous males have the favic defect.[106] In modern Greece, hereditary G6PD deficiency is present in all the oldest settlements, but its distribution is not uniform. Surveys made in Greece during the 1960s provide a sense of the magnitude of its presence. The frequency of the defect ranges from 2 percent to 12 percent depending upon the region. The areas in which it surpasses 10 percent are the plains of the Peloponnesus, Epirus, and Thessaly. By contrast, favism is relatively rare in Asia Minor and in mountainous areas.[107] S. A. Doxiadis has drawn attention to the prominence of the deficiency in newborns hospitalized in Athens.[108] There is a fine study by C. A. Kattamis based on 506 cases of favism in children who were treated from 1956 to 1966 at the Pediatric Clinic in Athens. It shows the extent of the disease's pathological manifestations and the prevalence of the Mediterranean variant (B−).[109] A study undertaken by this same investigator among the people of Rhodes confirms reports by Italian physicians who had noted the prevalence of favism in the Dodecanese in 1930.[110] The frequency of G6PD deficiency among Rhodian men is higher than 30 percent. It is also very high on the island of Cyprus. Such concentrations of favism on islands, likewise observed in Sardinia, Sicily, and Corsica, could be the result of a certain genetic segregation among these populations, of a greater degree of consanguinity in island peoples than in those of the mainland.

How can one explain the maintenance, not to say the progress, within a given population of hereditary traits like this, which at first sight offer grave biological disadvantages? Why are they not eliminated by natural selection? The geographic distribution of the genetic trait expressed by G6PD deficiency largely corresponds to that of the ancient malarial endemic, exactly like the distribution of sickle cell anemia or the various thalassemias. This is sometimes true even for distribution within a district. So, for instance, among boys in the region of Arta (Epirus), the frequency of the favic enzymopathy varies according to the exposure of the region to malaria in the past: much more common among the inhabitants of the plain than those of the mountains.[111] Accordingly, it seems wise to apply to the genetics of this defect the hypothesis of balanced polymorphism invented by J.B.S. Haldane and developed by A. C. Allison in connection with sickle cell anemia. According to this hypothesis, the maintenance at a high rate of this erythrocytic enzymatic deficiency would be ascribable to the selective advantage it provides in zones of malarial endemic.[112] The research of L. Luzzatto, U. Bienzle, and others shows that in men (of necessity hemizygous for traits linked to the X chromosome), the G6PD deficiency does not at all increase resistance to malaria, but that heterozygous women (especially those of type B+A−) do benefit from an evident protection when exposed to malarial infestation.[113] A mathematical model can be constructed showing how such an advantage is enough to balance in demographic terms the deleterious effects of favism. Nevertheless, the correlation between the prevalence of this enzymopathy and the intensity of the malarial endemic in antiquity is not always satisfactory. Among African Jews, for instance, it does not correspond to the requirements of the theory.[114] The hypothesis that introduces malaria into the history of favism as yet offers only a partial solution to the problem it is intended to resolve.

Nor should we forget that the heterogeneity of the G6PD deficiency and its interaction with hereditary hemoglobinopathies infinitely complicates the history of favism.[115] Even in Greece, where the B− variant is largely dominant and where the "Mediterranean phenotype" of the idiosyncrasy appears homogeneous, current research reveals unexpected complexities.[116] Numerous minor variants of the G6PD deficiency have just been described. They are named after the place in which they were found: Athens, Attica, Corinth, Orchomenos, Levadia, Thessaly, Karditsa, and so forth. The genesis of these variants should not be confused with that of the "Mediterranean" mutation in the strict sense of the term. The latter especially interests the medical historian of the Greek world: the frequency of the B− type (as against the other alleles responsible for the erythrocytic enzymopathy in whites) and also its particular geographical distribution force us to acknowledge at once its antiquity and its place of origin. Mediterranean favism goes back at least to the archaic period of Greek civilization.

Has modern science, then, unexpectedly discovered an empirical justification for the ancient prohibition against eating broad beans? At the moment I am posing this question rhetorically I will pose it again in a more appropriate form after examining the work of modern exegetes on this strange piece of ancient history.

Modern Opinions on the Pythagorean Prohibition

From the rebirth of classical studies in the fifteenth century until the nineteenth century, countless humanists glossed the tabu against eating broad beans. Taking up the explanations of ancient authors, they defended those that suited their predilections without really strengthening or embellishing them with new arguments.[117] Since physicians firmly maintained that eating these beans was harmless, the prevailing opinion was that the underlying reason for abstinence from them in the Pythagorean tradition was mystical or symbolic. For Neoplatonists, gnostics, and followers of similar philosophical systems, nothing was more natural than reference to cosmogonic myths, to the passage of souls into the beans, and to the mystical correspondence between this plant and the human body. On the other hand, for authors of an Aristotelian persuasion and for partisans of modern rationalism, the most comfortable approach was that of Aristoxenus. One simply denied the dietetic nature of the prohibition, preferring to assert its sexual or political significance. Some commentators gladly thought it originated in the resemblance of the broad bean to a testicle and claimed that it was a symbol of the moral law limiting sexual relations. The political explanation, given prestige by the cautious approval of Plutarch, stressed the use of broad beans in the election of magistrates in Greek city-states. For instance, after citing the expression "Abstain from broad beans!" Kurt Sprengel, the famous physician, botanist, and founder of pragmatic medical historiography, says, "Probably Pythagoras wished by these words to divert his disciples from seeking political office, so that they would thereby remain more attached to his own order."[118] A similar view on the political significance of the Pythagorean rule was given credence among German philologists thanks to a monograph by A. B. Krische.[119]

However, belief in the real harmfulness of broad beans does not seem to have been lacking in Greek folklore. During a study of popular representations of the causes of infantile mortality, Richard and Eva Blum came across several Greek peasants who were convinced that broad beans are dangerous to infants and children, causing sickness or death. According to the Blums, "This belief is widely held and its historical importance is attested to by the doctrine of Pythagoras that proscribed the eating of beans."[120] Is this really a survival of the Pythagorean teaching in the unlettered world of the Greek countryside? I do not believe so. Given the genetic conditions in some Greek communities, the danger was only too real. The harm in broad beans was probably discovered many times over by mothers attentive to the food and health of their children. Knowledge acquired this way gets transmitted orally from one generation to the next without help from any philosophical tradition. Balkan folk medicine, which has only recently begun to disappear, rejoiced in a mixture of empiricism and magic that in many ways resembled the Presocratic mentality; as such it was rich in observations that did not conform to the imperatives of scientific medicine. So nothing prevented Greek peasants from noticing that a food that was usually well tolerated could also be a poison. But physicians were unwilling to see in that anything other than superstition, since they were blinded by a concept of determinism that was at once very effective and overly simple.

In an encyclopedia article written at the end of the nineteenth century, F. Lenormant summarized current historical understanding of the prohibition, which he attributed to the tradition of the Orphic mysteries. For him, the key to the problem was provided by Aulus Gellius: the word *kúamos* originally refers to the genitals of animals and not to broad beans. Abstinence from such beans can only have a symbolic meaning. Lenormant insists on the analogy of this ritual and moral precept to the prohibition against eating pomegranates for Athenian women participating in the Thesmophoria and the one against eating celery for priests during the Corybantic mysteries. The analogy is instructive, since these customs have symbolic links with bloody mythological events.[121] But Charles Daremberg, the physician who was chief editor of the *Dictionnaire des antiquités grecques et romaines,* in which Lenormant's article appeared, could not keep himself from adding to it the following remark, which is imbued with the positivist's faith: "Surely at the heart of all these legends there is a simple rule of hygiene, like the rule about the abstinence from the meat of the pig among the Hebrews, on which ancient superstition embroidered a wide variety of themes." A rational interpretation of another kind was proposed in 1904 by E. Bourquelot of the Society of Biology in Paris, then a shrine to the experimental method and metaphysical agnosticism of men like Claude Bernard and Charles Robin. First Bourquelot states that the Pythagoreans abstained from eating animal flesh. According to him, that was because of the doctrine of the transmigration of souls. But they also abstained from eating broad beans, which were a food much enjoyed by Mediterranean peoples. Clement of Alexandria's explanation is inadequate: he attributed to broad beans the property of making women sterile, but then Pythagoras had no grounds for denying them to men. So Bourquelot cites the passage in the play of Lucian in which Pythagoras relates that cooked broad beans, when exposed to the light of the moon for a certain number of nights, give off blood:

> This explanation [writes Bourquelot] does not appear as ridiculous today as it did to Lucian. Apparently people must have observed the spontaneous development on cooked broad beans of one of those chromogenic microbes whose cultures so

resemble bloodstains that one can understand how people in antiquity might have made this mistake. The fact struck Pythagoras, who saw it as proof of the animal nature of the broad bean.

Faithful to his experimental method, Bourquelot studied these phenomena in the laboratory:

For that purpose, I did not think it necessary to expose the cooked beans to moonlight; but I did innoculate them with a well-known chromogenic bacillus, Kiel's bacillus. So I can report that the conditions which permit one to obtain abundant production of red spots are exactly those Pythagoras describes. The raw broad beans must be shelled and cooked; otherwise, it is not possible to succeed, or one can only be partially successful. The best technique is, after having moistened and then sterilized the beans at 110°, to put them in the oven at 33° for 24 hours, and then leave them at room temperature (18–20°). At the end of eight days, the beans will be covered with bloody spots.

Bourquelot concludes that "by an altogether natural association of ideas, the bloody broad beans of Pythagoras recall the bloody hosts [of the Catholic Eucharist] that were so disturbing to look at 1,800 or 2,000 years later."[122]

The positivism of Daremberg and Bourquelot had no audience, at least during the first half of the twentieth century. All research in that period is marked by the work of Sir James George Frazer on tabus and their links with totemism,[123] and by the work of Erwin Rohde on the concept of the soul and the cults related thereto.[124] In the light of comparative ethnological studies carried out by British anthropologists (E. B. Tylor, J. G. Frazer, and others), the prohibition against touching broad beans seemed like a classic food tabu based on primitive totemic representations. The code of superstitious maxims attributed to the sage Pythagoras goes back, says Frazer, to a much more distant past and reflects in symbolic form the assumptions of a lost and forgotten sociocultural context.[125] This set of notions from cross-cultural anthropology soon received the support of psychoanalysis. First one digs up the roots of rites and myths, and then one understands their special unconscious logic. Masterfully exploited by Salomon Reinach,[126] elaborated in a series of monographs,[127] and cited in handbooks on the history of medicine or of science in general,[128] such psychosocial accounts reach their height in penetrating studies by the philologist Armand Delatte[129] and the philosopher Marcel Detienne.[130] Reinach recalls Daremberg's remark and even takes the trouble to cite it completely, the better to denounce his purpose and insist on the futility of utilitarian explanations of tabus: "This error is instructive, since it is typical of many others like it that are not only anachronistic but also put the cart before the horse; they see superstition as a corrupt form of science, when science is its distant descendant or even its posthumous child, if superstition can ever be said to die."[131] It is an arrogant, unacceptable point of view. A goodly number of modern "superstitions" are indeed corruptions of the science of an older age. Still, it is true that magical thought, which is the subject under discussion here, is not the corruption of a prior science. In that, Reinach is correct, but he imputes to Daremberg an idea that is not his, and in doing so he does not even advance his own point of view: the chronological priority of magical thought does not mean that it cannot contain empirical, utilitarian knowledge. In a word, superstition is not necessarily all "false," any more than science is absolutely and completely "true."

Pythagoras's fellow citizens planted broad beans, and Reinach concludes that "this plant was not considered impure or unhealthy, but sacred instead." The tabu necessitated that it not be killed by being eaten or trod upon, since it was considered one of man's totemic ancestors. That is the underlying sense of the Orphic verse that likens the act of eating broad beans to gnawing one's parents' heads: "The ancients did not understand this prohibition and devised extravagant ways to account for it, and the more extravagant they were the more they were hygienic and utilitarian."[132] Jean Larguier de Bancels also believes that Pythagoras and his followers "adopted or revived by means of a symbolic prohibition an old ritual whose original sense had long since been lost." It was a tabu of Indo-European origin. Even flatulence, which the ancient authors mention in their discussions of eating broad beans, can have its symbolic aspect. Larguier de Bancels translates the view of Diogenes Laertius a little differently from the way I have above: it was necessary to abstain from broad beans "because, being windy, they participate in the nature of the soul." Broad beans are animate, and so likened to animals, since they possess breath. He also draws attention to the Indo-European theory of the psychic pneuma, which implies close conceptual relations between the soul, the air breathed, and flatulence.[133] Besides, according to the psychoanalyst E. Jones, breath is only a symbolic displacement of flatulence, and, more important, the notion of the soul in the last analysis derives from the internal sensations that an infant has of gas trapped in the belly.[134]

Armand Delatte notes that ancient observations about broad beans alternate between awe and dread, which are the two poles of a single sphere of confused impressions that the Greek language represents by the term *hierós* 'sacred.' This word was applied to "anything loaded with a powerful, supernatural fluid, alternately religious and magical, whose touch can be either beneficial or harmful."[135] So the attitude toward the broad bean is "ambivalent," as is to be expected with a tabu. Delatte classifies the ancient texts on this subject and arranges them in such a way that "once they are examined in the light of the customs and beliefs called totemic" they constitute a unique system of explanation for the superstition:

> If it were possible to express the latent and confused reasoning that guided the primitive mentality at God knows how distant an era, here is how it could be formulated: leguminous plants and especially the broad bean, which is the most

widespread and often used of them in human food, produce, during digestion, flatulence, which disturbs certain mental functions (the clear perception of dream visions). So broad beans contain winds that have an unfavorable effect; however, the souls and, in particular, the souls of the dead, which are usually considered harmful, are also winds, so broad beans contain the souls of the dead. By what mysterious route? That is what they struggled to explain, apparently in a less distant era, first by establishing a relation between the theories about the return of souls to the earth for reincarnation and the observation of the special shape of the plant's stem; and then—and this is the contribution of those who enjoy finding original causes, which is already a habit of mind in "primitive" peoples—by inventing the cosmogonic myth about the common origin of broad beans and men. A single practical conclusion flows naturally from this: eating broad beans is criminal cannibalism; and just touching them is a defilement and a danger, like touching a cadaver.[136]

Here is another long citation from a work by Marcel Detienne that is so lively I prefer not to paraphrase:

For strict vegetarians, every blood sacrifice is a murder and ultimately an act of cannibalism for which their horror is expressed by way of the broad bean. In fact, this legume is at the antipodes of spices, the marvellous food of gods and the Golden Age. Thanks to a stalk without nodes and by virtue of affinities with the rotten, the broad bean establishes the same direct communication with the world of the dead as spices establish with the world of the gods to which they belong through their solar quality and dessicated nature. But in the Pythagorean system of thought, the broad bean is still more. It is a being of flesh and blood, the double of the man at whose side it grows and from whose rotten compost they both feed. As a result, say the Pythagoreans, it is the same crime to eat a broad bean as to gnaw one's parents' heads. Proof of it is produced by a set of experiments known to Pythagorean tradition. A broad bean is placed, for its mysterious cooking, in a pot or closed container that is then hidden in manure or buried in the ground. After a more or less lengthy period of gestation, the bean transforms itself either into female genitals with a child's scarcely formed head attached to them or into a human head whose features are already recognizable. In these experiments, the pot is a womb entrusted with the task of revealing the broad bean's true nature. But it can already be discovered by taking a half-eaten or slightly squashed broad bean and placing it in the sun for a moment or two. Immediately a smell arises which is said to be either the smell of sperm or that of blood shed in a murder. The Pythagoreans are explicit: eating broad beans is feeding on human flesh, is devouring the most marked type of meat . . . The broad bean is indeed the most marked source of generation in the plant world, to the extent that it appears as a mixture of blood and genitals in the fantasies of the Pythagoreans. But the prohibition against tasting it only restates in more urgent terms the hackneyed tabu against eating meat or spilling the blood of a living being.[137]

Detienne also notes that the egg, the heart, and the broad bean occur together, as for the disciples of Orphism or Pythagoreanism,

in one and the same list of prohibitions that a cultic regulation from Smyrna dated to the second century A.D. enumerates for the initiates of Dionysos Bromios: don't approach the altars wearing black clothing, don't strike the victims that cannot be sacrificed, don't serve eggs in the banquets honoring Dionysos or burn the heart (of the victim) on the altars, and abstain from mint, which accompanies the accursed race of broad beans. But the horror provoked by these leguminous plants in this Dionysiac context receives a novel justification that the regulation suggests be told to the mysteries' initiates: broad beans were born from Titans, the murderers of Dionysos.

The originality of this text, according to Detienne,

does not lie in the way it combines Orphic precepts with Pythagorean tabus while giving them a certain Dionysiac flavor. It lies instead in the way it overdetermines parallel motifs of different origin, for example, by inventing a Titanic origin for broad beans. These vegetables are not only the nocturnal, bloody doubles of the human plant, whose consumption is tantamount to cannibalism; broad beans are themselves born from the primordial beings who were promoted to the rank of ancestors of carnivorous humanity by their anthropophagic behavior.[138]

Clearly, Detienne has learned his lesson well from Georges Dumézil and Claude Lévi-Strauss. It would also have been interesting to look at the role of the raw and the cooked in the mythemes about broad beans from a structuralist point of view. I should also point out a central notion in his discussion: "overdetermining parallel motifs." Characteristic of the logic of dreams, overdetermination slips in everywhere in magical thought; I will return to it later.

Depth psychology, the sociological approach, and structuralism all in turn offer keys for the constantly renewed interpretation of ancient texts. Their insights are dazzling; the conclusions made by specialists in anthropological analysis of myths dominate the field. Alongside them are only a few rare and timid attempts to complement, never replace, the magico-cultural and structuralist interpretations of the Pythagorean tabu by a dietetic justification of it in medical terms. To Joseph Schumacher, for instance, the prohibition against eating broad beans has its "natural explanation" in the application of the general Pythagorean rule whereby one should eat in conformity with the nature of the human body, and avoid foods that swell the belly and cause concern.[139]

Once favism became visible to medical eyes as a real disease, the link between it and Pythagorean teaching was made, at first in a marginal and superficial way in specialized medical studies that were totally unknown to historians of the ancient world. Had the doctors finally found the true sense of this "simple rule of hygiene" that Daremberg suspected lay behind the legend? To my knowledge, the first to take up the question from this point of view, with appropriate knowledge both of historical sources and the medical discoveries, was the Greek physician Solon Veras. In an account given in May 1939 to the Hellenic Society of Pediatrics in Athens, he reviewed the principal evidence on the prohibition against broad beans in antiquity, stressed the magical or simply dietetic nature of the ancient justifications of it, and came to the conclusion "that no proof existed in accounts from the past of a real knowledge of favism by Greek writers."[140] There is no doubt that Veras is correct: nothing in the historical documentation at our disposal allows us to infer any clinical knowledge of incidents of favism. But Veras does not take account of the fact that all that documentation is second-hand and informs us only indirectly and very poorly of the actual lore of the first Pythagoreans.

The debate began anew once the intrinsic cause of favism had been unearthed. The tabu against broad beans could, it was suggested, be explained on the simple supposition that Pythagoras himself or one of his associates had G6PD deficiency and was aware from direct experience of the crises of favism.[141] This hypothesis was constructed on the basis of very little evidence, without an in-depth study of the problems it poses. In two recent publications, the medical explanation of the Pythagorean tabu is vigorously criticized with arguments that go beyond those of Solon Veras. Moreover, the two are unaware of each other and do not know or cite the work of Veras. The first of them, M. Enrique Laval, a philologist from Chile, claims to have heard from a doctor friend that Pythagoras knew of favism. Wishing to be sure about it, he examined both modern medical publications as well as Greek and Roman texts and came to the conclusion that "neither Pythagoras nor any other philosopher or physician believed that eating broad beans or inhaling the fragrance of their flowers could damage one's health; the prohibition against eating them is religious, and probably linked to the doctrine of the transmigration of souls."[142] The second authority, Constantin Ballas, a physician from Athens, discusses the subject with barely concealed contempt for his overly rational colleagues. He dismisses them in a footnote: "In an attempt to find 'hidden medical knowledge' almost everywhere, some contemporary historians of medicine have claimed that most of the Pythagorean akousmata are plain hygienic rules; this quite naive interpretation doesn't deserve any serious consideration."[143]

This is an easy way out of the problem, too easy in fact. We should avoid the false reasoning that has been mechanically repeated since Salomon Reinach and that tacitly presupposes that a genuinely mythological motivation for a custom will not consist in something hygienic or generally utilitarian. The mutual exclusivity of two kinds of determinism, one mythological and the other utilitarian, is not at all proven; it is even unlikely to be true. The overdetermination in myth is not restricted to the sociocultural and psychological register. It is indeed possible that apparently contradictory explanations are actually complementary and work on different levels. This was known in antiquity, and people did not deprive themselves of combined justifications.

In concluding this review of modern opinions, I should stress the success of the anthropological analysis of the broad bean prohibition. It does indeed resonate with totemism. The proof of its magical/religious nature is provided by an examination of the overall role of the *súmbola* and *akoúsmata* of the Pythagoreans. However, analytic procedures that have been useful in decoding the tabu on the mythological level have also taught us that in this domain the discovery of a single reason for something does not necessarily exclude others.

Concluding Questions

The reality of favism on the one hand and the legendary Pythagorean teachings about broad beans on the other pose pressing questions for a methodology that seeks to integrate medical history with epistemology and the history of daily life. In the hope that the clear formulation of such questions is a step toward answering them, I would pose them as follows:

1. Did the favic genetic defect exist in the ancient population of the Mediterranean?

2. If the answer to question 1 is yes, how did it come about that the disease was not observed by physicians prior to the nineteenth century?

3. Was the prohibition against eating broad beans dictated or at least prompted by the actual observation of hemolytic incidents in Egypt, the Greek colonies in Italy, or in Greece itself? In other words, did the Egyptian priests, Pythagoras, and Empedocles know about the favic idiosyncrasy even in a vague way?

4. If the answer to question 3 is yes, why is the tradition silent with regard to such knowledge?

I do not hesitate to answer yes to the first of these questions. The current geographical distribution of the favic defect cannot be well explained according to the rules of population genetics unless we admit the ancient existence of this mutation in the Mediterranean. The rates of favic defect seem to evolve relatively slowly, at least in the absence of significant migrations. For obvious reasons the eating of broad beans should lead to the selective elimination of favism. However, field observation shows that the persistence of a high frequency of the enzymopathies linked to G6PD deficiency is compatible with the presence of broad beans in the standard diet. In Iran, there is almost no G6PD deficiency among the Zoroastrians, who represent the oldest layer of the current population, while the deficiency rate among Moslems is greater than 7 percent. True favism is rare there. It is worth noting that the broad bean probably originated in that part of the world or at least that its consumption there goes back to the remote past.

The maintenance of a high rate of the favic defect appears to be linked to the falciparum type of malarial endemic; it is then a consequence of balanced polymorphism, as was explained above. Pure favism does not come from Asia. Its cradle is North Africa or Magna Graecia, and the zone of malignant tertian fever passes through them. The malarial endemic in Sicily is attested from the start of the historic period. Even a legendary tale about Empedocles speaks of it.[144] The city of Croton, center of the first Pythagorean community, was known to be particularly salubrious,[145] but that does not mean that malaria was not rampant in the vicinity.[146]

In sum, these are my reasons for believing that the favic defect was present at the dawn of classical civilization precisely where the prohibition against eating broad beans was first articulated. Favic incidents must have taken place in antiquity in that region, since their triggering cause was also present there. For the ancient Greeks, as for the Romans after them, broad beans were a basic food cultivated everywhere as far back as anyone knew:[147] "Phainias in his treatise *On Plants* says, 'When they are fresh, we put bitter vetch, broad beans, and chickpeas in appetizers; when they are dry, we serve them boiled or almost always roasted.' "[148] Eaten fresh and raw as snacks, broad beans were also a main dish when served boiled.[149] Some storing and cooking techniques significantly modify their toxicity for persons who suffer from favism. There is a large number of recipes for preparing the beans that reduce the danger. Such recipes first appeared in the eastern Mediterranean and in the course of time became widespread.[150]

As for the second question, I have outlined an answer to it in the first part of this chapter. There were epistemological obstacles that hindered the free growth of knowledge. Science sharpens perceptions in one direction only by blinding it in others. It is not an accident that the discovery of favism in the nineteenth century was effected not by the medical elite but by provincial practitioners who were open to folklore and relatively free from the dominant medical ideology. It is also no accident that current research on this enzymopathy is being carried out by veteran scientists in highly specialized institutions. Science sets aside certain facts only to take them up later on at another level of development. They are the facts that at a given point in time trouble the accepted conceptual framework and run counter to what since Thomas Kuhn has been called the scientific paradigm. They are conjured away, made invisible by an intellectual selection process that takes place below the level of the proper processes of critical elimination and conscious, logical scrutiny.

In the past physicians saw acute jaundice, the appearance of blood in the urine, and other symptoms of favism, but they refused to see them as causally linked with broad beans. In this instance they were blinded by an absolute demand for deterministic coherence. In the eyes of a Greek physician or naturalist of the fifth and fourth centuries B.C., the harmlessness of broad beans was proven by daily, irrefutable experience: a person who eats broad beans does not fall ill from them; at worst he or she gets bloated and sleeps poorly. If someone does fall ill after a meal of broad beans, that proves nothing. Science had unmasked the fallacy in the rule *post hoc ergo propter hoc*. In this way it could always preserve the coherence of its causal chains. So in terms of Hippocratic nutritional science, it was established that everyone can eat broad beans with impunity, at least from the point of view of physical health. To be sure, the notion of an individual disposition, a particular *phúsis,* was already well developed, but with a significant limitation. In the doctrinal perspective of humoral pathology, a disposition is the result of a special mixture of the components of the body, an apparent individual state that is visible to the clinical eye. In a disease like consumption, for example, the disposition is revealed by external tokens, by a habitus phthisicus. There is nothing of the kind for favism: the individual intrinsic state is perfectly hidden, given the limits of ancient investigative technique.

According to the recent opinion of Salomon Katz, "Deeper knowledge about susceptibility to favism should have developed, and in such a way as to reduce its deleterious effects to a minimum. And yet it turns out that favism is still a widespread disease throughout the [Mediterranean] region."[151] If the broad bean, says Katz, had only negative effects, humans would have ceased to use it. Since "evolution has provided no implicit or explicit knowledge of its toxicity," the blindness should be counterbalanced by a biological advantage. To explain what he represents as an "evolutionary paradox," Katz formulates the hypothesis that in those individuals not sensitive to its dangerous hemolytic effects, the broad bean had antimalarial properties similar to but less potent than those of synthetic antimalarials:

> The broad bean has been eaten since Neolithic times and it is clear that neither tabus nor treatment techniques have been enough to diminish the number of cases of favism. Although the broad bean is an important agricultural product in the Mediterranean basin, it remains difficult to explain its continuous use given the rates of morbidity and the high mortality that it produces in individuals with G6PD deficiency. Accordingly it seems likely . . . that the fact that its use confers a cumulative resistance to malaria constitutes a supplementary selective advantage. More specifically, several kinds of active components in broad beans that have been shown to be responsible for crises of favism in subjects deficient in G6PD actually increase the sensitivity of red blood cells to oxydants in normal individuals, and they do so without toxic side effects.[152]

Malaria, then, promotes the maintenance of the favic defect, while eating broad beans combats malaria. At least, that is the hypothesis, which is indeed attractive but as yet lacking in experimental proof.

As for the hereditary aspect of favism, E. Giles has shown that in Indo-Europeans transmission of any trait linked to the X chromosome was made invisible by exogamy and the patrilineal, patrilocal system of kinship. It was very hard to perceive the relation between a disease transmitted by mothers and a line of descent based on fathers.[153]

The third question is the heart of the matter. A secure answer seems to me impossible, but I tend toward a nuanced yes. In the absence of proof, we have to rely on clues. The Pythagoreans were extremely attentive to the effects of food on the state of the organism. The tradition is unanimous on the subject, and it attributes to Pythagoras and his immediate followers extensive research in this domain.[154] The master from Samos is said to have been a vegetarian himself and the inventor of a meat diet for athletes: "Of all forms of medicine, [the Pythagoreans] understood dietetics above all. In that they showed themselves to be very fastidious. They were the first to try to understand the signs of the relation between exercise, food, and rest. They were among the first to provide explanations and advice about the preparation of food."[155] We have seen the importance of mythological links between broad beans, blood, and death. The most distinctive symptom of favism is hemoglobinuria, which at times can cause sudden, spectacular death. Moreover, Pythagoras and Empedocles did not yet have an epistemological obstacle, a fundamental prejudice, to make favism "invisible." Here I touch upon the fourth and final question. The essential element of an answer to it occurs in a statement by Plutarch: "Philosophy was rife with visions, fables, superstitions when he [Socrates] received it from Pythagoras and Empedocles; it was possessed, and he trained it to get in step with reality and pursue truth by means of sober reason."[156]

The magical thought of the Presocratic thinkers is known to us only through the filter of their rationalizing successors. We know nothing of the real rootedness of Pythagoras's teaching in his personal experience of life. We know only a few bits of his teachings in any case, and they are only what writers of the fourth century B.C. chose to transmit. As exegetes, those writers were poorly informed (considering the esoteric nature of the philosophical sects) and also, they were firmly committed to retrieving the great figures from the past and giving them a new, corrected image, in tune with a new scientific morality. When I cited the evidence of Alexander Polyhistor above, I observed that the prohibition against eating broad beans had to do with a sacred dietetics that was linked to the idea of ritual purity, not health. Although nowadays these conceptual domains are clearly distinguished, was such a distinction really valid in the archaic period of Greek civilization? After taking a close look at the Pythagorean prohibitions reported by Alexander, I would say that although all are tabus and as such religious, a good number of them can *also* be justified on hygienic grounds.

In 1975, in my seminar at the Ecole Pratique des Hautes Etudes, I offered an explanatory schema that divided this historical process into three phases:

1. Observation of crises of favism and their imprecise interpretation by a largely "magical" mentality (Pythagoras, Empedocles).

2. Abandonment of this belief by the rationalizing mentality of thinkers like Hippocrates or Aristotle. The harmfulness of broad beans is such a complex phenomenon that medical experience on an elementary level does

not confirm it; it was therefore relegated to the domain of superstition that people tried to demythologize (Aristoxenus, Cicero, Plutarch, Aulus Gellius); for millennia, then, it was "invisible" to the learned.

3. Modern discovery of the particular modalities of favism and partial rehabilitation of the ancient tabu.[157]

Chapter Ten

POROTIC HYPEROSTOSIS, HEREDITARY ANEMIAS, AND MALARIA

It may be surprising to find a single chapter embracing such disparate pathological states as a peculiar morphological modification of ancient skulls, a group of hereditary blood abnormalities, and a fever caused by parasites.[1] But the combination is not a random one; any single part of this medico-historical triptych illuminates the other two. I also wish to demonstrate herein the usefulness of interdisciplinary research on problems of biological history: in writing this chapter I have had recourse to discoveries in paleopathology and modern clinical medicine, recent achievements in genetics and molecular biology, the historical exegesis of ancient texts, the examination of art objects, and historical geography.

From the time of the first systematic paleopathological investigations, the presence of a very strange sort of lesion has been observed on ancient bones from various parts of the world. It was mysterious for the simple reason that no one was able to identify it with any current disease entity in a truly persuasive way. The lesion consists of porous zones disposed bilaterally and almost symmetrically on the cranial vault. The surface of the affected areas, which resembles pumice stone, is rough, pitted with small cavities, and sometimes covered by a thin latticework of bone. Histological examination reveals that the diploë is enlarged, has rarefied zones and restructured trabeculae; the outer table is thinned down, hollowed out, and often disappears altogether in a newly formed bone mass; the inner table is unchanged. The preferred locale for such lesions is the parietal bones and the frontal bone. They can extend to the temporal, occipital, and sphenoid bones or even to the long bones of the axial (ribs) and appendicular skeleton. Localization on the upper walls of the eye sockets is not rare.

The first description of this curious osteopathy was made by Hermann Welcker, who studied it in 1885 on skulls from Peru, Java, Tuscany, and Africa. He was struck by the cribrate or riddled appearance of the eye sockets and named the lesion "cribra orbitalia." Influenced by R. Virchow's ideas about "pathological races" and "degenerate" peoples, Welcker thought this morphological state was a racial characteristic, an inherited abnormality due to excessive development of the blood vessels.[2]

Symmetrical porosity of the cranial vault was also observed on a Dayak skull, on a very ancient Egyptian one, and then on bones excavated in Nubia.[3] J. Saint-Périer thought the lesions syphilitic on a child's skeleton he found in 1913 amid the debris of a Gallo-Roman building at Souzy-la-Briche near Etampes. In the light of current knowledge, the "circular exostoses projecting outward from a surface riddled with channels perpendicular to a surface of newly formed bone," localized on the parietal bones and the eye sockets, accompanied by thickening of the diploë but with the inner table intact—all this cannot be the consequence of syphilitic osteitis, but belongs instead to the same nosological group as the porotic hyperostosis on ancient American and Egyptian skulls. The child whose skeleton was found at Souzy-la-Briche cannot have been older than 8 years of age at the time of death, while the Roman ruins in which it was buried date approximately from the fourth century A.D.[4] Unfortunately, old descriptions like this one suffer from a low level of general knowledge in osseous pathology. They can be used today only with the greatest caution. At the time, fine interpretation of X-rays of bone lesions was still in its infancy.

In 1914, Aleš Hrdlička gave a fairly detailed description of cranial porosity in the pre-Columbian Indians of Peru. He attributed a special paleopathological significance to this bone state and called it "osteoporosis symmetrica." By his lights, symmetrical osteoporosis was a disease *sui generis* that affected American Indians living along the coast. Everything seemed to suggest that it was a childhood disease whose issue was often fatal. He did observe lesions of the same sort on the skulls of adults, but they were less serious and even seemed "scarred" or marked by a repair process. Probably they were victims of the disease who had escaped death during an acute infantile phase and even considered themselves cured, though they kept the anatomopathological consequences for the rest of their lives. Hrdlička was correct in observing that these cranial lesions were not in fact a localized disease but the only remaining signs of a "systematic disorder" whose other consequences were lost on tissue less resistant to the passage of time.[5]

In 1929, Herbert U. Williams confirmed the majority of Hrdlička's conclusions. He also studied the histological and radiological aspects of this osteopathy on the skeletons of Anasazi children in Utah and Arizona, explaining their lesions as a functional hyperplasia of the bone marrow.

He drew attention to the morphological affinity of these bone lesions with others that had just been described in some anemic children.[6] At the same time, S. Moore was stressing the similarity between the cranial lesions in a kind of hereditary anemia and those of a cranial osteopathy among the ancient Maya.[7] E. A. Hooton (1930) demonstrated the extraordinary frequency of this disease in Indians of the Yucatán peninsula: two-thirds of the children in Chichén Itzá were seriously affected by it.[8] In France, Léon Pales diagnosed this kind of osteoporosis in 1930 on some fragmentary children's parietal bones from the Neolithic period (the dolmen of Boujassac in Lozère). They had previously been considered syphilitic, on the authority of J. Parrot.[9] I have examined these specimens (Musée de l'Homme, Prunières Collection, inv. nos. 17229 and 17230). Syphilis can be ruled out. A diagnosis of symmetrical osteoporosis is plausible but uncertain, since the bone fragments are too small to reconstruct the exact topography of the cranial lesions. The work of R. L. Moodie has filled out our knowledge of osteoporosis in Egypt.[10] A few cases have been described among black Africans and the Chinese. Finally, in 1946 J. L. Angel reported the frequency of osteoporosis on prehistoric skulls from Greece, but at first he thought it just a sign of malnutrition.[11]

The expression "symmetrical osteoporosis," which has been used by most experts since Hrdlička, is inappropriate and should be eschewed. It does not correspond to the anatomopathological reality and, moreover, it generates a regrettable confusion with senile, endocrine, and nutritional osteoporosis.[12] Osteoporosis in the strict sense of the word is marked by thinning down and rarefaction of the osseous trabeculae without any accompanying osteoplastic activity. However, the paleopathological lesions under discussion here consist above all of a thickening of the bone structure. Osteoporosis of the medullary space is just a secondary aspect of hyperactivity in that organ. Accordingly the term "hyperostosis spongiosa cranii" (H. Mueller, 1934) has been suggested,[13] but I prefer "porotic hyperostosis," a term invented by the American anthropologist J. L. Angel during his paleopathological investigations of Mediterranean archaeological remains.[14]

Although I think it judicious to drop the term and the notion of symmetrical osteoporosis, I do not accept the current habit of totally confounding under one name the porous zones of the cranial vault and those in the orbital region of the frontal bone. Without a solid proof of the etiological identity of these two manifestations, I prefer to keep Welcker's old expression, "cribra orbitalia," exclusively to designate the orbital localization. My position agrees with that of D. S. Carlson, G. J. Armelagos, and D. Van Gerven, who stress the difference between "osteoporotic pitting" (a mild form of osteoporotic affection of the vault), "spongy hyperostosis," and "cribra orbitalia."[15]

In any case, all these names aim merely at a condensed anatomopathological definition. They do not contribute to the problem of the idiopathic disease with or without secondary diseases that these bony lesions betoken or, more precisely, whose aftereffects they are. In the past, paleopathologists first thought of artificial deformations of the skull, then of rickets and syphilis. Nowadays, the latter diagnosis can be confidently ruled out, since X-ray analysis reveals morphological peculiarities that differentiate porotic hyperostosis from the osseous lesions that are produced by the infectious activity of the treponeme. The same is true for primitive osteoporoses and osseous lesions of toxic and endocrine origins. They have radiological characteristics that are indeed distinct from those found on ancient skulls affected by porotic hyperostosis.[16] Hrdlička imagined some toxic factor but was unable to specify what kind. Wood Jones suggested that the "cranial ulcerations" of the ancient Nubians were caused by their carrying heavy water jars on their heads.[17] Under the influence of E. A. Hooton, anthropologists at times confuse this disease with osteoporosis of nutritional origins.[18] That is certainly a mistake, but the possibility remains that porotic hyperostosis is linked to malnutrition by another physiopathological process. Vitamin D deficiency may be responsible for it, at least in part.[19] Experienced pathologists have said as recently as 1955 that anatomical examination of affected skulls does not in itself allow us to decide whether the disease is a kind of rickets, or a hemolytic anemia, or a combination of the two.[20]

H. U. Williams was the first to hint at the right solution by comparing X-rays of porotic hyperostosis with those of the lesions that had just been discovered in children suffering from hereditary anemias. For S. Moore, the analogy between this paleopathological affection of the cranium and sickle cell anemia merited detailed investigation. Despite these insights, Williams went astray and ended up with a hypothesis that is both ingenious and fallacious: that the pressure produced on the occiput of a baby resting on a head board could produce passive venous hyperemia and that it, along with disturbances due to vitamin deficiency, results in symmetrical osteoporosis of the skull.[21] Subsequently, Léon Pales returned to the initial hypothesis of Toldt and Adachi and combined it with Williams's. He explained this disease as the result of pressure exerted on the skull of newborns in an effort to deform it artificially for ritual or aesthetic reasons. Any such action on the skull of a newborn, says Pales, "produces venous stasis and, as a result of the changes in blood pressure, a hypervascularization of certain cranial regions, in particular the diploë and the outer table."[22] No concrete clinical observation was evoked in support of this etiology. In 1951, H. E. Sigerist still cited the opinions of Williams as the best explanation of porotic hyperostosis.[23] However, a much more plausible solution was already within the grasp of medical historians.

Clinical Picture and Physiopathology of the Thalassemias

In 1925, Thomas B. Cooley and Pearl Lee, physicians in Detroit, discovered a strange kind of anemia through clinical observations in five children. They defined a distinctive syndrome consisting of a drop in circulating red cells, pronounced enlargement of the spleen along with slight liver enlargement, skin discoloration, and osseous lesions primarily on the skull. From the start, Cooley was struck by the mongoloid facial appearance and significant bone changes in his patients. He thought their anemia was congenital but not hereditary.[24] He and his colleagues subsequently refined the morphology of the red cells in these anemics: of unequal size, they are poor in hemoglobin, which is often concentrated in their middles (so-called target cells). It soon became clear that this type of anemia is familial. The Americans suffering from it were almost all of Mediterranean stock, that is, they were the sons and daughters of Greek and Italian immigrants.[25] The Italian physicians F. Rietti (1925), E. Greppi (1928), and F. Micheli (1929) described some relatively benign hemolytic syndromes that subsequent researchers associated with Cooley's anemia to constitute a single disease entity called thalassemia.[26]

The term "thalassemia," which was proposed in 1936 by G. H. Whipple and W. L. Bradford, is an inept contraction of the word "thalassanemia," devised in 1934 by J. Comby on the pretext that the anemia in question was proper to inhabitants of the Mediterranean basin. As G. W. Corner, one of George Whipple's co-workers in Rochester, remembers it, the word *thálassa* was chosen to associate Cooley's anemia with the Mediterranean. The inspiration came from lingering schoolboy memories of the exclamation Xenophon imputed to his soldiers when they found themselves finally before the sea. Apparently, it had been forgotten that the *thálatta (sic)* in question was the Black Sea and not the Mediterranean. Because of a certain euphony, no doubt, the term "thalassemia" will live on, although its etymology and semantics can hardly be justified. The sea, *thálassa,* has absolutely no role in the pathogenesis of this anemia, which, moreover, is not even limited to the Mediterranean region. According to the formation rules in modern medical terminology, thalassemia should be a pathological state marked by the presence of sea water in the circulatory system. The reality is somewhat different. Once more, usage has triumphed over morphological principles.

The basic disturbance in thalassemia is an inborn error of hemoglobin metabolism. The error is embedded in a nonsexual chromosome and is transmitted from generation to generation like a dominant Mendelian trait whose strongest expression is in homozygotes.[27] Some of those who suffer from the disease have hemoglobin F in their blood (a fetal type that is not produced in normal adults) alongside the usual hemoglobins A and A_2. In others, the quantity of hemoglobin A_2 is increased relative to hemoglobin

A. In still other, rarer cases, the appearance of special hemoglobins has been reported. In short, there are several thalassemias, not a single disease entity defined by a single molecular lesion. For the historian of diseases, that is an important fact, for it justifies an explanation of its origin in several foci. According to current hypotheses, the mutations that originate the thalassemias affect regulatory, not structural genes. Some thalassemias slow down the synthesis of the alpha hemoglobin chain, as distinct from others that act on the delta or the beta chain. In β-A_2 thalassemia, the synthesis of hemoglobin A is reduced, so the amount of hemoglobin A_2 in circulating blood is relatively increased. The β-F type is expressed by the persistence of hemoglobin F after an individual's fetal stage. In alpha thalassemias, there are abnormal hemoglobins (H and Bart's) in the blood.[28]

The severe clinical form, *thalassemia major* or Cooley's anemia, occurs in homozygous children, in whom the genetic trait is inherited from both parents. It makes its presence known early, first insidiously, through extreme exhaustion, irregular fever, sallow or yellowish skin, growth retardation, and, at times, pain in the left hypochondrium. The fully developed clinical picture is dominated by symptoms resulting from hemolysis (anemia, jaundice, brown pigmentation), enlarged spleen, bouts of fever, and deformed facial features (mongoloid facies). Thalassemic children have an enlarged skull with lumps in the frontal and parietal regions, a broadened forehead, prominent cheekbones, slant eyes set far apart, a large, subsident nose, and a projecting upper jaw.[29] Death in childhood or adolescence is the usual lot of homozygous victims. By contrast, those who inherit the trait from only one parent reach maturity without particular difficulty. The heterozygous forms are expressed clinically as mild disturbances (thalassemia minor or the Rietti-Greppi-Micheli syndrome) that can regress and even become latent (thalassemia minima or Silvestroni-Bianco microcytosis).

In all persons who suffer from thalassemia, there is hyperplasia of the bone marrow, which compensates for the diminished longevity of red cells by increased hemopoietic activity. The radiological signs of thalassemia were outlined by Cooley but not precisely defined until about thirty years ago. Modifications of the cranial vault are very pronounced in homozygous patients and more restrained, though still evident, in heterozygous ones. The diploë is thickened and contains clear zones; it forces back the outer table, which is often thinned down and riddled with holes. The marrow's hyperactivity demands a supplementary vascularization that is provided by hyperplasia of the periostal zone and produces a porous appearance on the bone surface. The trabeculae take on a radiating form perpendicular to the inner table; sometimes they end in a "hair-on-end" pattern.[30] In homozygotes, the hair-on-end pattern appears less frequently than one might imagine after reading the earliest observations. In fact, it is frequently lacking and only shows up late. In heterozygotes, by contrast, who do not present severe clinical symptoms, it is relatively common.[31]

The X-ray just described coincides perfectly with that of porotic hyperostosis.[32] However, it is not a pathognomonic sign of thalassemia. It is only the nonspecific expression of bone marrow hyperactivity. The localization of porous zones in patients with thalassemia corresponds to the localization characteristic of some ancient skulls with hyperostosis. In its minor forms, the lesions are restricted to the cranial vault (sometimes with thinning down of the cortex of the long bones), while thalassemia major does not spare the facial bones or the long bones of the appendicular skeleton, in which the cortex is reduced, the medullar space enlarged, and there is osteoporosis as well as a reticulated disposition of the trabeculae in the metaphyses. Some authors attribute an almost pathognomonic value to the thickening of the temporal bones and the upper jawbones with inhibition of the pneumatization of the mastoid cellules and the maxillary sinuses.[33]

Other Hereditary Anemias

Another hemoglobinosis similar to thalassemia but characterized by the presence of sickle-shaped red cells (drepanocytes or sickle cells) in peripheral blood also produces bone modifications linked to bone marrow hyperactivity. It could, at least in some cases, be the cause of lesions on ancient skulls. Drepanocytosis or, to use its more common name, sickle cell anemia—the all too common barbarism "sicklemia" should be avoided—was described for the first time by James B. Herrick of Chicago as the result of a microscopic examination of the blood of an anemic black.[34] That first observation dates back to 1905, but the publication of the case, extraordinary for its time, dates from 1910.

First detected among blacks in the United States, sickle cell anemia was later discovered in black Africa as well as the Mediterranean along with an important focus in southern India. Because of a mutation that is transmitted from one generation to the next, the individuals afflicted with sickle cell anemia synthesize an abnormal hemoglobin, called hemoglobin S. So the disease is a "molecular" one.[35] Hemoglobin S is distinguishable from hemoglobin A only through a structural detail: in position 6 of the beta chain, glutamic acid is replaced by another amino acid, valine. That suffices to endow the hemoglobin molecule with a particular instability. Under certain environmental conditions, it crystallizes in the erythrocytes and makes them take on an elongated shape resembling a sickle or a holly leaf. These sickle-shaped red cells stick to one another and can inhibit local circulation. Moreover, their longevity is reduced relative to that of normal red cells.[36]

Hemoglobin S occurs in 50 to 100 percent of the red cells in homozygotes and in 20 to 40 percent of them in heterozygotes. Persons born from the union of two parents with the defect suffer from childhood on (severe anemia, jaundice, progressive weight loss, bouts of fever, splenomegaly, growth anomalies, thrombotic accidents, painful bones, abdominal crises, ulcers on the legs). Only exceptionally do they survive beyond puberty. By contrast, heterozygous carriers of the gene of this disease have only a handful of minor complaints.[37]

The osseous modifications that accompany this disease are due to bone marrow hyperplasia, exactly as with thalassemia. So it is not surprising that the morphology of the lesions is practically the same in both anemic affections being discussed here. Nevertheless, among those stricken with sickle cell anemia, radiological examination of the skeleton reveals several significant peculiarities, in particular, areas of infarction with necrosis in the small bones of the hand and, for adolescents or adults, osteoporosis of the vertebrae.[38]

Some other hereditary anemias that are much rarer (at least nowadays) may be responsible for osseous reactions similar to porotic hyperostosis: scherocytosis, elliptocytosis, and hemoglobinopathy C. In these ailments the lesions are moderate and do not attain the severity of a thalassemia. Favism, a genetic flaw that is widespread in Greece and southern Italy, can also be the cause of a chronic anemia that sometimes produces cranial lesions.[39] We now know that even a microcytic hypochromic anemia, if prolonged, can induce porotic hyperostosis in children. This hematological syndrome is not inherited; it is an iron deficiency anemia caused by environmental factors. A drop in serous iron results either from a lack of the mineral in food or from its loss through chronic intestinal hemorrhages. In the latter event, iron deficiency anemia is usually the result of a parasitic ailment (ankylostomiasis, schistosomiasis, tapeworm infestation, amebic dysentery, and so forth). Since the histological and radiological picture of bone damage due to iron deficiency anemia can mimic exactly that of a thalassemic or drepanocytosic osteopathy, it is that much more important to single out physiopathological and epidemiological features that distinguish among them. Lack of iron only stigmatizes children's bones, and its results are practically restricted to the skull. Although this type of anemia occurs often in children nowadays, its osseous complications are seen only rarely. This means that the appearance of porotic hyperostosis in a case of iron deficiency anemia must depend on one or more additional factors. According to recent clinical observations, the concomitant factors may be protein deficiency or rickets. Maternal malnutrition during pregnancy and premature birth seem to favor the osseous lesion. In some historical settings, all the factors just mentioned can be interconnected to form a complex of nutritional distress.[40]

So there is an astonishing multiplicity of possible causes for porotic hyperostosis. The list could be made still longer by adding to it several pathological states that produce the same kind of X-ray: polycythemia vera, some congenital cardiopathies, and so forth. The inevitable conclusion is that all pre- and protohistoric skulls having such lesions were not necessarily afflicted with one basic disease and do not necessarily share a common etiology. To make possible a differential diagnosis in specific cases, one can imagine a variety of criteria: morphological differences that take account of the state of all the bones in a skeleton, biochemical peculiarities, the frequency of affected skulls in a given site and their geographical distribution, data on the sociobiological conditions of the population in question, and so forth.

In children who have died as a result of Cooley's anemia (homozygous type), one should find thickening of the facial bones, osseous invasion of the paranasal sinuses including the mastoid cellules, exaggerated development of the zygomas, and, in particular, osteoporotic foci in the long bones sometimes accompanied by precocious fusion of the epiphyses. Contrary to Cooley's first observations, in homozygous thalassemics there are more often lesions of the appendicular skeleton without effects on the skull than the reverse. The most consistent signs are thinning of the cortex of the long bones and a reticulated appearance at the level of the elbow. Poynton and Davey have pointed out certain aspects of the teeth that are characteristic of thalassemia, but they have not yet been used by paleopathologists for a differential diagnosis of porotic hyperostosis.[41]

As for sickle cell anemia, it becomes probable when there is osteoporosis of the vertebrae along with necrotic foci in the appendicular skeleton. The sure absence of noncranial osseous lesions reduces the possibility of thalassemia major and of sickle cell anemia and increases the possibility of thalassemia minor or iron deficiency anemia. The importance of complementing the paleopathological examination of a skull with a methodical inspection of the whole skeleton cannot be overstated. Such an inspection is conclusive only after X-rays are made of all available long bones. In some ancient populations, for instance, in central Europe or in Nubia, cribra orbitalia occur fairly frequently without any other manifestations or porotic hyperostosis. According to recent research, it seems more and more likely that in such cases the main etiological factor is iron deficiency. That hypothesis seems to coincide best with current understanding of the living conditions in such populations and, moreover, it agrees well with observations on the etiology of this osseous lesion in apes.[42]

But it is also apparent that a certain uniformity in the reaction of bone marrow to very different physiopathological situations requires that in paleopathology the etiological diagnosis of such states not be founded exclusively on the examination of isolated skeletons. We must take into account archaeological data on socioeconomic well-being, nutrition, rites, and customs, nor should we forget to consider carefully all available demographic data and direct or indirect proof of the presence or absence of various parasitic diseases.[43] Nor is the frequency of affected skeletons in a specific necropolis a minor diagnostic factor. When it surpasses a certain threshold, sporadic diseases like congenital cardiopathy can no longer be contemplated. Differential diagnosis must then be oriented either toward inherited endemic diseases like thalassemia or toward acquired ones, such as iron deficiency anemia with a specific, common cause in a given population, and ailments of infectious origin. In the case of thalassemia, there must be severe cases in which long bones are affected as well as milder ones with moderate and isolated lesions on the skull. Moreover, the relation between the frequency of these two forms of the disease, one homozygous and the other heterozygous, should not be far from that predicted by population genetics (Hardy and Weinberg's distribution).

In a diachronic study of populations over a specified area, one would expect the incidence of porotic hyperostosis, insofar as it reflects chronic anemic states, to be inversely proportional to parameters that reflect the overall well-being of the general population, such as longevity, fertility, or abundance of food. The reversal of this relationship, that is, a positive correlation between these parameters and the frequency of porotic hyperostosis, could be understood as a sign favoring the etiological diagnosis of thalassemia or of some other nondeficient, hereditary anemia. I will show below how John Lawrence Angel's research points to exactly this positive correlation during certain periods of the ancient history of the Mediterranean.

In the future, further refinements in differential diagnosis will be made possible by the quantitative chemical microanalysis of the bones.[44] A still more decisive method would be the biochemical analysis of hemoglobin molecules preserved in mummified tissue or even, perhaps, along the byways of the spongy portions of skeletons. For instance, a paleopathological diagnosis of thalassemia could be confirmed by the presence of isoleucine (a component of hemoglobin F) in red blood cells once they are isolated by microchemical means, or, alternatively, by their form when imagined by a scanning electron microscope.

Distribution of Thalassemias and Hypotheses on Their Origin

Today the thalassemic trait is probably spread throughout all of mainland Greece as well as the islands.[45] It poses a serious public health problem. A single statistic can make its dimensions clear: during the seven years from 1948 to 1955, two pediatric hospitals in Athens admitted 421 children (representing about 2 percent of all hospitalizations in these institutions) with Cooley's anemia. They were homozygous cases with severe clinical symptoms and very high mortality.[46] Relatively high frequencies of thalassemia have been reported among the native inhabitants of several villages in Attica, in the Peloponnesus (Sparta, Corinth, and so forth), in the southern portions of mainland Greece (Thebes, Missolonghi), in Thessaly and Epirus as well as among inhabitants of the islands (Cephalonia, Zante, the Euboea, Mytilene, Samos, Crete, Rhodes, and so on). The rate of healthy carriers of the trait varies between 5 and 10 percent, roughly speaking, except for the Ionian islands and Rhodes, where the frequency is as high as 14–16 percent.[47] Systematic examination of a group of 1,500 soldiers from various parts of Greece has made it possible to establish an approximate national average of heterozygotes without overt problems: 7.7 percent.[48]

These data relate to beta thalassemias and especially to the so-called Mediterranean type, β-A_2, which is the predominant one. Nevertheless, it is true that the other forms exist alongside these: in Greece, the thalassemic gene is not uniform.[49] Type F, which is well known in Asia and reported in Africa, is rare in Greece. The alpha thalassemias that are common in the Far East are exceptional in the eastern Mediterranean. It is significant that the β-A_2 thalassemia is fairly evenly distributed in mainland Greece, while the other types occur chiefly in restricted foci.

There is one place where several hereditary anemias meet: the region of Arta in Epirus. For a very long time malaria was rampant in the flatlands there. According to G. R. Fraser and his co-workers,[50] the inhabitants are carriers of beta thalassemia (10 percent), alpha thalassemia (5.4 percent), delta thalassemia (9.7 percent),[51] favism (10.8 percent), and sickle cell anemia (9.3 percent). By virtue of the examination of 3,650 soldiers from all over Greece, Klonakis and his co-workers reported the presence of sickle cell anemia in a heterozygous state among 0.45 percent of their sample. This average does not speak to the real situation obtaining in Greece, since the sickle cell trait is concentrated in certain areas that are ancient zones of the malarial hyperendemic. For instance, I can cite two foci: the peninsula of Chalcidice, where 23.5 percent of the inhabitants are carriers of sickle cell anemia;[52] and the region of Lake Copais in Boeotia, with 20 percent.[53] For the opposite state of affairs, compare Rhodes, which has a high rate of thalassemia but is practically free of sickle cell anemia.

Thalassemic hereditary anemias are not just the prerogative of Mediterranean peoples.[54] They were discovered by an American physician among children living in North America; according to Neel, the frequency of carriers of the defect in New York in 1945 was slightly higher than 4 percent. However, the defective gene does not occur in American Indians of unmixed breed or in descendants of the Anglo-Saxon and Spanish colonizers of America. Australia and Japan appear to be free of it. In most

European countries, for example in mainland France, in Germany, or in the Scandinavian countries, there are sporadic cases whose origins are obscure. They could be a matter of immigration or recent mutations.

In Asia the situation is different indeed. Just as happened before with the discovery of the Mediterranean endemic, thalassemia among the Chinese was first reported among immigrants in the United States (L. P. Foster, 1940), then confirmed by Chinese physicians working amid native populations. Today, there can be no doubt about the magnitude and antiquity of its Asian foci. Moving from east to west, one can see that the Mediterranean focus extends at least to the edge of the Caspian Sea. Thalassemic defects are common in Iraq, Iran, Georgia, and Azerbaidzhan. Then there is a gap that may as easily be due to the inadequacy of hematological data about that part of the world as to the actual absence of hereditary anemias there. The situation in Afghanistan is poorly known, but the research of A. G. Maratchev, unknown in the West, reports the presence of thalassemia in Tadzhikistan and Uzbekistan.[55] From Pakistan and India on eastward, the rates become significant again.

Outside the modern Greek state but within the domain of the ancient Hellenic world, thalassemia is very common on Cyprus (16–20 percent, including both Greek and Turkish Cypriots), and widespread in Turkey (especially along the coast of Asia Minor), Macedonia, and around the Greek settlements in Dalmatia and Italy. The distribution of the thalassemic defect in Italy is especially well documented thanks to the research of Ezio Silvestroni and Ida Bianco. They examined close to 50,000 individuals between 1945 and 1959. Thalassemia is common in four regions: Sardinia (10–20 percent and even, in Carbonia, as high as 27 percent), Sicily (especially its southern coast, where the rate reaches 11 percent), the coastal regions of the southern part of the peninsula, especially Calabria and Puglia (5–12 percent), and finally, though at first sight paradoxically, in the Po delta, between Ferrara and the Adriatic coast (8–22 percent). In the rest of Italy, the distribution of thalassemia is fairly uniform and moderately common (0.4–5.0 percent). Most of the cases reported outside of these foci originally stem from the four regions.[56] Since the current havens of thalassemia correspond exactly to areas in which Greek colonization of Italy was particularly intense, Silvestroni and his co-workers have suggested that Italian thalassemia was a disease with Greek origins. Thalassemia is also found in Malta (4–7 percent) and in North Africa (particularly Tunisia and Egypt, though the figures are still uncertain). It occurs in the western Mediterranean, for instance in Corsica, Portugal, and in some Spanish provinces (Valencia, Galicia, the Balearic Islands). All these cases consist in small foci to which immigrants from the eastern Mediterranean may well have brought their thalassemic genes.

Thalassemic regions have been reported in the Punjab, in the region of Madras, in Bengal, and in Sri Lanka. But the defect seems relatively uncommon in Burma and in the parts of India not mentioned above. China is assuredly much affected, but the exact distribution of thalassemia within that huge land is unknown. It is believed to be more common in the southern provinces than in the north.

Soviet publications like the handbook of geographic pathology by A. P. Avtchin (1972) say nothing about thalassemia in Mongolia. I know of no study confirming that thalassemia is common or even present in modern Mongolia. That is a fact that should not be neglected in discussions of the origin and historical migrations of thalassemia. On the other hand, thalassemia is frequently encountered in Thailand, Cambodia, Vietnam, Laos, and Indonesia. According to Lucien C. Brumpt, it was imported from China: the genetic defect is absent from Khmers not interbred with Chinese.[57] Sporadic cases have been published from the Philippines and Borneo. Finally, I mention the still unsolved problem of the presence of thalassemia (and of pseudo-thalassemias) in black Africa, especially in Zaire. Here I share the reservations of Brumpt, Lancaster, and Lehmann. The types in question do not correspond genetically to the Eurasian beta thalassemias.

In my presentation on the distribution of this disease outside of the Mediterranean, I have not cited frequency figures. If we set aside some doubtful claims, they vary between 1 and 10 percent (heterozygous carriers as a percentage of the whole population). But the figures in question have been obtained on such differing samples and by such a variety of procedures that they do not all merit equal credence. The notion of statistical comparability among them is but an illusion.

I have not taken the variety of forms of thalassemia into account because of uncertainties in this regard in the documentation that I have been able to consult. From existing surveys it is tempting to conclude that in the thalassemic zone that stretches from the Mediterranean to Southeast Asia, all the genetic forms of thalassemia and especially thalassemia β-A_2 are represented everywhere, though with incidences varying from place to place. Alpha thalassemias are more widespread in the Far East than in Europe and Asia Minor.

Since the nature of the thalassemias was first understood, people have suggested ways to account for their distribution. Numerous authorities have sought to prove that thalassemia is a racial trait that appeared once in the history of humankind. Its current distribution should then be explicable in terms of interbreeding and migration. According to Ignazio Gatto, Cooley's anemia is a pathological hereditary trait that arose by mutation in a human group that lived in Europe during the Upper Pleistocene.[58] From this so-called paleo-insular group that peopled southern Italy and Greece before the Mediterranean race, the genetic defect spread throughout the Mediterranean. Gatto's main argument is the discovery in the cave of San Teodoro in Sicily of Paleolithic skulls that, according to him, bear thalassemic lesions. That paleopathological diagnosis is, as I will show below, far from convincing. The localization of the initial mutation in time and space proposed by Gatto seems to me utterly arbitrary. Moreover, the Asian foci are inexplicable on his hypothesis.

According to Edward C. Zaino, thalassemia was born more than 50,000 years ago in a Mediterranean valley to the south of Italy and Greece that is now submerged.[59] He justifies his choice by the fact that the place in question is near the zones where the degree of thalassemia is now highest. Zaino says that the original valley must have lain to the south of these countries, since thalassemia is rare in Yugoslavia, which lies between them. He can be reproached for a methodological error and an error of fact. First, it is not inevitable that the locale of a mutation so distant in time be in the neighborhood of those areas that nowadays have the highest frequency of it. Second, surveys by G. R. Fraser have proved that thalassemia is not rare in Dalmatia and that it has a continuous distribution from Greece along the Adriatic shoreline and the Po delta probably extending northward into Hungary.[60]

But Zaino's theory has one advantage: his imaginary valley bridges Europe and Africa and thus makes more likely certain hypothetical migrations of the genetic defect. Since he interprets as thalassemic all the osteoarchaeological cases of porotic hyperostosis that I have spoken of in earlier parts of this chapter, in particular the skulls from Nubia, South America, and the Far East, Zaino has to face up to the awesome task of explaining the routes for such a dissemination of thalassemia. In his opinion, the mutation took place during the third glaciation of Würm. Once the glaciers melted, the inhabitants of the flooded valley emigrated to Greece, Italy, and North Africa. From there, the thalassemic gene migrated toward the east, into Turkey, Mesopotamia, India, and China. The possibility of a second mutation taking place somewhere in Indochina is entertained but considered unlikely. From China, the defect took a northward route along the Pacific coasts of Asia and finally across the Bering Strait onto the American continent. In passing Zaino asserts that thalassemia was perhaps the mysterious scourge that caused the disappearance of the Maya. It is surprising that this person, who bases all the first part of his hypothesis on the persistence of thalassemia among current populations, is in no way embarrassed in the second half of his study by the total absence of the pathological gene among modern American Indians.

A more serious hypothesis has been put forth by two physicians from Marseille, André Orsini and Louis Badetti. They use theories on the origin of races to situate the thalassemic mutation in time and space. Avoiding risky business like small-scale migrations and interbreeding, they do not take a small ethnic group like the paleo-insular group or a single Greek tribe as their point of departure. Instead, they suggest that thalassemia "affected selectively a very broad racial grouping, which explains its diffusion."[61] The mutation took place in "short, dark dolichocephalics" before this Mediterranean racial complex, as defined by H. Vallois, split into three races: Mediterranean, Indo-Afghani, and South Oriental. At first sight, the superposition of current thalassemic zones over the area of expansion of these dark dolichocephalics is striking. However, the hypothesis does not stand up well to testing anthropogeographic criticism.[62] The main stumbling blocks are Chinese thalassemia (that of the north is unexplained while that of the south calls for the interbreeding of a Mongolian racial group with Indo-Afghani elements) and the rarity of the genetic defect in the western Mediterranean.

Thalassemia: Greek or Mongolian?

Before the discovery of Asian foci, the simplest and probably also the most satisfying solution was to attribute the thalassemic mutation to the Greek "race." This hypothesis was first put forth by authorities in the 1930s who were not yet worried about the Far East (J. M. Baty and V. Chini, among others). It was revived and elaborated by the Italian investigators Ezio Silvestroni, Ida Bianco, and Nereo Alfieri.[63] In order to avoid the confusions that mark current discussions of this subject, I resolve the so-called Greek hypothesis into three elements, which are the answers to three distinct problems: (1) the historical period and geographic localization of the first mutation; (2) the spread of the genetic defect over the Mediterranean; and (3) its transmission into the Far East.

As to the first, proponents of the Greek hypothesis do not take a clear position. Was the mutation produced in Greece among some pre-Hellenic people, or among the Dorians after their invasion, or on Greek soil after the great migrations of the twelfth century B.C.? The latter seems the preferred view, but it is couched in vague terms. It seems to me improper to speak of a Greek "race" when referring to the Greek people of the protohistoric period, which in my view was the result of complex interbreeding. If we accept the conclusions of J. L. Angel, which are based on paleopathological research to be discussed below, thalassemia in Greece dates from the Mesolithic period or even from the end of the Paleolithic period. It is therefore prior to the formation of the Greek people.

The power of the Greek hypothesis resides in the second point: Hellenic colonization accounts well for the spread of the thalassemic gene in the Mediterranean basin. It is especially convincing for the distribution of thalassemia in Italy and on the Dalmatian coast. The two usual objections to it can easily be dismissed. The presence of the defect in places that were not actually colonized by Greeks can be explained either by undoubtedly real individual migrations or by the interbreeding of Greeks with Roman settlers who became secondary carriers of thalassemia. The main argument of those opposed to this theory, namely, the absence or rather the rarity of the defect in certain regions where Greeks were very active over a long period of time (the south of France, Catalonia), appears serious but is not. Since the thalassemic gene is a pathological trait subject to natural selection, it could have been eliminated by then in specific zones under particular environmental conditions. Unfortunately, we still have very little solid information about the environmental factors that exert negative pressure or those that favor the thalassemic defect. Malaria, which will be discussed shortly, cannot be the only exogenous cause.

The Greek hypothesis is vulnerable when it comes to the third issue. According to Silvestroni and his co-workers, the soldiers of Alexander the Great brought thalassemia to India, and from there it passed into China on the silk routes. That thalassemia reached western Asia poses no problems to the historian, but it is more difficult to account for its diffusion in the Far East. It is certain that commercial links existed between China and the Mediterranean well before the period of the Mongolian conquest. In population genetics, the time factor is as important as the space factor. One only need introduce a single gene into the pool for it to proliferate, if the environmental conditions are favorable and if there is enough time. Instead of seeking the solution to the problem in great historical migrations, it is possible to adduce exchanges on the individual level—but then we need to allow more time. Clearly, the arrival of a single thalassemic gene has the same effect as a mutation. Nothing prevents us from asserting that one did arrive, for instance, in the Bronze Age (a period during which there was a certain unity of style and technical execution in various objects from China and the Mediterranean, according to the studies of O. Janse). To be sure, such an assertion is purely speculative, arbitrary, and without scientific value. Nevertheless, I am playing this guessing game in order to show that, biologically speaking, the genetic identity of the European and Chinese foci is not impossible, and that the transmission of genes from one region to the next could have happened in a historically invisible way.

Some researchers have tried reversing the general direction of the hypothetical migration of thalassemia. The point of departure for this was a clinical observation, namely, the mongoloid facies of thalassemic children, which was noted in the very first studies by Cooley. This pathological aspect of the face was studied mainly by the pediatrician J. Caminopetros, who observed it in his Greek patients. His first thought was the possibility of an Asiatic ancestry to the disease. In his article on erythroblastic anemia in the eastern Mediterranean, Caminopetros honestly but reluctantly recognized that clinical and radiological investigations "tend to rule out a racial etiology for the mongoloid facies in patients afflicted with erythroblastic anemia, in other words, its hereditary transmission going back to the Mongol race. On the other hand, they justify considering the mongoloid facies and in general the deformation of the bones of the head in erythroblastic anemia as the result of the effect of the disease on bones."[64]

Subsequent research fully confirmed Caminopetros's prudent conclusion. The mongoloid facies is not linked to specific genetic factors but results from osseous alterations caused by a hemolytic disease.

But Caminopetros did not turn from the road once taken. According to him, thalassemic children had other Asiatic racial attributes, chiefly Mongolian eyes and a blue spot in the sacral region. In some of these patients, the family history brought to light Chinese or Mongolian ancestry that was not so remote. So Caminopetros believed he was entitled to conclude that "interbreeding with the Mongol race plays a role in the etiology of the disease." In my opinion, his argument has no probative value. It is true that, as against the facies, slanted eyelids, an epicanthus, and the sacral spot are traits independent of hereditary anemia, and as a result their frequency in thalassemics could be an important sign of racial mixture. However, no study until now has confirmed the existence of a significant statistical correlation between these morphological peculiarities and the thalassemic defect. Their presence among Caminopetros's patients is indeed due to the recent interbreeding that his family histories confirm; but as we now know, that is just an exceptional circumstance that does not occur in the majority of carriers of the thalassemic gene in the eastern Mediterranean.

But the Mongolian hypothesis got a second wind from the research of Lucien Brumpt in Southeast Asia. In Cambodia and Vietnam, thalassemia "seems to exist in populations that have undergone crossbreeding with the Chinese."[65] Then why not also attribute to the Chinese responsibility for the dissemination of the trait in Europe? However, anthropogeographic considerations made it necessary to relegate the Chinese to an accessory role and to thrust the Mongols into the limelight as primary carriers. According to Brumpt, thalassemia is a "sinemia," or better still, a "mongolemia." "I consider thalassemia a Eurasian hemopathy brought by the Mongols, who first spread it into South China five centuries before Christ. Then the Chinese disseminated it throughout Southeast Asia. In Europe, after Atilla, the Huns entered the service of the Byzantines as mercenaries and scattered it in all their Mediterranean garrisons. The geographic distribution of thalassemia corresponds to the map of the Byzantine Empire at its apogee."[66] Jean-François Pays espoused this view and tried to buttress it with historical and genetic speculations.[67] The discovery of thalassemia in China and Iran, Brumpt and Pays aver, "did not upset those who cling to the theory that the Mediterranean basin was the cradle of the thalassemic defect; none of them was amazed that subjects with thalassemia major persisted in presenting a Chinese facies, though they had every right in the light of their hypothesis to discover in such individuals a Hellenic profile or the Roman gaze immortalized in so many masterpieces."[68] This is eloquent, but it does not rest on a single valid scientific argument. Without a statistical analysis of precisely defined racial traits, it is rash to assert, as they do, that other than being a pathological manifestation, the thalassemic facies represents "the resurgence of certain anthropological traits proper to the Mongol race." The contention seems to me most unlikely. Why would racial traits that are not recessive be manifested only in patients with thalassemia major? To my knowledge, it has not been maintained that they occur in heterozygous carriers of the genetic defect.

This is not the place to discuss the historical details with which Brumpt and Pays try to orchestrate the Eurasian diffusion of thalassemia; they only serve to conceal a faulty substructure. First of all, we should recall that the thalassemic defect, as common as it is among modern Greeks, has not been proven to exist among the Mongols of Gobi or Altay. The notion of such a recent introduction of the abnormal gene into the Mediterranean basin "to the gallop of Mongolian cavalry and under the canvas of the lumbering wagons of the Hun"[69] does not accord well with current rates in the gene pool, especially for mainland Greece, which cannot be considered a backwater.

The difficulties become still greater if we suppose, along with P. Bugard, that "the current distribution of thalassemia in Greece is a vestige of Turkish domination."[70] Selective action favoring the thalassemic gene, whether due to malaria or to other, still unknown factors, could not then have had enough time to produce frequencies higher than 7–10 percent. I add, finally, that some paleopathological and archaeological indices favor the presence of the thalassemic gene in the eastern Mediterranean at least prior to the Hellenistic period (statuettes from Smyrna) and probably before the Neolithic period. In this regard, it is surprising that Brumpt and Pays were ignorant of the research of Angel that will be discussed below.

Why search so obstinately for a single origin to thalassemia? "Unitarian" hypotheses do not account for the diversity of the thalassemias. It may well be that each of several genetically different forms had its own geographic distribution. If so, their superposition, which could produce a picture like the one described above ("Current Frequency of Hereditary Anemias in the Eastern Mediterranean"), makes it impossible to sort them out at this point in time. Theoretically, it is inadmissible that thalassemias β-A_2, F, and alpha all derive from a single historical mutation. The hypotheses that feature a single origin, Greek or Mongol, should nowadays be restricted to the most common beta variant. But even then, is it not possible that the current distribution results from several mutations in different zones? On that reading, the Mediterranean and Asiatic foci would be independent of one another. For Brumpt and Pays, that is "a facile solution" that must be rejected because of a theoretical obstacle: "Since a mutation is actually almost always the result of chance, the chance that it took place at any particular place and at any particular time are practically the same. It would then become difficult to explain why the thalassemic defect is absent from Australia and America . . . despite identical climatic and ecological conditions obtaining both in Europe and Asia."[71] This is faulty reasoning, since the identity of the ecological conditions in thalassemic areas and the rest of the world needs to be proven, not assumed. Moreover, the "randomness" of mutations is governed by the laws of thermodynamic stability acting on the genome, and their appearance can follow a certain order. In light of the most recent genetic studies, the hypothesis of an origin for beta thalassemia in several foci seems to me the only satisfactory one. Biochemical variants were individualized even with the "Mediterranean" type.

Some isolated cases of thalassemia minor, reported when the disease was being investigated in regions where it is extremely rare, lead one to suspect the existence of mutations that are independent of the historical mainstream. In fact, O. Tönz and his co-workers had the extraordinary good luck to discover a new mutation: a young Swiss girl with all the biochemical traits appropriate to a heterozygous carrier of thalassemia β-A_2, but whose parents (their parenthood was confirmed by careful genetic analysis), sister, and brothers are completely normal hematologically.[72] According to Tönz's calculations, at least five centuries must pass for such a mutation to occur in a population the size of modern Switzerland. To be sure, this makes it an exceptional event, but from the historical perspective that we are taking here it is a sufficiently common event to exempt us from believing in the more or less arbitrary hypotheses about genetic links between the Mediterranean and the Far East.

Another important fact has been reported only during the past few years: a particular form of glucose-6-phosphate dehydrogenase deficiency, the B(−) variant of favism, has a global distribution that corresponds to that of beta thalassemia (eastern Mediterranean, western Asia, India, Southeast Asia). This seems to raise once again the question of genetic migrations between Europe and the Far East. But that would be to misstate the problem once more. The essential question is, How has it come about that neither the thalassemic defect nor the favic one was carried northward? Clearly, the opportunities for such a migration were not lacking. But it is not enough that an abnormal gene simply be introduced into part of the world for it to attain statistical significance. Its maintenance is guaranteed only by environmental factors that favor it—an issue to which we will return in the discussion of malaria.

The restriction of the main variant of favism and of all forms of thalassemia (whose origin, of necessity, is due to several independent mutations) to the well-defined "Eurasian ribbon" must be the result of some specific ecological factors. The selecting action of environment is as decisive as that of the chromosomic substratum, and historical reality was forged by their interaction.

Distribution and Origin of Sickle Cell Anemia

The zone of maximum frequency of sickle cell anemia, in which heterozygous and homozygous carriers number 25 percent of the population, resembles a large belt that stretches across western Africa, Equatorial Africa (from the Sahara and from the Sudan to Zambezi), and Madagascar to Sri Lanka and southern India. Among some African tribes the frequency rises to 30 or 40 percent (for instance, in Togo). The disease also occurs in lower concentrations in Egypt, Italy, and Greece, and among American blacks.[73] Unlike thalassemia, which from the standpoint of molecular pathology lacks nosological unity, sickle cell anemia is due to a simple mutation of the genetic program for cell structure, not for regulation. The hypothesis of a unique mutation, or at least of a very restricted number of mutations, seems better founded here than in the case of thalassemic defects.

Everything points to the fact that this ancient mutation took place within a black community and that the presence of hemoglobin S in persons of other races is due to interbreeding at some early date. The mountain people of the south of India who carry this gene do have some Negroid traits. However, there are substantial difficulties in explaining the transmission of the sickle cell gene as far as India. Hermann Lehmann and Marie Cutbush thought that the trait derived from a Veddit population that had lived in the Arabian peninsula during the Mesolithic period. From this source, the gene traveled in two directions, toward the heart of Africa and also toward India. For Lehmann and Cutbush, the transport of the sickle cell gene from Africa is impossible because of the absence of certain hematological traits—particularly the *He* and R_0 *(cDe)* antigens proper to blacks—in the present inhabitants of southern India.[74] According to Peter Brain, the spread of the trait into Africa took place at a relatively late date, around the beginning of the Christian era, and followed the same path as the spread of zebu husbandry.[75]

Some researchers, particularly E. C. Bucchi, believe that extant sickle cell anemia results from two independent mutations, one African, the other Asiatic.[76] Whatever the case may be, one mutation or two, African or Arabic, the introduction of the trait into Greece must have been linked to the immigration of blacks from Africa. The autochthonous origin of Greek sickle cell anemia has been suggested, but in our present state of knowledge, nothing supports the assumption that a supplementary mutation took place there. J. Bernard and J. Ruffié attribute the introduction of hemoglobin S into Greece "to the invading armies and the black soldiers they hired."[77] That introduction probably dates back to classical antiquity.[78]

The Role of Malaria

The geographic zones in which the several thalassemias are common and those in which high frequencies of sickle cell anemia have been observed, when taken together, strikingly overlap those parts of the ancient world in which falciparum or malignant tertian malaria raged in historical times. After a clever suggestion by the famous physiologist and geneticist John B. S. Haldane,[79] the notion that hereditary anemias could depend on malarial infestation took root. If these defects do provide a specific protection against malaria, it would be easy to understand how it can happen that such a harmful gene is not eliminated by natural selection but rather maintains itself at amazingly high frequencies among certain populations. In 1954, Anthony C. Allison was the first to show that areas with a great number of persons affected by sickle cell anemia coincided with ancient malarial regions, and also that attacks of malaria were less common and featured more benign symptoms in heterozygous carriers of hemoglobin S than in normal individuals.[80] In a strongly malarial area, the loss that the sickle cell gene causes the population through the heightened mortality of homozygous carriers is compensated for by the advantage it offers heterozygotes in the form of a better defense against the severest form of malaria. That is just one aspect of the general biological phenomenon that geneticists call "balanced polymorphism."[81] Mathematical models reveal how, in a hyperendemic area, accrued mortality and diminished fertility in the normal population produce progressive increases in the proportion of defective individuals. The rates increase from one generation to the next until they stabilize at a balanced value that depends on the degree of malarial infestation. When the selection pressure of malaria declines, the rate of sickle cell anemia slowly diminishes, from one generation to the next; it constitutes a portion of the genetic load that is on the way to extinction.[82]

The same explanation was applied to the thalassemias, to hemoglobinosis E, and to the glucose-6-phosphate dehydrogenase (G6PD) deficiency (R. Cepellini, H. Lehmann, L. Brumpt, A. G. Motulsky, and others). In all these "inborn errors of erythrocytic metabolism," falciparum malaria is the external factor responsible for their heightened frequency in well-defined geographical areas.[83]

In regard to sickle cell anemia, the hypothesis that makes the selection pressure of malaria responsible for its survival gains confirmation on a daily basis. The same is not true for the thalassemias. Epidemiological investigations on this subject have not provided conclusive results.[84] Investigations carried out in Sardinia (U. Carcassi and R. Cepellini, 1957;

M. Siniscalco et al., 1959) and in the region of Ferrara (C. Menini, 1970) favor a correlation between the two pathological states.[85] In other countries, the results have been contradictory. In Greece, several detailed studies have confirmed the concentration of hemoglobinosis S and favism in areas where malaria was once prevalent, but for thalassemia the correlation has not been so plain.[86] The situation in the Arta (Epirus) region is particularly interesting in this regard. There is a kind of historical experiment taking place there. The valleys were strongly malarial until 1946, while those in the mountainous regions did not suffer from the disease. Rural communities in the whole region cling to a sedentary and fairly archaic way of life. A systematic examination of four groups of boys from different zones within it (two groups from the villages of the valleys, and two in places without malaria) showed that sickle cell anemia and G6PD deficiency are indeed more frequent in the first two groups (favic gene: 17.6 percent and 16.4 percent; sickle cell gene: 14.3 percent and 6.4 percent) than in the two others (4.4 percent and 2.8 percent for the former; no cases of sickle cell anemia). For thalassemia, the differences are not significant: 13.2 percent and 15.2 percent in boys from the valleys, 10.1 percent and 9.7 percent in the other two groups.[87] Hasty conclusions are inappropriate: this evidence neither confirms the hypothesis about the influence of malaria on the genetic survival of thalassemia, nor does it refute it. The simultaneous presence of sickle cell anemia and several thalassemic variants is an embarrassment, since competition between these diseases makes interpretation of the data difficult. We know that sickle cell anemia and thalassemia β-A_2 tend to exclude one another, probably because of the clinical severity of the heterozygous thalasso-drepanocytic combination.

Falciparum malaria is not necessarily the only external factor that comes into play in the establishment of a balanced polymorphism of sickle cell anemia and the thalassemias. Factors still unknown and suspect ones like amebiasis, iron deficiency, and endogamy, must also be taken into consideration.

The Distribution and Paleopathological Significance of Porotic Hyperostosis

Ancient cases of porotic hyperostosis have been reported in the following geographical areas: Greece proper and neighboring regions with mixed populations (Macedonia, Anatolia, Cyprus), Italy (particularly the south and the Po delta), France, and Hungary; Egypt (especially Nubia) and tropical Africa; India, Indonesia, China, and Japan; South America (especially Incaic Peru), Central America (Mayan Guatemala and Mexico, especially in the Yucatán peninsula) and North America (pre-Columbian Indians whose bones have been exhumed in several American states, especially Arizona, New Mexico, Utah, Arkansas, Florida, Illinois, and New

York). Despite numerous excavations and conscientious paleopathological examinations, no typical example of porotic hyperostosis is known to exist on bone remains from Scandinavia, Great Britain, Germany, or the Slavic countries. In France, of the two cases that have been described, one comes from the Mediterranean zone and is of Neolithic date, and the other concerns a subject found in a Roman context. There is no trace of this osteopathy in northern Europe or in Siberia. On bones exhumed in the Soviet Union that were rich in mongoloid traits, Rokhlin never observed lesions that could be interpreted as induced by chronic anemia.[88] This does not accord well with the hypothesis of Caminopetros and of Brumpt on the role of the Mongols in the introduction of the thalassemic gene into Europe.

There is a danger of confusing porotic hyperostosis with other osteoporoses not accompanied by medullar hyperplasia. In my opinion, certain isolated forms of cribra orbitalia (without concomitant lesions on the cranial vault or the postcranial skeleton) that occur in Egypt as well as on medieval Europeans derive from states of nutritional deficiency and perhaps even from an inflammatory affection of the eye. In a study of 285 skulls exhumed in Nubia, D. S. Carlson and his co-workers interpret cribra orbitalia as a sign of secondary anemia brought on by intestinal parasitism, lack of iron, chronic diarrhea, and an abundance of childbirths. They stress that the paleopathological evaluation of these lesions in the ancient population should take account of several biological and ecological variables.[89] Indeed, anemia can have a wide variety of causes. In Egypt, the role of schistosomiasis, an anemia-causing disease *par excellence,* must not be forgotten. And it is not at all impossible that cribra orbitalia and mild forms of porotic hyperostosis are at least in part linked to malaria by way of the anemic states that it causes. In that case, malignant tertian malaria is not the only thing to blame. In the same vein, Calvin Wells found cribra orbitalia on 6 percent of 200 Anglo-Saxon skulls he examined. As for a diagnosis of their etiology, he hesitates between a deficiency disease and an ophthalmic infection.[90]

According to a communication by A. Marcsik and F. Kósa at the twenty-fourth International Congress on the History of Medicine (Budapest, 1974), cribra orbitalia were present on 19 percent of the adult skeletons and 58.8 percent of the infantile ones that had just been exhumed from the Avar cemetery in Sükösd. The lesions resemble those found on the Nubian skulls: they do not show the characteristics of a hereditary anemia but probably result from a nutritional deficiency. By contrast, a medieval skull from Kiszombor (Hungary) whose racial origins have not been specified does have modifications on its vault that could be due to some form of hemoglobinosis.[91] Another lesion that could be confused with symmetrical osteoporosis of the vault is bilateral thinning of the parietals (the "carpet-bag skull"). Hrdlička's terminology has created the possibility of a confusion between porotic hyperostosis and this specific osteopathy, which cannot have any hematological significance. As an example, I cite the cranial anomaly of the mummy of Thutmoses III or that of an aged woman who lived in Berkshire (England) during the Roman period.[92]

Within these specifications and limitations, the geographical distribution of porotic hyperostosis is essentially identical to the combined distribution of the thalassemias and sickle cell anemia, which, in turn, is the same as the historical zones of strong infestation with falciparum malaria. To be sure, these distributions are only superposable for the Mediterranean, African, and Asiatic foci. The New World is a separate problem; the history of malaria in pre-Columbian America is a battleground.[93] It is very likely that malarial infestation was introduced on that continent only after the Spanish Conquest. Whatever the case may be, the hematological traits of American Indian tribes do not entitle us to hypothesize the existence of hereditary hemoglobinoses in the New World before the Spanish expeditions and the institution of the slave trade.

Since porotic hyperostosis of the cranial vault has no single etiology, there is no need to interpret similar lesions from different geographical locations in the same way. The absence of foci of osteoporosis in the postcranial bones of American skeletons, long ago stressed by Hrdlička, points to a hypochromic, nonhereditary anemia that could be due, for instance, to prolonged lactation associated with nutritional deficiencies, or to a parasitosis involving chronic blood loss. Several important paleopathological investigations of the spread of porotic hyperostosis among the pre-Columbian American Indians have recently been undertaken, above all by Mahmoud Y. El-Najjar. In his latest study, a sample of 3,361 skulls from various zones on the American continent served to establish the distribution of frequencies according to cultural grouping, age, and gender. Significant distinctions were reported. They clearly favor a hypothesis that explains the lesions of the cranial vault or the eye sockets as the consequence of a nutritional lack of iron and proteins combined with attacks from infectious diseases beginning in childhood. The decisive factor seems to be an almost exclusive dependence on corn for food and some traditional ways of cooking it.[94] Currently available data refute Zaino's hypothesis, discussed above, according to which the Mayas disappeared because of thalassemia.

The Osteoarchaeology of Mediterranean Porotic Hyperostosis

A diagnosis of thalassemia was suggested by Ignazio Gatto in 1948 for the bone remains of five individuals dating from the Upper Paleolithic period that were found by Paolo Graziosi in the cave of San Teodoro near Aquedolci in the province of Messina (Sicily).[95] Skeleton 5, which is not well preserved, showed signs of osteoporosis on the vertebrae and the epiphyses of the long bones. Moreover, the general appearance of the skulls, particularly the enlargement of their zygomatic arches, recalled the facies that Gatto had noted in parents of his thalassemic patients. So he concluded that thalassemia had existed among the aboriginal inhabitants of Sicily even prior to the Greek colonization of the island.[96]

But the lesions reported on the bones from the cave of San Teodoro do not correspond exactly to the consequences of bone marrow hyperplasia. The descriptive portion of Gatto's own article leads one to doubt the basis of his diagnosis. In 1973, Antonio Ascenzi reexamined skeleton 5 from this paleolithic site. He discovered that its diploë is perceptibly enlarged but in a way that suits senescence rather than hemopathy. Radiological examination gives no indication of anemia. The advanced age of the person in question is unfavorable to a diagnosis of thalassemia, a disease that is only rarely survivable. As for osteoporosis in the spinal column and the long bones, it can be explained as a consequence of old age and arthrosic changes in the joints.[97]

During archaeological investigations at Valle di Treba (1922) and Valle Pega (1953) in the Po delta, bone remains of the ancient inhabitants of the Greco-Etruscan town of Spina (fifth to third centuries B.C., approximately) were brought to light. Enrico Benassi and Antonio Toti reported the presence on them of stigmata that they attributed to thalassemia: enlargement of the diploë of the cranial vault, prominent cheekbones, and "wide mesh" osteoporosis on the epiphyses of the long bones. Unfortunately, the osteological material from Spina is exiguous compared with the corresponding archaeological finds, a state of affairs that is as much a consequence of the destructive effects of salt water from the lagoon as of the underwater archaeologists' mistakes—they are more interested in art objects than human remains. As a result, the paleopathological data do not lend themselves to statistical analysis. Relying on historical evidence of the role of Greeks in the colonization of Spina, Benassi and Toti have inferred that their paleopathological study is another argument in favor of the Silvestroni-Bianco hypothesis on the Greek origins of Italian thalassemia.[98]

A definite Italian case of porotic hyperostosis was presented by A. Ascenzi at the First French Paleopathology Colloquium (Lyon, 1973). The skull is of an adolescent aged 13 or 14, and it has the exemplary pathological morphology: frontal and parietal bumps, "hair-on-end" X-ray profile, and typical cribra orbitalia. Unfortunately, it derives from a relatively recent era: the skull was found in a medieval "cave-church" from Gravina in Puglia.[99] In order to shed light on the question of the origin of the thalassemic defect on Italian soil, A. Ascenzi and P. Balistreri performed a systematic examination of the human remains found on archaeological excavations in Lucania, a region in Italy whose colonization by Greeks is well known. In 227 skeletons from various periods (ranging from the eighth century B.C. to modern times), they found 4 cases of porotic hyperostosis, 3 of which go back to the High Middle Ages and one to antiquity. The three medieval cases come from the same locale, Venosa Trinità. The bone lesions of these three individuals are fairly typical for the skull, but in the postcranial skeleton, the stigmata that suggest thalassemic bone marrow reactions are lacking. Of the fourth individual, only an incomplete, damaged skull remains. It was exhumed from a tomb in the necropolis of Policoro, ancient Heracleum, which is dated archaeologically to the third century B.C. The person in question may well be a Greek settler, but unfortunately paleopathological analysis does not justify a firm conclusion that he suffered from thalassemia. The lesions on the cranial vault of this adult male consist only in a spongy enlargement of the parietal diploë without the characteristic striation of the outer edge. Ascenzi draws conclusions cautiously from his investigation: given the present state of knowledge, paleopathology does not elucidate the problem of the origin of Italian thalassemia. To progress in this field, new research is necessary, and it must take account of all parts of the skeleton and consider the possibility of establishing family links between subjects examined. It must give the greatest attention to the bone remnants of children.[100]

Following Ascenzi's recommendations, Gino Fornaciari and Francesco Mallegni surprised specialists by identifying traces of thalassemia on bones from an Etruscan region. During excavations at San Giovenale near Tarquinia in 1958, Swedish archaeologists discovered a group of tombs from the third century B.C. containing three well-preserved skeletons. On two of these (one of a woman aged 16 or 17, the other of a child around 5), researchers from the Center of Paleopathology of Pisa reported porotic hyperostosis on the cranial vault, cribra orbitalia, and osteoporosis of the vertebrae and the long bones. The details of the lesions, especially in the young woman, correspond perfectly to a diagnosis of thalassemia major.[101]

We owe the discovery of porotic hyperostosis in Greece to John Lawrence Angel, an anthropologist at the Smithsonian Institution. In his report on the first results of an anthropometric study of skeletons exhumed by J. L. Caskey's team at Lerna in the Argolid, Angel states that "the problem of cranial osteoporosis is still unsolved" and reports, as a puzzling and relatively frequent syndrome, combined porosities on the inner surfaces of vault bones.[102] At first, the nutritional origin of this lack of proper ossification seemed fairly plausible. In the Scandinavian countries, internal porosities in the skull had been described and interpreted as signs of malnutrition. Angel also set out on that route but took a different turn. Although in 1964 he still has a question mark in the title of an article on thalassemia in Greece,[103] the hesitation is missing in a newer publication on the same subject (1966),[104] and certitude marks his monograph on the ancient population of Lerna. Porotic hyperostosis on the skulls of Greece, according to Angel, is a sign of thalassemia or sickle cell anemia, and therefore its frequency is a precious index of the level of malarial infestation.

That is also the way he understands the pores and bumps on the inner table: they are the osseous expression of an initial overabundance in newborn homozygous thalassemics.[105] However, the overall progress of knowledge in this domain and an enriched personal experience led Angel to retreat somewhat, or rather to take a more qualified position. In his latest publications, he admits that an iron deficiency anemia can and even should be responsible for part of the Mediterranean cases of porotic hyperostosis.[106] While recognizing that the current state of paleopathological research does not enable us to distinguish between a hereditary and an iron deficiency etiology for these osseous lesions, Angel remains convinced that the main role belongs to thalassemia, at least as far as the eastern Mediterranean is concerned. His opinion rests on the diachronic and geographical correlation between the frequencies of porotic hyperostosis and the degree of severe malarial infestation, as well as on the statistical preference of the lesions for the skeletons of infants.

From 1937 to 1977, Angel examined the osseous remains of 2,334 individuals (1,750 adults, 584 infants and children) from the territory of the ancient Greek world (Greece proper, western Turkey, and Cyprus). He was able to determine topographic and diachronic frequencies of porotic hyperostosis that seem significant. The severest cases of the ailment are in infants, except for a few strong reactions on adult skulls from the Neolithic period. On infants' skulls, the thickening of the diploë is especially significant at physiological ossification points. Transverse sections of the skull reveal a complete restructuring of the diploë with radial canals and without visible traces of the outer table. The sphenoid, maxillary, and malar bones are often thickened as well, with signs of medullar hyperactivity. As an example, I can cite the case of a girl about 2 years of age whose facial skeleton contains spongy tissue in places where it is usually lacking (tomb no. 133 from Lerna). However, on the ancient Greek bone remains we do not find modifications comparable in severity to those that occur in certain modern thalassemic children. In the case just mentioned from Lerna (skeleton of tomb no. 133), porotic hyperostosis of the skull is accompanied by a disturbance in the overall development of the body and by spongy hyperplasia of the two femurs and several ribs.[107] Analogous postcranial lesions have been observed on some bones from Nea Nikomedia and from Cyprus (in particular the ulna of a child about 5 years of age, no. 40-3 CCB from Bamboula, which shows a thin new cortex and weblike trabeculae around an "inner shell" representing the unmodeled earlier bone).[108] At Bamboula, near the Cypriot salt marshes, a Bronze Age tomb was found containing four typical cases of porotic hyperostosis.[109] It was therefore a familial disease, either hereditary or due to an external pathogenic factor that acted selectively on the members of a single family.

In Greece and its environs, porotic hyperostosis seems to have had a predilection for marshy regions. The most striking example is its presence in Lerna, on the fertile Argive plain, whose swamps play a role in the legendary history of Greece. An archaic narrative situated the marshy habitat of the Hydra there, the horrible, seven-headed serpent. Without wishing to follow the reasoning of those who see this monster as the personification of malaria and Hercules' labor to slay it as an attempt to sanitize the area, I mention the legend only as an indicator of the importance of the swamps of Lerna and their dangerous reputation. In the same region, on the coast of the Gulf of Nauplia, lies the Franchthi Cave, where 2 adult skulls (of 6 examined) and 1 child's (of 3) bear signs of a hematopoietic hyperplasia. These osseous remains belong to the Mesolithic archaeological layer (about the eighth millennium B.C.) and are among the oldest examples of such an affection.[110]

The frequency of porotic hyperostosis is very high in two Early Neolithic cemeteries: Çatal Hüyük (about 7000 B.C.) in the plain of Konya in Anatolia, and Nea Nikomedia (about 6000 B.C.) in the coastal zone of Macedonia, at the time a very marshy region. In the former, the frequency of affected adult skulls is at 43 percent (of a total of 165 examined); in the latter, it is about 60 percent (of 45 examined). The first site is significantly less affected than the second—that is especially clear from a comparison of the bone remains of infants and children. Of 40 children in Çatal Hüyük, only 2 show the typical signs of porotic hyperostosis and 7 have relatively slight traces of it (in sum, 22.5 percent); but of 23 children's skeletons from Nea Nikomedia, 4 have marked signs and 9 slight ones (in sum, 56.5 percent). In adult samples from Nea Nikomedia, there are some especially severe cases of this osteopathy. Çatal Hüyük stands at an altitude of 900 meters, which may well explain why the endemic was less serious there than at Nea Nikomedia, which lies in the midst of a marshy delta.[111] Porotic hyperostosis is relatively rare and mild on bones from Neolithic villages established in insular, rocky regions without standing water nearby. For instance, at Khirokitia, an Early Neolithic site in Cyprus, the rate is at only 11 percent, and the cases have slight traces, in a sample of 36; at Kephala, a Late Neolithic site on the Cycladic island of Cea, the frequency dips below 7 percent (2 slight cases of 32 examined).[112] During the Late Neolithic period and the Early Bronze Age, the frequencies of porotic hyperostosis retreat in all archaeological sites in the Mediterranean, but the rate always stays much higher where the habitat is flat and humid (for instance, about 50 percent of the skulls found from this era at Corinth, near the marshy water channels) than when it is rocky and mountainous (for instance, ll percent of the skulls in Karataş in Lycia).[113]

During recent excavations at Lerna in the Argolid, all the skeletons of a necropolis were examined, and for the first time in Greece, not just in order to obtain values for anthropometric parameters but also for a systematic study of pathological modifications. Of 157 skeletons from the main part of this huge prehistoric cemetery—it belongs to the Middle Bronze Age, about 2000–1600 B.C.—Angel found 10 cases (6.4 percent) with well-developed porotic hyperostosis and 22 with slight traces of it. In sum, a fifth of the population of Lerna seems to have been affected by the disease. The distribution by gender is not significant; that by age deserves mention: of 73 adult skulls, 11 cases of porotic hyperostosis were discovered (3 severe cases); on 84 infants' and children's skulls, there were 21 cases with marked lesions, of which 7 were especially severe. According to Angel, these 7 infantile skeletons (Lerna nos. 10, 61, 71, 103, 133, 136, and 204) "very likely show results of homozygous thalassemia."[114]

Of a total of 31 Early Neolithic infants' and children's skulls from the Greek world that can be given proper paleopathological examination, there are 4 cases (14 percent), according to Angel, that are severe enough to correspond to the homozygous form of thalassemia. Of 116 infants' and children's skulls from the Middle Bronze Age, there are 9 (8 percent) that may be such homozygotes. From these numbers, Angel generated gene frequencies. Hardy and Weinberg's formula makes it possible to determine the probable percentage of thalassemic heterozygotes. If we consider that only a part, at most half, of heterozygous carriers of the genetic defect suffer anemic disturbances capable of affecting the osseous system, these numbers show that the percentage of mild forms of thalassemia in adults should have been about 20 percent for the Early Neolithic populations and a little less for the Bronze Age. This result is not too distant from real observations on bone remains from the Middle Bronze Age, especially as regards the population of Lerna, but it does not at all accord with the frequencies based on adult skeletons from Nea Nikomedia and Çatal Hüyük. So Angel concludes that more than half of the Neolithic cases of porotic hyperostosis must have a nonhereditary anemia as their cause. Unfortunately, paleopathological examination of osseous lesions does not yet permit a differential diagnosis between the homozygous and the heterozygous forms of thalassemia. This situation and also the still fairly restricted number of skeletons examined combine to deprive this type of statistical analysis of truly convincing conclusions.

Recently, two German specialists published a minute paleopathological analysis of the osseous remains of a young woman that were exhumed at Tiryns in the Argolid in a geometric tomb (900–700 B.C.). Although in this case there are no traces of cranial hyperostosis, the presence of cribra orbitalia and of a generalized symmetrical osteoporosis of the postcranial skeleton fully justifies a diagnosis of thalassemia.[115] For the classical period of Greek history (about 650–300 B.C.), Angel was able to examine 151 adult skeletons and 30 skeletons of infants and children. In this series, only a single adult skeleton has the typical signs of porotic hyperostosis, and no skeleton has well-developed lesions. Slight traces appear in 7 percent of the adults and 13 percent of the infants and children (some of which have only cribra orbitalia).[116] These data, which are to be interpreted either as the result of a decline in the malarial endemic or as an indication of good nutrition, suggest a great improvement in the conditions of daily life in comparison with the prehistoric period.

There is crying need for a systematic search for porotic hyperostosis on bone remains from ancient necropolises in Yugoslavia, both along the Adriatic coast and inland, particularly in Macedonia. The results of those paleopathological investigations, whatever they may be, will have considerable importance for hypotheses on the origin and expansion routes of the hereditary anemias.

Hemoglobinoses in the Art and Literature of Ancient Greece

Not long ago, readers of the venerable scientific correspondence section of the *British Medical Journal* were urged to respond if they knew of medical observations about sickle cell anemia or thalassemia prior to those by J. B. Herrick (1905). Dr. W. T. Menke reported to his colleagues at the time that the oldest description of a hemoglobinosis occurs, in his opinion, in the Hippocratic corpus, in chapter 32 of the treatise *Internal Affections*.[117] A literal translation of this text follows:

> Another sickness of the spleen. It comes on mainly in the springtime and is caused by the blood. The spleen becomes engorged with blood, which evacuates into the stomach. Shooting pains in the spleen, the breast, the clavicle, the shoulder, and beneath the shoulder blade. The body's coloration resembles lead. Sores form on the leg and become large ulcerations. The discharges with the feces are bloody and bluish green. The belly hardens and the spleen is like a stone. This one is more murderous than the one before, and few survive it.[118]

According to Menke, this passage refers to thalasso-drepanocytosis, that is, to the clinical expression of the chromosomic state that typifies the simultaneous presence in a single individual of the genes of thalassemia and sickle cell anemia. In fact, the clinical picture provided by a Greek physician of the classical period does resemble certain forms of thalasso-drepanocytosis (or, perhaps, a homozygous form of sickle cell anemia),[119] and actually there is no reason to oppose such a diagnosis. However, several other diseases can furnish the same symptoms as those in the Hippocratic account. This text can be considered an indication of the existence of hereditary anemias in ancient Greece, but its ambiguity prevents us from using it as a proof of the fact. Sickle cell anemia once seemed to me recognizable in a passage from the *Epidemics* (book 7, chapter 52), in which the Hippocratic writer describes two cases of a fatal disease of children marked by abdominal pains, thinning down, and a strange affection of the cranial vault. On reflection, I would now explain this observation by a diagnosis of hereditary xanthomatosis.

There is also a third passage in the Hippocratic corpus that could relate to hemoglobinosis and deserves mention in this context, namely, section 332 of the *Coan Prenotions*: "At the age of 7, weakness and discoloration, labored breathing while walking, and a craving for dirt herald corruption of the blood and its resolution."[120] An anemic syndrome seems to lurk behind these lapidary phrases. Is it a hereditary one, specifically, a form of thalassemia? The geophagy recalls instead a secondary anemia, a deficiency disease. One called pica provokes a perverse craving for inedible substances, especially soil. Modern studies have shown that it is associated with dietary iron deficiency.[121] The link is etiological, in that either iron deficiency anemia is expressed by such behavior, or because eating everything produces the deficiency in question.

Artworks provide an unhoped-for argument in favor of the presence of thalassemia in ancient Greece. While examining terra cotta figurines from the Hellenistic era in the Louvre for a study of the artistic representation of diseases that I have begun with Danielle Gourevitch, I was surprised to come across some children's heads with mongoloid facies and the stigmata of thalassemia.[122] Seven statuettes of this type come from Smyrna; one was found at Troy. The heads have swollen faces with hypertrophied zygomatic arches and symmetrical protuberances on the fronto-parietal parts of the skull, and the base of the nose is crushed. They resemble to an extraordinary degree the heads of homozygous thalassemic children in Greece and Turkey nowadays. Several other specimens of Smyrnean sculpture prove that the artist's goal was the sculptural reproduction of an actual pathological state, not an imaginative search for the "grotesque."

The Evolution of Malaria in the Eastern Mediterranean

In studying the morbidity of ancient populations, it seems reasonable to admit as a working hypothesis that a correlation exists between the frequency of cranial porotic hyperostosis and the degree of malarial infestation. The correlation may result from relationships between malaria and hereditary hemoglobinoses as well as more complex relations between the conditions of daily life, secondary anemias, and the malarial endemic. The results of J. L. Angel's research are summarized in the accompanying table (Table 2), which gives the diachronic distribution of the frequencies of porotic hyperostosis on skeletons from Greece and Asia Minor. Admitting that this distribution of frequencies reflects, if only in crude terms, the evolution of malaria in the eastern Mediterranean, one is struck by the existence of three periods of hyperendemic: the Neolithic period, the Roman era, and the time of the Turkish occupation and the beginnings of Greek independence. The corresponding low points are first in the Paleolithic period, then toward the end of the Dark Ages (that is, right before the so-called "Greek miracle"), and the Byzantine period.

TABLE 2. *Frequencies of Porotic Hyperostosis in the Greek World*

Period	Approx. Chronological Limits	Adults			Infants and Children			Total	
		Traces*	Typical Lesions*	No. Cases Examined	Traces*	Typical Lesions*	No. Cases Examined	Traces*	No. Cases Examined
Paleolithic		2**	—	50	—	—	—	2	50
	9000								
Mesolithic		17	16	6	33	0	3	33	9
	7000								
Early Neolithic		33	10	165	25	9	75	40	240
	5000								
Late Neolithic		18	3	63	9	5	22	19	85
	3000								
Early Bronze Age		11	1	332	7	5	163	11	495
(Doric invasion)	2000								
Mid. Bronze Age		11	1	169	16	6	148	17	317
	1500								
Late Bronze Age		8	1	215	10	1	81	9	296
	1100								
Early Iron Age		6	1	114	16	0	51	10	165
	650								
Classical period		5	1	151	13	0	30	7	181
	300								
Hellenistic period		12	1	138	22	0	9	14	147
	A.D. 150								
Roman period		24	1	100	—	—	3	24	103
	600								
Byzantine period		10	2	87	8	8	12	13	99
	1400								
Turkish occupation		45	2	53	—	—	3	45	56
	1800								
Nineteenth century		36	1	200	—	—	—	37	200
	1900								

SOURCE: J. L. Angel, "Porotic Hyperostosis in the Eastern Mediterranean," *MCV Quarterly* 14 (1978): 10–16.
*These figures represent percentages.
**These are dubious cases.

Looking at the distribution of these frequencies over time, it is not just the highs and lows that are arresting, but also the historical moments when a rise begins. These are the points at which the equilibrium of the pathocoenosis is broken, and they must be grasped and explained. According to the table, then, malignant forms of malaria invade in the Mesolithic period, and again during the classical period, and finally there is a recrudescence of the endemic after the fall of the Byzantine Empire. For historical times, this overall reconstruction of malarial infestation in Greece agrees with conclusions that can be drawn from literary evidence. For the oldest periods, it is in harmony with paleoparasitological and anthropogeographical considerations.

Malaria is a disease that left its mark on the history of Greece and Italy. It was certainly responsible for severe economic, social, and even political disturbances. A portion of Hippocratic medicine (for instance, the theory of critical days) can be understood only in terms of the prevalence of malaria in the classical Greek pathocoenosis. But malaria is not a disease native to the Balkans or the Italic peninsula. Its cradle was very likely tropical Africa. According to L. J. Bruce-Chwatt and P. F. Mattingly, the equatorial zone of Africa more than any other place on earth favored contact between hominids and the insects that are vectors of the various species of *Plasmodium*.[123] At first, these microbes could not have been exclusive parasites of humans, since small groups of isolated hunters could not have assured their survival. The first human malaria persisted only because there was a reservoir of hematozoa among other primates. It is possible that during a large part of the Paleolithic period, the disease sustained itself only in a very few foci of tropical Africa and the Far East. There are good reasons for believing that malarial infestation radiated from Africa toward Mesopotamia, and that it propagated along the Nile Valley up to the banks of the Mediterranean. Climatic changes, a demographic surge, and the beginning of agriculture combined to favor that propagation.[124]

It is important to keep in mind that malaria is not etiologically a unitary disease. Its history is complicated by the fact that several different species can cause it. They all belong to the genus *Plasmodium,* but are not identical morphologically, nor do they provoke the same symptoms, nor do they all necessarily have the same ancient pedigree. Humans nowadays are affected by four species of parasites: *Plasmodium vivax* (causal agent of vivax or benign tertian malaria, which predominates in temperate climates), *Pl. malariae* (agent of quartan malaria), *Pl. ovale* (agent of ovale malaria, a benign tertian form that is relatively rare and confined to tropical Africa), and *Pl. falciparum* (agent of falciparum or malignant tertian malaria). Specialists in the biology of Haemosporidia, the group to which the genus *Plasmodium* belongs, believe that *Pl. vivax* and *Pl. malaria* go back to the

Pliocene, a period of the Tertiary era, where they lived in some kind of association with the ancestors of humans. These species, or rather their ancestors, must have been relatively well adapted to severe climatic conditions. The affection they caused was of long duration, and they were able to survive despite the small size and wide dispersion of human populations. By contrast, *Pl. falciparum,* which is more sensible to cold and more devastating to its host, may be a more recent mutation, dating from the last, interglacial phases of the Pleistocene era.[125]

Only falciparum malaria can be related to porotic hyperostosis. A Paleolithic skull with a significantly enlarged diploë was found in the Petralona Cave in Chalcidice.[126] A diagnosis of thalassemia is far from certain, and even if it were, that would prove nothing about the antiquity of falciparum malaria, since the anemic mutation in humans must have preceded the one in *Plasmodium*. Other cases have been described on bone remains from an epi-Paleolithic necropolis at Taforalt in Morocco.[127] Their significance is unclear. In the Greek world, porotic hyperostosis assuredly appeared in the Mesolithic period and attained remarkable frequency in the beginning of the Neolithic period. The hypothesis that the eastern Mediterranean was invaded by falciparum malaria at the time can benefit from geological data on a rise in temperature and archaeological evidence on the beginnings of agriculture and sedentary life in low-lying, moist regions. *Pl. vivax* and *Pl. malariae* need an ambient temperature of at least 15° C to achieve sporogeny in hematophagous mosquitoes; *Pl. falciparum* must have a temperature higher than 18–19° C to survive. In the Paleolithic period, the stages of glaciation must have eradicated them from the European continent, if in fact they had gotten that far. But before the end of the Pleistocene and the beginning of the Holocene, that is, around 8300 B.C., the average temperatures in southern Europe rose to their current values. The expansion of agriculture in Greece during the eighth century B.C. may well have fomented malarial infestation, not just by creating conditions that were especially favorable to the transmission of its pathogenic agents, but also simply because of the demographic upswing and the concentration of persons in fertile, that is, hot and humid, zones. It is highly likely that at that time vivax and quartan malaria extended their endemic zones to the north, and falciparum malaria began laying waste to the Aegean basin.

Though he realizes that climatic changes taking place on the verge of the Neolithic period made for the spread of malaria into a large portion of Europe, Julian de Zulueta maintains that all during the Neolithic period and the Bronze Age the number of benign instances of this disease in Europe and particularly in Greece was relatively small and that its malignant form could not survive there. His argument is based on some traits of Anopheles mosquitoes, vectors of the disease, and their distribution in Europe. Experiments by P. G. Shute, C. Ramsdale, and de Zulueta himself have shown that the hematophagous species that is most important for the maintenance of the malarial endemic in southern Europe, *Anopheles atroparvus,* resists infection by the tropical strains of *Pl. falciparum.*[128] The preferred vectors of malign tertian malaria are *A. labranchiae* and *A. sacharovi.* Although it is true, says de Zulueta, that these two species still exist today along the northern banks of the Mediterranean, they did not reach the Aegean basin, Italy, and Spain until after the massive deforestation of these lands in the Hellenistic and Roman periods. Current distribution of *A. sacharovi,* he suggests, is the result of relatively recent diffusion by way of sea trade. So prehistoric Europe suffered only a little, if at all, from malaria, and it was completely spared the terrible ordeal of a falciparum endemic. Even the presence of thalassemia in preclassical Greece is called into question by this argument.[129]

Actually, we know nothing about the presence or the absence of the species *A. labranchiae* and *A. sacharovi* in the prehistoric eastern Mediterranean. It is altogether possible that the rise in temperature that characterized the end of the glacial age and took effect well before the flowering of Neolithic civilization incited the immigration from North Africa of *A. sacharovi* and *A. superpictus,* both of which were perfectly capable of transmitting *Pl. falciparum.* But there is no need to make this supposition, since *A. atroparvus,* or even *A. superpictus,* could have served as the vector of falciparum malaria in those days. Attempts to infect *A. atroparvus* with current Indian and African strains of *Pl. falciparum* regularly fail, but its infection with Italian or Rumanian strains easily succeeds. All this points to the split between tropical and European strains of *Pl. falciparum* and the antiquity of their geographical segregation from one another.

The disease that resulted from the first contact of the peoples of prehistoric Greece with this especially virulent germ must have been murderous. That helps to explain the astonishing success of the thalassemic gene, which offered an unhoped-for protection to its heterozygous carriers. Beginning in about 5000 B.C., the frequency of porotic hyperostosis and probably as well the degree of malarial infestation steadily diminish. And this improvement in public health was not interrupted, as it might have been, by the influx of new peoples, by destructions and political disturbances. The retreat of malaria seems to have been linked to a significant drop in sea level, to the drying up of wetlands, to the perfection of agricultural techniques, and to more judicious selection of ploughland. It was a complex event some of whose main features still elude us. In any case, Mycenaean civilization apparently did not suffer from malaria, and several intersecting clues suggest that at the beginning of the archaic period, falciparum malaria had completely disappeared from the majority of Greek lands, leaving the field open to the benign forms of the disease.

In a series of remarkable studies, William Henry Samuel Jones (1876–1963) took advantage of new ideas formulated by specialists in the epidemiology of malaria (he was especially inspired by the work of Sir Ronald Ross and Angelo Celli) and of his profound acquaintance with ancient Greek literature to validate the following two theses:

1. In early times, malaria, if it existed at all, was sporadic, rare, and not severe in its clinical manifestations; it spread into Greece only after 500 B.C., during the classical period—in Attica, for instance, it was introduced in about 430 B.C.

2. The malarial endemic "fell like a blight upon many fertile districts of Greece"; it ruined health and changed people's nature, depopulating lands essential for economic survival and, from the beginning of the Hellenistic period to the beginning of the twentieth century, it never ceased raging on; it was the decisive factor in the fall of classical civilization.[130]

The first of these is based on the silence of literary sources prior to the fifth century B.C. and on some general considerations. Jones maintains, for instance, that the principal Greek city-states are situated in zones that were especially exposed to malaria, which proves that their sites were chosen before the existence of the malarial endemic. Hesiod seems ignorant of the disease.[131] Between him and Theognis, that is, from the eighth to the sixth century B.C., the silence of literary witnesses is total.[132] Theognis, a didactic poet from Megara, mentions in passing the term *ēpíalos* 'fever with chills,' which in most later texts refers to a bout of malaria.[133] There is an allusion to malaria in Herodotus, but not on Greek territory. Aristophanes is the first figure in nonmedical Greek literature to speak clearly of fever accompanied by chills as a significant event in daily life. In the *Wasps,* a comedy composed in 422 B.C., it is spoken of on three occasions. There is another mention of it in the *Archarnians* (about 425 B.C.).[134] Jones concludes that the Athenians of the last quarter of the fifth century B.C. had special reasons for being interested in malaria, since it was a relatively new disease in Attica.[135] He asserts that after Aristophanes and notably at the time Plato was composing the *Timaeus,* the term *puretós* designated a paroxysm of malarial fever (that is, not fever in the general sense) in the ordinary language of Athenians and in almost all nonmedical literature.[136] The introduction of the cult of Asclepius in Athens near the end of the fifth century could also betoken the deterioration of public health, says Jones.

This first thesis of his was well received and has been widely disseminated. It now constitutes what some handbooks consider a secure historical truth. However, the opposite view has also been vigorously defended by several experts. Its main partisans are physicians with actual experience of the ravages of malaria in Greece.[137] For them, this disease is especially suited to that land and must have always flourished there: it arrived when people did. However, although malaria existed in Greece from the most remote times, it did not necessarily manifest itself with the same intensity throughout history. In prehistoric times, it is admitted that its scope was restricted; later on, certain factors provoked endemic upswings that enlarged infestation zones and made the clinical picture more severe.[138] By supposing that one of these upswings began in the classical period, the historical and philological arguments of Jones are rehabilitated. What remains is to account for a hyperendemic at this critical moment in Greek history. In Jones's perspective, everything is explained by the arrival of the Anopheles mosquito and of a specific hematozoon on virgin soil. Those who believe in the great antiquity of malaria in Greece instead see the cause either in ecological factors (especially deforestation[139] by human hands or a change in climate linked to great geophysical cycles[140]) or in factors related to the biology of the germ that cause it to undergo cyclic variations of its virulence.[141]

What I have said above is enough to show why nowadays we must find more subtle and complex explanations that combine and supersede both the traditional form of the hypothesis about the constant presence of malaria and the simple notion of its introduction *de novo*. In any event, we have no choice but to treat the problem in a wider framework than that of Greece and to consider the plurality of hematozoic parasites, their biological history and that of their vectors, human migrations, archaeological data, and finally, recent discoveries in paleoclimatology and the physics of the planet. Most of Jones's conclusions still evoke our assent, but on condition that his hypothesis of the first introduction of malaria into Greece be replaced by that of the reintroduction of falciparum malaria. Jones neglected prehistory and did not take into account the difference between the various malarial germs.

There can be no doubt as to the presence, at the time of Hippocrates, of vivax, quartan, and falciparum malaria (the bilious remittent fever as well as the invasive pernicious form). Writings in the Hippocratic corpus are imbued with clinical experience based on the observation of patients with these diseases. Malarial cachexia is well described in some treatises and, especially in *Airs, Waters, and Places,* causally related to stagnant water. Notice is taken of the wizened appearance and the intellectual and moral weakness of those who live near swamps. The author of the Aristotelian *Problemata* notes that they age prematurely. From the end of the fifth century, malaria is the disease *par excellence* in the Greek world. But its frequency and the variety of its clinical manifestations obscure its nosological unity. It is made into a host of different diseases. Associated with typhoid fever and dysentery, malaria is the source of clinical pictures that are both varied and impressive.

We know now how a malarial hyperendemic can mark and transform the pathology of a whole population. That is what started to happen with Greek patients in the classical period; it was surely an essential characteristic of the Hellenistic pathocoenosis.[142] But it is not easy to determine at what point in Greek history malaria took this turn for the worse. Was it just at the birth of Hippocratic medicine? Was it one or two centuries earlier? For the moment, the answer to these questions cannot profit from paleopathological research, given the low number of skeletons from the period that have been examined and their imprecise dating. Even if we assume that the frequency of porotic hyperostosis gives a good approximation of the degree of malarial infestation, it must be admitted that a substantial time lag should separate these two pathological phenomena. Arguments from immuology seem to me to favor the idea of a reintroduction of falciparum malaria shortly before the composition of the first book of the *Epidemics.* In addition to the philological and historical clues proposed by Jones, I can point to the severity and peculiarity of several cases of malaria described in the Hippocratic corpus. For Athens, there is the surprising way events unfolded during the Sicilian expedition.[143] Falciparum malaria occasionally took the form of a pestilential disease, and it is not impossible that its commonness contributed to the triumph of the concept of miasma over that of infection; it also may have been responsible for the success of fumigations. Without actually "purifying" the air, fumigations do get rid of the mosquitoes. The introduction of black bile into the system of the cardinal humors may have been due to clinical experience with malignant malaria, too. Jones draws attention to the role that the neglect of irrigation and other agricultural works during the Peloponnesian War may have played in the diffusion of malaria throughout Attica.[144] Moreover, the Sicilian War could have been responsible for the transmission of a virulent form of *Plasmodium falciparum* from Syracuse to Athens.

Once it had developed during the classical period, the falciparum infestation took on amplitude during the Hellenistic period and reached its apogee during the Roman era. For Jones, malaria depopulated Greece and made its inhabitants morose, pessimistic, and apathetic.[145] The Periclean Age did not keep its promises of a brilliant and triumphant future, but the fault for that lay in a disease that broke the life force of the Greek people. Pausanias seems to have voiced the same sentiment, without, however, making clear to what disease he was ascribing the failed power of the Greek city-states.

It is certain that a hyperendemic of malignant malaria can have catastrophic consequences for the birthrate, death rate, and overall vigor of a people. Contemporary medical geography offers dazzling proofs of that. Nevertheless, Jones's second thesis was heartily criticized by those who believe that the economic, demographic, political, and moral degradation of Greece is entirely due to social factors. For them, the expansion of the malarial endemic is more an effect than a cause of social disorder: the decline of city life brought on the disorganization of agriculture, the extension of swampland, the multiplication of mosquitoes, and thus the recrudescence of malaria.[146] In any case, a vicious circle links malaria, depopulation, poverty, and political disorder. Once the process has started, it matters little which element came first. Deforestation, the decline in agricultural techniques, and the neglect of hydraulic works were all important factors in the diffusion and intensification of malaria from the beginning of the Hellenistic era. There was also the rising level of the sea and the change in climate, which was becoming ever more hot and dry. However, all the factors just mentioned came into play after the fifth century B.C. They cannot, therefore, account for the first recrudescence of malaria in the time of Hippocrates, but only its subsequent extent.

Chapter Eleven

THE HIPPOCRATIC CONCEPTION OF DISEASE

An Exemplary Clinical Report

The seven books in the Hippocratic corpus called *Epidemics* include several series of clinical descriptions.[1] These lists of ancient patients, with the dry, precise descriptions of suffering they entail, are of priceless historical interest, since they have served as models for generations of practitioners. Few nowadays have direct knowledge of the clinical histories of Hippocratic patients, but it remains true that all doctors know them and benefit from them indirectly via the traditions of medical education. In their terminology, logical structure, standard analytic procedure, and effort to escape as much as possible from doctrinal underpinnings, the clinical observations stored in the *Epidemics* are still a model of the way in which the Western physician looks at a patient and reports his findings.

The Case of Philiscus

Here is the first case in the list of fourteen patients that constitutes a kind of appendix to the first book of the *Epidemics.*[2]

Philiscus lived near the wall; he went to bed; the first day he had an acute fever, sweating; a miserable night (1).[3]

Second day, an overall worsening; in the evening, after an enema, good bowel movement; a calm night.

Third day, in the morning and until the middle of the day, he seemed without fever; then, toward evening, acute fever, sweating, thirst, and his urine was black (2); miserable night, completely restless (3), confused about everything (4).

Fourth day, generally worse, black urine, a better night, urine color improved.

Fifth day, around midday, a slight dripping of unmixed blood from the nose (5);

varied, irregular urinations, containing rounded, floating particles in suspension resembling sperm; no deposit. After a suppository, a little excrement with wind (6). Miserable night; cat naps; talking, rambling; extremities everywhere cold, impossible to get them warm again; black urine; brief drowsiness near dawn; no voice; cold sweats; extremities livid.

He died around the middle of the sixth day. Toward the end, deep, infrequent breathing, as though he was trying to recall it (7). The spleen stuck out, forming a rounded swelling; cold sweats through to the end. The exacerbations on even days.

Before proceeding with a modern medical interpretation of this clinical case, some details of my translation need to be justified. Also, its spatial and temporal coordinates *qua* historical account need to be specified as well as its significance in the context of ancient medicine.

I have translated the Greek text as it was established by Hugo Kuehlewein[4] and revised by W.H.S. Jones,[5] but I have also taken into account Littré's apparatus criticus and Galen's commentaries.[6] Translation of an ancient text into a modern language is a work of approximation that necessitates interpretation and choice. The better to grasp the various ways in which the details of this Hippocratic text may be understood, I have consulted, besides the esteemed bilingual edition of Emile Littré,[7] several other French translations,[8] some German[9] and English translations,[10] and an Italian translation as well.[11] My version partly reflects the clipped and elliptical style of the original. The Hippocratic writer artfully joins precise content to concise form. Translation into a modern language requires more words, either to say the same thing as the Greek or in order to interpret and clarify it. An explanation of several details follows:

1. In the description of the initial stage of Philiscus's disease, the punctuation of the Greek text varies from one manuscript to the next, which allows for different interpretations of the sequence of symptoms. I have followed the punctuation of Littré that agrees with the way Galen presents the events in his commentary, as follows: "The fever was acute on the first day; then came sweating, which in no way arrested it; the night was miserable. A new exacerbation arrived on the second day."

2. For a medical evaluation of this case, it is especially important to determine the exact meaning in context of the word *mélana,* used three times to designate a specific appearance to the urine. I have translated *oûra mélana* as "black urine," in agreement with the accepted interpretation (Foesius, Littré, Daremberg, Fuchs, Jones). However, the adjective could also have a vaguer meaning and imply grayish or just dark-colored urine. Such is the opinion of Müri and Diller, who translate "Harn dunkel," like Martiny's "urines foncées." In this instance, it seems to me an excessively and unjustifiably cautious translation. There is such a thing as black urine. Since the most common meaning of the Greek adjective is medically possible, it is in principle preferable to secondary meanings. On most occasions when the Hippocratic writers speak of "black urine," they are

referring to hemolytic syndromes.[12] Returning to the case of Philiscus, I note that the translation "black urine" seems inevitable, partly because of its consistency with the overall clinical picture, and partly because of one of Galen's remarks. According to his commentary, the appearance of "black urine" on the third day is a fatal sign that betokens the seriousness of Philiscus's disease and allows one to predict rapid death. It would be hard to admit that such a statement refers to urine that was only dark-colored.

3. Despite their authority and number, I have not followed the scholars who translate *ouk ekoimḗthē* as "did not sleep" or "without sleep" (Littré, Fuchs, Jones, Diller, and others). A lack of rest is not the same thing as an absence of sleep, as is well shown by Daremberg in his commentary on the passage.[13]

4. To account for the psychic disturbances that the patient suffered on the third day, Littré wrote that he "eut des hallucinations sur toute chose" [hallucinated everything]. In my opinion, that goes beyond the Greek expression *pánta parékrouse*. From a medical standpoint, it is clear beyond doubt that the ramblings that often come up in *Epidemics,* I and III, have nothing to do with psychotic disturbances. They are states of confusion with toxic origins, that is, mental disturbances or delirious behaviors that take place under high fever (for instance, during a malarial paroxysm or in the acute phases of salmonellosis or shigellosis). Hallucinations are rare among them, and besides, they are always rooted in states of mental confusion. Littré's translation (or Fuch's "Hallucinationen") does not agree with the medical interpretation and can be justified neither by the etymology of *parékrouse* nor by its usage in other classical texts. Other, more satisfactory translations have been suggested, such as "divagations de toute sorte" [all sorts of ramblings] (Bourgey); "délire complet" [utter delirium] (Martiny); "delirious on all subjects" (Adams); "completely out of his mind" (Jones); "völlig besinnungslos" [totally insensate] (Müri); "ganz von Sinnen" [altogether out of his senses] (Diller); and "perse del tutto la ragione" [deprived of all reason] (Vegetti). I have opted for "confusion about everything," which keeps to the relatively vague meaning of the Greek.

5. On the fifth day, Philiscus had, according to Littré, "a small epistaxis of very black blood," or on my interpretation, a "slight dripping of unmixed blood from the nose." I did not wish to introduce into the translation a Greek technical term (epistaxis) in a place where the Greek author himself avoids it and says instead *apò rhinôn éstaksen* 'dripped from his nostrils.' Other than this small formal difference that I mention only in passing, there is a divergence semantically concerning the quality of what drips from the nose. The hemmorhage is said to be *ákrēton*. At first sight, the sense seems clear: "unmixed blood," that is, "pure," without anything else mixed in. P. Berrettoni[14] remarks that from Homer onward this

word is usually used to designate substances such as wine not diluted with water (see in this regard *Epid.*, VI, 6, 7). In a medical context, it may take on a more technical meaning and relate to a "raw," that is, undigested state of fecal matter or humors. But Littré instead argues for a different translation, citing Galen, who recommends that *ákrēton* here be translated "dark black." I do not accept this explanation, at least on the level of translation. The only thing that can be said concerning this passage in Philiscus's history is that "unmixed blood," especially without a mixture of "breath" or of bile, looks like "black blood." However, we have to be very cautious about such assertions: an anachronistic grafting of Galenic physiology onto Hippocratic clinical description can easily lead to historical misinterpretation.

6. The administration of a suppository on the afternoon of the fifth day of the disease produced the evacuation of *phusṓdea smikrá*. I have translated these words "a little excrement with wind." Bourgey speaks of "weak emission of gas." In the translation of a text from antiquity, is it permissible to use the technical term "gas," which was invented in the seventeenth century by J. B. van Helmont to denote a concept not formulated until his time? This term carries with it connotations that are alien to the pneumatic chemistry of antiquity. Albeit hesitantly—I am inhibited by notions of purism in scientific terminology—Bourgey's translation of *phusṓdea* seems to me perhaps acceptable even though I believe the work more probably implies flatulent stools rather than flatulence without either solid or liquid stools. In regard to this same passage, Diller is surely mistaken when he speaks of blood loss accompanying defecation ("Stuhl unter Blutungen"). The introduction of intestinal hemmorrhage into the clinical history of Philiscus's disease would be very important in a discussion of the modern diagnosis of this case if it were based on a valid historical or philological argument. But Diller's text probably results from a typographical error, with the correct version being "Stuhl unter Blähungen."

7. Toward the end of this account, the Hippocratic writer notes that Philiscus's breathing was "deep and infrequent, as though he was trying to recall it." Deep and infrequent breathing immediately suggests Kussmaul's dyspnea, but the expression *hṓsper anakaleoméno* indicates that it is rather paroxystic dyspnea of the Cheyne-Stokes type, a deep and noisy respiration that gradually diminishes and gives way to an apnea that can last as long as 20–30 seconds. During the apnea, one has the impression that the patient has forgotten how to breathe; then he catches his breath, as though by a conscious effort.

According to Galen's comments,[15] which are cited by Foesius and Littré, the word *anakaleoméno* in this context should be taken in the sense of the verb *anamimnḗskomai* 'remember, recall,' and the phrase translated "comme si le malade se souvenait de respirer" [as though the patient was remembering to breathe] (Littré), "comme chez quelqu'un qui ne respire que par souvenir" [like someone who only breathes when he remembers to] (Daremberg), "as though he were recollecting to do it" (Jones), or "wie einer, der sich immer darauf besinnen muss" [like someone who always has to remember] (Diller). This interpretation, in my opinion, does not deform the clinical reality of what is meant on the level of observation, but it still colors it by means of a dubious analogy. Galen's remarks are not self-evident. There is no difficulty in dispensing with the notion of "remembering," since the metaphorical description of Cheyne-Stokes breathing is all the more striking if we stick to the usual meaning of the verb, namely, to bring back someone or something.[16] Classical authors used this term to denote an invocation, a determined effort to summon someone or something (such as a dead soul from Hades). So I have tried to express in my translation the idea that the patient recalled his breath with a special effort. These two interpretations are in a way complementary. Vegetti combines them by commenting in a footnote on his translation ("quasi dovesse richiamarlo" [as though he had to recall it]): the patient "was forgetting" how to breathe and had to replace the automatic breathing process with a conscious effort.[17] Other interpretations of this passage have been proposed, for instance, "wie bei einem, welcher wieder zur Besinnung kommt" [like someone returning to consciousness] (Fuchs), "wie wenn er wieder zum Leben käme" [as if he were returning to life] (Müri), and "comme dans quelqu'un qui revient d'une défaillance" [like someone reviving from a blackout] (Martiny). To me they seem unacceptable.

The Place and Date of the Disease of Philiscus

By a fortunate coincidence, the exact place and approximate date of Philiscus's galloping disease can actually be determined: Thasos, a city on the island of that name in the northern Aegean, during the last decade of the fifth century B.C. It is usually accepted that books 1 and 3 of the *Epidemics* are the most authentic of the Hippocratic documents, that is, they began to take shape starting in the fifth century under the hand of Hippocrates (460–377 B.C.) himself or of an itinerant physician belonging to the Coan guild of Asclepiadae.[18] The results of modern historical and philological research do not refute the opinion of Galen, who says that Hippocrates himself wrote the oldest kernel of the *Epidemics*, especially the clinical observations and the *katastáseis* that are found in the first and third books of this "nosographic catalogue." In Hippocratic parlance, a *katástasis* (conventionally translated "constitution") is the climatic and pathological make-up of a whole year in a given place.[19] It denotes distinctive climatic conditions and a fixed set of prevalent diseases. The first book of the *Epidemics* consists of three constitutions, all of which refer expressly to the island of Thasos and to years that are very close to one another and are probably even successive. After them, the book consists of a series of individual cases that begins with the case history of Philiscus. The third book of the *Epidemics,* closely tied to the first in form and content, contains two lists of patients and another, fourth constitution, for which no place name is given. Although there is no rule about the relation between the sequence of constitutions and the individual case histories, the case of Philiscus can be attributed with certainty to the third constitution of Thasos. There are two proofs of it. First, Philiscus is recalled by name as an example of the patients who died during the third year despite having had a nosebleed, which was thought to be a sign favorable to the outcome of an ardent fever.[20] Second, his personal history is probably the basis for the generalized description of the malignant disease that dominated Thasos during the year of the third constitution.[21]

Philiscus is said to have lived close to the fortification wall of Thasos. As the result of archaeological research, we know the placement of that wall, whose reconstruction began around 411 B.C. That date, by the way, provides a *terminus post quem* for the arrival of the Hippocratic writer.[22] It is worth noting, in anticipation of the medical conclusion of my study, that the place is well suited to the propagation of mosquitoes.

In the catalogue of Thasian *theōroí,*[23] there occurs the name of a certain Philiscus the son of Aristocleides who, according to Deichgräber,[24] may well be the same person as the Hippocratic patient. In Thasos, the *theōroí* were high magistrates who held office for three years. Philiscus may have done so around 410, probably from 411 to 408 B.C. If this identification is correct, we must suppose that he succumbed to his disease around the end of that period or shortly thereafter. The dating of the column of the list with Philiscus's name is uncertain. Against the opinion of Fredrich expressed in the edition just cited of the Thasian inscriptions, Pouilloux dates the column in question to the fourth century B.C. (between 390 and 360).[25] On that hypothesis, it is no longer possible to identify our patient with the magistrate Philiscus.[26]

The Meaning of Kaûsos *in Hippocratic Medicine*

The Hippocratic description of the sufferings of Philiscus is not accompanied by a diagnosis; the disease in question is not named. The omission is intentional. The writer wished to make his account as objective as possible, so he refused to introduce a name that would be a result of conceptual analysis, not just the clinical reality. But it would be incorrect to conclude from this that Hippocrates did not countenance the intellectual process of diagnosis and that he forswore the naming of diseases. The author of this medical record knew that in the ancient system of disease entities, Philiscus's disease was a particular kind of *kaûsos.* That is what he calls it himself when he uses this case history to describe some traits of the third yearly constitution of Thasos.

From the viewpoint of modern pathology, what exactly was the fever that ancient physicians called *kaûsos,* or, in Latin, *causus*? It has become customary to translate this term "ardent fever" (French "fièvre ardente," German "Brennfieber"),[27] but that only displaces the problem, since the expression is not part of modern medical vocabulary. Actually, the Greek word *kaûsos* is not translatable into a modern term because it refers to a superseded notion that has no equivalent in modern conceptualizations of disease. *Kaûsos* is a clinical entity defined by a kernel of obligatory symptoms and a surrounding haze of optional ones. Its fundamental elements are acute fever that appears abruptly, intense thirst, coated tongue, insomnia, transient states of confusion, abdominal distress, and "bilious" excrements. The fever can be continuous or remittent. The patient's body is "cold on the outside and warm within,"[28] which means that the subject's sensation of fever is stronger than what the physician feels when he places a hand on the patient's body. At times the limbs are cold, and they can become livid. Among optional symptoms, the Hippocratic writers most often mention the following: nosebleed, mild jaundice, diarrhea, spleen enlargement, parotitis, bilious vomit, whitish or black urine, and deposits on the eyes and mouth. *Kaûsos* tends to transform itself into *peripneumonía.* It does not spare children and can bring on convulsions in them. Although it is an acute, febrile disease, *kaûsos* often appears sporadically. It is observed occurring in winter as well as in the heat of summer; the summer and fall forms can be very severe.[29]

This clinical picture is easily recognizable as a form of toxic-infectious febrile dehydration affecting particularly the central nervous system and the digestive system. The origin of such a disease is certainly microbial, but states similar to this one can be brought on by various germs. Several concrete cases of *kaûsos* described in the Hippocratic corpus suggest hypothetical diagnoses[30] that vary from one patient to the next: salmonellosis, malaria, rickettsial infection, acute food poisoning, puerperal septicemia, and, less securely, leptospirosis, relapsing fever, and acute appendicitis. So *kaûsos* is not a disease *sui generis* but a nonspecific syndrome. Renate Wittern is right to say that " attempts to identify it with a definite disease entity in modern nosology have ended in failure."[31] At times through retrospective diagnosis we can recognize the true nature of a specific case of *kaûsos,* but it is methodologically incorrect to persist in making a specific pathological identification of it when we are dealing with texts in which this disease name has general value.

From the Middle Ages up to the nineteenth century, physicians thought they recognized Hippocratic *kaûsos* in febrile diseases as varied as malignant intermittent fever, typhoid, typhus, ephemera, "bilious fever," and, against the epidemiological evidence, even plague and yellow fever.[32] In 1803, Jean-Baptiste Germain posed the problem of the modern sense of *kaûsos* very nicely, but the nosography of acute fevers was still in such a confused state that he had to content himself with comparing the ancient descriptions of it with observations by his contemporaries of diseases that a modern clinician can recognize as typhoid fever and the other salmonelloses.[33] The notion becomes more precise in Francis Adams, who sees Hippocratic *kaûsos* as "the bilious remittent fever of Sir John Pringle" (an obsolete clinical entity whose essential component was typhoid fever).[34] Emile Littré and Emile Beaugrand compare *kaûsos* "with the pseudo-continuous bilious fevers of tropical lands as described by African army physicians or the British in India" (translated into modern medical parlance, the reference here is to invasive forms of falciparum malaria).[35] Obstinately desiring to preserve the nosological unity of *kaûsos,* Carl A. Wunderlich avers that, when all is said and done, no modern disease corresponds to the clinical picture provided by Hippocrates, so the disease in question must have become extinct over the course of time.[36]

Twentieth-century medical historians were forced to break up the ancient concept and differentiate the identifications according to context. W.H.S. Jones says that Hippocratic *kaûsos* designates a group of several infectious diseases, with typhoid fever leading the way.[37] Georg Sticker distinguishes between *kaûsos* proper and *puretòs kausṓdēs:* the first is "Fleckfieber" (exanthematic typhus, rickettsiosis) and the second "Rückfallfieber" (relapsing fever or borreliosis).[38] Sir William MacArthur asserts that at least one form of *kaûsos* described in *Epidemics,* I, greatly resembles modern relapsing fever and that Thasian *kaûsos* should also include epidemic typhus.[39] Each of the identifications given here has some truth in it, but the whole undertaking is faulty from the start. *Kaûsos* is certainly the name of a disease for Greek physicians, but in terms of underlying nosological realities, it is a syndrome with multiple etiologies whose only unity lies in a common pathogenetic mechanism, namely, a particular disturbance in the body's water and electrolyte equilibrium.

For ancient practitioners, *kaûsos* was a disease in the strongest sense of the word.[40] Galen is anxious to insist that it is a disease and not just a symptom,[41] but that is already evident from some of the Hippocratic texts, in particular the treatise *Affections* and the Appendix to the *Regimen of Acute Diseases.*[42] The author of this appendix firmly believes in the etiological unity of *kaûsos;* for him, it is a special improper mixture of bile that was overheated after having been drawn through the small vessels. This same physician, or rather the group of physicians who profess the ideas he is codifying, distinguishes between two clinical forms of *kaûsos;* the distinction was later adopted and developed by some Greek medical writers of the Roman period and their Byzantine and Arabic successors.[43] Although at first this subdivision did not affect the unitary etiological explanation, later authors had a tendency to reduce one of the two forms of *kaûsos* to disturbances in bile and the other to those in phlegm.

At the beginning of the tenth century, Rhazes classified Hippocrates' *kaûsos* among the tertian fevers, a decision that doubtless reflects his own experience with malarial infestation in the Near East.[44] That famous Persian physician studied and commented on the Hippocratic text concerning Philiscus. The translation of it that he gives appears to be a good one.[45] His interpretation of the symptoms tends toward an implicit diagnosis of an especially brutal intermittent fever. It may be that his decision to classify Hippocratic *kaûsos* with the tertian fevers was influenced precisely by his knowledge of the case history of Philiscus.

Hippocratic Prognosis and Its Relationship to Diagnosis

It has been said that Hippocrates dismissed diagnosis and was interested only in prognosis. That method is supposed to be especially apparent in the "authentic" treatises of the Coan School, to which group the text under discussion belongs. Thus Monique Vust-Mussard does not hesitate to declare that

> the purpose of *Epidemics,* I and II, is to teach physicians to form a correct prognosis, one that will allow for appropriate treatment and will show them how to take account of the diverse elements at their disposal, how to relate the patient's habits, the symptoms he/she presents, the disease, the climate . . . In fact, as numerous signs suggest, the orientation of *Epidemics,* I and III, is heavily toward prognosis. They make it possible for Hippocrates to reveal what diseases a physician in certain atmospheric conditions can expect and how regularly such diseases will recur. This interpretation alone accounts for the specific character of Hippocratic medicine, in which prognosis has the central role while diagnosis as it is now conceived is not utilized.[46]

This opinion is widespread among current specialists in Greek medicine. But the idea that Hippocrates consciously wished to dispense with diagnosis has been blown out of proportion by O. Temkin and several classical philologists who are well versed in textual analysis but have no personal experience of the practice of medicine (Deichgräber, Edelstein, Diller, and others).[47]

There is certainly some truth in the assertion that the author of the *Epidemics* held prognosis more dear than diagnosis. More precisely, I would say that he preferred statements in prognostic form to statements in diagnostic form. But we should not overestimate the importance of this preference on the practical level and start to believe that the Hippocratic physicians actually abandoned the art of diagnosis. The opposition between these two modes of clinical investigation is clear and complete only in abstract formulations. It gets blurred once we look at the concrete intellectual strategies of physician confronting patient. In truth, modern diagnosis implies prognosis, and Hippocratic prognosis is partly diagnosis in disguise. In that it offered an immediate way to verify the professional know-how of an itinerant practitioner, the prognostic art of the Coan physicians certainly had a specific social usefulness; but from the standpoint of medical logic, its main role was taxonomic. Prognosis gave the physician a simple and effective way to distinguish and articulate typological regularities in the jumble of a still very crude nosological taxonomy. It was the way in which Hippocrates sought to differentiate and classify the complex and confusing clinical reality that lay before him. As a tool for making subdivisions and nosological comparisons, Hippocratic prognosis functioned the way diagnosis does for modern physicians. With the help of his prognostic method, Hippocrates pretended to "discover beforehand and, in the presence of the sick, to reveal the present, the past, and the future" (*Prognostic,* 1). Foresight is not the only goal. The Hippocratic method should enable the physician to make judgments about the patient's present status and also his past. Essentially, it was a matter of recognizing the diachronic regularity of diseases.

The subtle logic of the Greek natural philosophers shattered the rigid framework of the ontological concept of disease that characterized archaic medicine and replaced it with a dynamic interpretation of all pathology. For Hippocrates, disease is not a being but a process. It consists of a disturbance in the equilibrium of the body's humors, a dynamic upset of the organism's natural harmony. So disease should be studied and described in its temporal dimension.[48] Clearly, from this standpoint, there are diseases beyond counting. However, they do have structural traits that make it possible to group them; there are pathological events that recur in a determined sequence. Prognosis is probably the most flexible way of grasping their structural regularities in the temporal dimension, so it is the preferred way, if not the only one. Actually, none of the writers in the Hippocratic corpus was really able to abandon the classificatory method of traditional diagnosis.

To perfect his nosology through prognosis, Hippocrates divides the clinical forms of an acute disease into those that cure it and those that end badly, that is, in relapse, or by becoming chronic, or in death. In the course of the disease, he observes events whose importance is not plain to the uninitiate but that he notes with care so as to relate them to the outcome. For instance, Hippocrates remarks that in the cases of *kaûsos,* blood loss via the nose is an auspicious sign, while black urine betokens approaching death. By interpreting the message that these signs relate, Hippocrates takes into account the whole individual history of the patient, the chronological sequence of pathological phenomena, and especially the exact day on which each clinical change took effect.[49] For example, when a patient sleeps on the stomach, that is a bad sign, but only if it was not customary before he or she fell ill. Sweats are good or bad depending on the number of the day in the sequence on which they appear and the chronological relationship between the sweat and the bout of fever or its end. In the Hippocratic dynamic vision of nosological reality, signs that function as precursors, discovered as such through minute clinical observation, actually play the role of differential symptoms.

Let us consider how our author proceeds to elicit nosological teaching from the case of Philiscus. For instance, in his description of the third constitution of Thasos, he writes as follows:

> In the beginning of spring, the ardent fevers began, and they continued until the equinox and through the summer. Now those who fell ill in springtime or early in summer in most cases got well, though a few died; but when fall came and with it the rains, the affection turned dangerous, and more patients died. The course of the ardent fevers was such that patients who bled copiously and properly from the nose were the most likely to survive. In this constitution I do not know a single case that proved fatal when proper bleeding occurred. In fact, Philiscus, Epaminon, and Silenus, who died, had only slight nosebleeds on the fourth and fifth days, in small quantities, and they died. Most of the patients had chills before the crisis came, especially those who had not suffered a bleeding.[50]

For the Hippocratic physician, one feature of the case history of Philiscus was surprising and instructive, because it seemed to contradict a general rule: in the course of the disease, he had an epistaxis and despite that favorable sign, he died. The physician sought for and found an explanation: the epistaxis in a patient sick with *kaûsos* is auspicious only when it is copious and occurs on a favorable day. Instead of falsifying the rule, observation of this case confirms it, but the price is a restrictive modification of the rule.

In a third stage of medical reasoning by the author of the *Epidemics,* a model description of the disease detached itself from a series of similar clinical reports. This changeover from the description of a concrete case associated with a patient's name and address, to a syndrome that is so generally conceived as to dispense with comments about individuals, can be illustrated by a comparison between the case history of Philiscus and the description of the autumnal form of *kaûsos* in the third Thasian constitution. Here is the Hippocratic passage:

> The patient afflicted with ardent fever showed early signs that indicate a fatal issue. From the start there was acute fever with slight chills; insomnia, thirst, nausea, some sweats on the forehead and the collarbones, but never on the whole body; frequent nonsensical talk, fears, depression, very cold extremities, toes and hands, especially the latter. Exacerbations occurred on even days. In most cases, the pain was very severe on the fourth day; the sweats were usually cold; it was impossible to warm up their limbs, which remained livid and cold; they ceased being thirsty. Their urine turned black, and was small in quantity, and thin; bowels were constipated. In none of the patients with these symptoms was there a nasal bleeding,

only a slight loss of blood. No one had a relapse, but all died on the sixth day, sweating.[51]

Although this description has a broad scope, it is undoubtedly modeled on the notes the physician took over the course of Philiscus's disease, which were then filled out by observation of similar cases. In comparing these two passages from *Epidemics,* I, one about a patient and the other about a disease, one cannot help noticing a number of resemblances in form and content that, as Monique Vust-Mussard correctly points out, "are unquestionably too striking to be attributed to coincidence or chance."[52] However, the logical process by which the Hippocratic physician constructs his clinical picture only appears to be a matter of pure induction. His glance is not as "virginal" or "objective" as numerous historians of medicine say it is. Actually, his nosography is organized on the basis of the various theoretical presuppositions and risky hypothetical generalizations that also underlie his nosology.

The Hippocratic effort ends up with concise judgments, aphorisms even, on the supranosological reality in the sequence of pathological events. Here is an example of them from *Prorrheticon,* I: "Sweating, especially on the head, in acute diseases, with pain, is bad, especially when the urine is black; if dyspnea is added, that is bad."[53] An aphorism from *Prognostic* likewise stresses the fatal significance of black urine.[54] Since that treatise is probably by the same author as the first book of the *Epidemics,* the clinical experience accumulated by this itinerant physician during his stay in Thasos must have either confirmed or been the basis of his apprehensions about patients presenting this symptom.

Blackwater Fever: The First Case in History

In ten of Hippocrates' patients,[55] the urine is described as black. All suffered from a very severe febrile ailment. In terms of modern diagnoses, one can entertain several possibilities depending on the special features of each case, including first malaria and septicemia, then relapsing fever, leptospirosis, and typhoid fever. Only three of the ten patients escape death. I omit from consideration patients whose urine shades toward black *(hupomélana)* or whose sediment or suspensions are blackish. Hippocrates had reason to fear the appearance of black urine in patients suffering from acute fevers. In the majority of cases in which ancient physicians encountered urine of that color, it was due to the presence of reduced hemoglobin. The clinical context makes it possible to exclude alkaptonuria, melanuria in the strict sense, and porphyrinuria. Confusion with simple hematuria is possible, at least in some specific cases. However, it does not seem to me likely in the patients whose sufferings are related in *Epidemics,* I and III.

The Hippocratic physicians recognized perfectly well and explicitly noted the presence of blood in urine, particularly in the course of diseases they attributed to the kidneys. I should stress that "black" urine left no deposit, unlike the majority of urines called "red" or "shading toward black." That is an important differential sign. Another misunderstanding to avert would be, in my opinion, considering as hemoglobinuric dark brown urine, which is easily described as "black"; actually, its color is due to a urobilinuria that can arise, for instance, from an attack of typhoid. In sum, hemoglobinuria is the pathological phenomenon that best corresponds to the Hippocratic "black urine," and that entitles us to consider it an expression of a hemolytic crisis.

In order to diagnose the idiopathic disease that brought on the hemolytic crisis in Philiscus, it is useful to recall the circumstances and symptoms by expressing them in modern medical parlance. This Thasian fell ill at the beginning of the rainy season, in fall or toward the end of a summer that, according to Hippocrates, was marked by an unusual drought and by intense and unremitting heat. The climate and geographical structure of this region, an insular coastal plain looking out on the nearby shore of Thrace, favored vectors of all sorts of swamp hematozoa. With its saline soil and typically Mediterranean coastal ecosystem, this part of the island of Thasos has all the traits of the biotope that M. Sorre has characterized as "a bioclimatically determined pathogenic complex."[56] The *kaûsos* of Philiscus did not arise sporadically, but, as Hippocrates notes in the third constitution, it was the exacerbated form of an endemic disease.

Stricken by a sudden, rising fever, Philiscus is forced to remain bedridden from the start of his sickness. He perspires freely, but his temperature does not fall. He suffers throughout his body; then the fever becomes remittent, with paroxysms like those of tertian fever. During the attacks, he is agitated and confused; when they remit, he is weak and drowsy. From the third day on, he suffers from thirst and a coated tongue. He is constipated, which is treated with an enema and laxatives. On the third and fourth days, his urine becomes black. (It should be noted that the Hippocratic physicians do not observe urine right after micturition.) Then the urine becomes clear but with whitish flakes, an attenuation that lasts barely a day, after which it becomes black again. On the fifth day, there is a mild nosebleed. During the last days of the disease, the limbs become cold and livid, and there are cold sweats, Cheyne-Stokes respiration, and significant spleen enlargement. Six days after the first bout of fever, the patient is dead.

I recognize this as the first description in history of malarial hemoglobinuria or blackwater fever. It is very likely that the patient's quick demise was caused by acute renal failure. In that case, his Cheyne-Stokes breathing was due to uremia. I hasten to add that this diagnosis of Philiscus's disease is couched in broad terms that are nowadays outdated. Malarial hemoglobinuria or blackwater fever is a severe, paroxystic hemolytic syndrome that is often fatal; it occurs in victims of *Plasmodium falciparum*. My diagnosis is of a clinical entity recognized in the nineteenth century that is now being split up into several pathological states with similar symptoms that are probably caused by differing pathogenic mechanisms.

There are writers, such as Galen and the Byzantine physicians Theophilus Protosparathius (seventh century) and Johannes Actuarius (fourteenth century), who mention as a fatal symptom the appearance of black urine in certain acute febrile states (at times there is mention of jaundice and an enlarged spleen). But their remarks are so vague that it would be rash to insist on interpreting them by a modern diagnosis, especially because it is hard to distinguish the personal clinical experience of these writers from what they repeat of traditional Hippocratic lore.

In the modern era, the earliest certain descriptions of this disease go back to the first half of the nineteenth century. First a few cases were observed by French and British physicians among inhabitants of the west coast of Africa; later there were reports by local practitioners in the United States and Greece.[57] This pernicious form of malaria was first conceived as a clinical entity *sui generis* during the third quarter of the nineteenth century. Physicians in the French navy on the Comoro Islands and in Madagascar isolated the syndrome under the name "fièvre pernicieuse ictérique" [pernicious icteric fever] (Lebeau, 1847, in his report on the health service on Mayotte). Once the close link to malaria was recognized, the main thrust of differential diagnosis was to distinguish this fever from "vomito negro" or yellow fever. Three sets of symptoms were especially scrutinized: (1) remittent or unremitting high fever; (2) jaundice and bilious vomiting; and (3) black urine.[58] The strange urine color was attributed to massive renal hemorrhage, but some colonial physicians expressed doubts as to the origins of this pigmentation. Nineteenth-century medical terminology takes account of the malarial character of this disease as well as its trilogy of symptoms. But there is no name that prevails for the majority of physicians.[59]

The first modern publication of a certain case of blackwater fever in Greece dates from 1858. The clinical observation was made over a decade before by A. Antoniades in Nauplia in the director of the School of Agriculture in Tiryns.[60] From then on the disease was reported fairly often in the main wetland regions of continental Greece and the Peloponnesus, less often in Crete and Cephalonia, and rarely among inhabitants of the Aegan islands. Numerous sporadic cases have been described, but there have also been true epidemics of malarial fevers with a predominance of the hemoglobinuric type over all other pernicious complications. In the last century, such epidemics took place, for instance, in Phthiotis in 1858–

59, in 1864–66, and in 1870. Perhaps one can even speak of a real recrudescence of this disease in Greece during the second half of the nineteenth century. "This type of malaria," writes Stéphanos in 1884,

> was apparently relatively rare or unknown around the first few years of Greek independence in many places where it is relatively common today. Many older physicians are certain that they only observed it for the first time in the past few years. The evidence from these Greek practitioners is not trivial, but one must be careful not to draw hasty conclusions from it, since their reports coincide with the introduction of a new form of Western medicine in Greece and with the nosological recognition on a global scale of blackwater fever.[61]

Whatever the case may be, blackwater fever did not disappear from Greece in the twentieth century, and the highs and lows of its frequency in modern times seem to correlate with variations in the degree of malarial infestation.

Modern Greek physicians were the first to bring to light some etiological factors and to clarify the real nature of black urine. In his article of 1858, Antoniades was already citing the opinion of some of his Greek colleagues who had observed massive "hematurias" in malaria victims taking quinine; they wished to reduce the new nosological entity to an intolerant reaction to chemotherapy. Antoniades rejects the hypothesis and asserts that there can be "hematurias" of nonmedicinal origin during bouts of malaria.[62] In a lecture published in 1859 but delivered in Paris the same year that Antoniades' article was published, S. Verettas took the lead in extolling the pathogenic explanation of blackwater fever in terms of the selective toxic action of quinine. He had observed in his own father a special sensitivity to the drug whose chief manifestation was the production of blackish urine. According to Verettas, blackwater fever was the prerogative of malaria sufferers who were subject to repeated bursts of fever and had been vigorously treated with extracts of cinchona bark.

Observation of the undesirable consequences of antimalarial chemotherapy spread. Even leading lights like S. Tommaselli and R. Koch did not hesitate to consider blackwater fever as the intoxication by quinine of an organism previously weakened by chronic disease. In retrospect, a significant source of error in these opinions on the cause of malarial hemoglobinuria, especially in Greece, was confusion between it and the hemolytic crises caused by glucose-6-phosphate dehydrogenase (G6PD) deficiency.

At the same time as they found proof of the triggering action of quinine in numerous cases of malarial hemoglobinuria, some Greek malaria specialists at the end of the nineteenth century, particularly Karamitsas, Koryllos, and Palladios, did note that identical attacks also took place in the absence of quinine chemotherapy. According to Karamitsas and Corre, another sporadic cause of these attacks was the exposure of a chronic malaria patient to moist cold.[63] In 1878, Karamitsas realized that the black urine of these patients contained not blood proper but free hemoglobin from the intravascular destruction of red blood cells.[64]

To explain the clinical features of blackwater fever, some raised the possibility of a specific etiology. According to them, it was a disease radically different from malaria, produced by a special germ (they tried to identify it with certain species of *Babesia,* spirochetes, and chlamydia), and tied to malaria only by ecological and secondary epidemiological circumstances. But these attempts at explanation ended in total failure.[65] In 1892 two Italian researchers, E. Marchiafava and A. Bignami,[66] described *Plasmodium falciparum* and distinguished between malignant tertian malaria or falciparum malaria and quartan malaria. It was shown soon thereafter that blackwater fever mainly arises in patients infested with falciparum hematozoa.[67]

In the twentieth century, knowledge of malarial hemoglobinuria is becoming complex. The most recent handbooks of hematology and malaria admit that the pathogenesis of its hemolysis is as obscure as ever. Nowadays, the disease has been reduced to a syndrome, since there is good reason to deny the unity of the pathogenic mechanism of hemolysis. In the nineteenth century and the beginning of the twentieth century, it was asserted that malarial hemoglobinuric crises occurred above all among indigenous inhabitants of hyperendemic zones. Current handbooks have a different opinion: that the complication is more frequent in persons who have recently arrived in endemic zones, for instance, among Europeans landing in regions where tropical diseases rage. On the one hand, experience has shown that the administration of quinine and other analogous medications can trigger a hemolytic crisis in patients with malaria. But on the other, careful observations, such as those made during World War II, have shown that there are bouts of falciparum malaria accompanied by severe hemolysis that cannot be attributed to the intervention of chemotherapy. Besides, the discovery of enzymatic deficiencies and the progress of our knowledge on immunological mechanisms have laid the groundwork for a deeper understanding of malarial hemoglobinuria.

To impose some order on this chaotic situation, it was necessary to revise the nosological content of blackwater fever or malarial hemoglobinuria in the broad sense. In recent publications by French specialists, a firm distinction is drawn between at least three disease entities that differ from one another in their pathogenesis as well as their clinical characteristics. Each of these entities, however homogeneous it may be from the standpoint of symptoms, is not necessarily produced by a single physiopathological process. The three entities are as follows: (1) the acute hemolytic syndrome in which hemoglobinuria immediately follows chemotherapy; it is basically linked to a hereditary deficiency of erythrocytic glucose-6-phosphate dehydrogenase; (2) the nonmedicinal hemolytic syndrome, which occurs during an attack of invasive falciparum malaria; and (3) malarial hemoglobinuria in the strict sense, arising in chronic malaria patients usually, but not necessarily, after a quinine treatment and manifesting itself by the classical profile of blackwater fever, with liver and spleen enlargement and massive hemoglobinuria.[68]

Concerning the first of these syndromes, I should stress that it is not a purely coincidental encounter of three independent factors (hereditary enzymatic deficiency, malarial infestation, and quinine treatment). In 1957, Motulsky showed that a falciparum malaria endemic favors, by the phenomenon of balanced polymorphism, the frequency of inherited red cell enzymopathies. According to U. Bienzle (1972), the biological advantage of glucose-6-phosphate dehydrogenase deficiency resides in the accrued resistance of heterozygous women to malarial infestation. Whatever the case may be, this defect was and still is widespread in Greece and Italy. To be sure, in the classical age in the Mediterranean there was no use of antipyretics derived from cinchona bark or, still less, from 8-aminoquinoline; but we should not forget that broad beans, which were consumed as food and not for therapeutic reasons, can induce hemolytic crises in deficient individuals.[69]

Most of the recent explanations of the pathogenic mechanism of classical malarial hemoglobinuria are inspired by the autoimmunization hypothesis proposed in 1946 by J. Gear.[70] According to it, certain individuals who are particularly sensitive or who find themselves in "immuno-allergic" situations that are still poorly understood develop autoantibodies that act against their own antigenic constituents. In support of the existence of autoantibodies in the blood of such individuals, one can point to the positive results of Coombs' test. It has been suggested that the presence of parasites changes the antigenic structure of individual erythrocytes and that the parasite and its host both contribute to the formation of the hemolytic factor. It may also be true that malarial hemoglobinuria is an acquired enzymopathy. Probably it is necessary to invoke a third factor to explain the triggering of the hemolytic crisis: it can be quinine, but it seems to me that in our present state of ignorance, there are insufficient reasons to restrict still further the definition of blackwater fever by excluding cases in which chemotherapy does not intrude as a secondary factor.

Modern Diagnosis of the Disease of Philiscus

Since it is not my task to unravel the tangled web of current hypotheses about the mechanics of hemolysis in infectious disease, now is the moment to return to the main theme of this chapter, Philiscus's disease. The Hippocratic presentation of it is in perfect accord with the clinical profile of malarial hemoglobinuria, as sketched by nineteenth-century clinicians, except for two details, both of which relate to "bilious" disturbances. Philiscus does not seem to have suffered from jaundice or vomiting, and this presents an especially troubling problem in historical pathology: what significance should be given to silence about certain phenomena? Does the omission of a symptom necessarily signify its absence? There is no need to take literally the rhetorical claim that W.H.S. Jones made about Hippocrates' "clinical histories": "Nothing irrelevant is mentioned; everything relevant is included."[71] It is probably more true to historical reality to believe, with R. Joly, that the Hippocratic descriptions contain insignificant details, since "by the very inadequacy of his knowledge of causes, the writer is constrained to put everything on the same level of significance," and "above all, one should set aside the idea that *Epidemics,* I and III, are devoted to purely objective observation. Several *a priori*'s reveal themselves: even observation . . . depends on a fleeting state of mind."[72]

In an area infested with malaria and amid a population whose skin was tanned by the sun and sea air, a slight case of jaundice could easily escape notice if someone was not carefully looking for it; only a pronounced case would impress itself on an objective observer. But the same is not true of vomiting, a symptom to which Hippocrates attributed great importance and one he would have not failed to notice if Philiscus had suffered from it. In the course of the generalized description of this disease (the *kaûsos* of the third constitution), nausea is not forgotten. However, in studying the evidence favoring the existence of blackwater fever in ancient Greece, I prefer to hold to concrete cases and avoid reference to a synthetic description that may actually be an amalgam of what we now consider several diseases.

H. Foy and A. Kondi[73] propose a diagnosis of blackwater fever for five other cases in *Epidemics,* I and III (Silenus, Hermocrates, Pythion, Heropythus, and Apollonius). Putting aside Philiscus for the moment, the only Hippocratic case in which the diagnosis seems justified is that of Pythion. Hermocrates' disease is probably leptospirosis icterohemorrhagica (Weil's disease). As for Silenus, Heropythus, and Apollonius, the most likely diagnoses are invasive malaria and typhoid fever. In summary form, here are the disease symptoms mentioned by Hippocrates in the case of Pythion, who lived on Thasos near the sanctuary of Heracles: acute intermittent or remittent fever of the tertian type, sudden onset, chills, weakness, periodic coldness in the extremities, short intervals of mental confusion, shorter than normal breathing, nausea, vomiting, heaviness in the stomach, black urine without sediment, death on the tenth day of the disease.[74]

Vomiting is a common but not obligatory symptom of blackwater fever. Its absence in the case of Philiscus is not material to a differential diagnosis. Since the hemolysis that occurs in this disease is generally intravascular, the jaundice that accompanies it is generally mild. It appears only after the transformation of free hemoglobin into bilirubin. All other things being equal, the mention of flamboyantly yellow skin coloration in an ancient clinical description suggests Weil's disease rather than malarial hemoglobinuria.

The Hippocratic description of Cheyne-Stokes respiration is concise and beyond doubt.[75] In modern medicine, this type of dyspnea was described by the Irish physicians John Cheyne (1818) and William Stokes (1854) in patients suffering from heart failure. Near the end of the century, Sir William Osler, one of the most famous American physicians of the time, observed this type of breathing in a patient suffering from an acute hyperthermia that was soon fatal. The diagnosis of the living patient was just "heat stroke"—a sad mistake for such a clever clinician—but the autopsy showed malignant malarial infestation and thus established a link between that etiology and the clinical observation of Cheyne-Stokes breathing.[76] Subsequent investigations have shown that in such cases the paroxystic dyspnea is due to uremia resulting from acute renal failure, which is very common in blackwater fever or in malignant falciparum malaria.[77]

What diagnoses for Philiscus's case have been proposed up to now by medical historians? In the beginning of the nineteenth century, Hippocratic commentators likened the febrile diseases reported in *Epidemics,* I and III, to nosological entities that are obsolete today but correspond to various clinical forms of typhus and typhoid fever. The case of Philiscus was interpreted as a special variant of typhoid.[78] Then advances in colonial medicine improved knowledge of tropical diseases, and E. Littré, relying on the works of M. Maillot, W. Twinint, and J. Johnson, was able to assert in 1840 that "Philiscus's disease as related by Hippocrates has nothing to do with typhus or typhoid fever." Instead, it is "a remittent fever from the tropics."[79] A glance at the history of the disease of a soldier named Devos, whose case is cited by Littré as the modern counterpart of Philiscus's, is enough to confirm that his diagnosis corresponds to what is now called pernicious malaria.[80] In 1859, Carl A. Wunderlich, in his handbook on the history of medicine, expressed the *consensus omnium* that Philiscus's disease is a classic example of malaria.[81] A retrospective diagnosis of malarial hemoglobinuria was proposed above all by Greek physicians of the second half of the nineteenth century. In 1861, A. Antoniades, who provided the first modern description of this syndrome in Greece (see above), drew attention to the resemblance between his own observations and the Hippocratic descriptions. C. Stéphanos remarked with caution that "hemospherinuric malarial fever" was "perhaps observed by Hippocrates on Thasos (*Epidemics,* I, third constitution, first patient)."[82] J. P. Cardamatis supported his identification with enthusiasm as well as sound knowledge of the subject.[83] But difficulties began to arise with the hypothesis of the obligatory intrusion of quinine to trigger the hemolytic crisis. In 1909, in his ground-breaking monograph on the role of malaria in Greek history, W.H.S. Jones refused to accept the existence of this syndrome in the Hippocratic writings on the grounds that the ancient Greeks were ignorant of treatment by extracts from cinchona bark. In the case of Philiscus he opts for simple malignant malaria. This argument is lame and was soundly criticized by H. Foy and A. Kondi[84] and by H. Scott;[85] even so it reappears from time to time in recent publications.

There is no doubt that it would be impossible to contemplate a diagnosis of blackwater fever for Philiscus if by definition that name were restricted to hemoglobinuric crises brought on in malaria victims by the administration of certain medications. That is not where the problem lies. The issue is whether some Hippocratic descriptions, in particular the cases of Philiscus and Pythion, correspond more closely to the modern symptomatology of malarial hemoglobinuria than to a severe attack of "bilious remittent" malaria. It is conceivable that without quinine the triggering substance was something eaten—for instance, broad beans. In a recent work, M. Martiny made the following remarks on Philiscus's case: "Amid the various acute ailments possible, a severe form of invasive malaria could provide this clinical profile."[86] This verdict is a reaffirmation of the cautious opinions of Jones and Littré. In my opinion, the enlarged spleen, the periodic drops in fever, and the seriousness of the urine modifications make a diagnosis of blackwater fever more likely than one of invasive malaria.

The two possibilities considered here both view *Pl. falciparum* as the main pathological agent. But there is the rare medical historian who casts doubt on that etiology for Philiscus's disease. According to G. Sticker, his is a case of typhus recurrens, that is in modern medical parlance, an especially severe form of relapsing fever (borreliosis). Since the patient died on the sixth day, which is usually crucial in that disease, its main symptom, the recurrence of the febrile state, could not manifest itself, but Sticker believes that his diagnosis is justified if other Hippocratic texts are taken into account.[87] I reject this way of amalgamating cases. It is necessary first to prove the nosological identity of descriptions that relate to different patients, not to presuppose it. In Philiscus's case, taken in isolation, the following characteristics are clearly against an identification with relapsing fever: the remittence of his hyperthermia (not a fever on a continuously high level, as seen in the initial phase in patients afflicted with relapsing fever); the color of his urine; the absence of severe muscular and joint soreness; a swollen spleen that seems soft instead of hard.

A physician who is otherwise very sensible, R. E. Siegel has suggested exanthematic typhus, but indirectly: he proposes it not explicitly for Philiscus but in connection with the generalized description of his disease included in the third constitution of Thasos.[88] That is really attempting the impossible, and to do it Siegel has to resort to subterfuge. In citing the passage from Hippocrates, he quietly replaces a key phrase ("exacerbations on even days") with an ellipsis (. . .) and tries vaguely in his comments to explain this periodicity in the fever as the irregular remissions that mark the fever curve during the first ten days of an infection with *Rickettsia prowazekii*. There is a single point in favor of Siegel's hypothesis, the coldness and lividity of the extremities. Against it, there is a decisive detail: the exanthem that regularly appears on the fourth or fifth day of exanthematic typhus is mentioned neither in the case history of Philiscus nor in the generalized description of the *kaûsos* of which he perished. In any case, other, more likely alternatives can be imagined, such as Weil's disease, acute miliary tuberculosis, or a severe form of streptococcal septicemia. Nor should we dismiss the possibility of a strange coincidence: a crisis of favism in a patient suffering from falciparum malaria.

In conclusion, exegesis of the case history of Philiscus provides strong evidence in support of the existence of falciparum malaria in the eastern Mediterranean toward the end of the fifth century B.C. Information and considerations of another type also point to its recrudescence and, in come areas of Greece, to its introduction at this time. This recrudescence and the concomitant observation of "melanuric" fever are probably not unrelated to the transformation in the concept of black bile that was taking place right at the time that the main treatises of the Hippocratic corpus were being composed.[89] Just like favism, blackwater fever was probably present in Greece for at least the 2,500 years between Hippocrates and the nineteenth century, even though it was invisible to the eyes of physicians owing to a combination of sociological and doctrinal factors. The lot of this Thasian man makes me suspect that blackwater fever could well be the clinical expression of malarial infestation encountering a still unidentified enzymopathy. At this juncture, however, the historian of medicine must hand the matter over to the clinicians and experimenters who live in the present and for the future.

Chapter Twelve

THE CONSTITUTION OF A WINTER IN THRACE

The "Cough of Perinthus"

The Hippocratic report on what has been called, since Littré, the "cough of Perinthus" is a basic text that should be considered a paradigm in any historical, philological, or medical study of Greek epidemiology in the classical period, alongside the "plague of Athens" and the *katastáseis* of Thasos.[1] This narrative, part of the sixth book of the *Epidemics,* is very carefully composed and of exceptional richness from a clinical standpoint.[2] I append a translation of it:[3]

Coughs began around the winter solstice, fifteen or twenty days after there had been frequent changes in the south wind, the north wind, and the snow wind (1). Some [of these coughs] lasted a short time, others long; then there were frequent pneumonias (2). Before the equinox (3), most had a relapse, usually on the fortieth day counting from the start [of the illness]. In some, the relapse was hardly severe and its crisis was mild; in others, the throat was inflamed, and in others there was angina (4); in some, there were paralyses (5), and others, especially children, had trouble seeing at night (6). The pneumonias were not very severe (7). Trouble seeing at night (8) replaced coughing in those who subsequently coughed a little or not at all; sore throats were not severe, especially in those who saw poorly at night (9). Anginas and paralyses (10) brought with them hard, dry [sputum], or little and slightly concocted, or in some highly concocted (11). Those who had used their voice a lot or suffered a chill were finally stricken (12) mostly with angina (13). Those who exerted themselves with their arms had paralyses only in their arms. Those who rode horseback or who walked a lot or who tired out their lower limbs in some other way had paralytic disturbances (14) in their loins or lower limbs; also aches and pains in their thighs and legs (15). The harshest and most violent [coughs] brought with them paralyses (16). All this happened in patients with relapses, rarely in the first stage. In several patients, the coughing subsided in the middle (17) without stopping altogether; and it came back during the relapse.

In those who lost their voice in fits of coughing (18), most did not even have fever and a few had a very little bit. None of them suffered at all from pneumonia or paralysis; they had no other symptoms than the crisis in their voice (19). Problems with night vision arose in the same way as those that arose after other initial manifestations (20). They mainly affected children; as for eyes, especially those whose eyes were black with lightly colored spots and small pupils, generally those in which black was dominant (21). There was a preference for people with big eyes, not small ones; most of them had black, straight hair. Women did not suffer the same way from the cough; only a few had the fever, and of those, very few fell victim to pneumonia; they were old people, and all recovered. I attributed (22) that (23) both to the fact that they do not go out like men (24) and to the fact that, even in other diseases, they are not affected the way men are (25). Only two free-born women had anginas (26), which were benign to boot. Slave women were more severely affected, among whom there were some violent cases that soon proved fatal (27). However, many men were stricken, and some were cured, while others perished. As a rule, the disease was benign and bearable for those who merely couldn't swallow (28), but it was troublesome and long-lasting in those who also spoke indistinctly; among those who in addition suffered from swollen veins in their temples and neck (29), it was pernicious; finally, it was a very grave disease in those whose breathing was elevated (30), since they had the fever. The train of morbid symptoms was as I have just described it; those described at the beginning appeared without those described afterward, but the later symptoms did not occur without the earlier ones. The quickest to die were those who were overcome by a feverish chill. In all these patients, nothing was gained either by massage (31), or purging the abdominal cavity, or bleeding, all of which I attempted. I even tried making an incision beneath the tongue (32); and to some I administered medication orally (33). These diseases persisted throughout the summer along with many others that burst on the scene. First (34), during the drought, painful ophthalmias predominated.

Commentary on the Hippocratic Text and Its Translation

Every modern translation of an ancient text like this one is actually only an interpretation. It is therefore incumbent on me to explain and to try to justify my version. I have taken Littré's edition of the Greek text as my point of departure, along with his apparatus criticus and a collaction of the two best manuscripts, *Marcianus* 269 (M) and *Vaticanus* 276 (V).[4] The sixth book of the *Epidemics* was the subject of commentaries by Galen, Palladius, and John of Alexandria.[5] Galen's commentary is by far the most important, but unfortunately the part on the description of the "cough of Perinthus" was not preserved in its original version. Some editions of the works of Galen contain a Latin translation of this part of his remarks; but we should not be fooled—that text is a forgery from the sixteenth century. However, we now have at our disposal a modern German translation of the medieval Arabic version of Galen's commentary.[6] As for the two Alexandrian commentators from the end of the sixth century, Palladius and John, the former's work is available to us in a well-edited Greek text, while we have the latter's by way of a recent critical edition of it in a Latin version.[7] As for translations of this Hippocratic passage into modern languages, I have consulted those of Littré, Puschmann, Fuchs, and Kapferer.[8]

Explanatory remarks on several details of the Hippocratic account follow:

1. The epidemic cough appeared right at the start of winter, after an autumn marked by frequent weather changes. Puschmann is incorrect in translating the passage to mean that the epidemic began "the fifteenth or twentieth day after the solstice." It is important to keep in mind that these events took place in northern Greece, where the climate is colder than on the Mediterranean islands that were probably the homeland of the physician who wrote this report. It is easy to understand why the Arabic translator of this lemma in the works of Galen interpreted the snow wind as an "icy wind." In connection with this information about the winds, Galen theorizes that when the south wind shifts to the north, it is especially harmful to the head, since it is uncovered. He explains the pathogenesis of all the forms of sickness that will be mentioned in the Hippocratic text as stemming from an extreme cold that descends from the head and becomes fixed in the throat, the lungs, the eyes, or the limbs. The south wind gathered up the moisture in the head, and the north wind impeded it from being properly dissipated, whence, says Galen, the catarrh, the cough, the pneumonia, the sore throat, the vision problems, and the paralyses.

2. *Peripneumonía* is presented in this account as a complication arising immediately after the initial disease and not as a relapse. For the now conventional translation of the ancient Greek word *peripneumonía* or *peripleumonía* (Latin *peripneumonia*) by the modern term "pneumonia," see above, Introduction, "Semantic Constants and the Difficulties of Retrospective Diagnosis," and chapter 4, "The Oldest Medical Evidence on Purulent Inflammation of Internal Organs."

3. The spring equinox takes place on March 21 or 22. According to Galen, the reading in the old manuscripts was both "before the equinox" and "after the equinox." The former agrees better with the interval between the initial disease and the relapse mentioned in the next clause.

4. In Greek, the term is *kunángkhai*. It can be translated "anginas," in the general sense of a strangling pain. I will return to this issue. This passage is especially instructive in regard to it since it draws a clear distinction between *kunángkhai* and inflammation of the throat, *phárunges ephlégmēnan*. Puschmann's translation ("Rachenentzündung" [sore throat] as against "Halsentzündung" [laryngitis]) is false medically and a theoretical anachronism, since the Hippocratic writers did not yet make the distinction that modern anatomy does between the pharynx and the larynx.

5. The Greek has *paraplēgikgá*, but that is not modern paraplegia. For the Hippocratic writers, it is indeed paralysis of the limbs, but without specifics as to which.

6. I understand Hippocratic *nuktálōepes* to mean night blindness. That agrees with Galen's and Palladius's commentaries, which are very explicit about it, but it is not the opinion of Littré or still less that of Fuchs, who relies on a statement in *Prorrheticon,* II, to support his translation of *nuktálōps* as "day blindness." To confirm his preconceived diagnosis and cut this Gordian knot with a single stroke of his pen, Puschmann states that it is merely a case of photophobia ("die Lichtscheu im Allgemeinen") probably caused by influenza. This view does not stand up to critical analysis of the ancient evidence on *nuktálōps;* and medical arguments make the translations of Littré and Fuchs very unlikely.

7. Another possible translation is that they were of short duration. In any case, this statement seems to contradict what was just said on the importance of the pneumonias that followed the coughs. Palladius explains correctly that the contradiction is just an apparent one, since only in relapse were the pneumonias minor.

8. Here, the text of the *recentiores* (with the exception of C, a sixteenth-century manuscript that usually matches V) and the vulgate is corrupt; instead of *nuktálōpes* there is discussion of *phárunges,* which from a medical standpoint is clearly not harmonious with the context. Galen's commentary has a lacuna at this point; Palladius and John speak of "nyctalopia" in reference to this passage. Careful examination of the M manuscript (f. 422v) proves that the error goes back to its scribe: he skipped a passage and began his phrase with the word *phárunges,* which is repeated a little farther down in the Hippocratic text; then he realized what he had done but only partially corrected his mistake. The result is that M and its apographs omit *nuktálōpes* while the word *phárunges* appears in them twice instead of once. The correct reading can be restored from the V manuscript.

9. I cannot follow Littré here, who translates "sore throats that were mild and less than the nyctalopias."

10. The word *paraplēgiká* was eliminated by Puschmann, who found it troublesome on his medical interpretation. According to him, the word is lacking in Palladius, which is incorrect. Puschmann read Littré's apparatus incorrectly. It says "Pall. n'a rien sur cette phrase" [P. has nothing on this sentence], that is, as opposed to John of Alexandria, he does not comment on it. According to Galen, paralyses were mentioned here, even though the context cannot relate to them if his medical theory is the right one.

11. Since this sentence is elliptical in Greek, my translation is of necessity a conjecture. What do the two adjectives *sklērà kai xērá* and the verb *anágousai* refer to? According to Foes's Latin translation, they should refer to the anginas and paralyses: *anginae autem et partium siderationes aut durae aut siccae erant aut parvae et raro matura educentes.* Littré does not accept this interpretation. He construes the adjectives with sputum and refers the verb to the cough, a word that is to be understood: "The writer was able to omit [it] the more easily since it was the chief phenomenon of this

epidemic and as such was always present to mind." From this argument results the following translation: "The anginas and paralyses declared themselves in the coughs which brought up hard, dry matter, or little and slightly concocted, or even in some cases highly concocted." My translation is fairly close to Littré's, but it differs from it by refusing to introduce in explicit terms the notion of the cough. I am inspired mainly by Galen's remarks, where he speaks of dry, hard matters, or slightly concocted ones, that are rarely, though sometimes profusely, spit up. Although I know of this remark only via the Arabic and German versions, it is certain that the solution adopted there goes back to Galen himself. He clearly affirms that the terms in this sentence refer to sputa that are associated only with angina, not paralysis.

12. The tradition recognized two variants to this passage: according to the first, the patients were stricken with angina, but according to the second, they died of the disease. This divergence was already in existence in the time of Galen, who considers the former reading correct, though he stresses that the angina was indeed malignant.

13. According to Galen, the Hippocratic writer is insisting on his discovery. The humors that derive from the head have a predilection for the organs that were previously weakened. There is a general formulation of this clinical observation in *Aphorisms* (IV, 33).

14. John of Alexandria explains that the expression *akrasíai paraplēgikaí* denotes paralytic impotence. Littré translates it "intempéries paralytique" [paralytic humoral disturbance], which construes the first term of the Greek expression as a derivative of *krâsis* 'mixture of humors.' The humoral disturbances in question are probably those expressed by the loss or substantive lessening of voluntary movement. According to Galen, the impotence in question is such that the patient lacks the strength needed to support himself on his legs and remain standing without wavering.

15. In drawing attention to this painful sensitivity, the Hippocratic writer provides us with key evidence for a differential diagnosis. Galen understood the importance of this observation. A total paralysis, he tells us, occurs when feeling and mobility are lost at one and the same time. He reports his own clinical experience that a limb that has lost its mobility can still be painful. We know that this dissociation actually exists in certain paralyses, for instance, in those that are due to diphtheria or poliomyelitis.

16. In Greek, the subject of this sentence is not given, a fact noted by all the commentators. Galen refers the sentence to the pains that were mentioned in the previous one, but he must then admit that the writer made a blunder when he used the feminine form instead of the masculine. Palladius basically agrees with Galen, and he tries to explain the unlooked-for feminine by understanding the synonym *odúnai* as standing in place of *pónoi*. Neither solution is satisfactory, for their medical content is dubious, even unlikely. Cornarius and Foes, followed by Littré and Fuchs, decided

to introduce the word *bêkhes* 'coughs' as the subject of the sentence. I join them.

17. By using the expression *en tôi mésōi,* the authory probably meant that the coughs subsided in the interval between the relapse and the initial phase of the disease. Other interpretations are possible. According to Fuchs, the cough increased in the middle of the relapse. Palladius understood something completely different, namely, that compared with other troubles, the cough was of middling severity.

18. The translation I have adopted here is Littré's. It seems to me that this passage is describing concisely a symptom that is encountered, for instance, in patients with whooping cough, namely, the sudden interruption of speech by coughing fits. The Arabic translation in the indirect tradition is really different: "in those whose voice is lost due to coughing." The Arabic translator, Hunain ibn Ishaq, took his cue from Galen's commentary on the passage. Galen explains that in these patients, since all the pathogenic matter is deposited near the larynx and trachea, the voice is ruined. If this interpretation is accepted, the disease is one marked not by sudden, unforeseen fits of coughing, but by a kind of laryngitis with aphonia.

19. It is worth stressing that the Hippocratic writer is now isolating very clearly a group of patients who suffered from a special type of cough that was relatively benign in both its accompanying symptoms and its outcome.

20. Littré translates, "like those arising from altogether different causes." At issue is the *próphasis,* an ancient notion customarily understood to mean "occasion" or "immediate cause." In the classical medical writings, this term usually keeps its original sense and indicates the initial aspect or the very first expression of a state, especially a state of disease.[9] That meaning applies here very well and elucidates the Hippocratic statement: the hemeralopias in relapse were not different from those that arose in the beginning of the disease. Littré's translation causes difficulties in the medical interpretation of the text, since its author allows for only one cause of night blindness.

21. I have tried to preserve the elliptical style of this sentence in my translation. This whole text is a set of notes. Greek physicians used writing to save the essence of their observations and thoughts in concise format; information committed to memory was to be transmitted by word of mouth as a supplement to the notes, to render them complete. According to Galen, the Hippocratic description is referring to the appearance of the eyes, which on this occasion tended to be afflicted with night blindness. An individual observation has been made over into a general rule, and Galen struggles to provide a physiopathological explanation of it. According to him, black eyes, small pupils, eyes that change color, and black, straight hair constitute a predisposition to night blindness because they are the outer signs of a moist temperament and, in particular, of an inborn

abundance of moisture in the head and the eyes. The same explanation had been given more succinctly but in almost identical terms in a treatise of Aristotle.[10] Galen certainly knew the passage, and moreover I think it not unlikely that Aristotle's theory of vision and its failings was inspired by the clinical reports of the Hippocratic physicians. In particular, it appears that Aristotle knew, either directly or indirectly, the observations contained in the sixth book of the *Epidemics*. Palladius is distancing himself from both Aristotle and Galen when he remarks in regard to this line that the eyes became black, the pupils small, and the eyeballs swollen under the influence of the ailment. On his interpretation, the Hippocratic description does not refer to the patients' state before the disease but instead to the way their eyes looked during it. Littré took a stand against Palladius and similar to Galen's, which was not yet known to Western scholars since it is preserved only in the Arabic version. I think it necessary to qualify both views: the Hippocratic writer did indeed have predisposition in mind and not the changes brought on by night blindness, but in practice he was unable to foretell who would be afflicted by this disease; so he had to base his observations on actual patients at the same time as he believed that they had had the traits given above before falling ill. He mistook what is actually a symptom of the disease for a normal somatic trait.

The Greek text contains a strange word: *hupopoíkila*. Galen seems to have understood this to mean that the eyes had changing colors. To a modern physician, that is nonsense. Littré translates, "of somewhat varied color." That is satisfactory from a lexical standpoint, but it introduces a certain contradiction, namely, that eyes susceptible to night blindness were at once black and variegated. To skirt the problem, Puschmann offered the following translation: "in den Augen erschien das Schwarze verschiedenartig gefärbt." If *hupopoíkila* really denotes shimmering eyes, or eyes with lightly colored spots, it may be the first notice of a distinguishing symptom of xerophthalmia, the organic side of night blindness. At the time Littré was translating the *Epidemics* and writing his commentary on them, little was known about the anatomopathological substratum of night blindness, and its etiology was completely unknown. In 1863 Bitot published the first description of the whitish or, rather, pearly gray, iridescent spots that he observed on the conjunctiva of undernourished children in a Bordeaux orphanage; he noted their correlation with disturbances in night vision.[11] Later on the real nature of these xerophthalmic spots was understood: they are the clinical manifestations of the cornea degeneration that, along with failing eyesight in weak light, is caused by vitamin A deficiency. In conclusion, it seems that the Hippocratic writer saw and noted in summary fashion Bitot's pearly spots, but that their presence was wrongly taken to be a normal somatic trait that was a predisposition to night blindness.

22. One should note the use of the verb in the first person singular.

The text is certainly an individual's handiwork, and it bears the marks of an original version composed when the events in question were not remote. Its author is a physician whose opinion has weight in the Greek intellectual community, a weight of which he is indeed conscious.

23. Littré's translation of this passage as "j'attribuai cette immunité" [I attributed this immunity] is a serious anachronism. Neither the term nor the concept of immunity in its modern medical sense existed in Hippocrates' time. The Greek text simply has the word *toûto* 'this thing.' Palladius believes that it refers to menstruation: the women were less subject to the cough, fevers, and pneumonia than men because they did not go out as much and because they benefit from menstrual purgation. Probably Palladius's strange interpretation stems from his desire to absolve Hippocrates of a reproach by Galen.

24. According to Galen, the author meant that women are less susceptible than men to bad weather and abrupt changes in air. The Hippocratic explanation is only partial, he says, because one should add the benefit accruing to women from menstruation.

25. This sentence looks like a marginal comment that later slipped into the text. It is missing from the V manuscript. But if it is an interpolation, it is an old one, since Galen knows of it.

26. According to Galen, Artemidorus Capito, an editor of the Hippocratic corpus, suppressed the word "two" here, but most commentators believed that it belonged in the original text.

27. By Galen's time two readings of this passage were known. The second of these was correctly translated by Littré: "dans les cas où elles furent violentes, elles causèrent très promptement la mort" [when they were violent, they were almost immediately fatal].

28. According to medical teaching in Galen's day, difficulty in swallowing was a very serious symptom. This text is therefore an embarrassment to him, and he resorts to all his skill in argument to explain why it is associated here with a mild ailment. In this case the advantage clearly lies with the relatively unsystematic, flexible theory of the Hippocratic observer.

29. The Greek word is *aukhḗn*. Its usual meaning is "nape of the neck." Curiously, the indirect tradition (Hunain ibn Ishaq) here speaks of "eyes." I translate the word "neck," since there are no blood vessels in the nape of the neck or the eyes that would be visible when swollen. For Galen, such swelling is a harbinger of suffocation. It occurs when bad humors are so abundant that they cannot be evacuated and overflow their place of abscession.

30. Exactly what is meant by the expression *pneûma xunemeteōrízeto?* It is some kind of breathing, but Littré calls it "elevated," Fuchs "superficial," and Puschmann "accelerated." According to Galen, breathing was elevated in these patients because of laryngeal constriction. In modern

medical terms, this means laryngeal dyspnea. There is no doubt that the Hippocratic account is an increasingly precise clinical picture of croup.

31. In the medieval manuscripts of the direct tradition, the text of this passage is obscure. The chief difficulty is to understand precisely what is meant by the expression *oudè anastásei.* And how should one translate the term *piezoménous* in relation to it? Foes thinks it has to do with the repressive effects of repercussive medications. Calvus understands *anástasis* to mean defecation, and he is followed therein by Littré, who, "without mistaking just how obscure this passage really is," decides to translate it as follows: "ces malades, que la présentation sur le siège ne fatiguait même pas" [these patients, who were not the least bit indisposed by the calls of nature]. From a medical standpoint this is really ridiculous, so Fuchs suggests we understand the passage to mean that the sick were tortured by the need to defecate. That translation suits the demands of logic, but it does violence to the Greek language. Cornarius tried another solution: suppress the words *oudè anastásei.* This is exactly what Hunain ibn Ishaq did in the Arabic translation of the Hippocratic lemma of Galen's commentary. His justification for doing so comes from the commentary itself. Galen says that there were two readings. I have adopted the one he dubs "ancient" and whose medical value he explains very clearly.

The Hippocratic writer is here alluding to the treatment of swollen tonsils by local massage: the physician used his fingers, which had been smeared with ointment. Since these porous glands had become swollen through the absorption of phlegmatic humor, massage was indicated in order to squeeze out the liquid. Galen states that he used this method himself in combination with the administration of astringents. Manual intervention should be prudent and moderate. It is useful, he says, when the swelling affects only the glands. If the throat itself is swollen, massage can actually be harmful. According to Galen, some editions of the Hippocratic text had another reading of the passage in question, to wit, that there was no use in torturing ("squeezing") the patients with "forbidden things." Those two words have always piqued commentators. Galen tells us that according to the "new physicians" (these are "the ones who lived after the death of Alexander"), it was a matter of abstaining from certain foods, but that the "ancient physicians" had taken no position on the subject.

32. The Hippocratic writer practiced a special form of bloodletting. Note the insistent, repeated use of the first person singular of the verb.

33. Littré translates "que je fis vomir" [whom I induced to vomit]. That is indeed simpler and clearer. But the Greek text has a lack of certainty that I wished to preserve by translating it as literally as possible. Usually, says Galen, *ánō epharmákeusa* means "I induced vomiting by medications," and when Hippocrates speaks of medicating "from below" and "from above" without further detail, the former implies the use of purgatives

and the latter the use of emetics. In this case, however, the usual interpretation runs up against a medical objection: to induce vomiting in a patient with a swollen throat who is in danger of suffocating is counterindicated. That is why Dioscorides, a Hellenistic editor of the text of Hippocrates, chose to replace *áno* by *káto*. If that is the correct reading, our healer purged his patients instead of making them vomit. Galen sees the virtue in ridding the text of vomiting, but he does not feel entitled to modify such a venerable document without a historical or philological motive. So he keeps the reading "from above" and mends the text by explaining that the Hippocratic writer is referring not to the use of emetics but to topical medications, especially gargling and the application of drugs to drive out phlegm through the nostrils.

34. This instance of *prôton* 'first of all' followed by a truncated clause and without a matching "second," shows that the narrative aborts and has not been preserved in its entirety. The only consolation is that, in beginning to speak of the summer, the author seems to have completed his statement on the diseases that ruled in winter and in spring over the space of a year in a specific Greek settlement.

The Author, Date, and Locale of this Epidemiological Report

Although this text contains no hint of the name of the place in which the Hippocratic physician made his observations, it is certain that the whole story is connected with the city of Perinthus. In a chapter from the same book of the *Epidemics,* there is talk of "a cough that visited Perinthus during the winter."[12] Moreover, in the Hippocratic treatise *Humors,* there is a remark that the pathological humors settle in parts that were abused before the outbreak of the disease, "as was the case with those who in Perinthus suffered from cough and angina."[13]

Situated on the Propontis, Perinthus was an important fortified port in Thrace. In the course of its troubled history, it changed its name to Heracleum. Today it is known as Eregli, a Turkish town on the Sea of Marmora. The town of Perinthus is mentioned by name seven times in the Hippocratic corpus. The oldest of the citations is probably the one in Section 3 of book 2 of the *Epidemics,* in which there are descriptions of the diseases observed and treated by a group of physicians immediately upon their arrival in Perinthus near the solstice of a certain year—which year, we are not told. A passing remark in the same book stresses the influence of the regularity of the seasons on the nature of diseases: an aphorism of broad applicability is illustrated "by what is seen at Perinthus." Three other citations concern patients who are said to be inhabitants of Perinthus: a certain Antigenes, his wife, and a swarthy patient who lived in the home of Temenes' niece.[14] Antigenes' wife was among the patients visited by the Hippocratic physicians at about the time when the cough afflicted the Perinthians. Her case is very strange from a medical standpoint, but for the moment it interests us only because it seems to offer a way to date the stay in Perinthus of the author of the notes about the cough.

The consultation in question took place at about the same time as two extraordinary natural events that were noted by the itinerant physician in a kind of preamble to his clinical report: "At the winter solstice, the appearance of a rather large star; the fifth and sixth days thereafter, an earthquake."[15] Littré relates this text to a notice in Aristotle that "in the archonship of Eucles, the son of Molon, at Athens, a comet appeared in the north in the month of Gamelion when the sun was in the winter solstice."[16] Two men named Eucles were archons at Athens, one in 426, the other in 402. Historians of astronomy and modern commentators on Aristotle favor 427–426 B.C. as the date of the appearance of this comet. That is also the opinion of Littré, who furthermore recalls that during the winter of 427–426, according to Thucydides, there was a recurrence of the "plague" at Athens and earthquakes were felt in Attica, Euboea, and Boeotia.[17]

After the philological and historical analyses of Deichgräber, however, Littré's dating became very troublesome, because the group consisting of *Epidemics,* II, IV, and VI, appear to be later than the group consisting of *Epicemics,* I and III, which is dated around 410 B.C. That is why Grensemann, who considers 400–399 B.C. as the *terminus post quem* of *Epidemics,* IV, identifies the "rather large star" in the Hippocratic text with the comet of 373–372 B.C.[18] Just like Littré, Grensemann relies on the authority of Aristotle, but he evokes another passage in which there is talk of "the great comet that was seen at the time of the earthquake in Achaea and the coastal flood . . . This large star appeared in winter during the frost and when the weather was calm in the west, under the archonship of Asteius."[19] This really seems to refer to the winter of 373–372, as Gundel allows, but it is worth noting that in the astronomical lists of Pingré and Bigourdan, this same comet is dated to 371 B.C.[20]

Di Benedetto disputes Grensemann's argument and returns to Littré's view. According to him, the star seen at Perinthus was the same as the comet seen at Athens under the northern sky in January of 426 (the month of Gamelion began that year on the day that corresponds to January 13 of our calendar). Di Benedetto's choice is due to his conviction that, from a doctrinal standpoint, the group *Epidemics,* II, IV, and VI, is older than the group *Epidemics,* I and III.[21]

Looking closely at both sides of this dispute and putting aside all other considerations about the Hippocratic texts, I find myself forced to admit that there is no sound reason to identify one as against the other of

Aristotle's comets with the large star of Perinthus. Actually, the situation is even more uncertain. For the period from 450 to 350 B.C., no other comet observation was recorded in historical documents in the West,[22] but we are not entitled to think that written records exhaustively mirror the reality of astronomical phenomena observable in Greece during the time. For example, we know by calculation that in 392/391 B.C. Halley's Comet returned, but nothing is said of it in the ancient sources. That date happens to be very well suited to our Hippocratic report. Unfortunately, the description there is couched in such vague terms that we cannot be sure if it is really reporting a comet and not a supernova or even a simple nova. The Hippocratic writer only speaks of an *astḗr ou smikrós* 'no little star,' not a *komḗtēs astḗr* 'long-haired star,' as Aristotle calls it. He does not tell us if the star in question was fixed or moving in relation to other stars, nor does he indicate its place among the constellations or give any information on the length of time during which it was seen. If the Hippocratic star was a nova or a supernova, which is perfectly compatible with the text, no chronological conclusions can be drawn.[23]

Ingenious philologists have sought to date *Epidemics,* II, IV, and VI, by using various other clues, such as names that could relate to persons known from other sources. A patient is said to come from the village of Medosades.[24] Xenophon in the *Anabasis* mentions a certain Medosades to whom Seuthes, king of Thrace, ceded some villages not far from Perinthus. Xenophon's narrative on this subject is linked to the return to Greece of the 10,000, and Deichgräber therefore infers that the story told in *Epidemics,* IV, 45, must be later than 400/399 B.C.[25] It seems to me that Deichgräber's interpretation arbitrarily fixes this *terminus post quem* at too late a date. Xenophon simply says that in 400/399 the Greek army supplied itself "in the villages that were given to Medosades by Seuthes." The account suggests that they were ceded prior to the army's encampment in the region.[26] Consequently, the *terminus post quem* should be put back a few years, to the time of Seuthes' rise to power around 410–405 B.C.

If the Cyniscus mentioned in *Epidemics,* IV and VI, is the same person as the Spartan who, according to Xenophon, commanded in the Thracian Chersonnese, the Hippocratic reports on him should be dated to around 400 B.C. But the identification is very uncertain. There is also a patient who is identified as "coming from Alcibiades'" (but the phrase could also mean "coming from Alcibiades").[27] He was probably a member of the retinue of an important personage.[28] Deichgräber does not hesitate to allow that the reference is to the famous Alcibiades, who in fact spent time in the vicinity of Perinthus until 404 B.C. Surprisingly, the celebrated philologist concludes that "we must assume that this event and along with it the accounts in *Epidemics,* II, IV, and VI, took place a little after 399."[29] It is a doubly surprising conclusion, since on the one hand, Alcibiades had already been assassinated by that date and the posthumous use of his name in the context of the Hippocratic report would be very strange; and second, fixing the date of one account in no way demands that all other medical observations in these three books of the *Epidemics* be contemporary to it and, still less, that they all be later than it.

In my opinion, the upshot of Deichgräber's arguments, if the identifications he proposes are accepted, is that the case history in book 4 that mentions the village of Medosades must be dated sometime after 410–405 B.C., and that the mention in book 2 of Alcibiades is prior to 404 B.C. It is even possible to accept the date 399 as a *terminus post quem* of the story about the village of Medosades without fearing, as Deichgräber does, that it prevents us from accepting the date 404 as the latest for the story of Alcibiades' man. The contradiction disappears if we admit that the "medical files" gathered up in *Epidemics,* II, IV, and VI, were made over a series of years. A date accepted as the *terminus post quem* for one specific case history also secures, to be sure, the chronological limit of the composition of the whole of book 4, and perhaps also that of books 2 and 6 in their current form,[30] but it would be a mistake to apply it to each medical observation in the 2–4–6 group.

Accordingly, we can say that the "cough of Perinthus" may well have been observed before the end of the fifth century, but it is unlikely that it occurred much before or much after 400 B.C.[31] It is known that Perinthus joined the revolt of the colonies against Athens in 411 and that it was reconquered in 410 by Alcibiades. According to Oberhummer, a specialist in the history of Perinthus, the acute epidemic fever mentioned in the second book of the *Epidemics* arose at around this time, if not even earlier.[32] This summer fever certainly preceded the epidemic winter cough, but by how much we do not know: it could be a single year, a few years, or even more. But we do know that the appearance of the summer fever coincided with the arrival in Perinthus "around the time of the summer solstice" (that is, in the second half of June) of a group of itinerant physicians.[33] Who were they? The tradition is unanimous in associating them with the medical center at Cos. Could Hippocrates himself have been their leader? My analysis of the chronological clues does not exclude the possibility, and some circumstances even make it relatively plausible. I think it is a reasonable hypothesis that the description of the summer fever and that of the winter cough of Perinthus go back to the same author as the one who compiled *Epidemics,* I and III. The latter texts are generally thought of as among the most authentic: they derive from Hippocrates himself or from a Coan physician who was his close contemporary.[34] To be sure, this attribution is not necessarily correct for all the clinical observations and medical notes that make up *Epidemics,* II, IV, and VI, in their current form.

To a modern reader, the heterogeneity of *Epidemics,* II, IV, and VI, is surprising. F. Robert's description is apposite: "A formless mass of disordered notes, some of which had previously been carefully edited, implying the desire to produce a real book, but the vast majority of which are unchanged from the rude state they were in when jotted down by a physician returning from a patient's bedside."[35] I do not believe in their unity of authorship, if by "author" is understood the physician who actually stood beside patients and noted his clinical observations and reflections and generalizing conclusions; but I freely admit the unity of the compiler of this whole. The contents of these three books are spread out before us like a collective dossier based on the personal experience of several practitioners.

Nikitas has brought out some differences between books 2 and 6 as against book 4. They are a matter of diction and style (for instance, the use of articular infinitives, adjectives in *-ōdēs,* more or less learned expressions, and turns of phrase in more or less high style) as well as some nuances in their teachings and in the way medical observations are used. Since he did not wish to see that such differences could also be detected between the several chapters within each of the three books, Nikitas concluded that book 4 is the most recent in its group and that its author was a second-rate physician capable only of applying a fixed doctrine to what he observed instead of making new inferences from it.[36] But this attempt to split the group 2–4–6 did not convince specialists. F. Robert explains the differences mentioned above as the result of "a more or less advanced state of work in the same author" and, naturally, the part whose form is the farthest from final form, namely book 4, seems to him to be the oldest part of the whole.[37]

Although Robert and Di Benedetto may be right in refusing to separate book 4 from books 2 and 6, the arguments in this whole debate reveal deep inconsistencies in the composition of the texts in question. It seems to me that books 2, 4, and 6 of the *Epidemics,* constitute a mosaic in which the lines that separate the various pieces do not correspond to the traditional book division. By means of a sophisticated study of the addresses of the patients, Robert was able to show that from books 1 and 3 to books 2, 4, and 6, there is an observable reduction in the interest of the physician in the habitat of each patient, a drift away from the etiological teachings espoused in *Airs, Waters, and Places* and toward those found in the treatise *Humors.* There is no way of mistaking the author (or, to put it more cautiously, the editor) of books 2, 4, and 6 for the author of books 1 and 3. However, this demonstration loses in value if there is a distinctive feature limited to a part of books 2, 4, and 6, in particular the general descriptions that rise above the individual case histories and integrate them into epidemiological profiles.

But that is exactly the case for the two chapters II, 3, 1, and VI, 7, 1. In the midst of a formless mass, they stand out; their formal perfection contrasts sharply with the unfinished notes and hasty clinical remarks that surround them. The method used for describing the diseases that prevailed in Perinthus during the summer and winter of one or two years around 400 B.C. is exactly the same as the distinctive intellectual procedure that makes the *katastáseis* of Thasos so valuable. Between the two chapters just cited and the epidemiological descriptions in books 1 and 3, there is an extraordinary similarity in style, composition, and above all in medical teaching and "research program."[38] From my analysis, which primarily takes into account the effectiveness of the investigative techniques and the quality of the medical content, the two "constitutions" of Perinthus are in no way inferior to those of Thasos.[39] There are two possible explanations for this similarity: either all these texts had the same author, or the observations at Perinthus are the work of a disciple or close collaborator of the author of books 1 and 3. If the latter is true, it must be admitted that the disciple's genius for research and acute clinical observation was not less than his master's.

According to Galen, learned men in Hellenistic and Roman times attributed books 1 and 3 of the *Epidemics* to Hippocrates. It was commonly held that their form was particularly pure since the Coan master himself had prepared them for publication.[40] Littré says there is no reason to doubt this important contention. As for books 2 and 6, Galen aligns himself with the majority of ancient commentators, who held that they contain personal notes by the great master that his son, Thessalus, edited, having found them on his father's hides or tablets. Unfortunately, Thessalus filled them out with his own abundant store of notes.[41]

A reading of books 1 and 3 reveals that Cyzicus on the Propontis was the furthest from home that Hippocrates ventured, and probably also the last place he visited to practice his art during the time-frame of the two books. But Perinthus also lies on the Propontis, right across from the peninsula on which Cyzicus was situated. What could be more natural for traveling physicians than to pass from one to the other of these cities? If we accept that Hippocrates left Thasos in 408 B.C. (a date made credible by the patient research of Dugand) and that he subsequently visited Cyzicus, his arrival at Perinthus, a nearby port city and as such a likely stopover, could not be sooner than the summer of 407 and was probably a bit later.[42]

A Retrospective Diagnosis of the "Cough of Perinthus"

When Emile Littré published his edition of *Epidemics,* II, IV, and VI, in 1846, he committed an error that has made retrospective diagnosis of the disease of Perinthus difficult if not impossible; until recently, it even led astray the philological exegesis of these books as a whole. His error was in supposing there was one disease of Perinthus, that is, that the description in VI, 7, 1, refers to one specific epidemic disease. Supposing that to be true and that the disease in question was very special and rare, Littré brought to bear on this one historical event scattered notes and observations that had in common the mention of certain symptoms. He sketched a synthetic pathological profile and was proud he had reconstituted it using many remarks scattered throughout the Hippocratic corpus:

Several passages that were very obscure are elucidated by simple cross-reference; some very short case histories that are barely skeletal become completely intelligible once they are fleshed out with the *general description* to which they must be referred; isolated fragments come together under a single heading; seeing the way remarks and facts *all belonging to a single affection* are scattered about, we can understand the nature of these notes that were taken by the Hippocratics and that have survived to our day under the rubric of the books of *Epidemics;* three aphorisms (*Aph.*, IV, 31, 33, 54) are attached to them that were inspired by *the disease of Perinthus,* and we can thus witness the research of the Hippocratics and the elaboration of their ideas.[43]

In short, Littré took VI, 7, 1, to be the description of an epidemic in the sense that term had in the medical language of the nineteenth century (which is essentially the same as that of our own time) and not in the sense proper to the Hippocratic writings themselves. In the Hippocratic corpus, the word "epidemic" designates the totality of diseases observable in a given place during a given time.[44] A disease that is said to be epidemic, for instance, the epidemic cough, is a disease that visits a region from time to time; its appearance is strictly linked to the change of seasons and to climatic variations.

Analysis of the medical content of this text in the light of modern epidemiological knowledge proves beyond doubt that the Hippocratic description of the "cough of Perinthus" has nothing to do with a particular, specific epidemic in the modern sense of the word; rather, it refers to what is conventionally called an "epidemic constitution." The Hippocratic writer is offering an overview of the climatic conditions and the seasonal endemic and epidemic diseases that prevailed in Perinthus over a specific winter and spring. So the "cough of Perinthus" is analogous, not to the "plague of Athens," but to the "constitutions" of Thasos. I contend that the Hippocratic description refers to a harmonious ensemble of pathological phenomena, in other words, to a historical moment in the pathocoenosis.

From this standpoint, it is possible to foresee the difficulties that awaited any attempt at a retrospective diagnosis of the "cough of Perinthus." At least in his first publication on the subject, Littré did not hesitate to choose a solution that most historians of medicine today would consider a sad, evasive admission of ignorance: that Hippocrates had observed and described an epidemic disease unknown to modern medicine. In his words:

In my reading I have found *nothing resembling the epidemic of Perinthus,* that is, an affection that most often presents itself as a cough that falls into remission, then relapses and in its relapsing form is accompanied by either nyctalopia, anginas, or paralytic weakness in the limbs, or else it attaches itself to a preexisting fever and produces feebleness or abscesses in the limbs as well as deposits in the ears. Accordingly, until we are better informed, it is necessary to group this disease with those *epidemics of which no other example exists;* it swells the list of such diseases, which are already rich in singular features; and in this respect, it is of real interest to historical pathology.[45]

When he wrote these lines, Littré was still unaware of the existence of diphtheritic paralyses. Actually, such paralyses had been mentioned by W. Piso in the seventeenth century and by C. W. Hufeland in 1811. But not until 1855, when a certain Dr. Herpin, a physician in Tours, was himself affected by paralytic complications of a diphtheritic infection, did Pierre Bretonneau, at that time the leading authority on diphtheria, reveal to the world in precise detail the existence of this relatively common clinical feature.[46] At the time that he was preparing his edition of the Hippocratic text on the cough of Perinthus, Littré could only have known of Bretonneau's previous article on diphtheria (1826), a masterly work in which the disease was accurately described for the first time as a properly defined, specific, contagious clinical entity; but a discussion of the relapses accompanied by paralysis of the soft palate and the limbs did not yet exist.[47]

Though buried in work, Emile Littré, tireless master of positivistic philosophy, classical philology, and French lexicography, still succeeded in keeping up with the progress of medical science. He read the clinical lessons of Trousseau and the monograph of Maingault, and so modified his diagnosis of the epidemic of Perinthus.[48] In 1861, in a number of the *Gazette médicale de Paris,* he declared that it could no longer be considered an extinct disease. Its symptoms—fever, angina, and cough with consecutive, not concomitant, paralyses affecting mobility (first of the soft palate, then of the limbs) and perception (notably, disturbed vision)—suggested, not to say guaranteed, that the disease in question was diphtheria.[49] Shortly after the appearance of this journal, Littré took up the subject for the third time in the last look back ("Dernier coup d'oeil") that accompanied the final volume of his edition of the works of Hippocrates. There he says that the retrospective diagnosis of diptheria is indeed alluring to a modern physician, but he no longer considers it obligatory. Having consulted a monograph by Gubler, a leading authority at the time, Littré had learned of the existence of paralyses that followed nondiphtheritic fevers.[50] Here are his final reflections and conclusions on the subject:

Once I had identified everything in the Hippocratic corpus that pertained to this epidemic and realized by a retrospective diagnosis that it was not a series of disjointed accidents relating to various pathological states but connected accidents linked to a single pathological state, I stopped and could go no further . . .

Today the additional information I was awaiting has arrived. In the world of science, when facts are unique, they trouble the mind merely because of their isolation. But when they become part of a group of facts, and their links with something more general can be glimpsed, one is reassured, and one gains confidence in the clarity that such connection brings. That is the case for the epidemic of Perinthus, since new research on consecutive paralyses in diphtheria or fevers or certain inflammations has made it possible to order the disease described by Hippocrates alongside others described by modern authorities . . .

These are the four principal traits of the disease: the appearance, during more or less advanced convalescence, of paralysis of the soft palate, followed by paralysis of the limbs and impairment of vision in various degrees and in various forms . . .

In a related observation, the Hippocratic writer, who was disturbed by the complications that were arising, took the trouble to say that neither the face nor the intelligence underwent alteration. Apparently, he feared some brain affection or other; but when he saw that there was none, he also understood the link between what he called "the cough" and the paralyses. Nor did he allow himself to be fooled by the minimal relationship that seemed to exist between the original stage of the disease and its sequels. His guiding principle was to consider all the phenomena that occurred in the epidemic as tied to each other. The cough, the nyctalopia, the paralyses, the angina, even the pneumonias (for he noted several that were concurrent with the disease), all appeared to him as a whole springing from a single cause, which in the event was a single constitution. Thence came the confidence with which he recognized what was before him, not as paralyses of encephalitic origins, but as paralyses due to the influence of environment . . .

Poor speech articulation and difficulty in swallowing suggest paralysis of the soft palate, which is the ordinary sign of invasive diphtheritic paralysis. And if it were true that nyctalopia and consecutive paralysis were exclusive symptoms of diphtheria, it would be difficult to disregard the similarity between the epidemic of Perinthus and diphtheria. But the problem is more complex.

The study of consecutive paralyses has just taken a further step. In an important report, Dr. Gubler has shown that impaired vision and paralyses can occur consecutively after convalescence in fevers, inflammations, even simple sore throats, and that basically even though these complications are more common in diphtheria than anywhere else, in diphtheria they are the specific expression of a general rule . . .

If we return to the epidemic at Perinthus with that in mind, it is certain that its arrival was signaled by cases of nyctalopia and consecutive paralysis that occurred after the remission and then the relapse of a cough. Although the cough in question was severe, with violent expectoration of dry matter and fatal, suffocating anginas, it remains to be seen whether the disease was diphtheritic, since consecutive complications, as Gubler has shown, are not exclusively diphtheritic. So we must stop at the most general level, at which they are recognized as being part and parcel of the chief acute diseases. Accordingly, we must consider the epidemic of Perinthus as just another instance of that fact. The Hippocratic writer has preserved for us an important page in medical history: twenty-two centuries ago a physician noted the connection of an acute disease with consecutive paralysis and nyctalopia. This observation, which proves the consistency of organic reactions over an extensive period of time, was buried in obscurity because a mind alive to the relation between original effects and consecutive ones was lacking for so long.[51]

Read a century later by a professional historian of medicine, this lengthy citation from Littré, for all its clarity, subtlety, and precision, immediately calls for criticism. First there is the methodological error discussed above: all the pathological states mentioned in *Epidemics,* VI, 7, 1, are not necessarily the result of a single disease in the modern sense of the word. To be sure, it is appropriate to attempt a reduction of the diagnosis to a single clinical entity, but it is not necessary to be obstinate. If the structure of the medical description points toward a plurality of clinical profiles, it is dangerous to wish to impose upon them at all costs a unitary and simplistic nosological account. In the case of the *katástasis* of Perinthus, the complexity of the underlying pathological events is apparent, at least in the view of a twentieth-century physician. But Littré's historical setting forced him to disregard this complexity. The concurrence of several diseases was of no interest to him, since it would essentially nullify the logical procedure of Hippocrates. Littré is overjoyed that the establishment of "epidemic constitutions," a method that he sees as typical of Hippocrates of Cos and opposed to the "Cnidian" nosology, provides such unexpectedly important results as the discovery of etiological links between angina and paralysis. "True Hippocratic medicine" triumphs through its unifying, global quality, which is the one Littré retains as a model for his own medico-historical research.

My two other criticisms are the direct result of subsequent advances in medical knowledge. The diphtheritic toxin can in fact bring on accommodation paralysis and oculomotor weakness, but the specific disturbances that result from it—notably, eyestrain, double vision, and strabismus—are not to be confused with weak night vision. Although night blindness has been reported in the course of some modern diphtheria epidemics, it is now established that it is due to a concomitant vitamin deficiency that does not belong to the diphtheritic infection itself. Littré understands the "nyctalopia" of this Hippocratic text as a poorly defined vision impairment, which offers him two advantages: he does not have to decide between the two classic, contradictory senses of this term (thus avoiding the need to amend *Prorrh.*, II, 33) and in addition he can easily include it with the symptoms of diphtheria. Today, this interpretation seems to me untenable. The text of *Epidemics,* VI, 7, I, says explicitly that troubled vision arose especially in those patients who coughed a little or not at all and who suffered from mild sore throats. In a diphtheritic intoxication of the eye muscles, the Hippocratic writer would no doubt have noticed just the opposite, namely, a heightened frequency of disturbed vision in those who previously had suffered severe laryngitis or pharyngitis. If we carefully examine the five Hippocratic passages that speak of "nyctalopia," sound medical reasons emerge for restricting the retrospective diagnosis to night blindness in the modern sense of the word, more exactly, to the acquired form of night blindness, which is a defect in the eye's adaptation to darkness that results from vitamin A deficiency.[52] Danielle Gourevitch has just confirmed this identification by a very precise philological investigation.[53] Moreover, it is worth stressing that the Hippocratic physicians knew of and described in different terminology the pathological states produced by paralysis of the eye muscles.[54]

My third and final criticism of Littré's opinion concerns the limb paralyses consecutive upon nondiphtheritic fevers. Specifically, he cites a clinical observation by the British physician Eade published in 1859 in the *Lancet:*

the man in question was "down for a month with influenza," recovered, then got sick again and had symptoms of paralysis exactly like those observed in diphtheria.[55] According to Littré, this case belongs with others like it collected in Gubler's monograph. He adopts Gubler's opinion that paralytic complications consequent upon fevers and anginas are not specific, that even in diptheria they are "just a special instance of a general rule." But that is incorrect. The paralyses described by Gubler do not arise after any given infection but, if we exclude diphtheria, they only otherwise arise in the presence of a neurotropic virus. Significantly, true influenza does not result in disturbed mobility and sensibility. Reading today the nineteenth-century clinical histories referred to by Littré, I recognize some cases of acute idiopathic polyneuritis (otherwise known as the Guillain-Barré syndrome) and, in particular, an outbreak of poliomyelitis with paralytic complications in western Europe right at a time when the general health was improving.

A retrospective differential diagnosis between diphtheritic paralysis and that caused by a neurotropic virus is not impossible to achieve. In the first place, the massive occurrence of paralytic disturbances, even in the form of small epidemics in a region like that of ancient Greece, is itself a point in favor of diphtheria. As a rule, the Guillain-Barré syndrome arises sporadically. For very specific epidemiological reasons, poliomyelitis could not have brought about numerous, grouped cases of paralysis in a place with the demography and hygiene of fifth-century Greece. Epidemic encephalitis has to be considered; I will discuss it further below. The set of symptoms makes it possible to distinguish effectively diphtheritic paralyses from viral ones. We will see how the clinical profile of the latter is a poor fit to the Hippocratic description of the cough of Perinthus.

Such considerations as these would have quieted Littré's doubts. The upshot is that the "cough of Perinthus" was indeed diphtheria or, to put it more precisely, among the diseases mentioned in *Epidemics,* VI, 7, 1, there were several cases of diphtheria. A neurologist, Achille Souques, has adduced additional arguments in favor of this hypothesis. According to him, a long and strange clinical description included in book 2 of the *Epidemics,*[56] whose meaning was obscured by the Hippocratic writer's obsession with the position of cervical vertebrae, is actually a report of a diphtheria epidemic.[57] Littré took the description literally and believed that "the vertebrae of the neck projected forward" in these patients, a notion that led him to postulate a diagnosis that is totally unacceptable to modern medicine.[58] There is no such thing as "a spontaneous luxation of the cervical vertebrae" that is an acute fever occurring epidemically. If we shed this error and interpret the so-called projection of the vertebrae as swollen cellular tissue between the spinal column and the posterior face of the pharynx, then no other disease than diphtheria is recognizable in the minute Hippocratic description of tonsilitis with immediate, severe symptoms (angina, submaxillary lymphatic reaction, difficulties in swallowing, speaking, and breathing, fever, neck deformity, and so forth) and its paralytic aftereffects (paralysis of the soft palate, occasional paralysis of the limbs, and difficulty standing up). It is even possible that the observation logged at *Epidemics,* II, 2, 24, was made at Perinthus and that it has a direct link with the *katástasis* of *Epidemics,* VI, 7, 1, but of this we have no proof. The kinship between the two is certain: the pathological events that they describe cannot be distant from one another either in time or in space. Given that, the diptheritic nature of the anginas and paralyses at Perinthus becomes still more likely.[59]

However, diphtheria cannot by itself account for all aspects of the "cough of Perinthus." What about the pneumonia, for instance? Ever since the first half of the nineteenth century, epidemiologists[60] were conceiving the possibility that the winter epidemic at Perinthus had the same nature as a Roman plague that they thought was simultaneous to it (dated by Livy 341–342 A.U.C., that is, 407–406 B.C.).[61] It was thought to be an influenza epidemic, since "many fell ill, but few died." It must be stressed that Livy's account is not precise about a single symptom of the disease. Moreover, at the time of Littré's edition of Hippocrates, the clinical profile and epidemiology of influenza were very poorly understood. A correct and almost exhaustive symptomatology of it was first established during the pandemic of 1889–90. In several European cities the incidence was said to be 40–50 percent, and from 0.5 to 1.2 percent of the population died—which speaks clearly of its importance. Naturally, the epidemic reached Greece, and an Athenian physician, Gerasimos Phokas, who fought it on his own turf, recalled the epidemic of Perinthus and did not fail to relate the Hippocratic description to the epidemiological experience he had just lived through.[62] His identification of the "cough of Perinthus" with influenza was enthusiastically accepted by esteemed clinicians like Alexandre Laboulbène in Paris and renowned medical historians like Theodor Puschmann of Vienna.[63] And their opinion should not be taken lightly, since they were able to benefit from direct, fresh knowledge of a specific pandemic of so-called Asiatic influenza. Phokas was an anticontagionist, and even in 1892, well after the work of Pasteur, he still thought that the Hippocratic remarks on the epidemiological role of climatic changes were perfectly relevant to an influenza epidemic. The main argument of those who favor this diagnosis is the overall impression created by the clinical picture that Hippocrates sketches. The following symptoms and complications of influenza are found in the Hippocratic description: cough, the fever curve, weakness and pain in the limbs, loss of voice, angina, pneumonia. "Nothing is missing," exclaims Phokas, expressing surprise at Littré's ignorance. "Nothing is missing, not the etiology, not the diversity of phenomena that mark the various forms of influenza."

But things are never that simple. The elements of the "cough of Perinthus" that favor a diagnosis of influenza are not pathognomonic. With regard to the "pneumonias" that were relatively mild and whose outcome was not serious, it is proper to think of viral bronchopneumonias rather than pneumococcal or streptococcal ones, but the diagnosis cannot be restricted to the influenza virus. Besides, in the influenza epidemics of 1889 and 1918, patients did indeed suffer from serious and dangerous pneumonias that were caused by bacterial superinfection. Some details of the Hippocratic text are even less relevant to true influenza. How can one explain relapses on the fortieth day? Phokas obscures the issue by discussing the nature of the troubles and not the moment they appeared. The "nyctalopia" has to be transformed into photophobia, if the symptoms of influenza are to be recognized at all costs. Another dubious argument: the predominance of male victims of the disease. As for the paralyses, their connection with influenza rests on a confusion with other diseases that present the same syndrome, namely poliomyelitis and encephalitis.

In 1923, Angelika G. Panayotatou, a physician/hygienist in Greece, posed the following question: "According to the observations of modern science, . . . couldn't this epidemic [the cough of Perinthus] be related to epidemic encephalitis?" The question is rhetorical, since it is accompanied by arguments that favor a positive answer. Panayotatou singles out the paralyses, the eye problems, and the cough as decisive symptoms of epidemic encephalitis.[64] Writing in 1923, she has in mind a very specific disease, the encephalitis lethargica of von Economo, which appeared in Europe in severe epidemic form during World War I. Small epidemics were reported in several countries, with Greece among them, up until the end of the 1920s. Apparently, this disease no longer exists. No one had doubted that it is viral, but the virus responsible was never isolated. Other viral forms of encephalitis have been proven to exist. Their clinical profile is so varied that a specific diagnosis is impossible without recourse to laboratory tests. Current medical belief is that certain viral forms of encephalitis, particularly those originating from mumps, herpes, or enteroviruses, should have cropped up from time to time in the ancient Mediterranean population. Still, none of the diseases described in antiquity really corresponds to encephalitis lethargica. In particular, the "cough of Perinthus" is a poor fit to such a diagnosis. The Hippocratic text makes no mention of lethargy, convulsions, or Parkinsonian tremor. Paralysis set in not immediately, but after a relatively long interval. Eye problems discussed in the text concern vision, not eye movement. And as for the cough and angina, they have specific qualities that can just as easily (if not more easily) be referred to other diseases like diphtheria and influenza.

To Henri Favier, the disease of Perinthus is dengue, a viral fever. Although this disease exists nowadays in the Mediterranean, its set of symptoms hardly resembles the Hippocratic picture. To begin with, dengue does not produce a cough or angina. It has a fairly typical way of unfolding that only partly matches the Hippocratic data. The author of this surprising identification realizes that "if we are content to compare [the symptoms of dengue] as a whole with the description of the disease of Perinthus in the sixth book of the *Epidemics,* the analogies are hard to grasp; but if we study the observations in the second and fourth books, by way of which the description in the sixth was constituted, numerous analogies appear."[65] Favier's hypothesis does not stand up to medical or textual analysis.

An enthusiastic specialist in infectious diseases, Edward Wilberforce Goodall, allows that the clinical description in two passages of the *Epidemics* (VI, 7, 1, and VI, 7, 10) "sounds very like influenza," but he isolates some cases of "paraplegia" in them that he feels "suggest acute poliomyelitis."[66] His opinion is not shared by an American physician, John Rodman Paul, the author of a monograph on the history of infantile paralysis. According to his study of the Hippocratic texts, acute anterior poliomyelitis is recognizable only in the description of acquired clubfoot (*Art.,* 62).[67] I pass rapidly over the hasty and arbitrary judgment of Arcangelo Ilvento, who sees the events at Perinthus as "an episode of typhoid fever or exanthematic typhus."[68] Most historians of medicine nowadays look askance at this Hippocratic evidence and opt either for diphtheria, or influenza, or a combination of the two.[69] In the last analysis, the diagnosis of diphtheria nowadays seems unshakable, but that of influenza remains problematic for the lack of basic epidemiological information about Perinthus. Here is what the virologist Pierre Lépine says about the matter:

> Nothing permits us to assert that influenza did or did not flourish in antiquity. People have singled out a description in the sixth book of the Hippocratic *Epidemics* of a contagious disease that raged five centuries before Christ in the north of Greece . . . The clinical description reminds one of influenza, whose symptoms it recalls; but the lack of precise data on the incidence of the disease in the population as a whole, on the duration of its evolution, and on the mortality rate, prevents us from eliminating with certainty another disease with an etiology different from influenza, such as an adenovirus infection or para-influenza.[70]

I had already been immersed in the complexity of this *katástasis* of Perinthus, both in the philological exegesis of the text and in the modern medico-historical commentaries, when I came across an eighteenth-century study that surprised me for its originality and the exactness of its assertions. In a way, it anticipated my own conclusions. In a report to the Société Royale de Médecine in Paris, Dr. Chamseru referred to *Epidemics,* VI, 7, and stated, "The picture Hippocrates offers indeed resembles what happens every year in La Roche-Guyon." At first sight, such a comparison between classical Greece and rural France near the end of the *ancien régime* brings a smile to one's lips, but what follows proves that his opinion is not unfounded.[71] For Chamseru, Hippocratic "nyctalopia" is "night blindness," a disease that he knows well from having observed it regularly each spring in a poor district in France. His zeal for the study of Hippocrates led him to collate manuscripts in the Bibliothèque du Roi, where he discovered that the codex R 2254 contains a negative in the definition of "nyctalopia" that occurs in *Prorrheticon,* II. So it really concerns "those who do not see at night." From his own medical experience, Chamseru concluded that the omission of the negative in most of the manuscripts "could only have originated in a copyist's error."[72] The "cough of Perinthus," according to him, was not the result of a single disease:

> These winter coughs no doubt answer to several degrees of cough that we moderns distinguish by name, as rheum, whooping cough, catarrh . . . Some of them were afflicted with paraplegia, a disease inappropriately confused with paralysis and hemiplegia, that was peculiar to the district that Hippocrates was observing, and that we believe was a kind of rheumatic enfeeblement, very similar to the Indians' beriberi . . . The text of Hippocrates relates the progress of other diseases of the same constitution, and specifically sore throats which carried off several victims in a few days and which Galen called pestilential. Actually, one recognizes therein, with as much likelihood as in the Syriac ulcers of Aretaeus, the signs of gangrenous or malignant angina, of which we had several examples last winter [that is, in 1784–85] in Paris and various provinces of the realm.[73]

So Chamseru contends that the epidemic constitution of Perinthus is composed of several diseases, the main ones being, to give them their modern names, night blindness, influenza syndrome, whooping cough, bronchopneumonia, beriberi (or another form of polyneuritis), and diphtheria. The diagnosis of whooping cough, passed over by more recent commentators, seems perfectly reasonable for a group of diseases that are isolated from the rest in the Hippocratic account: those "who lost their voice in fits of coughing" and who had no fever whatever, or very little, and suffered neither pneumonia nor paralysis. Chamseru does well to distinguish the paralyses of Perinthus from apoplexy, but, since he knows nothing of the existence of postanginal diphtheritic paralyses, he offers a risky hypothesis: beriberi. In his day, it was a disease practically unknown in Europe. However, evidence on the nutritional habits of ancient Greece in no way favors the diagnosis of a lack of thiamine. Beriberi in Perinthus seems out of the question. But there may have been B group avitaminoses (or rather, hypovitaminoses) that facilitated the neurological complications of infectious diseases.

Some Individual Case Histories from Perinthus

In the welter of *Epidemics,* II, IV, and VI, several passages contribute to a better appreciation of the nature of the "cough of Perinthus." But they must be cautiously used. Relying on a certain similarity of symptoms, Littré and Deichgräber associated *Epidemics,* VI, 7, 1, with various other

Hippocratic texts. "Once I grasped the essential trait of this epidemic as the author had represented it to himself," writes Littré, "that is, a cough and paralyses consecutive to it, it was possible for me to discover several scattered passages which, in relation to it, provide added information."[74] The procedure is as seductive as it is dangerous. It assumes that the Hippocratic account in *Epidemics,* VI, 7, 1, is restricted to a single disease. Furthermore, the disease must be a kind whose epidemic expression is both rare and localized. Otherwise, we have no right to interpret isolated symptoms as "debris" from the "cough of Perinthus," that is, as observations that of necessity relate to a specific place and a specific year. Littré's first impression, that the epidemic disease in question was exceptional and extinct, served to justify his way of relating texts, but he should have become more cautious once he came up with the diagnosis of diphtheria. In those days in rural Greece, it could only have held sway as an endemic spreading sluggishly, heating up now and then. Isolated cases and even other small epidemics must have occurred in the vicinity. The same reasoning applies to viral diseases like influenza, which as a rule sweep over very large areas and return at irregular intervals as small epidemic spurts in the wintertime.

Since the group of itinerant physicians making observations over one winter in Perinthus was especially struck by certain symptoms—in particular, a relapsing cough and instances of paralysis after angina—they and their disciples cannot have failed to speak of them on other occasions. Mention of the "cough of Perinthus" in the treatise *Humors* leads me to believe that the *katástasis* of VI, 7, 1, served as a model text for pupils to imitate.[75] So it may well be that even within *Epidemics,* II, IV, and VI, the references to it are not contemporaneous with it.

In three successive groups of the seven Hippocratic books called *Epidemics,* I believe there is a change in overall structure that reveals an evolution in method. First, in books 1 and 3, the *katastáseis* are plainly inferred from concrete cases that are catalogued apart in lists (those lists are incomplete); then, in books 2, 4, and 6, there are, side by side, *katastáseis,* then aphorisms of broader scope, then concrete clinical descriptions that illustrate the two previous categories of medical discourse instead of preceding them on the level of investigative method; and last, in books 5 and 7, there remain only some vestigial *katastáseis* buried in the presentation of actual cases and, though the casuistry has become richer and more varied than before, there is a failure to formulate new, general rules of prognosis (and, by implication, of diagnosis).

As for the "cough of Perinthus," it is impossible to prove with certainty that any concrete case reported in the Hippocratic writings was used to define the "epidemic constitution" of VI, 7, 1, that is, that it was prior to it from either a logical or a chronological standpoint. However, even though the links of certain passages with the "cough of Perinthus" are not as direct as has been maintained, a medical historian can infer supplementary information from them concerning the diseases present in northern Greece at the time of Hippocrates and use that information indirectly for retrospective diagnosis.

Let us look closely at a specific instance in which an identification with the "cough of Perinthus" was made without sufficient justification and probably incorrectly:[76] "The female who had her right arm and left leg paralyzed following a cough (she coughed only briefly and insignificantly) suffered no other change, nothing in her face or her intelligence. Not very severe. On the twentieth day things took a turn for the better, at about the same time as the patient had her period, perhaps for the first time, since she was a young girl."[77] In this clinical report, the principal fact is the crossed paralysis of one side's arm and the other's leg. Described here for the first time in the history of medicine, this peculiar detail distinguishes the pubescent girl's case from all the diseases that make up the "cough of Perinthus." Although a cough is mentioned in the story, that is only to emphasize its distinct insignificance. We are not told anything about the space of time between the cough and the appearance of the paralysis. To be sure, the physician who composed this report was especially attentive to the cough-paralysis sequence. Supposing that the link between relapsing cough and paralysis was not discovered until the "cough of Perinthus," then this particular observation must have followed the composition of the *katástasis* in VI, 7, I. To me that seems very likely, but not proven, since it is not impossible that the discovery of postanginal paralysis preceded the masterly description of it in *Epidemics,* VI, 7, I. Given the insignificance of her upper respiratory problems, the peculiar location and relative mildness of her paralysis, and also the ways in which it was cured, it is possible to exclude diphtheria as a diagnosis for this young girl. The disease in question might be acute anterior poliomyelitis,[78] but probably the most likely diagnosis is conversion hysteria.[79] The physician's distrust concerning anamnesis, expressed in connection with the patient's menarchy, says a good deal about the customs of this society. From a medical standpoint, the remark about the absence of change in the face or intelligence of the patient is a valuable sign that betrays the broad clinical experience of this particular physician. Without it, one would have diagnosed an organic brain lesion.

Here is the passage that, more than any other in the Hippocratic corpus, resembles cases included in the *katástasis* of Perinthus: "Among the patients who were coughing, those who worked with their arms, like the child who twisted withes and the son of Amyntas, had only their right arms paralyzed. In both cases, that ended, and then they suffered, having the cough. Those who rode horseback or walked, in the loins, in the thighs. Most were dry, and if not, strong in any case."[80] My translation of this Hippocratic account differs a good deal from those of Littré and Fuchs. The difference is due in part to emendation of the text, and in part to the preservation of obscurities that are inherent in its clipped style. The first sentence is not without ambiguities concerning the age and social position of the victims mentioned, since *paîs* can mean "child" as well as "slave," and *ho Amuntéō* is a vague expression that can refer either to a member of Amyntas's household or specifically to his son. Beginning with the second sentence, the text can be interpreted and completed in such a way as to make it resemble the account of Perinthus as closely as possible, for instance, "in both cases . . . *the cough* ended, then they suffered *from paralysis,* having the cough *once more.* Those who rode horseback or who walked *had paralyses* (or, alternatively, *had pains*) in their loins and thighs. Most *of the coughs* were dry, and if not, in any case they were strong."

In comparing this passage from *Epidemics,* IV, 50, with the analogous part of VI, 7, 1, one cannot help being struck by certain similarities in the symptoms mentioned and especially in the words used to describe them. For Littré and Deichgräber, there was no doubt whatever about their having a common source. As far as they are concerned, *Epidemics,* IV, 50, simply reports observations made during the "epidemic" of Perinthus. Since it is a more concrete description, it is somewhat prior to the composition of *Epidemics,* VI, 7, 1, or, at the very least, contemporary with it. This conclusion is troubling to Nikitas, however, who, after a detailed philological examination, concludes that IV, 50, is a kind of generalized reprise of VI, 7, 1. For him, the former is later than the latter, though it derives from observation of the same pathological event.[81]

In my opinion, the common historical origin of the two texts in question is in no way proven. To begin with their medical content, it is neither apparent nor even likely that the two reports derive from observations made during a single epidemiological event. Philological comparison obliges one to conclude that the author of one knew the other's formulations, or else that they are both by the same author. It is easier to explain the situation if we assume that *Epidemics,* VI, 7, 1, is older than IV, 50. It is not necessary to conclude, as Nikitas does, that the latter is an extract in more generalized form of a prior description that has come down to us piecemeal through VI, 7, 1. On the contrary, IV, 50, appears, medically speaking, to be a first observation made by someone whose knowledge of VI, 7, 1, provided him with vocabulary and an orientation. It appears as though the author of IV, 50, was anxious to make known what he had observed in a similar situation to the *katástasis* in VI, 7, 1, and to make even more clear the relationship between coughing, physical exertion, and paralysis. This method of investigation is exactly the same as the one that the author of the account of Philiscus of Thasos used to study the clinical importance of an epistaxis occurring in the midst of an acute attack of fever. In *Epidemics,* IV, 50, the circumstance that engages the writer's interest is that the paralysis is restricted to the right arm. Both patients "worked with their arms," but "had only their right arms paralyzed." Nothing of the kind was noticed during the "cough of Perinthus," though it is just the sort of observation that the Hippocratic physicians highlight in general epidemiological presentations. So here is a new fact that was not observed within the framework of the *katástasis* in VI, 7, 1, and it was important to bring it to light in order to refine the prognosis. What is said about patients who walked or rode looks like a repetition or confirmation of previous experience. Finally, I point out that most of the coughs in the *katástasis* of Perinthus do not seem to have been severe; on this minor point, the two texts also seem to diverge.

The symptoms enumerated in *Epidemics,* IV, 50, are too summarily presented to allow for a retrospective diagnosis. The disease could be poliomyelitis, diphtheria, the Guillain-Barré syndrome, and so forth. Both victims were very young, but they are spoken of in a vague way that leaves one wondering about their age. Some philologists and historians relate the following story to IV, 50: "Preferably the positions that give relief; like the person who wove or twisted withes with his hand and suffered intense pain when lying down, but by grasping an ankle over his head was soothed."[82] From the standpoint of its medical content, this case has nothing to do with the previous ones. The only common feature is the patient's type of work, an activity that was certainly not rare in Greek villages. The problem here is not motor function (the pain is relieved by grasping an ankle), but a painful condition in the arm. By translating the Greek word *huperodunéōn* [very painful] 'souffrant cruellement,' Littré adopted literary rather than technical language that happens to facilitate his interpretation of the case as a paralysis of the arm related to those in Perinthus. Actually, the diagnosis of this very sharp pain is not difficult: it is an occupational cramp.[83]

The sixth book of the *Epidemics* contains a paragraph that is situated not far from the *katástasis* of VI, 7, 1, and is surely related to it. It looks like an afterthought by the person who observed the "cough of Perinthus." The nosological conceptualization process is identical to the one that marks the first and third books of the *Epidemics* and the treatise *Prognostic:* observation of specific cases and meteorological conditions, classification of clinical profiles and their integration into *katastáseis,* and, finally, differentiation of syndromes through prognosis. After writing his composite sketch (VI, 7, 1), the same physician continues to elaborate the empirical data in two complementary directions: by generalizing them (formulation of rules in the form of "aphorisms") and by limiting them (formulation of exceptions). Both tendencies emerge clearly from the following text:

For consumptives, the fall is bad. So also the spring, when the leaves of the fig tree are as long as crow's feet. In Perinthus, most [fared poorly]. The accompanying cause was a cough that stayed through the winter. The same thing happened for the other chronic diseases, whose presence was confirmed where heretofore it had been unclear. Nevertheless, there were chronic diseases in which that did not happen, for instance, in those with kidney pains and also in some other patients, like the one I was brought to by Cyniscus.[84]

The sentence that adverts to the events at Perinthus is puzzling. It cannot be made out unless one looks at the aphorism it exemplifies, the one right before it, which speaks to the exacerbation of consumption.[85] Littré suggests that this text be read in the light of accounts in *Epidemics,* IV, 47; IV, 49; II, 2, 9; and IV, 53. I think an association willful for the first two citations, likely for the third, and practically certain for the last. The patient whom Cyniscus brought this physician to see suffered from an acute disease that grew worse on the seventh day and better on the fourteenth.[86] The Hippocratic description of his case suggests pneumonia or an influenza syndrome.

Epilogue: Diseases Present in Perinthus around 400 B.C.

The clinical profile of the "cough of Perinthus" can be understood in the framework of modern pathology only if its unity is broken. Among the various nosological elements of which it is constituted, one can recognize some viral diseases (influenza syndrome caused by rhinoviruses and enteroviruses, perhaps influenza in the strict sense, too), bacterial infections (notably, severe forms of diphtheria and pulmonary tuberculosis as well as a small-scale epidemic of whooping cough), and deficiency diseases (above all, vitamin A deficiency, whose pathognomonic expression is night blindness; perhaps also B and C hypovitaminoses).

Did influenza in the strict sense of the term, "the last great plague," flourish in the Mediterranean in classical times? To attempt an answer to this question, it is necessary to consider not only the varied clinical aspects of the influenza syndrome but also the results of recent research on the properties of the influenza virus, the cyclical variations in the immunological relations between it and humankind, the regular recurrence of influenza pandemics, and the role played therein by demographic density and animal stocks. The germ of this disease, *Myxovirus influenzae,* which was isolated in 1933 by Smith, Andrewes, and Laidlaw, provokes a potent immune reaction in humans that determines the halt of its great epidemic waves. However, the reaction is not enough actually to eliminate the disease, since the virus undoes the immunological defenses by a continual hybridization process between human strains and those that are parasitic in animals. Influenza is a disease of domesticated animals and of birds that live in provimity to mankind. In modern times, the general rule is that the periodic genetic recombination of the human influenza virus takes place in Asia, in the vast frontier lands between Siberia and western China. There the pandemic waves arise and proceed with astonishing speed to infect in cycles all of humanity. Not a single historical influenza epidemic began in the Mediterranean—even the so-called Spanish epidemic is wrongly named, since it, too, came from Asia.[87]

We now have precious historical information about influenza from serological archaeology. It has been proven, for instance, that the pandemic of 1889 had the same immunological properties as the "Asian flu" pandemic of 1957, which followed the "Spanish" one. The Asiatic and Spanish types alternate with some regularity. Every sixty or seventy years, one gives way to the other, and each cycle is broken around the midpoint by an influenza pandemic brought on by a change of immunological subtype. Going back in time, it is possible to apply the modern epidemiological schema to former epidemics with the features of influenza, but no earlier than the fourteenth century.[88] The cyclical scheme seems to be invalid for antiquity, and at least in the case of Rome, a city whose plague records are relatively complete, the absence of regularity cannot be explained away by a lack of historical sources.

To a historian of medicine reading the current literature on influenza, the relevant point is that its clinical manifestations are not specific. No description of symptoms, then, can guarantee its retrospective diagnosis. Instead, the course of its epidemics and their periodicity are the disease's characteristic signs. The description of the "cough of Perinthus" corresponds in part to the influenza syndrome, but we know today that a wide variety of viral infections can produce such a syndrome. The overall nature of the epidemiological events at Perinthus is not at all favorable to a diagnosis of influenza. Three other texts have been cited to support the presence of this disease in ancient times. They are from three historians of Rome, Dionysius of Halicarnassus, Livy, and Cassius Dio, and they concern plagues that ravaged the city in about 488, in 412/413 (or 407/406), and in 43 B.C.[89] But in fact all three accounts are so laconic and vague that no retrospective diagnosis is possible. The *Myxovirus influenzae* has such genetic suppleness that it is sure to have undergone profound changes since antiquity. Its ancestor in classical times was not necessarily as pathogenic for humanity as the strain that decimated the world's population in 1918. It is even legitimate to wonder whether the demographic density in Hippocratic times was great enough to sustain the germ in its virulent form.

It is certain that the ancient Greeks and Romans suffered from coryza or the common cold.[90] The Hippocratic writers were careful to note that a runny nose is unfortunate when it occurs alongside some other disturbances, particularly in the lungs.[91] But these symptomatic coryzas are not colds in our sense of the word. The true "head cold" is described in the *Ancient Medicine*. This text informs us that coryza is one of those things "that everyone often experiences and will continue to do so," and also that the Hippocratic physicians consider it a kind of model to use in explaining the notion of crisis. Right when the cure begins, an abrupt change takes place in the organism: what flows from the nose becomes thicker, and the inflammation subsides.[92] The author of the treatise *Airs, Waters, and Places* considers colds a physiological purging of the brain that must take place when winter ends in spring; without them there is a risk of serious disease, especially hemiplegia.[93]

In modern societies, coryza or acute rhinitis is as trite as can be, a common disease that is an embarrassment in several ways. It is a benign affection for which there is no means of cure or prevention. Strictly speaking, it is not a disease at all, but a syndrome that can belong to the clinical profile of a specific disease like influenza, whooping cough, poliomyelitis, and others, or it can stand alone in a variety of forms affecting the several levels of the respiratory tract. Experience and common opinion tell us that its main cause is the weather, that people more often catch cold after a local or general chill. For medical science, chills are only a factor that favors this ailment, not something sufficient or indispensable to its occurrence. The necessary condition for the common cold is a viral infection. Nowadays we know of at least a hundred viruses that can cause it. They belong to the *Myxovirus, Adenovirus, Enterovirus,* and especially *Rhinovirus* groups. Contemporary Western man is subject to such an infection an average of two to four times a year.

Although the cold has been a relatively common affection since classical times, it is reasonable to wonder if its frequency in the past was as great as it is now. No statistical comparison is possible, but it is interesting to note, as a token of the lower incidence of colds in ancient times, the absence of allusions to acute rhinitis in Greek and Roman comic writers. They only mention runny noses in the elderly.

Whooping cough or pertussis, a disease caused by the bacillus *Hemophilus pertussis* (discovered in 1906 by J. Bordet and O. Gengou), is older than most manuals of the history of medicine allow. For chroniclers and physicians of the past, it was often an inapparent disease, since it usually kills newborns and young children. Because of that, whooping cough was confused with other, undifferentiated causes of infant mortality.

As I indicated earlier, none of the diseases described in antiquity corresponds to encephalitis lethargica (von Economo's disease), but it is certain that several other forms of viral encephalitis appeared early on in the history of the Mediterranean world. In particular, there are notable dermatological accounts that testify to the ancient existence of the *Herpesvirus* group.[94] We now know that a viral agent of the herpes group is the cause of two diseases that are very different in their clinical manifestations: chickenpox and herpes zoster (shingles). The former is a generalized disease that probably corresponds to the viral primo-infection, while the latter is the localized manifestation of a nervous lesion that seems to be due to late reactivization of the latent virus. In a passage in the Hippocratic corpus, there is talk of "herpetic eruptions above the groin, developing toward the side and the pubis."[95] A modern physician could not find a more concise way to describe certain typical forms of herpes zoster. We must suppose, then, that chickenpox was also a disease that the Hippocratic physicians encountered in the exercise of their art. In modern times, it is the mildest of the fevers that cause skin eruptions, but it can take on severe forms and produce fatal respiratory and neurological complications, especially when there is a secondary bacterial infection. Although the traditional view of medical historians is that chickenpox was unknown in Hippocratic times,[96] I think that the new interpretation of a Hippocratic text by Paul Potter is plausible. According to him, there is a nosological description in *Diseases,* III, that essentially corresponds to chickenpox with a bronchopneumonic complication.[97] What favors this diagnosis is chiefly the moment when the exanthema appears and its exclusive localization on the back and chest. Under the epidemiological conditions of archaic and classical Greece, there is no need to think of chickenpox as exclusively a childhood disease.

There is no reason to believe that the ancient inhabitants of the Mediterranean knew of measles and rubella, two infectious, eruptive diseases that are extremely contagious and caused by specific viruses very close to the one that causes mumps. Measles is thought to have existed in China from time immemorial, but no trace of it is to be found in Greek and Roman documents. However, the presence of mumps (epidemic parotitis brought on by a paramyxovirus) in the Greek city-states is known from a local epidemic of it observed on the island of Thasos in about 410 B.C.[98] The mention of orchitis following parotid swelling guarantees the diagnosis. That the majority of victims were adolescents proves that mumps was no longer a new disease there.

If acute anterior poliomyelitis (Heine-Medin disease, caused by viruses of the *Poliovirus* group) did exist in the Greco-Roman world, it must have been endemic, about the way it was recently in the Near East or Latin America: a generalized, immunizing infection in children, with a few serious paralytic cases. It is a well-known paradox that the great prevalence of this viral disease goes hand in hand with its clinical invisibility. Some Hippocratic descriptions of paralyses that occur after a catarrh syndrome could relate to poliomyelitis, but the diagnosis is very dubious. They are better explained as diphtheritic intoxication or even, in one case (*Epidemics,* II, 2, 8), as conversion hysteria. There is no certain classical reference to the acute phase of poliomyelitis, but it is possible that the disease was responsible for some chronic deformities. That is probably true for the porter named Ruma whose stele is preserved in the Ny Carlberg Glyptotek in Copenhagen. The atrophy of his lower right limb looks exactly like a result of poliomyelitis.[99] So this Egyptian monument from the Pharaonic period makes likely the existence of poliomyelitis in the whole Mediterranean from the archaic period on. However, it is far from certain that this disease is the cause of the foot deformities described in the Hippocratic corpus, particularly those in chapter 62 of the treatise *Joints*. John R. Paul, the greatest specialist in the history of poliomyelitis, believes such a diagnosis,[100] but in my opinion he has let himself be misled by the English translation of the Hippocratic work in question. The author of *Joints* speaks of congenital clubfoot and clubfoot acquired through trauma, and he appears to be ignorant of clubfoot acquired through paralysis.[101]

The paralyses observed at Perinthus were flaccid, and certainly the result of damage to peripheral neurons. An Aristotelian text proves that spastic paralysis was also known in antiquity. In the *Nicomachean Ethics,* the conflict between reason and impulse in an incontinent man is illustrated by an analogy to the body: the soul, says Aristotle, finds itself exactly in the same situation as the body of some paralyzed persons whose "crippled limbs, that they wished to move to the right, instead swing to the left."[102] This passage allows us to recognize the existence in classical Greece of Little's disease, that is, of spastic paraplegia with clubfoot and scissor gait as the result of a precocious encephalic affection.[103]

As for the anginas that the Hippocratic writer describes during his stay in Perinthus, it should be made clear that the term *kunángkhē* (or *sunángkhē*) in ancient medicine designates "any obstacle to breathing or swallowing in a body-part, whether it be the back of the throat, above the lungs, or in the stomach."[104] Basically, it is a constrictive discomfort that can result from a local infection of the oropharynx and the larynx as well as a disease of the bronchi or of the heart. What I have just said clarifies the pathological situation for a modern physician, but it also introduces into the explanation of the ancient term some anachronistic concepts and some connotations that it cannot have borne: the Hippocratic writers were not only ignorant of the role of heart ailments in angina pectoris, they did not even distinguish between the oropharynx and the larynx. More recent physicians, especially Aretaeus and Galen, made that distinction perfectly clear, but no one in antiquity succeeded in understanding symptoms originating in the heart. Clinical descriptions from the classical period include various ailments under the term *kunángkhē,* including membranous pharyngitis, pharyngeal and peritonsillar abscess, ulcerative-necrotic pharyngitis, herpetic pharyngitis, and diphtheria of the pharynx and larynx, to say nothing of tuberculosis of the upper respiratory tract and angina pectoris. (There is an important infectious disease that appears to be excluded from this list: scarlatina or scarlet fever. No certain case of it is known in Europe before the last centuries of the medieval period.)

Diphtheria seems to dominate ancient descriptions of angina. It is a fairly contagious acute disease caused by a specific microbe, *Corynebacterium diphtheriae* or the Klebs-Löffler bacillus (discovered in 1883 by E. Klebs). The germ first attacks the upper respiratory tract and produces a sore throat with a characteristic formation of false membranes covering the tonsils and obstructing the larynx. It secretes a toxin that can damage tissues far from its original focus and so create myocardial lesions, paralyses, digestive disturbances, and so forth. In modern times, before its treatment with serum (1890), diphtheria was a scourge in Mediterranean countries. In the prevalence and severity of its forms, it was particularly devastating in Egypt, Syria, and Greece. Aretaeus of Cappadocia, who has provided us with a masterful description of diphtheritic sore throat, explains that the disease was called Egyptian or Syrian ulcers, since it was particularly rampant in those two lands.[105] Aretaeus's account dates from the first century B.C. It was followed by some very pertinent observations made by Rufus of Ephesus and Aetius of Amida. But the history of diphtheria in Greece is older still. Aphorisms 24 and 31 of the Hippocratic treatise *Dentition* concern this disease, since the first asserts that "in ulceration of the tonsils, the presence of something resembling a spider's web is not good," and the second speaks of the voice change that appears when such ulcerations extend over the uvula.[106] The subject here is the appearance of paralysis of the upper palate after an ulcerous sore throat, a phenomenon carefully noted by the ancient writer in its clinical consequences but poorly understood in its anatomical extension. In my opinion, the second type of angina described in the Appendix of the *Regimen of Acute Diseases* definitely includes, among other throat ailments, laryngeal diphtheria, just as the first type of angina described in *Diseases,* II, contains, among other forms of pharyngitis, pharyngeal diphtheria.[107] This reinforces the credibility of the diagnosis of diphtheria in the framework of the "cough of Perinthus."

One final word on the subject of Hippocratic "night blindness": its origins in nutritional deficiency are evinced in the therapeutic success of ingesting raw beef liver.[108] Diseases do not associate with one another in an arbitrary way. We now know that nonspecific wintertime infections of the upper respiratory tract are aggravated by the lack of vitamin A. In ancient societies, night blindness regularly occurs in the presence of bronchitis and sore throat. Vitamin B deficiencies facilitate the neurological complications of toxic-infectious diseases. Chronic alcoholism (that is, consumption of wine accompanied by a low-protein diet) is not a negligible factor for a true etiological appreciation of the "epidemic constitution" of Perinthus. To be sure, Hippocrates does not breathe a word about it, but that is because the cultural acceptability of such a diet made it intellectually invisible. Finally, I add that Bretonneau long ago stressed that cases of diphtheria are exacerbated during an epidemic of influenza syndrome.[109]

How is it that a practitioner of the eighteenth century, Dr. Chamseru, had clearer vision in his interpretation of the "cough of Perinthus" than all the physicians and philologists who succeeded him? The reason is that, unlike Littré and most recent commentators, Chamseru avoided the mistake of fixing his gaze in a single direction, of insisting on the preservation of the nosological unity in the modern sense of pathological specificity. He also, by virtue of his personal experience in a rural environment not yet tainted by the Industrial Revolution, was able to grasp another kind of unity in the Hippocratic picture: the balance of symptoms in the seasonal appearance of a pathocoenosis.

Chapter Thirteen

A DIALOGUE BETWEEN A PHILOLOGIST AND A PHYSICIAN

It has been my privilege to collaborate with Fernand Robert, a professor of ancient Greek literature and civilization at the Sorbonne, in the preparation of an edition of the *Epidemics* for the *Collection des Universités de France.* Our collaboration began shortly after the Hippocratic colloquium at Strasburg in 1972, in which we were both participants. The colloquium had allowed philologists and physicians interested in Hippocrates to meet and judge the benefits of working together. As far back as 1933, K. Deichgräber had concluded a fundamental work on Hippocrates with an appeal in that vein: henceforth, he asserted, philologists need to call on physicians for help if they are to progress in their study of the Hippocratic corpus in general and of the *Epidemics* in particular.[1]

This chapter faithfully reproduces, with minimal changes to suit the conventions of written exposition, selected parts of the actual dialogue we held as we prepared the edition (with commentary and translation) of *Epidemics,* VII.[2] The point is not so much to publish secure results before a work in progress is completed—since the paleographic research is in progress, there has not as yet been a review of some more recent manuscripts, to say nothing of the questions posed by Arabic and Latin traditions—as to bring out the problems encountered, to illustrate the method followed, and to show how the work of both participants is intertwined in the translation and even in the choice of variants to retain in establishing the Greek text.[3]

Among the texts that we have already studied together, we chose (1) a short but complete text that allows for detailed discussion; (2) a very long, remarkable text—we could only touch upon its highlights; (3) several concise texts that are so rich in content that the modern physician can fairly easily postulate a diagnosis within the framework of modern pathology; and (4) a group of texts in which it is possible to show, from either a philological or a medical standpoint, that the original account of the observation has come down to us in truncated form.

A Case of Chronic Tetanus

I offer below a translation of chapter 8 of book 7 that we have agreed upon and that we intend to justify. It is based on the Greek text edited by Littré,[4] which was carefully checked and revised on the basis of current knowledge of the Hippocratic manuscript tradition.

In the woman who lived over the Gates, already elderly, there was a slight fever, and, at the moment when it was about to end, a pain in the nape of the neck extending down the back to the loins; she did not have complete control of these areas; moreover, clenched jaws, and squeezing the teeth together too hard to let a probe pass through; her voice articulated badly because her body was inert, without movement and without strength; but she was conscious. With fomentations and lukewarm mead, she improved on about the third day; and then, with barley gruel and soup, she returned to good health. Took place at the end of autumn.

Our discussion follows:

Robert: For this text we have only one ancient manuscript, which is M, since there is a very long lacuna in V (it stretches from chapter 5 to chapter 11).[5] The M manuscript allows for several solutions here that accentuate the rapid, somewhat telegraphic style. Our translation should keep the look of notes taken in haste or, more precisely in this case, of slips put in final form with an extreme concern for conciseness. The place where Littré proposed a conjecture (*epi toùs* instead of *heōutoùs*) has the same impossible reading in M as Littré found in the manuscripts that he knew. His conjecture is an excellent one, and setting it next to the actual reading is enough to explain how the mistake happened. As for the rest, the problems in the text or in the translation will depend—I say this from the outset—on the medical interpretation. It is appropriate, then, to ask you now whether or not you can propose a diagnosis on the basis of Littré's text.

Grmek: This case contains an excellent description of trismus, a tonic spasm of the muscles of mastication.[6] We can exclude a local ailment of the mouth and the temporo-mandibular joint because of the patient's generalized illness. This particular symptom can occur during an epileptic fit, in the last stage of rabies, during strychnine poisoning (for instance, with nux-vomica) or, and above all, as the basic sign of infection with *Clostridium tetani*. In this case, the clinical picture is certainly not that of a grand mal epileptic fit. Rabies and strychnine poisoning can also be eliminated on the basis of the absence of agitated movement and clonic spasms. The patient is calm, immobilized, with consciousness intact, not shaken by convulsions, agitated, or delirious. Her return to health would also tell against a diagnosis of rabies or massive poisoning.

A single possibility remains: tetanus. This disease definitely existed in classical Greece. Three other case histories in this same book relate to it (*Epidemics,* VII, 36–38).[7] In all three, Littré proposed it as the diagnosis. Why does he not do so for the one that interests us here? Probably because of the rapid and apparently complete cure. In Littré's time, attenuated and chronic forms of tetanus were poorly understood. Besides, Littré did not even know that it was an infection and so defined "tetanus" only in clinical terms. His diagnosis of "tetanus" always corresponds to acute tetanus in modern terms, usually a fatal form of the disease unless there is a particular medical intervention. I mention in passing that the Hippocratic physicians used the term *tétanos* to designate a pathological concept that in some contexts overlaps the disease we call by that name and in others does not.[8]

This particular case is a chronic tetanus. Painful contractions along the nape of the neck and the back are very characteristic of it, and this writer describes it in precise, lapidary style. Three days after a brief and harsh attack that is preceded by a fever and features spasms, immobilization of the whole body, and voice deformation, the symptoms begin to recede. The convalescence in this disease is long and marked by frequent remissions. So we may well ask ourselves about the actual duration of this particular observation. Was the physician really able to follow the patient's progress after the stated period? Was he an itinerant physician who never stayed very long in the places where his patients resided? Tetanus must be preceded by a wound, but none is mentioned in this account. However, in these relatively benign forms of tetanus, the wound can be minimal and the incubation period very long (from ten to thirty days). So it's not surprising that the Hippocratic physician did not see a relation between the physical trauma and the paroxystic state.

R.: In book 7, there can be two reasons for an unfinished observation: you know that books 7 and 5 seem to me to have been copied at different dates by two medical teachers or even students from a file in which each took the observations or the parts of observations that interested him and left the rest.[9] That is the first reason why an observation can be unfinished, but your study here shows that missing links, like the wound and its incubation, or the convalescence, can be part of the original observation itself. It is not that the writer (that is the term we must reserve for the person who prepared the file, calling the persons to whom we owe book 7 in its present state an editor) was a poor observer (the whole book is proof to the contrary). In the conditions he worked under, there were limits to the duration of his observation, either, as you suggest, because he was an itinerant physician, or simply because the patients at the time were not as thin-skinned as they are now and so would not have had recourse to a physician except when they suffered a great deal. There are other cases in which the physician lets us know that he himself was not present at the outset of a disease.[10]

Let's get into the details. For the word *trákhēlos,* I understand that you do not always accept the translation "neck." Here, is it "neck" or "nape of the neck"?

G.: For medical reasons, it is clearer to translate this term here as "nape of the neck," since probably we can consider the nape as part of the neck, and in this case we risk misleading the reader if we do not, because the word "neck" nowadays designates especially the anterior and lateral portions of it. For another example, see *Epidemics,* VII, 5, where the discussion is of the sign of meningitis, so it must be "nape of the neck."

R.: Besides, from the standpoint of the language, I can offer no objection. From the Liddell-Scott-Jones dictionary, I learn that in Plato *trákhēlos* is probably distinguished from *aukhḗn* 'nape of the neck,' but that *aukhḗn,* used in *Prognostic,* 23, is glossed as *trákhēlos* by Galen.[11] So the medical interpretation must rule the day. For the peace of mind of Hellenists, however, it would be best to explain this in a note once and for all at the first instance of *trákhēlos* translated "nape of the neck," then to cross-refer to it explicitly every time we translate it as such.

G.: Littré, who was a physician and a philologist, was certainly correct in translating the word *rákhis* here as "back" and not "spine."

R.: Again, it's the physician who must decide how to render *ou pánu engkratès toúton:* since *ou pánu* can mean "not at all" or "not completely," with the first meaning explicable as a litotic use of the second, as when we say that someone is not very nice, meaning that the person is not nice at all. So should we say here that the patient "has absolutely no control over these areas" or that he "does not have complete control" over them?

G.: That he "does not have complete control" over them: the patient is not suffering from a true paralysis, and the physician seems to me to be carefully distinguishing these symptoms from the absolute impossibility of voluntary movement.

R.: Now we are faced with the biggest problem. To be sure, we accept Littré's correction *epi toùs.* But right after *pareînai,* M adds the two words *ouk ên* to the text of the *recentiores* that Littré used. The effect is to change both the grammatical construction and the meaning. Were it not for these two words, we would translate "clenched jaws, and squeezing the teeth together too hard to let a probe pass through." "Squeezing" is a translation of the word *epí* that gives it the value of a second verb coordinated with "clenched," even if we can say that *xunēgménai* is to be understood with *kaí*; and the construction "too hard to" governs the infinitive *pareînai,* an epexegetic infinitive. But if we add *ouk ên,* the sense will be "and it was not possible to pass anything over the teeth larger than a probe." The infinitive *pareînai* is then a complement to *ouk ên*. Clearly it is no longer possible to render *epí* by "squeezing," and a real weakness of this solution is that the words "pass anything over" suit only the lower jaw! But the main problem is that the teeth are no longer as tightly clenched as they were in the first translation, since now the probe can pass. It is incumbent on us to pay careful attention to all the ancient readings that were unknown to Littré and to prefer them whenever possible. Is there a medical way to accept the version in M? And what exactly is this probe?

G.: It's a metallic probe with the shape of a knife whose blade is dull and whose handle ends in a small ball, whence its name (*mḗlē,* which recalls the Greek word for apple). Such probes have been found in excavations.[12]

As for the jaws, in this disease they are very tightly clenched, and Littré's text and translation are satisfactory. If it were absolutely necessary to accept the reading in M, I would have to imagine that this practitioner—I'm sure he tried to insert his probe, I can see him doing it—finally succeeded because the woman was old and in Greece dentition was often poor; plausible, but still!

R.: Let's not go too far. It happens often enough that the oldest manuscripts provide an absurd reading and that the later ones restore the text, whether because a good corrector had the ingenuity to discover the right reading or because it occurred in an old manuscript otherwise unknown to us.[13] So we're perfectly entitled not to idolize the M manuscript, the more so since this error is of a known type. The construction without *ouk ên* is perfectly good Greek, if a bit weak, and someone who did not understand it thought he was making the text clearer by adding to it. So we can stick with Littré here.

As for the patient's voice, the change that the disease produces and that is designated by the word *psellḗ* cannot be stuttering, since Aristotle draws a distinction between *psellós* and *traulós* 'stuttering.'[14]

G.: And in tetanus the voice does not stutter. It is distorted and hoarse instead. Littré is wrong here. Stuttering is a symptom of psychological or neurological origins, but what is affected here are muscles in the larynx and the glottis. The voice is intelligible but very distorted.

R.: It remains for us to interpret the word *paraleluménon*; I really hesitate to speak, as Littré does, of paralysis, although that is the French (as well as the English) word derived from it, since it is clear that the writer is searching for the proper term. As little as purely stylistic issues concern him (which, by the way, does not prevent him from being unconsciously artistic, given his powers of observation), he would not have started a list of three words with the harshest and most precise one. And you have just brought out how careful he is to avoid confusion with paralysis in the strict sense of the term; it is significant that his effort in this regard is particularly plain just before he uses a word that, if transcribed as such into French or English, would introduce the very notion he is at pains to avoid.

G.: Yes, I do not like the word "paralysis" here at all, since it suggests hemiplegia or something similar. The body in such cases of tetanus is immobile but not really paralyzed.

R.: Having in mind the definition of *paralúo* in Bailly's school dictionary as "relâcher les muscles d'un côté du corps" [relax the muscles on one side of the body], I thought of translating it "without muscles, without movement, without strength."

G.: Uh-oh! Above all, don't speak of muscles, because the Hippocratics never gave them a role in movement, which to them was produced only by bones and ligaments.

R.: So much for that ineptitude. I had in mind an expression that was also as untechnical as possible, even a little familiar. Looking at it another way, what is the difference for modern medicine between paralysis and the state described here?

G.: Paralysis is the impossibility of voluntary movement, but here there is immobility without it necessarily being impossible to move when desired. This is something not situated on the level of the central nervous system. It's a difficulty in the transmission of the nervous impulse, or a disposition to avoid pain.

R.: How about translating it "inert"?

G.: I'd have no objection.

R.: So when I ask you, as I just did, to define for me a difference between two modern notions, the concern is to understand and make understood a difference between them that the ancient observer also perceived, just as when we were speaking of the difference between *psellós* and stuttering. Someone may object to our rejection of the word "paralysis" here because the ancient observer did not have the notion "nervous impulse." But we are not imputing to him a concept that was unknown to him. It can happen that the Hippocratic writer uses a word from our vocabulary in a sense that is technical for him but not the same as its modern technical sense, or, again, it can happen that we believe that a term designates for him just what it designates for us, but that our belief is mistaken. In both instances, it is likely without being absolutely inevitable that we would use the modern term and add a note to avoid any confusion in the reader's mind. A note is also obligatory when we do not translate it with the modern term, to explain why not. Such a note would be necessary here to explain why we do not translate the word *paralúō* as "paralysis" in our sense, on the grounds that the author is struggling to express something that he knows to be different from paralysis, as his successive approximations demonstrate. In practice, a note is always necessary except when the old and new senses of the word in question coincide perfectly.

A Case of Typhoid Fever

From the lengthy observation of Hermoptolemos's wife, which takes up two and a half pages in Littré, I append a translation that the two of us have agreed upon and whose detail we will not take up as we did for VII, 8.[15] Instead the discussion is intended to show the way we are able to work together on the commentary to such texts.

In Hermoptolemos's wife, wintertime, fever, headache; when she drank, as if it was hard to swallow; she got up and said that her heart was being crippled; her tongue was livid from the outset. First manifestation taken for the result of a chill after bathing; awake night and day; after the first days, when asked, not only her head, as before, but her whole body was suffering. Thirst, sometimes intense, sometimes moderate. From the fifth and sixth days to the ninth, she was almost raving, then she began talking to herself in incomplete phrases; drowsiness with it; sometimes, she tried to grasp the plaster wall with her hand, or she would apply a cool pillow from beside her head to her chest; from time to time she kicked off her bedclothes. In her right eye was the characteristic spot of blood, and a tear; urine, with the appearance that is always bad in children. Stools at first yellowish, then watery and the same color. On the eleventh, the heat seemed to diminish and at times the thirst ceased, to the extent that if nothing was given her she did not ask. Moments of rest, after the initial stage, occurred satisfactorily by day, but at night she did not sleep, and she suffered at night especially. On the ninth, her belly was disturbed, watery substances, on the tenth as well; the days previous, fits of rage, whining like a small child, outcry, frights, looks in every direction every time the drowsiness broke. On the fourteenth, it was a job to take and hold her just for a moment, she was jumping and shrieking with all her might as though smitten with horrible pain and terror; afterward, she was again calm, drowsy and sluggish without seeing and at times without even hearing; she switched frequently from one state to the other, from tumult to calm, almost the whole day. The following night, she excreted some bloody substances, somewhat viscous, then again somewhat muddy, and after that, of a very pronounced leek green, or black. On the fifteenth, brusque movements, and some frights; and her shouting grew fainter, but the exasperation, the anger, the weeping continued if one did not rush to do what she wished. As soon as the first few days passed, she again began to recognize persons and objects, and the spot on her eye was gone. But her folly, her incoherence, her shrieking, followed by the slipping into drowsiness I spoke of above, kept up. She could hear only irregularly, at times perfectly even if one whispered, at other times one had to speak loudly; feet always as warm as the rest of her body until her last days. The sixteenth, less severe. The seventeenth, though she was in a more moderate state than the other days, she curled herself up in a ball like someone shivering, and her fever went up. Great thirst; other things as before; there was shaking in her hands, and she shook her head; bruises around the eyes and hostile looks; the thirst was violent. As soon as she drank, she asked for more; she would grab the container, and drink all at once; you couldn't take it away from her again; tongue dry, bright red, and the whole mouth and lips were dry, ulcerous; possessed by the shakes, she would put her hands to her mouth and nibble them, and whatever you offered her to chew or swallow, she would gulp down and swallow greedily and furiously; her look was angry. Three or four days before the end, shivering would come over her at times, so that she curled up, covered herself up, and gasped for breath; contractions, the legs; chills in the feet; thirst as ever; getting up to relieve herself either to no purpose or for the sake of a little thin stuff, exerting herself for a short time. The last day, the twenty-third, eyes wide open in the morning, quick glances all around, at times she was calm, and without covering herself or dropping off. Toward evening, the right eye moved as though it saw or wanted something, from an exterior angle toward the nose; she recognized and answered a question posed to her; she began to stutter, and because of the shrieking, her voice was broken and hoarse.

R.: Surely this is one of the most beautiful texts in Greek, and its movement is remarkable, as well as the quality of its observed details; a work of art, even if no artistic intention is apparent in it. It may be that I have thrust one upon it by translating the patient's own words at the beginning of the text "her heart was being crippled"; there are not enough attestations of the verb *giuóō* for us to know with certainty if the overuse of this word, whose proper meaning is "amputate" but which ended up meaning "weaken," had reached the point where we should here speak of a simple "weakness" in the heart. The physician has taken the trouble to note that it was the patient's own word, and I think that is a sign in favor of an expressive translation of a word that he thought striking.[16] Everywhere else the prevailing aesthetic is simplicity.

There are two older manuscripts at our disposal here, M and V, at least from the word "first manifestation" (*próphasis*) on, in the second sentence. That is where the long lacuna in V ends. The differences from Littré's text that can be established on the basis of their readings are relatively insignificant: an otiose mention of the eleventh day after the tenth in the phrase concerning the ninth day and those following it, and an absurdity (visitors who recognize the patient, rather than the other way around) in the sentence after the fifteenth day—again a case of a reading in the newer manuscripts that is superior to the older ones, though we should not come to think of that as a general circumstance.

The word *próphasis* is used in the beginning, remarkably, in its strictly etymological sense, to mean the first phenomenon to appear in a developing process. Its causal sense developed from this one in all thinkers, especially medical ones, who did not waste words and who wished to scrutinize a reality that was visible and tangible.[17] We particularly refrain from searching for a causal connotation in this term as the result of our regrettable tendency always to translate it "pretext" or "immediate cause," as though there were another, more profound one. Actually, for this writer, there is no cause at all. The issue is to discover what is the first phenomenon that is definitely part of the process he is trying to describe. Neither the bath nor the chill is such a phenomenon, which must be the first attack of fever that follows them. As for this phenomenon, he only knows of it by *dóxa: edókei* 'was taken for.' The physician was summoned once the fever had already lasted for some time. It can also be considered likely that, since the first observation properly speaking (it is the first one dated in relation to the onset of the disease) was on the fifth day, the dates are recorded from the *próphasis* on. Considering the importance of these dates in the description and in Hippocratic doctrine, that is an essential item to determine.

In response to your constant urging, I have, needless to say, avoided translating the Greek word *kôma* as "coma" as Littré does, since in almost every instance it designates a state in which the subject remains conscious.[18] I proposed "torpor" and we finally agreed on "drowsiness." It should really be made a rule that whenever a Greek word has a precise meaning in the translation that is radically different from the sense in which it was used by the Greek medical writers, the word must not be translated as its cognate in the language of the translation. But we are now in your territory—I think I have gone as far as I can without a medical interpretation, which is . . . ?

G.: Two aspects of the narrative—the remarkable description of movements that Galen calls "carphology" (gathering bits of straw),[19] and the states of confusion, the "mild delirium," which, in this patient, alternates with *maníē* 'rage, wildness, folly'[20]—suggest, at the outset, three different infectious diseases: typhoid fever, a common type of septicemia, or a meningococcemia. But the color of the stools, the yellow ochre that is characteristic of typhoid and is still used as a diagnostic sign nowadays, points us in the right direction. In all its aspects, this passage is a beautiful description of typhoid fever.[21] Or rather we should call it salmonellosis, since without bacteriological analysis there is no way to distinguish between typhoid fever in the strict sense, caused by *Salmonella typhi,* and some other diseases caused by the germs of the same genus (paratyphoid fevers).[22]

Intermittent deafness is common in this context. It is due to a bacterial injury of the brain and not to ear lesions. The observation about the patient's feet is noteworthy: it is there because the physician is trying to establish a differential diagnosis. In exanthematic typhus—its clinical manifestations were known to the Hippocratic physicians, who thought of them as particularly deadly forms of acute fever—there are often complications in the extremities. Moreover, by his silence with respect to a certain symptom, the author gives away the differential diagnosis in question: he makes no mention of an exanthema. Actually, it is a symptom of both typhoid and typhus, but in the former it is very unobtrusive (lenticular spots that are often hardly visible, and then only through a careful search of covered parts of the body), while in the latter it cries out for attention (purple spots that turn brownish). So the typhic state in Hermoptolemos's wife is not a rickettsiosis. The purple eruptions it produces would not have escaped the attention of this particular clinician, while the light rash accompanying typhoid fever could have no special significance to him, nor would it arouse his interest enough for him to mention it.

There is another interesting omission: enlargement of the spleen. The physician's silence with regard to this symptom, which he considers minor, does not always denote its absence in a patient. If the issue of spleen size never comes up in this case, that is of no consequence for the diagnosis I have proposed, since its enlargement in typhoid is soft, painless, and not necessarily palpable. Modern medicine knows it from percussion, a procedure unknown to the ancient physicians.

Without treatment, a typhoid victim's fate is usually decided around the end of the third week of the disease. At that point, the fever falls, the delirium lessens, and slow recovery can begin. That is what happened to Hermoptolemos's wife, but her organism was not really able to recover, and she fell prey to disturbances of her hydric and electrolytic metabolism (note the red tongue, the split lips, and the appearance of her face). The chills stem from septicemic attacks. An intestinal hemorrhage, which is a very common complication in salmonelloses, signals the end.

In this whole description, there is but one surprising remark: the movement of her right eye on the day of death. Usually, one eye does not move without the other. If the observation is to be taken literally, there was paralysis of the left eyeball, a fairly rare occurrence. In any case, it is the first known description of nystagmus. To my mind, the words used are simply an elliptical way of describing the direction of the nystagmus in both eyes, since the rhythmic jerk in only one eyeball is directed toward the nose.[23]

R.: That's a likely possibility, in view of the willfully elliptical style of this writer. He may well have thought it pointless to specify the movement of the other eye. Would you let me quibble with you a little over the expression "differential diagnosis"? It's just a matter of which words to use. What delights the modern reader of *Epidemics,* VII, is to construct a diagnosis from the elements that are so remarkably well described by the ancient observer. For him, on the other hand, there is no talk at all of diagnosis, and if, rarely, he mentions the name of a disease, he never once asks himself if a patient is suffering from one disease instead of another. In this respect, he remains strictly within the tradition of the treatise *Prognostic,* whose last chapter says, in essence, "If you complain that in my work there are not enough names of diseases, you are mistaken, since they are all there"—this despite the fact that he actually provides very few. Even so, it is also true that this physician does do what you say he does, that is, he carefully notices one symptom or another because experience has taught him about different cases in which the foreseeable processes were distinct. In all this, it seems clear that his way of thinking was the best one possible before the existence of microbes and viruses became known.

G.: As you say, our disagreement is only an apparent one. And since we are discussing ways of thinking that our writer forbids himself to engage in, I am also struck by the consistency with which he avoids speaking of causes. For once, however, in the text in question, he has allowed himself to mention one, since it seemed so obvious to him: I mean where he says that toward the end, the patient's voice became hoarse as the result of having cried out. But, alas, he is mistaken! Her voice was hoarse not from crying out, but from a specific infection of the larynx caused by the bacillus. It's an utterly typical symptom.

R.: The patient's cries constitute a structuring motif in the account and left a lasting impression on the physician's mind. Or rather, her cry, since the word is always in the singular in the text. I wished to draw attention to it by translating the word *boḗ* with the word "clameur" [outcry]. To stress the vivid impressions engraved in this observer's memory, it was also important to render the meaning of the Greek definite article when he speaks of "the" spot of blood and not "a" spot, even though he had not spoken of it previously. There is no reason to hesitate to add, as I have, the word "characteristic" to reproduce what is in fact a consistent sense of the Greek article—not that it was characteristic of the disease (which would be to reason like a diagnostician and contradict what we have just said), but characteristic of this patient. I would not be so bold as to translate the article's force here with "this spot of blood that struck me so" or "that bothered me so much," but that is really what's being said. Translating it "her" spot of blood would be inadequate, not clear enough.

Four Concise Case Histories

R.: A text can be much shorter than this account of typhoid and still be complete. I know how much you admire chapter 116 of this same seventh book for the concision with which it describes a case of breast cancer in a few lines:

> In a woman, at Abdera, a carcinoma developed on the breast; its appearance was so: a bloody *ikhṓr* flowed from the nipple; once the flow stopped, she died.[24]

G.: Modern medicine confirms the diagnosis of *karkínōma* proposed by the Greek physician.[25] The case in question was probably an epithelioma. Breast cancer, with typical lymphatic spread and cachexia, is well described in another text from the Hippocratic corpus.[26] Indeed, it looks as though then, as now, it was a relatively common disease in women of a certain age. A famous patient at the end of the sixth century B.C., Queen Atossa, daughter of Cyrus and wife of Darius, is thought to have suffered from it. Herodotus tells us that she "had a tumor (*phûma*) on her breast that burst open and was slowly spreading."[27] However, the complete cure that was effected without mutilation of the breast by the physician Democedes of Croton leads one to suppose that Atossa's disease was a mastitis, not a malignant tumor. In fact Herodotus, who is always very precise in his choice of technical terms, avoids speaking of cancer in this instance and instead uses the term *phûma,* which can designate an abscess as well as a neoplasm.[28] As for the *ikhṓr,* the word signifies the sero-purulent discharge from a wound, the exudation from a sore, the juice of animal flesh, and so forth, that is, what flows when fleshy parts of the body are liquefied (to be sure, this last part of the definition is not a description of reality but the way the ancient Greeks represented it to themselves); recent philological research has shown that even in Homer the word *ikhṓr* refers to such a liquid and not to "the blood of the gods," as is commonly thought.[29]

R.: Here are three other case histories from the seventh book of the *Epidemics.* They appear to me to pose no problem whatever from the standpoint of modern medical interpretation:

In the commander of the large ship, whose right forefinger, bone and all, had been crushed by the anchor, an inflammation appeared, a dry gangrene, and some fever. He was mildly purged on the fifth day. The bouts of fever subsided then as well as the pain. A part of the finger fell off. After the seventh day, an *ikhṓr* came out properly. Afterward, he said that with his tongue he wasn't succeeding in explaining everything. Prediction: the backward spasm is on its way. The jaws began clenching, then it went to the nape of his neck; on the third day, he was totally convulsed backward, with sweating; on the sixth day after prediction, he died.[30]

The prorrhḗsis (prediction) seems clearly to mean what we usually call the prognosis, but the word *prognṓstikon* has a broader sense in Greek and in the Hippocratics in particular. In my opinion, we should avoid translating *prorrhḗsis* "prognosis," as Littré does. By inserting the words "is on its way," I am restoring in this text an expression that occurs in its parallel passage in *Epidemics,* v. Its presence here is, to my mind, guaranteed by the existence, in M and the vulgate, of an unintelligible addition to the text adopted by Littré (his text was based on V).

At Cardia, in Metrodoros's little boy, after a toothache, dry gangrene of the jaw, horrible overgrowth of flesh on the gums; there was moderate suppuration; the molars and the jawbone became detached.[31]

The man wounded in the head with a stone thrown by a Macedonian had a cut over his temple equivalent to a scratch; when struck he had seen stars and fallen. On the third day, he stopped talking; a fever, not very high; beating temples, as from mild heat; he heard nothing, was not conscious, would not stay still; perspiration on the forehead and from below the nose to the chin. He died on the fifth day.[32]

G.: The first of these three cases is a perfect description of tetanus.[33] The expression "backward spasm" is unusual, but it corresponds to the root meaning of the word in the text, *opisthotónos.* This word made its way unchanged from Greek into modern medical parlance to designate the phenomenon under discussion in this case, namely, the tonic contraction of all posterior muscles along the spine. To keep it in a modern translation of the text would imply that the original used highly technical language, which is untrue. Needless to say, the physician's prediction of opisthotonos and death is a triumph of the Hippocratic method of clinical observation.

The expression "dry gangrene" gives a good sense of the pathological reality referred to by the words *sphákelos* and *sphakelismós*. In the first history, it is an osseous gangrene of traumatic origin, and in the second, a necrosis of the facial bones caused by noma. Noma is an ulcerative and gangrenous stomatitis occurring in undernourished children. It is actually a complication of infectious diseases that cannot occur without gross weakening of the immune system. There was a time when noma was widespread in Europe, but nowadays it is never seen in the industrialized world. Three other cases of the same type are described in *Epidemics,* IV, 19, and V, 4. They should be considered an indication of the low level of infant hygiene, particularly in times of crisis (wars, food shortages).

In fact the third history, a remarkable analysis of the stages of dying in a case of intracranial hemorrhage, does introduce war. Information like this about combat with a Macedonian and, in the case that follows this one in book 7, on the death of a warrior wounded at Delos by a javelin—is it of any use in dating these texts?

R.: Books 5 and 7 were certainly composed during times of war; but war is hardly unusual in the history of Greece. Still, these two books are unusual in the Hippocratic corpus and among the *Epidemics* for reporting actual war wounds; and there is talk of battles on Delos and Datos. Several details seem to fit the historical situation that may have obtained around and about 357 B.C.[34]

Cases of Epilepsy, Pneumonia, and Amebic Dysentery

R.: The case histories we have looked at up to this point appear complete, but here is proof that other texts have been cut short:

For Anechetos's boy, the same thing: wintertime, giving himself a rubdown, he had gotten warm at the fireplace in the bathhouse and suddenly got epileptic convulsions. Once the convulsions subsided, he started looking around, not yet conscious, but the next morning, after coming to, he was again seized: a convulsive state, but not much foaming at the mouth; the third day, only some bits of speech; and the fourth, he could only express himself by movements of the tongue, his voice faltered, he was unable to speak and stopped at the beginning of words. On the fifth day, his speech was very disturbed; the convulsions came on, and he was not in possession of his senses; then, when all that ceased, his speech only barely returned to a normal state.[35]

On the sixth day, the account comes to an end in words that Littré translates as follows: "Le sixième, ayant été mis à l'abstinence de tout, décoction d'orge et boisson, il n'eut rien et ne fut pas repris" [the sixth day, put on abstinence from everything, gruel and drink, he had nothing and was not taken again]. The Greek text Littré translated is as follows: *hektaïōi aposkhoménōi pántōn kaì rhophēmátōn kaì potoû, oudén, kaì ouk éti elámbanen.* Here is the text as we now have it from M and V: *hektaíōi aposkhoménōi pántōn, kaì rhuphḗ matos kaì potoû oukéti elámbanen* (a text that Littré knew in almost exactly this form by way of C, a sixteenth-century manuscript that is almost always an exact copy of V and what he called the vulgate). This text from the oldest manuscripts has to be translated, "the sixth day, put on abstinence from everything, he did not even touch gruel or drink." And we can be sure that this text is authentic. Why? Since we can see so clearly how one text became the other. The text in M and V could in no way conclude the account. So the physicians who were using it around the end of the Middle Ages urged the copyists to tease a conclusion out of it somehow, rather than abandon the reader on some bland detail of the patient's treatment and in ignorance of the final outcome. In C attempts are still being made to clean it up. The first step was to add the word "nothing," "none of," rather than understand the construction of the verb "take" with the genitive (as in "take of the drink" = "take some/any drink"); once the word "nothing" was added, it acquired the sense of a complete sentence without a verb and was taken to mean "nothing more," that is, that the patient had no more attacks; finally, the verb "take" received a new subject, an understood subject that was no longer the patient but instead the disease itself: "(the disease) took him no more." These shorthand phrases are not at all improbable given our author's elliptical style, but it is also perfectly natural to think that the phrase originally had the form it still does in the old manuscripts. Or is it that the conclusion of the account was stated clearly enough in its first words: "For Anechetos's boy, the same thing"? But what is "the same thing"? One would be hard put to discover any specific resemblance between this account and the one that precedes it. Nor am I reluctant to believe that the expression is further proof that we do not have the whole text, or even that the account that preceded our chapter 46 in the original collection was not necessarily the one in our chapter 45.

G.: Epilepsy was of great interest to the physicians of the classical age.[36] The Hippocratic treatise the *Sacred Disease,* which was certainly earlier than this text, is specifically about epilepsy and tries to desacralize it. The case you have just cited shows how the clinical study of epileptic states was still intriguing physicians. The gaps that philological inquiry discovers in chapter 46 coincide with silences in the description from a medical standpoint and with the problems it poses. In other chapters as well, one gets the impression that the narrative has been truncated or abridged; for instance, in chapter 13.

R.: Here's a translation of it:

The shopkeeper from outside the walls, the one with pneumonia,[37] his belly let loose right away. On the fourth day, lots of sweat; the small fever seemed to have stopped; small cough, almost nothing. The fifth, sixth, seventh days, the fever took over. Sweat on the eighth. The ninth, his vomit was yellow. The tenth, his stool was compact, infrequent. Around the eleventh, relieved. Around the fourteenth, cured.[38]

G.: This history begins on the fourth day, without providing any indication of what took place previously: the editor (he was probably not in fact the one, you call the writer, who made the original reports) cut everything that had come before by using, flatly, the name of a disease, giving a diagnosis, which is against his custom, and calling the patient "the one with pneumonia." This editor is eager to get to what interests him: diarrhea in a case of pneumonia.

Likewise, in observation number 55, the usual clinical report on the beginning of the disease is lacking.

R.: So it is. Here is this particularly concise chapter:

In Cleotimos's shoemaker, whose bowels had been loose for a long time, a fever came over, and a swelling in the form of an abscess on the liver descended to the lower abdomen; bowels remained loose, then another abscess on the liver rising along the hypochondrium. He died.[39]

G.: No information on the patient's initial state; nothing about his urine; and likewise, no precise chronological information. Even the way of saying that a tumor develops "on the liver" is inconsistent with the usual form of such descriptions, in which the writer describes what he sees and not what he imagines within the body. How does he know that this tumor develops on the liver rising along the hypochondrium? Are we to imagine a dissection, or even an operation? It is assuredly not our writer's custom to make us worry about the conditions under which he knows what he is observing—he who is so careful to distinguish clearly between what he has learned by *dóxa,* by hearsay, as against what he reports as his own observation. It is hard to imagine him resorting to exceptional investigative methods without telling us about them; it is much easier to imagine that the editor meddled with the account after it was written, giving a summary of his interpretation of the case in order to cut out a part of the original that didn't interest him.

Despite the case's abbreviated presentation, a retrospective diagnosis does not seem to me impossible. Chronic diarrhea and abscess of the liver suggest one thing: amebic dysentery. The ameba in question, *Entamoeba hystolytica,* is a parasite common to all primates. It is ubiquitous and found often in Greece to this day. Sensitized by this example, I think I recognize it in several other passages in the Hippocratic corpus (particularly in *Epidemics,* III, and the *Coan Prenotions*). It even seems to me that the disease of Theodoros's wife (or daughter) in *Epidemics,* VII, 24, is nothing other than a suppurating hepatitis of amebic origin.

R.: So the signs of cuts in the descriptions in book 7 confirm our suspicion that this whole book is only the vestige of a collection of observations that was once much richer. Long after the collection was first made, perhaps even during the second century B.C.,[40] some student or teacher of medicine chose the pieces that have come down to us and threw out those he thought useless for his studies or his teaching. But he still left us with a good deal of it, so that today it interests us more than many other texts in the corpus, not only because the quality of the observations is remarkable, but also because here, the philologist is almost on virgin ground. Despite Littré's perspicacious, positive judgment, nineteenth-century scholars and our contemporaries as well have generally continued to leave book 7 outside the purview of their research. In doing so they have made themselves abiding victims of the distrust that Galen showed it long ago.

G.: My interest in this text is enlivened by the relatively pure state of the observations it contains—they are as free as possible from the general concepts (on the correlation between "meteorology" and diseases) that are telling in *Epidemics,* I and III, but muted here. At times these ancient facts seem to lie before me like a patient on a hospital bed.

Notes

Introduction

1. This discussion restates some ideas presented at the First Hippocratic Colloquium held in Strasburg, 1972. See M. D. Grmek, "La réalité nosologique au temps d'Hippocrate," in *La collection hippocratique et son rôle dans l'histoire de la médecine* (Leiden, 1975), pp. 239–55.

2. For the history of the concept of disease, see E. Berghoff, *Entwicklungsgeschichte des Krankheitsbegriffes,* 2d ed. (Vienna, 1947); W. Riese, *The Conception of Disease, Its History, Its Versions, and Its Nature* (New York, 1953); G. Canguilhem, *Le normal et le pathologique,* 3d ed. (Paris, 1966); M. D. Grmek, s.v. *Bolest* [Disease] in *Medicinska Encicklopedija,* 2d ed. (Zagreb, 1967), 1: 490–529; P. Diepgen, G. P. Gruber, and H. Schadewaldt, "Der Krankheitsbegriff, seine Geschichte und Problematik," in *Handbuch der allgemeinen Pathologie* (Berlin, 1969), 1: 1–50; D. D. Copeland, "Concepts of Disease and Diagnosis," *Persp. Biol. Med.* 20 (1977): 528–38; and A. L. Caplan, H. T. Engelhardt, and J. J. McCartney, eds., *Concepts of Health and Disease* (Reading, Mass., 1981).

3. For example, we can cite the works of Danielle and Michel Gourevitch on the representation of diseases on clay statuettes of the Hellenistic era. See especially "Terres cuites hellénistiques d'inspiration médicale au Musée du Louvre," *Presse Méd.* (1963), pp. 2751ff, and "Témoins d'argile," *Abbotempo* 1 (1965): 16–21. The authors of these remarkable studies have succeeded in identifying the following pathological states: acromegaly, achondroplasia, senile cachexia, leprosy, hydrocephalus, ascites, umbilical hernia, hemorrhoids, facial paralysis, trismus, eyelid ectropion, rhinophyma, elephantiasis of the leg, torticollis, gibbosity, and the Klippel-Feil syndrome (fusion of the cervical vertebrae). Although the material in question is later than mine, I stress the value of this research from the standpoint of method. In classical and archaic Greek art, bodily deformation appears much less frequently than in Hellenistic statuettes, but that could be due to aesthetic sensibility rather than the absence of the diseases. Nevertheless, the fact that goiters are never represented in Greek pictorial or plastic art is revealing and confirms other signs of the absence of endemic hypothyroid cretinism.

4. Such an approach is taken by C. G. Gruner in his *Morborum Antiquitates* (Breslau, 1774), and followed by A. Hirsch, *Handbuch der historisch-geographischen Pathologie,* 2d ed., 3 vols. (Stuttgart, 1881–86); J. D. Rolleston, *The History of Acute Exanthemata* (London, 1937); A. Pazzini and A. Baffoni, *Storia delle malattie* (Rome, 1950); W. R. Bett, ed., *The History and Conquest of Common Diseases* (Norman, 1954); and many others. Even the most recent authors do not stray from the beaten path: E. H. Ackerknecht, *Geschichte und Geographie der wichtigsten Krankheiten* (Stuttgart, 1963); F. Henschen, *The History and Geography of Diseases* (New York, 1966); and M. Sendrall et al., *Histoire culturelle de la maladie* (Paris, 1980).

5. M. D. Grmek, "Préliminaires d'une étude historique des maladies," *Annales*

E.S.C. 24 (1969): 1437–83; an updated German translation of this article is to be found in A. E. Imhof, ed., *Biologie des Menschen in der Geschichte* (Stuttgart, 1978), pp. 79–96. The first public use of this term was in my contribution to a discussion at a medical colloquium in London in 1966. See F.N.L. Poynter, ed., *Medicine and Culture* (London, 1969), pp. 119ff.

6. See G. Herdan, "The Mathematical Relation between the Number of Diseases and the Number of Patients in a Community," *J. Roy. Statist. Soc.,* A, 120 (1957); 320–30; C. B. Williams, *Patterns in the Balance of Nature and Related Problems in Quantitative Ecology* (London and New York, 1964); and N.T.J. Bailey, *The Mathematical Theory of Infectious Diseases and Its Applications,* 2d ed. (London, 1975); see also J. Atchison and J.A.C. Brown, *The Log Normal Distribution* (London, 1957).

7. Hesiod, *Works and Days,* ll. 109–15, trans. H. G. Evelyn-White (Cambridge and London, 1914; rept. 1977), p. 11.

8. *Works and Days,* ll. 174–82, pp. 15–17.

9. Since the Renaissance, we speak of her box, not jar.

10. Hesiod, *Works and Days,* ll. 90–100, p. 9.

11. In this regard, see R. M. Frazer, "Pandora's Diseases, *Erga* 102–104," *Gr. Rom. & Byz. Stud.* 13 (1972): 235–38, and A. Casanova, *La famiglia di Pandora. Analisi filologica dei miti di Pandora e Prometeo nella tradizione esiodea* (Florence, 1979).

12. Plato, *Republic,* 405c–406c.

13. Celsus, *Prooemium,* 4–5, trans. W. G. Spencer (London and Cambridge, 1935; rev. and rept. 1948), p. 5.

14. For constants in diagnostic procedures and in the description of symptoms, see C. Habrich, F. Marguth, and J. H. Wolf, eds., *Medizinische Diagnostik in Geschichte und Gegenwart* (Munich, 1978), especially the contributions of G. Preiser, "Diagnôsis und diagignôskein. Zum Krankheitserkennen im Corpus Hippocraticum," pp. 91–99, and R. Wittern, "Zum Krankheitserkennung in der knidischen Schrift *De internis affectionibus,*" pp. 109–19.

15. We consider a retrospective diagnosis adequate if it takes account of all the symptoms mentioned, explains the chief ones, and contradicts none of them; it should also accord with epidemiological conditions brought to light by medical historians. But such a diagnosis is not necessarily the only one possible. Most ancient clinical accounts are lacking from the viewpoint of modern medicine and could wear several labels from modern pathology. Modern diagnosis proceeds from the symptom to the fundamental lesion and its etiology, a procedure that introduces a high risk of error. On this subject, see M. Bürger, *Klinische Fehldiagnosen,* 2d ed. (Stuttgart, 1954), and J. A. Jaquez, ed., *The Diagnostic Process* (Ann Arbor, 1964). The margin of error in diagnosis in a modern, well-equipped hospital ranges from 20 to 40 percent, as confirmed by autopsy. See V. Munck, "Autopsy Finding and Clinical Diagnosis," *Acta Med. Scand.,* suppl., 266 (1955); P. Gallo and F. Nardi, "Sul divenire della patologia umana," *Recenti progressi in medicina* 61 (1976): 413–49; and L. Goldman et al., "The Value of the Autopsy in Three Medical Eras," *New Eng. Jour. Med.* 308 (1983): 1000–1005.

16. As I have shown for several diseases of the spine: M. D. Grmek, "Die Wirbelsäule im Zeitgeschehen," *Med. Welt* 25 (1974): 70–76. For a broad overview of this important feature of the natural history of diseases, one can consult R.M.J. Harper, *Evolutionary Origins of Disease* (Barnstaple, 1975). Those modern biologists who offer such an explanation of anatomical and physiological imperfections and the origin of some diseases consider it a product of Darwinism. However, it has been used since antiquity in the context of creationism. In the third century B.C. the Stoic philosopher Chrysippus posed the question "whether the diseases of man happen in accord with nature," and his answer was that "it was not part of

nature's initial design to subject man to disease, since that was totally incompatible with the author of nature, who engendered all that is good. But since he was creating and placing in the world many great things that were both useful and fitting, some drawbacks arose that were inseparable from the creation process. Such drawbacks were made by nature because of inevitable linkages." For instance, says Chrysippus, "when nature was fashioning the body of men, fineness of structure and the thing's own advantage dictated that the head be formed of very thin and minute bones. But as a result of thus heeding the advantage of the chief part, there was an exterior drawback. The head was poorly protected and easily broken by slight blows. Likewise diseases and pains came into the world along with health" (Aulus Gellius, *Noctes Atticae,* VII, 1).

17. V. Capecchi, "Quelques réflexions sur la préhistoire du pied bot congénital," *Actes du Congrès Ass. Europ. Paléopath.* (Caen, 1980).

18. *Art.,* 62, and *Genit.,* 10. For ancient ideas on the etiology of this deformity, see M. Michler, *Die Klumpfusslehre der Hippokratiker* (Wiesbaden, 1963), pp. 44–52.

19. See especially *Aer.,* 14; *De morbo sacro,* 2; *Prorrh.,* II, 5; Aristotle notes that "deformed children are born from deformed parents: the lame sire the lame, the blind the blind," *Hist. anim.,* VII, 585b.

20. See S. Ghinopoulo, *Pädiatrie in Hellas und Rom* (Jena, 1930). For the elimination of crippled children, see M. Moissidês, "Le malthusianisme dans l'Antiquité grecque," *Rev. d'Hist. de Droit* 47 (1969): 177–97.

21. Such is the view of N. Rothschild, *Ueber das Alter der Hämophilie* (Berlin, 1882). See M. Schachter, "L'histoire de l'hémophilie: Quelques précisions," *Bull. Soc. Franç. d'Hist. Méd.* 27 (1933): 101–5; H. Häfliger, *Zur Geschichte der Hämophilie, unter besonderer Berücksichtigung der Schweiz* (Basel and Stuttgart, 1969); and G.I.C. Ingram, "History of Haemophilia," *Jour. Clin. Path.* 29 (1976): 469–79.

22. Hippocrates, *Hemorrhoids* (Littré, VI, 436–44), text and translation by R. Joly (Paris, 1978). See S. Glaser, "Hippocrates and Proctology," *Proc. Roy. Acad. Med.* 62 (1969): 380ff.

23. See E. D. Baumann, "De Diabete Antiquo," *Janus* 37 (1933): 257–70; H. Schadewaldt, *Die Geschichte des Diabetes* (Frankfurt, 1971); and C. L. Gemmill, "The Greek Concept of Diabetes," *Bull. New York Acad. Med.* 48 (1972): 1033–36.

24. F. Merke, "Die Eiszeit als primordiale Ursache des endemischen Kropfes," *Schweiz. Med. Wschr.* 95 (1965): 1183–92.

25. For example, see W. Doerr, K. Kohn, and H. H. Jansen, *Gestaltwandel klassischer Krankheitsbilder* (Berlin, 1957); M. Moser, ed., *Diseases of Medical Progress* (Springfield, 1964); and M. Howe, *World Geography of Human Disease* (New York, 1977).

26. C. Nicolle, *Destin des maladies infectieuses* (Paris, 1933). See also R. Dubos, "The Evolution of Infectious Diseases in the Course of History," *Canad. Med. Assoc. Jour.* 79 (1958): 445–51, and A. Cockburn, *The Evolution and Eradication of Infectious Diseases* (Baltimore, 1963).

27. See J. du Boulay, *Portrait of a Greek Mountain Village* (Oxford, 1974).

28. R. and E. Blum, *Health and Healing in Rural Greece* (Stanford, 1965).

29. *Acut.,* 5, 1 (Littré, II, 226; Joly, 37).

30. This word is omitted in most editions, notably in Joly's. It is the reading of the oldest manuscript of this text (*Marcianus gr.,* 269).

31. *Acut.,* 5, 1–2 (Littré, II, 226), after the translation by R. Joly (Paris, 1972), pp. 37–38. The translation is the same as his except in the names of the diseases, where I have preferred to transliterate rather than translate. Although his rendering of *pleurîtis* as "pleurisy" is defensible, that of *phrenîtis* as "encephalitis" I consider an anachronism.

32. Plato, *Alcibiades,* II, 139e.

33. *Epid.*, I and III. See below, chapter 12.

34. *Aer.*, 3–4 (Littré, II, 14–22), from *Hippocrates,* vol. I, trans. W.H.S. Jones (Cambridge and London, 1923; rept. 1948), pp. 75–78.

35. Hierocles and Philagrios, *Philogelos,* no. 94. See the now standard edition of A. Thierfelder (Munich, 1968).

36. M. D. Grmek, "Histoire des recherches sur les relations entre le génie et la maladie," *Rev. Hist. Sci.* 15 (1962): 51–68. For bibliography, see J. B. Gilbert and G. E. Mestler, *Disease and Destiny: A Bibliography of Medical References to the Famous* (London, 1962).

37. To be sure, there are critical situations when the health of a military leader or a political figure can have important historical consequences. As for the princes and the great political figures of the past, one cannot be too careful in forming a judgment on the bearing their diseases may have had on history. Usually the literature on this subject is too anecdotal. In France, it has found a wordy spokesman in Dr. Auguste Cabanès, who tried to justify his method (*L'histoire éclairée par la clinique*) [Paris, 1921]). But it was impossible for him to go beyond the stage of research into "curiosities" and the "medical indiscretions of history."

38. Emile Littré had defined historical pathology as "a still embryonic science whose development will be one of the intellectual duties of the twentieth century."

39. The bibliography on epidemics and history is immense. There are more than 100 titles on the "Great Plague."

Chapter One: Literary Reflections of Pathological Reality

1. In particular, E. Rosner, "Terminologische Hinweise auf die Herkunft der frühen griechischen Medizin," in *Medizingeschichte in unserer Zeit (Artelt Festschrift)* (Stuttgart, 1971), pp. 1–22. See also R. Stromberg, *Griechische Wortstudien: Untersuchungen zur Benennung von Tieren, Pflanzen, Körperteilen und Krankheiten* (Göteborg, 1944); J. Pokorny, *Indogermanisches etymologisches Wörterbuch* (Bern and Munich, 1948–1969); H. Frisk, *Griechisches etymologisches Wörterbuch* (Heidelberg, 1954–72); P. Chantraine, *Dictionnaire étymologique de la langue grecque: Histoire des mots* (Paris, 1968–80).

2. An important list of *nomina morborum* is given by Galen, *Meth. med.*, II, 2 (Kuhn, X, 81–85). For a more complete thesaurus of these terms, see J. E. Hebenstreit, *Exegesis nominum Graecorum quae morbos definiunt* (Leipzig, 1751).

3. To be sure, the origin of several terms in pathology is unknown. Rosner, "Hinweise" (above, n. 1), pp. 14ff., mentions among doubtful cases *hubós* 'hunchback' and *dothiēn* (abscess on the body surface; perhaps a Mediterranean term derived from viticulture, like Latin *furunculus*); according to him, the word *mílphōsis* 'loss of eyelashes' is non–Indo-European. Moreover, the terms *ánthrax* and *eskhára* have been thought to be of Egyptian origin, but even if the theory is correct, originally neither term had anything to do with pathology (*ánthrax* is first used only in the sense "burning coal"and *eskhára* in the sense "hearth, fireplace"). See P. V. Ernštedt, *Egipetskie zaimstvovaniya v grečeskom yazyke* (Moscow and Leningrad, 1953), pp. 21–24, 26ff.

4. Rosner, "Hinweise" (above, n. 1), p. 14.

5. For the overall picture, see J. Chadwick, *The Decipherment of Linear B* (Cambridge, 1958), and S. Hiller and O. Panagl, *Die frühgriechischen Texte aus mykenischer Zeit* (Darmstadt, 1976). Of fundamental importance is the work of M. Ventris and J. Chadwick, *Documents in Mycenaean Greek,* 2d ed. (Cambridge, 1973); see also L. R. Palmer, *The Interpretation of Mycenaean Greek Texts* (Oxford, 1963).

6. See W. H. Hein, "Die Bedeutung der Entzifferung des Linear B für die

Arzneimittelgeschichte," *Pharm. Zeitung* 106 (1961): 1145–48, and C.P.W. Warren, "Some Aspects of Medicine in the Greek Bronze Age," *Medical History* 14 (1970): 364–77.

7. Very probably the word *i-ja-te,* which occurs on PY Eq 146 in a nonmedical context, represents the Mycenaean form of the Homeric term *iatēr* 'doctor.' See Ventris and Chadwick, *Mycenaean Greek* (above, n. 5), p. 123, and C. Gallavotti and A. Sacconi, *Inscriptiones Pyliae ad Mycenaeam aetatem pertinentes* (Rome, 1961), p. 66. Palmer, *Mycenaean Greek Texts* (above, no. 5), p. 422, accepts the identification as well.

8. Landau, *Mykenisch-griechische Personennamen* (Göteborg, 1958), esp. the chapter "Körperliche Eigenschaften," pp. 190–93.

9. Tablet reference: KN Dx 6059. See ibid., p. 192.

10. Unless stated otherwise, the translations cited and the references given are from Richmond Lattimore, trans., *The Iliad of Homer* (Chicago, 1951) and *The Odyssey of Homer* (New York, 1965).

11. For an overall perspective on the Homeric epics, see F. Robert, *Homère* (Paris, 1950); F. Buffière, *Les mythes d'Homère et la pensée grecque* (Paris, 1956); W. Schadewaldt, *Von Homers Welt und Werk,* 3d ed. (Stuttgart, 1959); A.J.B. Wace and F. H. Stubbings, *A Companion to Homer* (London, 1963); Ch. Mugler, *Les origines de la science grecque chez Homère: L'homme et l'univers physique* (Paris, 1963).

12. For medical themes in the Homeric poems, see especially J. F. Malgaigne, *Etudes sur l'anatomie et la physiologie d'Homère* (Paris, 1842); Ch. Daremberg, *La médecine dans Homère* (Paris, 1865); O. Körner, *Die ärtzlichen Kenntnisse in Ilias und Odyssee* (Munich, 1929); A. Botto-Micca, *Omero medico: Medici, ferite e medicina in Omero* (Viterbo, 1930); H. Buess, "Mediko-chirurgisches in Ilias und Odyssee," *Dtsch. Med. Wschr.* 81 (1956): 1818–22; H. Sigerist, *History of Medicine,* vol. 2, *Early Greek, Hindu, and Persian Medicine* (New York, 1961); K. Mitropoulos, "Homerou Iatrika," *Platon* 14 (1962): 145–76; A. Albarracin Teulón, *Homero y la medicina* (Madrid, 1970); and A.H.M. Kerkhoff, "La médicine dans Homère: Une bibliographie," *Janus* 62 (1975): 43–49.

13. Körner, *Die ärtzlichen Kenntnisse* (above, n. 12), pp. 3ff. See also T. D. Seymour, *Life in the Homeric Age* (New York, 1963), and M. I. Finley, *The World of Odysseus* (New York, 1954; rev. ed. 1965).

14. In addition to the publications cited above, n. 12, see also O. Braumüller, *Krankheit und Tod bei Homer* (Berlin, 1879); W. H. Friedrich, *Verwundung und Tod in der Ilias* (Göttingen, 1956); F. M. Pontani, *La morte degli eroi* (Florence, 1975); and B. Moreux, "La nuit, l'ombre et la mort chez Homère," *Phoenix* 25 (1971): 95–105.

15. It is difficult, even impossible, to translate the Homeric terms *psukhḗ,* thumós, and *phrénes* correctly into a modern language. Much ink has been spilled in quest of their meaning. From the viewpoint of the history of ideas, it is useful to read what Daremberg, *La médecine* (above, n. 12), pp. 53–59, thought in the last century and what B. Snell writes nowadays; see *Die Entdeckung des Geistes: Studien zur Entstehung des europäischen Denkens bei den Griechen* (Hamburg, 1948; rev. ed. Göttingen, 1975); B. Simon, *Mind and Madness in Ancient Greece* (London, 1978); and especially M. McDonald, "Terms for Life in Homer," *Trans. St. Coll. Phys. Philadelphia* (1982), pp. 26–58.

16. For example, see the description of the death of Patroclus (*Iliad* 16.805–63), of Lykaon (21.49–85, 95–127), and of Hector (22.319–66).

17. *Iliad* 16.480–507.

18. *Iliad* 5.584–89.

19. *Iliad* 22.365–67.

20. *Odyssey* 11.218–22. This is our translation, which differs from the standard

French translation by V. Bérard (Paris, 1955–56) and from that of Lattimore in the translation of *thumós* (Bérard: "âme"; Lattimore: "spirit") and *psukhḗ* (Bérard: "ombre"). It should also be stressed that the word *înes* designates fibrous tissues, chiefly tendons but also nerves and ligaments. Bérard's translation of "fury of fire" as "énergie de la brûlante flamme" is unacceptable to me for its anachronistic connotations.

21. *Iliad* 9.408–9.

22. See Daremberg, *La médecine* (above, n. 12), pp. 57ff., and A. Nehring, "Homer's Descriptions of Syncopes," *CP* 42 (1947): 106–21.

23. *Iliad* 5.696, 5.309, and 14.418.

24. *Iliad* 23.466; *Odyssey* 24.345.

25. *Odyssey* 10.557–60.

26. *Odyssey* 3.276–83.

27. Cf. *Odyssey* 17.251.

28. *Iliad* 24.612. For Artemis's other interventions, see *Iliad* 6.428 and 21.483, as well as *Odyssey* 20:61.

29. The term *loimós,* usually translated "plague," occurs in *Iliad* 1.61. The epidemiological content of this Homeric narrative is obscured by the mythologizing of reality. See Heraclitus, *Quaestiones Homericae,* 7; F. Buffière, *Les mythes d'Homère et la pensée grecque* (Paris, 1956), pp. 130 and 195–99; F. Berheim and A. A. Zenner, "The Sminthian Apollo and the Epidemics among the Achaeans at Troy," *Trans. Amer. Philol. Assoc.* 108 (1978): 11–14.

30. *Odyssey* 11.198–203. Again, our translation, since we differ from Lattimore (and, for that matter, Bérard) in the passage concerning the consumptive disease.

31. *Iliad* 6.211.

32. *Odyssey* 4.611.

33. In the *Iliad* and the *Odyssey* there is some evidence about bodily needs, food, and so on, but despite what is often alleged, no true preoccupation with hygiene. See L. Moulé, "L'hygiène dans les poèmes homériques," *Bull. Soc. Franç. Hist. Méd.* 17 (1923): 350–77, and R. Lorenz, *Beiträge zur Hygiene bei Homer* (Munich, 1976).

34. Hesiod, *Works and Days,* ll. 695–705, in *Hesiod, Homeric Hymns, and Homerica,* trans. H. G. Evelyn-White (Cambridge and London, 1914; rept. 1977). Eugenic exhortations abound in Theognis, the sixth-century poet from Megara, who invokes the wisdom of animal husbandry to justify his preference, in a wife, of race (*génos*) over wealth: see especially ll. 183–92. Not all the poetry ascribed to Theognis is agreed to be as old as the sixth century, however.

35. *Odyssey* 7.112–21, 8.245–49.

36. *Odyssey* 15.405–11.

37. Herodotus, *The Histories,* trans. A. de Sélincourt (Baltimore, 1954; rept. 1968), IX, 122, p. 599.

38. In particular, *Airs, Waters, and Places.* For an excellent analysis of the birth of this medical-geographic notion, see W. D. Smith, "Physiology in the Homeric Poems," *TAPA* 97 (1966): 547–56.

39. *Iliad* 1.247–48.

40. *Iliad* 2.216–20.

41. See below, chapter 2, n. 88.

42. *Iliad* 2.266.

43. *Odyssey* 19.246–48; *Odyssey* 2.15–16; *Iliad* 10.316; *Iliad* 1.594 and 18.394–405; *Odyssey* 8.307. Cf. Körner, *Die ärztlichen Kenntnisse* (above, n. 12), p. 17.

44. *Iliad* 2.594–600. The blinding of the lyre-player Thamyris is figured on an Attic hydria of the fifth century B.C. (Oxford, Ashmolean Museum no. 530). Greek

vase-painting also illustrates the blinding of other legendary personages: the kings Phineas and Oedipus (see, for instance, British Museum E291, E302, and G105).

45. *Odyssey* 10.492ff.

46. *Odyssey* 8.63–64. Other blind singers are mentioned by Hesiod and Euripides.

47. Cf. Maximus of Tyre, *Diss.,* 38, 1, and Porphyry, *Quaest. Hom. ad Od.,* ed. H. Schrader (Leipzig, 1882), II, 72.

48. *Hymn to Apollo,* 172. Cf. Thucydides, III, 104.

49. Proclus, *Vita Homeri,* 16–18, *apud* A. Severyns, *Recherches sur la Chrestomathie de Proclos* (Paris, 1963), 4:68. According to modern studies, *homēros* is an institutional term signifying any member of a group characterized by solidarity. Thence it came to designate a hostage responsible for others, a guide for a blind person, and even, perhaps, a singer interpreting an author's works. See L. Deroy, "Le nom d'Homère," *Antiquité Classique* 41 (1972): 427–39.

50. According to [Plutarch,] *De vita Homeri,* 1, 2 (C. Müller, *Frag. Hist. Graec.,* I, 227).

51. Plato, *Phaedrus,* 243a.

52. Hellenistic and Roman copies of the bust of Homer are kept in the archaeological museumsin Rome, Naples, Florence, Modena, and Bonn. The Louvre has a Hellenistic terra cotta replica of it (D1549). See R. and E. Boehringer, *Homer: Bildnisse und Nachweise* (Breslau, 1939), and G.M.A. Richter, *Portraits of the Greeks* (London, 1965), pp. 45–56. On the iconography of Stesichorus, the old blind hunchback, see R. Heidenreich, "Eine Dresdener Mantelstatue," *Arch. Anz.* (1972), pp. 570–83.

53. Cicero, *Tusculan Disputations,* V, 39, 114.

54. Proclus, *Vita Homeri,* 47–49, *apud* Severyns, *Recherches* (above, n. 49), 4: 72.

55. Lucian, *Verae historiae,* II, 20.

56. Dio Chrysostom, *Orat.,* 36.

57. See in particular *Suda* s.v. *Homēros.*

58. Pausanias, *Description of Greece,* IV, 33, 7, and II, 33, 3.

59. Heraclides Ponticus, *De rebus publicis,* 32, in C. Müller, *Frag. Hist. Graec.,* II, 222.

60. [Herodotus], *Vita Homeri,* 7.

61. Among modern publications on this subject, there are an anonymous article entitled "La cécité d'Homère," *Chron. Med.* 12 (1909): 680, and the studies of A. Esser, "Augenkrankheiten berühmter Persönlichkeiten in der Antike," *Med. Welt* 14 (1940): 894, and *Das Antlitz der Blindheit in der Antike,* 2d ed. (Leiden, 1961), p. 10.

62. For the identification of the Egyptian term *nehat* in *Papyrus Ebers* with trachoma, see B. Ebbell, *Alt-ägyptische Bezeichnungen für Krankheiten und Symptome* (Oslo, 1938), p. 26. It is generally accepted that this form of granular conjunctivitis was a scourge of Pharaonic Egypt. See G. Lefebvre, *Essai sur la médecine égyptienne de l'époque pharaonique* (Paris, 1956), pp. 74ff. The presence of trachoma in Greece is attested from the first appearance of texts in Greek on eye disease. The Hippocratic treatise *Vision* recommends some reasonable and relatively simple measures for the treatment of granulations on the eyelids (*De visu,* 4; Littré, IX, 156). The most recent editor of the text, Robert Joly, is surely correct to state, in his commentary on this chapter, that it "undoubtedly deals with the granulations of trachoma" and "is very judicious in its information and advice" (Hippocrates, *Des lieux dans l'homme* [Paris, 1978], p. 170). This work probably dates from the beginning of the fourth century B.C., and the disease in question was not considered a novelty in Greece at that time. See also M. Meyerhof, *The History of Trachoma Treatment in Antiquity and during the Arabic Middle Age* (Cairo, 1936).

63. See the famous analysis in Snell, *Die Entdeckung* (above, n. 14), pp. 13–18.

64. H. J. von Schumann, "Phänomenologische und psychoanalytische Untersuchung der Homerischen Träume: Ein Beitrag zur Klärung der umstrittenen Blindheit des Dichters," *Acta Psychother.* 3 (1955): 205–19.

65. According to the famous British politician William Ewart Gladstone, whose argument was taken up and developed by the ophthalmologist Hugo Magnus and the philologist Lazarus Geiger, the Homeric Greeks had not attained the perfect color perception characteristic of modern man. This strange idea was the result of an erroneous application of Darwinism and some ill-founded philological reasoning. See W. E. Gladstone, *Studies on Homer and the Homeric Age* (Oxford, 1858), 3:457–96. With much conviction but little success, W. Schultz defended the hypothesis that the Greeks were color-blind, that is, hereditarily blind in the blue and green portion of the spectrum (*Das Farbenempfindungs-system der Hellenen* [Leipzig, 1904]). For the refutation, see Körner, *Die ärtzlichen Kenntisse* (above, n. 12), pp. 52ff., and especially the study by M. H. Marganne, "Le système chromatique dans le corpus aristotélicien," *Etudes classiques* 46 (1978): 185–203.

66. He listed the following localizations: dome of the skull 6, forehead 7, temple 3, auricular region 8, orbital region 1, nose 1, mouth 1, jaws 2, throat 6, nape of neck 10, decapitation 2, clavicular region 4, sides of the chest 1, front of the chest 9, upper chest 1, mammary region 10, heart 1, hypochondrium at the level of the diaphragm 1, middle of belly 5, flank and lower belly 10, umbilical region 2, groin 1, liver 4, back 9, rear shoulder 3, front shoulder 9, shoulder removal 1, arm removal 1, arm 2, forearm 5, wrist 2, buttock 3, hip 1, thigh 3, knee 2, back of the knee 1, calf 1, ankle 1 (Daremberg, *La médecine* [above, n. 12], pp. 76–77).

67. Instead of Daremberg's 140 wounds whose placement is clearly specified, Frölich counted 147.

68. H. Frölich, *Die Militärmedizin Homer's* (Stuttgart, 1879), pp. 56–60.

69. See especially Körner, *Die ärtzlichen Kenntnisse* (above, n. 12), pp. 86ff.; Botto-Micca, *Omero medico* (above, n. 12), pp. 59–63; T. Mildner, *Chirurgie und Wundbehandlung vor Troja* (Traunstein, 1962). For the most recent and most complete list of wounds, classed topographically from head to toe, see A. Albarracin Teulón, "La cirugia homerica," *Episteme* 5 (1971): 83–97.

70. *Iliad* 5.297–317, 431–70, 512–18.

71. *Iliad* 16.738–42.

72. *Iliad* 5.584.

73. See Seymour, *Life in the Homeric Age* (above, n. 13), pp. 620ff., and Albarracin Teulón, "La cirugia" (above, n. 69), pp. 95ff.

74. *Iliad* 16.345–50.

75. *Iliad* 17.293–98.

76. *Iliad* 16.411–14 and 569–80.

77. *Iliad* 11.349–60.

78. *Iliad* 5.309–10.

79. Probably this is why Frölich, wrongly, did not include it in his table. If we also include the case of Euryalos, discussed below, and Eumelos's accident during a chariot race (*Iliad* 23.391–97), the *Iliad* contains three descriptions of head wounds without fatal consequences, only one of which is due to warfare.

80. Daremberg (*La médecine* [above, n. 12], pp. 60–62) made this diagnosis long ago.

81. *Iliad* 23.687–98.

82. See Daremberg, *La médicine* (above, n. 12), pp. 62–64; Botto-Micca, *Omero medico* (above, n. 12), p. 60; and above all Albarracin Teulón, "La cirugia" (above, n. 69), pp. 89ff., and E. Prim, "Hals, Nase und Ohr in Ilias und Odysee," *Zeitschr. Laryng. Rhin. Otol.* 43 (1964): 330–43. In Frölich's statistical table, decapitations and

some wounds in which the weapon reaches the skull by way of the neck are classed as head wounds. This is why the number of neck wounds in Frölich is relatively smaller than in statistics compiled by more recent historians.

83. *Iliad* 22.324–29. In connection with Hector's mortal wound, it is noteworthy that previously, in single combat with Ajax, he had a narrow escape: of all the epic heroes, he is the only certain survivor of a neck wound, a superficial cut that made his black blood ooze up (*Iliad* 7.260–63).

84. Carotid hemorrhage is surely the cause of sudden death when the weapon reaches the neck "by jaw and ear" (*Iliad* 16.606ff.; cf. also 13.177–81 and 671ff.). Antilochus kills Thoon straightaway by cutting clean through "the entire blood vessel / which runs all the way up the back till it reaches the neck" (*Iliad* 13.545–49). Here the Homeric anatomy is caught in error, since there is no important vessel running along the back of the trunk. This can only be a lesion of the carotid (or, possibly, the brachio-cephalic trunk artery or the internal jugular vein), with the "dorsal vessel" being in that case, clearly, the aorta. An imaginary dorsal vessel is also mentioned in the Hippocratic corpus. Körner and, more recently, Kudlien defend the empirical basis of this vascular lesion in Homer, against Friedrich who speaks of "Scheinrealismus" in regard to it. See F. Kudlien, "Zum Thema Homer und die Medizin," *Rh. Mus.* 108 (1965): 293–99.

85. *Iliad* 20.480–83. See also 14.49 and 11.145–47, 259–61.

86. A particularly well-aimed and forceful spearcast could skirt the shield and pierce the bronze or iron mail, as in the case of the Trojan Alcathoos (*Iliad* 13.438–44). Stabbed in the middle of his chest by a spear, "he cried out then, a great cry, broken, the spear in him, / and fell, thunderously, and the spear in his heart was stuck fast / but the heart was panting still and beating to shake the butt end / of the spear." Although the penetration of the spear's point through the coat of mail is plausible, the enormous power of the heart to transmit vibrations through the heavy spear haft belongs to the poet's imagination.

87. Cf. *Iliad* 11.577–79; 13.411ff.; 17.347–49; 20.460–72.

88. See L. Schönbauer, "Die Chirurgie bei Homer," *Neuburgers Festschrift* (Vienna, 1948), pp. 436–39.

89. Daremberg, *La médecine* (above, n. 12), pp. 69ff.; Albarracin Teulón, "La cirugia," (above, n. 69), pp. 91ff.

90. *Iliad* 11.380–82.

91. *Iliad* 5.537–40; see also 5.615–17, 16.463–65, and 17.516–24.

92. *Iliad* 13.567–75.

93. *Iliad* 4.527–31.

94. *Iliad* 16.81ff.

95. *Iliad* 5.65–68.

96. Such was the opinion, long ago, of Malgaigne, *Etudes* (above, n. 12), p. 17. The *Iliad* contains the description of a wound with exactly the same trajectory for a different weapon, an arrow (13.650–54). One of the descriptions could be an imitation of the other.

97. See Daremberg, *La médecine* (above, n. 12), pp. 70–72, and Albarracin Teulón, "La cirugia," (above, n. 69), pp. 86ff. and 92ff. For wounds of upper limbs, see especially H. Lipschutz, "Hand, Arm, and Shoulder Trauma in the *Iliad*," *Surgery* 51 (1963): 833–36.

98. *Iliad* 8.324–29. Our translation, which differs from that of Lattimore in the interpretation of *par' ômon, kairión,* and *neurên* (1. 328). In book 22 Homer uses an analogous, but not identical, expression to describe the place where Achilles wounds Hector mortally, where the collarbone separates the shoulder from the throat. The wound of Teucer is more lateral than Hector's, a fact that agrees completely with the pathological results of both wounds.

99. *Iliad* 5.73–75.

100. *Iliad* 11.267–68.

101. *Iliad* 11.396–98.

102. Already in A. Brendel, *De Homero Medico* (Wittenberg, 1700); then, for example, the works of Frölich (above, n. 68) and A. Floquet, *Homère médecin*, thesis (Paris, 1912).

103. Körner, *Die ärtzlichen Kenntnisse* (above, n. 12), pp. 88–89.

104. Körner's arguments were refuted by E. Fuld, "Quelques remarques sur les sciences naturelles et médicales dans Homère," *Rev. étud. hom.* 2 (1932): 10–17.

105. See Frölich, *Die Militärmedizin* (above, n. 68), pp. 61–68; Seymour, *Life in the Homeric Age* (above, n. 13), pp. 623ff.; and especially O. Schmiedeberg, *Ueber die Pharmaka in der Ilias und Odysee* (Strasburg, 1918), as well as G. Majno, *The Healing Hand* (Cambridge, Mass., 1975), pp. 141–52.

106. It is true that the *Iliad* speaks of the ulcerated sore on the leg of Philoctetes, which arose as a chronic complication from snakebite, but the treatment of it is described in a summary by Proclus of the *Little Iliad*, not in the great epics. In any case, this wound is of a magical character.

107. For instance, *Iliad* 4.190, where Agamemnon tells Menelaus that a doctor will palpate and medicate his cut, a superficial, belt-high wound of the trunk. Strangely, this word never occurs in the *Odyssey.*

108. See chapter 4, p. 125.

109. The Greek word *traûma* is not attested before Herodotus. It designated a bodily wound but also a material loss.

110. I use this term in a restricted sense, of the permanent alteration of a function in the absence of an ongoing pathological process.

111. To be consulted in this connection area A. Semelaigne, *Etudes historiques sur l'aliénation mentale dans l'Antiquité* (Paris, 1869); R. Ganter, "Psychopathologisches aus Homer," *Münch. Med. Wschr.* 72 (1925): 1924–26; J. L. Heiberg, *Geisteskrankheiten im klassischen Altertum* (Berlin and Leipzig, 1927); J. Mattes, *Der Wahnsinn im griechischen Mythos und in der Dichtung* (Heidelberg, 1970); and especially Simon, *Mind and Madness* (above, n. 15). We leave aside a long list of writers from S. Freud to O. Rank and G. Devereux who took the ancient literary texts as points of departure for psychoanalytical interpretations.

112. Cf. B. Lincoln, "Homeric *lússa*: Wolfish Rage," *IF* 80–81 (1975–76): 98–105. For the antiquity of rabies, see Aristotle, *Hist. anim.*, 604a, and a vase in Boston, Museum of Fine Arts no. 00.346.

113. *Iliad* 17.695. See also *Odyssey* 4.704, where the stupefaction of Penelope is the subject.

114. *Iliad* 5.10, 241.

115. See E. D. Baumann, "De asthmate antiquo," *Janus* 38 (1934): 139–62, and H. Schadewaldt, *Geschichte der Allergie,* vol. 2, *Heufieber und Asthma bronchiale* (Munich, 1980), pp. 188–94.

116. *Iliad* 8.181–83 and 9.243.

117. *Odyssey* 14.480–502 and 17.22–25.

118. *Odyssey* 5.453–57 (slightly modified from Lattimore).

119. *Odyssey* 9.410–12. According to one recent commentator, the passage alludes to cholera (Seymour, *Life in the Homeric Age* [above, n. 13], p. 626). There is no real basis for this diagnosis.

120. Celsus, *De medicina,* praefatio, 3. For the distinction in archaic Greek thought between external wounds amenable to medical treatment and internal diseases of divine origin, see F. Kudlien, *Der Beginn des medizinischen Denkens bei den Griechen* (Zurich and Stuttgart, 1967), pp. 89–91.

121. *Iliad* 1.10.

122. See P. Lain Entralgo, "Die Krankheit in den Dichtungen Homers," in *Heilkunde in geschichtlicher Entscheidung* (Salzburg, 1950), pp. 35–47; Sigerist, *History of Medicine* (above, n. 12), 2: 20–24; and G. Preiser, *Allgemeine Krankheitsbezeichnungen im Corpus Hippocraticum* (Berlin and New York, 1976), pp. 89–91.

123. See H. Oldelehr, *Seekrankheit in der Antike* (Düsseldorf, 1977), pp. 14ff.

124. *Odyssey* 14.252–56.

125. *Thesmophoriazusae,* 882.

126. Semonides, *Women,* 54. See Oldelehr, *Seekrankheit* (above, n. 123), pp. 1–3. The modern word "nausea" is derived, by the intermediation of classical Latin, from the word *nautía* (root *naûs* 'ship').

127. Daremberg, *La médecine* (above, n. 12), p. 86.

128. *Odyssey* 5.394–97.

129. *Iliad* 13.666–70.

130. *Odyssey* 11.201.

131. Hesychius identifies the Homeric *tēkedṓn* with *phthísis* in later authors, and *Suda* as well as Pollux puts the two terms in the same class. See B. Meinecke, "Consumption (Tuberculosis) in Classical Antiquity," *Ann. Med. Hist.* 9 (1927): 379–402.

132. Sophocles, *Antigone,* 819.

133. Euripides, *Alcestis,* 204 and 236.

134. *Iliad* 22.31.

135. Brendel, *De Homero Medico* (above, n. 102).

136. Daremberg, *La médicine* (above, n. 12), pp. 91ff.

137. See W.H.S. Jones, *Malaria: A Neglected Factor in the History of Greece and Rome* (Cambridge, 1907), pp. 23ff.

138. F. Robert, *Homère* (Paris, 1950), p. 208.

139. Hesiod, *Works and Days,* 496–99, trans. H. G. Evelyn-White (Cambridge, 1914; rept. 1977). See also the critical edition and commentary on this text by M. L. West, *Hesiod's Works and Days* (Oxford, 1978).

140. See W. Schiller, "Das Hungerödem bei Hesiod," *Janus* 25 (1921): 37–44.

141. *Works and Days* 240–45, 533–36.

142. Plutarch, *Banquet of the Seven Sages,* ch. 14.

143. With the sole exception of certain words occurring in the Pseudo-Hesiodic fragments on the Proetides.

144. Jones, *Malaria* (above, n. 137), p. 25.

145. Hesiod, *Works and Days,* 100–104; see also West *ad loc.*

146. It is a process that apparently begins in the framework of a magico-religious conception of the world and is enabled by the integration of magical causality into the natural order of things. That much was well shown by H. Fränkel, *Dichtung und Philosophie des frühen Griechentums,* 2d ed. (Munich, 1962), p. 130, and developed by G. Preiser, *Krankheitsbezeichnungen* (above, n. 122), pp. 91ff. I cannot subscribe to the opinion of U. von Wilamowitz-Moellendorf, who thought that Hesiod "rejects all attempts to reduce disease to natural causes" in the lines cited (*Erga* [Berlin, 1928], p. 53), or of G. Lanata, according to whom Hesiod's diseases are "silent figures utterly immune to natural causality" (*Medicina magica e religiosa popolare in Grecia fino all'età di Ippocrate* [Rome, 1967], p. 30). The distinction between natural and magical causality should not be retrojected by our analysis into a system of thought in which precisely the confusion between the two was of fundamental importance.

147. Alcmaeon, fr. 4 (Diels-Kranz); text transmitted by Aetios Doxographos, *Placita,* V, 30, 1. See H. Diels and W. Kranz, *Fragmente der Vorsokratiker,* 6th ed. (Berlin, 1951), 1:215ff. This central passage is actually a reconstruction by Diels from several variants. The difference between the short and the long versions is far from

negligible, since in the former *monarkhía* signifies the domination of a single quality, while in the latter it signifies the domination of one quality over its opposite. Contrary to accepted opinion, I believe that *isonomía* signifies equilibrium among all the qualities and not equality within each pair of opposed qualities.

148. In this context, the word *hierós* should not be understood in the sense of a link with the cult of a divinity but in that of participation in supranatural and mysterious phenomena.

149. See Preiser, *Krankheitsbezeichnungen* (above, n. 122), pp. 47, 51, 82–85, and 87–89.

150. *De morbo sacro,* I, 1–3 and 10 (Littré, VI, 352–53). This translation differs from those of Littré, Daremberg, and Joly. It is based on the critical edition of the Greek text by H. Grensemann, *Die hippokratische Schrift "Ueber die heilige Krankheit"* (Berlin, 1968), p. 60.

151. See Lanata, *Medicina magica* (above, n. 146), and above all the masterly monograph of O. Temkin, *The Falling Sickness,* 2d ed. (Baltimore, 1971).

152. *De morbo sacro,* II, 4 (Littré, VI, 364; Grensemann, 68).

153. The Hippocratic writer militating against this name hasn't yet at his disposal another technical term for the disease. See Grensemann, *Die hippokratische Schrift* (above, n. 150), pp. 5ff.

154. Herodotus, III, 33, trans. A. de Sélincourt (Baltimore, 1954; rept. 1968). Cf. T. S. Brown, "Herodotus' Portrait of Cambyses," *Historia* 31 (1982): 387–403.

155. Heraclitus, fr. 46 D-K (Diels and Kranz, *Vorsokratiker* [above, n. 147], I: 161).

156. See M. Marcovich, *Heraclitus* (Merida, 1967), p. 575.

157. Diogenes Laertius, *Vitae philosophorum,* IX, 3, after the translation by R. Genaille (Paris, 1965), 2: 163.

158. Ibid., IX, 5.

159. I cite him from Archilochus, *Fragments,* ed. F. Lasserre and A. Bonnard (Paris, 1958)(L-B). I have also used E. Diehl, *Anthologia Lyrica Graeca,* fasc. III, 3d. ed. rev. E. Beutler (Leipzig, 1952) (D); M. Treu, *Archilochos, griechisch und deutsch* (Munich, 1959); and J. Tarditi, *Archilochus* (Rome, 1968). See also the article by J. N. Dambassis, *Epet. Etair. Kyklad. Melet.* (1968), pp. 672–81.

160. Archilochus, fr. 93 L-B (60 D).

161. Archilochus, fr. 236 L-B (from Philoxenos, *Anecd. Oxyr.*, I, 164).

162. C. Daremberg, *Etat de la médecine entre Homère et Hippocrate* (Paris, 1869), p. 5.

163. See F. Lasserre, *Les epodes d'Archiloque* (Paris, 1950).

164. *Schol. Theocr.*, II, 48.

165. *Pap. Oxy.*, 2313, frs. 13 and 14.

166. Archilochus, fr. 27 L-B (42 D).

167. A. Bonnard in Archilochus, *Fragments* (Paris, 1958), pp. 9ff.

168. The poet says (fr. 105 L-B) that he lived off "those figs" and food "gotten from the sea."

169. Daremberg, *Etat de la médicine* (above, n. 162), pp. 5ff.

170. Archilochus, fr. 198 L-B.

171. Archilochus, fr. 200 L-B.

172. Archilochus, fr. 85 L-B, and see Jones, *Malaria* (above, n. 137), p. 26.

173. Archilochus, frs. 245, 249, and 266 L-B.

174. T. Reinach and A. Puech, *Alcée; Sapho* (Paris, 1938). See especially the famous poem of Sappho (fr. 2) that was translated and commented on by Boileau in his *Traité du sublime*.

175. See, for example, Anacreon, fr. 428 Page; Theocritus, 30, 30; Prodikos, fr. 84 B 7 D-K. Among the medical writers who thought of love as a disease, the most significant are Soranus, Galen, and Oribasius. For secondary sources on this sub-

ject, see H. Crohns, "Zur Geschichte der Liebe als Krankheit," *Arch. Kult. Gesch.* 3 (1905): 66–86; M. M. Mesulam, "The Diagnosis of Love-sickness: Experimental Psychopathology without a Polygraph," *Psychophysiology* 9 (1972): 546–51; M. Clavolella, *Malattia d'amore dall'Antichità al Medioevo* (Rome, 1976); and A. Giedke, *Die Liebeskrankheit in der Geschichte der Medizin,* diss. (Düsseldorf, 1983).

176. Even in Homer, wine "clouds one's reason." For the signs of drunkenness, see *Odyssey* 14.466–69 and 21.293–98. The effect of wine on the soul is expounded on at great length and with remarkable literary erudition by Galen in his treatise *Quod animi mores*. See J. O. Leibowitz, "Acute Alcoholism in Ancient Greek and Roman Medicine," *Brit. Jour. Addiction* 62 (1967): 83–86, and G. Preiser, "Wein im Urteil der griechischen Antike," in G. Völger, ed., *Rausch und Realität* (Cologne, 1981), pp. 296–303.

177. Theognis, *Poèmes élégiaques,* ed. and trans. J. Carrière (Paris, 1975), II. 211ff.

178. *Bulletin épigraphique,* no. 385 (1978). See C. Meillier, "Un cas médical dans une inscription funéraire," *Zschr. Pap. Epig.* 38 (1980): 98.

179. Diogenes Laertius, 1, 81. See Reinach and Puech, *Alcée; Sapho* (above, n. 174), 190.

180. O. Masson, *Les fragments du poète Hipponax* (Paris, 1962). For example, see frs. 32 and 33.

181. Hipponax, fr. 36 Masson (29 D). Later, Aristophanes exploits the theme of the blindness of the god of wealth.

182. Hipponax, frs. 10, 34, 59, 12, and 26 Masson (11, 25, 55, 15, and 39 D).

183. Hipponax, fr. 118 Masson (X + XII D). The text is in *Pap. Oxyr.* 2176. See Masson, *Hipponax* (above, n. 180), pp. 84–86 and 162–66.

184. Daremberg, *Etat de la médecine* (above, n. 162), p. 6.

185. *Pap. Oxyr.* 2174, fr. 4.

186. Hipponax, fr. 73 Masson (1 + 71 D).

187. Masson, *Hipponax* (above, n. 180), p. 143.

188. "A slave's head is never straight, it is always bent and sits on a slanting nape. Rose or hyacinth never sprang from squill" (Theognis, *Poèmes élégiaques,* 1, ll. 535–37).

189. Theognis, *Poèmes* (above, n. 177), II. 173ff. The term *ēpíalos* designates fever in general or, according to Hesychius, in particular the shudder that precedes its onset. It is also the name of an evil spirit that causes nightmares. According to Jones, *Malaria* (above, n. 137), pp. 27ff., the word is associated with attacks of malaria.

190. Theognis, *Poèmes* (above, n. 177), 1, ll. 1122ff.

191. E. Benveniste, "La doctrine médicale des Indo-Européens," *RHR* 130 (1945): 5–12.

192. Pindar, *Pythian,* 3, 47–53, from *The Odes of Pindar,* trans. R. Lattimore (Chicago, 1947; rept. 1959), pp. 53ff.

193. See. D. Brandenburg, *Medizinisches bei Herodot* (Berlin, 1973); A. Corlieu, *Etude médicale sur la retraite des Dix-Mille* (Paris, 1878); and H. Cosson, *Etude sur les allusions médicales chez Xénophon,* thesis (Paris, 1966).

Chapter Two: Paleopathology

1. See M. A. Ruffer, *Studies in the Palaeopathology of Egypt,* ed. R. L. Moodie (Chicago, 1921). This Anglo-French doctor gave a new meaning to the neologism proposed in 1892 by R. W. Shufeldt to denote the study of pathological clues in animal fossil remains (cf. "Notes on Palaeopathology," *Popular Science Monthly* 42 (1892); 679–84). A pioneer in paleopathological research on Egyptian bones and

mummies, Ruffer was professor of bacteriology in Cairo and a world-famous epidemiologist. He stayed in Greece during World War I, where he participated in the organization of the health services of the Allied armies. He was interested in Greek paleopathology but published nothing on the subject because his life was abruptly cut short: returning by ship from Salonika, he died on the open sea, the victim of a torpedo attack. For the story of his life, see W. E. Swinton, "Sir Marc Armand Ruffer, One of the First Palaeopathologists," *Canadian Medical Association Journal* 124 (1981): 1388–92.

2. J. F. Esper, *Ausführliche Nachricht von neuentdeckten Zoolithen unbekannter vierfüssiger Thiere* (Nuremberg, 1774). For the beginnings of paleopathology, see H. E. Sigerist, *History of Medicine,* vol. 1, *Primitive and Archaic Medicine* (New York, 1951), pp. 38–42.

3. R. L. Moodie, *Palaeopathology: An Introduction to the Study of Ancient Evidences of Disease* (Urbana, 1923); L. Pales, *Paléopathologie et pathologie comparative* (Paris, 1930). This work, a doctoral thesis in medicine, is of exceptional scope and significance.

4. Pales *Paléopathologie,* p. 4. Indeed, Pales uses paleopathological evidence to draw conclusions about the etiology and pathogenesis of certain diseases (notably tooth decay, spondylitis, temporo-maxillary osteoarthritis, and cranial osteoporosis).

5. See the update and bibliography published by Sigerist, *History of Medicine* (above, n. 2), pp. 45–101 and 532–39. For European paleopathology, see especially G. Wilkie, *Die Heilkunst in der europäischen Vorzeit* (Leipzig, 1936).

6. E. H. Ackerknecht, "Palaeopathology," in A. L. Kroeber, *Anthropology Today* (Chicago, 1953), p. 120.

7. For an overview, see M. D. Grmek, "Metodi nuovi nello studio delle malattie antiche," in *Annuario della Enciclopedia della Scienza (Scienza e Tecnica 1975)* (Milan, 1975), pp. 71–84. See also L. von Karolyi, "Palaeopathologie (Aufgaben, Objekte, Methodik, gegenwärtiger Stand)," *Sudhoffs, Archiv* 54 (1970): 398–422. Among recent handbooks, worth recommending are D. Brothwell and A. T. Sandison, eds., *Diseases in Antiquity* (Springfield, 1967); R. T. Steinbock, *Paleopathological Diagnosis and Interpretation* (Springfield, 1976); and D. J. Ortner and W. G. Putschar, *Identification of Pathological Conditions in Human Skeletal Remains* (Washington, D.C., 1981).

8. H. A. Harris, *Bone Growth in Health and Disease* (London, 1933), and C. Wells, "Les lignes de Harris et les maladies anciennes," *Scalpel* 177 (1964): 665–71.

9. See P. Stastny, "HL-A Antigens in Mummified pre-Columbian Tissues," *Science* 183 (1974): 864. For HLA associations with disease, see J. Dausset and A. Svejgaard, *HLA and Disease* (Copenhagen, 1980), and D. C. James, "HLA-B 27 in Clinical Medicine: Historical Reflection on the Discovery of the Disease Association," *Brit. Jour. of Rheumatology* 22, no. 4, suppl. 2 (1983): 20–24.

10. See A. Savicki et al., "Presence of Salmonella Antigens in Feces from a Peruvian Mummy," *Bulletin of the New York Academy of Medicine* 52 (1976): 805–13.

11. See J. Jansen and H. J. Over, "Observation on Helminth Infections in a Roman Army Camp," *Proc. First Intern. Congress Parasit.* (Rome, 1966), 2: 791; A. W. Pike, "Recovery of Helminth Eggs from Archaeological Excavations," *Nature* (London) 219 (1968): 303ff.; P. J. Wilke and H. J. Hall, *Analysis of Ancient Feces: A Discussion and Annotated Bibliography* (Berkeley, 1975).

12. See A. MacKie et al., "Lead Concentration in Bones from Roman York," *Jour. Archaeol. Soc.* 2 (1975): 235–37; J. E. Ericson et al., "Skeletal Concentration of Lead in Ancient Peruvians," *New England Journal of Medicine* 300 (1979): 946–51.

13. See J. L. Angel, "The Bases of Paleodemography" *American Journal of Physical Anthropology* 30 (1969): 427–37, and "Paleodemography and Evolution," ibid. 31 (1969): 343–54.

14. V. Møller-Christensen, "Osteo-archaeology as a Medico-historical Auxiliary Science," *Med. History* 17 (1973): 411–18. I prefer the term "osteoarchaeology" to "paleo-osteology," which has also been proposed for this field.

15. H. Schliemann, *Mycènes,* trans. J. Girardin (Paris, 1879), p. 68.

16. See E. H. Acknerknecht, *Rudolf Virchow* (Stuttgart, 1957), pp. 187–91.

17. See H. Schliemann, *Ilios, ville et pays des Troyens* (Paris, 1885). The book's preface is by Virchow. In several places, it testifies to the active participation of Virchow in Schliemann's work and to the friendship that united them. An appendix (pp. 964–70) contains a medical report by Virchow, "Pratique médicale en Troade (1879)." The discussion revolves around malaria, tuberculosis, and injured workers. Two of Virchow's observations deserve comparison with clinical descriptions in the Hippocratic corpus: malarial spleen enlargement in children and geophagy in an anemic child. For Virchow's Mediterranean trip, see also his own accounts in *Zschr. für Ethnologie* 11 (1879): 179ff., 204–17, 254–81.

18. R. Virchow, *Alttrojanische Gräber und Schädel* (Berlin, 1882).

19. R. Virchow, "Ueber alte Schädel von Assos und Cypern," *Abhandl. K. Preuss. Akad. Wiss. zu Berlin: Phys.-math. Cl.* 24 (1884), 11, pp. 1–55.

20. R. Virchow, "Schliemann's letzte Ausgrabung," *Sitz.-Ber. K. Preuss. Akad. Wiss. zu Berlin* (1891), pp. 819–28; R. Virchow, "Ueber griechische Schädel aus alter und neuer Zeit, und über einen Schädel von Menidi der für den des Sophokles gehalten wird," *Sitz.-Ber. K. Preuss. Akad. Wiss. zu Berlin* (1893), pp. 677–700.

21. C. Stephanos, "Grèce: Géographie médicale," in *Dictionnaire encyclopédique des sciences médicales,* ed. A. Dechambre (Paris, 1884), 4th series, 10: 363–581.

22. Ibid., pp. 432–33.

23. Ibid., pp. 433ff. In modern skulls cranial capacity varies greatly, with the average at about 1500 (±250) cc. It should be stressed that despite numerous dedicated attempts, no correlation has ever been established between the volume or weight of the brain (anatomical data that are easily measured and tied to cranial capacity) and its intellectual potential or individual intelligence or the level of cultural development (themselves theoretical values that are difficult if not impossible to determine and quantify). The brainpan of fossil *Homo sapiens* is essentially unchanged in modern man. If Kant had an enormous cranial capacity (1740 cc.), it is also true that Leibniz's was not more than 1422 cc., which is at the average Virchow established for male skulls in Greece. According to recent anthropological measurements, the cranial capacity of the ancient Greeks is about the same as that of other European peoples. G. de Morsier (*Essai sur la genèse de la civilisation scientifique actuelle* [Geneva, 1965]) has tried hard to explain the cultural progress of humanity by brain mutation. According to him, in the course of 30,000 years, *Homo sapiens* has undergone "two evolutionary cerebral mutations," the first taking place "around 6,000 years ago in a well-defined region of the Middle East" (the "crescent of Neolithic civilization") and the second "500 years ago at the end of the 15th and the beginning of the 16th century in a well-defined territory of central and western Europe" (this is the "circle of scientific mutation"). G. de Morsier has had the incredible effrontery to devise a "biological" history of the progress of human thought in which the "Greek miracle" is erased and short-circuited by a pseudo-scientific trick.

24. I. G. Koumaris, "Sur quelques variations des os des crânes grecs anciens," *Anthropologie* 29 (1918): 29–36.

25. H. E. Sigerist, *History of Medicine,* vol. 1 (above, n. 2).

26. C. M. Fürst, *Zur Anthropologie der prähistorichen Griechen in Argolis* (Lund, 1930) (*Lunds Univ. Årsskrift,* n.s., sec. 2, 26, no. 8 [1930]), and *Zur Kenntnis der Anthropologie der prähistorischen Bevölkerung der Insel Cypern* (Lund, 1933) (*Lunds Univ. Årsskrift,* n.s., sec. 2, 29, no. 6 [1933]).

27. E. Breitinger, "Die Skelette aus den submykenischen Gräbern," in W. Kraiter and K. Kubler, *Kerameikos,* vol. 1, *Die Nekropolen des 12. bis 10. Jahrhunderts* (Berlin, 1939), pp. 223–61.

28. See especially J. L. Angel, "Skeletal Changes in Ancient Greece," *American Journal of Physical Anthropology,* n.s., 4 (1946): 69–97, and "Some Problems in Interpretation of Greek Skeletal Material: Disease, Posture, and Microevolution," ibid., n.s., 12 (1954): 284ff.

29. Cf. J. L. Angel, "A Racial Analysis of the Ancient Greeks," *American Journal of Physical Anthropology,* n.s., 2, no. 4 (1944). See also his work on the population of Lerna (n. 31, below), p.6.

30. Angel, "Skeletal Changes" (above, no. 28), p. 69.

31. The principal publications of John L. Angel containing osteoarchaeological analysis, listed by site, are "Classical Olynthians," in D. M. Robinson, *Necrolynthia: Excavations at Olynthus* (Baltimore, 1942), pt. II, appendix, pp. 211–40; "Skeletal Material from Attica," *Hesperia* 14 (1945): 279–363; "Troy: The Human Remains,"in C. W. Blegen, *Troy* (Princeton, 1951); "The Human Remains from Khirokitia," in P. Dikaios, *Khirokitia* (London, 1953), pp. 416–30; "Human Biological Changes in Ancient Greece, with Special Reference to Lerna," *Yearbook Amer. Phil. Soc.* (1957), pp. 266–70; "Appendix on the Early Helladic Skulls from Aghios Kosmas," in G. E. Mylonas, *Aghios Kosmas* (Princeton, 1959), p. 169–79; "Human Skeletal Remains at Karataş," *American Journal of Archaeology* 70 (1966): 255–57, and 72 (1968): 260–64, and 74 (1970): 253–59 (henceforth Angel, "Karataş"), "Human Skeletal Material from Franchthi Cave," *Hesperia* 38 (1969): 380–81; *The People of Lerna: Analysis of a Prehistoric Aegean Population* (Princeton and Washington, D.C., 1971); "Early Neolithic Skeletons from Catal Hüyük: Demography and Pathology," *Anatolian Studies* 21 (1971): 77–98; "Late Bronze Age Cypriotes from Bamboula," in J. L. Benson, *Bamboula* (Philadelphia, 1972); "Human Skeletons from Grave Circles at Mycenae," in G. E. Mylonas, *O Tafikos Kyklos B tou Mykenou* (Athens, 1973), pp. 379–97; "Early Neolithic People of Nea Nikomedea," in E. Schwidetzky, *Die Anfänge des Neolithikums vom Orient bis Nordeuropa* (Cologne, 1973), pp. 103–12; "Early Bronze Age Karataş, People and Their Cemeteries," *American Journal of Archaeology* 80 (1976): 385–91 (henceforth Angel, "Karataş People"); "Ancient Skeletons from Asine," in S. Dietz, *Asine* II, *Excavations East of the Acropolis 1970–1974* (Copenhagen, 1982), fasc. 1, pp. 105–38. This scholar's bibliography was published in the *American Journal of Physical Anthropology* 51 (1979): 509–16.

32. R. P. Charles, "Etude anthropologique des nécropoles d'Argos, contribution à l'étude des populations de la Grèce antique," *Bull. Corresp. Hellén.* 82 (1958): 258–313 (henceforth Charles, "Argos I"); *Etude anthropologique des nécropoles d'Argos, contribution à l'étude des populations de la Grèce antique* (Paris, 1963) (henceforth Charles, *Argos* II); Anthropologie archéologique de la Crète (Paris, 1965); J. Dastugue, "Grotte de Kitsos (Lavrion). IV. Les ossements humains pathologiques," *Bull. Corresp. Hellén.* 98 (1974): 749–54; J. Dastugue and H. Duday, "Les ossements humains pathologiques," in N. Lambert, ed., *La grotte préhistorique de Kitsos* (Paris, 1981). The other publications will be cited as they come up in the subsequent discussion.

33. J. L. Angel, "Patterns of Fractures from Neolithic to Modern Times," *Anthrop. Kozlemenyek* (Budapest) 18 (1974): 9–18.

34. See T. W. Jacobsen, "17,000 Years of Greek Prehistory," *Scientific American* 234 (1976): 76–87, esp. pp. 81ff., and Angel, "Franchthi Cave" (above, n. 31), pp. 380ff. In the Petralona Cave in Chalcidice the skull of a fossil hominid was discovered that is at least 200,000 years old. It is well preserved, thanks to a thin layer of

stalagmite around it, and it hasn't a trace of disease or wounds. It does not concern us at the moment, though, since the specimen in question is not *Homo sapiens.*

35. Angel, "Karataş, People" (above, n. 31), p. 385.

36. Angel, "Mycenae" (above, n. 31), pp. 380–82.

37. Angel, *People of Lerna* (above, n. 31), pp. 42 and 91, pl. 2.

38. Ibid., pp. 58ff. and pls. 13 and 22.

39. See the whole treatise *De capitis vulneribus* (Littré, III, 182–260) and in particular chs. 8 and 16. It is instructive to consult the commentaries of J. E. Petrequin, *Chirurgie d'Hippocrate* (Paris, 1877), 1: 412–558, and the modern medico-historical analyses of E. Iversen, "Wounds in the Head in Egyptian and Hippocratic Medicine," in the festschrift volume *Studia orientalia Johannis Pedersen dicata* (Copenhagen, 1953), pp. 163–71, and of E. S. Gurdjian, *Head Injury from Antiquity to the Present* (Springfield, 1973).

40. Charles, *Argos* II (above, n. 32), pp. 35 and 66, pl. 10, fig. 4.

41. Angel, "Skeletal Material from Attica" (above, n. 31), pp. 301 and 303, fig. 6.

42. Virchow, "Assos und Cypern" (above, n. 19), pp. 25, 26.

43. See the works of Angel on Lerna, Çatal Hüyük, and Karataş. On the skull from Asine, see Fürst, *Argolis,* (above, n.-26), p. 123, pl. 8, and Angel, "Ancient Skeletons from Asine" (above, n. 31), p. 109. P. M. Fischer noted a fracture of the lower jaw that healed remarkably well on a Bronze Age Cypriot skull from Trypes near Dromolaxia (*Opuscula Atheniensia* 13 [1980]: 140).

44. Angel, *People of Lerna,* p. 61, and "Human Biological Changes," p. 269 (both above, n. 31).

45. Angel, "Çatal Hüyük," p. 91 and pl. 4, and "Ancient Skeletons from Asine," p. 109, fig. 15, (both above, n. 31).

46. See A.J.B. Wace, *Mycenae: An Archaeological History and Guide* (Princeton, 1949), p. 117, and Angel, "Mycenae" (above, n. 31), p. 381.

47. *Fract.*, 1 (Littré, III, 414), trans. E. T. Withington, *Hippocrates* (London and Cambridge, 1928; rept. 1948), 3: 95.

48. For classical knowledge of the treatment of fractures, see E. J. Gurlt, *Geschichte der Chirurgie und ihrer Ausübung* (Berlin, 1898); A. Benedetti, *Traumatologia al tempo di Ippocrate* (Rome, 1969); A. Roselli, *La chirurgia ippocratica* (Florence, 1975).

49. Angel, "Çatal Hüyük (above, n. 31), pp. 91, 94; pl. 4.

50. Angel, *People of Lerna* (above, n. 31), pp. 44, 91; pl. 26.

51. Breitinger, "Die Skelette" (above, n. 27), p. 236.

52. Angel, *People of Lerna* (above, n. 31), p. 42. In Corinth, there was a local hero in the protogeometric period (ninth century B.C.), a man of about 45, tall, broad-shouldered, with a fractured right hand, bad teeth, and marked degenerative joint disease (E. Vermeule, *Aspects of Death in Early Greek Art and Poetry* [Berkeley, 1977], pp. 206ff.).

53. Angel, "Çatal Hüyük" (above, n. 31), pp. 91, 94; pl. 4.

54. Fürst, *Argolis* (above, n. 26), p. 123, fig. 52.

55. E. Vermeule, *Greece in the Bronze Age* (Chicago and London, 1954), p. 9, pl. 1.

56. Angel, "Mycenae" (above, n. 31), p. 384.

57. Angel, *People of Lerna* (above, n. 31), p. 44.

58. Angel, "Çatal Hüyük" (above, n. 31), p. 94 and pl. 4.

59. Angel, *People of Lerna* (above, n. 31), pp. 50, 92; pl. 26.

60. Ibid., p. 58. I will take up the paleopathology of purulent inflammations in chapter 4, which is devoted to the historical reality concerning pyogenic microbes and the sequelae of nonspecific infections.

61. See especially E. Guiard, *La trépanation crânienne chez les Néolithiques et chez les Primitifs modernes* (Paris, 1930); Sigerist, *History of Medicine* (above, n. 2), 1: 101–13; J. Dastugue, "Le diagnostic des trépanations empiriques du crâne," in *Travaux et documents du Centre de paléoanthropologie et de paléopathologie* (Lyon, 1975), t. 2, vol. 2, pp. 71–79.

62. Angel, "Çatal Hüyük" (above, n. 31), p. 91.

63. A. D. Tsouros, "Ereuna sé proïstoriká pathologiká ostâ: tó kranío toû Arkhámōn," *Anthropos* (Athens) 1, no. 1 (1974): 55–60.

64. Y. Sakellarakis and E. Sapouna-Sakellaraki, "Drama of Death in a Minoan Temple," *National Geographic Magazine* 159 (1981): 205–22.

65. Charles, *Argos II* (above, n. 32), pp. 67–69.

66. *De capitis vulneribus* (Littré, III, (182–260), especially chs. 11, 30, and 31. See J. E. Petrequin, "Recherches historiques sur l'opération du trépan chez les anciens et en particular sur la trépanation dans la contusion du crâne d'après Hippocrate," *Bull. Soc. Chir. de Paris* (1867), pp. 155ff.

67. Angel, "Karataş," p. 256, and "Karataş People," p. 385 (both above, n. 31).

68. Angel, *People of Lerna* (above, n. 31), pp. 43ff. and pl. 5.

69. Angel, "Mycenae" (above, n. 31), pp. 380, 391; pl. 248.

70. Angel, "Ancient Skeletons from Asine" (above, n. 1), p. 109.

71. Charles, "Argos I" (above, n. 32), pp. 310ff.

72. L. Münter, *Das Grab des Sophokles* (Athens, 1893).

73. The spokesman for Münter's opponents was P. Wolters. For a resumé of the first polemics, see R. Virchow, "Ueber den vermeintlichen Sophokles-Schädel und über die Grenze zwischen Anthropologie und Archäologie," *Zschr. für Ethnol.* (*Verh. Berl. Ges. Anthrop.*) 26 (1894): 117–25. Münter's hypothesis has not found its way into the handbooks and reference books.

74. Virchow, "Ueber griechische Schädel" (above, n. 20), pp. 687–95.

75. The anecdote of the gluttonous high liver who is killed by a fatal grape, which is too symbolic to be true, is also told of Anacreon and Pietro Aretino. As for Sophocles, the *Vita* tells two other versions of his demise: he perished while reading from one of his tragedies—a long tirade made him lose his breath—or he died from joy on learning that he had won a literary contest. None of the three versions stands up to historical criticism. The only thing known from a reliable source is that he "died well, without having to suffer indignity" (Phrynichus, fr. 31). On this subject see J. Labarbe, "La mort tragique de Sophocle," *Bull. Classe Lettr. Acad. Roy. Belgique* 55 (1969): 265–92.

76. See M. S. Gazzaniga, *The Bisected Brain* (New York, 1970); R. W. Sperry, "Lateral Specialization in the Surgically Separated Hemispheres," in F. O. Schmitt and F. G. Worden, eds., *The Neurosciences: Third Study Program* (Cambridge, Mass., 1974), pp. 5–19.

77. Plutarch, *Pericles,* 3, 3–4, in *The Rise and Fall of Athens: Nine Greek Lives by Plutarch,* trans. lan Scott-Kilvert (Baltimore, 1960; rept. 1966), p. 167.

78. T. Fay, "The Head: A Neurosurgeon's Analysis of a Great Stone Portrait," *Expedition* (Philadelphia) 1, no. 4 (1958–59): 12–18.

79. L. A. Schneider, *Asymmetrie griechischer Köpfe vom 5. Jh. bis zum Hellenismus* (Wiesbaden, 1973).

80. The main arguments in favor of it are in F. Studniczka, "Das Bildnis Menanders," *Neue Jahrb. klass. Altertumsgesch.* 21 (1918): 1–31. For a more recent and more complete study, see M. Bieber, *The History of the Greek and Roman Theater* (London, 1961), pp. 82–92. Other scholars have thought they recognized the head as Virgil's, but it is hardly likely that the statue is of Roman origin.

81. *Suda,* s.v. *Menandros*; Phaedrus, *Fabulae Aesopiae,* V, 1, 12; Alciphron, *Epistulae,* IV, 18, 4. See S. Charitonidis, L. Kahil, and R. Ginouvès, *Les mosaïques de la*

maison de Ménandre à Mytilène (Berne, 1970) (*Antike Kunst,* Beiheft 6), pp. 27–28 and pl. 1; J. I. Bungarten, *Menanders und Glykeras Brief bei Alkiphron,* thesis (Bonn, 1967).

82. Angel, "Skeletal Changes" (above, n. 28), pp. 75 and 81–82; *People of Lerna* (above, n. 31), pp. 87ff.

83. Angel, "Mycenae" (above, n. 31), pp. 380ff.

84. N. G. Gejvall and F. Henschen, "Two Late Skeletons with Malformations and Close Family Relationship from Ancient Corinth," *Opuscula Atheniensia* 8 (1968): 179–93.

85. See G. Bräuer and R. Fricke, "Zur Phänomenologie osteoporotischer Veränderungen bei Bestehen systemischen hämatologischer Affektionen," *Homo* 31 (1980): 198–211.

86. Louvre Museum D 1178. See D. and M. Gourevitch, "Terres cuites hellénistiques d'inspiration médicale au Musée du Louvre," *Presse Méd.* (1963), p. 2751, fig. 3, and M. D. Grmek, *La médecine grecque classique* (Memento thérapeutique Latéma 1974) (Paris, 1974), pl. 9. The syndrome was described for the first time in *Nouvelle iconographie de la Salpêtrière* 25 (1912): 280–85. For the typical appearance of those so handicapped and accompanying disorders, see P. C. Windle-Taylor et al., *Ann. Otol. Rhin. Lar.* 90 (1981): 210–16.

87. For the archaeological description of this figurine, see A. N. Stillwell, *Corinth,* vol. 15, pt. 2, *The Potter's Quarter: The Terracottas* (Princeton, 1952), p. 143. For medical commentary, see T. Skoog, "A Head from Ancient Corinth," *Bull. Hist. Dent.* 19 (1971): 50–54.

88. For the osteoarchaeological diagnosis of the two cases, see C. S. Bartsocas, "Stature of Greeks of the Pylos Area during the Second Millennium B.C.," *Hippocrates Magazine* 2, no. 2 (1977): 157–60, and "An Introduction to Ancient Greek Genetics and Skeletal Dysplasias," *Progr. Clin. Biol. Res.* 104 (1982): 3–13. The relevant text of the *Iliad* concerning Thersites is cited in chapter 1, above, p. 24. For its medical interpretation, see C. S. Bartsocas, "Kleidokraniaki dysostōsis par' Omirō" *Arch. Hellin. Paid. Hetair.* 36 (1973): 107–9.

89. Charles, "Argos I" (above, n. 32), pp. 280 and 311.

90. Angel, "Skeletal Changes" (above, n. 28), p. 82.

91. Angel, *People of Lerna* (above, n. 31), pp. 52, 55, and 92, pl. 24.

92. Hippocrates, *Art.*, 51–59 and 62. See P. Bade, "Hippokrates und die angeborene Hüftverrenkung," *Acta chir. Scand.* 67 (1930): 34–42, and M. Michler, *Die Klumpfusslehre der Hippokratiker: Eine Untersuchung von De articulis* (Wiesbaden, 1963) (*Sudhoffs Arch. Gesch. Med., suppl. 2*). Dislocation of the hip is well depicted on an Etruscan or Hellenistic bronze statuette (Klejman Collection, New York). Beginning in the classical period, clubfoot appears on Greek vases in representations of Hephaestus's return to Olympus (Vienna 3577; Athens NM 664; Rhodes 10,711; Florence 4209; etc.).

93. For detailed documentation on this problem, see M. D. Grmek, "La paléopathologie des tumeurs osseuses malignes," *Histoire des sciences médicales* 9, no. 1 (1975–76): 21–50.

94. Specimen no. 1474 in the National Archaeological Museum in Florence. The case was presented by L. Capasso to the Third European Congress of the Paleopathological Association at Caen (1980).

95. Several scholars have incorrectly supposed that they recognized cancer on certain fragmentary reliefs and marble busts and on terra cotta figurines (e.g., Louvre D 586 and D 1146; Metropolitan Museum C.S. 1434). Some took for a tumor what is just a fruit being held close to the chest. The absence of a breast on an ancient bust is insufficient evidence for the diagnosis of an amputation performed as treatment for cancer, since it could well be a mythological representation

(an Amazon) or mammary aplasia. The only cases in which a cancer diagnosis should be taken seriously remain a Hellenistic marble bust with a damaged left breast and a terra cotta statuette from Smyrna with deep ulceration of the mammary region. Both cases were brought to light by Theodor Meyer-Steineg, who tells us that the second was kept at the Museum of the Evangelical School of Smyrna. The photographs Meyer-Steineg took of these two objects have often been reproduced, but I do not know where the objects themselves are now. The same is true for the clay head of a boy with a globular tumor on his right eye. Obtained by Meyer-Steineg on the island of Cos, it has not been seen since the last world war. See T. Meyer-Steineg, *Darstellungen normaler und krankhaft veränderter Körperteile an antiken Weihgaben* (Jena, 1912), and E. Holländer, *Plastik und Medizin* (Stuttgart, 1912). According to G. Uschmann (1970), what remains of Meyer-Steineg's collection has been given to the Institute of Pathology at Jena. The Museum of Tarentum has a figurine that, judging by photographs, resembles the one published by Meyer-Steineg and suggests a diagnosis of sarcoma of the eye socket or of retinoblastoma. See A. Galeone, "Stati patologici nell'arte greca," *Atti Mem. Accad. Stor. Arte San.* 4 (1938): 332, fig. 3.

96. Angel, *People of Lerna* (above, n. 31), pp. 51, 89, and 92; pl. 24.

97. Gout is mentioned twenty-two times in the Hippocratic treatises and appears in them as an everyday disease whose nature and symptoms need no account. The oldest case of gout known to history is that of Hieron, tyrant of Syracuse (died ca. 466 B.C.), as mentioned in Pindar *Pyth,* I, 90.

98. *Alcibiades,* 2, 140a.

99. Elliott Smith and F. Wood Jones, "The Pathological Report," *Bull. Arch. Survey of Nubia* 2 (1910).

100. C. Wells, "A Palaeopathological Rarity in a Skeleton of Roman Date," *Medical History* 17 (1973): 399ff.

101. Although Pliny the Elder (*Natural History,* XXVI, 100) considers gout in Italy "an ailment of foreign origins," i.e., a poisonous gift from the Greeks, for Lucian (*Pro merc. cond.*, 31 and 39) its spread is due to the Romanization of the world, and for Seneca (*Epist.,* 95) it is the result of moral decay, especially gluttony.

102. C. Wells, "Prehistoric and Historical Changes in Nutritional Diseases and Associated Conditions," *Progress in Food and Nutrition Science* no. 11 (1975): 729–79, esp. pp. 758–60.

103. See M. M. Boross and J. Nemeskéri, "Ein bronzezeitlicher Nierenstein aus Ungarn," *Homo* 14 (1963): 149ff. Paolo Orsi, former director of the Archaeological Museum in Syracuse, has said in a private letter that he has seen, during one of the many excavations in Sicily, a large urinary stone. This statement, disclosed by W. Ebstein (*Janus* 5 [1900]: 333), is extremely vague, lacking any indication of the location or the date of the tomb in question.

104. Angel, "Mycenae" (above, n. 31), p. 383.

105. J. L. Angel, "Skeletal Material from Attica" (above, n. 31), pp. 308ff.

106. Herodotus, IX, 83.

107. Plutarch, *Pyrrhus,* 3; Pliny, *Natural History,* VII, 69; Tzetzes, *Chil.*, III, 950; and Valerius Maximus, I, 8, 12. See C. S. Bartsocas, "Complete Absence of the Permanent Dentition: An Autosomal Recessive Disorder," *American Journal of Medical Genetics* 6 (1980): 333ff. A similar malformation exists in a skull from Monte Cassino. On a mandible from Mycenaean Pylos there is a smooth bony surface where the teeth should be, except for one canine tooth and the socket of the other. Cf. S. Marinatos,"Pylos Excavations," *Praktika tis en Athenais Archaiol. Etair.* (1966), pp. 195–209.

108. Herodotus, VII, 117. The same author (I, 68) relates the discovery in Tegea of the bones of a man who measured 7 cubits (10 feet!). Considered the remains of

Orestes, they must have been fossilized bones of a giant animal from the Pleistocene. See G. Huxley, "Bones for Orestes," *Greek, Roman, and Byzantine Studies* 20 (1979): 145–48.

109. A typical example is the statuette in the Louvre numbered D 1176. The overall appearance of the face is characteristic of the disease. See, on this subject, M. and D. Gourevitch, "Terres cuites" (above, n. 86), p. 2751, fig. 2, and Grmek, *La médecine grecque* (above, n. 86), pl. 8. I am not convinced of the diagnosis of acromegaly for most of the terra cotta figurines cited as examples of its artistic representation. Likewise, I do not agree with Gerald D. Hart, who believes he has identified this disease on coins struck with the image of Ptolemy I Soter ("The Diagnosis of Diseases from Ancient Coins," *Archaeology* 26 [1973]: 127).

110. See the publications of F. Regnault, P. Richer, H. Meige, A. Galeone, D. and M. Gourevitch, C. Wells, and C. S. Bartsocas. In collaboration with Danielle Gourevitch, I am preparing a critical reexamination of Greco-Roman pathological iconography.

111. H. Grimm, "Ueber Rachitis und Rachitis-Verdachtsfälle im ur- und frühgeschichtlichen Material," *Zschr. ges. Hyg.* 18 (1972): 451–55, and Wells, "Prehistoric and Historical Changes" (above, n. 102), pp. 756ff.

112. W. Ebstein, "Ueber das Vorkommen der Rachitis im Alterthum," *Janus* 5 (1900): 332–37.

113. G. Regöly-Mérei, "Paleopathological Examination of Skeletal Finds in the Roman Period and Description of Diseases in Greek and Roman Medical Texts," *Medical History in Hungary* (1970), pp. 58ff.

114. In a study of pathological traits in the work of statuette sculptors from Asia Minor, Jean-Martin Charcot and Paul Richer have drawn attention to heads with "the most diverse kinds of skull deformations," which are "placed on the deformed torsos of rickets-sufferers" (*Les difformes et les malades dans l'art* [Paris, 1889], p. 9). Specifically, they mention a statuette of a young man "endowed with the thinnest legs" and a "chest rounded like a hunchback." The terra cotta in question is Louvre D 573. It was found in Pergamum, and Simone Besques's catalogue (3:96) dates it to the second century B.C. I have examined it and believe that the diagnosis of rickets is only one among many possibilities. The "rickety" appearance of a Hellenistic terra cotta in the collection of P. M. de la Charlonie is more convincing (Musée Archéologique Municipal de Laon, inv. no. 37.376). The diagnosis of rickets for an Etruscan votive torso from Lucera is not compelling, despite E. Greco, "La patologia nella antichità classica attraverso lo studio degli ex-voto anatomici," *Il Policlinico* 67, sez. prat. (1960): p. 1248.

115. For instance, see Soranos, *Gyn.*, I, 112, and II, 43–45, and Galen, *De san. tuenda*, 7.

116. Herodotus, III, 12, trans. A de Sélincourt (Baltimore, 1954; rept. 1968), p. 178. The battle of Papremis took place in 460 B.C. at the time of the Egyptian uprising against the Persian satrap Achaimenes.

117. Actually, following Coray, Littré, and Hirsch, some philologists and historians associate certain passages in the Hippocratic corpus with scurvy (especially *Int.*, 46, and *Epid.*, VII, 47), but that interpretation must be forcefully rejected. First of all, what nineteenth-century scholars understand by "scurvy" does not completely overlap with current notions of the vitamin C deficiency disease from a clinical or etiological point of view. An ulcerous, gangrenous affliction on the mouth is not necessarily scurvy, and when it is linked with chronic spleen enlargement (as often in classical accounts) a diagnosis of malarial cachexia is much more likely than vitamin deficiency. The "bloody intestinal obstruction" (*eileòs haimatítēs*) in *Int.*, 46, is certainly not scurvy (*pace LSJ* s.v., which is inspired by Littré's translation of the passage [VII, 282, in his edition]) but a toxic purpura. In the case

of Kleokhos (*Epid.*, VII, 47), Littré's interpretation is untenable from the mere fact that the patient took excessive amounts of honey. He suffered from either a blood disorder or an inflammation of the lymphatic vessels accompanied by an infectious ulcerous stomatitis.

118. Strabo and Pliny tell how the Roman armies were struck by an epidemic that made their mouths stink, was caused by water of poor quality, and could be treated by a certain plant (Pliny, *Natural History*, XXV, 3; Strabo, *Geogr.*, 16). The information about symptoms given by these authors is so meager that it supports either a diagnosis of scurvy or one of infectious stomatitis. For the details, see M. D. Grmek, "Les origines d'une maladie d'autrefois: Le scorbut des marins," *Bull. Inst. Océanogr. Monaco,* special no. 2 (1968), pp. 505–23, esp. p. 508.

119. Wells, "Prehistoric and Historical Changes" (above, n. 102), pp. 756ff.

120. See M. Baudouin, "La préhistoire du rhumatisme chronique: La plus vieille maladie du monde," *Méd. Internat.*, no. 2 (1923), pp. 43–48; Pales, *Paléopathologie* (above, n. 3); H. Grimm, *Vorgeschichtliches, frügeschichtliches und mittelalterliches Fundmaterial zur Pathologie der Wirbelsäule* (Leipzig, 1959) (*Nova Acta Leopoldina* 21, no. 142); H. Buess and H. Koelbing, *Kurze Geschichte der ankylosierenden Spondylitis und Spondylose* (Basel, 1964), (*Documenta Geigy, Acta Rheumatologica,* no. 22).

121. J. B. Bourke, "A Review of the Paleopathology of the Arthritic Diseases," in Brothwell and Sandison, *Diseases* (above, n. 7), pp. 352–70; C. M. Cassidy, "Arthritis in Dry Bones: Diagnostic Problems," *Henry Ford Hosp. Med. Journal* 27 (1979): 68ff; A. Cockburn et al., "Arthritis, Ancient and Modern: Guidelines for Fieldworkers," ibid., pp. 74–79.

122. The disease is known in French as *arthrose*. Certain French writers use *ostéo-arthrite hypertrophique dégénerative* as a synonym, but this expression is considered inappropriate by eminent rheumatologists. In fact, the term *arthrite* should be reserved for inflammatory processes involving the synovial membrane. For up-to-date knowledge on rheumatic ailments, see S. de Sèze et al., *Le diagnostic en rhumatologie* (Paris, 1978), and W. N. Kelley et al., *Textbook of Rheumatology* (Philadelphia, 1981).

123. For example, see R. D. Jurmain, "Stress and the Etiology of Osteoarthritis," *Amer. Jour. of Phys. Anthro.* 46 (1977): 353–66.

124. W. M. Krogman, "The Skeletal and Dental Pathology of an Early Iranian Site," *Bull. Hist. Med.* 8 (1940): 28–48.

125. Angel, "Çatal Hüyük" (above, n. 31), p. 91 and pl. 2.

126. B. Alpagut, "Some Paleopathological Cases of the Ancient Anatolian Mandibles," *J. Human Evolution* 8 (1979): 571–74.

127. Angel, *People of Lerna* (above, n. 31), p. 52.

128. Dastugue and Duday, "Les ossements humains" (above, n. 32).

129. Fürst, *Argolis* (above, n. 26), p. 12 L.

130. Angel, *People of Lerna* (above, n. 31), p. 89 and pl. 24.

131. Ibid., p. 89. For a description of an occupational disease of the arm in the patients of Hippocrates, see below, chapter 12, the section "Some Individual Case Histories From Perinthus."

132. Charles, "Argos I," p. 311, and *Argos* II, p. 67 (both above, n. 32).

133. French authorities call this disease *spondylarthrose*; the majority of Anglo-American medical writers use the term "spondylitis."

134. See J. Forestier, F. Jacqueline, and J. Rotes-Querol, *La spondylarthrite ankylosante* (Paris, 1951), and J. Forestier and R. Lagier, "Ankylosing Hyperostosis of the Spine," *Clin. Orthoped.* 74 (1971): 65–83. The definition of Forestier's syndrome is recent. It calls for the revision of some earlier osteoarchaeological diagnoses, especially cases thought to be ankylosing spondylitis. In many cases of Forestier's

syndrome, one can see not just vertebral hyperostosis but also diffuse extraspinal osteophyte growth. Cf. D. Resnick et al., "Diffuse Idiopathic Skeletal Hyperostosis (DISH): Forestier's Disease with Extraspinal Manifestations," *Radiology* 115 (1975): 513–24. It appears that DISH is tied to metabolic factors such as obesity and diabetes.

135. See M. D. Grmek, "Die Wirbelsäule im Zeitgeschehen," *Med. Welt* 25 (1974): 70–76.

136. Fürst, *Argolis* (above, n. 26), pp. 14 and 122, fig. 49.

137. See p. 74.

138. Angel, "Mycenae" (above, n. 31), pp. 381ff., pl. 249.

139. Angel, *People of Lerna* (above, n. 31), pp. 58ff., pl. 25.

140. *Aff.*, 29 (Littré, VI, 240–42).

141. Fürst, *Argolis* (above, n. 26), p. 122.

142. Angel, *People of Lerna* (above, n. 31), pp. 88ff., pl. 25.

143. Angel, "Some Problems" (above, n. 28), p. 284.

144. Angel, "Çatal Hüyük" pp. 85 and 90. See also Angel, "Karataş" (above, n. 31), p. 253, where it is stated that this disease affects 66 percent of the men's vertebrae and 57 percent of the women's in the necropolis.

145. Angel, *People of Lerna* (above, n. 31), pp. 86ff.

146. Angel, "Osteoarthritis in Prehistoric Turkey and Medieval Byzantium," *Henry Ford Hosp. Med. J.* 27 (1979): 38–43.

147. See Angel, "Skeletal Changes" (above, n. 28), p. 82; *People of Lerna* (above, n. 31), p. 87; "Mycenae" (above, n. 31), p. 379. Dastugue and Duday ("Les ossements humains" [above, n. 32]) found Schmorl's nodule in a Neolithic thoracic vertebra from a cave near Laurion (*1726 Kitsos*).

148. See G. Bergmark, "Jehles och Scheuermanns ryggradförändringar bid antika skulpturer" ("Jehle's and Scheuermann's Deformations of the Spinal Column on Sculptures from Antiquity"), *Nordisk Medicin* 33 (1947): 325.

149. I use this term in its modern sense, to refer to acute or chronic joint diseases whose initial and principal lesion is an inflammation of the synovial membrane.

150. *Aff.*, 30 (Littré, VI 242). For rheumatism in ancient Greek medical literature, see especially A. Delpeuch, *Histoire des maladies: La goutte et le rhumatisme* (Paris, 1900), and A. Ruiz Moreno, *Las afecciones reumáticas en el Corpus Hippocraticum* (Buenos Aires, 1941). For the commonness of sore throats in antiquity, see below, chapters 4 and 12.

151. See J. M. Riddle, "Rheumatoid Arthritis," *Henry Ford Hosp. Med. J.* 27 (1979): 18–23, and Kelley et al., *Textbook of Rheumatology* (above, n. 122).

152. See Cockburn et al., "Arthritis, Ancient and Modern" (above, n. 121), pp. 77–79; T. Appelboom et al., "Rubens and the Question of the Antiquity of Rheumatoid Arthritis," *J. Amer. Med. Ass.* (1981), pp. 483–86; and D. E. Caughy, "The Arthritis of Constantine IX," *Ann. Rheum. Dis.* 33 (1974): 77–80.

153. C. L. Short, "The Antiquity of Rheumatoid Arthritis," *Arthr. Rheum.* 17 (1974): 193–205. His opinion is not shared by Ronald E. Domen, who cites medieval European and American cases of the disease and stresses the diagnosis in the Egyptian mummy mentioned above. See his attempt to set the record straight, "Paleopathological Evidence of Rheumatoid Arthritis," *J. Amer. Med. Assoc.* 246 (1981): 1899.

154. See P. Stastny, "Immunogenetic Factors in Rheumatoid Arthritis," *Clin. Rheum. Dis.* 3 (1977): 315–32, and V. Lemaire, "Polyarthrite rhumatoïde et système HLA," *Concours Méd.* 102 (1980): 1967–69.

155. See W. W. Buchanan, "The Contribution of History to the Study of the Aetiology of Rheumatoid Arthritis," *Med. Hist.* 23 (1979): 229ff.

156. L. L. Klepinger, "Paleopathological Evidence for the Evolution of Rheumatoid Arthritis," *Amer. J. Phys. Anthro.* 50 (1978): 119–22.

157. See *Paleopathological Newsletter,* no. 25 (March 1979), pp. 10ff., and no. 26 (June 1979), pp. 6ff.

158. L. Sokoloff et al., "Spinal Ankylosis in Old Rhesus Monkeys," *Clin. Orthop.* 61 (1968): 285–93.

159. See Forestier, Jacqueline, and Rotes-Querol, *La spondylarthrite* (above, n. 134); S. de Sèze and M. Phankim-Chapuis, "Naissance de la pelvi-spondylite rhumatismale," *Histoire de la Médecine* 10 (1960): 44–53; Buess and Koelbing, *Kurze Geschichte* (above, n. 120); D. A. Brewerton et al., "Ankylosing Spondylitis and HLA-B 27," *Lancet* 1 (1973): 904–7; C. V. Jimenez, "Ankylosing Spondylitis," *Henry Ford Hosp. Med. J.* 27 (1979): 10–13; D. G. Spencer, R. G. Sturrock, and W. W. Buchanan, "Ankylosing Spondylitis: Yesterday and Today," *Med. Hist.* 24 (1980): 60–69.

160. It was described and diagnosed by Léon Pales. See Buess and Koelbing, *Kurze Geschichte* (above, n. 120), p. 26.

161. See the review of their research by P. A. Zorab, "The Historical and Prehistorical Background of Ankylosing Spondylitis," *Proc. Roy. Soc. Med.* 54 (1961): 415–20.

162. See Bourke, "Paleopathology of the Arthritic Diseases" (above, n. 121), pp. 357–60.

163. E. Benassi, "I raggi x al servizio dell'archeologia," *Rivista Biellese* 10 (1955): 11–14.

164. *Art.,* 47 (Petrequin, II, 411).

165. See M. A. Ruffer, "Note on the Presence of Bilharzia haematobia in Egyptian Mummies of the Twentieth Dynasty (1250–1000 B.C.)," *Brit. Med. J.* 1 (1910): 16.

166. Angel, *People of Lerna* (above, n. 31), pp. 48 and 93.

167. See G. Regöly-Mérei, "Paläopathologische und epigraphische Angaben zur Frage der Pocken in Altägypten," *Sudhoffs Arch. Gesch. Med.* 50 (1966): 411–17.

168. The specimen was presented to the Colloquium in Paleopathology at Toronto, 1978.

169. J. Dastugue, "Pathologie des hommes fossiles de l'abri de Cro-Magnon," *Anthropologie* 71 (1967): 470–92.

170. P. L. Thillaud, "L'histiocytose x au Paléolithique (sujet n° 1 du Cro-Magnon)," *Anthropologie* 85 (1982): 219–39.

Chapter Three: Paleodemography

1. Aside from the publication of Angel cited in the previous chapter, see D. R. Brothwell, "Palaeodemography," in W. Brass, *Biological Aspects of Demography* (London, 1971), pp. 111–29; C. Masset, "La démographie des populations inhumées: Essai de paléodémographie," *L'Homme* 13 (1973): 95–161; and J. D. Willigan and K. A. Lynch, *Sources and Methods of Historical Demography* (New York, 1982).

2. The conclusions that follow are my own. They are inspired, in part, by the excellent article of J. L. Angel, "Health and the Course of Civilization as Seen in Ancient Greece," *The Interne* (1948), pp. 15–48. For an overall orientation, I have consulted chiefly F. Heichelheim, *An Ancient Economic History from the Palaeolithic Age to the Migrations of the Germanic, Slavic, and Arabic Nations* 3 vols. (Leiden, 1958–70); P. Lévêque, *L'aventure grecque,* 2d ed. (Paris, 1968); and K. W. Butzer, *Environment and Archaeology: An Ecological Approach to Prehistory* (Chicago, 1971).

3. See especially R. J. Rodden, "An Early Neolithic Village in Greece," *Sci-*

entific American 212 (1965): 82–90 (on Nea Nikomedia); J. Mellaart, *Çatal Hüyük: A Neolithic Town in Anatolia* (New York, 1967); F. L. Dunn, "Epidemiological Factors: Health and Disease in Hunter-Gatherers," in R. B. Lee and I. de Vore, *Man the Hunter* (Chicago, 1968); R. Tringham, *Hunters, Fishers, and Farmers of Eastern Europe, 6000–3000 B.C.* (London, 1971); and J. Cauvin, *Les premiers villages de Syrie-Palestine du IXe au VIIe millénaire avant J. C.* (Lyon, 1978). For some optimistic assessments, see M. Sahlins, *Stone Age Economics* (Chicago, 1972), and for a discussion of difficulties on the level of demography, see M. N. Cohen, *The Food Crisis in Prehistory: Overpopulation and the Origins of Agriculture* (New York and London, 1977). For the medical side, see especially T. A. Cockburn, "Infectious Diseases in Ancient Populations," *Curr. Anthro.* 12 (1971): 45–62. Cf. also S. Clarke, "Mortality Trends in Prehistoric Populations," *Hum. Biol.* 49 (1977): 181–86.

4. For the prehistoric periods in question, see E. Vermeule, *Greece in the Bronze Age* (Chicago, 1964); G. E. Mylonas, *Mycenae and the Mycenaean Age* (Princeton, 1966); and M. I. Finley, *Early Greece: The Bronze and Archaic Ages* (London, 1970). Sanitary conditions are analyzed by C. P. W. Warren, "Some Aspects of Medicine in the Greek Bronze Age," *Med. Hist.* 14 (1970): 364–77.

5. Warren, "Some Aspects" (above, n. 4), pp. 367–71; F. Schultze, "Reinlichkeit, Bad und Wäsche bei den mykenischen Griechen," *Münch. Med. Wschr.* 84 (1937): 743–45; and H. Schmidt-Ries, *Wasser für Hellas: Das Wasser in altgriechischen Raum* (Düsseldorf, 1956).

6. See Anthony M. Snodgrass, *The Dark Age of Greece* (Edinburgh, 1971), and Finley, *Early Greece* (above, n. 4).

7. According to Camp, Greece, and especially Attica, underwent a particularly harsh and long drought around 700 B.C. that would have caused famine, epidemics, and an abrupt rise in the death rate. This scholar's opinion is based on the relatively high number of abandoned wells in Athens at the time in question. See J. McK. Camp, "A Drought in the Late Eighth Century B.C.," *Hesperia* 48 (1979): 397–411. The arguments against this hypothesis are more convincing. Snodgrass points out that the number of sites and tombs in Greece points to an enormous upsurge of population, at least locally, in the two generations before 700 B.C. Between 780 and 720 B.C., the population of Attica increased by a factor of seven. See A. M. Snodgrass, *Archaic Greece: The Age of Experiment* (London, 1980).

8. Angel, "Health and Civilization" (above, n. 2), pp. 16–17. See F. Chamoux, *La civilisation grecque à l'époque archaïque et classique* (Paris, 1963), and J. Charbonneaux, R. Martin, and F. Villard, *La Grèce archaïque* (Paris, 1968).

9. F. Chamoux, *La civilisation* (above, n. 8); R. Flacelière, *La vie quotidienne en Grèce au siècle de Périclès* (Paris, 1959); G. Glotz, *La cité grecque,* rev. ed. (Paris, 1968); M. Austin and P. Vidal-Naquet, *Economie et société en Grèce ancienne: Périodes archaïque et classique* (Paris, 1976) (*Economic and Social History of Ancient Greece: An Introduction,* trans. and rev. M. M. Austin [Berkeley and Los Angeles, 1977]).

10. J. Burckhardt, *Griechische Kulturgeschichte* (1898–1902), ed. R. Marx (Stuttgart, 1941), 3: 136.

11. Angel, "Health and Civilization" (above, n. 2) p. 46.

12. Cf. W. H. McNeill, *Plagues and Peoples* (New York, 1976).

13. For the geography of ancient Greece, see the old but still commendable works of C. Neumann and J. Partsch, *Physikalische Geographie von Griechenland mit besonderer Rücksicht auf das Alterthum* (Breslau, 1885), and L. Lacroix, *Iles de la Grèce* (Paris, 1853). An exemplary summary statement in accord with modern geographical concepts is to be found in N. G. L. Hammond, "The Physical Geography of Greece and the Aegean," in A. J. B. Wace and F. H. Stubbings, *A Companion to Homer* (London, 1963).

14. The healthiness of the Greek climate and the importance of geographic

factors for the flowering of Greek civilization are well brought out by H. E. Sigerist, *History of Medicine* (New York, 1961), 2: 11–16 ("Archaic Medicine in Greece: The Setting").

15. Cf. Finley, *Early Greece* (above, n. 4), p. 6.

16. See E. Martini, *Wege der Seuchen* (Stuttgart, 1954), and McNeill, *Plagues* (above, n. 12).

17. Aristotle, *Meteor.,* 1, 14. For the notion of "malarial complex" and the influence of other pathogenic geographical factors, see M. Sorre, "Complexes pathogènes et géographie médicale," *Ann. Géograph.* 42 (1933): 1–18, and *Les fondements biologiques de la géographie humaine* (1951; rev. ed. Paris, 1971).

18. Plato, *Laws,* 707e.

19. See M. D. Grmek, "Géographie médicale et histoire des civilisations," *Annales E. S. C.* 18 (1963): 1071–97 (esp. pp. 1073ff.).

20. R. Joly, *Hippocrate* (Paris, 1964), p. 75. See also R. Joly, *Le niveau de la science hippocratique* (Paris, 1966), pp. 180–210.

21. See above, Introduction, the section, "The Greek Pathocoenosis in the Classical Period."

22. *Airs, Waters, and Places,* 23, in *Hippocrates* trans. W. H. S. Jones (London and Cambridge, 1946), 1: 131–33.

23. C. McEvedy and R. Jones, *Atlas of World Population History* (Harmondsworth, 1978), p. 19. See also E. S. Deevey, "The Human Population," *Scientific American* 203 (1960): 195–205, and R. H. Ward and K. M. Weiss, eds., *The Demographic Evolution of Human Populations* (London, 1976).

24. C. Renfrew, "Patterns of Population Growth in the Prehistoric Aegean," in P. J. Ucko et al., *Man, Settlement, and Urbanism* (London, 1972), pp. 383–99. See also W. A. McDonald and R. H. Simpson, "Further Explorations in Southwestern Peloponnese," *American Journal of Archaeology* 73 (1969): 123–77.

25. Renfrew, "Patterns of Population" (above, n. 24), pp. 394 and 397.

26. J. L. Angel, "Ecology and Population in the Eastern Mediterranean," *World Archaeology* 4 (1972): 88–105 (esp. p. 95).

27. J. L. Angel, *The People of Lerna* (Princeton and Washington, D. C., 1971), pp. 109ff.

28. See J. L. Angel, "The Bases of Paleodemography," *American Journal of Physical Anthropology* 30 (1969): 427–38. Unfortunately, statistics on fecundity among prehistoric populations, which are based on the state of scars on public symphyses, cannot be accepted as absolute values. It is preferable to consider them vague indicators of some demographic tendencies. The enthusiasm of anthropologists using this method must be set against the observations of forensic medicine, which views it with suspicion. See especially B. Herrmann and T. Bergfelder, "Ueber den diagnostischen Wert des sogenannten Geburtstrauma am Schambein bei der Identifikation," *Zschr. Rechtsmedizin* 81 (1978): 73–78.

29. The fundamental work on this subject remains J. Beloch, *Die Bevölkerung der griechisch-römischen Welt* (Leipzig, 1886; rev. ed. Rome, 1968). Important further considerations are in E. Cavaignac, *Histoire de l'Antiquité* vol. 2 (Paris, 1913), and especially P. Salmon, "La population de la Grèce antique," *Bulletin de l'Association Guillaume Budé,* 4th ser., 18 (1959): 449–76. It is interesting to note that, by calculations of Jardé based on the production and consumption of wheat, this degree of density represents a kind of biological limit. See below, at n. 107.

30. Salmon, "La population" (above, n. 29), pp. 457ff.

31. At about A.D. 310, Demetrius of Phalerum is said to have had a census done of the population of Attica. According to Ctesicles (Athenaeus, VI, 272b), the surprising and unlikely result was a count of 21,000 citizens, 10,000 resident aliens, and 400,000 slaves. On problems and new perspectives in demographic research

on antiquity, see J. N. Corvisier, "La démographie historique est-elle applicable à l'histoire grecque?" *Ann. Démog. Hist.* (1980), pp. 161–84.

32. Thucydides, II, 13 and 31.

33. Other than the works of Beloch and Salmon cited above, n. 29, see especially A. W. Gomme, *The Population of Athens in the Fifth and Fourth Centuries* B.C., (Oxford, 1933); G. Glotz and R. Cohen, *Histoire grecque,* vol. 2, *La Grèce au Ve siècle* (Paris, 1938); and M. H. Hansen, "The Number of Athenian Hoplites in 431 B.C.." *Symb. Osloens.* 56 (1981): 19–32.

34. Thucydides, II, 14–16.

35. Salmon, "La population" (above, n. 29), p. 453.

36. See A. Landry, "Quelques aperçus concernant la dépopulation dans l'Antiquité gréco-romaine," *Rev. Hist.* 177 (1936): 1–33, and J. Bérard, "Problèmes démographiques dans l'histoire de la Grèce antique," *Population* 2 (1947): 303–12. It is instructive to compare the reality of demographic problems with their image in the minds of learned men. In this connection, see J. Moreau, "Les théories demographiques dans l'Antiquité grecque," *Population* 4 (1949): 587–613.

37. Polybius, XXXVII, 9.

38. Some specialists guess that measles and influenza, if they are to maintain themselves, require an interacting community of approximately 500,000 members. Cf. G. J. Armelagos and A. McCardle, "Population, Diseases, and Evolution," *American Antiquity* 40, no. 2, pt. 2 (1975): 1–10.

39. See F. L. Black, "Infectious Diseases in Primitive Societies," *Science* 187 (1975): 515–18. Macfarlane Burnet has shown that the most likely origin of the measles virus is the germ resembling it that causes a certain disease in dogs. The smallpox virus is linked genetically to the group of pox viruses of domesticated animals, especially the cowpox virus. Since viruses are products of a degenerative evolution of the genes of bacteria or protozoa that cannot maintain themselves in free state, their continuing existence demands conditions favorable to immediate contagion, in particular significant population density. But the prerequisite applies only to the germs of acute diseases. Those viruses that live alongside humans without causing much harm can be transmitted vertically and originate in phylogenetic ancestors, not domestic animals. Most likely that is the case for the herpesvirus, and perhaps that of chickenpox and shingles. See M. Burnet, *Viruses and Man* (Harmondsworth, 1955), and the same author's chapter in G. W. Leeper, *The Evolution of Living Organisms* (Melbourne, 1962). See also G. de Beer, "Virus et préhistoire," *Archéocivilisation* 7 (1968): 1–3.

40. The determination of age at death from these skeletal remains is based on tooth eruption, formation of long bones, cranial suture closure, metamorphosis of the public symphysis, radiographic translucency of proximal femur and humerus, dental wear, and a variety of minor indicators. Substantial bias exists in the present methods of analyzing cranial sutures and pubic symphysis metamorphosis.

41. J. L. Angel, "The Length of Life in Ancient Greece" *J. Geront.* 2 (1947): 18–24. See also S. Jarcho, "The Longevity of the Ancient Greeks," *Bull. N.Y. Acad. Med.* 43 (1967): 941–43.

42. Cf. J. L. Angel, "Skeletal Changes in Ancient Greece," *American Journal of Physical Anthropology,* 4 (1946): 69–97 (esp. p. 72).

43. D. M. Robinson, *Necrolynthia* pt. 9 (Baltimore, 1942), 146–70.

44. Angel, "Length of Life" (above, n. 41), pp. 21ff.

45. See especially J. L. Angel, "The Bases of Paleodemography," *American Journal of Physical Anthropology* n.s., 30 (1969): 427ff., and his "Ecology and Population" (above, n. 26).

46. H. V. Vallois, "La durée de la vie chez l'homme fossile," *Anthropologie* 47 (1937): 499–532 (see also *Comptes rendues de l'Académie des Sciences* 204 [1937]: 60–62).

47. J. N. Biraben, "Durée de la vie dans la population de Columnata (Epipaléolithique oranais)," *Population* (1969), pp. 487–500.

48. Angel, "Ecology and Population" (above, n. 26), pp. 95ff.

49. Mellaart, *Çatal Hüyük* (above, n. 3).

50. J. L. Angel, "Early Neolithic Skeletons from Çatal Hüyük: Demography and Pathology," *Anatolian Studies* 21 (1971): 77–98.

51. Ibid., p. 78.

52. Angel, "Ecology and Population" (above, no. 26), pp. 95ff.

53. J. L. Angel, in M. J. Mellink, "Excavations at Karataş-Semayük and Elmali, Lycia 1969," *Amer. J. Archaeol.* 74 (1970): 245–59.

54. J. L. Angel, "Early Bronze Age Karataş People and Their Cemeteries," *Amer. J. Archaeol.* 80 (1976): 385–91.

55. See G. E. Mylonas, *Aghios Kosmas: An Early Bronze Age Settlement and Cemetery in Attica* (Princeton, 1959), pp. 169–79.

56. Angel, *People of Lerna* (above, n. 27), pp. 109ff.

57. See J. L. Angel, "Human Skeletons from Grave Circles at Mycenae," in G. E. Mylonas, *O tafikos kyklos B tou Mykenou* (Athens, 1973), pp. 379–97.

58. R. P. Charles, "Etude anthropologique des nécropoles d'Argos," *Bull. Corresp. Hell.* 82 (1958): 258–313, esp. pp. 307ff.

59. R. P. Charles, *Anthropologie archéologique de la Crète* (Paris, 1965), pp. 208ff.

60. V. V. Caramalea et al., "Contributi paleodemografice la studiul unor communitati tribale din epoca bronzului de pe teritoriul Rominiei," *Probleme Antrop.* 7 (1963): 243–61.

61. M. S. Senyürek, "The Duration of Life in the Chalcolithic and Copper Age Population of Anatolia," *Anatolia* 2 (1957): 95–110.

62. Angel, "Bases of Paleodemography" (above, n. 28), pp. 429–31.

63. See C. Wells, "Ancient Obstetric Hazards and Female Mortality," *Bull. N.Y. Acad. Med.* 51 (1975): 1235–49.

64. For these tables and their use, see L. Henry, *Manuel de démographie historique* (Geneva and Paris, 1967).

65. B. E. Richardson, *Old Age among the Ancient Greeks* (Baltimore, 1933).

66. Ibid., p. 234.

67. V. G. Vallaoros, "E méoē diárkeia tḗ zōḗa eís tḗn arkhaían Helláda," *Praktiká tḗs Akadḗmias Athḗnō̂n* 13 (1938): 401–9.

68. J. C. Russell, "Late Ancient and Medieval Populations," *Trans. Amer. Phil. Soc.*, n.s., 48, pt. 3 (1958): pp. 24–30.

69. M. Hombert and C. Préaux, "Note sur la durée de la vie dans l'Egypte gréco-romaine," *Chronique d'Egypte* 20 (1945): 139–46. For a more detailed analysis by site, see B. Boyaval, "Remarques sur l'indication d'âge de l'épigraphie funéraire grecque d'Egypte," *Zschr. Pap. Epig.* 21 (1976): 217–50.

70. For example, see A. R. Burn, "Hic Breve Vivitur: A Study on the Expectation of Life in the Roman Empire," *Past and Present,* no. 4 (1953), pp. 2–31; R. Etienne, "Démographie et épigraphie," *Atti III Congr. Intern. Epigr. Gr. Rom.* (Rome, 1959), pp. 414–19; J. D. Durand, "Mortality Estimates from Roman Tombstone Inscriptions," *Amer. Jour. Sociol.* 65 (1960): 365–73; and M. Clauss, "Probleme der Lebensalterstatistiken aufgrund römischer Grabinschriften," *Chiron* 3 (1973): 395–417.

71. L. Henry, "La mortalité d'après les inscriptions funéraires," *Population* 12 (1957): 149–52, and "L'âge au décès d'après les inscriptions funéraires," *Population* 14 (1959): 327–29. See also the excellent study by K. Hopkins, "On the Probable Age Structure of the Roman Population," *Popul. Stud.* 20 (1966): 245–64, and the conclusions of B. Boyaval, "Epigraphie antique et démographie: Problèmes de méthodes," *Rev. Nord* 59 (1977): 163–91.

72. Aristotle, *Politics,* IV, 16, 1334b–1335a.

73. Thucydides, II, 20.

74. See A. H. M. Jones, *The Athenian Democracy* (Oxford, 1957; rept. Baltimore, 1986), pp. 82ff., and O. W. Reinmuth, *The Ephebic Inscriptions of the Fourth Century, Mnemosyne,* suppl. (1971).

75. M. D. Grmek, *On Ageing and Old Age* (The Hague, 1958) (Monographiae Biologicae, V, 2), and "Le vieillissement et la mort," in *Encyclopédie de la Pléiade: Biologie* (Paris, 1965), pp. 789–99.

76. *Iliad* I.247ff (trans. R. Lattimore).

77. *Iliad* XXIII. 627ff.

78. Thucydides, II, 36.

79. Thucydides, VI, 12.

80. See above, p. 107. For the argument between Nicias and Alcibiades, its relationship to transgenerational conflict, and the use of medical metaphors in political discourse, see J. Jouanna, "Politique et médicine: La problématique du changement dans le Régime des maladies aiguës et chez Thucydide (livre VI)," in *Hippocratica* (Paris, 1980), pp. 299–319.

81. See Grmek, *On Ageing* (above, n. 75), p. 30.

82. Psalms 90:10.

83. Herodotus, III, 22ff.

84. Censorinus, *De die natali,* 14, 12, and 15, 1–2. Plato himself died on the eve of his eighty-first year.

85. For the dubious longevity of the ancient Greek philosophers, see L. Jerphagon, "Les mille et une morts des philosophes antiques," *Revue Belge Philol. Hist.* 59 (1981): 17–28.

86. See Grmek, *On Ageing* (above, n. 75), pp. 32–38, and A. Sauvy, *Les limites de la vie humaine* (Paris, 1961).

87. Fragment of a stele from Lycia (*Suppl. Epigr. Gr.,* II, 690). We decline to take into account two late funerary inscriptions from Egypt, one of which, of Panopolitan origin, gives the age of the deceased as 115, and the other, whose origin and interpretation are both uncertain, as 117. There is also a late Greek epitaph in Rome that specifies the deceased's age as 110.

88. See G. Maspero, *Les contes populaires de l'Egypte ancienne,* 4th ed. (Paris, 1911), pp. 32–34.

89. Censorinus, *De die natali,* 17, 4. See the edition by G. Rocca-Serra (Paris, 1980), p. 23.

90. These figures were drawn from various publications of J. L. Angel. For an overall perspective and a comparison of the situation in Greece with that among the populations of Egypt, see J. L. Angel, "Biological Relations of Egyptians and Eastern Mediterranean Populations during Pre-dynastic and Dynastic Times," *J. Hum. Evol.* 1 (1972): 307–13.

91. Angel, *People of Lerna* (above, n. 27), p. 85; C. S. Bartsocas, "Stature of Greeks of the Pylos Area during the Second Millennium B.C.," *Hipp. Magazine* 2 (1977): 157–60; and M. J. Becker, "Human Skeletal Remains from Kato Zakro," *Amer. J. Archaeol.* 79 (1975): 271–76.

92. Angel, "Mycenae" (above, n. 57), p. 386.

93. According to the anthropologist Robert P. Charles, "Greek artists had conceived a plastic ideal either from pure aesthetic rules or under the spell of artistic canons in vogue in other schools or according to models taken from outside the ethnic type most common among themselves" (Charles, "Argos" (above, n. 58), pp. 274ff.). For the anthropometric traits of Greek statues, see M. Clementelli and A. Jalongo, "La formula corporea nella scultura dell'antica Grecia," *Riv. Anat. Artistica* (Rome) 1, nos. 3–6 (1967): 43–54.

94. For an overview, see S. and J. Brommer, *Die Ernährung der Griecher und Römer* (Munich, 1943); D. R. and P. Brothwell, eds., *Food in Antiquity* (London, 1969); and P. J. Ucko and G. W. Dimbleby, *The Domestication and Exploitation of Plants and Animals* (London, 1969). As for the paleopathological aspects of nutrition, there is an excellent update and critique by C. Wells, "Prehistoric and Historical Changes in Nutritional Diseases and Associated Conditions," *Progress in Food and Nutrition Science* 1, no. 11 (1975): 729–79.

95. Sahlins, *Stone Age Economics* (above, n. 3), provides convincing arguments in this regard.

96. Cf. Cohen, *Food Crisis* (above, n. 3).

97. At least that is the opinion of most of those who have recently discussed the question. See Brothwell and Brothwell, *Food in Antiquity* (above, no. 94); the section by J. Yudkin and N. A. Barnicot in Ucko and Dimbleby, *Domestication and Exploitation* (above, n. 94); and W. A. Stine, "Evolutionary Implication of Changing Nutritional Patterns in Human Populations," *American Anthrop.* 73 (1971): 1019–30.

98. *Iliad* 19.160–66. See M. Primiero, "L'alimentazione nei poemi omerici," *Riv. Stor. Med.* 17 (1973): 17–24.

99. Plato, *Republic,* 372a–c, trans. P. Shorey.

100. *Republic,* 372c–d. The Hippocratic corpus, in particular the treatise *Diet,* contains precious information on the nutritional hygiene of Greeks during the classical period.

101. *Republic,* 405c–d.

102. See P. T. Makler, "New Information on Nutrition in Ancient Greece," *Klio* 62 (1980): 317–19.

103. R. Van Reen, ed., *Idiopathic Urinary Bladder Stone Disease* (Washington, D.C., 1977).

104. Cf. E. L. Prien, "The Riddle of Urinary Stone Disease," *J. Amer. Med. Assoc.* 216 (1971): 503–7; Van Reen, *Idiopathic Bladder Stone Disease* (above, n. 103), and Makler, "New Information" (above, n. 102), p. 319.

105. *Airs,* 9; *Morb.,* IV, 55; *Progn.,* 19; *Epid.,* VI, 3, 7; *Aph.,* III, 26. See E. Lesky, "Zur Lithiasis-Beschreibung in Peri aerōn," *Wien. Stud.* 63 (1948): 69–83, and "Die Lithiasis im Altertum, eine ausgesprochene Kinderkrankheit," *Zschr. Kinderheilk.* (1948), pp. 250–59.

106. *Morb.,* IV, 55 (Littré, II, 600).

107. A. Jardé, *Les céréales dans l'Antiquité grecque* (Paris, 1925), p. 142.

108. See H. Brabant, "La denture humaine à l'époque néolithique," *Bull. Soc. Roy. Belg. Anthrop.* 79 (1968): 105–41, and Wells, "Prehistoric Changes" (above, n. 94), pp. 741–44.

109. Becker, "Skeletal Remains" (above, n. 91), pp. 271–76.

110. Charles, "Argos" (above, n. 58), pp. 278–80.

111. Angel, *People of Lerna* (above, n. 27), p. 90.

112. Angel, "Çatal Hüyük" (above, n. 50), p. 90.

113. Angel, *People of Lerna* (above, n. 27), p. 90.

114. Other factors can intervene (sexual differentiation in eating habits or in tasks involving chewing) to invert the usual contrast: for instance, at Çatal Hüyük strong dental abrasion occurs in 31.4 percent of the women and only 29 percent of the men.

115. Strong dental abrasion on teeth from the Greek necropolis of Pithekussai on the island of Ischia in Italy actually begins in childhood (eighth and seventh centuries B.C.). See F. R. Munz, "Die Zahnfunde aus der griechischen Nekropole von Pithekussai auf Ischia," *Archaeol. Anz.* (1970), pp. 452–75. It is worth noting that infant mortality there was especially high and average longevity low, judging

in particular from skeletons of this colony belonging to the eighth-century B.C. stratum.

116. A. J. Clement, "Caries in the South African Ape-man," *Brit. Dent. Jour.* 101 (1956): 4–7. On tooth decay in the prehistoric populations of *Homo sapiens,* see H. V. Vallois, "La carie dentaire et la chronologie des hommes préhistoriques," *Anthropologie* 46 (1936): 201ff.

117. See H. Euler, *Die Zahncaries im Lichte vorgeschichtlicher und geschichtlicher Studien* (Munich, 1939), and C. Wells, "Prehistoric Changes" (above, n. 94), pp. 730–38.

118. See J. L. Angel, "Greek Teeth, Ancient and Modern," *Human Biol.* 16 (1944): 283–97, and *People of Lerna* (above, n. 27), p. 90; and C. Wells, "Prehistoric Changes" (above, n. 94), pp. 732–34. According to Angel's initial research, the frequency of decayed teeth in the Greek Neolithic reached 12 percent, but the figure must be lowered as a result of subsequent studies of teeth at Nea Nikomedia and Çatal Hüyük.

119. Angel, "Mycenae" (above, n. 57), p. 307, and *People of Lerna* (above, n. 27), p. 90.

120. C. M. Fürst, *Zur Anthropologie der prähistorischen Griechen in Argolis* (Lund, 1930), p. 122, and Charles, "Argos" (above, n. 58), p. 309.

121. H. G. Carr, "Some Dental Characteristics of the Middle Minoans," *Man* 60 (1960): 119–22.

122. See n. 118.

123. E. Nyqvist, "Human Teeth from Kition," *Opuscula Atheniensia* 13 (1980): 185–88. See also P. M. Fischer, ibid., pp. 139–48.

124. E. Benassi and A. Toti, "Osservazioni sulle ossa rinvenute negli scavi della necropoli di Spina," *Atti Mem. Accad. Stor. Arte San.* II, 24 (1958): 16–28; and Munz, "Die Zahnfunde" (above, n. 115).

125. Pseudo-Aristotle, *Problemata,* XXII, 14, 931a. Hippocrates blamed certain kinds of nutritional debris for causing tooth decay; see G. Cootjans, "Le problème étiologique de la carie dentaire dans l'Antiquité," *Revue Belge Stomat.* 52 (1955): 677–88.

126. D. M. Hadjimarkos and C. W. Bonhorst, "Fluoride and Selenium Levels in Contemporary and Ancient Greek Teeth in Relation to Dental Caries," *Nature* (London) 193, no. 4811 (1962):177ff.

127. H. Duday, "La pathologie dentaire des hommes de Kitsos," in N. Lambert, ed., *La grotte préhistorique de Kitsos* (Paris, 1981).

Chapter Four: Common Purulent Inflammations

1. For an overview of the history of the concept of infection, see especially T. Puschmann, *Die Geschichte der Lehre von der Ansteckung* (Vienna, 1895); O. Temkin, "An Historical Analysis of the Concept of Infection," in *Studies in Intellectual History* (Baltimore, 1953), pp. 123–47; and M. D. Grmek, "Le concept d'infection dans l'Antiquité et au Moyen Age," *Rad. Jug. Akad.* (Zagreb) 384 (1980): 9–55. For the history of ideas concerning the infection of wounds, see G. Majno, *The Healing Hand: Man and Wound in the Ancient World* (Cambridge, Mass., 1974). The writers of the Hippocratic corpus were not ignorant of the clinical manifestations of the suppurating infection of wounds and excelled in the description of diseases that nowadays are considered infectious. There are medical-historical publications on this aspect of the Hippocratic texts, for instance M. Soulangas, *Etude sur Hippocrate, son oeuvre, ses idées sur l'infection et les moyens antiseptiques* (Paris,

1894); G. Sticker, "Fieber und Entzündung bei den Hippokratikern," *Arch. Gesch. Med.* 22 (1929): 313–43, 361–81, and ibid. 23 (1930): 21–25, 92–100; and R. E. Siegel, "Epidemics and Infectious Diseases at the Time of Hippocrates," *Gesnerus* 17 (1960): 77–98. However, the idea of the propagation of diseases by contagion is missing from the Hippocratic texts, and clinical phenomena of this kind are explained therein by an appeal to endogenous factors or the special conditions in a given environment.

2. The double staining method invented by Hans Gram makes it possible to divide bacteria into two groups: gram-positive ones that retain the first (violet) dye, and gram-negative ones that, when discolored by alcohol, retain the second (red) dye.

3. See J. W. Schopf et al., "Electron Microscopy of Fossil Bacteria Two Billion Years Old," *Science* 149, (1965): 1365–67; E. S. Barghoorn, "The Oldest Fossils," *Scient. Amer.* 224 (1971): 30–42; J. W. Schopf, "L'ère de la vie microscopique," *Endeavour* (French-language edition) 34, no. 122 (1975): 51–58.

4. R. L. Moodie, *Palaeopathology* (Urbana, 1923); for the critique of his interpretation, see Majno, *The Healing Hand* (above, n. 1), pp. 16 and 473.

5. Ju-kang Woo, "Mandible of Sinanthropus Lantianiensis," *Curr. Anthrop.* 5 (1964): 98–101.

6. See J. Enselme, *Mort et maladies à l'aube de l'humanité* (Lyon, 1973), pp. 144ff.

7. L. Pales, *Paléopathologie et pathologie comparative* (Paris, 1930), pp. 187–90; H. E. Sigerist, *History of Medicine,* vol. 1, *Primitive and Archaic Medicine* (New York, 1951), p. 49; C. Wells, *Bones, Bodies and Disease* (London, 1964), pp. 76ff.

8. See R. Hare, "The Antiquity of Diseases Caused by Bacteria and Viruses," in D. Brothwell and A. T. Sandison, *Diseases in Antiquity* (Springfield, 1967), pp. 115–31 (esp. p. 123).

9. M. A. Ruffer, "Remarks on the Histology and Pathological Anatomy of Egyptian Mummies," *Cairo Scient. J.* 4 (1910): 3–7.

10. J. L. Angel, *The People of Lerna* (Princeton and Washington, D.C., 1971), pp. 50 and 91–92, pl. 24.

11. R. P. Charles, "Etude anthropologique des nécropoles d'Argos," *Bull Corr. Hell.* 82 (1958): 310, and *Etudes anthropologiques des nécropoles d'Argos* (Paris, 1963), p. 66.

12. Cited from D. G. Rokhlin, *Bolezni drevnih lyudei* (Moscow and Leningrad, 1965), p. 93.

13. Angel, *People of Lerna* (above, n. 10), pp. 55 and 84.

14. The archaeologist Alan J. B. Wace first pointed out the case of this Mycenaean aristocrat in 1949, suggesting that he had "suffered from a septic wound of the jaw" (A.J.B. Wace, *Mycenae: An Archaeological History and Guide* [Princeton, 1949], p. 117). Purulent inflammations on Mycenaean jawbones were also reported by C. M. Fürst, *Zur Anthropologie der prähistorischen Griechen in Argolis, Lunds Univ. Årsskrift,* n.s., sect. 2, 26, no. 8 (1930): 122. A detailed description of the pathological state of the jawbone of *59 Myc.* was given by Angel in G. E. Mylonas, *O Tafikós Kúklos B toû Mykēnou* (Athens, 1973), pp. 381ff., pl. 245.

15. See J. L. Angel, "Appendix on the Early Helladic Skulls from Aghios Kosmas," in G. E. Mylonas, *Aghios Kosmas* (Princeton, 1959), p. 169; Angel, *People of Lerna* (above, n. 10), pp. 39, 42, 50, 52, 84, and so forth, and pl. 22; J. Dastugue and H. Duday, "Les ossements humains pathologiques," in N. Lambert, ed., *La grotte préhistorique de Kitsos* (Paris, 1981); Charles, *Etudes anthropologiques* (above, n. 11), p. 66.

16. H. G. Carr, "Some Dental Characteristics of the Middle Minoans," *Man* 60 (1960): pp. 119–22.

17. J. L. Angel, "Skeletal Material from Attica," *Hesperia* 14 (1945): 279–363.

18. For the problem of the antiquity of gonorrhea, see below, chapter 5, the section "Gonorrhea, Spermatorrhea, and Leukorrhea."

19. P. Chantraine, *Dictionnaire étymologique de la langue grecque* (Paris, 1974) 3: 952.

20. Aristotle, *De gen. anim.*, IV, 8 (777a7).

21. Cf. Plato, *Phaedo,* 96b, and Pseudo-Galen, *Def. medicae,* 99 (Kühn, XIX, 373).

22. J. Bollack, *Empédocle* (Paris, 1969), vol. 3, 2, p. 539. The false translation is widespread, since it was recommended by H. Diels and W. Kranz, *Die Fragmente der Vorsokratiker,* 6th ed. (Berlin, 1951), 1: 337, fr. 68. In order to sustain it, Kranz had to emend the word *gála* 'milk' in the manuscripts of Aristotle and replace it with the word *haîma* 'blood,' an arbitrary change in the sense of Aristotle's statements.

23. Aristotle, *loc. cit.* (above, n. 20).

24. For the "putrefaction" of the humors in an organism as a pathogenic factor, see especially R. Wittern, *Die hippokratische Schrift De Morbis I* (Hildesheim, 1974), pp. 18, 28, 32, 36, 38, 48, 52, 80, 82, 90, and so forth (for the Hippocratic text), and p. 195 (for Wittern's remarks on the meaning of this family of words). See also *Prorrh.*, I, 99. For Hippocratic *sêpsis* as the physiological process of digestion, cf. *Aff.*, 84; *Vict.*, III, 80; *Anat.*, I. See A. Foesius, *Oeconomia Hippocratis* (Frankfurt, 1588), p. 562. P. Chantraine, *Dictionnaire étymologique* (above, n. 19), p. 592, is surely correct in relating the substantives of the *pûon* family to the verb *pûthomai* 'rot,' but from the viewpoint of the history of ideas it is an error to translate, as he does, the Hippocratic expressions *sarkopúon* as "infected flesh" and *émpuos* as "infected." The correct translation is "purulent," or even "putrid," but not "infected," since the Hippocratic concept (or even the Aristotelian one) of pus has no connection with the idea of infection either in the sense of defilement or in that of the transmission of an agent.

25. For example, *Morb.*, I, 19 and 29; *Vet. med.*, 18; *Aph.*, II, 40; *Acut.*, 38. See Foesius, *Oeconomia* (above, n. 24), pp. 492 and 504.

26. *Epid.*, III, 4. I adopt the text of Jones (I, 242), not Littré.

27. *De alimento,* 52 (Joly, 147).

28. See Foesius, *Oeconomia* (above, n. 24), p. 544, and M. P. Dumini, *Le sang, les vaisseaux, le coeur dans la Collection hippocratique,* thesis (Paris, 1983).

29. *De capitis vulneribus,* 14 (Littré, III, 20; Petrequin, I, 474–75).

30. The correctness of this Hippocratic observation is stressed by E. D. Churchill, "Healing by First Intention and with Suppuration: Studies in Wound Healing," *J. Hist. Med.* 19 (1964): 193–214 (esp. p. 199).

31. See, for instance, *Epid.*, VI, 5, 6: "In wounds, the blood flows in."

32. *Ulc.*, 26 (Littré VI, 430; Petrequin, I, 310–11).

33. *Morb.*, IV, 50, 4 (ed. R. Joly [Paris, 1970], p. 107).

34. *Fract.*, 31 (Petrequin, 206–7).

35. See F. Kudlien, *Der Beginn des medizinischen Denkens bei den Griechen* (Zürich and Stuttgart, 1967), pp. 49 and 72ff.

36. Majno, *The Healing Hand* (above, n. 1), p. 183.

37. For instance *Aph.*, VI, 20; *Flat.* (Littré, VI, 106 and elsewhere).

38. In the Hippocratic texts, the term *spasmoí* does not necessarily signify contractions. It also designates extensions; the word refers to a state of tension. See Wittern, *Die hippokratische Schrift* (above, n. 24), p. 197.

39. *Morb.*, I, 14 (Littré, VI, 162; Wittern, 32) and 17 (Littré, VI, 170; Wittern, 44).

40. *Morb.*, I, 15 (Littré, VI, 164; Wittern, 36).

41. Cf. *Progn.*, 7, 17, 18, and 22; *Aph.*, VII, 44, 45; *Praen. Coacae,* 403 and 404.

42. *Epid.*, VI, 3, 4 (Littré, V, 294). My translation is perceptibly different from the one Littré suggests.

43. Herodotus, *Histories,* III, 64–66, trans. A. de Sélincourt (Baltimore, 1954;

rept. 1966), pp. 201–3 (replacing, as translations of *esápē,* the words "gangrene" and "mortification" by "decay" and "putrefaction").

44. Herdotus, *Histories,* VI, 136 (again with the words "gangrene" and "mortification" replaced by words signifying putrefaction).

45. Herodotus, *Histories,* VI, 134, my translation. The verb *spasthênai* here must mean "break" or "fracture," not "twist" or "dislocate" as others translate it. See L. W. Daly, "Miltiades, Aratus, and Compound Fractures," *Amer. J. Philol.* 101 (1980): 59ff., who refers to the case of Aratus of Sicyon, a Greek general of the third century B.C. who broke his leg, underwent several incisions, and for a long time carried out his military duties from a litter (cf. Plutarch, *Vita Arati,* 33).

46. For the local and general symptoms of wounds, see for instance *Morb.,* IV, 48 (Joly, 103–4).

47. The Greek word is *spasmós* 'tetanus.'

48. *Artic.,* 63 (Petrequin, II, 472–75).

49. *Mochl.,* 30 (Petrequin, II, 594–97).

50. For instance *Epid.,* V, 26, 45, and 65 (Littré, V, 224, 234, and 244); *Epid.,* VII, 61 (Littré, V, 426). See Majno, *The Healing Hand* (above, n. 1), pp. 196–98.

51. *Artic.,* 55 (Petrequin, II, 446–47), trans. E. T. Withington, in *Hippocrates,* vol. 3 (London 1928), p. 329. Cf. also *Mochl.,* 21.

52. See K. E. Müller, *Die Geschichte der entzündlichen Knochenerkrankungen und ihrer chirurgischen Behandlung* (Düsseldorf, 1938).

53. For a general description of this disease, see *Morb.,* II, 7 and 24 (Littré, VII, 14–16 and 38), and for concrete cases, for example, see *Epid.,* V, 97, and VII, 35 (Littré, V, 256 and 402). In the citation from the Hippocratic book *Diseases,* this form of bone caries is designated by the word *terēdṓn,* whose primary application is to a wood borer's drilling and piercing. Is this technical term based simply on a morphological analogy between decayed bone and worm-eaten wood, or does it represent the traces of a very old etiological hypothesis?

54. *Epid.,* I, 13, 9 (Littré, II, 704).

55. *Epid.,* V, 45 (Littré, V, 234).

56. Cf. *Praen. Coacae,* 196; *Progn.,* 23; *Aph.,* V, 23; *Epid.,* III, 3–4. See E. W. Goodall, "Infectious Diseases and Epidemiology in the Hippocratic Collection," *Proc. Royal Soc. Med.* 27 (1934): 526.

57. Cases of gas gangrene are described in one of the *katastáseis* of Thasos (*Epid.,* III, 4 [Littré, V, 70–76]). See C. E. Kellett, "The Early History of Gas Gangrene," *Ann. Med. Hist.* 1 (1939): 452–59; and M. Sussmann, "A Description of Clostridium Histolyticum: Gas Gangrene in the *Epidemics* of Hippocrates," *Med. Hist.* 2 (1958): 226ff.

58. See below, chapter 13, the section "Four Concise Case Histories," for a discussion of tetanus in *Epid.,* VII, 36.

59. For instance *Epid.,* II, 1, 1, and perhaps *Epid.,* III, 7. See B. Ebbell, *Beiträge zur ältesten Geschichte einiger Infektions-krankheiten* (Oslo, 1967), p. 44.

60. *Epid.,* V, 61 (Littré, V, 240–42). In a parallel description of the same case (*Epid.,* VII, 33 [Littré, V, 402]), there is the additional detail that the patient's eyes were greenish. For the historical circumstances of this wound, see F. Robert, "La bataille de Délos (Hippocrate, Epidémies, V, 61 and VII, 33)," *Bull. Corresp. Hell. Suppl.,* I, *Etudes déliennes* (1973), pp. 427–33. Other cases of peritonitis are described in *Epid.,* V, 98–99, and *Epid.,* VII, 29–30. The presence of ileus (severe intestinal blockage) is a noteworthy sign of traumatic peritonitis. For a medical commentary, see Majno, *The Healing Hand* (above, n. 1), p. 193.

61. For the first form of pharyngitis (*kunángkhē*), see *Morb.,* II, 11 and 30 (Littré, VII, 18, and 48); for the second, *Morb.,* II, 9 and 28 (Littré, VII, 16 and 46); and for

Ludwig's angina (*hupoglōssís*) see especially *Morb.*, II, 31 (Littré, VII, 48). Specific cases are described in *Epid.*, I, 13, case 5; and *Epid.*, III, 1, 2, cases 6 and 7.

62. Cf. *Morb.*, III, 2 (Littré, VII, 120; Potter, 70–72). For other passages on this disease, see A. Courtade, "L'otologie dans Hippocrate" (Paris, 1904) (from the *Arch. Intern. Laryng.*), pp. 4–11.

63. *Epid.*, VII, 5 (Littré, V, 373–76).

64. See especially *Morb.*, II and III. There are some useful remarks in A. Souques, *Etapes de la neurologie dans l'Antiquité grecque* (Paris, 1936), pp. 72–79.

65. See E. Bazin, *La pneumonie, la pleurésie et la phtisie chez les médecins de la période gréco-romaine* (Paris, 1891), and A. Souques, "La douleur dans les livres hippocratiques," *Bull. Soc. Franç. Hist. Méd.* 32 :(1938): 178–86.

66. *Morb.*, III, 15 (Littré, VII, 136–38; Potter, 82–85). See the medical commentary in P. Potter's edition (Berlin, 1980), pp. 118–19. For other descriptions of this disease, see for example *Morb.*, II, 47 (Jouanna, 178–83), and *Acut. (sp.)*, 31 (Littré, II, 456–64; Joly, 83–84). The excellent study by G. Preiser should also be consulted: "*Peripleumoniē* in den Schriften der knidischen Aerzteschule," in *Medizingeschichte in unserer Zeit* (Stuttgart, 1971), pp. 31–35.

67. See for instance *Morb.*, III, 16 (Littré, VII, 142–56; Potter, 86–96). A general historical sketch is given by A. Baffoni, *Storia delle pleuriti da Ippocrate a Laennec* (Rome, 1947).

68. *Morb.*, II, 59 (Littré, VII, 92; Jouanna, 198ff.)

69. See Barbillon, "L'empyème hippocratique," in *Etudes critiques d'histoire de la médicine* (Paris, 1930), pp. 36–43; A. Souques, "La pleurésie et l'empyème hippocratiques," *Presse Méd.* (1938), pp. 425–27; and R. E. Siegel, "Clinical Observation in Hippocrates," *J. Mount Sinai Hosp.* 31 (1964): 295–97.

70. An excellent description in *Aff. int.*, 14–17 (Littré, VII, 202–10). See E. Desnos, *Histoire de l'urologie* (Paris, 1914); E. D. Baumann, "Ueber die Erkrankungen der Nieren und Harnblase im klassischen Altertum," *Janus* 37 (1933): 34–47, 65–83, 116–21, and 145–52; and M. D. Grmek and R. Wittern, "Die Krankeit des attischen Strategen Nikias und die Nierenleiden im Corpus Hippocraticum," *Arch. Intern. Hist. Sci.* 26 (1977): 3–32.

71. See H. Fasbinder, *Entwicklungslehre, Geburtshülfe und Gynäkologie in den hippokratischen Schriften* (Stuttgart, 1897), and P. Diepgen, *Die Frauenheilkunde der Alten Welt* (Munich, 1937), pp. 187ff. and 212–25.

72. *Epid.*, I, cases 4, 5, and 11; *Epid.*, III, 2d list, cases 2 and 14. See also *Mul.*, I, 35–41.

Chapter Five: Syphilis

1. For a recent bibliography of the state of the question, see F. Guerra, "The Dispute over Syphilis: Europe versus America," *Clio Medica* 13 (1978): 39–61. This author favors the autochthonous origins of European syphilis in the fifteenth century. The arguments of the "Americanists" are well condensed by F. E. Rabello, "Les origines de la syphilis," *Nouvelle Presse Médicale* 2 (1973): 1376–80. He stresses the "sharp contrast between [anti-Americanist] hypotheses, which are at times anecdotal and cute, and the impressive weight of facts that support the nonexistence of syphilis [in Europe] before Columbus."

2. Especially important in this regard are J. Rosenbaum, *Geschichte der Lustseuche im Alterthume* (Halle, 1839), and J. K. Proksch, *Die Geschichte der venerischen Krankheiten* (Bonn, 1895). Both these monographs are remarkable for the historical documentation assembled in them, but they must be used with the greatest care,

since their interpretation of those sources is not critical enough and no longer corresponds to modern medical knowledge.

3. For a critique of the so-called classical descriptions of this disease, see I. Bloch, *Der Ursprung der Syphilis,* 2 vols. (Jena, 1901–11), and E. Jeanselme, *Histoire de la syphilis* (Paris, 1931). Even Socrates' snub nose on busts has been considered a proof of the existence of syphilis in his day. In this regard, see B. Springer, *Die genialen Syphilitiker,* 2d ed. (Berlin, 1926), p. 61; G. Milian, "Socrate hérédo-syphilitique," *Paris méd.,* suppl., 14 (1913): 597–603; and especially the critical review of W. Fahlbusch, "War Sokrates mit angeborener Syphilis behaftet?" *Derm. Wochenschr.* 107 (1938): 1067–79. The snub nose can be a simple anatomical variation (that is probably the case for Socrates' nose, which, though it lacked the beauty of Cleopatra's, was not necessarily the sign of a disease), but it can also result from a pathological collapse of the nose. An event of this sort is actually described in the Hippocratic texts (*Epid.,* IV, 19, and *Epid.,* VI, 1, 3; Littré, V, 156 and 266). It is true that nowadays syphilis, both congenital and tertiary, is the most common cause of this type of nasal deformity, but that is not sufficient reason for us to follow the authors who interpret the central collapse of the nose as a pathognomonic sign of syphilis and who cite the Hippocratic corpus as evidence for the antiquity of the disease (for instance, J. Wright, *The Nose and Throat in Medical History* [Philadelphia, n.d.], p. 45, and R. Kapferer, *Hippokrates-Fibel* [Stuttgart, 1943], p. 127). The syphilitic snub nose is chiefly caused by the destruction of the nasal septum by vascular disturbances, while the Hippocratic text speaks of a consuming ulceration that causes the collapse of the nose in a child by "the exit of a bone from the roof of the mouth." One can suppose in this case a perforation of the hard palate by tertiary syphilitic inflammation, but the observations of the ancient Greek physician do not lend themselves to this diagnosis, since the ulceration in question is so extensive that it makes the upper incisors fall out and even some lower teeth. This is noma (gangrenous stomatitis), not syphilis (see chapter 13, below, the section "Four Concise Case Histories," for a discussion of noma in *Epid.,* VII, 113). A relatively recent paper suggests that the final illness of the Roman general Sulla was syphilis (see T. F. Carney, "The Death of Sulla," *Acta Classica* 4 [1961]: 64–79); the identification of this case of "phthiriasis" with syphilis rests on an argument that is medically unacceptable.

4. See T. B. Turner and D. H. Hollander, *Biology of the Treponematoses* (Geneva, 1957).

5. E. H. Hudson, *Non-venereal Syphilis: A Sociological and Medical Study of Bejel* (Edinburgh and London, 1958); "Treponematosis and Man's Social Evolution," *Amer. Anthrop.* 67 (1965): 885–901; "Christopher Columbus and the History of Syphilis," *Acta Tropica* 25 (1968): 1–16.

6. C. J. Hackett, "On the Origin of the Human Treponematoses," *Bulletin W.H.O.* 29 (1963): 7–41; "The Human Treponematoses," in D. Brothwell and T. A. Sandison, *Diseases in Antiquity* (Springfield, 1967), pp. 152–69.

7. Hackett, "Human Treponematoses" (above, n. 6), pp. 161 and 165.

8. D. R. Brothwell, "The Real History of Syphilis," *Science Journal* 6 (1970): 27–33.

9. T. A. Cockburn, "The Origin of the Treponematoses," *Bulletin W.H.O.* 24 (1961): 221–28, and *The Evolution and Eradication of Infectious Diseases* (Baltimore, 1963), pp. 152–74.

10. J. D. Oriel and T. A. Cockburn, "Syphilis: Where Did It Come From?" *Paleopathology Newsletter,* no. 6 (1974): 9–12.

11. See H. C. Raven, *The Anatomy of the Gorilla* (New York, 1950); A. Fribourg-Blanc and H. H. Mollaret, "Natural Treponematoses of the African Climate,"

Primates in Medicine 3 (1968): 110–18. The first author states the existence of a syphiloid cutaneous disease in apes, and the two others have detected anti-treponematic antibodies in the blood and treponemes living in the popliteal lymph nodes of African apes.

12. V. Møller-Christensen, "Evidence of Tuberculosis, Leprosy, and Syphilis in Antiquity and the Middle Ages," *Proc.* XIX *Intern. Congr. Hist. Med. (Basel, 1964)* (Basel, 1966); "Venerische und nichtvenerische Syphilis," in *Medizinische Diagnostik in Geschichte und Gegenwart* (Festschrift für H. Goerke) (Munich, 1978), pp. 226–34.

13. For the criteria that should be the basis of the paleopathological diagnosis of treponematoses, see especially C. J. Hackett, "An Introduction to Diagnostic Criteria of Syphilis, Treponarid, and Yaws (Treponematoses) in Dry Bones, and Some Implications," *Virchow's Archiv für Pathol. Anatomie und Histologie* 368 (1975): 229–41, and "Diagnostic Criteria of Syphilis, Yaws, and Treponarid (Treponematoses) and of Some Other Diseases in Dry Bones," *Sitzungsbericht. Heidelberger Akad. Wiss., Med.-nat. Kl.* (1976), pp. 339–470.

14. Hudson, "Treponematosis," (above, n. 5), p. 899.

15. See H. U. Williams, "The Origin and Antiquity of Syphilis," *Archives of Pathology* 13 (1932): 779–814 and 931–83; S. Jarcho, "Some Observations on Disease in Prehistoric North America," *Bull. Hist. Med.* 38 (1964): 1–19; C. W. Goff, "Syphilis," in Brothwell and Sandison, *Diseases* (above, n. 6), pp. 279–94; N. G. Gejvall and F. Henschen, "Anatomical Evidence of pre-Columbian Syphilis in the West Indian Islands," *J. Occup. Therap.* 25 (1971): 138–57; M. Y. El-Najjar, "Human Treponematosis and Tuberculosis: Evidence from the New World," *Amer. J. Phys. Anthr.* 51 (1979): 599–618. In several cases, carbon 14 dating makes it certain that the bones in question are really pre-Columbian (twelfth to fourteenth century); cf. D. Brothwell and R. Burleigh, "Radiocarbon Dating and the History of Treponematoses in Man," *J. Archaeol. Sci.* 2 (1975): 393–96.

16. T. D. Stewart and O. Spoehr, "Evidence on the Paleopathology of Yaws," *Bull. Hist. Med.* 26 (1952): 538–53.

17. See Hackett, "Diagnostic Criteria" (above, n. 13), pp. 230 and 238.

18. For a critical evaluation of the old research on this subject, see H. E. Sigerist, *History of Medicine* (New York, 1951), 1: 54–56. The medieval cases from Siberia described by D. G. Rokhlin and preserved in his museum in Leningrad have been discredited by recent examinations (performed by V. Møller-Christensen and by me). In the case from Spitalfields (London) published by D. Brothwell (*Digging Up Bones* [London, 1972], p. 137, pl. 5), the diagnosis is certain but the date of the specimen is not. There has been a diagnosis of "hereditary syphilis" on Neanderthal remains deposited in the British Museum (cf. D. J. Wright, "Syphilis and Neanderthal Man," *Nature* [London] 229 [1971]: 409); the diagnosis is a fantasy based on dubious criteria. An extraordinary case was presented by Eliane Spitery at the Third European Congress of the Paleopathological Association held at Caen in 1980: in question is a male skull from the private collection of S. Gagnière (Marseille) with the typical signs of gangosa (rhino-pharyngitis mutilans). The diagnosis of tertiary yaws seems most likely, but the history of this museum specimen is troubling. It seems to have been found in a Roman cemetery at Arles in 1839. Precise documentation of the location and conditions of the find are lacking. It might be the skull of a Roman soldier, as an old label has it, or it might be a later intrusion. An African origin cannot be ruled out, despite the absence of Negroid anthropometric traits. It would be very useful to submit this skull to modern dating methods, particularly carbon 14 dating. The diagnosis of bejel proposed by F. Kail and A. de Froe (*Hantarzt* 4 [1953]: 82) for a sixth-century skeleton from Iraq seems to me uncertain and unlikely.

19. See in this connection the studies by L. Glück and J. Fleger. A survey of syphilitic endemics in modern times can be found in G. Solente, "Les principales endémies de syphilis," *Presse Médicale* 69 (1961): 2363–65.

20. E. H. Ackerknecht, *Geschichte und Geographie der wichtigsten Krankheiten* (Stuttgart, 1963), p. 107, and F. Henschen, *The History and Geography of Diseases*, trans. J. Tute (New York, 1966), p. 87.

21. Rosenbaum, *Geschichte der Lustseuche* (above, n. 2), translated into English from the French version, *Histoire de la syphilis dans l'Antiquité* (Brussels, 1847), pp. 37–38. This work enjoyed great success before the public (there were seven German editions and translations into several languages), and it was accepted with enthusiasm by specialists. Karl Sudhoff, the leading historian of medicine at the beginning of the twentieth century, wrote an encomiastic review of it and dubbed it "unsterblich," immortal! See H. T. Koch, "Julius Rosenbaum (1807–1874) als Medizinhistoriker," *NTM* (Leipzig) 18 (1981): 84–90.

22. Ibid., pp. 181–84, 196–98, and elsewhere.

23. Ackerknecht, *Geschichte und Geographie* (above, n. 20), p. 107; M. L. Brodny, "The History of Gonorrhea among the Greeks and Romans," *Trans. Amer. Neisser. Med. Soc.* 3 (1937): 92–106. In the cuneiform texts of Mesopotamia, there is talk of venereal diseases. Though syphilis cannot be identified, gonorrhea seems probable. On this subject, see R. Labat, "Geschlechtskrankheiten," in *Reallexicon der Assyriologie* (Berlin, 1971), 3: 221–23.

24. Henschen, *History and Geography of Diseases* (above, n. 20), p. 87.

25. Pazzini, "De amatorum morbis," *Boll. Istit. Stor. Ital. Arte San.* 10 (1930): 1–18 and 131–54, and "Ancora sulla blenorragia degli antichi," *Atti Mem. Stor. Arte San.* (1983), pp. 85–90.

26. H. St. H. Vertue, "Enquiry into Venereal Disease in Greece and Rome," *Guy's Hosp. Rep.* 102 (1953): 277–302, and J. D. Oriel, "Gonorrhea in the Ancient World," *Paleopath. Newsletter,* no. 4 (1973).

27. The basic reference is Leviticus 22:4 in the Septuagint. The medical texts usually cited for the ancient existence of the gonococcus are as follows: Hippocrates, *Epid.*, III, 7; *Morb.*, II, 51; *Aph.*, IV, 82; and *Mul.*, I, 24, and II, 116; Celsus, *De med.*, VI, 18; Aretaeus, *De diut. morb.*, II, 5, and *De cur. diut. morb.*, II, 5; Galen, *De locis affectis,* VI.

28. Oriel, "Gonorrhea" (above, n. 26).

29. For instance, *Epid.*, VI, 8, 29; *Aff. int.*, 43; *Morb.*, II, 51; and *Genit.*, I.

30. *Morb.*, II, 51 (Littré, VII, 78–80; Jouanna, 188).

31. See M. D. Grmek and R. Wittern, "Die Krankheit des attischen Strategen Nikias und die Nierenleiden im Corpus Hippocraticum," *Arch. Intern. Hist. Sci.* 26 (1977): 3–32.

32. *Aph.*, IV, 82. See also *Aph.*, VII, 57, and *Praen. Coacae*, 463.

33. See below, chapter 11, "The Place and Date of the Disease of Philiscus."

34. So Jones for the Greek word *pollá,* which could also be translated, as by Littré, "frequent, common."

35. *Epid.*, III, 7 (Littré, III, 84), trans. W.H.S. Jones, *Hippocrates* (Cambridge and London, 1948), 1: 247. See also *Epid.*, III, 3, 3 (Littré, III, 70; Jones, I, 241).

36. J. Hirschberg, *Geschichte der Augenheilkunde im Alterthum* (Leipzig, 1899), p. 70.

37. Rosenbaum, *Histoire de la syphilis* (above, n. 21), p. 255.

38. H. Behçet, "Ueber rezidivierende aphthöse, durch ein Virus verursachte Geschwüre am Mund, am Augem, und an den Genitalien," *Derm. Wochenschr* 105 (1937): 1152–57.

39. See A. Feigenbaum, "Description of Behçet's Syndrome in the Hippocratic Third Book of Endemic Diseases," *Brit. J. Ophthalm.* 40 (1956): 355–57.

40. For example, see *Morb.*, IV, 55; *Epid.*, II, 3, 5; *Epid.*, VI, 2, 2; *Aph.*, IV, 55.

41. *Lysistrata,* 987–88.

42. Galen, *Meth. med.*, VIII, 8, 6 (Kühn, X, 580).

43. *Mul.*, I, 24 (Littré, VIII, 64).

44. Galen, *De loc. aff.*, VI (Kühn, VIII, 441; cf. also Kühn, IX, 267). See P. Diepgen, *Die Frauenheilkunde der Alten Welt* (Munich, 1937) (*Steckel's Handbuch der Gynäkologie,* XII–1), p. 199, and R. E. Siegel, *Galen on the Affected Parts* (Basel, 1976), pp. 192ff.

45. *Mul.*, II, 116–20 (Littré, VIII, 250–62).

46. *Mul.*, II, 116 (Littré, VIII, 250–52); based on Littré's translation.

47. Diepgen, *Die Frauenheilkunde* (above, n. 44), p. 198.

48. M.-T. Fontanille, *Avortement et contraception dans la médicine gréco-romaine* (Paris, 1977), p. 158.

49. *Aph.*, III, 24 (Littré, IV, 496). For an aphthous mouth as a bad omen in pregnant women, see *Praen. Coacae,* 504 and 533 (Littré, V, 700 and 706). To be sure, it is impossible for us to distinguish aphthae in the mouth that have viral origins from those due to thrush, but the insistence in ancient sources on the commonness of this disease in newborns points to mycosis. In my opinion, the two diseases coexisted in antiquity. Hippocratic knowledge of thrush is generally accepted by historians of pediatrics, who find corroboration in the writings of Soranus, Celsus, Aretaeus, and Galen. See D. Ghinopoulo, *Pädiatrie in Hellas und Rom* (Jena, 1930), pp. 57ff., and A. Peiper, *Chronik der Kinderheilkunde,* 2d ed. (Leipzig, 1955), p. 23.

50. *In Hipp. Aph. comm.*, III, 25 (Kühn, XVII, B 627). See also *Def. med.*, Kühn, XIX, 441, and the lexicons of Hesychius and Erotianus. Etymologically linked to the verb *háptō* 'enflame, join, seize,' the term *aphtha* does not apply to deep, stubborn ulcerations (whence the distinction, in *Epid.*, III, 7, between *aphthṓdea* and *helkṓdea* in the mouth) nor to blistering ulcerations (whence the distinction between them and *phlúktainai* 'blisters' in the ancient gynecological texts).

51. *Nat. mul.*, 60, 86, and 100 (Littré, VII, 398, 408, and 416); *Mul.*, I, 34 (Littré, VIII, 82); *Praen. Coacae,* 518 (Littré, V, 704).

52. *Morb.*, II, 50 (Littré, VII, 76).

53. See J. Jouanna's note in his edition: *Hippocrate, Maladies* II (Paris, 1983), p. 254.

54. *Praen. Coacae,* 518 (Littré, V, 704).

55. See below, chapter 7.

56. In the Hippocratic corpus, the term *hérpēs* designates some serious dermatoses that recall herpes zoster (shingles), herpes circinatus, or even perhaps the eruptions of smallpox, as the famous dermatologist Robert Willan thought. In my opinion, we should think of them as indicating a cutaneous lesion having a certain appearance, a kind of serpiginous ulcer, rather than a disease proper. None of the uses of this word in the medical literature of the classical period refers to genital herpes in the modern sense. See T.S.L. Beswick, "The Origin and Use of the Word Herpes," *Med. Hist.* 6 (1962): 214–32.

57. *Nat. mul.*, 108 (Littré, VII, 422). See also *Mul.*, I, 90 (Littré, VIII, 214–18).

58. See especially *Mul.*, II, 173 (Littré, VIII, 354).

59. *Epid.*, VI, 8, 21 (Littré, V, 352).

60. *Mul.*, I, 40 (Littré, VIII, 96–98).

61. *Ulc.*, 14 (Littré, VI, 418; Petrequin, I, 292).

62. Celsus, *De medicina,* V, 28, 14B, trans. W. G. Spencer (London and Cambridge, 1983; rept. 1953), 2: 161.

63. See J. D. Oriel, "Anal and Genital Warts in the Ancient World," *Paleopath. Newsletter,* no. 3 (1973).

64. *Nat. mul.,* 66 and 83 (Littré, VII, 402 and 406). See also Galen, *Meth. med.,* V (Kühn, X, 325).

65. Diepgen, *Die Frauenheilkunde* (above, n. 44), p. 217, and H.-J. von Schumann, *Sexualkunde und Sexualmedizin in der klassischen Antike* (Munich, 1975), col. 34.

66. Pliny the Younger, *Epistolae,* VI, 24. The case was recently well discussed by A. Keaveney and J. Madden in *Hermes* 107 (1979): 499ff., who refute the diagnosis of syphilis proposed in Pauly-Wissowa, *Real Encyclopädie der Altertumswissenschaft,* 15: 1026.

67. Celsus, *De medicina,* VI, 18, 2. Cf. W. R. Bett, *A Short History of Some Common Diseases* (Oxford, 1934), p. 35.

68. According to Palladius, *Hist. Lausiaca* (Migne, *Patrologia Graeca,* XXXIX, col. 1091). See E. Jeanselme, "Le chancre mou existait-il à l'Alexandrie au IVe siècle?" *Bull. Soc. Franç. Hist. Méd.* 14 (1920): 233–38.

69. Flavius Josephus, *Against Apion,* II, 13.

70. *Mul.,* II, 115 and 122 (Littré, VIII, 248 and 258). See also *Mul.,* II, 176, where the symptoms of purulent endometriosis are prominent.

71. Herodotus, III, 149.

Chapter Six: Leprosy

1. For the history of this research, see V. Møller-Christensen, "New Knowledge of Leprosy through Paleopathology," *Intern. Jour. Leprosy* 33 (1965): 603–10, and J.G. Andersen, "Studies in Mediaeval Diagnosis of Leprosy in Denmark," *Danish Med. Bull.* suppl. 9, 16 (1969): 1–124.

2. L. Glück, "Die Lepra der oberen Atmungswege und Verdauungswege," *Mittheilungen und Verhandlungen der Intern. Lepra-Conferenz zu Berlin* 1 (1897): 1–93.

3. V. Møller-Christensen, *Bone Changes in Leprosy* (Copenhagen, 1961), and *Leprosy Changes in the Skull* (Odense, 1978).

4. V. Møller-Christensen, "Evidence of Tuberculosis, Leprosy, and Syphilis in Antiquity and the Middle Ages," *Proc.* XIX *Intern. Congress History Med. (Basel, 1964)* (Basel, 1966), pp. 229–37.

5. See G. Elliott Smith and F. Wood Jones, "Report on the Human Remains," *Archaeological Survey of Nubia, Report for 1907–1908,* vol. 2 (Cairo, 1910); G. Elliott Smith and D. E. Derry, "An Anatomical Report," *Archaeological Survey of Nubia,* Bull. 6 (1910); V. Møller-Christensen and D. R. Hughes, "An Early Case of Leprosy from Nubia," *Man* 62 (1966): 242–45; and Andersen, "Studies in Mediaeval," (above, n. 1), pp. 49 and 79.

6. T. Dzierzykray-Rogalski, "Paleopathology of the Ptolemaic Inhabitants of Dakleh Oasis (Egypt)," *Jour. Hum. Evol.* 9 (1980): 71–74.

7. These cases (except for the last two) were published by D. Brothwell, C. Wells, and V. Møller-Christensen. In this connection see D. Brothwell and A. T. Sandison, *Diseases in Antiquity* (Springfield, 1967), p. 303. Since the publication just cited, leprous lesions were diagnosed on the lower extremities of a skeleton found at Dorset in a Roman necropolis of the fourth century A.D. See O. K. Skinsnes, "An Ancient Briton Adds to the Story of Leprosy," *Intern. Jour. Leprosy* 44 (1975): 387ff. However, this diagnosis, which is based exclusively on the "lollipop" appearance of the phalanges, is uncertain, as E. Jonquières (*Inter. Jour. Leprosy* 45 [1977]:66) has remarked in responding to Skinsnes's publication. Another British case, from Poundbury (about A.D. 400), is also doubtful to the extent that the diagnosis relies only on vague, noncranial lesions. Cf R. Reader, "New Evidence for the Antiquity of Leprosy in Early Britain," *Jour. Archeol. Sci.* 1 (1974): 205–7.

8. Brothwell and Sandison, *Diseases* (above, n. 7), p. 302.

9. J. L. Angel, "Human Skeletal Remains at Karataş," *Amer. Jour. Archaeol.* 74 (1970): 256.

10. See I. Bloch, "Zur Vorgeschichte des Aussatzes," *Verh. Berliner Ges. Anthrop.* 31 (1899): 205–16 (esp. pp. 210 and 214ff.).

11. F. E. Hoggan, "The Leper Terra-cotta of Athens," *Jour. Hellen. Stud.* 13 (1892): 101–3.

12. Louvre Museum, terra cotta figurine E 17. The diagnosis of leprosy was posited by F. Regnault, "Les figurines antiques devant l'art et la médecine," *Medicina* (Paris) 4 (1907): 26ff. See the description and photographic reproduction in S. Besques, *Musée Nationale du Louvre, Catalogue raisonnée des figurines et reliefs en terre cuite grecs, étrusques, et romains* (Paris, 1972), 3: 95, and pl. 120h. This object can be compared with another terra cotta from Troy, dating from the first century A.D., Louvre E/D 567, where the deformity of the nose is insufficient evidence of a leprous ailment. In the *Histoire générale de la médecine* published under the direction of M. Laignel-Lavastine (vol. 3 [Paris, 1948]), there is a photograph of a Hellenistic figurine in the Louvre that, according to the caption, represents a leper. The terra cotta in question, which comes from Smyrna and is catalogued at the Louvre as D 1469, does indeed call to mind leontiasis, but such a diagnosis is not justified: the presence of a single eye on the forehead proves that it is a caricature of the Cyclops Polyphemus.

13. Besques, *Musée du Louvre, Catalogue raisonnée* (above, n. 12), 3: 222, and pl. 303h. The figurine is numbered E/D 1681.

14. Louvre E/D 1793, E 144, and E/D 1823. See Regnault, "Les figurines" (above, n. 12), pp. 26 ff., and Besques, *Musée du Louvre, Catalogue raisonnée* (above, n. 12), 3: 234, pls. 311m, 312d, and 313k. The head E 144 shows all the signs of rhinoscleroma. These are just a few representative examples; over twenty figurines of this type are known.

15. Greco-Roman Museum of Alexandria and Fouquet Antiquities Collection no. 455. See A. Panayotatou, "Terres cuites d'Egypte de l'époque gréco-romaine et maladies," *Actes VIe Congrès Intern. Hist. Méd.* (Leiden and Amsterdam, 1927), pp. 41–47, esp. figs. 28a and 28b.

16. Panayotatou, "Terres cuites" (above, n. 15), p. 45.

17. Benaki Museum, Athens, inv. no. 12599.

18. Archeological Museum of Dijon, ex-voto no. 97 (Catalogue of S. Deyts). See R. Bernard and P. Vassal, "Etude médicale des ex-voto de la Seine," *Rev. Archéol. de l'Est* 9 (1958): 332.

19. Rockefeller Museum, Jerusalem; see M. Yoeli, "A *Facies Leontina* of Leprosy on an Ancient Canaanite Jar," *Jour. Hist. Med.* 10 (1955): 331–35.

20. See, in this regard, Dharmendra, "Leprosy in Ancient Indian Medicine," *Intern. Jour. Leprosy* 15 (1947): 424–30; M. Schär-Send, "Die Lepra in der altindischen Medizin und Gesellschaft," in H. M. Koelbing et al., *Beiträge zur Geschichte der Lepra* (Zürich, 1972), pp. 11–33; and above all, J. Filliozat, *La doctrine classique de la médecine indienne,* 2d ed. (Paris, 1975).

21. Susruta, *Nidānasthāna,* v, 12–14. Cf. Filliozat, *La doctrine* (above, n. 20), pp. 82 and 103.

22. See especially *Nidānasthāna,* v, 7. Cf. Schär-Send, "Die Lepra," 1972, (above, n. 20), pp. 19–23, and Filliozat, *La doctrine* (above, n. 20), p. 95.

23. *Nidānasthāna,* v, 26.

24. In this regard I refer the reader especially to the law code of Manu and the political treatise of Kautiliya.

25. *Huang-ti Nei-ching* (Yellow Emperor's Manual), Sû-wen, XII, 42, after the French translation by A. Husson (Paris, 1973), p. 197.

26. See K. Chimin Wong and Wu Lien-teh, *History of Chinese Medicine* (Tientsin, 1932), pp. 103–5; Liu Mu Chih, "Data on Leprosy in Chinese Medical Literature and Historical Records," *Chin. Jour. Derm.* 4 (1956): 3ff.; P. Huard and M. Wong, *La médecine chinoise au cours des siècles* (Paris, 1959), pp. 19–20, 24, and 61; Lu Gwei-djen and J. Needham, "Records of Diseases in Ancient China," in Brothwell and Sandison, *Diseases in Antiquity* (above, n. 7), pp. 222–37, esp. p. 233.

27. *Lun yü,* VI, 8.

28. K. Chimin Wong and Wu Lien-teh, *History* (above, n. 26), p. 103, and Lu Gwei-djen and Needham, "Records," (above, n. 26), pp. 236ff.

29. *Pap. Ebers,* no. 877. For the most recent version of his argument in favor of the identification of leprosy in this papyrus, see B. Ebbell, *Beiträge zur ältesten Geschichte einiger Infektionskrankheiten* (Oslo, 1967), pp. 68–84. For a critique, see H. Grapow et al., *Grundriss der Medizin der alten Aegypter* (Berlin, 1958), IV/1: 288; Andersen, "Studies in Mediaeval" (above, n. 1), pp. 10–14; and Koelbing et al., *Beiträge* (above, n. 20), pp. 35ff.

30. See K. Sudhoff, "Die Krankheiten *bennu* und *sibtu* der babylonisch-assyrischen Rechtsurkunden," *Arch. Gesch. Med.* 4 (1911): 353–69; H. E. Sigerist, *History of Medicine* (New York, 1951), 1: 381 and 398; J. V. Kinnier Wilson, "Leprosy in Ancient Mesopotamia," *Rev. Assyr. et Archéol. Orient.* 60 (1966): 47–58. The antiquity of the isolation of persons affected by certain diseases in this region is confirmed by a letter of Zimri-lim, king of Mari in the eighteenth century B.C. See A. Finet, "Les médecins au royaume de Mari," *Ann. Inst. Philol. Hist. Orient.* 14 (1954–57): 123–44, esp. p. 129.

31. VAT 7525, col. 2, ll. 42–45. Wilson, "Leprosy," (above, n. 30), and F. Köcher and A. L. Oppenheim, "The Old-Babylonian Omen Text VAT 7525," *Arch. für Orientforsch.* 18 (1957): 62.

32. *Rev. Assyriol.* 71, (1967): 190. Cf. also S. G. Browne, *Leprosy in the Bible* (London, 1971). I note that it is incorrect to introduce into the discussion of Mesopotamian leprosy the absence of paleopathological proof, since the number of specimens that has been examined from this region is still too small.

33. Leviticus 13:2–46. See the detailed analysis of this text in J. Preuss, *Biblische-talmudische Medizin,* 3d ed. (Berlin, 1923), pp. 369–90.

34. For studies subsequent to Preuss, see E. Jeanselme, *La lèpre* (Paris, 1934), pp. 12–16; R. G. Cochrane, *Biblical Leprosy,* 3d ed. (Glasgow, 1963); I. Goldman, "White Spots in Biblical Times," *Arch. Derm.* (Chicago) 93 (1966): 744–53; I. Simon, "La dermatologie hébraïque dans l'Antiquité et au Moyen Age," *Rev. Hist. Méd. Hébr.* 27, no. 110 (1974): 149–54, and ibid. 28, no. 111 (1974): 7–14.

35. Exodus 4:6, Numbers 12:10b; 2 Kings 5:27.

36. E. V. Hulse, "The Nature of Biblical Leprosy and the Use of Alternative Medical Terms in Modern Translations of the Bible," *Palestine Exploration Quarterly* 107 (1975): 87–105.

37. Preuss, *Biblische-talmudische Medizin* (above, n. 33), p. 372.

38. For example, see Andersen, "Studies in Mediaeval," (above, n. 1), p. 15.

39. Flavius Josephus, *Contra Apion,* I, 26–32, 34, and 35.

40. *Contra Apion,* I, 26 (esp. sec. 229).

41. Tacitus, *Histories,* V, 3; Justinus, *Historia Philippicae,* XXXVI 2; Diodorus Siculus, XXXIV, 2.

42. Flavius Josephus, *Contra Apion,* 1, 31 (especially secs. 281–82).

43. Herodotus, 1, 138.

44. Aeschylus, *Choephoroi,* 279–82. See J. Dumortier, *Le vocabulaire médical d'Eschyle et les écrits hippocratiques,* 2d ed. (Paris, 1975), pp. 80–83.

45. P. Chantraine, *Dictionnaire étymologique de la langue greque* (Paris, 1974) 3: 630–31.

46. Nicander, *Theriaca,* 156 and 262.
47. *Morb.,* I, 3 (Littré, VI, 144).
48. *Aph.,* III, 20 (Littré, IV, 494).
49. *Epid.,* VI, III, 23, and *Hum.,* 20 (Littré, V, 304 and 500).
50. *Epid.,* II, I, 7 (Littré, V, 78).
51. *Alim.,* 20 (Littré, IX, 104). See K. Diechgräber, *Pseudo-Hippokrates Ueber die Nahrung* (Wiesbaden, 1973), pp. 28 and 35. This is a late treatise probably dating from the first century A.D..
52. *Liqu.,* 4 (Littré, VI, 128). The use of salt is recommended for leprous nails.
53. *Epid.,* II, V, 24 (Littré, V, 132).
54. See Koelbing et al. *Beiträge,* (above, n. 20), pp. 40ff.
55. *Prorrh.,* II, 43 (Littré, IX, 74).
56. *Hum.,* 17 (Littré, V, 498).
57. *Epid.,* V, 17 and 19 (Littré, VI, 246).
58. *Aff.,* 35, (Littré, VI, 246).
59. Theophrastus, *Sweat,* 14; *Characters,* 12.
60. Aristotle, *Problemata,* VII, 8 (887a).
61. Pausanias, *Description of Greece,* V, 5, and *Suda,* s.v. *Lepreon.* There may have been a temple of *Zeus Leukaios* in his town, but it is possible that the name in the textual tradition of Pausanias is simply a corruption of *Zeus Lukaios.* On sulfurous springs, see Stéphanos in *Dictionnaire des sciences médicales* (Paris, 1884), 4th ser., 10: 530ff.
62. See in particular *Prorrh.,* II, 43. Plato mentions among the diseases caused by phlegm one that "dapples the body with white spots" (*Timaeus,* 85a).
63. *Praen. Coacae,* 502 (Littré, V, 700).
64. See Aristotle, *Hist. anim.,* 518a; *De gener. anim.,* 784a. Concerning Atossa, daughter and then wife of Artaxerxes, king of Persia from 404 to 358 B.C., Plutarch says that "her father loved her so much that, once she had become his wife, he felt not the slightest disgust for her when her body was taken over by an *alphós*" (*Life of Artaxerxes,* 23, 7). The example is an instructive one because it concerns the Persian court, where contracting *lépra* or *leúkē* in their Herodotean sense meant banishment. That the disease Plutarch calls *alphós* was benign is proven by the rest of the story of Atossa: she became her brother-in-law's lover and outlived her father-husband despite his exceptional longevity.
65. *Prorrh.,* II, 43 (Littré, IX, 74).
66. See Littré, IX, 74, n. 7 of the *apparatus criticus.*
67. The critical edition of the text of this letter is by E. Drerup (Leipzig, 1904); for a commentary and the dating of it, see K. Schwengler, *De Aeschinis Quae Feruntur Epistolis* (Giessen, 1913).
68. Oribasius, *Collectio medica,* XLV, 28. For Straton, see M. Wellman, *Philologische Untersuchungen,* XIV, 24, and Kind, s.v. *Straton,* in Pauly-Wissowa, *Real-Encyclopädie,* 2d ser., vol. IV/1, col. 316.
69. After the French translation by Bussemaker and Daremberg, *Oeuvres d'Oribase* (Paris, 1876), 4: 63ff.
70. Such is the opinion of the leprologist Andersen, "Studies in Mediaeval" (above, n. 1), p. 43.
71. According to chapter 13 of the Pseudo-Galenic treatise *Introductio seu medicus* (Kühn, XIV, 757), some authorities used the term *elephantíasis* in a generic sense, proposing to include in it six particular forms of diseases, namely, *elephantíasis* (in the narrow sense), *leontíasis, ophíasis, lépra, alōpekía,* and *lṓbe.* Since *alōpekía* (a disease that, from the Pseudo-Galenic description, may be related to Aristotle's *leúkē*) and *ophíasis* certainly have nothing to do with the leprosy complex proper, the same thing can be stated with regard to *lépra,* and there is therefore no need to see this

classification as an attempted nosological identification of "leprosy" in the Hippocratic sense with "leprosy" in the modern sense. Nevertheless, it may be true that this text, which is attributed to Galen and was much appreciated in the Middle Ages, contributed to the false explication of the classical nosological terminology and to the confusion from which the history of leprosy has long suffered. See Koelbing et al., *Beiträge* (above, n. 20), pp. 47 and 55.

72. According to Aristotle, "In the disease called *satyríasis*, . . . as the result of an abundance of humor or of breath that has not undergone coction and penetrates into the parts of the forehead, the face resembles that of another animal or a satyr"; *De generatione animalium*, 768b, after the edition and French translation by P. Louis (Paris, 1961), p. 150. The traditional explanation (see the Liddel-Scott-Jones lexicon s.v. *saturíasis*, II, and the note in Louis's edition) is that the deformity that makes the disease's victims resemble satyrs is the development of frontal exostoses. However, J. Jouanna and J. Taillardat ("Une vox nihili," *Rev. Etudes Grecques* 93 (1980): 132) have well shown that this notion is only a poor interpretation of a text in Galen; through comparison with passages in the Hippocratic corpus it is possible to deduce that the deformities in question were swelling near or under the ears.

73. Lucretius, *De rerum natura*, VI, 1114ff.

74. Celsus, *De medicina*, III, 25. Galen says that in his time *elephantíasis* was very common in Alexandria, rare in Germany and Mysia, and unknown among the Scyths (Kühn, XI, 142).

75. Pliny, *Natural History*, XXVI, 1 (trans. W.H.S. Jones, vol. 7, [London and Cambridge, 1956], p. 265).

76. Pliny, *Natural History*, XXVI, 5 (Jones, p. 271).

77. Plutarch, *Quaestiones conviviales*, VIII, 9.

78. In this regard, see the excellent analysis of Plutarch's text by C. Mugler, "Démocrite et les dangers de l'irradiation cosmique," *Rev. Hist. Sci.* 20 (1967): 221–28.

79. Aretaeus of Cappadocia, *Signa chron.*, II, 13. See the edition of the Greek text by K. Hude, *Corpus Med. Graecorum*, II, 2d ed. (Berlin, 1958), pp. 85–90, and the modern medical commentary in Andersen, "Studies in Mediaeval" (above, n. 1), pp. 30–40, and Koelbing et al., *Beiträge* (above, n. 20), pp. 43–54.

80. Aretaeus, *Signa chron.*, II, 13, 19 (Hude, pp. 89 ff.).

81. For instance, Galen still passionately defends the Hippocratic theory that pestilences were due to miasmata and could not pass from one human to the next. Nevertheless, Aretaeus points out and adopts the popular notion that plague victims and lepers are both to be avoided, since sickness is transmitted to healthy people by the breath of the ill. With regard to the treatment of leprosy, he says that "we fear cohabitation and communal life with them no less than if they were victims of plague; the infection (*baphé*) is easily transmitted by breath" (*Cura chron.*, II, 13, 1 [Hude, 168]).

82. This Saint Lazarus, the medieval patron of lepers, is a Biblical figure, an ulcerous pauper who begged at the gate of the evil rich man (*Luke* 16:19–31); he is not to be confused with the brother of Martha who, in the *Gospel according to John*, was miraculously brought back to life.

83. See G. Kurth, *La lèpre en Occident avant les Croisades* (Paris, 1899); E. Jeanselme, "Comment l'Europe au Moyen Age se protégea contre la lèpre?" *Bull. Soc. Franç. Hist. Méd.* 25 (1931): 1–155; E. Jeanselme, *La lèpre* (Paris, 1934); J. Cougoul, *La lèpre dans l'ancienne France* (Bordeaux, 1943); W. Dörr, *Ueber den Aussatz im Altertum und in der Gegenwart* (Heidelberg, 1948); R. G. Cochrane, "The History of Leprosy and Its Spread throughout the World," in R. G. Cochrane and T. F.

Davey, eds., *Leprosy in Theory and Practice* (Bristol, 1964); H. Schadewaldt, "Zur Geschichte der Lepra," *Hautarzt* 20 (1969): 124–30.

84. See S. N. Brody, *The Disease of the Soul: Leprosy in Medieval Literature* (Ithaca and London, 1974).

85. See Koelbing et al., *Beiträge* (above, n. 20), pp. 62ff.

86. For statistical data about leprosy and its geographical distribution, the authority is P. Harter, *Précis de leprologie* (Paris, 1968), and thereafter, the recent epidemiological bulletins of the World Health Organization and reports of international conventions on leprosy. As for Greece, leprosy was still relatively common there in the nineteeth century: in 1840 and 1843, official statistics recorded a little more than 150 cases, to which must be added 1,000 lepers on the island of Crete. To be sure, these figures are low. The centers of the disease were the northern part of Corfu, in Gortynia, in the southern part of Euboea, and on the islands of Lesbos, Thera, and to repeat, Crete. See C. Stéphanos, "Grèce," in *Dictionnaire des sciences médicales,* published under the direction of A. Dechambre (Paris, 1884), 4th ser. 10: 529ff. It is not uninteresting to note that, according to Caelius Aurelianus (*Acut.,* III, 18) the physician Themison (first century) noticed the commonness of leprosy in Crete.

87. D. Zambaco Pacha, *La lèpre à travers les siècles et les contrées* (Paris, 1914); G. Barbézieux, "Contribution à l'étude de l'histoire de la lèpre: La lèpre dans la plus haute antiquité," *Janus* 19 (1914): 132–49.

88. R. Chaussinand, *La lèpre* (Paris, 1954).

89. T. A. Cockburn, "Infectious Diseases in Ancient Populations," *Current Anthropology* 12 (1971): 42–62, esp. p. 48.

90. See A. Basset, "La lèpre, son intérêt dans l'étude de l'épidémiologie et de la pathologie générale," *Concours Médical* 93 (1971): 5627–37.

91. See, for instance, Andersen, "Studies in Mediaeval" (above, n. 1), p. 45, and S. G. Browne, "How Old Is Leprosy?" *Brit. Med. Jour.* (1970), pp. 640ff.

Chapter Seven: Tuberculosis

1. My late friend Charles Coury relied on his twofold expertise in tuberculosis and in history to create *Grandeur et déclin d'une maladie: La tuberculose au cours des siècles* (Paris, 1972). For the ancient history of tuberculosis, nothing has yet equaled the documentation in the sumptuous monograph by J. Jedlička, *Vyvoj fthiseologie, nauky o tuberkulose* (Prague, 1932); this work is in Czech, which means that it is hardly known and never used. As for other studies of the history of this disease around the world and through time, I cite M. Piéry and J. Roshem, *Histoire de la tuberculose* (Paris, 1931); A. Castiglioni, *History of Tuberculosis,* (New York, 1936); R. Bochalli, *Geschichte der Schwindsucht* (Leipzig, 1940); R. Burke, *An Historical Chronology of Tuberculosis,* 2d ed. (Springfield, 1955).

2. For osteoarchaeological diagnosis of tuberculosis, see D. Morse, "Tuberculosis," in D. Brothwell and A. T. Sandison, eds., *Diseases in Antiquity* (Springfield, 1967), pp. 249–71; T. Steinbock, *Paleopathological Diagnosis and Interpretation* (Springfield, 1976); and M. A. Kelley and M. Y. El-Najjar, "Natural Variations and Differential Diagnosis of Skeletal Changes in Tuberculosis," *Amer. Jour. Phys. Anthrop.* 52 (1980): 153–67; D. J. Ortner and W. G. J. Putschar, *Identification of Pathological Conditions in Human Skeletal Remains* (Washington, D.C., 1981), pp. 141–75.

3. See Morse, "Tuberculosis" (above, n. 2), p. 250.

4. L. Pales, *Paléopathologie et pathologie comparative* (Paris, 1930), p. 226;

V. Møller-Christensen, "Evidence of Tuberculosis, Leprosy, and Syphilis in Antiquity and the Middle Ages," *Proc. XIX Intern. Cong. Hist. Med.* (Basel, 1966), pp. 229–37; P. Sager, M. Schalimtzek, and V. Møller-Christensen, "A Case of Spondylitis Tuberculosa in the Danish Neolithic Age," *Danish Med. Bull.* 19 (1972): 172–80.

5. P. Bartels. "Tuberkulose (Wirbelkaries) in der jüngeren Steinzeit," *Arch. Anthrop.* 34 (1907): 243–55.

6. See C. Wells, *Bones, Bodies, and Disease* (London, 1964), p. 97.

7. G. E. Smith and M. A. Ruffer, "Pott'sche Krankheit an einer ägyptischen Mumie aus der Zeit der 21. Dynastie (um 1,000 v. Chr.)" *Krankheitserreger,* fasc. 3 (Giessen, 1910).

8. See A. J. E. Cave, "The Evidence for the Incidence of Tuberculosis in Ancient Egypt, " *Brit. Jour. Tub.* 33 (1939): 142; D. Morse et al., "Tuberculosis in Ancient Egypt," *Amer. Review Resp. Diseases* 90 (1964):524–41; A. P. Leca, *La médecine égyptienne au temps des Pharaons* (Paris, 1971), pp. 233ff.; and J. B. Bourke, "The Palaeopathology of the Vertebral Column in Ancient Egypt and Nubia, " *Med. History* 15 (1971): 370.

9. It is a small wooden statuette representing a man with a high thoracic kyphoscoliosis and an angular projection of the sternum (Musées Royaux de Bruxelles, no. E 5850). For its description and arguments in favor of the diagnosis of tuberculosis, see F. Jonckheere, "Le bossu des Musées Royaux d'Art et d'Histoire de Bruxelles," *Chronique d'Egypte* 23 no. 45 (1948): 24-35. His opinion is not shared by Leca, *La médecine égyptienne* (above, n. 8), p. 235, according to whom "nonspecific kyphoscoliosis can result in a similar deformity." Another example of a figurine with Pott's disease was published by B. Schrumpf-Pierron, "Le mal de Pott en Egypte 4,000 ans avant notre ère," *Aesculape* 23 (1933): 295.

10. Michael R. Zimmerman has succeeded in demonstrating the presence of acid-resistant bacilli in the vertebrae and extravasated blood in the lungs of a child mummy. See M. R. Zimmerman, "Pulmonary and Osseous Tuberculosis in an Egyptian Mummy," *Bull. New York Acad. Med.* 55 (1979): 604–8.

11. Coury, *Grandeur et déclin,* (above, n. 1), p. 10.

12. R. Campbell Thompson, "Assyrian Prescriptions for Diseases of the Chest and Lungs," *Rev. Assyr.* 31 (1934): 8–22.

13. See P. Cordier, "Histoire de la médecine indienne: La phtisie pulmonaire," *Ann. Hyg. Méd. Colon.* 15 (1912): 255–66 and 535–48; D. V. Subba Reddy, "Tuberculosis in Ancient India," *Bull. Hist. Med. Hyderabad* 2 (1972): 156–61.

14. See T'ao Lee, "Tuberculosis in Ancient China," *Chin. Med. Jour.* 61 (1942):272–80.

15. D. Morse, "Prehistoric Tuberculosis in America," *Amer. Rev. Respir. Dis.* 83 (1961): 489–504. See also Morse, "Tuberculosis," pp. 257ff.

16. See especially J. G. Roney, Jr., "Palaeoepidemiology: An Example from California," in S. Jarcho, ed., *Human Palaeopathology* (New Haven, 1966), pp. 101–3; M. J. Allison, D. Mendoza, and A. Pezzia, "Documentation of a Case of Tuberculosis in Pre-Columbian America," *Amer. Rev. Respir. Dis.* 107 (1973): 985–91; M. Kelley, *Paleopath. Newsletter,* no. 26 (June, 1979), p. 4; M. Y. El-Najjar, "Human Treponematoses and Tuberculosis: Evidence from the New World," *Amer. Jour. Phys. Anthr.* 51 (1979): 599–618; J. Buikstra, ed., *Prehistoric Tuberculosis in the Americas* (Evanston, 1981).

17. C. Coury, *La médecine de l'Amérique précolombienne* (Paris, 1969), pp. 84ff.

18. Ibid., p. 14.

19. Ibid., p. 194.

20. J. L. Angel, "Problems in Diagnosis," *Annual Meeting of the Paleopathological Association* (Toronto, April 1978).

21. See A. Krause, "Tuberculosis and Public Health," *Amer. Rev. Tub.* 18 (1928): 271–73.

22. Odyssey XI. 171–74 and 198–203; V.394–97; *Iliad* XIII. 663–72. Sophocles, *Antigone,* 819; Euripides, *Alcestis,* 204 and 236.

23. Aside from the general bibliography on the history of tuberculosis cited above in n. 1, see the following publications, which are devoted to the history of the disease in classical antiquity: B. Meinecke, "Consumption (Tuberculosis) in Classical Antiquity," *Ann. Med. Hist.* 9 (1927): 379–402; E. D. Baumann, "De phthisi antiqua," *Janus* 34 (1930):209–25 and 255–72; H. Gertler and D. Schultz, "Antike Aussagen zur Schwindsuchtsfrage," *Zschr. Tuberk.* 122 (1964):282–89.

24. See H. Frisk, *Griechisches etymologisches Wörterbuch* Heidelberg, 1969), 2: 1014–16, and P. Chantraine, *Dictionnaire étymologique de la langue grecque* (Paris, 1980), IV/2: 1201.

25. Herodotus, VII, 88, trans. A. de Sélincourt (Harmondsworth, 1954; rev. and rept. 1976), p. 471.

26. Meinecke, "Consumption" (above, n. 23), p. 381.

27. F. Kudlien, *Der Beginn des medizinischen Denkens bei den Griechen* (Zürich and Stuttgart, 1967), p. 110.

28. It could as easily be hemoptysis as hematemesis; classical medical texts use derivatives of the verb *emeō* to designate without distinction vomiting and spitting.

29. *Morb.,* I, 3 (Littré, VI, 144). See R. Wittern, *Die hippokratische Schrift De morbis* I (Hildesheim and New York, 1974), pp. 9 and 10.

30. K. Deichgräber, "Zur Milchtherapie der Hippokratiker (Epid. VII)," in *Medizingeschichte in unserer Zeit (Festschrift Artelt)* (Stuttgart, 1971), p. 50, n. 10.

31. Pseudo-Galen, *Definitiones medicae,* 261 (Kühn, XIX, 419). See C. Daremberg, *Oeuvres choisies d'Hippocrate,* 2d ed. (Paris, 1855), p. 264, and Wittern, *Die hippokratische Schrift* (above, n. 29), p. 194.

32. *Morb.,* II, 49. This *phthōē* is a long-term disease, according to the statement in *Morb.,* I, 3. However, it can be cured (if the disease is treated from the start), which creates a semantic problem, since then the disease is not properly a subclass of *phthísis* in *Morb.,* I, which must be fatal.

33. *Aff. int.,* 10 (Littré, VII, 188–90). See L. Bourgey, *Observation et expérience chez les médecins de la Collection hippocratique* (Paris, 1953), p. 149, and Coury, *Grandeur et déclin* (above, n. 1), p. 16.

34. *Aff. int.,* (Littré, VII, 192). After the translation by Bourgey, *Observation* (above, n. 33), p. 149, except for the passage on the morning cough. According to Littré, "The cough especially lays low old people." For correction of this passage, see R. Wittern, "Zur Krankheitserkennung in der knidischen Schrift De internis affectionibus," in *Medizinische Diagnostik in Geschichte und Gegenwart* (Munich, 1978), p. 109.

35. *Aff. int.,* 12 (Littré, VII, 192–94.)

36. *Morb.,* II, 48 (Littré, VII, 72). After the translation by Jacques Jouanna, based on his critical edition of the Greek text, *Maladies II* (Paris, 1983), pp. 183ff.

37. *Morb.,* 49 (Littré, VII, 74–76). After the translation by Jouanna, *Maladies II* (above, n. 36), pp. 185ff.

38. *Morb.,* 50 (Littré, VII, 76; Jouanna, 186).

39. In this regard, see R. E. Siegel, "Clinical Observations in Hippocrates: An Essay on the Evolution of the Diagnostic Art," *Jour. Mt. Sinai Hosp.* 31 (1964):285–303, esp. p. 295. The morning cough is also mentioned in *Aff. int.,* 11 (see above, n. 34).

40. See A. Baffoni, *Storia delle pleuriti da Ippocrate a Laennec* (Rome, 1947).

41. Swelling of the fingertips with curving of the nails, noticed by the Greek physicians and not ignored since, is still an indicator, as puzzling as it is reliable, of

severe disturbances in the organism. The physiopathological mechanism in question is unknown; in the diagnosis of pulmonary tuberculosis, they are not pathognomonic, since they occur in conjunction with a variety of intrathoracic disorders. Pulmonary suppuration remains their principal etiology, however, whence the old proverb about the examination of the lungs beginning at the fingertips. See C. Coury, *L'hippocratisme digital* (Paris, 1960), and "Le signe du doigt hippocratique," *Pagine Stor. Med.* 12, no. 2 (1968) 3–12.

42. *Aph.*, V, II (Littré, IV, 536), after Daremberg's translation.

43. *Praen. Coacae,* 426 (Littré, V, 680). Subsequently, Celsus, Caelius Aurelianus, Aretaeus, and others repeat this text. See W. D. Sharpe, "Lung Disease and the Greco-Roman Physician, *Amer. Rev. Respir. Dis.* 86 (1962): 178–92.

44. *Praen. Coacae,* 427 (Littré, V, 680).

45. *Praen. Coacae,* 428 (Littré, V, 680). Cf. *Aph.*, V, 12 and 14.

46. *Praen. Coacae,* 425 (Littré, V, 680). Cf. *Aph.*, V, 13.

47. *Loc. Hom.*, 14 (Littré, VI, 302–8).

48. *Morb.*, I, 19 (Littré, VI, 174–76; Wittern, pp. 48–52).

49. Galen, *Comm. in Hipp. Epid.*, VI, 13 (Kühn, XVII, 855). Celsus translates *phûma* by *tuberculum,* at least when the Greek word applies to formations located in the lungs that are manifested by coughing up blood (*De medicina*, IV, 5). See also H. Dönt, *Die Terminologie von Geschwür, Geschwulst, und Anschwellung im Corpus Hippocraticum* (Vienna, 1968).

50. Daremberg, *Oeuvres choisies* (above, n. 31), p. 282.

51. See especially the analysis by W. Pagel, "Die Krankheitslehre der Phthisie in den Phasen ihrer geschichtlichen Entwicklung," *Beitr. Klin. Tuberkl.* 66 (1927): 66–98.

52. Aristotle, *Parva naturalia,* 478b. See the text edited and translated by R. Mugnier (Paris, 1953), pp. 130ff. I should note that Aristotle, in describing a disease of cattle called *kraûros,* mentions that "the signs of this disease are hanging ears and loss of appetite; death comes quickly, and on dissection, the lung appears rotten" (*Hist. anim.*, VIII, 23, 604a).

53. *Epid.*, I, 3 (Littré, II, 604–10), in *Hippocrates,* trans. W. H. S. Jones (London and Cambridge, 1923), I: 148–50.

54. For the definition of *katástasis,* see below, (chapter 9, the section "The Place and Date of the Disease of Philiscus."

55. Daremberg, *Oeuvres choisies* (above, n. 31), p. 457.

56. It is amusing to see two radically opposed opinions on the frequency of consumption in the Greek world of this time. Bruno Meinecke asserts that "Hippocrates describes consumption so often and so fully that we are forced to the conclusion that it must have been very prevalent already in his days" (*Annals of Medical History* 9 [1927]: 381). Another, no less competent, specialist states that "although there are these references to the disease [phthisis], one cannot say that they occupy a leading place in Hippocratic writings, and we may assume that, though tuberculosis affected the Greeks of Hippocratic days, it played no very evident or particular part in the incidence of disease" (J. Fraser, "Tuberculosis," in W. R. Bett, *A Short History of Some Common Diseases* [London, 1934], p. 17). I favor Meinecke's opinion. The number of times consumption is mentioned in the Hippocratic corpus is less significant than the content of certain passages, especially those in the *Epidemics.* It is also essential to keep in mind the frequency and bearing of texts that refer to pleurisy, empyema, and other diseases whose etiology is at least partially tuberculous.

57. It is likely that in this regard popular opinion surpassed professional knowledge. The orator Isocrates alludes to the common belief that chronic consumption is contagious (*Aegin.*, XIX, 29).

58. *Aph.*, v, 9 (Littré, iv, 534). The same statement can be found in *Praen. Coacae*, 431. According to *Aph.*, vii, 88, the ages most vulnerable to consumption are from 18 to 30. See also *Aph.*, iii, 29, which speaks of hemoptysis and consumption as diseases that prevail among young people.

59. *Praen. Coacae*, 513 (Littré, v, 702).

60. *Prorrh.*, ii, 7 (Littré, ix, 24). This statement is based on correct observation but incorrect inversion of the causal chain: amenorrhea is the effect, not the cause, of tuberculous disease.

61. *Aer.*, 4, (Littré, ii, 22).

62. *Morb. sacr.*, 5 (Littré, vi, 364; Grensemann, p. 68).

63. *Prorrh.*, ii, 5 (Littré, ix, 20).

64. *Epid.*, iii, 14 (Littré, iii 96–98).

65. *Prorrh.*, ii, 7 (Littré, ix, 24).

66. G. Sée, *De la phtisie bacillaire des poumons* (Paris, 1884), p. 137.

67. *Epid.*, vii, 49 (Littré, v, 418). The same account occurs also in *Epid.*, v, 103 (Littré, v, 258). Translation after an as yet unpublished edition by Fernand Robert.

68. Translated in accord with the text given in the V manuscript: *apohrémpsies hupopuōdées*. Littré reads: *apohrémpsies puōdées*.

69. Littré translates "la phtisie s'établit" [consumption took hold], a rendering that in the context seems to me more satisfactory from a medical viewpoint. But to reach this version, he has to eliminate the word *kaì* in the phrase *phthísis kaì katéstē*. However, that word is attested in both M and V and the *recentiores*.

70. See P. Diepgen, *Die Frauenheilkunde der antiken Welt* (Munich, 1937), pp. 265 and 267.

71. *Epid.*, vii (Littré, v, 378). My translation of this case history follows the as yet unpublished critical edition by Fernand Robert.

72. The Hippocratic physicians did not know about taking the pulse, but they understood the value of visually marking the beat of the temporal artery.

73. Celsus, *De medicina*, iii, 22.

74. Aretaeus of Cappadocia, *Signa chron.*, i, 8. See the commentary by C. Coury, "La pathologie pulmonaire dans l'oeuvre d'Arétée de Cappadoce," *Presse Méd.* 70 (1962): 655–57. When Laennec made his magisterial description of pulmonary tuberculosis in the nineteenth century, he did not omit to recall "the coughing, dyspnea, purulent sputa, hectic fever, hemoptysis, marasmus, in sum, the totality of symptoms whose image Aretaeus traced with terrifying realism" (R. T. H. Laennec, *De l'auscultation médiate* (Paris, 1819), 1: 57).

75. See especially Sharpe, "Lung Disease" (above, n. 43), and Gertler and Schultz, "Antike Aussagen" (above, n. 23).

76. Aretaeus, *Signa chron.*, i, 8.

77. Plutarch, *Life of Aratus*, 52. The association of consumption with poisoning seems to have been a popular belief in the Hellenistic and Roman periods. In this connection, see the epitaph of Thermion, who died in Alexandria in the first century (E. Bernard, *Inscriptions métriques de l'Egypte gréco-romaine* [Paris, 1969], no. 46).

78. Plutarch, *Life of Cleomenes*, 30. See Baumann, "De phthisi antiqua" (above, n. 23), p. 271. In this particular case the diagnosis of pulmonary tuberculosis is likely. But it seems to me arbitrary to interpret as such the *phthísis* that, according to Diogenes Laertius, iv, 20, made off with the Platonic philosopher Polemon of Athens in his declining years.

79. Aelianus, *Frag.*, 99; *Suda* s.v. *phthôē*.

80. This iconographic representation of consumption is only known to us from writen evidence (*Suda* s.v. *Theopómpos*). In this connection, see E. and L. Edelstein, *Asclepius* (Baltimore, 1945), 1: 262ff. According to Pausanias, in the sanctuary of Delphi there was a "sculpture in bronze of a chronic invalid" who was "utterly

wasted away and reduced almost to the state of a skeleton" (*Descriptio Graeciae,* x, 2, 6). See H. Pomtow, "Delphische Neufunde. III. Hippokrates und die Asklepiaden in Delphi," *Klio* 15 (1917): 303–38, and F. Chamoux, "Perdiccas," in *Hommages à Albert Grenier* (Collection Latomus), 58 (1962): 386–96. In 1844, a bronze statuette presenting an emaciated youth was found in the Aisne, near Soissons. Long inaccessible, it was finally acquired by a public collection (Dumbarton Oaks, Research Library, no. 47.22). A Roman copy of a Greek work from the Hellenistic era, its withered body, emaciated face, and feverish stare are presented with great skill. The inscription "PERDIK . . . " on the base of the drapery leads one to believe that the person wasting away could be Perdiccas, sick with love. In that case the statue is a pendant to the Delphic *ex voto.* However, G. M. A. Richter maintains that the inscription alludes to Perdrix, a lame Athenian merchant taunted by Aristophanes (*Catalogue of Greek and Roman Antiquities in the Dumbarton Oaks Collection* (Cambridge, 1956), p. 32). Is this tuberculous consumption, pining away from love, or clubfoot with accompanying decline? The three diagnoses are not mutually exclusive, but it is, unfortunately, impossible to consider the statue a deliberate iconographic representation of pulmonary consumption. Since this disease is not marked by any external pathognomonic stigma, it is not enough to see an artistic image of a withered person in order to consider it a representation of tuberculosis. Likewise doubtful are the emaciated invalid on the Roman mosaic from Lambridi (Gsell Museum in Algiers) and the Hellenistic statue of the so-called "young consumptive" from the Fayûm (Cairo Museum). For the latter, see P. Perdrizet, "Le mort qui sentait bon," *Annuaire Inst. Philol. Bruxelles* 2 (1934): 719–27.

81. *Iámata,* case 33 (*Inscr. Graecae,* IV^2, 122). See R. Herzog, *Die Wunderheilungen von Epidauros* (Leipzig, 1931), p. 106, and Edelstein and Edelstein, *Asclepius* (above, n. 80), 1: 227.

82. Celsus, *De medicina,* III, 22.

83. Pliny the Younger, *Epistolae,* v, 19, 6. This treatment of pulmonary tuberculosis by change of climate may explain a strange find: the corpse of a young girl of the Roman aristocracy that was mummified in Egypt during the second century and exhumed in 1964 at the crossroads of the Via Cassia and the Via Grottarossa in Rome. See U. Scamuzzi, "Studio sulla Mummia di bambina cosidetta Mummia di Grottarossa," *Riv. Stud. Class* 12 (1964): 264–80. An appropriate paleopathological examination of the mummy could confirm or refute the hypothesis.

84. Pliny the Younger, *Epistolae,* VII, 9. See in this regard E. F. Leon, "A Case of Tuberculosis in the Roman Aristocracy at the Beginning of the Second Century," *Jour. Hist. Med.* 14 (1959): 86–88.

85. The term "tuberculosis" was invented only in 1832 (by J. L. Schönlein). First adopted in German, the word did not enter French medical literature until 1854. Although Laennec was the pathfinder in this slow trek toward the unity of tuberculosis, his anatomoclinical intuition did not really prevail until the advent of bacteriology.

86. *Aph.,* VI, 46 (Littré, IV, 574).

87. *Art.,* III, 41 (Littré, IV, 178–80); my translation follows, except in one detail, that of E. T. Withington, trans., *Hippocrates,* vol. 3 (Cambridge and London, 1928; rept. 1948), *Joints,* 41, pp. 279–81. Where he renders the word *próphasis* "origin," I prefer "first appearance."

88. See R. H. Major, "How Hippocrates Made His Diagnoses," *Intern. Record Med.* 170 (1957): 482; M. Michler, "Die Krüppelleiden in De morbo sacro und De articulis," *Sudhoffs Arch. Gesch. Med.* 45 (1961): 321–23, and Coury, *Grandeur et déclin* (above, n. 1), p. 62.

89. Not all the hunchbacks represented in works of art from antiquity are tuberculous. The diagnosis can only be considered if the hunchback is at right angles. Unfortunately, that is not enough. I have already stressed that an angular hump on a sculpted or painted figure does not secure the diagnosis of vertebral tuberculosis. However, such a diagnosis becomes plausible when the prevalence of tuberculosis in the society is proven independently. The Louvre has several Hellenistic terra cotta torsos from Smyrna that present angular kyphoses (inv. D 1177, D 1214, D 1216, D 1223, and so on). In the Greco-Roman Museum in Alexandria, there are oil-lamps and a statuette representing hunchbacks. The British Museum owns an ivory statuette, a Greek work of the first century, that represents a man with Negroid features whose spine is very curved (Townley Coll. 1594–4.15.2). Also worth mentioning is an Etruscan mirror with a drawing of a hunchbacked, emaciated man on it (Tarquinia Museum).

90. *Aph.*, VI, 35 (Littré, IV, 572).

91. *Epid.*, VII, 19 (Littré, V, 390–92).

92. For the general appearance of this epitaph, its historical vicissitudes, and a translation into French, see D. Gourevitch, "Une observation pédiatrique pour épitaphe," *Echo médical* 26, no. 145 (1968): 14. The diagnosis of tuberculosis is well defended by B. Meinecke, "A Quasi-autobiographical Case History of an Ancient Greek Child," *Bull. Hist. Med.* 8 (1949): 1022–31. The most recent study, which includes a very careful medico-historical analysis and abundant bibliography, is the thesis of H. D. Klitsch, *Eine inschriftliche Krankengeschichte des 3. Jht. n. Chr.: Das Grabgedicht für den fünfjährigen Lucius Minicius Anthimianus* (Erlangen and Nuremberg, 1976).

93. *Gland.*, 7–8 (Littré VIII, 562, ed. Joly (Paris, 1978). pp. 117ff.

94. See Bourgey, *Observation et expérience* (above, n. 33), p. 73.

95. *Prorrh.*, II, 11 (Littré, IX, 32). In this connection, see S. Ghinopoulo, *Pädiatrie in Hellas und Rom* (Jena, 1930), pp. 17 and 82ff.

96. *Praen. Coacae,* 502 (Littré, V, 700).

97. *Aph.*, III, 26 (Littré, IV, 498).

Chapter Eight: Leprosy and Tuberculosis

1. The conclusions of this chapter were presented to the Third European Colloquium of the Paleopathological Association at Caen (1980).

2. For more complete information, see C. Gernez-Rieux et al., "Les mycobactérioses humaines," *Actes du XVIe Congrès Nat. de la Tuberculose* (Bordeaux, 1970), pp. 1–70.

3. A. Cockburn, *The Evolution and Eradication of Infectious Diseases,* (Baltimore, 1963), pp. 38, 73, 219–20.

4. Ibid., pp. 73 and 221ff.

5. R. Hare, "The Antiquity of Diseases Caused by Bacteria and Viruses," in D. Brothwell and A. T. Sandison, eds., *Diseases in Antiquity* (Springfield, 1967), pp. 115–31 (esp. p. 127).

6. Ibid., p. 117.

7. The oldest mention of it occurs in Aristotle, *Parva naturalia,* 478b, and *Hist. anim.*, 604a. See chapter 7, n. 52. More recent descriptions that also happen to be more secure are given by Latin authors, especially Columella, *De re rustica,* VI, 14, and Vegetius, *Mulomedicina,* II, 45. I should also mention the evidence from Aretaeus of Cappadocia (*Signa chron.*, II, 13) on the frequency of tubercles in the flesh of sacrificial animals. This important observation is usually misunderstood

and neglected because Aretaeus inserts it in his chapter on leprosy. For the general history of this disease, see J. Francis, *Bovine Tuberculoses* (London, 1947).

8. See K. J. Donham and J. R. Leininger, "Spontaneous Leprosy-like Disease in a Chimpanzee," *Jour. Infect. Dis.,* 136 (1977): 132–36.

9. I refer to the situation in the nineteenth century and not to current Greece, since it is especially instructive to look at epidemiological conditions prior to the introduction of chemotherapy, sanitary techniques, massive urbanization, and the admixture of populations, all of which nowadays upset the "natural history" of infectious diseases.

10. See above, chapter 6, n. 86.

11. C. Stéphanos, "Grèce. Géographie médicale," in *Dictionnaire des sciences médicales,* ed. A. Dechambre (Paris, 1884), 4th ser., 10: 531.

12. For the existence of a natural resistance factor (probably of genetic origin) for the leprosy bacillus, see A. Rotberg, "Résistance et lèpre," *Bull. Ass. Lépr. Lang. Franç.* (1968), pp. 141–44.

13. See J. Poirier, *Recherches sur les réactions à la lépromine en milieu lépreux et non lépreux,* thesis (Paris, 1944); A. Basset, "La lèpre, son intérêt dans l'étude de l'épidémiologie et la pathologie générale," *Concours Médical* 93 (1971): 5627–37 (esp. pp. 5628ff.).

14. See especially J. Lowe and F. McNulty, "Tuberculosis and Leprosy: Immunological Studies," *Leprosy Review* 24 (1953): 61–90, and H. Floch, "La réaction de Mitsuda rendue positive par une primo-infection tuberculeuse est-elle accompagnée d'une immunité relative anti-lépreuse?" *Bull. Soc. Path. Exot.* 47 (1954): 771–75.

15. R. Chaussinand, "Tuberculose et lèpre, maladies antagonistes. Eviction de la lèpre par la tuberculose, *Jour. of Leprosy* 16 (1948): 431-38, and "Quelques remarques concernant la théorie de l'antagonisme entre tuberculose et lèpre," *Acta tropica* 21 (1964):82–87.

16. See M. D. Grmek, "Préliminaires d'une étude historique des maladies," *Annales E.S.C.* 24 (1969): 1478.

17. Starting in 1964, the World Health Organization organized a trial vaccination of children against leprosy with BCG in Burma. By the end of March 1973, the trial had covered 28,220 children below the age of 14. During this period (1964–73) there were 768 new cases of leprosy recorded in the control population, of which 343 were in children who were vaccinated and 425 in children who were not. So the protective effect of vaccination was about 20 percent. The highest degree of protection (38 percent, which is a statistically significant number in this context) was observed in children not older than 4 years of age at the beginning of the trial. In other age groups, the degree of protection was not statistically significant. The official report concludes that "it seems unlikely that BCG vaccination can modify the current or future manifestations of leprosy in similar (to Burma) regions." See L. M. Bechelli et al., "BCG Vaccination of Children against Leprosy," *Bull. W.H.O.* 51 (1974): 93–99.

18. See for instance Basset, "La lèpre" (above, n. 13), pp. 5632ff., and P. Harter, *Précis de la léprologie* (Paris, 1968), p. 38.

19. D. L. Weiss and V. Møller-Christensen, "An Unusual Case of Tuberculosis in a Medieval Leper," *Dan. Med. Bull* 18 (1971): 11–14. G. A. Hansen himself found tuberculosis to be the most common cause of death among leprosy patients in nineteenth-century Norway. It may be that tuberculosis did protect some people from leprous infection at the same time as it killed the lepers themselves. W. H. Jopling examined 500 leprous patients and none had a history of tuberculosis before contracting leprosy; 3 of the patients contracted it afterward ("Clinical Aspects of Leprosy," *Tubercle* 63 [1982]: 295–305).

20. See R. and E. Blum, *Health and Healing in Rural Greece* (Stanford, 1965).

21. In 1938, when the general mortality in Greece had already gone down to 13.3 (it was around 30 in previous decades), the figures for officially declared causes of death were, for every 1,000 deaths that year, 150.7 from "pneumonia," 70.3 from tuberculosis of the respiratory tract, 52.8 from infantile diarrhea and enteritis, and 30.1 from malaria. In 1948, among the inhabitants of Athens, respiratory tuberculosis was officially the cause of 180 of 1,000 deaths over the year. It is worth adding that at the same period and in the same population, extrapulmonary tuberculosis had 25 victims for every 1,000 deaths.

22. R. and J. Dubos, *The White Plague: Tuberculosis, Man, and Society* (Boston, 1953).

23. M. Lurie, *Resistance to Tuberculosis: Experimental Studies in Native and Acquired Defensive Mechanisms* (Cambridge, 1964).

24. M. Castels et al., "Les bacilles tuberculeux de type africain," *Rev. Tub. et Pneum.* 32 (1968): 179.

25. See W. Hennig, *Phylogenetic Systematics* (Urbana, 1966); D. L. Hull, "Contemporary Systematic Philosophies," *Ann. Rev. Ecol. Syst.* 1, (1970): 19–54; D. Guinot, "Examen des théories actuelles de la classification zoologique," *Hist. Phil. Life Sci.* 1, (1979): 119–38 (contains an important bibliographic essay).

26. J. Grober, "Zur Urgeschichte der menschlichen Tuberkulose," *Med. Klin.* 49 (1954): 670–73.

27. This is a probable, not a certain, conclusion. The *presence* of a disease on both sides, that is, in the Old and the New World, constitutes a real proof of its prior origin, but the absence of its existence on the American side only supports a presumption of its posterior origin. Some germs could have existed in the Old World but not have been transmitted as such onto the American continent by prehistoric migrants. Drawing attention to this state of affairs, Stewart has devised the concept of a "cold screen" that would explain the filtering out of germs during their journey through Siberia and Alaska. See T. D. Stewart, "A Physical Anthropologist's View of the Peopling of the New World," *South-west Journ. Anthrop.* 16 (1960): 259–73. Nevertheless I note that a "cold screen" could not affect the mycobacteria.

28. Tuberculosis does not seem to affect nomads; it is present in an endemic state only among sedentary peoples. See A. J. Perzigian and L. Widmer, "Evidence of Tuberculosis in Prehistoric Populations," *Jour. Amer. Med. Ass.* 241 (1979): 2643–46.

Chapter Nine: The Harm in Broad Beans

1. This chapter was originally published in *History and Philosophy of the Life Sciences* 2 (1980): 61–121; it appears here with additions and some modifications.

2. This formulation of the prohibition against broad beans is preserved in several authors from antiquity, for instance, Plutarch, *De educatione puerorum,* 17; Diogenes Laertius, *Vitae philosophorum,* VIII, 23; Porphyry, *Vita Pythagorae,* 44; Iamblichus, *Vita Pythagorica,* 109. For the general meaning of the Pythagorean *súmbola,* see Iamblichus, *Vita,* 103–5; I have used L. Deubner's critical edition (Leipzig, 1937) and the revised and annotated edition of M. von Albrecht (Zürich and Stuttgart, 1963).

3. The chapters on Pythagoras, Empedocles, and the Neopythagoreans in H. Diels and W. Kranz, *Die Fragmente der Vorsokratiker,* 6th ed. (Berlin, 1951), are indispensable. As for modern publications on the personality and achievement of Pythagoras, the historical reality of the brotherhood at Croton, and the roots of

Neopythagoreanism, I would mention especially A. Delatte, *Etudes sur la littérature pythagoricienne* (Paris, 1915); I. Lévy, *Recherches sur les sources de la légende de Pythagore* (Paris, 1926); K. von Fritz, *Pythagorean Politics in Southern Italy* (New York, 1940); W. Burkert, *Weisheit und Wissenschaft, Studien zu Pythagoras, Philolaos, und Platon* (Nuremberg, 1962) (*Lore and Science in Ancient Pythagoreanism,* trans. E. L. Minar [Cambridge, 1972]); C. J. de Vogel, *Pythagoras and Early Pythagoreanism* (Assen, 1966); and B. L. Van der Waerden, *Die Pythagoreer, religiöse Bruderschaft and Schule der Wissenschaft* (Zürich, 1979).

4. The basic doxography on the subject was gathered by Aulus Gellius, *Noctes Atticae,* IV, II, 1–12.

5. See A. de Candolle, *Origine des plantes cultivées* (Paris, 1883), pp. 253-57. According to research by the school of N. I. Vavilov in Leningrad, the cradle of the broad bean is West Asia (V. S. Muratova, 1931).

6. *Iliad* XIII. 589.

7. Theophrastus, *De causis plantarum,* IV, 14.

8. The author of *De mulierum affectibus* uses the broad bean (specifically, the seed) as a unit of size to specify the dosage of medications. He is at pains to make it clear that he is speaking of a "Greek seed" (*Mul.,* 46; Littré, VIII, 106) in one case and of an "Egyptian broad bean" in the other (*Mul.,* 181; Littré, VIII, 364). The "Egyptian broad bean" is also mentioned in *Acut. (sp.),* 53 (ed. Joly, 92). I disagree with the opinion of Littré who, following the Renaissance commentators and acceding to the authority of J. H. Dierbach, thinks that certain attestations of *kúamos* without modifiers in the Hippocratic treatises designate the "Egyptian broad bean" (identified with *Nymphaea nelumbo).*

9. Dioscorides, *Materia medica,* II, 105 and 106. For the modern identification of the plants at issue, see J. Berendes, *Des Pedanios Dioskurides Arzneimittellehre* (Stuttgart, 1908), p. 209.

10. This opinion is still maintained by J. H. Dierbach, *Die Arzneimittel des Hippokrates* (Heidelberg, 1824), pp. 20ff. See the discussion in A. Benedicenti, *Malati, medici e farmacisti* (Milan, 1947), I: 93ff.

11. Pliny, *Natural History,* XVIII, 30, 12. See J. André, *Lexique des termes de botanique en latin* (Paris, 1956), s.v. *Faba.*

12. See for example "Pythagore et les haricots," *Chronique médicale* 27 (1920): 244ff.; 28 (1921): 185 and 375–77; 33 (1926): 184–87; 34 (1927): 88–90 (contains the question of a doctor from Alger on the real hygenic value of the Pythagorean precept according to which "one must abstain from beans" and the answer of Dr. A. Lebeaupin to the effect that it cannot be beans, followed by a discussion on the dangers sometimes posed by the consumption of common broad beans and also of toxic European beans).

13. *Chronique médicale* 33 (1926): 185–87.

14. See for example Dioscorides, IV, 68.

15. Empedocles, fr. 141 (D-K I, 368); text transmitted by Aulus Gellius, *Noctes Atticae,* IV, II, 9.

16. Callimachus, fr. 126 Pfeiffer; text transmitted by Aulus Gellius, *Noctes Atticae,* IV, II, 2.

17. Cicero, *De divinatione,* I, 62.

18. Iamblichus, *Vita Pyth.,* 109.

19. Diogenes Laertius, VIII, 19; see also *Suda* s.v. *Pythagoras.*

20. To be found in Diogenes Laertius, VIII, 33.

21. Artemidorus, *Onirocriticon,* I, 68.

22. Porphyry, *De abstinentia,* IV, 16; see also Diogenes Laertius, VIII, 33.

23. Pausanias, *Descriptio Graeciae,* I, 37, 4. Also according to Pausanias, in Ar-

cadia it was said that Demeter provided all vegetables except broad beans (*Descriptio Graeciae,* VIII, 15, 1).

24. Gregory of Nazianzus, *Orationes,* XXIII, 535; Rufinus, *In Greg. Naz. Orat.,* IX, 10; Didymus according to *Geoponica,* II, 35, 8; Plutarch, *Symp.,* II, 3, 1. See *Orphicorum fragmenta,* fr. 291 Kern.

25. *Geoponica,* II, 35, 8.

26. See W. Rathmann, *Quaestiones Pythagoreae Orphicae Empedocleae,* thesis (Halle, 1933), and K. Kerényi, *Pythagoras und Orpheus,* 3d ed. Zürich, 1950).

27. L. von Schröder, "Das Bohnenverbot bei Pythagoras und im Veda," *Zschr. Kunde Morgenland* 15 (1901): 187. This opinion is qualified by several more recent authorities, for instance A. C. Andrews, "The Bean and Indo-European Totemism," *Amer. Anthrop.* 51 (1949):274–92.

28. See de Candolle, *Plantes cultivées* (above, n. 5), p. 254. Admittedly, in the *Susrutasaṃhitā (Sūtrasthāna,* XLVI, 19–20) there is a discussion of the dietetic properties of several kinds of *shimva,* a term usually translated "broad bean," but the seeds in question come from other legumes than *Vicia faba.*

29. Herodotus, II, 37 (trans. A. de Sélincourt, rev. A. R. Burn [Harmondsworth, 1972; rept. 1976], p. 144). Some similar information probably based on this can be found in Diodorus Siculus, I, 89; Plutarch, *Symp.,* VIII, 8, 2 and *De Is. et Osir.,* 5; Porphyry, *De abstinentia,* II, 25.

30. For specimens discovered in tombs and for the mention of the broad bean in hieroglyphic texts, see V. Loret, *La flore pharaonique,* 2d ed. (Paris, 1892), p. 93. A significant quantity of broad beans was offered by Ramses III to the priests of Memphis and Heliopolis. The botanical determination of the seeds found by archaeologists is not at issue, but there is controversy about the precise meaning of the Egyptian term *iwrj.t,* which is usually translated "broad bean." Recent lexica (Erman-Grapow, Cerny, Charpentier) identify the term not with Greek *kúamos* but instead with *dólikhos* 'calavance' (*Vigna sinensis* Endl.). There is no Egyptian text that forbids the eating of a legume or pronounces one harmful.

31. Isocrates, *Busiris,* 28; Herodotus, II, 123.

32. Herodotus, II, 123 (trans. Sélincourt, p. 178); see also II, 81, and IV, 95.

33. According to Origenes, *Contra Celsum,* V, 41.

34. According to Aulus Gellius, *Noctes Atticae,* IV, 11, 12.

35. Tertullian, *De anima,* 31, asserts that Pythagoras forbade his disciples to walk across a field of broad beans.

36. Diogenes Laertius, VIII, 45. See also *Anthologia Palatina,* VII, 122.

37. Diogenes Laertius, VIII, 39. Diogenes also relates a similar story from Hermippus to the effect that Pythagoras was killed by Syracusans unhappy with the help he had given the Agrigentans. The details that interest us are not changed in this variant; death results from the fact that the philosopher, while fleeing, "arrived at a field of broad beans that he did not wish to cross." See also *Suda,* s.v. *Pythagoras.*

38. Iamblichus, *Vita Pyth.,* 189–94.

39. This text comes from a lost work by Aristotle himself or one of the collaborators to whom he entrusted the task of studying the Pythagorean tradition. It is cited from Diogenes Laertius, VIII, 34.

40. Iamblichus, *Vita Pyth.,* 109.

41. Plutarch, *Symp.,* II, 3, 1, and Clement of Alexandria, *Stromata,* III, 3.

42. Pliny, *Natural History,* XVIII, 118–19. The offerings for the dead mentioned by Pliny were made during the archaic rites of the Lemuria.

43. Lucian, *Somnium (Gallus),* 5–6.

44. Lucian, *Vitarum auctio,* after the French translation by L. Humbert.

45. *Geoponica,* II, 35, 6. The same information can be found in Pliny, who speaks of the "mournful letters on the flower of the broad bean" (*Natural History,* XVIII, 119).

46. Porphyry, *Vita Pyth.,* 44.

47. Plutarch, *De educatione puerorum,* 17.

48. Iamblichus, *Vita Pyth.,* 206.

49. Aulus Gellius, *Noctes Atticae,* IV, 11, 4–5.

50. Aulus Gellius, *Noctes Atticae,* IV, 11, 10.

51. Artemidorus, *Onirocriticon,* I, 68.

52. Cicero, *De divinatione,* I, 62; see also Aulus Gellius, *Noctes Atticae,* IV, 11, 3.

53. Pliny, *Natural History,* XVIII, 118.

54. Diogenes Laertius, VIII, 23.

55. *Geoponica,* II, 35, 3–4. See also Tertullian, *De anima,* 48.

56. Clement of Alexandria, *Stromata,* III, 3. In the *Geoponica,* the broad bean is accused of making livestock infertile.

57. The context of this phrase is something as follows: "When will I be served, along with vegetables dressed in greasy lard, this bean, Pythagoras's sister?" (Horace, *Satires,* II, 6, 63). The Latin word *cognata* does not just mean "sister" but also and always specifies a blood relation.

58. See J. Jouanna, "Présence d'Empédocle dans la Collection hippocratique," *Bull. Assoc. Guill. Budé* 44 (1961): 452–63.

59. *Regimen,* II, 45, 1 (trans. W. H. S. Jones, *Hippocrates* (Cambridge and London, 1943), 4: 315).

60. *Acut. (sp.),* 64 (Littré, II, 518), and *Epid.,* II, 6, 7 (Littré, V, 134). In these cases it is the broad bean as such that is recommended as medicine. Other Hippocratic passages stipulate the therapeutic use of the "Egyptian" bean, that is, the seeds of the pink lotus.

61. Dioscorides, II, 105.

62. *Epid.,* VII, 82 (Littré, V, 436–38).

63. *Acut. (sp.),* 47 (Littré, 484–86; Joly, 89).

64. *Epid.,* II, 4, 3 (Littré, V, 126), and *Epid.,* VI, 4, 11 (Littré, V, 310). My translation is perceptibly different from Littré's. I wish to thank J. Jouanna for collating this passage in the manuscripts of the Hippocratic corpus.

65. For the subsistence crisis in Ainos, see J. M. F. May, *Ainos, Its History and Coinage* (Oxford, 1950). For the dating of *Epidemics* II–IV–VI, see chapter 12, the section "The Author, Date, and Locale of this Epidemiological Report."

66. Galen, *In Hippocratis libros I et II Epid. commentaria, ad loc.* The passage concerning Ainos is known only in the Arabic translation; see the edition of E. Wenkenback and F. Pfaff, *Corpus Medicorum Graecorum,* V, 10, 1 (Leipzig and Berlin, 1934), pp. 338–40. See also the commentary on the parallel passage in *Corp. Med. Graec.,* V, 10, 2, 2, ed. Wenkenbach and Pfaff (Berlin, 1956), p. 219.

67. See Dierbach, *Arzneimittel* (above, n. 10), pp. 41ff., de Candolle, *Plantes cultivées* (above, n. 5), pp. 85ff.; and the Liddell-Scott-Jones *Greek-English Lexicon* s.v. One should not follow R. Joly in his edition of the treatise *Regimen.* He rejects Littré and translates *órobos* (II, 45, 2) by the French word *vesce,* a term with too broad a meaning if it applies to all plants of the genus *Vicia,* or too imprecise if it is limited to common vetch (*Vicia sativa*). The identification of *órobos* with bitter vetch is supported by descriptions in Theophrastus and Dioscorides.

68. Dioscorides, II, 108.

69. Pliny, *Natural History,* XXII, 153.

70. Galen, *In Hippocratis libros I et II Epid. commentaria* (above, n. 66), p. 339.

71. A. Cantani, "Latirismo (Lathyrismus) illustrato da tre casi clinici," *Il Morgagni* 15 (1873): 745–65.

72. See J. C. Huber, "Historische Notizen über den Lathyrismus," *Friedrich's Blätter für gerichtliche Medizin* (1886), pp. 34–36, and R. H. Major, "How Hippocrates Made His Diagnoses," *Intern. Rec. Med.* 170 (1957): 481.

73. B. Schuchardt, "Zur Geschichte und Casuistik des Lathyrismus," *Dtsch. Arch. Klin. Med.* 40 (1886–87): 312–41.

74. See J. Borg, G. Mazars, and B. Sacko, "A propos de la neurotoxicité de Lathyrus sativus, plante alimentaire et médicinale de l'Inde," *Les médecines traditionelles de l'Asie* (Actes du Colloque de Paris, 1979) (Strasburg, 1981), pp. 103–10.

75. J. André, *L'alimentation et la cuisine à Rome* (Paris, 1961), p. 38 (new ed. [Paris, 1981], p. 37).

76. Pliny, *Natural History,* XVIII, 103.

77. Anaxandrides, fr. 41, 43; Alexis, fr. 162, 12.

78. Particularly an amino acid, diaminopropionate. See E. D. Schilling and F. M. Strong, "Isolation, Structure, and Synthesis of a Lathyrus Factor from L. odoratus," *Jour. Amer. Chem. Soc.* 76 (1954): 2848; rept. in *Nutr. Rev.* 23 (1976): 242. See also Borg, Mazars, and Sacko, "A propos de Lathyrus" (above, n. 74); E. Massa, "An Overview of Lathyrism," *Rev. Neurobiol.* 18 (1972): 181–206; and I. E. Liener, ed., *Toxic Constituents of Plant Foodstuffs* (New York, 1980), pp. 239–63.

79. See M. Streifler and D. F. Cohn, "Chronic Central Nervous System Toxicity of the Chickling Pea (Lathyrus sativus)," *Clin. Toxicology* 18 (1981): 1513–17.

80. "Favas verdes produsindo ictericia," *Revista Universal Lisbonese* (1843), p. 515.

81. A. Minà La Grua, *Sopra l'itterizia endemica e su le malattie ordinarie dei contadini di Castelbuono* (1856); cited and discussed by G. Sansone, A. M. Piga, and G. Segni, *Il favismo* (Turin, 1958), pp. 9ff.

82. See Sansone et al., *Il favismo* (above, n. 81), pp. 10ff.

83. G. Montano, "Del favismo o intossicazione fabacea," *Atti del XI Congr. Med. Internationale* (Rome, 1894), 3: 301–4.

84. See Mulè Bertolo, "Zàfara, o itterizia particolare prodotta dalle particelle odorifere della pianta fava," *Pratica del medico* (1901) (this article was originally published in 1873 in a local political journal of Caltanisetta).

85. In Sansone, Piga, and Segni, *Il favismo* (above, n. 81), p. 11.

86. Montano, "Del favismo" (above, n. 83), p. 304; see also Sansone, Piga, and Segni, *Il favismo* (above, n. 81), p. 14.

87. Especially worth citing are the research of Fermi in Sardinia (1905) and the critical review of prior research undertaken by A. Gasbarrini, "Su di una forma ancora insufficientemente conosciuta di anemia acuta febbrile con itterizia ed emoglobinuria (il favismo)," *Folia Clin. Chim. Microscop.* (Salsomaggiore) 4 (1912–14): 374–89.

88. This acid was to have been liberated into the organism from "cyanogenetic glucosides" that were supposed to exist in broad beans. See M. R. Marquet, *Intoxications alimentaires par certaines légumineuses: Gesses, fèves, haricots cyanogénétiques* (Paris, 1944). In reality, cyanhydric poisoning has only been reported after the ingestion of certain other beans (for example, *Phaseolus lunatus*). The hypothesis of this toxic mechanism as the fundamental phenomenon in favic idiosyncrasy was put forth by analogy, not as the result of direct observations on the broad bean itself.

89. A. Turchetti, "Forme poco frequenti di emoglobinuria da farmaci in corso di infezione malarica," *Riforma medica* 62 (1948): 325–28; this article is cited as a precursor by E. Beutler, "The Hemolytic Effects of Primaquine and Related Compounds," *Blood* 14 (1959): 103–39.

90. P. E. Carson et al., "Enzymatic Deficiency in Primaquine Sensitive Erythrocytes," *Science* 124 (1956): 484ff.

91. See W. H. Crosby, "Favism in Sardinia (Newsletter)," *Blood* 11 (1956): 91ff.; A. Szeinberg et al., "Studies on Erythrocytes" *Blood* 12 (1957): 603–13; W. H. Zinkham et al., "A Deficiency of Glucose-6-phosphate Dehydrogenase Activity in Erythrocytes from Patients with Favism," *Bull. Johns Hopkins Hosp.* 102 (1958): 169–75; P. Larizza et al., "L'individualità bioenzimatica dell'eritrocita favico: Sopra alcune anomalie biochimiche ed enzimatiche delle emazie nei pazienzi affetti da favismo e nei loro familiari," *Haematologia* 3 (1958): 251–59; G. Sansone and G. Segni, "Nuovi aspetti dell'alterato biochimismo degli eritrociti favici: Assenza pressochè completa della glucosio-6-P-deidrogenasi," *Boll. Soc. Ital. Biol. Sper.* 15 (1958): 327–29; U. Carcassi, *Eritroenzimopatie ed anemie emolitiche* (Pisa, 1959).

92. K. L. Roth and A. M. Frumin, "Studies on the Hemolytic Principle of the Fava Bean," *Jour. Lab. Clin. Med.* 59 (1960): 695–700. See J. Ducas, *Le déficit en glucose-6-phosphate déshydrogénase,* thesis (Nancy, 1961).

93. J. Y. Lin and K. M. Ling, "Studies on Favism: 1. Isolation of an Active Principle from Fava Beans," *Jour. Formosan Med. Ass.* 61 (1962): 484–89. For new research on these substances, see E. Bottini et al., "Presence in Vicia faba of Different Substances with Activity in Vitro on Gd–Med. Red Blood Cell Reduced Glutathione," *Clin. Chim. Acta* 30 (1970): 831–34; and J. Jamalian, "Favism-inducing Toxins in Broad Beans (Vicia faba)," *Plant Foods for Human Nutrition* 27 (1977): 207–11.

94. R. Lederer, "A New Form of Acute Hemolytic Anaemia: Baghdad Spring Anaemia," *Trans. Roy. Soc. Trop. Med. Hyg.* 34 (1941): 387–94.

95. See Ducas, *Le déficit* (above, n. 92), and A. Orsini et al., "Le favism," *Sem. Hôpit.* (Paris, 1961), pp. 557–70.

96. S. H. Boyer et al., "Electrophoretic Heterogeneity of Glucose-6-phosphate Dehydrogenase and Its Relationship to Enzyme Deficiency in Man," *Proc. Nation. Acad. Sci. USA* 48 (1962): 1868.

97. H. N. Kirkman et al., "Functionally Abnormal Glucose-6-phosphate Dehydrogenases," *Cold Spring Harbor Symp. Quant. Biol.* 29 (1964): 391.

98. P. R. McCurdy et al., "A Chinese Variant of Glucose-6-phosphate Dehydrogenase," *Jour. Lab. Clin. Med.* 67 (1966): 374.

99. A. Yoshida, G. Stamatoyannopoulos, and A. G. Motulsky, "Biochemical Genetics of Glucose-6-phosphate Dehydrogenase Variation," *Ann. N.Y. Acad. Sci.* 155 (1968): 868–79; E. Beutler, "Drug-induced Hemolytic Anaemia," *Pharmacol. Rev.* 21 (1969):73–103; J. C. Dreyfus, "Bases moléculaires des anomalies enzymatiques génétiques," *Biochimie* 54 (1972): 559–71; J. C. Kaplan, "Remarques sur les enzymopathies génétiques du globule rouge," *Biochimie* 54 (1972): 765–73; J. C. Kaplan, "Defective Molecular Variants of Glucose-6-phosphate Dehydrogenase and Methaemoglobin Reductase," *Jour. Clin. Path.* 27 (Suppl. Roy. Coll. Path. 8) (1974): 134–41; and G. Schapira et al., *Pathologie moléculaire* (Paris, 1975). An excellent, up-to-date overview by E. Beutler can be found in J. B. Stanbury, J. B. Wyngaarden, and D. S. Frederickson, *The Metabolic Basis of Inherited Diseases* (New York, 1978), pp. 1430–51.

100. B. Childs et al., "A Genetic Study of a Defect in Glutathione Metabolism of the Erythrocite," *Bull. Johns Hopkins Hosp.* 102 (1958): 21–37; E. Sartori, "On the Pathogenesis of Favism," *Jour. Med. Genet.* 8 (1971): 462–67; V. A. McKusick, *Mendelian Inheritance in Man,* 3d ed. (Baltimore, 1971).

101. See G. Stamatoyannopoulos et al., "On Familial Predisposition to Favism," *Amer. Jour. Hum. Genet.* 18 (1966): 253–63; Sartori, "Pathogenesis" (above, n. 100); E. Beutler, "Abnormalities of the Hexose Monophosphate Shunt," *Sem. Hemat.* 8 (1971): 311–47.

102. See Sansone, Piga, and Segni, *Il favismo* (above, n. 81); Ducas, *Le déficit* (above, n. 92); Orsini et al., "Le favisme" (above, n. 95); G. Lugassy, *Le déficit en glucose-6-phospho-déshydrogénase,* thesis (Paris, 1979), pp. 311–47.

103. S. A. Doxiadis et al., "Glucose-6-phosphate Dehydrogenase Deficiency, a New Etiological Factor of Neonatal Jaundice," *Lancet* (1961), I, pp. 297–301.

104. See chapter 10.

105. See Sansone, Piga, and Segni, *Il favismo* (above, n. 81); J. Bernard and J. Ruffieé, *Hématologie géographique* (Paris, 1966–72); M. A. Belsey, "The Epidemiology of Favism, *Bull. W.H.O.* 48 (1973): 1–13; Lugassy, *Le déficit* (above, n. 102); M. Benabadji et al., "Heterogeneity of G6PD Deficiency in Algeria," *Hum. Genet.* 40 (1978): 177–84.

106. See the publications cited above by G. Sansone, G. Segni, P. Larizza, U. E. Carcassi, M. E. Belsey, and others.

107. See C. Choremis, L. Zannos-Marioulea, and M.D.C. Kattamis "Frequency of Glucose-6-phosphate Dehydrogenase Deficiency in Certain Highly Malarious Areas of Greece," *Lancet* (1962), I pp. 17ff.; A. C. Allison et al., "Deficiency of Erythrocyte Glucose-6-phosphate Dehydrogenase in Greek Populations," Ann. Hum. Genet. 26 (1963): 237–42; G. Stamatoyannopoulos et al., "The Distribution of Glucose-6-phosphate Dehydrogenase Deficiency in Greece," *Amer. Jour. Hum. Genet* 18 (1966): 296–308.

108. Doxiadis et al., "Neonatal Jaundice" above, n. 103).

109. See C. A. Kattamis, "Some Clinical and Biochemical Aspects of Favism in Childhood," *Ann. Soc. Belge Méd. Trop.* 49 (1969): 289–304. In the decade following Carson's ground-breaking publication, more than 500 cases of favism were treated in a large pediatric hospital in Greece. To all appearances, this "epidemic" reflects changing medical knowledge and not nosological reality. The historian of medicine should ask himself what went on beforehand in the diagnosis and treatment of children with favism. By what means was this disease rendered "invisible"?

110. See C. G. Gasperini et al., "Osservazione sulle manifestazioni allergiche locali e generali nel favismo ed il favismo nell'Isola di Rodi," *Gior. Ital. Mal. Esot. Trop.* 4 (1931): 49, and C. A. Kattamis et al., "G6PD Deficiency and Favism in the Island of Rhodes (Greece)," *Jour. Med. Genet.* 6 (1969): 286–91.

111. G. R. Fraser et al., "Thalassemia, Abnormal Hemoglobins, and Glucose-6-phosphate Dehydrogenase Deficiency in the Arta Area of Greece," *Ann. N.Y. Acad. Sci.* 119 (1964): 415–35. See also Stamatoyannopoulos et al., "Distribution in Greece" (above, n. 107).

112. M. Siniscalco et al., "Favism and Thalassemia in Sardinia and Their Relationship to Malaria," *Nature* 190 (1961): 1179ff.; A. C. Allison, "Malaria and Glucose-6-phosphate Dehydrogenase Deficiency," *Nature* 197 (1963): 609; A. G. Motulsky, "Hereditary Cell Traits and Malaria," *Amer. Jour. Trop. Med. Hyg.* 13 (1964): 147–58. See also chapter 10, below.

113. U. Bienzle et al., "Glucose-6-phosphate Dehydrogenase and Malaria," *Lancet* (1972), I pp. 107–10.

114. Lugassy, *Le déficit* (above, n. 102), pp. 60–61 and 64.

115. See for instance U. E. Carcassi, "The Interaction between Beta-thalassemia, G6PD Deficiency, and Favism," *Ann. N.Y. Acad. Sci.* 232 (1974): 297–305.

116. Thanks especially to the work undertaken by G. Stamatayannopoulos et al., "Genetic Diversity of the 'Mediterranean' Glucose-6-phosphate Dehydrogenase Deficiency Phenotype," *Jour. Clin. Invest.* 50 (1971): 1253–61.

117. For an overview of the humanists' commentaries, see C. T. Menke, *De Leguminibus Veterum* (Göttingen, 1814), esp. the chapter entitled "Faba Pythagoricis Vetita." A reading of this particularly learned thesis in medicine highlights the

contrast between the abundance of traditional imaginings on this subject and the paucity of newer ideas.

118. K. Sprengel, *Versuch einer pragmatischen Geschichte der Arzneykunde* (Halle, 1792), vol. 1. In the French edition of this work (Paris, 1815, 1: 229) broad beans are mistaken for beans (*Phaseolus* sp.); the error lies with the translator, not Sprengel himself.

119. A. B. Krische, *De Societatis a Pythagore in Urbe Crotoniatarum Conditae Scopo Politico Commentatio* (Göttingen, 1830). See also C. Hölk, *De Acusmatis sive Symbolis Pythagoricis,* thesis (Kiel, 1894).

120. R. and E. Blum, *Health and Healing in Rural Greece* (Stanford, 1965), p. 78.

121. F. Lenormant, "Faba," in C. Daremberg and E. Saglio, *Dictionnaire des antiquités grecques et romaines* (Paris, 1896), 2: 947.

122. E. Bourquelot, "Remarques à propos des fèves de Pythagore," *C. R. Soc. Biol.* (Paris) 56 (1904): 861ff.

123. J. G. Frazer, *Totemism* (Edinburgh, 1887); *The Golden Bough* (London, 1890).

124. E. Rohde, *Psyche* (Freiburg im Breisgau, 1898); trans. from the 8th ed. by W. B. Willis (London and New York, 1925) and often reprinted.

125. See especially J. G. Frazer, *The Golden Bough,* 3d ed., (London, 1911), 1: 117–19, 214, etc.

126. S. Reinach, *Cultes, mythes, et religions* (Paris, 1905).

127. Especially J. Larguier de Bancels, "Sur les origines de la notion de l'âme à propos d'une interdiction de Pythagore," *Arch. Psychol.* 17 (1918): 58–66; A. Lebeaupin "Pythagore et les haricots" (above, n. 12), pp. 244ff.; L. Piniatoglou, "The Pythagorean Tabous," *Acta Greek Anthrop. Soc.* (1934), p. 36; M. Tierney, "A Pythagorean Tabu,"*Mélanges Boisacq* (Brussells, 1938), pp. 317–21; L. Bonuzzi, "Ancora su Pitagora e il suo influsso sulla medicina greca," *Acta Med. Hist. Pat.* 15 (1968–69): 9–16.

128. As examples, I cite H. E. Sigerist, *History of Medicine* (New York, 1961), 2: 96, and G. Sarton, *History of Science* (Cambridge, 1960), 1: 201.

129. A. Delatte, "Faba Pythagorae Cognata," *Serta Leodiensia* (Liège, 1930), pp. 31–57.

130. M. Detienne, "La cuisine de Pythagore," *Arch. Sociol. Rel.* 15, no. 29 (1970): 141–62; *Les jardins d'Adonis* (Paris, 1972) (*The Gardens of Adonis,* trans. J. Lloyd [Hassocks and Sussex, 1977]); *Dionysos mis à mort* (Paris, 1977) (*Dionysos Slain,* trans. M. and L. Muellner [Baltimore, 1979]).

131. Reinach, *Cultes, mythes, et religions* (above, n. 126), 1: 44.

132. Ibid., 1: 43–48.

133. Larguier de Bancels, "Sur les origines de l'âme" (above, n. 127), pp. 58–66. A like opinion is maintained by Andrews, "The Bean and Indo-European" (above, n. 27), p. 289, who finds the tabu's origin in the primitive experience of flatulence (which is felt as the presence of souls in the broad beans) and not of totemism.

134. See E. Jones, "Die Empfängnis der Jungfrau Maria durch das Ohr," *Jahrb. Psychoanal.* 6 (1914): 135.

135. Delatte, "Faba" (above, n. 129), p. 31.

136. Ibid., p. 56.

137. Detienne, *Dionysos Slain,* pp. 60ff. and 85 (French ed., pp. 146–47, 192) (above, n. 130).

138. Ibid., p. 86ff. (French ed., pp. 193–94). For the text of this cultic regulation, see F. Sokolowski, *Les lois sacrées de l'Asie Mineure* (Paris, 1955), no. 84. As for mint, which is still a condiment for broad beans in modern Greece, see G. Daux, "L'interdiction rituelle de la menthe," *Bull. Corresp. Hell.* 81 (1957): 1–5.

139. J. Schumacher, *Antike Medizin,* (Berlin, 1940), pp. 59–63.

140. S. Veras's account was published in Italian as "Il favismo era conosciuto

dai Greci antichi," in the book by Sansone, Piga, and Segni, *Il favismo* (above, n. 81), pp. 5–7. Among those who see a relationship between the Pythagorean tabu and favism, I especially mention T.H.D. Arie, "Pythagoras and Beans," *Oxford Med. School Gaz.* 11 (1959): 75–81. See also E. Lieber, "Favism in Antiquity," *Koroth* 5 (1970): 331–35, and "The Pythagorean Community as a Sheltered Environment for the Handicapped," in *Inter. Symp. Society, Medicine, and Law (Jerusalem, 1972)* (Amsterdam, 1973), pp. 33–41; and R. S. Brumbaugh and J. Schwartz, "Pythagoras and Beans: A Medical Explanation" *Class. World* 73 (1980): 421ff.

141. See Arie, "Pythagoras" (above, n. 140), and the letter by H. A. Waldron published in *Brit. Med. Jour.* (June 16, 1973).

142. M. Enrique Laval, "La prohibicion pitagorica de comer habas. Una nueva explication?" *Anal. Chil. Hist. Med.* 11 (1969): 79–97.

143. C. N. Ballas, "The Pythagorean Prohibitions," *Acta Congr. Inter.* XXIV *Hist. Artis Med.* (Budapest, 1976), 2: 1343–46.

144. Diogenes Laertius, VIII, 2, 70. See O. Bernhard, "Ueber Malariabekämpfung im klassischen Altertum," in *Neuburger's Festschrift* (Vienna, 1928), pp. 44–46.

145. See Strabo, *Geog.*, VI, 1, 2, and 2, 4.

146. In their studies of the history of malaria in Greece, W.H.S. Jones and P. Fraccaro stress the importance of the disease in southern Italy.

147. See André, *L'alimentation* (above, n. 75), p. 35.

148. Athenaeus, *Deipnosophistae,* 54ff.

149. Pliny, *Natural History,* XVIII, 118; see André, *L'alimentation* (above, n. 75), p. 36.

150. See Belsey, "Epidemiology of Favism" (above, n. 105), pp. 1–13.

151. S. Katz, "Un exemple d'évolution bioculturelle: La fève," *Communications* 31 (1979): 53–69 (esp. p. 57).

152. Ibid., p. 66.

153. E. Giles, "Favism, Sex-linkage, and the Indo-European Kinship System," *Southwest Jour. Anthrop.* 18 (1962): 286–90.

154. See de Vogel, *Pythagoras* (above, n. 3), pp. 232–44, and Schumacher, *Antike Medizin* (above, n. 139), pp. 57–63.

155. Iamblichus, *Vita Pyth.*, 163.

156. Plutarch, *De genio Socratis,* 580C. On the abandonment of the "miraculous" by thinkers after Socrates and especially on Plutarch's rationality, see the spirited discussion by H. Pourrat, *Le sage et son démon* (Paris, 1950).

157. "Rapport sur les conférences d'Histoire de la médecine et des sciences biologiques," *Annuaire de l'E.P.H.E., IV section, pour l'année 1975–1976* (Paris, 1975), p. 814.

Chapter Ten: Porotic Hyperostosis, Hereditary Anemias, and Malaria

1. Most of the material in this chapter was published in *Annales E.S.C.* (1975), pp. 1152–85. It has been revised to take account of new research, in particular, an inquiry by the Paleopathology Association (Detroit, 1977), a study of cribra orbitalia in Europe, an overview of Mediterranean research by J. L. Angel (1978), and the work of M. M. Wintrobe (1980). The section on the history of malaria is new.

2. See C. Toldt, "Ueber Welcker's Cribra orbitalia," *Mitt. Anthrop. Gesell. Wien* 16 (1886): 20, and H. Welcker, "Cribra orbitalia: Ein ethnologisch-diagnostisches Merkmal am Schädel mehrerer Menschenrassen," *Arch. Anthrop.* 17 (1888): 1–18. In this connection it is interesting to read Virchow's anthropological lucubra-

tions, "Ueber einige Merkmale niederer Menschenrassen am Schädel, *Abh. Preuss. Akad. Wiss., Phys. Kl., 2 Abth.* (1875), pp. 1–130. Virchow knew of symmetrical porous osteophytosis among American Indians; recent examination of a Peruvian skull in his old collection in Berlin has confirmed the diagnosis.

3. B. Adachi, "Die Porosität des Schädeldaches," *Zschr. Morph. Anthr.* 7 (1904): 373; F. Wood Jones, "Report on Human Remains," *Archeol. Survey of Nubia, Report for 1907–1908* (Cairo, 1910), pp. 1–375.

4. J. Saint-Périer, "Lésions osseuses d'un squelette d'enfant trouvé dans un milieu gallo-romain," *Bull. Mém. Soc. Anthr. Paris* 5 (1914): 31–36.

5. A. Hrdlička, "Anthropological Field Work in Peru in 1913; With Notes on the Pathology of Ancient Peruvians," *Smithsonian Inst. Misc. Coll.* 61 (1914): 1–69 (esp. pp. 57–60). For a historical estimate of this research, see S. Jarcho, *Human Palaeopathology* (New Haven and London, 1966), pp. 16ff.

6. H. U. Williams, "Human Paleopathology, with Some Original Observations on Symmetrical Osteoporosis of the Skull," *Arch. Path. Labor. Med.* 7 (1929): 839–902. The same parallel between symmetrical osteoporosis and familial anemia is made in the article by B. F. Feingold and J. T. Case, "Roentgenologic Skull Change in Anemias of Childhood; A Few Notes on Similar Findings among Skulls of Peruvian Indians," *Amer. Jour. Roentg.* 29 (1933): 194–202.

7. S. Moore, "Bone Changes in Sickle Cell Anemia, with Note on Similar Changes in Skulls of Ancient Maya Indians," *Jour. Missouri Med. Ass.* 26 (1929): 561–64.

8. E. A. Hooton, *The Indians of Pecos Pueblo: A Study of Their Skeletal Remains* (New Haven, 1930), esp. pp. 306–30; see also "Skeletons from the Cenote of Sacrifice at Chichén Itzá," in *The Maya and Their Neighbors* (New York, 1940), pp. 272–80.

9. L. Pales, *Paléopathologie et pathologie comparative* (Paris, 1930), p. 250 and pl. 43, 2.

10. R. L. Moodie, *Roentgenological Studies of Egyptian and Peruvian Mummies* (Chicago, 1931).

11. J. L. Angel, "Skeletal Changes in Ancient Greece," *Amer. Jour. Physical Anthrop.* 4 (1946): 69–97.

12. For example, see R. Fraser, "The Problem of Osteoporosis: A Critical Review," *Jour. Bone Joint Surg.* (1962), pp. 485–95.

13. H. Mueller, "Het voorkomen van de zgn. osteoporosis symmetrica cranii op Java en haar verband met de rhachitis," *Geneesk. Tijdsch. Neder. Indie* 74 (1934): 1084–93.

14. J. L. Angel, "Porotic Hyperostosis, Anemias, Malarias, and Marshes in the Prehistoric Eastern Mediterranean," *Science* 153 (1966): 760–63.

15. In particular, see D. S. Carlson, G. J. Armelagos, and D. Van Gerven, "Factors Influencing the Etiology of Cribra Orbitalia in Prehistoric Nubia," *Jour. Hum. Evol.* 3 (1974): 405–10. In an examination of 285 skulls from Nubia, they discovered just one case of the association of cribra orbitalia with porotic hyperostosis (of the cranial vault). The former ailment was reported in 21.4 percent of the specimens and the latter in 0.7 percent.

16. See especially W.G.J. Putschar, "Problems in the Pathology and Palaeopathology of Bones," in Jarcho, *Human Palaeopathology* (above, n. 5), pp. 56–65.

17. Hrdlička, "Anthropological Fieldwork" (above, n. 5), and Wood Jones, "Human Remains" (above, n. 3).

18. Hooton, *Indians* (above, n. 8), and the critical remarks of Jarcho, *Human Palaeopathology* (above, n. 5), p. 22.

19. See Mueller, "Het voorkomen van osteoporosis" (above, n. 13).

20. H. Hamperl and P. Weiss, "Ueber die spongiöse Hyperostose am Schädel aus Alt-Peru," *Virchows Arch. Path. Anat.* 327 (1955): 629–42.

21. Williams, "Paleopathology" (above, n. 6), p. 900.

22. Pales, *Paléopathologie* (above, n. 9), p. 250.

23. H. E. Sigerist, *History of Medicine,* vol. 1 (New York, 1951), p. 47.

24. T. B. Cooley and P. Lee, "A Series of Cases of Splenomegaly in Children with Anemia and Peculiar Bone Changes," *Trans. Amer. Ped. Soc.* 37 (1925): 29; T. B. Cooley et al., "Anemia in Children with Splenomegaly and Peculiar Changes in the Bones," *Am. Jour. Dis. Child.* 34 (1927): 347–63. For the history of this discovery, see W. W. Zuelzer, "Thomas B. Cooley (1875–1945)," *Jour. Pediatr.* 49 (1956): 642–50, and D. J. Weatherall, "Toward an Understanding of the Molecular Biology of Some Common Inherited Anemias: The Story of Thalassemia," in M. M. Wintrobe, *Blood, Pure and Eloquent* (New York, 1980), pp. 373–414.

25. See the bibliographical documentation in V. Chini and C. M. Valeri, "Mediterranean Hemopathic Syndromes," *Blood* 4 (1949): 989–1013. Cooley described what is now considered the homozygous, severe form of a hereditary anemia particularly widespread in certain Mediterranean lands. Its discovery was brought about with relatively unsophisticated technical means available to any physician. How did it happen, then, that this anemia was recognized as a disease *sui generis* by American physicians before being detected by physicians in Greece or Italy? Weatherall ("Thalassemia" [above, n. 24], p. 376) proposes a simple and convincing, if paradoxical, explanation: Cooley noticed the disease in Detroit since it was a rarity there and so represented something worth noting, while in Italy it escaped medical perception precisely because it was too familiar.

26. For the formation of this nosological concept, see G. H. Whipple and W. L. Bradford, "Mediterranean Disease—Thalassemia (Erythroblastic Anemia of Cooley)," *Jour. Pediatr.* 9 (1936): 279–311; G. Astaldi et al., *La talassemia; Morbo di Cooley e forme affini* (Pavia, 1951); R. M. Bannerman, *Thalassemia: A Survey of Some Aspects* (New York, 1961); and Weatherall, "Thalassemia" (above, n. 24), pp. 373–414. For the determination of the thalassemic trait, see D. Hammond et al., "Definition of Cooley's Trait or Thalassemia Minor: Classical, Clinical, and Routine Hematology," *Ann. N.Y. Acad. Sci.* 119 (1964): 372–89. For an up-to-date survey, see especially the monograph of D. J. Weatherall and J. B. Clegg, *The Thalassemia Syndromes,* 2d ed. (Oxford, 1972).

27. Definitive proof of the hereditary nature of thalassemia was provided by V. Angelini, "Primi risultati di ricerche ematologiche nei familiari de'ammalati di anemia di Cooley," *Minerva Med.* 28 (1937): 331ff., and J. Caminopetros, "Recherches sur l'anémie érythroblastique infantile des peuples de la Méditerranée orientale; Etude Anthropologique, étiologique et pathogénique; La transmission héreditaire de la maladie," *Ann. Méd.* 43 (1938): 27–61 and 104–25. The genetic details of this disease were laid out by W. N. Valentine and J. V. Neel, "Hematologic and Genetic Study of Transmission of Thalassemia (Cooley's Anemia; Mediterranean Anemia)," *Arch. Intern. Med.* 74 (1944): 185–96, and by H. Lehmann, "Variations in Human Hemoglobin Synthesis and Factors Governing Their Inheritance," *Brit. Med. Bull.* 15 (1959): 401–46. See also D. L. Rucknagel, "Current Concepts of the Genetics of Thalassemia," *Ann. N.Y. Acad. Sci.* 119 (1964): 463–49.

28. For clarification of the physiopathological mechanism of the thalassemias and their classification, see Lehmann, "Variations in Hemoglobin" (above, n. 27); P. Fessas, "Forms of Thalassemia," in J.H.P. Jonxis and J. F. Delafresnaye, *Abnormal Hemoglobins* (Oxford, 1959); A. Fiehrer, "Les nouvelles données sur les anémies méditerranéennes: Les bêta et alpha-thalassémies," *Rev. Path. Comp.* 64

(1964): 273–80; M. L. Freedman, "Thalassemia, an Abnormality in Globin Chain Synthesis," *Amer. Jour. Med. Sci.* 267 (1974): 256–65; G. Schapira et al., *Pathologie moléculaire* (Paris, 1975).

29. For the clinical picture and the facies of thalassemic children in modern Greece, see J. Caminopetros, "Recherches" (above, n. 27), pp. 27–61, and S. Charokopos, "Considérations sur l'anémie de Cooley chez l'enfant grec," *Pédiatrie* (Lyon) 10 (1955): 535–38.

30. See J. P. Caffey, "Cooley's Anemia: A Review of the Roentgenographic Findings in the Skeleton," *Amer. Jour. Roentg.* 78 (1957): 381–91; J. E. Moseley, *Bone Changes in Hematologic Disorders (Roentgen Aspects)* (New York and London, 1963); V. Bismuth and R. Benacerraf, "Etude radiologique des manifestations osseuses des anémies hémolytiques héréditaires," *Ann. Radiol. Sem. Hôp.* 10 (1967): 559–74. For the microscopic structure of the skull ("hair-on-end" pattern), see especially the old piece by L. Belloni and P. Fornara, "Istogenesi del cranio a spazzola nel morbo di Cooley," *Minerva Pediatrica* 7 (1955): 1638–45.

31. R. Lucot-Branlard, *Contribution à l'étude des lésions osseuses de la thalassémie*, thesis (Paris, 1969), and M. F. Tardivel, *Contribution à l'étude du diagnostic du trait thalassémique par la radiographie du crâne*, thesis (Paris, 1971).

32. See for example the articles by J. B. Moseley, "The Paleopathological Riddle of Symmetrical Osteoporosis," *Amer. Jour. Roentg.* 95 (1956): 135–42, and by J. L. Angel, "Porotic Hyperostosis or Osteoporosis Symmetrica," in D. Brothwell and A. T. Sandison, *Diseases in Antiquity* (Springfield, 1967), pp. 378–89.

33. Notably J. B. Moseley, "Radiographic Studies in Hematologic Bone Diseases: Implications for Paleopathology," in Jarcho, *Human Palaeopathology* (above, n. 5), pp. 121–30.

34. J. B. Herrick, "Peculiar Elongated and Sickle-shaped Red Blood Corpuscles in a Case of Severe Anemia," *Arch. Intern. Med.* 6 (1910): 517–21. For the history of this discovery, see the autobiographical account of J. B. Herrick, *Memory of Eighty Years* (Chicago, 1940). For a general sketch of the history of research on Herrick's disease in our time, see especially C. L. Conley, "Sickle-cell Anemia—The First Molecular Disease," in Wintrobe, *Blood, Pure and Eloquent* (above, n. 24), pp. 319–71.

35. The discovery of hemoglobin S and of its role in the physiopathology of an inherited disease was made in 1949 by Linus Pauling, H. Itano, S. J. Singer, and I. C. Wells. It represents a milestone in the history of contemporary medicine. See L. Pauling et al., "Sickle-cell Anemia: A Molecular Disease," *Science* 110 (1949): 138–42. This publication marks the debut of molecular pathology.

36. For the fundamental hematological aspects of sickle cell anemia, see B. J. Culliton, "Sickle-cell Anemia: The Route from Obscurity to Prominence," *Science* 178 (1972): 138–42; H. Lehmann and R. G. Huntsman, *Man's Haemoglobins* (Oxford, 1974); *Actes du Symposium sur la drépanocytose* (Abidjian, 1975); Schapira et al., *Pathologie moléculaire* (above, n. 28); H. F. Bunn et al., *Human Hemoglobins* (Philadelphia, 1977); Conley, "Sickle-cell Anemia" (above, n. 34).

37. For the clinical aspects of the disease, besides the publications cited in the previous note, see G. R. Serjeant, *The Clinical Features of Sickle Cell Disease* (Amsterdam, 1974). For its genetics, the basic discoveries are published in the following articles: W. H. Taliaferro and J. G. Huck, "The Inheritance of Sickle-cell Anemia in Man," *Genetics* 8 (1923): 594–98; J. V. Neel, "The Inheritance of Sickle Cell Anemia," *Science* 110 (1949): 64–66; A. C. Allison, "Population Genetics of Abnormal Human Haemoglobins," *Acta Genet.* 6 (1957): 430–34; and D. N. Rucknagel, "The Genetics of Sickle Cell Anemia and Related Syndromes," *Arch. Intern. Med.* 133 (1974): 595–610.

38. See K. R. Diebert, "Roentgen Changes in Sickle Cell Anemia," *Amer. Jour.*

Roentg. 82 (1959): 501–4; Moseley, *Bone Changes* (above, n. 30); and G. Charmot, "Aspect radiologique des lésions osseuses dans la maladie drépanocytaire," *Ann. Soc. Belge Méd. Trop.* 49 (1969): 199–204.

39. See chapter 9, above.

40. Luan Eng Lie Injo, "Chronic Deficiency Anemia with Bone Changes Resembling Cooley's Anemia," *Acta Haemat.* 19 (1958): 263–68; H. Burko et al., "Skull Changes in Iron Deficiency Anemia Simulating Congenital Hemolytic Anemia," *Amer. Jour. Roentg.* 86 (1961): 447–52; P. Lanzkowsky, "Radiological Features in Iron Deficiency Anemia," *Amer. Jour. Dis. Child.* 116 (1968): 16–29; P. Lanzkowsky, "Osseous Changes in Iron Deficiency Anemia—Implications for Paleopathology," in *Porotic Hyperostosis: An Enquiry* (Detroit, 1977), pp. 23–34.

41. G. Gurrarino and M. Erlandson, "Premature Fusion of Epiphyses in Cooley's Anemia," *Radiology* 83 (1964): 656–64; R. Lucot-Branlard, *Contribution* (above, n. 31); H. G. Poynton and K. W. Davey, "Thalassemia," *Oral Surg.* 25 (1968): 564–76.

42. H. Nathan and N. Haas, "On the Presence of Cribra Orbitalia in Apes and Monkeys," *Amer. Jour. Phys. Anthrop.* 24 (1966): 351–60; O. P. Hengen, "Cribra Orbitalia: Pathogenesis and Probable Etiology," *Homo* 22 (1971): 57–75; Carlson, Armelagos, and Van Gerven, "Cribra Orbitalia" (above, n. 15).

43. See especially J. Lallo, G. J. Armelagos, and R. P. Mensforth, "The Role of Diet, Disease, and Physiology in the Origin of Porotic Hyperostosis," *Hum. Biol.* 49 (1977): 471–83; L. M. Debra and G. J. Armelagos, "Paleoepidemiological Methods and Porotic Hyperostosis," *Paleopathology Newsletter,* no. 24 (1978), pp. 14–17.

44. Determination of the level of iron was used by a research team in Pisa on bone remains from Carthage. In a sample of 24 skulls dated to the third century B.C., of which 13 had cribra orbitalia, a direct relation was revealed between the presence of the lesion and a drop in the level of iron in the bones. The age and sex distribution of the cases of cribra orbitalia suggests a diagnosis of acquired iron deficiency anemia for this population. Cf. G. Fornaciari and F. Mallegni, "Cribra orbitalia in un campione de Punici di Cartagine," *Quad. Sci. Antrop.* (Padua) 5 (1980): 106–21, and G. Fornaciari et al., "Cribra Orbitalia and Elemental Bone Iron in the Punics of Carthage," *Ossa* 8 (1981): 63–77. Since iron is a factor in the synthesis of two amino acids, hydroxylysine and hydroxyproline, that are found in bone protein, it can be argued that their reduced concentration in skeletons with porotic hyperostosis supports a diagnosis of iron deficiency anemia. This was convincingly demonstrated by D. W. von Endt and D. J. Ortner, "Amino Acid Analysis of Bone from a Possible Case of Prehistoric Iron Deficiency Anemia from the American Southwest," *Amer. Jour. Phys. Anthrop.* 59 (1982): 377–85.

45. The basic data are in the following publications: Phaedon Fessas, "Hereditary Anemias in Greece," in J.H.P. Jonxis et al., *Abnormal Haemoglobins* (Oxford, 1959), pp. 260–66; B. Malamos et al., "Types of Thalassemia-trait Carriers as Revealed by a Study of Their Incidence in Greece," *Brit. Jour. Haemat.* 8 (1962): 5–14; N. A. Barnicot et al., "Haemoglobin Types in Greek Populations," *Ann. Hum. Gen.* 26 (1963): 229–36; J. Bernard and J. Ruffié, *Hématologie géographique* (Paris, 1966), 1: 89; N. Matsaniotis and C. Kattamis, "Thalassemias, a Social Problem in Greece," *Ann. Soc. Belge Méd. Trop.* 49 (1969): 223–30.

46. N. Spiropoulos et al., "Anémie méditerranéenne (érythroblastique) ou thalassémie ou anémie de Cooley et anémie à cellules falciformes," *Sang* 25 (1955): 610; Charokopos "L'anémie de Cooley chez l'enfant grec" (above, n. 29).

47. Matsaniotis and Kattamis, "Thalassemias" (above, n. 45).

48. Malamos et al., "Types of Thalassemia-trait Carriers" (above, n. 45).

49. See the publications of Barnicot et al. and Matsaniotis and Kattamis cited

above, n. 45, as well as A. Gouttas, "Anémies hémolytiques en Grèce," *Ann. Soc. Belge Méd. Trop.* 49 (1969): 185–92.

50. G. R. Fraser et al., "Thalassemia, Abnormal Hemoglobins, and Glucose-6-phosphate Dehydrogenase Deficiency in the Arta Area in Greece," *Ann. N.Y. Acad. Sci.* 119 (1964): 415–35. The numbers given in parentheses are indicative, not absolute. The distribution of anemic traits in this area is not homogeneous. A study by C. Choremis, L. Zannos-Marioulea, and M.D.C. Kattamis shows that the levels are different among inhabitants of the plains as against the mountain-dwellers ("Frequency of Glucose-6-phosphate Dehydrogenase Deficiency in Certain Highly Malarious Areas of Greece," *Lancet* [1962], I, pp. 17ff).

51. The delta trait, that is, the hemoglobinosis in which genetic error affects the production of the delta chain, was discovered in Greece by Phaedon Fessas in 1962.

52. See Barnicot et al., "Haemoglobin Types" (above, n. 45).

53. Choremis, Zannos-Marioulea, and Kattamis, "Frequency" (above, n. 50).

54. For the worldwide distribution of the thalassemias, see A. I. Chernoff, "The Distribution of the Thalassemia Gene: A Historical Review," *Blood* 14 (1959): 899–912; G. Sannie, *Répartition géographique de la thalassémie; Son interprétation*, thesis (Paris, 1964); Bernard and Ruffié, *Hématologie* (above, n. 45), 1: 88–89; Weatherall and Clegg, *Thalassemia Syndromes* (above, n. 26); and Weatherall, "Toward an Understanding" (above, n. 24).

55. A. G. Maratchev, "Gemoglobinopatii v Tadzhikistane," *Vestn. Akad. Med. Nauk* (1965), p. 86.

56. E. Silvestroni and I. Bianco, "The Distribution of Microcythaemias (or Thalassemias) in Italy," in Jonxis et al., *Abnormal Haemoglobins* (above, n. 45), pp. 242–59.

57. See L. C. Brumpt, "A propos de l'anémie de Cooley: Thalassémie ou sinémie?" *Bull. Acad. Nat. Méd.* 139 (1955): 333–36.

58. I. Gatto, "Sulla ereditarietà della malattia di Cooley," *Minerva Med.* 39 (1948): 194–98, and "Origine della thalassemia," *Pensiero Scientifico* 3 (1960): 413–19.

59. E. C. Zaino, "Paleontologic Thalassemia," *Ann. N.Y. Acad. Sci.* 119 (1964): 402–12.

60. G. R. Fraser et al., "Glucose-6-phosphate Dehydrogenase Deficiency, Abnormal Haemoglobins, and Thalassaemia in Yugoslavia," *Jour. Med. Gen.* 3 (1966): 35–41.

61. A. Orsini and L. Badettii, "Nosologie, étiologie et pathologie des thalassémies," *Rapports au XVe Congrès des Pédiatres de Langue française* (Marseille, 1955), pp. 1–130.

62. For such a critique, see J. F. Pays, *La thalassémie eurasiatique. Essai d'anthropopathologie* (Paris and Toulouse, 1971), pp. 136–40.

63. E. Silvestroni, I. Bianco, and N. Alfieri, "Sulle origini della microcitemia in Italia e nelle altre regioni della terra," *Medicina* (Parma) 2 (1952): 187–216.

64. See Caminopetros, "Recherches" (above, n. 27), p. 106.

65. Brumpt, "L'anémie de Cooley" (above, n. 56), p. 333. See also Thor Peng Thong, *La thalassémie au Cambodge* (Paris, 1958).

66. L. C. Brumpt, "Les splénomégalies chroniques africaines," *Rev. Sci. Méd.* 162 (1964): 78–87 (esp. p. 85).

67. Pays, *La thalassémie* (above, n. 62).

68. L. C. Brumpt and J.-F. Pays, "Signification anthropologique de la thalassémie eurasiatique," *Maroc Méd.* 52 (1972): 499–506.

69. Pays, *La thalassémie* (above, n. 62), p. 198.

70. P. Bugard, *L'état de maladie* (Paris, 1964), p. 99.

71. Brumpt and Pays, "Signification anthropologique" (above, n. 68).

72. O. Tönz et al., "New Mutation in a Swiss Girl Leading to Clinical and Biochemical β-Thalassemia Minor," *Humangenetik* 30 (1973): 321–27.

73. F. B. Livingstone, *Abnormal Hemoglobins in Human Populations* (Chicago, 1967); Bernard and Ruffié, *Hématologie* (above, n. 45), I: 72–77; and cf. the publications cited in n. 36, above.

74. H. Lehmann and M. Cutbush, "Sickle-cell Trait in Southern India," *Brit. Med. Jour.* (1952), I, pp. 404–5; H. Lehmann, "Distribution of the Sickle-cell Gene: A New Light on the Origin of the East Africans," *Eugenics Review* 46 (1954): 3–23; R. Singer, "The Origin of the Sickle Cell," *S. Afr. Jour. Sci.* 50 (1954): 287–91. On Lehmann's research, see especially Conley, "Sickle-cell Anemia" (above, n. 34), pp. 329–30.

75. See the articles by P. Brain in *Man* 53 (1953): 154, and *Brit. Med. Jour.* (1973), III, p. 294.

76. E. C. Bucchi, "Is Sickling a Veddit Trait?" *Anthropologist* I (1955): 25–29.

77. Bernard and Ruffié, *Hématologie* (above, n. 45), I: 72–77.

78. For contact between Greece and black Africa during the classical period, see especially A. Bourgeois, *La Grèce antique devant la négritude* (Paris, 1971).

79. J.B.S. Haldane, "The Rate of Mutation of Human Genes," *Proceedings of the VIIIth International Congress on Genetics* (Stockholm, 1948), *Hereditas,* suppl. (1949), and "Disease and Evolution," *Ricerca scientifica* 19 (1949): 68–76.

80. A. C. Allison, "Protection Afforded by Sickle-cell Trait against Sub-tertian Malarial Infection," *Brit. Med. Jour.* (1954) I, pp. 290–94.

81. The mechanism in question is well explained by A. G. Motulsky, "Metabolic Polymorphism and the Role of Infectious Diseases in Human Evolution," *Hum. Biol.* 32 (1960): 28–62; A. C. Allison, "Polymorphism and Natural Selection in Human Populations," *Cold Spring Harbor Symp. Quant. Biol.* 29 (1964): 137–49; and T. Dobzhansky, *Mankind Evolving* (New Haven, 1963). For general thoughts on this subject, see J. Bernard and J. Ruffié, "Origine du polymorphisme hématologique chez l'homme et dynamique des populations," *Annales E.S.C.* 34 (1979): 1324–43.

82. See especially the mathematical model proposed by S. L. Wiesenfeld, "Sickle-cell Trait in Human Biological and Cultural Evolution," *Science* 157 (1967): 1134–40.

83. H. Lehmann, "The Maintenance of the Haemoglobinopathies at High Frequency," in Jonxis et al., *Abnormal Haemoglobins* (above, n. 45), pp. 307–21; A. G. Motulsky, "Hereditary Red Cell Diseases and Malaria," *Amer. Jour. Trop. Med.* 13 (1964): 147–58.

84. A critical survey can be found in the thesis of D. Hesse-Turner, *Die Bedeutung der Thalassaemie und des Glucose-6-Phosphatedehydrogenase Mangels für die Pathologie und Epidemiologie der Malaria* (Tübingen, 1967).

85. See G. Montalenti, E. Silvestroni, and I. Bianco, "Nuove indagini sul problema della microcitemia," *R.C. Accad. Naz. Lincei,* 8, t. 14 (1959): 183–88, and C. Menini, "Osservazioni storiche sulla malaria nel Ferrarese, nei suoi rapporti con talassemia e favismo," *Episteme* 4 (1970): 234–40.

86. See the publications cited in n. 45, above, and the study by G. Stamatoyannopoulos and P. Fessas, "Thalassemia, Glucose-6-phosphate Dehydrogenase Deficiency, Sickling, and Malarial Endemicity in Greece," *Brit. Med. Jour.* (1964), I, pp. 875–79.

87. C. Choremis et al., "Three Inherited Red-cell Abnormalities in a District of Greece: Thalassemia, Sickling, and Glucose-6-phosphate Dehydrogenase Deficiency," *Lancet* (1963), I, pp. 907–9.

88. D. G. Rokhlin, *Bolezni drevnih lyudei* (Moscow, 1965).

89. Carlson, Armelagos, and Van Gerven, "Factors Influencing" (above, n. 15).

90. C. Wells, *Bones, Bodies, and Disease* (London, 1964), p. 114.

91. A. Marcsik and F. Kósa, "Pathological Aspects of Paleoanthropological Finds," *Acta Congressus Intern. Hist. Artis Med. (Budapest, 1974)* (Budapest, 1976), 2: 1301–7.

92. See T. Lodge, "Thinning of the Parietal Bones," in Brothwell and Sandison, *Diseases in Antiquity* (above, n. 32), pp. 405–16.

93. A good update can be found in F. L. Dunn, "On the Antiquity of Malaria in the Western Hemisphere," *Hum. Biol.* 37 (1965): 385–93, and J. de Zulueta and S. C. Ayala, "Malaria in Pre-Columbian America?" *Paleopathological Newsletter*, no. 23 (1978), pp. 12–15.

94. M. Y. El-Najjar, B. Lozoff, and D. J. Ryan, "The Paleoepidemiology of Porotic Hyperostosis in the American Southwest: Radiological and Ecological Considerations," *Amer. Jour. Roentg.* 125 (1975): 918–24; M. Y. El-Najjar et al., "The Etiology of Porotic Hyperostosis among the Prehistoric and Historic Anasazi Indians of Southwestern United States," *Amer. Jour. Phys. Anthrop.* 44 (1976): 477–88; and M. Y. El-Najjar, "Maize, Malaria, and the Anemias in the Pre-Columbian New World," *Yearb. Phys. Anthrop.* 20 (1976): 329–37.

95. P. Graziosi, "Gli uomini paleolitici della Grotta di San Teodoro (Messina)," *Riv. Sci. Preistor.* 2 (1947): 123.

96. Gatto, "Sulla ereditarietà" (above, n. 58).

97. A. Ascenzi, "Thalassémie et lésions osseuses. Avec discussion d'exemplaires paléopathologiques italiens," *Actes du Ier Coll. Franç. de Paléopath. (Lyon, 1973)* (Lyon, 1975), pp. 169–85.

98. E. Benassi and A. Toti, "Osservazioni sulle ossa rinvenute negli scavi della necropoli di Spina. Conferma all'origine razziale della talassemia," *Att. Mem. Accad. Stor. Arte San.*, 2d ser., 24 (1958): 16–28. See also P. Di Pietro, *Breve storia dell'ematologia* (Padua, 1958). It may be well to recall that Spina is in the region where F. Rietti made his first description of thalassemia minor.

99. Ascenzi, "Thalassémie" (above, n. 97).

100. A. Ascenzi and P. Balistreri, "Porotic Hyperostosis and the Problem of the Origin of Thalassemia in Italy," *Jour. Hum. Evol.* 6 (1977): 595–604; A. Ascenzi, "A Problem in Paleopathology: The Origin of Thalassemia in Italy," *Virchows Arch. Path. Anat.* 384 (1979): 121–30.

101. G. Fornaciari and F. Mallegni, "Iperostosi porotica verosimilmente talassemica in due scheletri rinvenuti in un gruppo di tombe del III secolo a.C. di San Giovenale (Viterbo)," *Quad. Sci. Antrop.* (Padua) 4 (1980): 21–50.

102. J. L. Angel, "Human Biological Changes in Ancient Greece, with Special Reference to Lerna," *Yearb. Amer. Philos. Soc.* (1957), p. 269.

103. J. L. Angel, "Osteoporosis: Thalassemia?" *Amer. Jour. Phys. Anthrop.* 22 (1964): 369–72.

104. Angel, "Porotic Hyperostosis" (above, n. 14).

105. J. L. Angel, *The People of Lerna: Analysis of a Prehistoric Aegean Population* (Princeton and Washington, D.C. 1971), pp. 77–84.

106. J. L. Angel, "Anemias of Antiquity: Eastern Mediterranean," in *Porotic Hyperostosis: An Enquiry* (Detroit, 1977), pp. 1–5; "Porotic Hyperostosis in the Eastern Mediterranean," *MCV Quart.* 15 (1978): 10–16.

107. Angel, *People of Lerna* (above, n. 105), p. 55.

108. Angel, "Porotic Hyperostosis" (above, n. 14), p. 762, and Brothwell and Sandison, *Diseases in Antiquity* (above, n. 32), pp. 380–81.

109. See J. L. Benson, *Bamboula* (Philadelphia, 1972).

110. J. L. Angel, "Human Skeletal Material from Franchthi Cave," *Hesperia* 38 (1969): 380–81.

111. J. Mellaart, *Çatal Hüyük: A Neolithic Town in Anatolia* (New York, 1967); J. L. Angel, "Early Neolithic Skeletons from Çatal Hüyük: Demography and Pathology," *Anatolian Studies* 21 (1971): 77–98; J. L. Angel, "Early Neolithic People of Nea Nikomedea," in I. Schwidetzky, *Die Anfänge des Neolithikums vom Orient bis Nordeuropa. Fundamenta.* (Cologne, 1973), pt. B, vol. 3, pp. 103–12; Angel, "Porotic Hyperostosis in the Eastern Mediterranean (above, n. 106).

112. Angel, "Porotic Hyperostosis in the Eastern Mediterranean" (above, n. 106).

113. M. J. Mellink and J. L. Angel, "Excavations at Karataş-Semayük in Lycia," *Amer. Jour. Archaeol.* 72 (1968): 243–63; Angel, "Porotic Hyperostosis in the Eastern Mediterranean" (above, n. 106).

114. Angel, *People of Lerna* (above, n. 105), p. 79.

115. G. Bräuer and R. Fricke, "Zur Phänomenologie osteoporotischer Veränderungen bei Bestehen systemischer hämatologischen Affektionen," *Homo* 31 (1980), 198–211.

116. Angel, "Porotic Hyperostosis in the Eastern Mediterranean" (above, n. 106), p. 11.

117. *Brit. Med. Jour.* (1973), I, p. 488, and II, p. 489.

118. *Aff. int.*, 32 (Littré, VII, 248).

119. The diagnosis of homozygous thalassemia suggested by P. Brain (*Brit. Med. Jour.* [1973], III, p. 294) does not seem to me acceptable, given the character and localization of the pain and the rarity of ulcerations in thalassemics.

120. *Praen. Coacae,* 333 (Littré, V, 656). This passage was mentioned in connection with thalassemia in studies by Caminopetros, "Recherches" (above, n. 27), Bannerman, *Thalassemia: A Survey* (above, n. 26), and Weatherall, "Toward an Understanding" (above, n. 24). Weatherall opts for a diagnosis of iron deficiency anemia and not thalassemia.

121. See especially P. Lanzkowsky, "Investigation into the Aetiology and Treatment of Pica," *Arch. Dis. Child.* 34 (1959): 140–8.

122. Louvre Museum, inv. nos. E/D 564 and E/D 1899–1905.

123. L. J. Bruce-Chwatt, "Paleogenesis and Paleo-epidemiology of Primate Malaria," *Bull. W.H.O.* 32 (1965): 363–87, and P. F. Mattingly, "Origins and Evolution of the Human Malarias: The Role of the Vector," *Parassitologia* 15 (1973): 160–72. The hypothesis that the first center for the evolution of simian and human malarias was not Africa but the jungles of Southeast Asia cannot be set aside. See G. R. Coatney et al., *The Primate Malarias* (Washington, D.C., 1971). From my point of view, it makes no difference; in either case, Africa was affected long before Europe.

124. Bruce-Chwatt, "Paleogenesis" (above, n. 123), pp. 377 and 384; P. F. Russell, *Man's Mastery of Malaria* (London, 1955); F. L. Dunn, "On the Antiquity of Malaria in the Western Hemisphere," *Hum. Biol.* 37 (1965): 385–93; L. J. Bruce-Chwatt and J. de Zulueta, *The Rise and Fall of Malaria in Europe* (Oxford, 1980).

125. P. C. Garnham, *Malaria Parasites and Other Haemosporidia* (Oxford, 1966), and P. F. Mattingly, "Evolution of the Malarias: The Problem of Origins," *Parassitologia* 18(1976): 1–8. For the current state of knowledge concerning malaria parasites and the clinical course, pathology, and epidemiology of malaria, see L. J. C. Bruce-Chwatt, *Essential Malariology* (London, 1980).

126. Angel, "Porotic Hyperostosis in the Eastern Mediterranean" (above, n. 106), p. 14.

127. D. Ferembach, *La nécropole épipaléolithique de Taforalt (Maroc Oriental); Etude des squelettes humains* (Rabat, 1962).

128. P. G. Shute, "Failure to Infect English Specimens of Anopheles Maculipennis var. Atroparvus with Certain Strains of *Plasmodium Falciparum* of Tropical Origin," *Jour. Trop. Med. Hyg.* 43 (1940): 175–87; J. de Zulueta, C. D. Ramsdale, and M. Coluzzi, "Receptivity to Malaria in Europe," *Bull. W.H.O.* 52 (1975): 109–11; Bruce-Chwatt and de Zulueta, *The Rise and Fall of Malaria* (above, n. 124), pp. 13–15.

129. J. de Zulueta, "Malaria and Mediterranean History," *Parassitologia* 15 (1973): 1–15; Bruce-Chwatt and de Zulueta, *The Rise and Fall of Malaria* (above, n. 124), pp. 13–16 and 34.

130. These ideas were first intuited by Sir Ronald Ross (1857–1932), who won the Nobel Prize in medicine for his research on the role of mosquitoes in the transmission of malaria. He conceived them during a trip to Greece. See R. Ross, "Malaria in Greece," *Jour. Trop. Med.* 9 (1906): 341–47. Not knowing how to document his historical conjectures, Ross enlisted his friend Jones, a classical philologist. See W.H.S. Jones, *Malaria, a Neglected Factor in the History of Greece and Rome* (Cambridge, 1907) (with a valuable introduction by Ross); "Malaria and History," *Ann. Trop. Med. Parasit.* 1 (1908): 529–46; "Dea Febris—A Study of Malaria in Ancient Italy," *Ann. Archaeol. Anthrop.* 2 (1909): 97–124; *Malaria and Greek History* (Manchester, 1909); "Ancient Documents and Contemporary Life, with Special reference to the Hippocratic Corpus, Celsus, and Pliny," in *Science, Medicine, and History (Essays in Honor of C. Singer)* (Oxford, 1953), 1: 100–110. See also P. Fraccaro, "La malaria e la storia degli antichi popoli classici," *Atene e Roma* 22 (1919): 57–88, and N. Toscanelli, *La malaria nell'antichità e la fine degli Etruschi* (Milan, 1927).

131. This is a significant fact because his homeland, Boeotia (especially the Lake Copais basin, which was a swamp at the time), fulfilled all the geographic conditions for rampant malaria. Actually, Hellenistic sources consider certain Boeotian locales like Onchestos to be fever centers. In Plutarch's time, this region of central Greece was devastated by malaria. See Jones, *Malaria and Greek History* (above, n. 130), pp. 25ff., 40, and 54.

132. This observation by Jones (ibid., p. 26) is absolutely true, but the argument he makes of it is vitiated by the extreme rarity of texts preserved from the period in question. Even the early date of the poetry attributed to Theognis is doubtful.

133. Theognis, 1, 174. See Jones, *Malaria and Greek History* (above, n. 130), and B. A. Van Groningen, *Théognis, Le premier livre, édité avec un commentaire* (Amsterdam, 1966), pp. 68–69.

134. Aristophanes, *Wasps,* 277, 281, and 812; *Acharn.,* 1165.

135. Jones, *Malaria and Greek History* (above, n. 130), p. 35.

136. Ibid., pp. 35 and 42–43.

137. See J. P. Cardamatis, "La malaria à Athènes depuis les temps les plus reculés jusqu'à nos jours," *Atti Soc. Studi Mal.* 8 (1907): 111, and "Du paludisme dans la Grèce continentale depuis les temps les plus reculés jusqu'à la période macédonienne," *Arch. Schiff. Trop. Hyg.* 19 (1915): 273–301; A. Cawadias, "Le paludisme dans l'histoire de l'ancienne Grèce," *Bull. Soc. Franç. Hist. Méd.* (1909), pp. 158–65; G. A. Livadas, "Malaria in Ancient Greece," *Riv. Parassit.* 20 (1959): 299–304.

138. It is worth recalling that at the time when Ross and Jones were publishing their historico-epidemiological hypotheses, malaria affected about a third of the population of Greece. Malaria-induced mortality was very high there, and the influence of the disease on economic and cultural life was especially devastating. On the history of malaria in Greece in modern times, see G. D. Belos, *L'histoire du paludisme en Grèce depuis l'Antiquité jusqu'à la découverte de Laveran* (Paris, 1933), and G. A. Livadas and J. C. Sphangos, *Malaria in Greece* (Athens, 1941).

139. As an example, see F. Regnault, "La décadence de la Grèce expliquée par la déforestation et l'impaludisme," *Presse Méd.* (1909), pp. 729–31, and "Du rôle du dépeuplement, du déboisement et de la malaria dans la décadence de certaines nations," *Rev. Scient.* 52 (1914): 46ff.

140. The American geographer Ellsworth Huntington provided the first detailed elaboration of the hypothesis that seeks to explain fluctuations in the malarial endemic in Greece by climatic cycles. Its recrudescence in Hellenistic times was due to the period of aridity that began around 300 B.C. See E. Huntington, "The Burial of Olympia: A Study in Climate and History," *Geograph. Jour.* 36 (1910): 657ff. For a contemporary view of the relation between malaria and climate in Greece, see especially G. Panessa, "Recenti studi di interesse paleoclimatologico riguardanti la Grecia," *Ann. Scuola Norm. Sup. Pisa,* 3d ser., III, 12 (1982): 1601–14.

141. See A. Celli, *Malaria* (London, 1900), and *Storia della malaria nell'Agro Romano* (Rome, 1925).

142. See Jones, *Malaria and Greek History* (above, n. 130), pp. 62–73; Kind, "Malaria," in Pauly-Wissowa, *Real-Encyclopädie,* 14 (1928), col. 830–846; G. Sticker, "Fieber und Entzündung bei den Hippokratikern," *Arch. Gesch. Med.* 20 (1928): 150–74; 22 (1929–30): 313–43, 361–81; 23 (1930): 40–67; G. Chairopoulos, *Le paludisme dans la Grèce antique,* thesis (Lyon, 1930); H. E. Sigerist, *History of Medicine,* vol. 2 (Oxford, 1961), pp. 328–32.

143. See chapter II, below, and M. Grmek, "Les ruses de guerre biologiques dans l'Antiquité," *Rev. Et. Grecques* 92 (1979): 141–63. Introduction of the falciparum type could have been brought about or facilitated by Xerxes' Persian army. For this hypothesis, see C. Laderman, "Malaria and Progress: Some Historical and Ecological Considerations," *Social Science and Medicine* 9 (1975): 587–94 (esp. p. 592).

144. Jones, *Malaria and Greek History* (above, n. 130), p. 76.

145. Ibid., pp. 95–100 and 132.

146. L. W. Hackett, *Malaria in Europe* (London, 1937), and E. H. Ackerknecht, *Geschichte und Geographie der Wichtigsten Krankheiten* (Stuttgart, 1963), p. 80.

Chapter Eleven: The Hippocratic Conception of Disease

1. The essence of this chapter was published in *Actualités hématologiques 1978,* 12th ser. (Paris, 1978), pp. 293–315.

2. *Epid.,* I, patient I (Littré, II, 682–84).

3. The numbers in parentheses refer to parts of the discussion in the next section of this chapter.

4. H. Kuehlewein, *Hippocratis Opera quae feruntur omnia* (Leipzig, 1894), I: 180–245.

5. W.H.S. Jones, *Hippocrates* (Cambridge and London, 1923), I: 146–211 (specifically, p. 186).

6. Galen, *In Hippocratis Epidemiarum librum primum commentaria* (Kühn, XVII, A. 1–302). Critical edition by E. Wenkebach and F. Pfaff, *Corpus Medicorum Graecorum,* V, 10, 1 (Leipzig and Berlin, 1934).

7. E. Littré *Oeuvres complètes d'Hippocrate* (Paris, 1840), 2: 598–717, esp. pp. 683–85.

8. Desmars, *Epidémiques d'Hippocrate* (Paris, 1767); C. Daremberg, *Oeuvres choisies d'Hippocrate,* 2d ed. (Paris, 1855), pp. 426–27; L. Bourgey, *Observation et expérience chez les médecins de la Collection hippocratique* (Paris, 1953), p. 200; and M. Martiny, *Hippocrate et la médecine* (Paris, 1964), p. 192.

9. R. Fuchs, *Hippokrates, Sämtliche Werke* (Munich, 1897), 2: 99–128; G. Sticker,

Hippokrates, Der Volkskrankheiten erstes und drittes Buch (Leipzig, 1923); R. Kapferer and G. Sticker, *Die Werke des Hippokrates* (Stuttgart and Leipzig, 1939), vol. II; W. Mueri, *Der Arzt in Altertum,* 3d ed. (Munich, 1962), p. 97; and H. Diller, *Hippokrates, Schriften* (Reinbek bei Hamburg, 1962), pp. 30–31.

10. F. Adams, *The Genuine Works of Hippocrates* (London, 1849 rept. Baltimore, 1939), pp. 111–12, and Jones, *Hippocrates* (above, n. 5), p. 187.

11. M. Vegetti, *Opere di Ippocrate* (Turin, 1965), p. 314.

12. In this regard, see the statement of A. Foesius, *Oeconomia Hippocratis Alphabeti Serie Distincta* (Frankfurt, 1588), col. 471.

13. Daremberg, *Oeuvres choisies* (above, n. 8), p. 461, n. 20.

14. P. Berrettoni, "Il lessico tecnico de I e III libro delle Epidemie ippocratiche," *Annali Scuola norm. Pisa* 39 (1970): 36.

15. Galen, *In Hippocratis* (above, n. 6), comm. III.

16. V. Langholf draws my attention to another Hippocratic passage in the *Use of Liquids* (Littré, VI, 118, 12), where the expression *khroiēn an kalēsai* means "to bring back the color of the skin."

17. Vegetti, *Opere di Ippocrate* (above, n. 11), p. 314.

18. See K. Deichgräber, *Die Epidemien und das Corpus Hippocraticum* (*Abh. Preuss. Akad. Wiss., Philol.-hist. Kl.,* no. 3) (Berlin, 1933; 2d ed., Berlin and New York, 1971).

19. For the Hippocratic notion of *katástasis,* see Jones, *Hippocrates* (above, n. 5), p. 141, and O. Temkin, "Die Krankheitsauffassung von Hippokrates und Sydenham in ihren Epidemien," *Sudhoffs Arch. Gesch. Med.* 20 (1928): 327–52.

20. Littré, II, 642.

21. Littré, II, 650–54.

22. J. Pouilloux, *Recherches sur l'histoire et les cultes de Thasos,* vol. I, *De la fondation de la cité à 196 avant J.-C.* (Paris, 1954), p. 249. See also J.-E. Dugand, "Hippocrate à Thasos et en Grèce du Nord," in *Corpus Hippocraticum (Actes du Colloque de Mons, 1975)* (Mons, 1977), pp. 233–45.

23. *Inscriptiones Graecae,* vol. XII, fasc. VIII, 1909, nos. 271 and 277.

24. Deichgräber, *Die Epidemien* (above, n. 18), p. 16.

25. See above, n. 22.

26. There is no need to keep silent about a further difficulty that Deichgräber does not take into account: the Hippocratic patient is once expressly referred to as the son of Antagoras (Littré, II, 665), while the *theōrós* with the same name is the son of Aristocleides. The commonness of the name "Philiscus" in Thasian epigraphy makes the identifcation fairly unlikely. It would be even easier, and completely gratuitous as well, to try to identify our patient with a certain Philiscus of Thasos nicknamed "The Savage," a recluse who indulged in apiculture. We know nothing of the man, except that he wrote a treatise on bees that was used by Hyginus and that is cited by Pliny the Elder (*Natural History,* XI, 9).

27. The term *kaûsos* is known to derive from the verb *kaíō* 'burn' and to belong to the same family as, for instance, the verb "cauterize" and the adjective "caustic." Besides Chantraine's *Dictionnaire étymologique,* p. 435, see the study by R. Strömberg, *Griechische Wortstudien: Untersuchungen zur Benennung von Tieren, Pflanzen, Körperteilen und Krankheiten* (Göteborg, 1944), p. 87.

28. *Aff.,* II (Littré, VI, 214).

29. The basic descriptions of this clinical entity are in *Epid.,* I, 9 (Littré, II, 650–52), *Acut. (app.),* I (Littré, II, 394–98, and Joly, 68–69), *Morb.,* II, 63 (Littré, VII, 96–98), and *Aff.,* II (Littré, VI, 214–18). For the latter two texts, one should consult the critical edition, translation, and philological commentary of J. Jouanna, *Hippocrate et l'Ecole de Cnide* (Paris, 1974), pp. 274–77, 286, and so forth. For other details on *kaûsos,* see Littré, *Oeuvres complètes* (above, n. 7). I, 612; II, 28, 50, 232,

368, 418, 600, 618–20, 636, 640–42, 685, 666; III, 60, 66, 70, 80, 90, 98, 102, 108, 118, 122, 130; IV, 496, 500, 522, 570; V, 72, 100, 168–70, 294, 380, 392, 408, 458, 462, 514, 530–32, 608–10, 716; VI, 144–46, 194, 200–202, 222; VII, 156–60.

30. For instance *Epid.*, I, patient 2; *Epid.*, III, first list, patients 10 and 12; second list, patients 1, 5, 7, 9, and 12; *Epid.*, VII, 10, 20, and 42.

31. R. Wittern, *Die hippokratische Schrift De morbis I* (Hildesheim and New York, 1974), pp. 190–91.

32. See the old bibliography in C. F. Fuchs, "Der Causos des Hippokrates," *Archiv des Vereins für wiss. Heilkunde* 2 (1866), and Sticker, *Hippokrates* (above, n. 9), p. 92.

33. J.-B. Germain, *Les Epidémies d'Hippocrate peuvent-elles être rapportées à un cadre nosologique?* thesis in medicine (Paris, 1803).

34. F. Adams, *The Seven Books of Paulus Aegineta* (London, 1844), 1: 260–62.

35. Littré, *Oeuvres complètes* (above, n. 7), pp. 566–71; E. Beaugrand, "Causus," in *Dictionnaire encyclopédique des sciences médicales* (Paris, 1874) 13:391–92.

36. C. A. Wunderlich, *Geschichte der Medizin* (Stuttgart, 1859), p. 9.

37. W.H.S. Jones, *Malaria and Greek History* (Manchester, 1909). To be sure, Jones admits that certain concrete Hippocratic cases of *kaûsos* are complications of malaria.

38. Sticker, *Hippokrates* (above, n. 9), pp. 91–93. The use of the terms *kaûsos* and *puretòs kausṓdēs* in the parallel versions of *Aff.*, II, and *Morb.*, II, 63, proves against Sticker that the two expressions are utterly synonymous.

39. W. MacArthur, "Historical Notes on Some Epidemic Diseases Associated with Jaundice," *British Medical Bulletin* 13 (1957): 146–49.

40. See in particular Strömberg, *Griechische Wortstudien* (above, n. 27), pp. 87–88.

41. Galen, *De atra bile*, 4 (*Corpus Med. Graecorum*, V. 4, 1, p. 76).

42. See n. 29, above.

43. Aretaeus of Cappadocia as well as Galen, Paul of Aegina, and Alexander of Tralles all describe *kaûsos* and distinguish two clinical forms of it, one "authentic" and the other "false." The split made by these late authors is not exactly the same as those in *Acut. (app.)*, 1. From the standpoint of modern differential diagnosis, none of these divisions is really useful.

44. See Adams, *The Seven Books* (above, n. 34), p. 261.

45. M. Meyerhof, "Thirty-three Clinical Observations by Rhazes (circa 900 A.D.)," *Isis* 23 (1935): 321–72, esp. p. 347.

46. M. Vust-Mussard, "Remarques sur les livres I et III des epidémies; Les histoires de malades et le pronostic," *Etudes de Lettres* (Lausanne), 3d, ser., 3 (1970): 67–69.

47. See Temkin, "Die Krankheitsauffassung" (above, n. 19). Fernand Robert has provided an excellent review of the role of prognosis in the relatively recent portions of the *Epidemics:* "La prognose hippocratique dans les livres V et VII des Epidémies," in *Le Monde grec (Hommage à Claire Préaux)* (Brussels, 1975), pp. 257–70.

48. See E. Vintró, *Hipócrates y la nosología hippocrática* (Barcelona, 1972), esp. p. 125.

49. For a formal analysis of the clinical observations attributed to Hippocrates, see P. Laín Entralgo, *La historia clínica*, 2d ed. (Barcelona, 1963), and Vintró, *Hipócrates* (above, n. 48), pp. 107–44. There have been attempts at critical analysis of these observations in the light of modern medical knowledge, notably by R. E. Siegel, "Clinical Observations in Hippocrates: An Essay on the Evolution of the Diagnostic Art," *Journal of the Mount Sinai Hospital* 31 (1964): 285–303.

50. *Epidemics*, I, 8 (Littré, II, 640–42; Jones, I, 167).

51. *Epidemics,* I, 9 (Littré, II, 650–54; Jones, I 173).

52. Vust-Mussard, "Remarques sur les Epidémies" (above, n. 46), p. 72.

53. *Prorrh.,* I, 39 (Littré, V. 520). The same text recurs in *Coac.,* 49.

54. *Progn.,* 12 (Littré, II, 142).

55. *Epidemics,* I, patients 1, 2, and 3; *Epidemics,* III, second list, patients 2, 3, 9, 10, 11, 13, and 14.

56. M. Sorre, "Complexes pathogènes et géographie médicale," *Annales de Géographie* 42 (1933): 1–18.

57. H. Scott, *History of Tropical Medicine* (London, 1939), 1:252–78; J.W.W. Stephens, *Blackwater Fever: Historical Survey and Summary of Observations Made Over a Century* (Liverpool, 1937).

58. See A. Guillon, "La fièvre bilieuse hémoglobinurique," in *Grandes épidémies tropicales* (Paris, 1935), 7: 60–75.

59. Fluctuation in the terminology reflects the uncertainties: the disease is called "pernicious melanuric remittent fever" (Duchassaing, 1850), "miasmatic haematuria" (Cummings, 1859), "bilious hematuric fever" (Barthélemy-Benoît, 1865; Veillard, 1867), "bilious melanuric fever" (Bérenger-Féraud, 1874), "black urine fever" (Pellarin, 1876), "hemospherinic paludal fever" (Karamitsas, 1882), "hemoglobinuric bilious fever" (Corre, 1883), "blackwater fever" (Easmon, 1884), "Schwarzwasserfieber" [blackwater fever] (Plehn, 1895), etc.

60. A. Antoniades, "Peri tôn haimorragiôn kaì idíōs tês haimatourías epì tôn dialeipóntōn puretôn," *Iatrikḕ Ephēmerís* 1 (1858–59): 161–63.

61. C. Stéphanos, "Grèce (Topographie médicale)," in *Dictionnaire encyclopédique des sciences médicales,* 4th ser. (Paris, 1884), 10:500.

62. See n. 60, above.

63. G. Karamitsas, "Perì elṓdous haimosphairinikoû puretoû (Athens, 1882); G. Karamitsas, "Sur la fièvre hémisphérinurique," *Archives de médecine navale* (1882), pp. 153–56.

64. See the publications cited in the previous note and Scott, *Tropical Medicine* (above, n. 57).

65. See Scott, *Tropical Medicine* (above, n. 57), 1: 266–69.

66. E. Marchiafava and A. Bignami, *Sulle febbre malariche estivo-autumnali* (Rome, 1892).

67. See for example Guillon, "La fièvre bilieuse" (above, n. 58), and B. Maegraith, *Pathological Processes in Malaria and Blackwater Fever* (Oxford, 1948).

68. For instance, G. Charmot and L. J. André, "Infection palustre et réactions immunitaires," *Médecine tropicale* 26 (1966): 115–30; F. Vachon et al., "Accès pernicieux palustre," in *Année en réanimation* 1 (1970): 105–70; G. Saimot et al., "Les Formes aiguës graves du paludisme," *Méd. mal. infect.* 1 (1971): 9–22.

69. See chapter 9, above.

70. J. Gear, "Autoantigens and Autoantibodies in the Pathogenesis of Disease with Special Reference to Blackwater Fever," *Trans. Royal Soc. Trop. Med.* 39 (1945): 301.

71. Jones, *Hippocrates* (above, n. 5), p. 144.

72. R. Joly, *Le niveau de la science hippocratique* (Paris, 1966), p. 220.

73. H. Foy and A. Kondi, "Researches on Blackwater Fever in Greece: Introduction and History," *Annals Trop. Med. Parasit.* 29 (1935): 383–93.

74. *Epidemics,* III, second list, patient 3 (Littré, III, 112–16).

75. See R. H. Major, "How Hippocrates Made His Diagnoses," *International Rec. Med.* 170 (1957): 479–85.

76. L. F. Barker, *A Study of Some Fatal Cases of Malaria* (Baltimore, 1895), pp. 6–8.

77. See for instance F. Vachon et al., "L'insuffisance rénale aiguë du paludisme pernicieux," *Nouvelle Presse Médicale* 2 (1973): 1035–39.

78. Cf. Germain, *Les Epidémies d'Hippocrate* (above, n. 33).

79. Littré, *Oeuvres complètes* (above, n. 7), 2:539–67.

80. Ibid., 2:543.

81. Wunderlich, *Geschichte der Médizin* (above, n. 36).

82. Stéphanos, "Grèce" (above, n. 61), p. 500.

83. J. P. Cardamatis, *De la fièvre hémoglobinurique observée en Grèce* (Athens, 1901).

84. Foy and Kondi, "Researches on Blackwater Fever" (above, n. 73).

85. Scott, *Tropical Medicine* (above, n. 57).

86. Martiny, *Hippocrate* (above, n. 8).

87. Sticker, *Hippokrates* (above, n. 9), pp. 90–91.

88. R. E. Siegel, "Epidemics and Infectious Diseases at the Time of Hippocrates: Their Relation to Modern Accounts," *Gesnerus* 17 (1960): 77–98.

89. See R. F. Timken-Zinkann, "Black Bile: A Review of Recent Attempts to Trace the Origin of the Teaching on Melancholia to Medical Observations," *Medical History* 12 (1968): 288–92.

Chapter Twelve: The "Cough of Perinthus"

1. The text of the first part of this chapter was given before the Third Hippocratic Colloquim (Paris, 1978). The second part has not been published before.

2. *Epidemics,* VI, 7, 1, (Littré, V, 330–36).

3. In this translation, the numbers enclosed in parentheses refer to the headings in the commentary that follows it. Word in square brackets are my own editorial comments.

4. After the appearance of my study in the acts of the Paris colloquium, D. Manetti and A. Roselli published a critical revision of the Greek text and an Italian translation of the sixth book of the *Epidemics* (Florence, 1982). Their work did not lead me to change my translation or conclusions.

5. Cf. W. Braeutigam, *De Hippocratis Epidemiarum Libri Sexti Commentatoribus,* thesis (Königsberg, 1908).

6. E. Wenkebach and F. Pfaff, *Galeni in Hippocratis Epidemiarum librum VI commentaria I–VIII* (Berlin, 1956), (*Corpus Medicorum Graecorum,* V, 10, 2, 2). The part concerning the "cough of Perinthus" occurs on pp. 386–401. It was translated into German by F. Pfaff from an Arabic text by Hunain ibn Ishaq. On this subject, consult F. Pfaff, "Die nur arabisch erhaltenen Teile der Epidemienkommentare Galens und die Überlieferung des Corpus Hippocraticum," *Sitzungs-Bericht. Berlin. Akad. Wiss.* (1931), p. 558. See also B. Alexanderson, "Bemerkungen zu Galens Epidemienkommentaren," *Eranos* 65 (1967): 118–45.

7. *Palladii scholia in Hippocratis de popularibus Morbis librum* VI, in F. R. Dietz, *Scholia in Hippocratem et Galenum* (Königsberg, 1834), 2: pp. 1–204 (repr. Amsterdam, 1966); and C. D. Pritchet, *Johannis Alexandrini commentaria in sextum librum Hippocratis Epidemiarum* (Leiden, 1975).

8. E. Littré *Oeuvres complètes d'Hippocrate* (Paris, 1846), 5: 331–37; Th. Puschmann, "Die Influenza im Alterthum," *Wien. Klin. Wschr.* 6 (1893): 239–42; R. Fuchs, *Hippokrates, Sämtliche Werke* (Munich, 1897), 2: 280–82; R. Kapferer (with the collaboration of G. Sticker), *Die Werke des Hippokrates,* vol. 2 (Stuttgart, 1939), pp. XII/75–XII/77.

9. Cf. F. Robert, "Prophasis," *Rev. Etudes Grecques* 89 (1976): 317–42.

10. Aristotle, *De generatione animalium,* V. 1; 780a. See S. Byl, *Recherches sur les grands traités biologiques d'Aristote* (Brussels, 1980), pp. 87ff. and 281.

11. Bitot, "Mémoire sur une lésion conjonctivale non encore décrite coïncidant avec l'héméralopie," *Gaz. Hebd. Méd. Chir.* 10 (1863): 284–88.

12. *Epidemics,* VI, 7, 10 (Littré, V, 342).

13. *Humors,* VII, trans. W.H.S. Jones, in *Hippocrates,* vol. 4 (London and Cambridge, 1931; rept. 1953).

14. *Epidemics,* II, 3, 1 (Littré, V, 100); II, 1, 5 (Littré, V, 74); II, 3, 11 (Littré, V. 114); VI, 21 (Littré, V, 160); and VI, 2, 19 (Littré, V, 286).

15. *Epidemics,* IV, 21 (Littré, V, 160).

16. Littré, *Oeuvres complètes* (above, n. 8), 5: 16–17; see Aristotle, *Meteorologica,* I, 6, 8.

17. Littré, *Oeuvres complètes* (above, n. 8), 5: 16–17; see Thucydides, III, 87.

18. H. Grensemann, "Die Krankheit der Tochter des Theodoros," *Clio Medica* 4 (1969): 72.

19. Aristotle, *Meteorologica,* I, 6, 9; 6, 10; and 7, 10. See also Diodorus Siculus, XV, 50, and Seneca, *Natural Questions,* VII, 16.

20. Gundel, s.v. *Kometen* in Pauly-Wissowa, *Real-Encyclopädie,* XXI, col. 1183; A. Pingré, *Cométographie ou traité historique et théorique des comètes* (Paris, 1783), 1: 259; G. Bigourdan, "Les comètes; Liste chronologique de celles qui ont apparu de l'origine à 1900," *Annuaire du Bureau des Longitudes* (1927), app. A.

21. V. Di Benedetto, "Principi metodici di Ep., II, IV, VI," in *Corpus Hippocraticum, Colloque du Mons* (Mons, 1977), p. 261.

22. See the lists of Pingré and Bigourdan cited above, as well as the work of A. S. Yamamoto, *Preliminary General Catalogue of Comets* (Kyoto, 1936). A comet appearing in 400 B.C. is mentioned in them, but that is probably the result of the incorrect interpretation of a late text.

23. Novas and supernovas are stellar explosions that appear irregularly in the sky. Their brightness can equal or exceed that of first-magnitude stars. On average, one supernova and ten very bright novas are seen in a century. For antiquity, the lists of such events are very incomplete. See D. H. Clark and F. R. Stephenson, *The Historical Supernovae* (Oxford, 1977).

24. *Epidemics,* IV, 45 (Littré, V, 186). For the critical edition of this text and a philological commentary, see V. Langholf, *Syntaktische Untersuchungen zu Hippokrates-Texten* (*Abhandl. Akad. Wiss., Mainz*) (Wiesbaden, 1977), pp. 106ff. and 164ff.

25. K. Deichgräber, *Die Epidemien und das Corpus Hippocraticum* (*Abhandl. Preuss. Akad. Wiss. Philol.-hist. Kl.,* no. 3) (Berlin, 1933), pp. 74ff. H. Grensemann has told me *per litteras* of his doubts concerning Deichgräber's conclusions.

26. Xenophon, *Anabasis,* VII, 1, 5; 2, 10 and 24; and, especially, VII, 7, 1–14.

27. Compare *Epidemics,* IV, 53, and VII, 7, 10, with *Anabasis,* VII, 1, 13.

28. According to Langholf, *Syntaktishce Untersuchungen* (above, n. 24), p. 15, this *Alkibiádēs* could also be a place name.

29. Deichgräber, *Die Epidemien* (above, n. 25), p. 75.

30. Book 4 differs from books 2 and 6 in some details of language, style, and method, but most philologists still maintain the compositional unity of the group 2–4–6.

31. I have a preference for the last decade of the fifth century B.C., even though, since Deichgräber, general opinion has favored the first decade of the fourth. Because of its being repeated in the handbooks, the relatively recent date of the "cough of Perinthus" appears as an established fact based on external historical evidence. Here is an eloquent example: in his monumental history of Greek literature, Albin Lesky states that the dating of *Epidemics,* II, IV, and VI, is based on the description of an epidemic that took place in Perinthus between 399 and 395.

A fine example of circular argument! See A. Lesky, *Geschichte der griechischen Literatur,* 3d ed. (Bern and Munich, 1971), p. 552.

32. E. Oberhummer, s.v. *Perinthus,* in Pauly-Wissowa, *Real-Encyclopädie,* XIX, 1, col. 806.

33. *Epidemics,* II, 3, 1 (Littré, V, 100, 1).

34. On this subject, see above, chapter II.

35. F. Robert, "Les Adresses de malades dans les Epidémies II, IV et VI," in *Collection hippocratique et son rôle dans l'histoire de la médecine,* Colloque de Strasbourg (Leiden, 1975), pp. 173–94, esp. p. 174.

36. A. A. Nikitas, *Untersuchungen zu den Epidemienbüchen II-IV-VI des Corpus Hippocraticum,* thesis (Hamburg, 1967; published 1968).

37. Robert, "Les adresses" (above, n. 35), pp. 174 and 184.

38. The similarity has not escaped the notice of philologists: see Deichgräber, *Die Epidemien* (above, n. 25), pp. 26 and 33.

39. According to Bourgey, the accounts of the epidemic constitutions of Perinthus and Thasos are "of the same order," but there is "greater mastery" shown in the latter. This judgment is the result of a common prejudice in favor of *Epidemics,* I and III; it is inspired by an overall judgment of the treatises and not a meaningful comparison of the actual texts in question. See L. Bourgey, *Observation et expérience chez les médecins de la Collection Hippocratique* (Paris, 1953), p. 38.

40. Galen, *De difficultate respirationis,* I, 8 (Kühn, VII, 854–55), and *In Hipp. Epid. librum VI commentaria,* praefatio (Kühn, XVIIa, 796; *CMG* V, 10, 2, 2, p. 5).

41. Galen, *De difficultate respirationis,* III, 1 (Kühn, VII, 890). See also the passages from Galen cited in the previous note as well as *De crisibus,* 2 (Kühn, IX, 859). Though he concedes the possibility that book 6 contains additions from other, post-Hippocratic authors, Galen is nevertheless convinced that its basic elements derive from original Hippocratic manuscripts revised by Thessalus (cf. *CMG,* V, 10, 1, p. 310, and V, 10, 2, 2, p. 5). He has the same opinion of book 2, but he considers book 4 to be at some remove from the actual teaching of Hippocrates himself. See Nikitas, *Untersuchungen* (above, n. 36), p. 15. I can add that the treatise *Presbeutikós* confirms the presence of Thessalus at the side of Hippocrates during his visit to Thessaly (Littré, IX, 418).

42. J.-E. Dugand, "Hippocrates à Thasos et en Grèce," in *Corpus Hippocraticum* (above, n. 21), pp. 233–45 (esp. p. 244). For the close geographic, political, and commercial links between Perinthus and Cyzicus, see Louis Robert, "Des Carpathes à la Propontide. VII. De Périnthe à Apamée, Cyzique et Claros," *Studii classice* (Bucharest) 16 (1974): 61–80.

43. Littré, *Oeuvres complètes* (above, n. 8), 5: 264. Italics mine.

44. I have borrowed this definition from F. Robert ("Les adresses" [above, n. 35]), who emphasizes the usage of the word in the plural and is obviously distressed by the need to consider the case of Perinthus as an exception. There is no valid medical reason to give this case a special meaning that conflicts with the semantic unity of the word "epidemic" and its derivatives in the Hippocratic treatises, but Littré's authority was such that his mistake was perpetuated in study after study, especially once it was reinforced by the statements of Deichgräber on the nature of the "Hustenepidemie" of Perinthus.

45. Littré, *Oeuvres complètes* (above, n. 8), 5: 265. Italics mine.

46. P. Bretonneau, "Sur les moyens de prévenir le développement et les progrès de la diphtérie," *Arch. gén. de méd.,* 5th ser. 5 (1855): 1–14; 6 (1855): 257–79.

47. P. Bretonneau, *Des inflammations spéciales du tissu muqueux et en particulier la diphthérite, ou inflammation pelliculaire* (Paris, 1826).

48. V.P.A. Maingault, *De la paralysie diphtérique* (Paris, 1860).

49. E. Littré, "De la diphtérite et de la paralysie consécutive à la diphtherite dans les oeuvres d'Hippocrate," *Gaz. méd. de Paris,* 3d ser. 16 (1861): 353–56.

50. A. Gubler, *Des paralysies dans leurs rapports avec les maladies aiguës, et spécialement des paralysies asthéniques, diffuses, des convalescents* (Paris, 1860).

51. Littré, *Oeuvres complètes* (above, n. 8), 10: ii–viii.

52. See N. Mani, "Die Nachtblindheit und ihre Behandlung in der griechischen-römischen Medizin," *Gesnerus* 10 (1953): 53–58.

53. D. Gourevitch, "Le dossier philologique du nyctalope," *Hippocratica* (Paris, 1979), pp. 167–87.

54. For example, *Epidemics,* IV, 12 (Littré, V, 150). In this regard, see J. Hirschberg, *Geschichte der Augenheilkunde im Alterthum* (Leipzig, 1899), p. 88.

55. Littré, *Oeuvres complètes* (above, n. 8), 10: vii.

56. *Epidemics,* II, 2, 24 (Littré, V, 94–98).

57. A. Souques, "Nature diphtérique des paralysies post-angineuses attribuées par les auteurs hippocratiques à la luxation spontanée des vertèbres cervicales," *Bull. Soc. Franç. Hist. Méd.* 27 (1933): 77–98; A. Souques, *Etapes de la neurologie dans l'Antiquité grecque (d'Homère à Galien)* (Paris, 1938), pp. 57–68.

58. Littré, *Oeuvres complètes* (above, n. 8), 5: 95.

59. A. Souques, "Nature diphtérique de l'épidémie de toux de Périnthe," *Bull. Soc. Franç. Hist. Méd.* 28 (1934): 151–55.

60. See F. Schnurrer, *Die Krankheiten des Menschen-Geschlechts historisch und geographisch beobachtet* (Tübingen, 1823), 1: 45; A. Corradi, *Annali delle epidemie occorse in Italia dalle prime memorie fino al 1850* (Bologna, 1865), 1: 18ff.

61. Livy, *History of Rome,* IV, 52.

62. G. Phokas, *Perì tês pár' Hippokrátei epidēmikēs Grípēs (Influenza)* (Athens, 1892).

63. A. Laboulbène, "Sur un mémoire de M. le Dr. Phokas: La grippe épidémique (Influenza) dans les écrits hippocratiques," *Bull. Acad. Méd.* (Paris), 3d ser., 28 (1892): 86–93; T. Puschmann, "Die Influenza im Alterthum," *Wien. Klin. Wschr.* 6 (1893): 239–42.

64. A. G. Panayotatou, *L'hygiène chez les anciens Grecs* (Paris, 1923), pp. 68–71.

65. H. Favier, "La dengue et la maladie de Périnthe," *Gaz. hebd. méd. chir.,* 2d ser. 23 (1886): 534–37 and 566–69 (esp. p. 536).

66. E. W. Goodall, "On Infectious Diseases and Epidemiology in the Hippocratic Collection," *Proc. Roy. Soc. Med.* 27 (1934): 525–34 (esp. p. 531).

67. J. R. Paul, *A History of Poliomyelitis* (New Haven, 1971), pp. 14–16.

68. A. Ilvento, *Storia delle grandi malattie epidemiche con speciale riguardo alla malaria* (Rome, 1938), p. 147.

69. See for instance F. Henschen, *The History and Geography of Diseases* (New York, 1966), p. 46; G. Rosen, *A History of Public Health* (New York, 1948), p. 31; W. I. Beveridge, *Influenza, the Last Great Plague* (New York, 1977), p. 25.

70. P. Lépine, "Les grandes épidémies de grippe," *Vie médicale* 51 (1970): 4151.

71. Chamseru, "Recherches sur la nyctalopie ou l'aveuglement de nuit, maladie qui règne tous les ans dans le printemps aux environs de La Roche-Guyon," *Mémoires de la Société Royale de Médecine* 8 (1786) (actually published in 1790): 130–78.

72. Ibid., p. 141.

73. Ibid., pp. 143–44.

74. Littré, *Oeuvres complètes* (above, n. 8) 10:ii. See also Deichgräber, *Die Epidemien* (above, n. 25), pp. 34ff.

75. Nikitas, *Untersuchungen* (above, n. 36), p. 141.

76. I have chosen this case just as an example. Among the clinical histories that, traditional opinion to the contrary notwithstanding, do not belong to the "cough of Perinthus," I can cite *Epidemics,* IV, 25, 36, 47, 51, 52; VI, 1, 12.

77. *Epidemics,* II, 2, 8 (Littré, V, 88). For the establishment of the Greek text, see Deichgräber, *Die Epidemien* (above, n. 25), p. 69, and Langholf, *Syntaktische Untersuchungen* (above, n. 24), p. 117.

78. A diagnosis suggested by Goodall, "Infectious Diseases" (above, n. 66), p. 531.

79. First considered in the last century, especially by Puschmann, "Die Influenza" (above, n. 63), p. 240, the diagnosis of neurotic paralysis is vigorously stated by I. Veith, *Hysteria, the History of a Disease* (Chicago, 1965).

80. *Epidemics,* IV, 50 (Littré, V, 190).

81. Nikitas, *Untersuchungen* (above, n. 36), p. 135.

82. *Epidemics,* VI, 3, 8 (Littré, V, 296).

83. The distinction between IV, 50, and VI, 3, 8, was well drawn by Nikitas, *Untersuchungen* (above, n. 36), pp. 132ff. I also owe the right diagnosis of the case in VI, 3, 8, to him; Galen in his commentary on the passage had already suspected it (*CMG,* V, 10, 2, 2, p. 149).

84. *Epidemics,* VI, 7, 9–10 (Littré, V, 342).

85. This way of interpreting the text agrees with Galen's commentaries (see above, n. 83, p. 433), as well as those of Palladius and Foes.

86. *Epidemics,* IV, 53 (Littré, V, 192–94).

87. See especially Beveridge, *Influenza* (above, n. 69); M. M. Kaplan and R. G. Webster, "The Epidemiology of Influenza," *Scientific American* 237 (1977): 88–106; and W. G. Laver, *The Origin of Pandemic Influenza Viruses* (New York, 1983).

88. For the chronology of the great influenza epidemics of the past, see above all E. S. Thompson, *Influenza, or Epidemic Catarrhal Fever* (London, 1890); J. F. Townsend, "History of Influenza Epidemics," *Ann. Med. Hist.* 5 (1933): 533–47; and G. Cavina, *L'influenza epidemica attraverso i secoli* (Rome, 1959). For the serological archaeology of influenza and the cyclical return of its epidemics, see N. Masurel, "De wederkomst van het varkens-influenzavirus," *Nederl. Tijdschr. Geneesk.* 120 (1976): 1123–25; M. Bader, "Influenza Cycles," *JAMA* 237 (1977): 2813; and especially Beveridge, *Influenza* (above, n. 69), pp. 77–79.

89. Dionysius of Halicarnassus, *Antiquitates Romanae,* VII, 68; Livy, *History of Rome,* IV, 52; Cassius Dio, *History of Rome,* XLV, 17. I consider it useless to include the evidence of Diodorus Siculus (XIV, 70) concerning the plague that smote the Carthaginian army before Syracuse in about 396/395 B.C., although Townsend, "History of Influenza" (above, n. 88), believes it was influenza. It is hard to believe that Townsend has read the original text of Diodorus, since it mentions symptoms that have nothing in common with the influenza syndrome.

90. The term *kóruza* sometimes refers to the humor that flows from the nose, sometimes to the flux itself, that is, the rhinorrhea (see Galen, *Comm. II in Progn.,* Kühn, XVIII, B, 180; *Sympt. caus.,* Kühn, VII, 263). When phlegm from the brain flows into the nostrils, that is *kóruza* in the strict sense; when it flows from the palate and then down the throat, it is called *katárrhos* (cold with pharyngitis); when the phlegm reaches the trachea, that is *brángkhos* (cold with laryngitis and tracheobronchitis). In this connection, see C. Daremberg, *Oeuvres choisies d'Hippocrate,* 2d ed. (Paris, 1855), p. 170.

91. *Prognostic,* 14 (Littré, II, 146), and *Praen. Coacae,* 393 (Littré, V, 670).

92. *Ancient Medicine,* 18 (Littré, I, 614; in Jones's edition, p. 46).

93. *Aer.,* 10 (Littré, II, 46); Jones, I, 100.

94. For the clinical mention of labial herpes and genital herpes, see above, chapter 5, "Other Diseases of the External Genitals."

95. *Praen. Coacae,* 618 (Littré, V, 728).

96. See for example Rosen, *History of Public Health* (above, n. 69); J. F. H. Broadbent, "The Acute Infectious Diseases," in W. R. Bett, *A Short History of*

Some Common Diseases (Oxford, 1934), pp. 8–9; and E. H. Ackerknecht, *Geschichte und Geographie der wichtigsten Krankheiten* (Stuttgart, 1963), p. 60.

97. *Morb.*, III, 7 (Littré, VII, 124–26). See P. Potter, *Hippokrates, Ueber die Krankheiten III* (Berlin, 1980), pp. 74–77 and 108.

98. *Epidemics*, I, 1 (Littré, II, 600–602). See E. Ebstein, "Klassische Krankengeschichten: II. Der Mumps bei Hippokrates," *Kinderärtzliche Praxis*, 2 (1931): 140–41.

99. O. Hamburger, "Un cas de paralysie infantile dans l'Antiquité," *Bull. Soc. Franç. Hist. Méd.* 10 (1971): 407–12.

100. Paul, *Poliomyelitis* (above, n. 67), p. 14.

101. See M. Michler, *Die Klumpfusslehre der Hippokratiker* (Wiesbaden, 1963) (*Sudhoffs Archiv. Beiheft 2*), p. 47.

102. Aristotle, *Nic. Ethics*, 1102b.

103. A.H.W. Adkins, "Paralysis and Akrasia in Eth. Nic.," *American Journal of Philology* 97 (1976): 62–64.

104. Daremberg, *Oeuvres choisies* (above, n. 90), p. 175.

105. Aretaeus of Cappadocia, *Signa ac.*, I, 9. See R. Bayeux, *La diphtérie depuis Arétée le Cappadocien jusqu'en 1894* (Paris, 1899); B. O. Hagedorn, *Die Diphtherie in ihrem geschichtlichen Aufbau* (Leipzig, 1919).

106. *Dent.*, 24 and 31; after the edition and translation by R. Joly (Paris, 1978), pp. 224–25.

107. *Acut (app.)*, 10 (Joly, 72–73); *Morb.*, II, 26 (Jouanna, 159–69). Diphtheritic sore throat is also described in *Morb.*, III, 10. In this connection, see Potter, *Hippokrates* (above, n. 97), pp. 76–79 and 110–11.

108. *De visu*, 7 (Joly, 171).

109. Bretonneau, "Sur les moyens," (above, n. 46), p. 7.

Chapter 13: Dialogue between a Philologist and a Physician

1. K. Deichgräber, *Die Epidemien und das Corpus Hippocraticum*, (*Abhandl. Preuss. Akad. Wiss., Philol-hist. Klasse*, no. 3) (Berlin, 1933; rpt. Berlin, 1971), pp. 16 and 172.

2. I hereby thank my friend for his permission to use the presentation we made together before the colloquium at Mons. See M. Grmek and F. Robert, "Dialogue d'un médecin et d'un philologue sur quelques passages des Epidémies VII," *Corpus Hippocraticum* (Mons, 1977), pp. 275–90. Although the first part of this chapter is the same as the presentation at Mons, the second part contains significant additions, including a translation and a medical commentary on several clinical histories that excel in the concision of their style and the astuteness of their medical observations.

3. I alone am responsible for the content and final form of this chapter, but I should perhaps stress that, although it represents a joint effort, the lion's share of the work was naturally the philologist's.

4. E. Littré, *Oeuvres complètes d'Hippocrate* (Paris, 1846), 5: 378–81.

5. M is *Codex Marcianus Graecus* 268 (tenth century), and V is *Codex Vaticanus Graecus* 276 (twelfth century).

6. A tonic spasm is a continuous muscular contraction, while a clonic spasm is a convulsion with a series of contractions.

7. Littré, V, 404–6. Parallel versions of these three case histories occur in *Epidemics*, V, 74–76 (Littré, V, 246–48). For the first of these cases, see the section "Four Concise Case Histories" in this chapter.

8. For instance, in *Morb.*, III, 12 (Littré, VII, 132; Potter, 80), "the tetanuses" *(hoi tétanoi)* that lay low a patient and produce trismus, strabismus, and paralysis

in the limbs correspond to the modern definition of the term, if not from the conceptual standpoint at least as regards the pathological substratum. The "tetanus" spoken of in *Acut. (app.),* 37, 1 (Joly, 85) is, by contrast, only a special affection of the hip.

9. This notion has been elaborated in F. Robert, "La prognose hippocratique dans les livres v and vii des Epidémies," *Le monde grec (Hommage à Claire Préaux)* (Brussels, 1975), pp. 257–70. It is much indebted to the notion of "Kollegheſte" or course notebooks used by Deichgräber in the book cited above (n. 1) and applied by him to several texts in the Hippocratic collection.

10. Such is the case for the wife of Hermoptolemos; see the section "A Case of Typhoid Fever" in this chapter.

11. Plato, *Phaedrus,* 253e, 2; Galen, in Kühn, xviii, B, 164.

12. For instance, see J. S. Milne, *Surgical Instruments in Greek and Roman Times* (London, 1907), pp. 51–83, pls. 11–14.

13. This important problem was the object of a stimulating, masterly discussion by Jean Irigoin at the Mons colloquium, "Le rôle des recentiores dans l'établissement du texte hippocratique," *Corpus Hippocraticum* (above, n. 2), pp. 9–17.

14. *History of Animals,* 492b, 32, and *Problems,* 902b, 22.

15. *Epidemics,* vii, 11 (Littré, v, 382–86).

16. After consulting the Hippocratic concordance prepared by G. Maloney and his Canadian team, I persist in this translation of *giuóō* by "cripple." Granted that a certain softening in the word's meaning took place in medical parlance, the usual translation of the word as "weaken" goes a little too far.

17. See F. Robert, "Prophasis," *Revue des études grecques* 89, (1976): 317–42.

18. Berrettoni's lexicon ("Il lessico tecnico del i e ii libro delle Epidemie ippocratiche," *Annali della Scuola normale sup. di Pisa* 39 [1970]: 90ff.), after providing "coma" as an initial translation of the word *kôma,* goes on to show the difference between *kôma* and sleep, since, in the former, consciousness is maintained.

19. The Hippocratic physicians were familiar with the automatic, unconscious, and continual gesturing that affects some patients with fever: they seem to search for nonexistent objects, grasp at their bedclothes, and tear out the threads of their blankets. The physicians saw these gestures, with good reason, as bad signs for the future, as likely precursors of death in patients who were delirious, victims of phrenitis, pneumonia, or any other kind of acute fever. See *Progn.,* 4, and *Prorrh.,* 1, 34. The term "carphology" (Gr. *karphología*), which was introduced as a modern medical term by Philippe Pinel, is used several times by Galen. He suffered an attack of fever with this symptom during his own childhood. See Galen, *Comment. I in Hipp. Progn.,* 23 (Kühn, xviii, B, 71–75), and especially *De loc. aff.,* iv, 2 (Kühn, viii, 226–27).

20. According to the *Suda,* there were three degrees of mental disturbance: the strongest was *paraphrosúnē* and the weakest *paralēros,* with *lēros* between the two.

21. In *Aff. int.,* 39–43 (Littré, vii, 260–74), distinctions are drawn between five diseases called *tûphos.* None of them really corresponds to typhoid fever, although we cannot rule out the possibility that the observation of actual cases of typhoid contributed to the formulation of these five clinical profiles that, to the eyes of a modern physician, are actually heterogeneous. The Hippocratic term *tûphos* has no equivalent in modern pathology and should not be rendered by the word "typhus." Typhoid fever was not understood as a clinical entity in classical antiquity. Instead, it was confused with various forms of phrenitis, *kaûsos,* and bilious fever. See G. Ongaro, "Evoluzione storica del concetto di tifo," *Riforma medica,* no. 6 (1967).

22. There can be no doubt as to the presence of salmonella infections in the ancient populations of the Mediterranean. I see the symptoms of salmonellosis in

several cases of *kaûsos* described in *Epidemics,* I and III. The tenth patient in *Epidemics,* I (the Clazomenean man who suffered from a strong, unremitting fever for forty days) is a good example (Littré, II, 704–8). For arguments in favor of the existence of salmonelloses in classical Greece, see E. W. Goodall, "On Infectious Diseases and Epidemiology in the Hippocratic Collection," *Proc. Royal Soc. Med.* (London) 27 (1934): 525–34 (esp. pp. 526–29).

23. The name "nystagmus" is given to slight, rhythmic, involuntary jerks of both eyeballs (rarely, of just one). There is a succession of jerks, with the alternation of a rapid jerk in one direction and a slower jerk that returns the eye to its original position. The direction is conventionally defined by the rapid one. Thus the Hippocratic writer is defining left, horizontal nystagmus. It is the sign of a lesion either in the inner ear or in the central nervous system (vestibular centers). Infections can be its etiology. This complication, then, agrees with the diagnosis of salmonellosis. I note in passing that the Greek word *nustagmós* occurs in ancient texts in a different sense from the one just given. It refers to the way a sleeping or drowsy person shakes his head. The general view has been that the first clinical descriptions of nystagmus date only from the eighteenth century. See G. Bilancioni, "Alcuni spunti sulla storia del nistagmo," *Boll. Ist. Stor. Ital. Arte San.* 11 (1931): 1–14.

24. *Epidemics,* VII, 116 (Littré, V, 462); parallel account in *Epidemics,* V, 101 (Littré, V, 258).

25. On the diagnosis of this case and the mammary cancer in antiquity, see P. Diepgen, *Die Frauenheilkunde der Alten Welt* (Munich, 1937), p. 237, and G. Grassi, *Storia dei tumori nella antichità greco-romana* (Rome, 1941), pp. 28–30.

26. *De mulierum affectibus,* II, 133 (Littré, VIII, 282); see also *Gland.,* 17 (Littré, VIII, 572).

27. Herodotus, III, 133.

28. Among the modern authors who opt for a cancer diagnosis, I can cite J. Körbler, *Geschichte der Krebskrankheit* (Wien, 1973), pp. 8–10. The opposite opinion has been put forth by A. T. Sandison, "The First Recorded Case of Inflammatory Mastitis: Queen Atossa of Persia and the Physician Democedes," *Medical History* 3 (1959): 317–22. A prudent position, very critical of the cancer diagnosis, was adopted by P. Menetrier and R. Houdry, "La guérison du cancer de sein de la reine Atossa," *Bull. Soc. Franç. Hist. Méd.* 15 (1921): 285–89.

29. See M-P. Duminil, "Le sens de *ichōr* dans les textes hippocratiques," *Corpus Hippocraticum* (above, n. 2), pp. 65–76; and, going beyond the medical context, J. Jouanna and P. Demont, "Le sens d'ichṓr chez Homère et chez Eschyle en relation avec les emplois du mot dans la collection hippocratique," *Revue des études anciennes* 83 (1981): 197–209.

30. *Epidemics,* VII, 36 (Littré, V, 404); parallel account in *Epidemics,* V, 74 (Littré, V, 246–48).

31. *Epidemics,* VII, 113 (Littré, V, 460–62); parallel account in *Epidemics,* V, 100 (Littré, V, 256–58).

32. *Epidemics,* VII, 32 (Littré, V, 400–402); parallel account in *Epidemics,* V, 60 (Littré, V, 240).

33. See S. Winkle, "Der Tetanos im Altertum," *Die gelben Hefte* 18 (1970): 916–28.

34. See F. Robert, "La bataille de Délos (Hippocrate, Epidémies, V, 61 and VII, 33)," *Etudes déliennes (Suppl. I du Bulletin de Correspondance Hellénique)* (Athens, 1973), pp. 427–33.

35. *Epidemics,* VII, 46 (Littré, V, 414).

36. For the history of epilepsy in antiquity, see especially O. Temkin, *The Falling Sickness,* 2d edition (Baltimore, 1971).

37. For the translation of Greek *peripneumonía* (or *peripleumonía*) by the modern term "pneumonia," see above, p. 307.

38. *Epidemics,* VII, 13 (Littré, V, 388).

39. *Epidemics,* VII, 55 (Littré, V, 422).

40. See A. Papanicolaou, *Glossikai éreunai épi tou Corpus Hippocraticum* (Athens, 1965).

Index